Insurance policies that practically everybody buys and nobody needs.

Page 388

Secrets of the successful test-takers. How to get much better scores.

Page 21

How to deduct all the interest on a personal loan without borrowing against home equity.

Page 467

How to double your chances of winning a sweepstakes.

Page 279

Get paid to take a dream vacation. Airfare. Hotels. Meals. Everything "on the house."

Page 207

Bottom Line
Books

www.BottomLinePublications.com

Contents

4 • MEDICAL SOLUTIONS

5 • IMPROVING YOUR APPEARANCE

6 • YOUR HOME

7 • YOUR CAR

8 • TRAVEL AND VACATIONS

9 • SPORTS AND RECREATION

10 • CONSUMER GUIDE

11 • PARTY AND ENTERTAINMENT GUIDE

12 • COLLECTING AND HOBBIES

13 • CREDIT CARDS

14 • PERSONAL MONEY MANAGEMENT

15 • INSURANCE AND YOU

16 • POINTS OF LAW

1

Family and Social Life

How to Make Better Friends and Be More Influential

Many people complain that it's harder than ever to make friends. And they're right. *Reason:* There are fewer opportunities for people to meet and interact.

Many of us spend our days involved with machines rather than people. We work with computers and go home and sit in front of the television.

Result: The time we spend with people is diminished and so are the opportunities to practice relating to others.

Also, our society has become more fast-paced. This means people have less time to get to know one another.

Example: In Nebraska where I grew up, people who first met would spend some time "rolling the cob." The term describes the way Nebraska farmers would sit around rolling a corncob under their feet and just talking about unimportant things. It was a way to slowly get to know the other person and develop a friendship.

People no longer have time for such a slow, easygoing process.

Sign of the times: At one time people handled disagreements by getting together and talking things out. Today they are more apt to hire lawyers to settle disputes, creating a litigious society that is costing us a fortune. In addition to all the *new* reasons that make it tough to make friends, the *old* reasons still apply.

Many people have trouble making friends because they're shy and think they shouldn't impose themselves on others. They feel standoffish, reluctant to push themselves forward to meet and get to know people.

Trap: We all have a *comfort zone*—an area in which it's relatively easy for us to relate to other people. This area is made up of people we

J. Oliver Crom, former president, Dale Carnegie & Associates, Inc., 290 Motor Parkway, Hauppauge, NY 11788. The company was founded by Dale Carnegie, pioneer of the self-development movement and author of *How to Win Friends and Influence People* (Simon & Schuster).

already know—our families, colleagues in business, old friends. Anything that forces us to move beyond that area causes discomfort and fear.

Example: At a meeting or party, most people immediately look around for someone they know to chat with rather than walk up to someone new and introduce themselves.

Although making friends and maintaining friendships involve a variety of skills, there are a few basics that anyone can follow…

•**Overcome shyness.** A big part of shyness is a lack of self-confidence. Before you can accept new friends, you have to learn to accept yourself. This calls for self-awareness—knowing both your strengths and your weaknesses and accepting them all.

Once you realize that you're a whole person—and that other people also feel awkward and unsure of themselves—it will be easier for you to make the first move. Inside everyone there's a confident, friendly person who wants to get out.

•**Banish fear.** Millions of people are more afraid of speaking to a group than they are of dying. *Reason:* They're sure they will only embarrass themselves or appear foolish.

But most people discover that once they stand up to address a group—or approach someone new to start a conversation—it isn't horrible or embarrassing at all.

What we really fear is the unknown. The way to overcome that fear is by doing the thing that scares you and keep doing it.

•**Broaden your thinking.** We all have a tendency toward pigeonhole thinking—applying what we know to just one part of our lives. But most of our skills can be used in different aspects of our lives.

Example: Many people take courses in order to enhance their public speaking skills. They're surprised to discover that what they learn also helps them to get along better with people.

The following tips on how to make friends come from Dale Carnegie's book, *How to Win Friends and Influence People…*

•**Don't criticize, condemn or complain.**

•**Give honest, sincere appreciation.**

•**Arouse in the other person an eager want.**

•**Become genuinely interested in other people.**

•**Smile.**

•**Remember that a person's name is to that person the sweetest and most important sound in any language.**

•**Be a good listener.** Encourage others to talk about themselves.

•**Talk in terms of the other person's interests.**

•**Make the other person feel important** —and do it *sincerely*.

June Marriages

June is still the favorite month of 12.3% of brides marrying for the first time. Among women remarrying, 10.2% choose July and another 10.2% choose December. *Most popular day:* Saturday (53%). *Least popular day:* Wednesday (4.2%). Religious ceremonies are chosen by 80% of first-time brides but by only 60% of women who are remarrying.

Put a Little Fun Into Your Marriage

Life is difficult—marriage even more so. To have a successful marriage, make sure you keep some fun in your marriage. Here are some ideas for you. But the possibilities are, of course, endless, and they are limited only by your loving imagination.

•**Start a scrapbook.** It helps you to relive the happy moments of your life together.

•**Buy a bulletin board.** Keep it in the kitchen or another room so you can leave funny and/or meaningful messages each day.

•**Serve each other breakfast in bed.** On odd Sundays, it's your turn…even Sundays, your mate's.

- **Buy a treat a day, large or small,** but with a light touch. *Examples:* Kiwi, a little American caviar, a red rose, some champagne, a trinket, a funny sign.

- **Make your home beautiful.** It should be a place that is fun to return to each night and to be in together away from the harsh world.

- **Buy something special for your house** that you can both enjoy. *Examples:* A piano, a video recorder.

- **Use satin sheets.** They are a treat for special occasions.

- **Make yourself look as good as possible.** Stay slim, trim and well-groomed.

- **Read aloud to each other.**

- **Buy subscriptions to your local theater group.** Go together or with close friends.

- **Enjoy sports together.**

- **Do things for each other.** *Examples:* Cut each other's hair, give each other massages, take care of each other's needs.

- **Start a hobby together,** such as collecting stamps or autographs.

- **Go to dancing school.** Learn special, fun dance steps that you can practice together.

- **Throw a big party** for your friends for absolutely no reason at all.

- **Plan a really special trip** in the coming year. Have fun planning it together.

- **Enjoy television together.** Subscribe to cable TV and see games and movies together.

- **Plan a treat a week.** One week, it's your treat…the other week, your mate's.

- **Buy a hot tub.**

- **Say nice things to each other.** See who can give the best and most compliments.

- **Make a ritual of dinner.** Replace paper napkins with linen napkins. Use sterling silver, fine china and candles. Drink good wine.

- **Become involved in community affairs together.**

- **Join a health club together** and work out daily.

- **Take a shower together.** It has great potential.

- **Allow plenty of time** for each partner to "do his or her own thing" alone.

Strategies for Feisty Couples

James L. Creighton, PhD, psychologist in Los Gatos, CA, who specializes in conflict resolution. He is author of *How Loving Couples Fight* (Aslan Publishing) and coauthor of *Getting Well Again* (Bantam).

It is a myth that happy couples never fight. In fact, many happy couples regularly disagree with each other.

What sets loving couples apart is that they disagree in loving ways. They don't let disagreements turn into nasty battles. And their "fights" strengthen, rather than hurt, their relationships.

Handling conflict in a healthy way is a skill that can be learned.

ACCEPT CONFLICT AS NORMAL

Trying to ignore disagreements or bury resentments doesn't get rid of them. It only allows them to grow below the surface. When we face conflict and deal with it openly, it's easier to let it go and move on. *Steps to take…*

- **Express what you *feel,* not what you *think.*** Couples who fight lovingly start by talking about how they feel, not about what they think is "wrong" with their partner.

They frame arguments by saying, "I'm hurt/angry/frustrated" rather than, "You're rude/sloppy/a jerk."

When one spouse does something that bothers the other, he or she says so *immediately.* But he describes the specific behavior —not his interpretation.

Example: "I was upset when you didn't return my call" expresses how the person feels. "I'm mad because you're inconsiderate" expresses what the person thinks.

It's tempting to blame your negative feelings on the other person's inadequacies. Resist this urge.

Attacking or accusing may make you feel temporarily powerful. But it erodes trust, creating emotional fallout that is very difficult to clean up.

- **Listen—rather than talk**—your way out of conflict. When someone is upset, the natural reaction is to try to talk him out of it. We do this by making excuses for the person…or trying to come up with solutions to the problem…or pointing out all the reasons why there's no need to be upset. But this response implies that the other person doesn't have a right to his feelings. So talking often makes matters worse.

In reality, all it takes to stop the person from being angry is to acknowledge how he feels.

Key to effective listening: After your partner has finished speaking, summarize the feelings and ideas that were just expressed. Don't evaluate whether those words are right or wrong…and don't try to "fix" anything. Just repeat what you've heard.

When you're first learning this technique, it can feel artificial or even patronizing—but it works very effectively.

Many of the couples I work with get around this by using the *five-minute rule.* Either partner can invoke this rule at any time.

How it works: One person has five minutes to speak without interruption. Then the other person has five minutes. If you can't decide who should start, flip a coin. Sometimes you both may need *another* turn to speak.

By the end of the second round, both people have usually gotten most of their frustration out of the way and can start discussing the problem more constructively.

FIGHT FAIRLY

Happy couples follow several unspoken rules that keep their small arguments from escalating into big ones…

• **Stick to the issue.** If he's mad because she's not ready to leave at the agreed-upon time, that's the subject the loving couple talks about.

They don't get sidetracked by accusations, such as, "You don't care how I feel" or, "One of us has to live in the real world."

They also don't keep bringing up past grievances. If an issue keeps coming up over and over, they'll talk about it—but not as a way of punishing each other when they're arguing about something else.

• **Don't hit below the belt.** Loving couples don't try to hurt each other by attacking sensitive areas, such as weight, job status, etc.

• **Don't drag other people into it.** Don't say things such as, "I'm not the only person who feels this way. Your sister and brother do, too."

Trying to bolster your side of the argument by bringing up someone else not only escalates the fight but also poisons your partner's relationship with that person.

Some couples find it helpful to make these rules explicit—and remind each other gently if one of them breaks a rule.

Don't turn these reminders into occasions to gloat. A simple reminder, such as, "Remember, we agreed not to do that" usually is enough.

Important: The best time to agree on rules is right after a fight, when you've cooled down enough to talk reasonably. The memory of the fight you just had—and how unpleasant it was not to be following the rules—will motivate you to do things differently.

HUDDLE TO SOLVE PROBLEMS

Sometimes just hearing each other out helps partners understand one another's point of view—and resolves the conflict. When that's not enough, happy couples work together to find a better way of dealing with the issue. *Problem-solving steps…*

• **Agree on what the problem is.**

• **Brainstorm alternative solutions.**

• **Agree on a solution that best meets your needs and those of your partner.**

• **Agree on a way to put the solution into practice.**

• **Evaluate how well the solution is working.**

If Your Spouse Returns to School

A spouse's return to school tests a marriage. The student develops new friendships or starts to regard the partner as an intellectual inferior. To make the process easier, enlist your mate's support before enrolling. Agree in advance to share household chores. Don't let all conversations center around school. Develop new activities with your partner to establish a fresh common ground. To keep your sex life healthy, set aside unbreakable dates for time alone together.

Internet "Affairs" and Your Marriage

Internet "affairs" can wreck a marriage—even if the people communicating over the Internet never actually meet. Internet relationships often begin in chat rooms or as E-mail on topics of professional or personal interest.

Trap: People you have not met face to face can be anything you want them to be. It's easy for those fantasies projected on them to seem better than reality—and they can wreak havoc on a marriage.

Danger signs: If you start to have romantic feelings about the person—or begin thinking that the person understands you better than anyone else.

Helpful: Consider counseling to help you understand the needs the cyber-relationship has been filling.

Betsy S. Stone, PhD, psychologist in private practice, Stamford, Connecticut.

How to Avoid Divorce

The late Clifford J. Sager, MD, psychiatrist and psychologist.

If one or both partners have definitely decided to get a divorce, there's usually no stopping them. If they are ambivalent, they should spend at least as much time considering the question of divorce as they did that of marriage. (If the courtship took a year, they should spend a year trying to stay together.) It's wise to get counseling or therapy if help is needed.

Two households can't be supported on the same amount of money and in the same style as one household.

Children may have problems at the beginning, but if the situation is handled well, the impact that divorce has on children can be minimized. *Important:* Parents should not denigrate each other or use their children as go-betweens. Both must give them time, attention and emotional support.

SYMPTOMS OF A TROUBLED MARRIAGE

Poor communication: Possibly due to lack of intimacy, of a sense of closeness, of being able to talk, of really being heard when you do talk, loss of sexual desire and a sense of not being understood.

Sexual infidelity: This is no longer a common cause of divorce, but often it is a sign that something is wrong with the relationship. Today people are more likely to accept some degree of infidelity. But it is always a sign of trouble in a previously monogamous relationship.

Children: Increasing use of children in struggles between adults.

Some people fail to make the shift from short- to long-term bonding. Short-term bonding is the initial period of being intensely in love. The partner isn't seen realistically. There is a strong sexual attraction and a desire to be with the loved one as much as possible. In long-term bonding, love is no longer a "sickness" but a more quietly satisfying feeling of caring and wanting to build together. The other person is seen more realistically and deficiencies are accepted. Some of the passion wears off, but it can be reawakened from time to time.

Motivation: You have to want to progress to long-term bonding and to accept the other person despite some shortcomings. It takes a lot of work to solve the problems of communication. For instance, you must want to communicate.

Example: A couple with an infidelity problem has to realize where they are in the short-term/long-term cycle. People who have to be intensely in love all the time go from one short-term relationship to another to get their "fix." Do they want to change? Although anger is a common cause of outside affairs, there are people who

5

need them. They may say, "I'm not taking anything away from you. This is the way I am." If the spouse can truly accept it, fine. But if the infidelity is sadly tolerated, the prospects for the marriage are poor.

First step in finding a solution: Once you know why things aren't working out, ask yourself whether you are contributing to the problem. It's easy to see what your spouse is doing wrong, but what are you doing that you should consider changing?

MOST LIKELY TO SUCCEED

Maturity: The best candidates for staying together (or for getting divorced) are the most mature. They know their own minds and are realistic in their expectations.

Good complementariness: The partners meet each other's emotional needs and dovetail well.

Mutual respect: The ability to compromise on both practical and emotional levels is necessary. *Example:* "I don't mind your being dependent on me at times because it's not that onerous. And when we're at a party, you always make sure I'm having a good time and not standing by myself." Some couples berate each other about personality traits they don't like. But not being able to lovingly accept such characteristics spells trouble.

Stay Friendly with In-Laws After the Divorce

To remain friendly with in-laws after the divorce, allow a cooling-off period before making contact. Then don't hesitate to make the first move. Get the approval of the family member who carries the most weight. Call a family meeting to bring resentments out into the open. Don't force your in-laws to take sides. Behave with them as you always have. Be patient—time is on your side. *Important:* Remember that your in-laws are your children's grandparents. Children need to be reassured that they won't lose other family members in the wake of a divorce.

How to Avoid the Alimony Trap

Lenard Marlow, JD, divorce mediator practicing in New York, and founder of Divorce Mediation Professionals, one of the oldest divorce-mediation facilities in the US. He is author of *The Two Roads to Divorce* (Xlibris Corp).

When a married couple finally decides to call it quits, both spouses usually feel a profound sense of failure and loss. Then the divorce proceedings begin, often bringing with them increasing levels of stress and anger that only make an already emotionally difficult situation worse.

But not every divorce has to be expensive or painful. In fact, a divorce can be mediated for less than what a divorce attorney charges.

AVOID HIRING SEPARATE LAWYERS

Divorce is not a legal problem. It is a personal problem with certain legal implications. The purpose of the divorce proceedings is to get it done, not to seek revenge.

The problem with hiring separate attorneys is that our legal system, by its very nature, is adversarial. Once put into motion, divorce proceedings take on a life of their own, usually at great financial and emotional cost to both parties.

How it works: Each attorney tries to get as much as possible for his/her client. A couple may believe they have hired two lawyers to negotiate a settlement, but negotiations do not begin for several months, to allow for "discovery" of financial conditions, often entailing "his and her" accountants, appraisers and auditors.

Trap: During this period, attorneys file orders of support and various motions that usually cause additional hurt and anger between the divorcing couple.

Inevitably, couples are swept into scenarios of distrust, pettiness, resentment and greed that are no longer within their control. Because both spouses usually have unrealistic expectations, the result is usually a settlement neither party feels is fair.

THE BENEFITS OF A MEDIATOR

Most divorcing couples can't communicate productively on their own. But given proper help, most divorcing couples are capable of deciding how to distribute their property and support their children, just as they did during marriage.

A professional mediator meets with both parties together. One spouse is never pitted against the other. The effort is to negotiate a fair settlement. *Benefits...*

• **Speed.** A mediator generally meets with a couple weekly. After about five to seven meetings, the parties reach the point at which an agreement can be drafted. Most divorce lawyers, on the other hand, don't even have their first meeting with each other in the first two months, while they are collecting information.

• **Cost.** Cost is a function of speed and complexity. The combined fee for a mediated agreement is usually less than the retainer that one spouse would have to pay just to initiate an adversarial proceeding, which is usually a fraction of the final fee.

All of a mediator's time is spent working out an agreement, while divorce lawyers spend much of their time filing and responding to pleas and motions.

• **Professionalism.** A mediator will inform the divorcing couple of all financial and child-custody issues and possible outcomes. These must be reviewed openly and provided for in the agreement. The mediator will also help the couple overcome impasses in their negotiations without needlessly pressuring either party.

Divorce lawyers, meanwhile, tend to overlook issues they believe may be detrimental to their own client.

• **Fairness.** The world of divorce is not different from the world of marriage—not everything is "fair." But two people who have worked to reach an agreement that both parties can live with feel far more satisfied with its fairness than a couple told by a judge how to conduct their affairs.

• **Closure.** *Divorce attorneys have a saying:* "Divorce never ends." That's because a drawn-out, acrimonious divorce can create painful repercussions far into the future—and take unresolved issues into subsequent marriages.

Mediators can help allow divorcing spouses to put the past behind them. A mediated divorce offers people a better chance to start anew.

How to find a mediator: Contact the Association for Conflict Resolution at 703-234-4141, 12100 Sunset Hills Rd., Reston, VA 20190, *www.acrnet.org*. You can also find a referral to mediators on the Web site, *www.mediate.com*. Or check your local *Yellow Pages* under "Mediation Services."

About half of all divorce mediators are therapists with expertise in matrimonial law and child custody. This is important only insofar as it applies to your particular needs.

Examples: If you have a complicated estate to distribute, you may prefer an attorney. If your primary struggle is over the kids, you may prefer a child-custody expert.

Note for couples beginning or in the midst of divorce proceedings: Couples may consult a mediator at any time during the divorce process, even if one or both spouses has already retained an attorney. But a mediated divorce is likely to be more complicated and time-consuming if lawyers are involved.

Single Parenting

Girls raised by their mothers without a father are stronger and more independent than those who are brought up in two-parent households. *Key:* Most children act the way their parents expect them to act. If a mother wants her daughter to be strong and independent, the daughter will develop these traits. *Insight:* Fathers often encourage their daughters to exhibit so-called feminine behavior. Daughters learn to act that way to please fathers rather than to emulate feminine mothers. *Role in society of a woman raised by a mother:* She is at no greater disadvantage in her relationships with men as any other woman.

Single parenting produces boys who are just as masculine and girls who are just as feminine as those in two-parent families. *Scholastic levels:* In the long run, both sexes do well after initial difficulties when parents separate.

Kathryn Black, PhD, professor emeritus of psychology, Purdue University.

How to Be a Good Stepparent

Barbara C. Freedman, CSW, director of the Divorce and Remarriage Counseling Center, New York.

Both partners in a remarriage usually have unrealistic expectations about their roles in the new marriage. As parents they are not prepared for the problems they will have to face when they get their collective children together through various custody and visitation arrangements. The children, of course, are not prepared for difficulties either.

Some people sail through the transition period, but for most there are many fantasies that can cause trouble. *Examples…*

• **Children expect the new parent to replace a deceased parent** or to provide something their custodial parent doesn't.

• **A stepparent who has never had children anticipates becoming an ideal mother** or father with an instant family.

• **Parents who have failed with their own children think they have a second chance.** But they may not really understand what the failure was about in the first place, and they often end up making similar mistakes.

It is not easy to adapt to new roles in the stepfamily. *Here are some of the problems that can arise…*

• **Children vie for seniority.** A girl who has been the oldest in one family finds that she is now number two or three. *Result:* Rivalry, jealousy, hurt feelings. The role of the new stepfather becomes difficult, too. He is sought after by all the children, which causes conflict between his loyalty to his own children and the need to relate to the stepchild.

• **Blood ties versus nonblood ties.** It is always more difficult to love, or even to get along with, someone else's children. A parent tolerates more inconvenience and conflict from a natural child than from a stepchild and suffers from feelings of guilt and hostility.

• **Differences in parenting style.** Watching one's spouse cope with a child in a way that you do not approve of can exacerbate an already tender situation. *Example:* A man who had long-standing problems with his adolescent son married a woman he thought would take care of these problems. She didn't consider it her role to be the disciplinarian. As she watched her husband tolerate abuse from his son, she began to lose respect for him.

Marriage and parenting are skills that one learns from parents. You blunder along, imitating or rejecting their behavior. But most people never had any role models for stepparenting. *Useful guidelines…*

• **New rules.** Families have different rules of conduct. Some rules have to be negotiated between the parents. It is helpful to establish times for the family to get together to work on decisions in which the children can be included.

• **Love is not instant.** While it is important for members of the family to be considerate and to allow one another space for self-expression, the pressure to love a new family can cause guilt and hurt feelings. Someday you may learn to love stepchildren, and they may learn to love you—but not necessarily.

• **Respect old ties.** A new stepfamily has many complicated connections with relatives. A natural parent and child have a unique relationship that may never be duplicated by stepparent and stepchild. People should not feel that a new family has to do everything as a group. Allow children time to be alone with natural parents, grandparents or other relatives.

• **Coparenting.** The basis for any successful remarriage is for ex-spouses to be as considerate of the children as possible. Conflicts between parents should be dealt with by them. Children should not feel they are included in these problems.

• **Divided loyalties.** Even the best stepparent can feel hostility from a stepchild for reasons that have nothing to do with the stepparent. It may arise from the child's feeling that the natural parent won't approve if he/she likes the new stepparent.

•**Children can love more than two adults as parents.** It's an enriching experience for a child to have more than two parents, two sets of grandparents, etc. The natural family should understand that it may be better for the child to develop a close relationship with someone in the stepfamily. Both sides should stand back and let children choose whom they want to love.

•**The couple relationship is primary.** This is the core of the new family unit despite the fact that each partner comes in with strong loyalties to their family of origin. Children have to know that the new couple is an unshakable combination and cannot be broken up (which they often try to do in order to get their own parents back together again). Seeing that the partners love and respect each other is an important role model.

•**Discipline.** You cannot discipline even your natural children unless you have a good relationship. It may take a year or two before this happens with stepchildren. In the meantime, the natural parent should be the disciplinarian for natural children. The authority of an absent natural parent should be vested in the stepparent. This must be made clear to the children.

•**Ironing out discipline policy.** Parents should discuss priorities and compromises. If they can't work out their differences, they should look into getting professional help.

To keep things in proper perspective, observe before acting. Then step in and do what you can. But don't expect too much. The romantic ideal of the nuclear family was never true, despite some ideal moments. It is the same with a stepfamily. There will be some wonderful times, but you should be prepared for the pain as well.

Skillful Parenting Pays Off

John Gottman, PhD, professor emeritus of psychology at the University of Washington and cofounder of the Gottman Institute, both in Seattle. He is author of *The Heart of Parenting: Raising an Emotionally Intelligent Child* (Simon & Schuster).

Many parents think of their children's intelligence in terms of academic achievement. While grades are important, so is a child's emotional intelligence—the ability to understand feelings and express those feelings appropriately.

Your child's emotional intelligence is critical because his/her ability to navigate the world of emotions determines success in all relationships with family, classmates and teachers—and later in adult life.

After conducting two 10-year studies of more than 120 families, I've concluded that there are five significant steps that parents can use to coach children to be more emotionally intelligent…

•**Recognize your child's emotions.** Many parents are keen observers of their children's behavior, but they don't always detect the emotions that are behind the behavior.

Example: If a child is scribbling on the walls or grabbing toys from another child, it's natural to focus on curbing the misbehavior.

But look as closely at the *why* as the *what*. Why is the child upset? Why is he angry?

Even when no misbehavior is involved, it's important to notice low-intensity emotions—such as sadness when a toy breaks—before they escalate into problems.

Helpful: To become more attuned to a child's feelings, parents need to be more aware of their own emotions first.

Think about how you handle worry…sadness…anger…and fear.

Are you temperamentally intense—or more easygoing? As you think about, and become more aware of, your emotional reactions, you'll be better able to decode your child's feelings and behavior.

•**See your child's emotions as opportunities for intimacy and teaching.** View a child's negative emotions as a chance to bond and teach, and you can turn negative situations into positive interactions.

By viewing behavior differently, children's anger, sadness and fear become more than just a reflection on you and your parenting style.

Helpful: When children are upset, comfort them and listen...and talk about how they feel rather than immediately moving to discipline them. This type of reaction lets children know they are understood, loved and valued.

Like coaching an athletic skill, our concern gives children a chance to practice how to express emotions and solve problems each time an occasion arises.

•**Listen carefully.** Listening means more than passively collecting information through your ears. It means tuning in to the child's current emotions by paying attention to his body language and facial expressions as well as to his words.

Then you're ready to see the situation from his perspective, and you can reflect his emotions back to him in soothing, noncritical words.

Example: At first, your responses may be a brief "Ummm,"..."Okay"...or "I see." But as you draw out your children, you can better assess their emotional situations.

You can also acknowledge their feelings by giving those feelings their proper names—"Sounds like you're anxious about..." or "You seem to be a little timid. Why?"

This part of emotional coaching shows your children that it is acceptable to feel the way they do...that you're interested enough to listen patiently...and that you believe they are able to cope.

By listening carefully, you also have refrained from jumping in with a ready-made solution. You haven't minimized or contradicted your children's genuine feelings by saying, "Don't feel bad. It will be all right if you..."

Instead, you have given your children a chance to express their emotions and, in the process, search for their own solutions to the problems at hand.

•**Help your children find words to name their emotions.** Words have power. When you help your children label their feelings, you give them some control of those feelings.

Naming emotions helps a child transform a scary or vague feeling into something real that can be defined and is normal.

Example: To a young child, jealousy may be an indistinct, unpleasant feeling. The child knows he doesn't like the fact that other children are being called on in school. But he hasn't yet reached the developmental milestone of abstract thinking, so he cannot identify his uncomfortable feeling.

If we use the term *jealousy* to name it, he learns that the amorphous feeling he has whenever other children are given special attention in class is acceptable. The feeling has a name. Other people know about it, and it's fine to feel that way.

Simply naming emotions will have a calming effect on children when they're upset.

By knowing and using the names of their feelings, they can learn to soothe themselves. Kids who learn this early in life are more likely to concentrate better, achieve more in school, enjoy good health and have better relationships with their peers.

Remember that children, like adults, experience mixed emotions. Children, however, don't know that unless we teach them.

Example: A child who is about to go off to camp may feel both proud of his independence and fearful that he'll be homesick. Parents can guide him by exploring his range of emotions and reassuring him that it's normal to feel two or more emotions at the same time.

•**Set limits on behavior** as you explore strategies to solve problems. If the emotion-of-the-moment is anger and the behavior is bopping a sibling on the head with a ball, you need to let the angry child know that hitting is absolutely unacceptable but feeling angry is acceptable.

Strategy: You might say, "Hitting isn't allowed," as you take the child away from the sibling. "I see you're pretty angry at Johnny, but you cannot hit people. Can you tell me why you're so mad at him? Maybe you would like to draw an angry picture to show me how you feel?"

Help your child try to find his own method of expressing emotions in acceptable ways.

Strict vs. Lenient Parenting

In a follow-up look at a group of adults whose mothers had been interviewed on parenting practices when the children were five years old, two patterns emerged.

The children who had been subjected to the strictest feeding schedules and toilet training had the highest need to achieve as adults.

The youngsters whose mothers were most permissive about sex and aggression (allowing masturbation and fighting with siblings, for example) showed the highest need for power as adults.

Practices the researchers expected to relate to adult characteristics did not show clear correlation in the study. How warm the mother was with the infant or how long the child was breast-fed, long assumed to be important to a child's well-being, did not match up directly with specific adult traits.

Study by psychologist David McClelland, Harvard University, reported in *Journal of Personality and Social Psychology*.

Encourage Expressiveness In Children

Fear of public speaking begins early. Parents may unwittingly make children feel foolish when they speak.

Helpful: Ask for children's opinions even when they are very young. Let them express negative as well as positive opinions. Avoid correcting or enlarging on everything they say. Encourage discussions at dinner. Tape-record children, and offer suggestions as they mature.

Clarissa Whitney, speech instructor, Santa Ana College, CA, quoted in *The Toastmaster*.

Temper Tantrums

A child's temper tantrum is best handled by simply walking away. This usually stops the display, as the child grows bored without the attention. Realize that tantrums are part of the process by which toddlers declare their individuality. Tantrums usually occur when the child is tired. Don't rush to the child and try to soothe him/her. This may make you feel better in front of onlookers, but it doesn't help. Don't automatically accept blame for the problem. Don't berate the youngster.

Best: Let the storm pass. Allow the child to have a nap, and don't mention the incident later.

Dennis Allendorf, MD, pediatrician, Columbia University Medical Center, and assistant clinical professor, NewYork-Presbyterian Hospital, both in New York City.

When a Child Needs a Therapist

Pearl-Ellen Gordon, PhD, child psychologist, New York City.

Children don't come to parents and say they need a therapist. They don't perceive the focus of the problem as themselves. They'll blame it on parents or school. Treatment revolves around helping children to see how they contribute to their problems.

Most children begin therapy because a teacher or school psychologist suggests it to a parent. Parents often do not recognize deviant behavior until the child goes to school. But many problems can be corrected if they are caught early.

Major tip-off: A child is arrested in development and is not doing what one would expect of a child in his/her age group.

Signs of poor emotional development…

• **A four-year-old in nursery school** cries and misses his/her mother.

• **An eight-year-old with no friends** comes home after school and watches television.

11

•**Rigid rituals.** The child's bedroom has to be a certain way. Particular foods must be served on certain nights.

•**Major sleep disturbances.** Frequent nightmares, waking in the middle of the night.

•**Lack of learning progress.** The child is not performing at grade level in school.

•**Psychosomatic illnesses.** Whatever the root cause, ailments are exacerbated by stress (ulcerative colitis, asthma, etc.).

When in doubt, ask the school psychologist or pediatrician to recommend a therapist. Don't bring the child in for the first visit. Request a consultation. In some cases there may not be anything wrong with the child. The parents may be the ones who need help.

Parents should use psychologists and psychiatrists more freely to help assess problems with children. *One answer:* More parenting centers where parents can go to ask questions and get guidelines about developmental progress.

Early Signs of Adolescent Drug Addiction

Boys who were both shy and aggressive in first grade are most likely to become abusers of drugs, alcohol and tobacco later in life, a study shows. These children were usually loners who did not participate in classroom activities and were hostile to their classmates and to school regulations. When these boys became adolescents, 45% smoked marijuana, 60% were heavy cigarette smokers, 18% drank hard liquor and 60% drank beer or wine. *Next most likely:* Boys who were aggressive without also being shy. *The least likely:* Those who were merely shy had the lowest percentages. Only 10% smoked marijuana as adolescents, 5% were heavy cigarette smokers, 20% drank wine or beer and none tried hard liquor.

A study of 1,200 youngsters by Sheppard G. Kellam, MD, senior research scientist and director of the Center for Integrating Education and Prevention Research in Schools at the American Institutes for Research, Washington, DC.

Great Gifts for Kids—Online

With a little quick searching, it's easy to find fun stuff on the Internet for all the kids in your life. *For example...*

Custom jigsaw puzzles: Puzzles are made from your favorite photos...can have pieces in animal shapes or other unusual forms. *http://jigsawpuzzle.com.*

Kids' products: Independent reviews of award-winning, age-appropriate books, videos, software, toys, etc. Includes toll-free numbers for ordering. *www.toyportfolio.com.*

Better Family-ing

When parents disagree *politely,* adolescents and young adults benefit mentally as well as emotionally. Effective communication among parents and offspring as well as between husbands and wives without the offspring present was associated with young adult adjustment. When parents criticize each other harshly, children are more likely to develop social and psychological problems such as anxiety, nervousness and substance abuse.

Clifford Notarius, PhD, professor of psychology, Catholic University, Washington, DC, and author of a three-year study of 54 families.

Better work at home—with a child around. Near your work area, set up your child's workplace. Include a craft desk with toilet-paper rolls, stickers, crayons, paper, glue, tape and similar items. *Schedule:* Set a timer for work time. While the timer runs, focus on work and have your child do the same. When the timer goes off, reset it for play time—and focus totally on your child. When the timer goes off again, return to work and reset it for the next play break. Decide how long to set the timer based on your child's age.

Teach kids to use the phone in case of emergencies. Children should learn their phone numbers—including the area code—as soon as they become verbal. They should know it is all right to dial 0 or 911 in an emergency, even before calling home. Teach them how to dial from various phones—home, cell, pay, hotel and business. Tell them to dial 911 and leave the phone off the hook if they are in danger—since emergency operators can trace the call rapidly.

Jan Wagner, founder, SAFE-T-CHILD, Austin, TX, and coauthor of *Raising Kids in an Unsafe World* (Avon Books).

More fun reading with young kids. Just talk about the pictures in a book. Skip over plots and the books' real text if children are not ready for them.

You don't have to read the whole book. Let your child's interest level guide you.

Read things you enjoy yourself. If you are not having fun, neither will your child.

Try adding movement or touching. *Example:* Bounce your child on your knee when the book says a pony trots.

Keep favorite books with you in a diaper bag, purse or glove compartment—to read when waiting at a restaurant or a doctor's office.

Nancy Hall, former contributing editor, *Parents,* 375 Lexington Ave., New York City 10017.

The Internet and Your Child

To block Internet sites that you do not want children to see, make sure they have plenty of good ones to visit. Try sites recommended by the American Library Association, *www.ala.org,* and Yahoo! Kids, *http://kids.yahoo.com.* Preview sites without your children. Bookmark favorites.

Filtering options: Some Internet services, such as America Online, offer optional control systems. Or try Cyber Patrol, *www.cyberpatrol.com,* or Net Nanny, *www.netnanny.com.* But remember that filters block some sites that are fine for most kids, such as Barenaked Ladies, a musical group popular with preteens.

John Edwards, high-tech consultant, Gilbert, Arizona.

Stay in Touch with Your Children When You Travel

The late Lee Salk, PhD, former clinical professor of psychology in psychiatry, New York Weill Cornell Medical Center.

The same principles of child rearing apply to parents who travel on business as to those who do not. These elements contribute to a child's emotional health and give him/her the skills to cope with life's problems later on.

FUNDAMENTALS

•**Options.** Children need to feel that they have choices. If other people make all their decisions for them, children lose their motivation, become depressed or angry and feel helpless. Being offered appropriate choices —which book to read at bedtime, for instance—gives children more motivation to learn. It helps them to make responsible decisions later on and to be less vulnerable to peer pressure.

•**Acceptance.** All children need to feel that they are accepted regardless of their strengths or weaknesses. Parents who are high achievers frequently put too much pressure on children. Rather than demand perfection, it is far more important for a parent to make sure a child feels successful at a realistic level.

•**Approval.** Children need someone to say, "That was a nice job." They also need to be aware of disapproval. Communicate when you are unhappy about something, too. Being a responsive parent doesn't mean you mustn't say no. Disapproval is a response, too.

If you're a responsive parent and feel comfortable giving your children choices, you have laid the groundwork for being able to meet your obligations even while you travel. Not being there to respond can be detrimental to your child, but parents can respond from wherever they are.

Here are some of the ways to stay in touch with your children…

• **Minimize time away.** Even if you travel a great deal, make it a rule not to be away from home for more than one week at a time.

• **Call children twice a day.** When you are away, bracket the day with one telephone call in the morning and another at night. Your presence is there even if you're not.

• **Plan children's time during your absence.** Before going on a business trip, try to set up the options your children will have while you're gone—a guest for dinner, an overnight visit at a friend's house. This allows you to participate in their lives even though you're not there. While you're away, you're not supervising or controlling but simply looking in to see what's going on.

• **Gifts should be special.** Parents shouldn't be expected to bring back gifts. If you find something special, then it's a surprise that says, "I was thinking of you." But bringing gifts every time you make a trip becomes a ritual. Kids who grow to expect a gift because they have always received a gift can become ambivalent about their parents' traveling. *The unfortunate lesson:* Materialistic values are more important than human values.

• **Take children along.** When possible, take your children with you. Missing a day or two of school is well worth it for the benefits of family closeness and the educational experience of travel. For longer trips, arrangements can be made with the school to bring lessons along and to do special projects. (In fact, the trip itself may provide the basis for a personalized school report.)

• **Communicate your feelings about separation.** Let your children know how much you miss them and that staying in hotels is a lonely business. When you telephone, say to your children, "I wish I were home with you."

• **When you return, let the children know how happy you are to be home.** It's nice if they can look forward to something special, like dinner out, to celebrate.

How to Talk With Your Child About Sex

The late Mary Steichen Calderone, MD, former medical director of the Planned Parenthood Federation of America and cofounder and president of SIECUS (Sex Information and Education Council of the US).

Parents who want to give their children mastery of the facts about sexuality have to start early in the child's life. That's when you should also begin to build the attitudes your children will need to enjoy themselves as sexual beings and respect the sexuality of others.

A child is born sexual, just as he or she is born with the capacity to walk and talk. Parents joyfully help children to develop their ability to walk and talk but rarely treat sexual pleasure the same way. Once you understand and accept your children's sexuality as normal and beautiful—the same as their other human endowments—you will be free to help them in their sexual socialization.

The process of socialization starts in infancy. You socialize your children in other natural functions such as eating. You praise them for using a spoon instead of plunging their hands into the cereal bowl and for other appropriate eating behavior.

A child also needs the guidance and support of parents in developing appropriate sexual behavior that fits in with the parents' own cultural norm and value system. *The beginning…*

• **Establish a sense of intimacy and trust** with a newborn by touching and holding. The cuddling, kissing and hugging should continue—do not stop when the child reaches three, when some parents feel awkward with physical demonstrations of affection, especially with boys.

• **When you start the game of naming parts of the body, include the sexual organs.** Avoidance of the area between the waist and the knees causes confusion and lays the groundwork for problems in adult life.

• **Don't interfere with a child's natural discovery and enjoyment of self-pleasuring.** Genital play is normal. At six or eight months, a child learns to put his/her hand where it feels good. Don't slap on a diaper, pull the hand away or look upset or disapproving. Leave the child alone. As the child gets older, teach what you consider to be appropriate behavior. You don't want your child masturbating in the supermarket or living room even at 15 to 18 months, so you pick up the child and, smiling, carry him/her to the bedroom. Explain that the place to pleasure yourself is in your own room with the door closed—that sex is good but should be private.

• **Parents need privacy, too.** *Tell children:* "When our door is closed, you don't come in without knocking and being invited. When we see your door closed, we'll do the same for you. Everyone likes privacy during sex games." This is when you can introduce the idea that sex games are something people who love and respect each other can play together.

• **Sex play between children is normal.** If parents banish the play, it will only drive the child underground. It's better to keep the lines of communication open and reinforce socially appropriate sexual play. *Inappropriate:* Sex play with someone older. Child molestation is more commonly practiced by someone who is in the family or known to a child than by a stranger. *The message:* You don't have to let anyone touch your body against your will. You are in charge, and you can say *no.*

Few parents are aware of how much sex education is transmitted before nursery school by attitudes and body language—how parents react to scenes on TV, the tone of voice or facial expression in sexual conversations or situations, significant silences.

Children delight in affection openly expressed between their parents. Withholding such demonstrations can indicate sexual hang-ups.

Don't avoid opportunities to discuss sex or to answer questions. Always speak only the truth. You may wish to withhold some of the details until later. Explain appropriate behavior outside the home. "In our family, we are open with each other about sex. But most other families don't talk about it the way we do. So we keep what we do private. It's a good thing to respect what other people believe."

A child who doesn't ask questions by the age of four or five has gotten the idea that the parent is either uncomfortable about sex or that sex is not an open topic. Or perhaps the child knows that he/she is not being given straight answers. Parents should be the ones to give children sexual information. Initiate a discussion. *One idea:* Tell your child about your own questions when you were the same age. If there is no response, try again another day to prove you're available.

Choose a time when you (or both parents) are alone with the child and have plenty of time. Be encouraging about behavior that is appropriate or shows maturation. Give recognition to a good line of thought. Respond positively even if you are criticized.

COMMON MISTAKES

The most damaging mistake is to associate sexual parts of the body with dirt, ugliness or sin. Guilt and shame transmitted about such a wonderful part of our human birthright will never be erased.

Parents should never lie, although they may find it necessary to tailor the truth to the level of the child. *Example:* To a three-year-old who asks, "Do you have to be married to have a baby?" the correct answer is, "No, you don't, but…" Then you go into your own value system about why marriage is important—on a level that a three-year-old can understand.

Talking with children about sex should be a shared responsibility. A harmonious front is important. Both parents should be clear on attitudes toward standards and rules and on what they agree and disagree on. If there are differences of opinion, call them that. Undermining the other parent shakes the child's confidence in the parent who's doing the undermining. Children trust parents who are for each other.

15

If you have laid the groundwork between birth and six or seven, you can take advantage of the major learning years until 12. Before puberty is when to pour in reliable information about sexually transmittable diseases, reproduction, etc. Keep the lines of communication open. Give opinions when they're asked for. Avoid judgments—they tend to close off discussions. Express your own values frankly and give sound reasons. Young people will respect them even if they don't share them.

How to Explain Death To a Child

Explaining death to a child of three or four years of age is best done with simple, direct sentences. *Example:* Explain that death is when a person is broken and no one can fix him/her—not a doctor, nurse or anyone. Young children know that badly broken toys cannot be repaired, so they can relate to this. Save more complex explanations for when the child is older.

Salk Letter

Finding the Right Books For Your Children

Teach children how to find books at their reading level. *Technique:* Tell the child to open the book near the middle and read from the top of any full page. If there are five words the child doesn't know before getting to the end of the page, the book is too hard.

Is Your Child Gifted? by Eliza Graue and David Graue (Oak Tree Publications).

Choosing a New Pet... Wisely

Susan Chernak McElroy, located in Jackson, WY, who has worked as a veterinarian's assistant, Humane Society educator, dog trainer, wildlife rehabilitator and zookeeper. She is author of *All My Relations: Living with Animals as Teachers and Healers* (New World Library).

Pick a pet with the same care you would use if adopting a child or getting married. Are you committed to taking care of it in sickness and in health?

FISH AND OTHER

Aquariums are mesmerizing. You can stare at the antics of fish all day.

Or you can put frogs or newts in an aquatic, aquarium-like setting.

Gophers are big enough to sit on your lap and play with you.

White rats are easy to care for—and deserve to be more popular. For affectionate companionship, they can't be beat. Rats know and adore their owners, answer to their own names and love to snuggle.

DOGS AND CATS

Find the best cats and dogs at your local animal shelter. Mixed-breed animals are usually far hardier and less costly than purebreds. Giving an animal a new lease on life provides a heartfelt sense of joy. *Factors to consider...*

•**Cats.** Although they love their independence, many cats will curl up near or on you. When you're sick, cats keep you company day and night. Unlike dogs, they don't have to be brushed, washed or walked.

•**Dogs.** A new puppy is fun, but it is usually high-strung and untrained. Older animals are mature and calm, often with good house manners. Which would suit you better?

Also consider size. For a pooch that can cuddle with you on the sofa or in bed, go small. Also, smaller dogs tend to live longer. If you want a dog to deter strangers, go big. The bigger the animal, though, the bigger the grocery bill.

BIRDS

Caged birds are great, especially in apartments and in nursing homes that ban dogs and cats.

Pound for pound, parakeets offer more features than other pets. They have a lovely song, can learn tricks and their names and live eight to 12 years. You can have their wings clipped and open the cage door. In a very short time you'll find them sitting on the edge of your plate and sharing your salad.

Parrots are extremely sociable and smart—some have the mental abilities of a five-year-old child.

When you've decided you want a parrot, find one that wasn't imported illegally. Find a veterinarian who practices avian medicine, and ask him/her what types of parrots to consider and for reputable sources.

LOOKING TO THE FUTURE

Older singles often write to me asking if they dare get a pet that would outlive them. I say yes, but do some advance planning. *Options…*

• **Find a family member to take the pet.** Shop together for an animal that pleases both of you.

• **Identify a neighbor or extended family member** who would assume responsibility.

• **Adopt an older pet from a humane society.** Grow old together.

The right way to give: Never give a pet you picked out as a present. *Acceptable:* A gift certificate to a pet shop with a note saying, "I want you to have an animal in your life. You choose."

Sex Education and Promiscuity

Sex education in school does not lead to promiscuity among teenagers. And young women who have had sex education are less likely to become pregnant than those who have not. These are the findings of surveys of teenagers. *Overwhelming conclusion:* There is no connection between sex education and sexual activity.

Family Planning Perspectives.

Family Time

Family mealtimes help asthmatic children by reducing their anxiety—so their lung function improves. Children with asthma often have separation anxiety—they worry about being away from their parents in case of a breathing emergency. Positive interaction at family meals reduces asthmatic children's worries and can help them breathe more easily.

Barbara H. Fiese, PhD, professor of human development and family studies, University of Illinois, Chicago, director of the university's Family Resiliency Center and leader of a study published in *Journal of Child Psychology and Psychiatry.*

When You Are Invading Your Child's Privacy

Howard M. Halpern, PhD, author of *Cutting Loose: An Adult's Guide to Coming to Terms with Your Parents* (Touchstone).

How much should parents know about their children's lives? The answer really depends more on how much the children are on their own than on age. Their lives become more and more their own business as they move away from parental supervision. Having an increasingly greater private life and knowing that you don't have to tell your parents everything is an essential part of growing up.

During the years when children are under your roof, the key to keeping track is dialogue. If communications are good, then you've developed a relationship in which children will want to share information with you that you should be aware of. If the relationship is sound and there are matters they don't want to share, they may have a good reason, and you should respect their privacy.

How to elicit information: When you are concerned about a serious issue, questions can work. *Better:* It's more of an invitation to open up if parents talk more about their feelings on what's going on in their own lives—being worried about this or embarrassed about that—or about feelings concerning something the child is experiencing. This helps create an atmosphere in which the child can talk about his/her feelings, too. *Particularly inviting:* A nonjudgmental parent.

Setting the stage: When you have something difficult to discuss with your children, do it in the car. No one can get up and walk out. You don't have to look at each other if that is a problem. Pick a trip that will last at least half an hour. Try not to ask questions.

Sometimes it is enough to give your opinion on a subject even if you elicit no information. *Example:* A divorced father with custody of his 16-year-old daughter had a conversation about her relationship with a boyfriend… "You and David are getting very close, and I think that's fine. I don't know how active a sex life you're having, but I hope you will delay a full sex life. I think you're too young for that. But whether in six weeks or six years you do go all the way, the one experience I don't want you to have is getting pregnant. I want you to feel free to come to me to ask for the name of a doctor."

Her response: "We're not doing anything like that now." A month or two later, she said she was having problems with menstrual bleeding and asked for the name of a gynecologist. The father had expressed what he wanted to say and had opened the door. The child didn't invite him in, but she certainly received the message.

How serious is the issue? Whether invasion of privacy is justified depends on the stakes. It is indefensible for parents to read a child's diary simply because they're curious about his/her sex life. If the problem is something that would be damaging to a child living under your roof, even if the child is 18, 19 or 20, you should intervene. *Example:* A parent who suspects that a child is getting involved

with drugs should search the child's room thoroughly.

Less serious problems: If the communication is good, the child might tell you about them. But a child who is on drugs may have a change in personality, and this will probably adversely affect a previously healthy relationship.

When and how you intervene depends on the severity of the issue and how it will affect a child's life. It also depends on what you can effectively do. *Examples…*

- **Movies.** Some parents might be concerned about sexuality or violence in films. They wouldn't want a 12- or 14-year-old to see a frightening or perverted horror film. They might, though, be more lenient about sex that isn't X-rated. *For this age group:* Strongly advise against an unsuitable film. Refuse to pay for it. If necessary, prohibit seeing it.

- **Friends.** If you're going to press a negative opinion, have a good reason. *Check yourself:* Do I object because this is not my preference for a friend? Do I think no one's good enough for my child? Am I afraid of competition? If the association is dangerous, you can refuse to allow the friend into your house, but it is impossible to police whom your child sees outside the house.

How much can a parent control a child? You can exercise more control of what goes on in the house than of what takes place outside. If you don't know that your child is getting drunk at parties, there's not much you can do. If your 15-year-old comes home drunk, you can say, "You're grounded. This has got to stop." If you pass a prohibition ("You're not to get high anyplace at any time"), obviously you'll have no way of enforcing it.

In general, keep the lines of communication open by expressing your own feelings and values. It may not always yield information, but at least it creates a receptive climate for exploring important issues.

School Sports Cautions

Pushing young athletes can result in "overuse" injuries such as stress fractures, tendonitis of the shoulder, bursitis of the hip and tennis elbow. These injuries in children were unheard of before the advent of organized sports programs after World War II. Even now, doctors rarely see these problems in youngsters who play sports among themselves without special coaching. (Children do not push themselves too hard.)

Most frequent cause of injury: Inappropriate or excessive training. Children are particularly susceptible to injury when they are tired or in pain.

Remedy: Make sure the coaches or trainers who work with your children are sensitive to this issue and that they have a proper perspective on what a sports program is really about.

Lyle Micheli, MD, director of sports medicine, Children's Hospital Medical Center, Boston, quoted in *The Ladies' Home Journal.*

Aspirin Can Be Dangerous

Aspirin given to children who have chicken pox or flu increases the risk of Reye's syndrome, a mysterious illness that sometimes follows viral ailments. *Symptoms:* Vomiting, fever leading to convulsions, coma and even death in about one-quarter of the cases.

US Department of Health and Human Services and the Centers for Disease Control and Prevention.

If Your Child Is Hospitalized

Parents of hospitalized children are now usually permitted (and often encouraged) to stay, even overnight, with the child in the hospital. This is a sharp departure from previous practice, when parents could visit only during visiting hours. *Why the change:* Parents provide continuity between the home and hospital. It is important that acutely ill children, especially the very young, don't see the hospital as a place of abandonment.

Why You Shouldn't Feed Honey to a Baby

Hold the honey for babies under one year of age. *Reason:* Even "pure" or "filtered" honey contains tiny amounts of bacteria. Although harmless to older children and adults, these can lead to infections and even botulism in an infant. *Symptoms:* Constipation, lethargy and feeding problems.

Vegetarian Times

Prevent Children's Ear Infections

Andrew Rubman, ND, founder and director, Southbury Clinic for Traditional Medicines, Southbury, Connecticut. *www.southburyclinic.com*

Most children's ear problems result from inflammation, not bacterial infection, so antibiotics will not help.

Danger: Use of antibiotics can increase the risk of infection by decreasing immune activity against common, normal oral bacteria.

Better for older children: Stir a teaspoon of salt into a half-cup of very warm water. Have the child sniff the vapor into his/her nostrils. Repeat until the ear pressure is relieved—often within a few minutes.

For young children: Place a very warm, wet cloth from the ear down along the side of the neck for five minutes, three times per day.

Consult your health-care provider if: Fluid is visible in the ear, or a greenish nasal discharge accompanies the earache, *or* the ear feels hot or appears very red, or the child has a fever.

To prevent ear problems: Stop giving children milk. Milk is the most allergy-provoking substance in the human diet and can aggravate ear problems. Cheese and yogurt are better tolerated, although still allergy-provoking.

Medicines Not to Give Your Child

Alcohol-based medicines can make children nauseous, confused or sluggish. If taken intensively for an extended period, they can even lead to heart and respiratory problems.

Trap: Alcohol is an unlabeled ingredient in many liquid antihistamines, cough syrups and anticolic medicines.

Advice: Ask your pediatrician to prescribe a nonalcohol-based alternative.

The late Jean Lockhart, MD, former director of the American Academy of Pediatrics, quoted in *Body & Soul.*

How to Deal with a Defiant Teenager

The late Clifford J. Sager, MD, psychiatrist and psychologist.

The problem of the teenager who defies parental authority is rooted in changes in the outside world as well as in the relationships in the home. In recent years we have seen a breakdown in discipline and a disruption of family authority. Family structures are not as strong as they were, nor are roles as well defined. Often there is conflict between parents. Increasingly, peer involvement has usurped family involvement.

In this society, with its breakdown of law and order, children are apt to see parents cheating on income taxes or using drugs. They know of illegal acts committed by people in the highest positions in the country. The attacks on September 11, 2001, and the proliferation of the nuclear bomb encourage children to ask, "What's the sense of it all?" They say to parents, "Who are you to tell us

what to do? Look at how you're living your life and how you messed up the world."

Even with these changes, adolescence is a period when children must separate from the family. At the same time, they still need guidance. Parents still need to know how to exercise the right proportions of flexibility and supervision. How parents set limits will influence their success in maintaining them. *Some suggestions…*

• **Parents should have their own standards,** but it's a good idea to check with other parents, and perhaps the school, about the prevailing views on curfews, use of alcohol and allowances. You can't always trust children to give you an accurate report of regulations observed in other families.

• **Both parents should agree on a course of action** and support each other. Kids will use every opportunity to take advantage of differences between parents.

• **Discuss the rules with children.** Explain your position calmly, and be prepared to back up your ideas. *Remember:* Things have changed a great deal since you were your child's age. Listen to your children carefully, particularly the oldest one, who usually has the toughest time because he/she is a trailblazer for those who follow.

• **Rules must be geared to the ability of the child to handle responsibility.** Development during adolescence is uneven not only physically but also emotionally. One child of 16 may be able to manage a flexible curfew, but another may not be mature enough.

If rules are being flouted, parents must first examine their own roles, expectations and motivations. Are they contributing to the problem? Are their demands arbitrary and unreasonable? *Examples…*

• **Bad language.** What kind of language do the parents use?

• **Rushing away from the dinner table**— not participating in family discussions. What is the dinner table ambiance? Is it one a child would want to get away from?

• **School grades.** Are parental expectations realistic?

Next, avoid hostile confrontation and open warfare. Create an atmosphere in which attitudes can be expressed and there is a positive feeling about learning, the intellectual spirit and the arts. The child should feel that home is a comfortable place and that his/her friends are welcome.

When stress periods come, and calls from the outside begin to run counter to family standards, the child has something to fall back on, a basis on which to make choices and parents to turn to.

Praise the child for what he is doing right before you tell him what he is doing wrong.

If a child is told he is bad, he begins to live up to that reputation and is more likely to get into trouble.

Defiant behavior is generally used to get attention or test limits.

Always deal with your child with understanding. Children react best to fairness. But it's all right to be angry if your anger is motivated by your concern for his safety. It is your job to protect him.

Don't impose restrictions you can't enforce.

Always give a warning.

Important: Don't deliver threats for punishment you're not able or willing to carry out.

Effective punishment requires the cooperation of both parents. What kind of punishment? Withholding part of the allowance or a planned trip or other treat is better than corporal punishment.

The punishment should fit the crime. Lesser matters (untidy rooms) may not call for the same approach as more urgent ones (drugs, alcohol).

Important: Do not discipline your child in front of other people, including siblings—and especially not in front of his friends.

Lethargy Can Be Caused by Allergies

Slothful teenagers may be allergic to common foods, not to work. In some youngsters, reactions to such staples as sugar, milk, corn, wheat or eggs can interfere directly with brain function, causing an inability to concentrate or think clearly. *Some signs beyond lethargy:* Nasal congestion, headaches, abdominal pains, pallor and dark circles under the eyes. *Test:* A special diet that eliminates certain foods, such as dairy, wheat or corn, from the child's meals. If dramatic improvement in health lasts more than 48 hours, an allergy seems likely. By reintroducing the youngster's regular foods one at a time, the source of the problem can be identified.

William G. Crook, MD, pediatrician, writing in *Medical Tribune.*

How to Get Better Test Scores

Dr. Harold T. Fox, former professor at Ball State University, Muncie, Indiana, and George A. Ball, business consultant.

There are several ways students can give their best effort when taking tests. *A few ideas...*

•**Keep current.** Prepare for tests as if they occurred without prior notice. Instead of memorizing the subject matter, paraphrase it and integrate it into your total store of knowledge. Most people do better on tests if they do not cram.

•**Be prepared.** Bring several pens and pencils to the test. Arrive a few minutes early. A little excitement may improve your performance, but do not let anxiety interfere with clear thinking. *Important:* Self-control.

•**Quickly scan the entire test at the start.** Ask the instructor immediately about any unclear phrasing. Be sure to follow all instructions exactly and to understand the criteria. *Example:* If a list is requested, do not compose an essay. Ask if wrong answers will be penalized. If not, guessing may improve your score slightly.

•**Mentally schedule your answers and set priorities.** For example, if the test lasts two hours, answer at the rate of 1% each minute. This pace gives you a little reserve time for the more difficult questions and for a complete review.

• **Study each question carefully and plan your answer.** Conserve time by avoiding repetitions. *Examples:* Label (do not write out) each question. Give as much detail as is requested but no more. Omit side issues, especially if they encroach on other questions. Do not write out the same answer to more than one question. Cross out wrong answers (instead of taking time to erase them). *Exception:* Computer-scored tests require complete erasures of mistakes.

• **Avoid dogmatic presentations.** In an essay on a controversial issue, give all sides before justifying your view. In an objective test, choices are usually wrong if they contain such words as *always* or *never*. A statement is false if any part of it is wrong.

• **Don't belabor the obvious.** For example, don't write that a company should set goals. *Instead:* Specify what goals are appropriate. Try to cover all bases, but do so briefly. Most teachers disdain padding.

• **Use clear expressions.** Define technical terms so that someone who is not familiar with them would understand. *Example:* Saying a computer's byte equals eight bits conveys nothing at all.

• **Allow time for review.**

• **Use the test as a springboard for further learning.** Don't blame the teacher or text if the grade you received is less than expected. Pinpoint and remedy the weakness.

• **Achievement test scores, not Scholastic Aptitude Test (SAT) ratings,** give the best indication of freshman-year college performance. Many top schools are now relying less on the SATs than on achievement tests in specific subjects and also recommendations from high schools.

Driver Education in School Is Not Enough

Driver-education programs in schools place teenagers behind the wheel for only 20 to 40 hours. Follow up by having one parent supervise the new driver for another 500 miles in light to medium traffic. Practice defensive maneuvers for 10 to 20 hours more in heavy traffic.

North American Professional Driver Education Association, Chicago.

Summer Jobs for Kids

Friends and relatives are the best source of help in finding summer jobs. Ask them for contacts or ideas.

Summer camps hire students for all sorts of jobs. *Usual requirements:* Camp experience, age 19 or older, and at least one year of college. Find out about job opportunities through the American Camp Association, 5000 State Road 67 North, Martinsville, IN 46151, on the Web at *www.acacamps.org*.

The National Park Service of the Department of the Interior provides summer jobs (and many winter jobs) annually. Applicants must be 18, provide a college transcript and be US citizens.

One useful approach: Advertise your services on local store and community-center bulletin boards. Two brothers kept busy painting houses (a very profitable enterprise) after putting up a note in a supermarket advertising their availability.

Many countries allow foreign students to work in temporary, seasonal jobs. The pay is usually low, but jobs can be interesting. *Example:* Working on the French grape harvest.

Here's How to Choose A Summer Camp

Laurie Edelman, former Executive Director, American Camp Association, New York section.

The best time to choose a camp for your child is the summer before. This enables you to visit a few prospective camps and see them in action. However, if this is not possible, begin your selection process in the fall for best results.

To learn about camps: Talk to friends, attend camp fairs, read advertisements and make use of the American Camp Association (ACA) guidance service, 800-428-2267. The guidance service will help you narrow your choices to three or four camps that are specifically appropriate to your child and your family's needs.

QUESTIONS TO ASK YOURSELF

• **Is my child ready for camp?** If he/she cries or behaves poorly when separated from you, or states firmly that he won't go, he's probably not ready for camp.

Helpful hint: Find out why the child doesn't want to go. Does he have false, preconceived ideas about going away to camp? If so, you may be able to change his mind, especially through a visit to camp during the summer.

• **What does your child want in a camp?** Consider his personality and take stock of his interests and the kinds of things he wants to learn and accomplish at camp. Then find a camp that will satisfy his interests, as well as what you want for him.

Example: If he likes to "hang out" and you want him to be active, seek a camp with structure and supervision but a variety of activities.

• **What is wanted in a camp?** Determine your child's needs, what he will tolerate and what he would be willing to give up.

Example: If your child won't swim in a lake, pick a camp with a pool. If your child enjoys a lake and wants to learn to water-ski or sail, look for a program that includes these activities.

• **How long will your child stay?** Pick the longest time period you can afford. *Reason:* A child adjusts better and learns and grows more the longer he is in the camp environment.

• **Should your child go to camp with friends or alone?** If you are considering sending your child with a friend, make sure both of them have the same interests—and that you and the other child's parents have the same criteria. Otherwise, one child will be unhappy. If your child wants to go alone, let him. One of the wonderful experiences camp provides is the chance to make new friends.

WHAT TO ASK PROSPECTIVE CAMPS' DIRECTORS

It's important to talk to camp directors before picking a camp to be sure it's a good match for your child. Eliminate a camp if any answers don't make sense or you are uncomfortable with the responses of the director.

• **What kinds of programs are available?** Parents who want their kids to have a fun, relaxing summer may prefer a recreational program. Those who want their children to learn something they can't during the winter may prefer an instructional program.

Example: On the tennis court at an instructional camp, campers are drilled on strokes and the emphasis is on proper form. At a recreational program, the emphasis is more on play than on drills.

• **What is a typical day like?** Have someone talk you through the program, including evening events. *Find out:* How much instruction is private and how much is in groups, which activities are required and which are elective, if your child can get as much as he likes of any one activity, who makes sure he gets to each activity and what types of trips might he take?

• **How many counselors and children are in each group?** How-do you recruit new counselors? What are your selection criteria? How old are the counselors?

Helping Children Gain Independence

The late Clifford J. Sager, MD, psychiatrist and psychologist.

Having the family all together for the holiday season may be cheerful, but togetherness can pall if it is overdone. And low starting salaries, high rents and a scarcity of apartments are keeping many young people at home and economically dependent on their parents well beyond graduation from college.

While some families welcome a return to lifestyles in which adult children, as well as grandparents, live together, the trend is potentially dangerous. Among other hazards, children fail to develop independence quickly enough when they live at home as adults. And the household and life-cycle rhythms are off.

Financial dependence on parents through the schooling period is directly proportionate to the slower maturing of young people today.

To help encourage independence, parents should...

•**Supplement their children's income at the outset** so that they can live in their own quarters. There is no substitute for the experience of having to manage a household.

•**Charge for room and board** if children must live at home. Some parents put this money aside as a stake for the child's marriage or business.

•**Put a time limit on living at home**—six months, a year or until the first salary raise. Whatever the arrangement, make it clear that independence is the goal.

Grown children's social lives often present problems to parents who matured in a different type of society. *But parents should not be afraid to set standards...*

•**If they are not comfortable when their children bring sex partners home,** they should say so. Making their feelings clear before a guest arrives avoids unpleasantness later.

•**Parents should not be afraid to ask grown children under their roof to help with chores** and with family obligations such as visiting relatives.

•**After children mature, some parents want to simplify their lives** by moving into a smaller house or apartment or closer to work. Do not be deterred by sentimental arguments the children pose. Independent parents foster independent children.

How to Improve Scores on Standardized Tests

Stanley H. Kaplan, founder of Kaplan Inc., 395 Hudson St., New York City 10014. *www.kaplan.com*

No matter how smart you are, no matter how well prepared, there are strategies you can use to improve your scores on any standardized test, including the SAT, GRE and MCAT.

WHAT TO DO

•**Get to know the test beforehand.** Every standardized test is different. *Important:* Read the test booklet provided by the testing firm to find out what subjects will be covered, the precise form questions will take and the directions. If you have to spend two minutes reading the directions when the test is in progress, you'll lose two minutes of valuable test-taking time.

•**Review the subjects that will be covered.** If the test you're planning to take has a mathematical section, bone up on math beforehand. Likewise with logical reasoning, science and so on. Start reviewing basic skills three or four months in advance.

•**Take practice tests.** Sample exams prepared and distributed by the testing organizations themselves are best. They will familiarize you with the material and give a fair indication of your actual exam score. If you are unhappy with your projected score, delay taking the exam until you have improved and are satisfied that you can do well.

•**Arrive an hour in advance.** If you're unfamiliar with the test site, make a trial run a few days beforehand.

•**Come prepared.** Bring your admission ticket, personal identification and six No. 2 pencils with dull points—they allow you to fill in the circles faster than sharp points and don't break as easily. If you're prone to headaches, bring an aspirin or your favorite analgesic.

• **Keep anxiety in check.** Cramming the night before the exam encourages anxiety. If you become anxious while you are taking the exam, breathe slowly and deeply. Get up and walk around during the break.

• **Use strategies.** Answer the short or easy questions first. Save the long reading passages for last.

If you have trouble with one question, put a mark by it in the test book and go on to the next question. Then go back if you have time.

In reading comprehension sections, some find it easier to scan the questions before reading the passage. This will clue you in on what to look for as you read.

If you finish the test early, go back over your answers.

• **Mark answers carefully.** Make sure the circle you're marking corresponds to the question you intend to answer. Many students mark column after column of circles only to discover they're ahead or behind where they should be.

Self-check: Every five questions, stop to make sure that the question and answer numbers correspond.

• **Know when—and when not—to guess.** A few tests penalize you for wrong answers (the SAT, for instance), others don't. Find out beforehand whether your test does.

On tests where there is no penalty for wrong answers, fill in every blank—no matter how unsure of the answer you are. On tests where there is a penalty, guess only if you can rule out at least one of the possible choices.

In some exams (the SAT for instance) questions at the beginning of each section are usually easier than those toward the end. As a result, if you arrive at a quick, easy answer on an early question, and that answer is listed among the multiple choices, chances are you have the right answer. But if you come up with a quick, easy answer on a question deep into the exam and that answer is among the multiple choices, watch out. There are no easy answers at the end of the test.

• **Don't let difficult questions rattle you.** If one section seems harder or less clear than most of the others, it could be an experimental section being used to try out new questions and will not count toward your score. Just do your best.

• **Don't panic!** If you think you bombed the test, notify the testing organization immediately (use overnight mail). For most tests you have a few days following the exam to ask that your test not be scored. You can take it again without penalty, although your record will show that you canceled a previous test.

If your test is scored and your performance falls shy of what you had hoped for, you can always take the test again. Most schools look only at the higher score. *Exception:* Most law schools average your scores.

College Applications

Florence Janovic, writer and marketing consultant.

The pressures and anxieties of first finding the right colleges and then filling out all the forms make a child's senior year in high school a difficult time for the entire family. Parents can offer support and assistance without adding to the turmoil if they are discreet.

• **Learn from your friends.** People who have recently gone through the application process have practical, first-hand information that is valuable. Find out which books they found most helpful (for example, *Fiske Guide to Colleges 2011* by former *New York Times* education reporter Edward B. Fiske, or Peterson's *Four-Year Colleges 2011*) and provide them for your child. Don't worry about your friends' personal biases about particular schools. Just pass on factual information about the housing crunch for freshmen at an urban college or the attitudes toward women at a formerly all-male campus.

• **Encourage an early deadline for finishing applications.** Thanksgiving is a good target date. Then the child can concentrate on his or her schoolwork before the end of the semester and keep his grades up. First-term senior-year grades are important to the colleges that will be considering them.

• **Make copies of all the finished applications** and correspondence. Most colleges acknowledge the receipt of completed papers with a postcard so you will know if anything is missing. If too much time passes without such an acknowledgment, you can call and check. Having a copy on hand will save time and trauma.

• **Consider early-action applications** or at least one or two schools with rolling admissions to get early decisions. Neither admissions policy commits the student to that particular campus, but knowing before April 15 that at least one school wants him can alleviate the pressure.

• **Talk to the high-school guidance counselor.** Be sure your child is applying to schools where he has a better than average chance of being accepted. One or two long shots are reasonable, but young egos are badly damaged by a series of rejections. Make sure there is at least one or two "safety" schools on your list, preferably with rolling admissions.

• **Budget for campus visits to potential colleges.** If time and money are a consideration, save the visits for after the acceptances come in and real choices have to be made. Be sure your youngster sees the college while it is in session. Admissions offices will arrange for dormitory stays and opportunities for going to class if your child doesn't know anyone at the school.

• **Don't be arbitrary.** A youngster's first choice may not work out, or it may prove to be a mistake. Let your child know now that he can transfer from one college to another with no loss of face. In fact, some colleges are easier to get into as a transfer student than as a freshman.

How to Visit Colleges

High school seniors who are touring colleges should make sure that their visits pay off. *Here's how...*

• **Find out as much as you can about the colleges before you go.** Check out their Web sites and explore them thoroughly. You can also see if your high-school guidance office has information.

• **Contact the colleges to request a view book,** a freshman class profile and other descriptive material.

• **Look for what the college doesn't, as well as what it does, tell you.** The college literature is promotional material designed to "sell" the institution. In this period of declining enrollments, many colleges are as image-conscious as Madison Avenue.

• **Seniors.** Talk with graduates of your high school who are attending the colleges you're interested in, and call neighboring high schools for the names of graduates attending these colleges. After you have written to a college for materials, a local representative of the college may call—usually an alumnus. Many representatives remain close to their alma mater and can be very helpful. Applicants should watch out for the occasional alumnus whose main source of information is a romantic memory of his/hers own undergraduate years.

• **High school students.** If possible, visit colleges during the summer after your junior year. It will help you to cut down your list. The admissions director will have more time to talk then than he/she will in the fall or winter, and visitors will find out how they react to the physical environment.

The two or three colleges at the top of your list should be visited in the fall or winter, preferably on a weekday so that you can attend a few classes. The admissions office will arrange overnight stays in an undergraduate's room, as well as a complete tour of the campus with a student guide.

At the interview, applicants should be open and candid. Don't try to impress the interviewer with a long list of questions that you should already have answered for yourself ("Is this a coed school?"). Concentrate on crucial questions to which you have no way of knowing the answers…"Are freshmen classes much larger than classes for upperclassmen?" "What happens on weekends—do most students stay or leave?" "Is the library crowded?"

If you know the field in which you want to major, go to that department and talk with the professors. They can give you a sure sense of what will be expected.

Most important: Spend an hour or more sitting in the student union building or some other gathering place where you can talk to students and ask them what they like best about the school—and what they think is wrong with it. This way, you can find out about social mores as well as courses and professors.

Financial Aid Wisdom

Dianne Van Riper, former assistant inspector general in the Office of Inspector General at the US Department of Education, Washington, DC. 800-872-5327. www.ed.gov

---

Stretching the truth to maximize financial assistance is riskier than most parents or students realize.

The penalty includes paying back up to three times the amount of aid you received and fines as high as $10,000 per lie. Cheats also may be arrested and charged with a felony.

Here are the most common ways that parents and students get into trouble on financial aid applications…

Trap: Using a dishonest college consultant. College consultants may charge several hundred dollars to help parents negotiate the student aid application maze. While most consultants are honest, a sizable minority are willing to bend or break the rules for clients.

When you sign the financial aid application that a consultant has prepared, you are legally certifying that you have reviewed the information, and it is accurate.

When choosing a consultant: Beware of those who "guarantee" to win your child student aid. There are so many variables involved in deciding which students are—and are not—awarded aid that guarantees are impossible.

Read and review the application instructions with the consultant. They're surprisingly clear and easy to understand. If you don't understand some of the instructions, call the college financial aid officer.

Trap: Underreporting household income. By law, colleges are required to verify the incomes that are claimed by 30% of the students who applied for financial aid. They usually do this by requesting copies of the families' tax returns.

But now, the US Department of Education has the authority to check all applications by matching them against the original tax data you provided to the IRS.

Trap: Claiming your child isn't your dependent. An independent child's student aid is based on his/her income, which can be meager.

There are very explicit requirements for a student to be declared independent. Applicants can access these rules from college financial aid offices…or at the US Department of Education Web site, *www.ed.gov.*

There are also rules for orphan or ward-of-the-state status.

Trap: Claiming more dependents than you actually have. Many cheats say they have more children than they actually do, to increase the amount of aid they receive. This information, too, will soon be checked against actual tax returns.

Trap: Falsely claiming that the child lives with the lower-earning parent, if you and your spouse are divorced.

Trap: A married college student who claims to be single or divorced so that his spouse's income isn't figured into the student aid calculation.

Trap: Falsely claiming that there are more members of the household in postsecondary education than are actively enrolled.

Interviewing for College

An unfavorable interview may work against a prospective college applicant. *Alternative:* Group-information sessions. These are usually best for the student who does not have specific, detailed questions about the college. *Reminder:* The student should have a personal interview if one is "recommended" but not required. Group-information sessions should be considered only when the personal interview is optional.

The Truth About Study Abroad

Wendy Williamson, director of Study Abroad at Eastern Illinois University, Charleston. She is founder of AbroadScout.com, which features articles about study-abroad issues, and author of *Study Abroad 101* (Agapy). *www.abroadscout.com*

Study abroad is a great way to expand a college education—but it can have implications that students fail to consider. *Here's what parents need to know...*

• **How much a study-abroad program costs** depends on the policies of your child's college, not just the price of the program. Foreign colleges often cost less than American schools, but some American colleges insist that their students who study abroad pay full US tuition anyway. That might mean paying $30,000 to attend a foreign school that charges only $5,000. This full-tuition policy is most common at pricey private American colleges. Most public universities simply pass along the cost of the foreign program, plus some fees.

If your child's college insists on full tuition, ask what policy applies when students enroll in foreign schools during the summer. Your student might not be required to pay inflated rates for summer programs abroad, and he/she even might be able to earn enough credits during affordable foreign summer sessions to graduate a semester early, meaning that you won't have to pay for the last semester at the expensive US school.

• **Financial aid varies.** Federal financial aid usually can be used to pay study-abroad costs. However, state and private college loan and scholarship rules do vary.

There also are scholarships available to help with study-abroad costs.

Examples: Rotary Club Ambassadorial Scholarships (go to *www.rotary.org*, click "Students and Youth," then "Educational Programs," then "Ambassadorial Scholarships")...Council on International Educational Exchange scholarships (*www.ciee.org/study/scholarships*).

• **Credits your child earns overseas might not count toward his degree.** Each US college and university has its own policy on the transfer of foreign credits. Confirm with the US school that credits will be transferable. Otherwise an additional semester of education—and tuition—might be needed to graduate.

• **Not all study-abroad locations are safe.** Students continue to study abroad in Kenya and Mexico, even though the US Department of State has issued personal-safety travel warnings for those countries.

Check the State Department Consular Information Sheets (*www.travel.state.gov/travel*) and the Centers for Disease Control and Prevention's Travel Notices (*www.cdc.gov*, then click "Travelers' Health").

• **Your health insurance might not fully cover your child overseas.** If necessary, supplemental coverage is available from many insurers, including HTH Worldwide (888-243-2358, *www.hthtravelinsurance.com*)...CMI Insurance Worldwide (800-586-0753, *www.cmi-insurance.com*)... and Cultural Insurance Services International (800-303-8120, *www.culturalinsurance.com*).

How to Sell Yourself Off The College Wait List

Frank Leana, PhD, former educational director, Howard Greene & Associates, educational consulting firm, New York City.

Instead of simply sending back the card telling the school admissions office that you want to remain on the wait list, include a letter restating your interest in the school and how you plan to make use of the facilities.

Example: A student planning to study journalism might mention his/her work on his high school's award-winning newspaper.

If possible, guarantee that you will attend the school if you're chosen. Schools hate it when wait-listed students turn them down. *Also tell the college...*

• **If you've been accepted by any other equally prestigious schools.**

• **About any new accomplishments since your initial application,** such as exemplary senior-year grades or additional recommendations.

Helpful: A follow-up call, one to two weeks later, to show your continued interest in attending.

Bottom line: By separating yourself from the rest of the wait-list crowd, you improve your odds of being moved nearer to the front of the line.

Better College Aid Strategy

Certain unsecured debts, such as consumer loans, credit card balances and personal loans, do not count when colleges determine how much aid to award. By paying off credit card and other debts, you reduce your net assets and automatically become eligible for more aid.

Example: If you have $20,000 in a money market fund but owe $5,000 on credit cards, colleges will value your assets at $20,000—not $15,000.

Homeowners: When calculating your assets, colleges are increasingly allowing you to exclude some equity in your home. But at many schools, paying off your mortgage to reduce available funds will not get you more aid.

Kalman Chany, president, Campus Consultants, Inc., an organization that assists families in maximizing financial aid, 1202 Lexington Ave., New York City 10028. *www.campusconsultants.com*

Eight Essential Skills to Improve Your Relationships

Redford Williams, MD, director of the Behavioral Medicine Research Center at Duke University, and Virginia Williams, PhD, cofounders of Williams LifeSkills Inc. *www.williamslifeskills.com*

Strong, positive relationships with friends and family certainly make life more pleasant.

But study after study has shown that good relationships also keep us healthy. Unfortunately, today's fast-paced lifestyles work against good relationships.

To the rescue: After years of research, scientists have identified eight distinct skills that are necessary to create and maintain strong relationships...

DECIPHERING THOUGHTS

If you fail to understand what you're thinking and feeling, you are likely to behave in ways that hurt others. You're not likely to get what you want, either.

Essential: Learn to pay attention to your inner life. Carry a small notebook for a few days, and use it to keep a log of daily events—and your reactions to them. Jot down bodily sensations...your emotions...and any words that run through your mind.

EVALUATING NEGATIVE THOUGHTS

Too often, we respond automatically to annoyances by shouting, withdrawing, etc. *To learn more effective ways of responding, practice asking yourself four fundamental questions...*

• **Is this situation important?** In many instances, merely asking yourself this question enables you to "let go" of anger.

• **Are my thoughts and feelings appropriate?** You have a right to your reaction, but it may not be in your interest to act on it.

• **Can this situation be changed?** Life is filled with negative circumstances we're powerless to change. Of course, some circumstances do lie within our control. It's crucial to be able to distinguish one from the other.

• **Would taking action really be worthwhile?** Standing up to a nasty boss might make you feel better. But are you willing to risk losing your job?

ACHIEVING ACCEPTANCE

If the answer to any of the above questions is "no," look for ways to live with the status quo. *Three strategies are especially helpful...*

• **Reason with yourself.** If you're upset by the actions of another person, don't assume that you know why he behaved that way. Instead, come up with alternative theories that might explain his behavior.

• **Distract yourself.** Read a magazine article. Hum your favorite song. Rearrange the living room furniture.

• **Meditate.** Calm yourself by focusing on your breathing. Silently repeat a soothing sound such as "peace" as you do.

SOLVING PROBLEMS

If you answer "yes" to all four of the fundamental questions, it's time to take action. *Use this problem-solving flow chart...*

• **Define the problem.** Consider the facts as objectively as possible. Decide which aspects of the situation you'd like to change.

• **Brainstorm ways to react.** Think of three or four realistic alternatives.

• **Make a decision.** Consider the positive and negative consequences of each action. Then choose the one that's likely to have the biggest payoff.

If the action you try fails to produce the desired outcome, repeat the chart...and try again.

BEING ASSERTIVE

Strong relationships involve a balance of giving and getting. If someone with whom you have a relationship does something that bothers you, you must be willing to speak up. *Here's how to proceed...*

• **Describe the bothersome behavior.** Be objective, not judgmental. "The first thing you did when you came home was to criticize me for being messy."

• **Explain how you feel.** "Right now I'm feeling hurt, angry and upset."

• **State your request.** "When you come home, I'd like your first comment to be affectionate—not critical."

Another part of assertiveness is learning to say "no." While it's fine to add "I'm sorry" or "I know how important this is to you," avoid complicated excuses.

IMPROVING COMMUNICATION

Real listening is rare. Most of us *think* we're listening when we're really just waiting for the other person to finish talking.

Using these simple techniques, most people can dramatically transform their conversations—and their relationships...

• **Don't interrupt.** Say nothing until the other person has finished speaking. Most people who try this for just one day are amazed to discover just how often they interrupt others.

• **Look interested.** Use attentive body language. Uncross your arms, lean forward and make eye contact.

• **Reflect back what you heard.** Restate the points or emotions that the speaker just expressed.

• **Be willing to be changed by what you hear.** Be open-minded. Don't pass judgment until you know all the facts.

How you speak is as important as how you listen. Saying "I like," "I feel," etc., is less likely to cause offense than telling the way things "are" or what's "wrong" with the other person.

BEING EMPATHETIC

To hone your empathy skills, think of an annoying habit of someone you're close to. Imagine you are that person, and describe his position using "I statements."

EMPHASIZING THE POSITIVE

Being positive doesn't necessarily mean being Pollyanna-ish. Having a good outlook can save relationships.

University of Washington psychologist John Gottman, PhD, taped interactions between newlyweds.

His findings: Marriages with at least five positive interactions for every one negative contact were most likely to last.

In addition to strengthening your relationships, this skill can boost your happiness. The happiest people aren't those who feel the most *intense* joy or excitement...but those who have mostly positive feelings all day long.

Choosing a Nursing Home Early

SmartMoney

Choose a nursing home far in advance so you don't have to scramble at the last minute to find a good one when it is needed for a loved one.

What to do: Contact your state long-term-care ombudsman for help finding facilities in your area (*www.ltcombudsman.org*). Narrow your list by using the data at *www.medicare. gov/nhcompare*, which provides information about health inspections, staffing, fire safety and other quality measures in nursing homes. Come up with about six possible choices. Then visit each facility several times, allowing plenty of time during each visit to get a sense of how a typical day goes. Do not announce your visits in advance, and do not judge a facility by your first impression—multiple lengthy visits are the best way to find out how the staff interacts with patients.

How to Select A Nursing Home

Placing a relative in a nursing home is a heart-wrenching ordeal. To ease the way, know when a nursing home is the only answer. *Deciding factors:* A loss of control of body functions, a loss of memory or an inability to perform the basic activities of daily life such as shopping, cleaning and dressing. People do not age physically and emotionally at the same rate.

Never coerce a person into a nursing home. Instead, open the decision for discussion. When possible, have the person accompany you when you shop for the proper home.

The nursing homes with the best reputations, highest staff-to-patient ratios and longest waiting lists are nonprofit. That is, they are run by churches, fraternal orders and charities. *Hitch:* Only about 25% of all homes are nonprofit. The majority of nursing homes are for profit, or proprietary. *Other differences among homes...*

• **Health-related facilities emphasize personal,** not medical, care. These are generally nonprofit homes.

• **Skilled nursing facilities are for patients with serious mental and physical disabilities.** Most of these places are proprietary.

Nonprofit homes usually charge a flat, high monthly fee with no extras for added services. Proprietary homes ask a lower monthly fee with extra payments for services. Always be certain that you understand the rates and service charges.

Many proprietary homes don't take Medicaid patients. The amounts paid by the state and federal health plans aren't always enough to cover the costs. Patients who have no money should be placed in a nonprofit home.

To select a home, start by asking the patient's physician, relatives and friends who have gone through a similar experience for information. Also, get information from the state departments of health and social services.

Begin the search to find a nursing home long before it becomes necessary. *Caution:* Many emotional problems among the elderly occur during the waiting period because of the stress of being in limbo.

Since this is an emotional experience, take a close friend with you when you inspect nursing homes. The person will look for things that you might forget.

WHAT TO SEEK IN A HOME

• **Good location.** The right home is close enough for convenient visits. Avoid places in run-down or dangerous neighborhoods. *Best:* A residential area with gardens and benches.

• **Well-lit, cheery environment.** Also, doors to the room shouldn't have windows. This is a home, not a hospital.

• **The home's affiliations with hospitals**

and associations. Find out how many patients are on Medicaid. If the number exceeds 50%, the home is not likely to provide adequate care.

•**A professional staff.** There should be a full-time or regularly visiting doctor with specialized knowledge in geriatrics. The total number of registered nurses, licensed practical nurses and nurses' aides should be at least 40% of the number of beds.

•**The residents.** Nothing speaks better for a nursing home than active, vital patients. Observe the staff to see if they treat residents with respect. Talk to the residents and ask for their complaints. *Bad signs:* If more than 3% of the residents are indoors at one time. If patients are still in bed or in bedclothes at 11 am. If many residents are catheterized to avoid linen changing. Ask what happens when a patient is hospitalized. Is the nursing home bed still available to him/her afterward?

•**Handrails in hallways and bathrooms.**

•**Smoke alarms in public areas and each room.** Ask to see the latest fire inspection report and note the date.

•**The dining room should be clean, bright and inviting,** with no dirty trays around. Are special diets adhered to?

•**The residents' rooms should be comfortable and attractively furnished.** Be sure the room can be personalized with pictures, plants, knickknacks. Drawers should be lockable.

•**Happy patients are those who are plugged into the outside world.** Newspapers and large-print books should be readily available. The home should show movies, bring in entertainers and provide outside trips. *Other necessary activities:* Gardening, workshops, education courses, lecture series and discussion groups. Find out about religious services and provisions for voting.

•**Special services should include visits by a licensed physical therapist** and workable therapy equipment that the patients can use. *Visits by other specialists:* Speech therapists for stroke victims, audiologists, dentists, psychiatrists, optometrists and podiatrists.

WHAT TO WATCH OUT FOR

•**Patients who are sedated** in order to keep them quiet.

•**The home asks for a large sum of money up front.**

•**Doctors who hold gang visits** (they see 40 to 50 patients during each call).

•**You are denied visiting rights** to the kitchen, laundry and/or library.

•**The Patient's Bill of Rights** isn't displayed.

Home Care Know-How

Peter J. Strauss, Esq., senior counsel in the law firm Epstein Becker & Green, PC, 250 Park Ave., New York City 10177. He is a fellow of the National Academy of Elder Law Attorneys and coauthor of *The Elder Law Handbook—A Legal and Financial Survival Guide for Caregivers and Seniors* (Facts on File).

Only the very rich can afford not to be concerned about the likelihood that some day they will need home care or nursing home care.

But the rest of us do have to worry about becoming incapacitated. And most of us would prefer to be cared for at home. *Questions we all have...*

•**How much does home care cost?**

•**Will Medicare pay for some of it?**

•**What quality of care can one expect** from the government?

•**Do I need a Medigap policy?**

•**What about a long-term-care insurance policy?**

MEDICARE

Medicare generally covers a very limited portion of the cost of care provided in the home. Although home care typically follows a hospital stay, Medicare does not make hospitalization a prerequisite for coverage.

As long as the care is necessary for treatment of an illness or injury, Medicare coverage applies. This coverage, however, includes only the items defined as "home health care benefits." *These include...*

•**Medical social services.**

- **Nursing care** (part-time or intermittent).
- **Medical supplies/equipment.**
- **Physical therapy.**
- **Occupational therapy.**
- **Speech therapy.**
- **Home health aides** (part-time or intermittent), but only if a skilled service—such as therapy—is provided also.

The benefits *must* be prescribed by a doctor and provided by a home-care agency that has been certified by Medicare.

- **Medicare does not cover everything.** For instance, Medicare limits coverage for part-time or intermittent home care—fewer than five days a week on an infrequent basis—to 28 hours per week. If continuing care is needed —care for a period of up to 21 days—then coverage can be for up to seven days a week, but only for up to 56 hours a week.

If a home health aide and nursing services are needed, the amount billed must be kept under 28 hours a week to be considered intermittent.

- **Medicare does not cover the cost of long-term care** or personal assistance care. Both of these are considered custodial-type care rather than medical care. This kind of care applies to those with chronic conditions, such as Alzheimer's disease, Parkinson's disease, etc., who need assistance with daily living activities (eating, bathing, getting in and out of bed, going to the bathroom, etc.).

- **Medicare does not cover the cost of housekeeping.** This is often needed by a person with a chronic condition.

MEDIGAP COVERAGE

Supplemental Medicare insurance—Medigap insurance—picks up only the amounts of Medicare-covered expenses that Medicare does not pay for, such as copayments and deductibles.

Medigap *does not* cover the cost of long-term care, since Medicare doesn't provide this coverage.

MEDICAID

Medicaid is a state/federal partnership program intended to serve the nation's most needy and vulnerable populations. Income limits for Medicaid eligibility are set separately by each state and the federal government pays a share of each state's Medicaid costs.

Some home care services, such as personal care services that help with the basic activities of daily living (ADLs), may be provided by the Medicaid program through what are called "Home and Community Based Services (HCBS) Waivers" as an alternative to institutional care.

Every state has at least one HCBS waiver. There is great variation in the scope and nature of services provided under the many different waivers, with some offering as many as 30 different services and some as few as one or two.

States have a great deal of leeway in administering their programs. For instance, they must review any transfer of personal assets a person may have made for less-than-fair-market value to other parties if they are trying to get Medicaid to help pay for care in an institution. This so-called "look-back" at asset transfers is not mandatory for those seeking home care, but many states are considering instituting such reviews in light of extreme fiscal difficulties and the increasing costs of Medicaid programs.

LONG-TERM-CARE INSURANCE

A growing number of older people are buying private insurance policies—long-term-care insurance—to cover the cost of nursing care. The policy should cover both care in a nursing home *and* care in their *own* home.

You can also buy policies that cover only in-home care or only nursing home care, but this is usually not wise.

Caution: Make sure a policy labeled a "nursing home policy" also includes coverage for at-home care.

These policies are expensive: They get more expensive the older you are when you buy them. *Best:* Buy them by the time you are in your 60s. Make sure you take an inflation rider!

CONSIDERATIONS

- **What is the extent of insurance coverage?** Some policies pay for home care only a fraction of what they pay for nursing home care.

- **What is the "triggering event"** for payment of expenses under the policy? Some policies pay much more quickly than others. Find out what the lag time is in policies you're considering.

Bottom line: Make sure that the level of coverage and the event that triggers payment are clearly spelled out in the policy.

TAX INCENTIVES

The tax law now provides breaks that defray some custodial care costs. A person needing home care can take an itemized deduction for "qualified medical expenses" to the extent that total expenses exceed 10% (7.5% if you are 65 or older) of adjusted gross income (AGI). *Deductible medical expenses include...*

• **Out-of-pocket medical costs,** including out-of-pocket payments to home health aides.

• **Medicare copayments** and deductibles.

• **Long-term-care insurance premiums** up to a dollar limit (depending on age).

• **"Long-term-care services"**—up to any amount—provided to a person who is chronically ill. The meaning of "long-term-care services" is liberally interpreted to include rehabilitative services and personal care services. This is so even though personal care service probably would not qualify as a deductible medical expense were it not a long-term-care service.

Taxes: Some part of the benefits provided under a long-term-care policy may be taxable.

Senior Aid

Now more than ever, seniors have helpful resources they can rely on. *For example...*

• **Weatherization Assistance Program.** Available at no charge to seniors who meet specific guidelines. The grant goes to the state, which allocates dollars to nonprofit agencies for purchasing and installing energy-related repairs. *Average value of weatherization services:* Over $2,500 per year.

Weatherization Assistance Program Branch, EE2K, US Department of Energy, 1000 Independence Ave. SW, Washington, DC 20585. *www1.eere.energy.gov/wip/wap.html*

• **The Eldercare Locator.** Provides access to an extensive network of organizations serving older people at state and local community levels. Services cover home-delivered meals, transportation, legal assistance, housing options, recreation and social activities, senior center programs and more.

Eldercare Locator, 800-677-1116 (Monday through Friday 9 am and 8 pm ET). *www.eldercare.gov*

Sex ?

How to Be a Better Lover

The secret to being a great lover is not necessarily a matter of knowing exotic techniques in the bedroom. It is more about developing an attitude of openness and curiosity—and making a commitment to keeping passion alive. *Here's how anyone can be a better lover…*

SHOW APPRECIATION

When we show appreciation, it creates good feelings, which draws us closer to our partner. Often we notice something about our partner that pleases us, but we don't think to say anything. Instead, speak up.

Example: "I really admire the way you stood up to your boss. That took guts."

Even better, tell others how proud you are of your partner, in your partner's presence. Champion your lover.

Example: "Have you heard about the fund-raising drive she organized? She did an amazing job." Bragging about other people isn't offensive if it is obvious that you take genuine pleasure in their achievements and aren't just trying to impress others.

Both men and women enjoy being told they are attractive. When she wears that dress that shows off her body, tell her how great she looks. When he steps out of the shower, tell him how sexy he is.

PAY ATTENTION

Pure, nondistracted attention is affirming and seductive. When your partner tells you about his/her thoughts, feelings, desires or just the things that happened that day, stop what you're doing and really listen. Don't keep tapping on your computer keyboard or have one eye on the television.

Another way to pay attention is to show that you are thinking of your partner. Make a cup of coffee for her while she is in the

Lou Paget, sex educator certified by the American Association of Sexuality Educators, Counselors and Therapists. Based in Los Angeles, she is host of the radio program *Sex Talk with Lou* and a regular speaker at national and international professional conferences. She is author of numerous books, including *The Great Lover Playbook* (Gotham). *www.loupaget.com*

shower, and clear the snow off her car. Call him during the day to tell him you love him and let him know about an article you read in the paper that you think he would find useful. Draw her a bath with lavender bath salts when she comes home from work.

BE ADVENTUROUS

Shake up your routine so that you see each other with new eyes. If you have fallen into the habit of cuddling on the couch and watching DVDs on the weekend, take a day trip instead or invite friends over for dinner. Exchange chores for a week.

Bring a sense of adventure to everyday events. Point out to each other the birds that are visiting the backyard bird feeder or the trees that are budding in your neighborhood. The ongoing accumulation of shared experiences, small and large, builds your shared personal history and increases intimacy.

PLAN CLOSENESS

Although planning may seem to work against adventure and spontaneity, the opposite is true. If you think about the times when so-called spontaneous sex happened, it was most likely possible because of planning—whether for a dinner date or a luxurious vacation. This planning doesn't necessarily mean planning sex—it means taking the time to create an environment conducive to intimacy.

TOUCH

Touching is the most powerful way to connect. It releases the "love hormone" *oxytocin.* The more you touch each other, the more you will desire each other. Give each other massages…cuddle first thing in the morning…pause for a full-body embrace as one of you is going out the door…take his arm or place your hand on the small of her back as you are walking…hold hands before going to sleep.

Be aware that men need to be touched two to three times more frequently than women to maintain the same level of oxytocin, according to a study by Swedish researchers.

AVOID PSYCHIC SEX

Many people believe that they should be able to intuit what will make a partner happy in bed. But it is dangerous to assume that you can figure out what your partner wants

without asking. You may wind up focusing on activities that you enjoy but that your partner does not and vice versa.

It is helpful to have this conversation in broad daylight so that you can see your partner's face and subtle reactions. If you are self-conscious about raising the topic, try doing so when you are lying down and snuggling, with low lighting—but not in the middle of sex. You can say, "You know, I was reading an article and realized that there are some things I don't know about what you enjoy in bed. I would love to know more, because I want to create that kind of pleasure for you. And I'd love to tell you about some things that sound exciting to me."

If your partner is shy and doesn't offer ideas, you could suggest a particular activity and say, "I thought this might be fun to try. Do you think you would like it, or is there a variation you might like more?"

If your lover has been touching you in a way that you don't enjoy anymore, speak in terms of your nerves and sensations. This keeps the information from feeling like a personal criticism. *Example:* "You know, it's almost like this has a different sensation for me—I might like it a little lighter or more on this side."

KISS CREATIVELY

Kissing is one of the least threatening, and most exciting, ways to vary your intimacy. But couples fall into a pattern where they essentially stop kissing or kiss in the same way, in the same places, time after time. Instead, experiment with playful Eskimo kisses (nose to nose)…kiss your partner's lips in a new way…explore your partner's body with your mouth.

One way to let your lover know what style of kissing you like is to begin kissing him/her the way you enjoy being kissed. Pause in mid-kiss and say, "Mmm, I love the way this feels." Then say, "Hey, would you show me what it feels like to be kissed by me just now?" Reinforce by saying, "Oh, do more of that."

STIMULATE YOUR SENSES

Engage all your senses—smell, hearing, touch, taste and sight. Light scented candles…play pulsating music or the song that was playing when you met…put fresh sheets on the bed…feed each other foods that you find aphrodisiacal (anything from oysters to chocolate-covered strawberries)…put a different-colored bulb in the bedside lamp.

Super Sex Every Time

Brigitte Mars, herbalist, founding member of The American Herbalists Guild and instructor at Naropa University, Bauman College and Boulder College of Massage Therapy, Boulder, Colorado. She has been practicing and teaching herbal medicine and nutrition for more than 40 years. She is author of *The Sexual Herbal: Prescriptions for Enhancing Love and Passion* (Healing Arts). *www.brigittemars.com*

Couples who enjoy sex regularly tend to live longer than those who rarely or never have sex. Sexual activity purges congestion from the prostate gland and relieves pain by stimulating the release of endorphins.

Yet millions of Americans struggle to have satisfying sex, or any sex, because of physical limitations. Medications can help with problems such as an inability to get erections or vaginal dryness, but they don't always work—and can carry the risk for side effects.

Better: Natural remedies that improve energy and libido as well as sexual performance. In my 40 years of specializing in herbal medicine, I have found them to be quite effective for many people. (The herbs and supplements noted here are readily available at most health-food stores and online.)

LUBRICATION

Vaginal dryness can be as problematic for a woman as erectile dysfunction is for a man. Women naturally produce less moisture (in the vagina, as well as in the eyes, skin and other parts of the body) as they get older. But it's one of the easiest sexual problems to correct—and without the use of store-bought, chemical-filled lubricants. Try one of the following remedies. If that doesn't work, try another until you find what works best for you.

•*Barley water.* Barley water is an emollient that also nourishes and strengthens vaginal tissues. Cook two cups of light pearled barley in 10 cups of water for two hours.

Strain, and reserve the water. Drink a glassful three or four times a day between meals for at least three weeks. If it helps, continue doing it. It can be kept in the refrigerator for up to three days. (You can use the leftover barley in soups and salads.)

•*Acidophilus.* Dryness is sometimes caused by an overgrowth of vaginal yeast. Before going to bed each night, insert a capsule of *acidophilus* into the vagina. It inhibits yeast and helps the vagina produce more lubrication.

Important: Don't use an enteric-coated capsule—it won't dissolve readily. Use an acidophilus gel capsule.

•*Chemical-free lubricant.* Mix one ounce of softenend cocoa butter with one tablespoon each of powdered *dong quai* (an herb in the parsley family), licorice root and marshmallow root, along with one tablespoon of powdered wild yam and two tablespoons of vitamin E oil.

Optional: Two drops of essential oil of rose for a pleasant aroma.

Roll the mixture into suppository shapes about the size of your little finger. Store them in a glass jar in the refrigerator for up to six months. Insert one in the vagina daily before bedtime.

LOW LIBIDO

If your sex drive is lower than you (or your partner) would like…

•*Eat black foods.* According to Traditional Chinese Medicine, the kidneys govern sexual vitality. Foods with natural black color, such as black olives, black sesame seeds, chia seeds and black beans, strengthen the kidneys and improve sexual energy and performance.

Bonus: Black olives and chia increase the production of *mucilage,* important for sexual lubrication.

•*Muira puama.* This is a South American herb that traditionally is used as an aphrodisiac and to improve erections as well as orgasms in men and women. It's a warming herb that increases circulation. If you have cold hands and/or feet, you probably have impaired circulation to the genitals as well. Muira puama can help.

Dose: One-half cup of muira puama tea… or 10 to 30 drops of tincture, mixed with an inch of water or taken straight, three times daily. Also available in capsules. Natives of South America sometimes apply the cooled tea directly to the genitals as a sexual stimulant.

• *DHEA,* an over-the-counter hormonal supplement that's converted to testosterone in the body, can increase libido and sexual responsiveness in women and men.

Important: Improper dosing can cause acne, the growth of facial hair in women and other side effects—including an increased risk for some cancers. Take DHEA only under the supervision of a doctor.

ERECTILE DYSFUNCTION

The arteries that carry blood to the penis are just slightly wider than the head of a pin. Even slight buildups of plaque (atherosclerosis) can impede circulation and make it difficult for a man to get and/or maintain an erection.

The same things that improve overall cardiovascular health, such as lowering cholesterol and blood pressure, can improve a man's ability to achieve an erection. *Also helpful...*

• *The Deer.* This is a Taoist exercise that removes energy blockages, stimulates hormone production and improves erections. Sit on the edge of the bed, and rub your hands to warm them. Hold the scrotum with one hand. With the other hand, massage right below the navel in a circular motion. Do it 81 times, then switch hands and rub in the other direction 81 times.

Follow this with 36 Kegel exercises, in which you tighten and then release the *pubococcygeus muscles*—the same muscles that you would use to stop urine in midstream.

• *Foot massage.* Once or twice a day, massage the entire foot, paying particular attention to the sides of the heels. The *meridians* (energy pathways) that support sexual potency run through this part of the foot.

• *Yohimbe.* Yohimbe bark extract is among the most effective natural products for improving erections. It increases blood flow to the genitals while at the same time impeding the flow of blood out of the penis—important for keeping an erection.

Dose: One cup of yohimbe tea...or 30 drops of tincture, mixed with an inch of

water or taken straight, 30 minutes to an hour before sex. Also available in capsules.

Caution: Yohimbe can elevate blood pressure and cause insomnia. It also interacts with many common drugs, including antihypertensives and heart and diabetes medications. Use it only under the supervision of a doctor and never more than twice a week.

• *Omega-3 fatty acids* enhance circulation and help the nervous system function better. Eat fish (such as salmon, tuna, sardines) twice per week or supplement with fish oil (follow directions on the label).

BETTER ORGASMS

Men and women who eat well, exercise regularly and are comfortable with their bodies experience better and more frequent orgasms. *Also helpful...*

• *Arginine.* An amino acid called L-arginine is a *vasodilator*, which means it helps to widen or open up blood vessels. Arginine cream can be applied to the clitoris or penis before sex to increase arousal and the intensity of orgasms. You also can take an oral capsule form to increase blood flow to sexual organs. Follow directions on the label.

Love in Middle Age And Beyond

Johnette Duff, Esq., certified family mediator and author of Love After 50: The Complete Legal and Financial Guide *(Legalines).*

Becoming involved in a serious relationship in middle age is more complicated legally and financially than it is for younger people...

• **There may be family members to care for**—*the children of prior marriages, exspouses, parents...*

• **The couple may have heavy financial obligations**—*alimony payments, child support...*

• **They may have piled up assets in which others have a stake.**

Examples: Pensions (one spouse has a legal interest in the other's pension)...business interests.

To avoid pitfalls that could undermine the relationship—the legal and financial issues the parties face must be thought through.

Should we marry...

Marriage has positive and negative financial consequences. A positive one is that marriage may entitle a nonworking spouse to employer-paid health coverage. *Other considerations...*

• **Responsibility for the support of the new spouse.** Obviously, those in a relationship help to support each other. But when you marry, this becomes a legal obligation that can create serious burdens for older people should one spouse need long-term nursing care.

• **Being responsible for the debts of your spouse.** Mature adults may have significant debt on credit cards, business loans or back taxes. Premarriage debts may become the responsibility of a new spouse.

• **Losing alimony payments from a previous marriage.** These payments often cease upon remarriage.

• **Losing Social Security benefits based on the earnings of a former spouse**...as long as you're married to your new spouse.

• **Being able to file a joint tax return.** For some couples, this may result in tax savings, while others may face a "marriage penalty" (paying more taxes than they would as singles living together).

...Or just live together?

State, as well as federal, law may affect the rights and obligations of an unmarried couple. *State law may...*

• **Make it illegal to live together**...even though this law is seldom enforced.

• **Recognize palimony rights**...should you decide to split up (although most states have enacted laws against this).

• **Recognize contracts**...including oral agreements made between the parties concerning property divisions, support or other financial arrangements.

While state law may not provide unmarried couples with the protections afforded married couples, people who decide to live together can create these protections through agreements or contracts.

Example: State law generally doesn't impose any support obligation on an unmarried person, but a couple can provide in a contract for continued support even if they decide to split up.

KEEPING EVERYONE HAPPY

For older individuals, there are usually more people to consider, as I mentioned earlier. There are former spouses, children from prior marriages and even grandchildren.

Often, concerns center on estate planning issues, such as who's going to get what.

Planning to keep everyone satisfied isn't easy, but it can be done. *Some approaches to consider...*

• **Don't rely on state law to determine who inherits what if you die without a will.** Under state law, someone you wanted to benefit may well receive nothing.

Example: State law does not provide any inheritance at all for a significant other who's not a legal spouse.

Protection: Make out a will spelling out who should get what when you die.

• **Use trusts to provide for more than one person.**

Example: Instead of giving the house to your companion, use a trust to give that person a lifetime interest in the house. When he or she dies, your children (or anyone else named in the trust) can inherit the home. *Impact:* Your mate has protection for life. The children are the ultimate beneficiaries of the house.

• **Review all beneficiary designations.** Retirement plans and IRAs allow individuals to name one or more beneficiaries. Well-considered designations can ensure that all parties get the protection you intended.

Example: A new spouse can be named as the beneficiary of a company pension plan, while children can be beneficiaries of various IRA accounts.

• **Use prenuptial agreements to spell out all your intentions.**

Example: Older spouses may each have sufficient assets so that they are willing to waive any legal claims they have to one another's estates.

KNOW WHERE YOU STAND

In making your decision about a long-term commitment and whether to do so under the umbrella of marriage, *be sure to...*

• **Get all the legal facts.** Be sure you understand the legal and financial ramifications of your decision.

• **Negotiate the terms of any arrangements you make.** Unless both parties are satisfied with the deal, it may not hold up later on.

• **Review your decisions with professionals.** Talk to an attorney about wills and other documents you may need in order to cement the arrangements you want. Talk to an accountant who can assess the tax impact of your decisions.

Sexual Habits of American Women

Think you know your partner? *Results from professional surveys might surprise you...*

• **Extramarital affairs.** In a *Cosmopolitan* poll, 54% said they fooled around, 21% in a poll conducted by *Ladies' Home Journal,* 34% in *Playboy,* and 43% in a survey by the Institute for Advanced Study of Human Sexuality. *Playboy*'s poll also showed that almost 65% of wives have had affairs by age 50.

• **Skill.** A majority of women think they are good at sex. *Playboy* found 80% who claimed they were skilled. Some 65% of those polled in the *Journal* rated themselves good to excellent. And 64% in the Institute poll admitted they were "great."

• **Frequency.** Most polls say that married women make love two or three times a week.

• **Orgasms.** Roughly half the women questioned said they had orgasms regularly.

• **Oral sex is practiced by more than 85% of the women questioned by *Cosmopolitan* and 95% of those by *Playboy.***

About one-half of married women incorporate it into their lovemaking.

• **Sex in public places is indulged in by about one-third of those polled by *Playboy.***

• ***Family Circle* found that 85% of wives are satisfied with their sex lives.**

• **One-third of the women polled by the Institute have had venereal disease or herpes.** About 91% use sex lotions or gadgets.

• ***Playboy* discovered that among young married couples,** wives play around more than husbands do.

Common Sexual Concerns

Judy Kuriansky, PhD, professor of clinical psychology, Columbia University Teachers College, fellow of the American Psychological Association and New York *Daily News* Sex & Romance columnist. She is author of several books on relationships, including *The Complete Idiot's Guide to a Healthy Relationship* (Alpha Books).

The act of sex should be the most natural thing in the world. But for some people, sex causes anxiety and concern. *There are several issues that are very common...*

AMONG MEN

• **Premature ejaculation.** The answer to this problem lies in learning to control the timing of ejaculation. This is easier than you think. You have to find the point at which you can no longer stop yourself from ejaculating. During masturbation, practice ways in which you can decrease or increase feelings of arousal. Discover which fantasies or behavior triggers your excitement and what diminishes it, and learn how to focus on the latter in order to postpone ejaculation. It's not a good idea to use the old-fashioned trick of thinking about baseball scores or work. Thinking about such totally nonsensual experiences is destructive to sexuality. Instead, focus attention on any sensation in your body, or minimal sensual thoughts—which at least keeps you in the realm of being sensual (but not at the peak of being excited).

• **Sexual deviations and fetishes.** Men are very much concerned with what they consider to be unnatural desires, such as the wish to be spanked by women. It arises from the need to be punished for feeling sexual, and also they need to be forced into sexuality as a way of avoiding responsibility for engaging in it. ("The devil made me do it.") Cross-dressing is the desire to put on women's clothes. Husbands and lovers who do this may keep the practice hidden or may be indulged by their partners until it becomes disturbing. A desire to put on women's clothes usually reflects sexual problems related to a desire, left over from childhood, to be "close to Mommy." (Mommy may not be near forever, but her clothes can be.) It may also be a sign of difficulty in integrating the passive "feminine" side of a man's nature with the active "masculine" side. *Example:* A man who has trouble expressing his passive side, as evidenced in the inability to cry, may find it easier to do so by putting on women's clothes.

• **A desire for more sexual aggressiveness from female partners.** A great many men wish that their wives or lovers would take the sexual initiative and behave less passively. *Theory:* If women could act out the more masculine side of themselves and thus come across to men in a more familiar way, physically and emotionally, far fewer men would have difficulties relating to women sexually. (This is borne out by homosexuals, who explain that what they get from relationships with men is missing from relationships with women.)

• **Erection problems** (failure to get or maintain erections). This is much more complex than premature ejaculation and more difficult to deal with. It is often complicated by emotional problems, such as insecurity or hostility to the partner, so psychological treatment, rather than special physical exercises, is usually required.

• **Penis size.** A very common concern, disguised with such euphemisms as "I have a handicap." (*Translation:* "I think my penis is too small.") The solution is to understand that physiologically the small penis is not a deterrent to sexual pleasure. It is important to find out what penis size means to you or your partner and the ways it affects your desire and pleasure.

AMONG WOMEN

• **Not having orgasms.** The first part of the solution is to learn not to focus on the missing orgasm—if it is missing. Studies show that at least half the women who think they don't have orgasms in fact do have them. *The dynamics:* They're looking for some ideal of an orgasm that they've heard about. *For the genuinely nonorgasmic:* This is relatively easy to overcome, often within a brief period of treatment that involves learning to achieve orgasm by yourself via masturbation. *Goal:* To learn to accept that sexual pleasure is for you, too, not just for men, as so many women have been brought up to think. After acquiring the capacity to accept the sexual pleasure she has learned to give herself, a woman can usually go on to the next step, the pleasure of orgasm with a male partner.

• **Conflict over the way they're treated in relationships with men.** Men are much more concerned with sexual performance and physical fears than are women. Women care far more about the psychological and emotional aspects of relationships than do men. *Most common conflict:* The still very common tendency among women to settle for "half a loaf" in a relationship, usually out of the mistaken belief that "That's all you can hope to get, so make do." The first step out of this trap is to refuse to accept such reasoning and to reject the false security of relationships that offer so little satisfaction.

• **Problems integrating the role of parent and lover.** It isn't only men who suffer from the madonna-prostitute complex (separating women into categories such as the "pure madonna" and the "sexy enticer"). Women can also suffer from this syndrome. *Example:* The woman who has a child and thus comes to feel that she isn't sexy and shouldn't feel sexy because she is now a mother. *Usual symptoms of the problem:* She avoids sex on the grounds of fatigue, a problem with the baby or concern over money.

Frequently asked by both sexes: Is it healthy to get involved in a sexual relationship with someone much older or much younger? *Answer:* There usually isn't a great deal wrong with these relationships. These couplings are often a holdover from incestuous childhood desires. When such desires are acted out by two adults, it can be taken as psychological information, but nothing else.

The Truth About Sexual Desire In Women

Leah Millheiser, MD, clinical assistant professor in the department of obstetrics and gynecology and director of the Female Sexual Medicine Program at Stanford University School of Medicine in Stanford, California.

Ever since an FDA advisory panel rejected the approval of a so-called "female Viagra"—the drug was deemed no more effective at increasing libido than a placebo—there's been some debate on the female libido.

Key issue: If a woman's desire for sex is low, is that necessarily a "dysfunction" that should be treated? *What women—and their partners—need to know…*

IS THERE A PROBLEM?

When it comes to libido, medical experts agree that there is no "normal" or "abnormal." Doctors diagnose a libido dysfunction only when there is a recurrent or persistent problem with libido that causes *personal distress to the woman.*

Therefore, if a woman has no sexual desire but is undisturbed by this fact, then no dysfunction exists. Alternatively, if a woman wants to have sex twice a week but is distressed because she used to want it more often than that, then the decrease in libido is a dysfunction for her.

To diagnose low libido: A woman needs to answer just one basic question—do *you* think you have a problem with your level of sexual desire?

Note: When a man and woman's desire don't match, it's called "desire mismatch," which is not truly a sexual dysfunction, though the partners may benefit from sex therapy.

CAUSES OF LOW LIBIDO

Not all doctors ask about their patients' sexual health, so any woman who experiences chronic or recurrent low libido should tell her gynecologist and/or primary care physician. *Most common causes…*

•**Health problems.** Some chronic diseases, such as diabetes and atherosclerosis (clogged arteries), can decrease blood flow—including that feeding the sex organs.

•**Medication use.** The side effects of many drugs may include a change in sexual desire and/or difficulty reaching orgasm.

Common culprits: Antidepressant drugs known as selective serotonin reuptake inhibitors (SSRIs), such as *fluoxetine* (Prozac) and *sertraline* (Zoloft)…and cholesterol-lowering statin medications, such as *atorvastatin* (Lipitor) and *simvastatin* (Zocor).

•**Psychosocial factors.** If a woman is in a relationship that is physically, emotionally or verbally abusive, her sexual desire can diminish. Past physical or sexual abuse can also lower libido. Any woman experiencing abuse should work with her doctor to create a plan to improve the relationship or leave it. Those experiencing current or past abuse may also benefit from therapy.

•**Partner's health issues.** If a woman with low libido has a partner who has a sexual dysfunction—such as low sex drive, erectile dysfunction or inability to orgasm—both partners can drag each other's desire down even further. Therefore, both people should be evaluated by a sex therapist.*

•**Hormone levels.** The primary male hormone (testosterone), which is also present in females, plays a crucial role in women's libido. Postmenopausal women, in particular, have decreased testosterone, which lowers libido and makes it more difficult to have an orgasm. Premenopausal women may experience lowered testosterone levels if they take birth control pills. Women taking testosterone need to be carefully monitored with blood tests every three to six months.

*To find a sex therapist or MD in your area who specializes in treating sexual dysfunction, consult the International Society for the Study of Women's Sexual Health, *www.isswsh.org.*

WHAT YOU CAN DO

It's important to work with your doctor to rule out underlying physical problems that may be leading to your low libido. *In the meantime, simple therapies may help…*

• **Reduce vaginal dryness.** Vaginal moisturizers—which are different from lubricants in that they are used two to three times a week, not just before sex—add moisture barriers in the vagina. This helps provide a layer of protection and comfort so that sex is not painful—a common complaint among women who experience vaginal dryness.

Recommended: KY Silk-E or Replens.** Follow label instructions. *Important:* You must use such vaginal moisturizers for at least two months before judging results.

• **Masturbate.** Yes, this simple action can be a powerful libido booster for women—partly because it turns out that sexual desire really is a "use it or lose it" function.

• **Use lubricants.** Sexual lubricants help make sex more comfortable—painful sex is a common cause of low libido.

Recommended: Pjur Eros Bodyglide, which is a silicone-based, glycerin-free product. This combination offers several advantages, including a reduced risk for yeast infections or vaginal inflammation, compared with products that contain glycerin.

**All the products mentioned in this section can be purchased from *www.drugstore.com*, which ships its orders in a plain box labeled only with the company name.

Sex After 50

Saul H. Rosenthal, MD, author of *Sex Over Forty* (Tarcher).

Middle age can be an opportunity to make sex better and more satisfying than ever before. *Basic reasons:* People of mature years have had more experience in lovemaking. (Research shows that many women don't experience a climax until they are in their 30s, though this is beginning to change as men learn more about orgasm.) The pressures of career building are less frantic,

leaving couples with more time to share.

The children have grown up and left home, giving adults more privacy and fewer demands on their time. And as men age, they lose the pressure to get right to intercourse and a quick climax. They can concentrate on a fuller sensual and sexual experience in lovemaking.

Most common mistakes about age and sex…

• **Believing that your sex life is essentially over by the time you're in your 50s.** Society tends to reinforce this notion with its emphasis on youth—the absence of advertisements showing older people as objects of sexual interest, for example. People behave according to the expectations that the culture sets for them and begin to give up on their sexual lives when they reach middle age. This is in many ways the equivalent of giving up on life itself.

• **Failing to understand that the physiological changes affecting sexual function are normal** and can be adapted to without the loss of a sex life. Middle-aged men suppose that these changes are signals that sex is (and is supposed to be) over for them. They become fearful that they can no longer function. Once this fear sets in, sexual function really is seriously affected. *Example:* Many men ages 55 to 60 or older worry when they don't get a spontaneous erection when seeing their partner undress as they did when they were 20 or 30.

But this does not mean sexual function is over for them. It only means that they now require more direct stimulation. Many men put off having intercourse until they get a spontaneous erection for fear their wives will think they have some sexual problem. Sex in these circumstances becomes less and less frequent, and this is what causes wives to be fearful that their husbands are no longer interested in them.

• **Believing that sex requires a climax every time.** As men get older, they need longer and longer periods between ejaculations. A man in his 60s may require a full day or even several days between ejaculations. This does not mean that he cannot enjoy intercourse and lovemaking in between. Sex partners get into serious trouble when they think climaxes are essential and that the male, particularly, must have one. (The man feels he must because his partner expects it. The woman feels that if he doesn't, he no longer cares for her.) You can enjoy all the sensations of sexual arousal without climax. Remember how pleasurable it was just to neck in the back of a car in your younger days, when mores were less permissive?

Lack of lubrication, the problem for aging women: Oral estrogen therapy can alleviate this condition. However, this should be discussed with your doctor as recent evidence has suggested that it increases the risk for breast cancer and other maladies.

The problem of impotence: Many factors can cause impotence. Contrary to the opinion that has prevailed since Masters and Johnson did their research, not all impotence is caused by psychological problems. New research shows that a variety of physical problems can cause impotence and that these are treatable. (Included are hormonal problems and vascular and neurological conditions.)

Impotence may be caused by medical or organic factors (rather than psychological ones) if…

- **Medications are being taken to lower blood pressure,** or antidepressants, tranquilizers, antihistamines or decongestants are being used.
- **Alcohol is being overused.** Alcohol has very strong negative effects on sexual functions, including possible long-term problems such as reduced production of the male hormone, decreased sperm production and reduced sex drive.
- **A major illness, especially diabetes,** thyroid disease or arteriosclerosis is experienced. Illness isn't necessarily the cause of erection problems but should be considered one possibility.
- **The man has lost his sexual desire** (as well as capacity).

Impotence is probably caused by psychological factors if…

- **There are firm erections under some circumstances** (waking at night or in the morning, during masturbation, etc.). This indicates that the physical mechanism is in good working order and that emotional factors are the more likely cause of impotence.

- **Firm erections are lost just before or after entry.** The odds here greatly favor an emotional cause.
- **The problem started suddenly,** over a period of a month or less. This is more likely to be an emotionally caused impotence, since physical problems affect sexual function more gradually. *Caution:* There are exceptions. Emotional causes are not always sudden in their effect. And medical causes can be sudden in their effect, especially if a new drug is prescribed.
- **The problem started after a very stressful emotional experience** (the death of a spouse, the loss of a job, a divorce, rejection by a partner).

Jump-Start Your Sex Life…Naturally

Chris D. Meletis, ND, executive director, the Institute for Healthy Aging. He is author of several books, including *Better Sex Naturally* (HarperResource), *Complete Guide to Safe Herbs* (DK Publishing) and *Instant Guide to Drug-Herb Interactions* (DK Publishing).

Well before erectile-dysfunction drugs, people relied on aphrodisiacs to increase sexual desire…boost stamina …improve performance…and increase pleasure. Many of these compounds owe their reputation to folklore, but several herbs and dietary supplements have proven sex-enhancing effects.

Good news: Products that improve sex naturally may be less likely to cause serious side effects than prescription drugs. Many strengthen the cardiovascular system and help regulate hormone production. That's as important for good sex as having an erection or being sufficiently lubricated.

Unlike *sildenafil*, sex-enhancing herbs and supplements aren't taken just an hour or so before sex. They're taken daily until there's a noticeable improvement in sexual performance.

At that point, some people take a pause to see if the herbs and supplements are no longer necessary. Others continue taking the preparations indefinitely.

Important: Use herbs and supplements only under medical supervision. That way you'll be sure to get the product and dosage that's right for you.

Caution: Fresh or dried herbs differ greatly in potency from batch to batch. Use capsules or tinctures, instead. They've been standardized to contain the proper amounts of active ingredients.

For better sex, try one of the following natural enhancers. Select the one that best suits your needs. Give each preparation a few months to work. If you see no effect, try another.

GINKGO BILOBA

Ginkgo* contains a variety of compounds that relax blood vessels and increase circulation to the brain and pelvic area.

For women, increased blood flow improves vaginal lubrication and sexual responsiveness.

For men, adequate blood flow is essential to achieve and sustain erections.

Typical dosage: *Capsules:* 40 mg to 60 mg of 24% standardized powdered extract three to four times daily. *Tincture:* 30 drops three to four times daily.

Side effects: Ginkgo may cause dizziness, headache or heart palpitations.

Caution: Ginkgo is a blood thinner and can increase the blood-thinning effects of aspirin and *warfarin* (Coumadin). Check with your physician before using ginkgo if you're taking either medication.

MUIRA PUAMA

Also known as "potency wood," this herb contains sterols and other compounds that boost levels of testosterone, a hormone that plays a critical role in sexual desire in women as well as men.

Muira puama* also contains volatile oils, including camphor and beta-carophyllene. They're thought to restore sex drive by stimulating nerves in the brain's pleasure center.

Typical dosage: 250 mg three times daily in capsule form.

Side effect: Muira puama may lower blood pressure by as much as 10%. Check with your doctor before using this herb if you have low blood pressure (hypotension).

*Before taking herbs, please consult your medical doctor or your naturopathic doctor.

GINSENG

This herb is an "adaptogen," meaning it helps the body compensate for extended periods of stress. Stress can cause sexual desire and performance to plummet.

These compounds also improve blood flow to the penis, help tissues use oxygen more efficiently and boost production of testosterone in men and progesterone in women.

Typical dosage: *Capsules:* 10 mg to 50 mg one to three times daily. *Tincture:* 30 to 60 drops daily.

Side effect: Ginseng may cause diarrhea …high blood pressure…sleeplessness.

ASHWAGANDA

A member of the pepper family, this herb contains *withanolides*, substances that increase the activity of testosterone and progesterone. Ashwaganda also relieves stress and anxiety.

Typical dosage: *Capsules:* 1,000 mg once or twice daily. *Tincture:* 60 to 90 drops two or three times daily.

Side effects: Because ashwaganda has antianxiety properties, it should not be used by anyone taking medications to treat anxiety and/or depression. The herb could intensify the drugs' actions as well as their side effects. Ashwaganda may also trigger miscarriages.

ARGININE

Taken in supplement form, this amino acid has been shown to relax smooth muscle contractions. This boosts arterial dilation, bringing more blood to the pelvic area.

The body uses arginine* to produce nitric oxide, a chemical needed to achieve erections. (Sildenafil works in part by making nitric oxide more readily available in the body.)

Typical dosage: 1,000 mg to 2,000 mg twice daily in capsule form. Take capsules between meals, since many foods contain lysine, an amino acid that counteracts arginine's effects.

Side effect: Don't take this herb if you get cold sores caused by the herpes simplex virus. Arginine stimulates viral replication.

FOR MEN ONLY

The herb *yohimbe* is approved by the FDA for treating impotence and low sex drive.

*Before taking herbs, please consult your medical doctor or your naturopathic doctor.

Yohimbe contains a compound called *yohimbine,* which helps dilate blood vessels in the penis. Most men who take yohimbe experience an increase in sexual desire within an hour.

Typical dosage: 15 mg to 25 mg daily in capsule form. Divide into several doses throughout the day to minimize side effects. Take smaller amounts at first—for example, 5 mg or 10 mg a day—then gradually increase the amount over several weeks.

Side effects: Elevated blood pressure, nausea, racing heart and anxiety. Use yohimbe only under medical supervision.

FOR WOMEN ONLY

The herb *dong quai* contains plant sterols that help correct estrogen deficiencies.

Studies suggest that dong quai can increase sexual desire as well as the intensity of orgasms.

Typical dosage: Capsules: 1,000 mg three to four times daily. *Tincture:* 45 to 60 drops two or three times daily.

Caution: Pregnant and lactating women should not use dong quai. The herb also increases sensitivity to sunlight.

Sex Therapy

Shirley Zussman, EdD, sex therapist and co-director of the Association for Male Sexual Dysfunction, New York City.

It isn't easy for couples who have sexual problems to seek out professional help. They're embarrassed. They believe that therapy takes years, costs more than they can afford and might not work. Sex therapy isn't cheap. But if you do have sexual difficulties with a loving partner, there's a good chance new techniques can help in a matter of a few months.

The most common problems: Lack of interest. Trouble with erections and orgasms. Pain, real or imaginary.

WHEN TO CONSIDER THERAPY

When the problem becomes so great that it jeopardizes the relationship and preoccupation with the problem becomes so overwhelming that work suffers and enjoyment of life wanes.

One spouse often knows instinctively when a problem reaches a critical point. When you say to yourself, "I can't go on like this anymore," you're usually telling the truth. *Especially dangerous to a relationship:* Trying to avoid the problem by drinking, abstaining from sex or turning to extramarital partners.

Another self-deception: Believing that only one partner has a problem. It may originate with the man or woman, but once one has a problem, both have a problem.

FINDING A THERAPIST

Since sex therapists are not licensed, anyone can claim the title. Occasionally unethical persons do. To find a reputable therapist, ask your physician or county medical society for a recommendation. The American Association of Sex Educators, Counselors, and Therapists (AASECT) publishes a directory of its members, for whom it sets education and training standards.

Most qualified therapists have degrees in a behavioral science (psychology, psychiatry) as well as training in sex therapy. Although sex therapy focuses primarily on sexual problems, a knowledge of psychology is essential because sexuality is so inextricably connected with total personality and life events.

Important first step: Get a medical examination to find out whether the problem is a physical one. Often it is, especially when the problem is pain during intercourse or difficulties during erection. If a sex therapist doesn't ask during the first visit whether you've had a medical exam or refer you for one, find another therapist.

FACTS AND MYTHS

In some states therapists often use a surrogate partner (a paid partner) during treatment. Someone experiencing sexual difficulties is taught how to overcome them during supervised foreplay and other sexual activities with the surrogate. But many therapists consider the use of a surrogate to be inappropriate.

If you're married, it's more effective to undergo therapy as a couple. *Reasons:* Since successful therapy may mean a change in sexual practices, your spouse will inevitably be involved. Moreover, many sexual difficulties, such as lack of interest and failure to be aroused, are often the result of a breakdown in communication between partners.

A typical session lasts one hour, and therapists usually recommend one session per week. Most difficulties can be successfully treated in three to six months.

Some people are helped significantly in a single session because they only think they have a problem. *Example:* A woman who fails to have an orgasm during sexual intercourse. Or a man who feels guilty when his partner fails to have an orgasm during intercourse. *The fact:* Most women do not have orgasms during intercourse.

EMOTIONAL REASONS FOR PROBLEMS

Lack of sexual interest, the most common problem, takes longer to treat. Therapists now recognize that although some declining interest is normal during a relationship, it's often aggravated by depression, stress or emotions that build up at home.

The new technique of sex therapists is to deal with these outside causes, with the specific goal of increasing sexual interest. The therapist may also recommend that a couple experiment at home with activities designed to heighten sexual interest. *Examples:* Different kinds of foreplay, verbal excitement, different positions during intercourse. Lack of interest often develops because a couple haven't been communicating their preferences in sexual activity to each other.

The most common mistake couples make is assuming that sex must always be spontaneous. Few things in life really are. Most couples don't think twice about making reservations at a restaurant, but they wince at the idea of scheduling sex. It works, say the therapists. And it's one of the simplest and most effective ways out of the problem.

Does Running Affect Sex?

Running can improve a man's sex life if he doesn't take it too seriously, according to recent surveys of runners. Those who clocked less than 35 miles a week reported increased sexual desire, more frequent sexual activity and greater sexual satisfaction. However, more than half the runners training for marathons and covering more than 35 miles a week admitted to sometimes feeling too tired for sex.

The Runner

Heart Attacks Don't End Your Sex Life

Older heart attack and stroke victims can usually resume sexual activity in three to four months without risk. Doing so may actually reduce the chance of another attack.

Sexuality in Later Life

Sensual Stimulation Misconception

A woman's breasts may not be erogenous. Alfred C. Kinsey found in his early sex studies that nearly half the women he interviewed were not sexually stimulated by having their breasts stroked. More recent studies have confirmed that women vary widely in the parts of their bodies that give them the greatest sexual satisfaction.

Michael Carrera, EdD, adjunct professor of community medicine, Mount Sinai Medical Center, New York City.

Delayed Desire

A minority of women feel their greatest sexual drive right before menstruation rather than midcycle. Doctors suggest both physical and psychological reasons. Physically, estrogen/progesterone stimulation may excite them. Psychologically, relief from worry about conception and an emotional need for affection may make them more open to sex.

Ewa Radwanska, MD, PhD, reproductive endocrinologist, Chicago, writing in *Medical Aspects of Human Sexuality.*

Not Necessarily Dull

The missionary position for intercourse (woman on her back, man on top) doesn't deserve its reputation for being boring and staid. Some men and women can't reach orgasm any other way. It rarely causes anxiety, since most people are very used to it. It permits a lot of face-to-face, torso-to-torso contact. It gives many men an intense orgasm.

Sleeping After Sex

Sleep following sex comes much more quickly to men than to women. A woman's body takes longer than a man's to return to a nonaroused state (10 to 15 minutes). If a woman has had no orgasm, the problem of getting to sleep can be even worse. Studies show a strong correlation between sexual frustration and insomnia. *Solution:* Patience, communication and trust between sexual partners.

Samuel Dunkell, MD, director of the Insomnia Medical Services, New York City.

Orgasms Don't Mean Better Sleep

It's commonly believed that satisfactory sex with orgasm leads to better sleep for both partners. But a recent experiment did not prove this. The sleep of volunteers who deprived themselves of sex with their wives for one week was compared with the sleep of those same volunteers following sexual satiation. *Result:* No difference in the quality of sleep, nor in how rested each person felt on awakening. *Upshot:* There are widespread individual differences in responses to orgasm. Some people even feel more energetic after sex.

Charles Fisher, MD, writing in *Medical Aspects of Human Sexuality.*

Drugs Ease Painful Orgasms

Pelvic pain that radiates to the inner thigh, bladder or rectum in the period preceding and during orgasm is experienced by many older men. Their ejaculatory intensity diminishes, and the time required until the next orgasm increases (in some cases up to several days). Small doses of testosterone (via prescription pills or shots) are often effective.

Medical Aspects of Human Sexuality

Headaches During Sex Can Be Treated

Orgasmic headaches are caused by sudden reduced blood flow to the brain during intercourse. They may be related to sudden sexual excitement or to outside factors such as extreme heat, drugs or alcohol. A history of migraine attacks frequently contributes.

Not related: Age or gender.

Pattern: Headaches usually don't occur often. Pain, which may be severe, lasts only a short time.

Preventive measures: Avoid alcohol and hot showers before intercourse. Take an aspirin an hour before sexual activity. Change sexual positions, or try an activity that produces less physical stress.

Important: See your doctor if orgasmic headaches occur often.

George W. Paulson, MD, professor emeritus of neurology and codirector of the Parkinson's Center of Excellence, Ohio State University College of Medicine & Public Health, Columbus.

Improve Sex During Menopause

Soy can be sexy for women going through menopause. Soy foods are full of natural plant estrogens. Eating three to four ounces of tofu daily—or drinking one cup of soy milk—can provide an estrogen boost that makes sex more pleasurable.

Julian Whitaker, MD, founder, Whitaker Wellness Institute, Newport Beach, CA, and author of *Shed Ten Years in Ten Weeks* (Diane Publishing Company).

When Condoms Prevent Disease and When They Don't

Condoms offer protection against some venereal diseases (gonorrhea, nongonococcal urethritis and yeast infections). They are less effective against herpes, venereal warts and chlamydia, which are small enough to pass through the pores of the condom. Condoms do not offer 100% protection against HIV, but they greatly lower the risk of transmission. If either partner has an active urethral infection or genital lesion, the only safe course is sexual abstinence.

Michael Carrera, EdD, adjunct professor of community medicine, Mount Sinai Medical Center, New York City.

Is the Pill Still Right For You?

Richard P. Dickey, MD, PhD, clinical professor and chief of reproductive endocrinology and infertility in the department of obstetrics and gynecology at Louisiana State University Medical School in New Orleans. He also is the founder of the Fertility Institute, which has three clinics in Louisiana, and author of *Managing Contraceptive Pill/Drug Patients* (EMIS). *www.fertilityinstitute.com*

We recently overheard a group of women, obviously friends in their 20s and 30s, talking about birth control pills—which types they had tried, which ones they liked, which brands had unpleasant or dangerous side effects. When was the last time *you* had such a conversation with your girlfriends…or with your doctor?

If you are heading toward menopause, you are due to have that discussion with your gynecologist, we were told by Richard P. Dickey, MD, PhD, chief of reproductive endocrinology and infertility in the department of obstetrics and gynecology at Louisiana State University Medical School.

Reason: Recent research provides surprising revelations about the benefits and risks of oral contraceptives. So if you are not taking "the Pill" now and thought that you were too old, you might want to reconsider. If you are on it, you need to make sure that it is still safe, given your lifestyle and medical history… and also make sure that the type you are taking has minimal side effects for you.

To minimize the risk for an unintended pregnancy, you should continue to use birth control until one full year has passed without a menstrual period. And despite what many women think, oral contraceptives do not delay the onset of menopause.

Here's what you need to know now about oral contraceptives…

The Pill recently celebrated its 50th birthday (like many of its users), and it is taking middle age quite well despite earlier fears that it might be detrimental to users' long-term health.

Evidence: A recent study in *BMJ* (*British Medical Journal*), which involved more than 46,000 women who were observed for up to 39 years, found a significantly lower rate of death from any cause among women who had ever used the Pill, compared with women who had never used it. Also, a study published in *Contraception* found that oral contraceptives strongly protected against death from uterine cancer and ovarian cancer. Surprisingly, many of these protective effects persisted for years after users stopped taking the Pill—which means that oral contraception often is a particularly good choice for women with a family history of uterine or ovarian cancer, Dr. Dickey said.

Good news for the perimenopausal: Combination estrogen/progestin oral contraceptives (the most common type) alleviate many annoying menopausal symptoms, including hot flashes, night sweats and vaginal dryness…and also may help midlife women maintain muscle tone in the pelvic floor, which is important for preventing incontinence.

Bonus: Oral contraceptives (particularly the low-dose type) often lighten perimenopausal menstrual periods or make them stop altogether.

All birth control pills are not created equal—different brands have different ratios of estrogen to progestin—so if one brand causes side effects for you, talk to your doctor about other options. For instance, Dr. Dickey said, developing migraines might mean that your pill has too much estrogen…developing depression, fatigue or increased appetite might suggest too much progestin.

Some studies indicate that being overweight interferes with the contraceptive effects of the Pill. To reduce pregnancy risk, overweight women may be advised against using a low-dose formulation and also should be careful to take their pills exactly as prescribed, Dr. Dickey suggested.

Important: Many drugs and supplements (including acetaminophen, antibiotics and St. John's wort) can interact with progestin, reducing the Pill's effectiveness. Be sure to tell your doctor about any medications or supplements you take.

Who should not use the Pill: If you are over age 35 and a smoker, oral contraception is not an option for you—there is a clear link between Pill users who smoke and an increased risk for breast cancer, cardiovascular disease and potentially life-threatening blood clots.

Also: Oral contraceptives containing estrogen are not appropriate for women with a history of heart disease, uncontrolled hypertension, blood clots or estrogen-dependent cancer. It is not that the Pill is believed to cause those conditions, Dr. Dickey said, but rather that it can exacerbate existing conditions. Some women with such conditions can take a progestin-only oral contraceptive, however, so discuss this possibility with your doctor.

Condoms Lessen VD Risk

Men who are exposed just once to a woman who has gonorrhea have a 22% to 40%

chance of contracting the disease. But some men won't catch it even after repeated exposure.

Why: They have antigonococci organisms in their urethras or residual immunity from previous infections.

To decrease risk: Use a condom.

Best Ways to Boost Your Sexual Fitness

The late Robert N. Butler, MD, founding president, International Longevity Center (*www.ilcusa.org*), former chairman, department of geriatrics and adult development, Mount Sinai Medical Center, New York City. He is coauthor of *The New Love and Sex After 60* (Ballantine).

Everyone knows that some medical conditions, including diabetes and hormone deficiency, can cause sexual difficulties ranging from impotence to lack of desire. It's also well known that many drugs, including antidepressants and blood pressure drugs, often produce unwanted sexual side effects.

What few people realize is that a significant number of sexual difficulties are not linked to a medical condition or medication.* *For these cases, keeping your body fit—with proper diet, exercise and rest—is the best solution…*

EAT SMART

Excessive dietary fat and cholesterol produce artery-clogging plaque that not only increases your risk for heart attack and stroke but also restricts blood flow to the genitalia. This can hinder a man's ability to achieve or maintain an erection and may also possibly reduce vaginal and clitoral sensitivity in women.

Self-defense: Consume no more than 30% of your daily calories as fat. Avoid saturated fat and trans-fats (abundant in fried foods and commercially baked goods). Choose unsaturated fats, which can be found in olive and flaxseed oils, nuts and fish.

Warning: Overindulging in alcohol can dampen sexual appetite and diminish sexual performance. Although alcohol lowers inhibitions, it's known to depress physical arousal.

*If you experience sexual difficulties, see your doctor for a thorough evaluation to rule out a treatable medical condition.

Eating until you're uncomfortably full can leave you feeling too bloated and sluggish for sex. To avoid unnecessarily straining the heart, it's advisable to postpone sex for a few hours following a heavy meal.

Heart attacks during sex are extremely uncommon. According to a study conducted at Harvard University, the risk for heart attack during sex among people who have coronary disease is 20 in one million.

GET MORE EXERCISE...

For the stamina and flexibility required to enjoy sex, you need to exercise. Brisk walking usually provides the best overall workout for people age 60 or older. Aim for 10,000 steps daily, five to six days a week (2,000 steps equals roughly one mile).

If that sounds daunting, consider that even relatively inactive adults average 3,500 steps a day. Simple changes—taking the stairs instead of the elevator or walking rather than driving to a store, for example—can add to that number substantially. That means a two- or three-mile walk may be all that's required to reach your overall goal.

...AND MORE SLEEP

At least half of all adults over age 50 suffer from sleep disturbances. Insomnia, illness, pain or frequent nighttime trips to the bathroom can interfere with sleep cycles, depriving you of sufficient rapid eye movement (REM) sleep—the kind associated with dreaming. Chronic sleep deprivation can leave you too exhausted for sex and may also lead to a deficiency of important hormones, including human growth hormone, which helps keep your body lean, fit and energized.

Important: After age 60, it's common to experience a sleep pattern that occurs when you fall asleep at dusk and awaken before dawn. This can disrupt your sex life, particularly if your partner maintains a traditional sleep schedule.

Fortunately, the problem can usually be reversed with regular sun exposure in the late-afternoon. Aim to get approximately 30 minutes of sun *without sunscreen* between 4 pm and 6 pm. This will not only correct sleep patterns, but also help prevent osteoporosis by triggering production of vitamin D in your skin.

Warning: Avoid unprotected sun exposure between 10 am and 2 pm, when harmful ultraviolet rays are most intense.

ADDITIONAL STRATEGIES

Improved nutrition, exercise and rest typically lead to more satisfying sex within a matter of weeks. *For more immediate results...*

- **Use visual, tactile stimulation.** Men, especially, are aroused by sexual images and touch. Turn down the lights and watch a steamy movie. Women may want to wear sexy lingerie. Share a gentle massage or engage in mutual stimulation.

- **Fantasize.** Imagining sexy scenarios can heighten arousal for both partners. Interestingly, however, one study showed that men's ability to fantasize may diminish with age. This may explain why men tend to rely on sexy pictures, videos and other visual aids.

- **Use lubricants.** Postmenopausal women, especially, may find their enjoyment of sex hampered by vaginal dryness. Water-based lubricants, such as Astroglide, can help. Oil-based lubricants may lead to vaginal infections.

- **Plan around arthritis pain.** A hot shower before sex can help reduce joint pain and stiffness. So can taking your pain medication 30 minutes before sex. If you suffer from osteoarthritis, try sex in the morning, before joints have a chance to stiffen or become inflamed. If you have rheumatoid arthritis, sex in the late afternoon or evening may be preferable, since symptoms often subside with activity.

- **Vary times and positions.** Don't get stuck in the rut of always having sex at night, in the missionary position. If you or your partner are too tired for sex at night, plan a morning or afternoon sex date. If one of you has a heart condition, hip or back pain, let that person take the bottom position, which requires less vigorous movement.

- **Practice seduction.** Good sex starts in the brain, which means it should begin hours before you actually arrive in the bedroom. Throughout the day, give your partner caresses, kisses and other outward signs of affection. Genuine intimacy is the best aphrodisiac.

Women's Infertility Can Be Predicted

Infertility in women can now be predicted with 95% certainty by chemical analysis, tests and a physical exam.

Point: A woman need not have a baby just to see if she can. When the tests determine her childbearing status, she and her husband are then free to delay having children if they decide to do so.

Stanley T. West, MD, chief, division of reproductive endocrinology and infertility, St. Vincent's Hospital and Medical Center, New York City.

Jockey Shorts Lower Sperm Counts

Athletic briefs may lower the sperm counts of men who wear them. The form-fitting underwear increases scrotal temperatures, which often leads to a reduction of sperm production. Men with impaired fertility sometimes try to avoid things that raise scrotal temperatures, such as hot baths.

Note: Even if the shorts lower sperm counts slightly, there is no evidence that they affect male fertility.

Stanley A. Brosman, MD, writing in *Medical Aspects of Human Sexuality.*

Age Is Not a Factor

Sperm count is reduced by poor health but not by aging. A recent study showed that healthy men between 60 and 88 had higher counts, with comparable fertilizing capacity, than a group aged 24 to 37.

Journal of Clinical Endocrinology and Metabolism

Surprising Cause of Infertility

Infertility in men is often caused by varicocele, an enlarged vein in the testicles.

Corrective procedure: A varicocelectomy. Done with local anesthetic, sometimes on an outpatient basis, the operation ties off the enlarged vein to reroute the blood flow.

Result: About 70% recovery rate (men able to impregnate their wives).

No one knows why this vein causes infertility. But it can affect the fertility of men in their 30s and 40s who were fertile in their 20s.

Natural Birth and Caesarean

Caesarean deliveries need not necessarily be repeated for subsequent births. Guidelines adopted by the American College of Obstetricians and Gynecologists give conditions for allowing women to choose vaginal delivery after an earlier Caesarean. *Among them:* A low transverse type of incision in the earlier operation. A single fetus with headfirst presentation, weighing less than eight pounds. A delivery room with equipment to monitor fetal heart rate and the uterus. Nonrepeating reasons for the earlier surgical delivery. However, in case of difficulties, the mother may have to have another Caesarean.

Is Exercise an Aphrodisiac?

Researchers and common sense have long held that exercise enhances health and makes people feel better about themselves and their bodies. This in turn makes them more sexually attractive and responsive. Now studies are suggesting that exercise is a potent stimulus to hormone production in both men and women. It may, in fact, chemically increase basic libido by stepping up the levels of such hormones as testosterone.

Whole Body Healing by Carl Lowe and Jim Nechas (Rodale Press).

3

Staying Well

The Only Workout You'll Ever Need

Research shows that moderate-intensity exercise at least three times a week can increase your life span by at least two-and-a-half years.

I've developed a five-day-a-week walking and toning program that takes less than one hour per day to perform. And you don't have to go to a gym to do it.

AEROBIC WALKING

On Monday, Wednesday and Friday, walk two miles in less than 30 minutes—15 minutes per mile.

You may have to work up to this quick pace. Begin with a 20-minute mile, and progress as you feel comfortable.

Be sure to get your doctor's approval before you start this program if you've been sedentary or have a history of heart disease or another medical condition. *Steps to take...*

• **Warm up by walking at a slow pace for one-quarter mile.**

• **Then spend five minutes stretching your hamstrings,** quadriceps and back and arm muscles. This will help to prevent musculoskeletal problems that can occur with any exercise.

• **Walk at your designated,** brisk rate for 30 minutes. Don't worry about checking your heart rate. Instead, keep count of your steps per minute.

To walk two miles in 30 minutes, shoot for a pace of at least 120 steps per minute (60 steps in 30 seconds). To start with a 20-minute mile, walk 90 steps per minute.

Keep your arms next to your body. Bend your elbows, and pump your arms at the same pace you move your legs. The faster you walk and the more you pump your arms, the greater the aerobic benefit.

Kenneth H. Cooper, MD, MPH, chairman and founder of The Cooper Aerobics Center, 12200 Preston Rd., Dallas 75230. He is an expert in preventive medicine and author of *Controlling Cholesterol the Natural Way* (Bantam).

• **Cool down for five minutes** to prevent lightheadedness or an irregular heartbeat. Sixty-five percent of severe cardiac events occur after a workout because blood has been diverted from the heart and pumped to the exercising muscles.

Walk slowly. After five minutes, take your pulse. If it is still over 120 (and you are under 40 years of age) or over 100 (and you are over 40 years of age), you may be exercising beyond your capacity. The next time you exercise, don't walk as fast or as far.

STRENGTH TRAINING

Developing adequate muscle mass is critical to your health. Otherwise you'll be weak—even if your heart is strong from aerobic walking.

The simplest and most convenient form of toning exercise is calisthenics. They use your body's weight and the force of gravity as resistance to build up muscle strength.

On Tuesday and Thursday, do 20 to 30 minutes of toning exercises. If you prefer to do toning exercises the days you walk, do them after aerobic activity.

Reason: If you perform calisthenics before aerobic activity, you'll build up an excessive oxygen debt in your body that will make it difficult for you to walk fast and may lead to earlier fatigue.

Try to work the main muscle groups—chest, arms, abdomen and thighs—each session. *Essential exercises…*

• **Pelvic tilts** strengthen your stomach and back. Lie flat on your back, and put your hands under your head. Bend your knees with your feet on the floor.

Tilt your pelvis by contracting your stomach muscles and pressing your lower back to the floor. Hold for a count of 10. Release. Repeat three times.

• **Hamstring and gluteal squeezes** strengthen the back of your thighs and buttocks.

Staying in the pelvic tilt position, lift your hips off the floor, but not your upper back. Squeeze your thigh and buttock muscles tightly. Lower and release. Work up to 20 repetitions.

• **Stomach crunches** strengthen your stomach and back. Lie flat on the floor with your knees pulled up to a 90-degree angle. Slowly lift your upper body off the floor using your stomach muscles.

Go only as far as the bottom of your shoulder blades. Lead with your chest and shoulders—not with your head. Work up to 30 repetitions.

Don't place your hands behind your head. You'll be tempted to use them to raise your upper body, and you'll risk straining your neck muscles. Fold them on your chest instead.

• **Quadriceps lifts** strengthen the front of your thighs. Lie on the floor with your arms at your sides.

Keeping the right leg straight and flat, bend the left knee and rest your foot on the floor.

Slowly raise and then lower your right leg, keeping it straight…your ankle flexed…and your toes pointing toward your head.

Progress to 20 repetitions. Then switch legs.

• **Pushups** strengthen your chest, shoulders and backs of the arms.

Lie on the floor, stomach down…hands under shoulders. Push up and rest your weight on your toes and hands. Keep your back, elbows and arms straight.

Lower your body to the floor using only your arms. Then raise your body off the floor using only your arms until your elbows are straight again. Work up to 20 repetitions.

THE BEST TIME TO EXERCISE

Early morning exercisers are the most consistent. Exercising before the evening meal or before the largest meal of the day has the greatest benefit, particularly if weight loss is desired.

Don't exercise until two hours after a heavy meal. Exercising sooner can cause heart problems. Also, don't exercise vigorously less than two hours before bedtime—to avoid affecting your sleep.

Personally, I find that working out for one hour starting any time after 5 pm but no later than 7 pm is optimal.

Most people tend to overeat at this time of day, and exercising keeps the appetite and caloric intake in check.

Also, exercising at this time of day stokes the metabolism for two hours. Your body will burn off calories more efficiently…the stress of the day will be relieved…and endorphins —feel-good chemicals that will put you in a pleasurable state of mind—will be released.

Making a Plan For Wellness

Passing an annual physical exam was once enough to satisfy most people about their health. But today an increasing number strive beyond that—for optimal health or the condition of "wellness," as it is known. Essential to achieving wellness is a plan that is both personal and practical. *How to set one up for yourself…*

•**Try to clarify your most important reasons for living,** and write them down in a clear and concise fashion.

•**With these in mind,** identify the health goals that bolster your chances of living longer and healthier. *Be specific:* Do not plan to lose weight but to lose 20 pounds in six months. *Other possible goals:* Lowering blood pressure by a specific amount, accomplishing a dramatic feat, such as riding the Snake River rapids or completing a marathon.

•**List supportive actions for each goal.** *Example:* Joining a fitness club, training for long-distance running.

•**Also identify the barriers to each goal** and how they can be overcome.

•**List the payoffs for each goal,** whether they are new energy at the office or more fun at the beach.

Virtually no one, however, can hope to stay on a wellness plan without support from friends or a system of benchmarks. Before starting the program, list the network of friends you can rely on for bicycle rides, tennis or other activities in the plan.

Once the plan is under way, set realistic quarterly benchmarks to track your achievements. A log or diary is usually helpful. *Pitfall:* Do not become so involved in the plan that you begin serving it rather than the reverse.

Best Exercise Machine

Jerome Zuckerman, PhD, president of Cardio-Fitness Systems, 345 Park Ave., New York City.

The stationary bicycle is safe, aerobic and noncompetitive. You can ride it rain or shine, and because you work out continually without pauses, you can work off more calories per minute than you would in a stop-and-start sport.

Men's Health, 33 E. Minor St., Emmaus, PA 18098.

SELECTING A STATIONARY BIKE

•**Durability is an important feature.** The more plastic there is in a bike, the less durable it is.

•**Besides a quality calibration component,** a good bike has a speedometer and an odometer.

•**The seat and handlebars should be adjustable.** *Correct seat height:* When the leg is comfortably extended, with the ball of the foot on the down pedal.

UNDERTAKING THE PROGRAM

•**Start each exercise period with stretching exercises to warm up.**

•**Take an easy workload** for the first three to five weeks.

•**Monitor your pulse rate.** It dictates when to increase the exercise level. *Example:* As you condition yourself to a given workload, your pulse rate will drop. That's the signal to step up the load by adjusting the calibration component.

•**Make up a workout schedule.** Three to five workouts a week is satisfactory.

•**Ignore the handlebars when pedaling the bike.** Sit upright with your arms folded or hanging down. If you have to grasp the handlebars when pedaling, it means you're working too hard. *Bonus:* When working out, you are free to read or watch TV.

•**Elevate your legs on the leg posts of the bike after completion of the exercise period.** *Alternative:* Lie down with legs raised. Or walk around the house for five to ten minutes. *Caution:* Without the cool-down period, you risk dizziness or worse.

Best Exercises for Elderly People

Exercise keeps the joints from becoming stiff and immobile and may even strengthen the bones themselves. *Reason:* The pull of muscles on bones often stimulates the bones to acquire calcium. *Best exercises:* Flexing and stretching. Gently bend, extend or rotate the neck, shoulders, elbows, back, hips, knees and ankles. *Best aerobic exercise:* Walking.

Also beneficial: Swimming, dancing, riding and using an exercise bicycle.

Muscles shrink only from disease or disuse, not from age. Any healthy muscle responds to exercise, no matter what the age of the person. *Point:* Exercise will maintain musculature, and even expand it, after the age of 50.

The Health Letter.

Exercise Payoff

Heart disease risk is significantly reduced with regular exercise. A National Institutes of Health (NIH) panel recommends that adults and children engage in moderate-intensity physical activity for at least 30 minutes on most days—preferably every day.

If you can't set aside a 30-minute period, you'll get similar benefits from three 10-minute sessions of walking, cycling, yard work, etc.

To stick with your regimen: Choose low-cost activities that you enjoy, feel safe doing and can access easily.

Russell Luepker, MD, professor and head of epidemiology, University of Minnesota School of Public Health, Minneapolis. He chaired the NIH Panel of Physical Activity and Cardiovascular Health.

"Space-Age" Exercise Equipment: Facts and Fantasies

The sophisticated machinery that has turned old-fashioned gyms into today's health clubs is designed to offer continual resistance during each of the movement exercises for which you use it. This is a much faster, more efficient way to build muscle strength than using weights, for example.

If you do all the exercises for all the muscle groups on a regular basis, would you be perfectly fit?

No. Strength and fitness are not equivalent. Although muscle strength is a component of fitness, you also need flexibility and heart-lung capacity. Stretching exercises make you flexible, and aerobic exercises such as running and bike riding build up your heart muscle and your lung capacity.

Can working out on these machines help you lose weight?

There is a common myth that strengthening exercises turn fat into muscle. It doesn't work that way. People who are overweight need to follow a calorie-restricted diet and do aerobic exercises, which trigger the body to use up fat. Working out on machines only builds up muscle under the fat layer. However, combining a weight-loss program with strengthening exercises can improve body tone as the weight comes off.

Are these machines safe to use?

You need to learn the proper technique for using each machine, including proper breathing, before you are allowed on the equipment alone. Poor form on the machines can lead to serious injuries. So can using the wrong weight settings.

Good rule of thumb: Use a weight setting that allows you to do eight to 12 repetitions comfortably. If you must struggle to get beyond five, the setting is too heavy. If you complete 10 without feeling any fatigue at all, it is too light. You will have to experiment with each machine to get the right setting. Then, from time to time, you can adjust the weights upward. But be cautious. Pushing yourself too hard not only invites injury but also discourages you from sticking to the program on a regular basis.

Great Exercise Gear

Gregory Florez, president and CEO, First Fitness, Inc., a Salt Lake City company that specializes in sports-and-fitness training and product-information education.

Having the right equipment can motivate you to work out. *Here's some gear to help you make the most of your fitness program...*

• **Weighted jump rope.** Jump ropes provide a terrific aerobic workout. This one has half-pound, removable weights tucked inside its cushioned handles to increase resistance, tone arms and help burn more calories. $15–$25*.

All-Pro weighted jump rope. Available at *www.paragonsports.com.*

• **Weighted padded nylon vest** has pockets to hold up to 40 half-pound weights to increase amount of calories burned while walking... running...hiking...or doing aerobics. Starting at $219.95.

Uni-Vest. *www.power-systems.com.* 800-321-6975.

• **Heart rate monitor.** A wireless wrist-watch-style monitor and a chest strap communicate via an infrared beam. Automatically determines heart rate at which your body burns calories most efficiently, so you can stay within that zone when exercising. Doubles as a watch...alarm...daily calendar...and stopwatch. $269.95.

Polar "RS400" heart rate monitor. 800-227-1314. *www.polarusa.com.*

• **Body fat/Body Weight Scale.** Uses a low-level electrical current to safely determine percentage of body fat. Step-on scale stores personal data for up to four people. Also measures body weight. $29.99 and up.

Tanita, 847-640-9241 to find a store near you that sells Tanita products. Available online at *www.tanita.com.*

*Prices are manufacturers' suggested retail.

Walking Mistakes

Gary Yanker, author of many books and audiotapes about walking, including *Walking Medicine: The Lifetime Guide to Preventive and Therapeutic Exercisewalking* (McGraw-Hill).

Although most of us have been walking since we were toddlers, at least 30% of all people still haven't learned how to walk correctly.

Whether you're walking for pleasure, walking for exercise or just walking to get from one place to another, it's important to walk properly.

Mistake: **Not maintaining proper posture.** Poor posture puts extra stress on joints, vertebrae and muscles, causing pain.

Correct: **Tuck your chin into your neck** so your ear, shoulder, hip and ankle form a straight line perpendicular to the ground when you're standing still. Then hold this position as closely as possible when you walk. This avoids undue stress on any one joint or part of your body.

Mistake: **Arching your back.** This causes lower back pain and shortens the length of your steps.

Correct: **Do a pelvic tilt.** Tuck your buttocks under your body and hold in your stomach while you walk. This will take conscious effort at first, but after a while, your stomach and buttocks will stay in automatically. Walking this way strengthens the back and the stomach muscles, which redistributes weight away from the lower vertebrae, eliminating back pain.

Mistake: **Keeping your arms still.** You lose almost half the exercise value of walking—increasing your heart rate and working your shoulder, back and arm muscles—by not moving your arms.

Correct: **Pump your arms.** Bend your elbows slightly for regular walking, and 90° for aerobic walking.

Guide the arms straight forward and back, hands rising as far as the chest—at least to the waist. Let the inside of your arms rub the sides of your body—you should hear your clothing rubbing.

Pumping your arms is an upper-body calisthenic—your shoulders, upper back and chest all get exercised. If you pump your arms during brisk or aerobic walking, it doubles the exercise value.

Mistake: **Walking duck-footed** (with the knees pointed out) or pigeon-toed (with the knees pointed in). This puts stress on the knees and ankles. They are hinge joints—made for forward, not side-to-side, motion. Stress causes knee and ankle pain.

Correct: **Walk with your feet parallel.** And use the heel-toe roll. Land the heel first and turn the ankle out slightly (the width of a finger). Then roll on the outer edge of the foot until you reach the toe. This aligns the lower and upper leg.

Mistake: **Walking with your feet too close together.** This makes it easy to trip and fall.

Correct: **Keep your feet hip-width to shoulder-width apart.**

Mistake: **Taking short steps.** This also reduces the exercise value of walking, and it causes the leg and hip muscles to tighten.

Correct: **By reaching further with each step**—and using arm pumping and the heel-toe roll—most people can lengthen their average step three to eight inches. Longer steps burn more calories, work leg muscles, raise heart rate, increase circulation, make you feel more energetic and increase walking speed.

Walk for Your Heart

Brisk walking keeps your mind sharp. But it also does more. Recently compiled results of a study involving 72,488 women aged 40 to 65 showed that as little as three hours of brisk walking a week reduced the risk of heart disease by as much as 40%. And...five hours of brisk walking cut the risk by 50%.

Important: To obtain this benefit, you must walk at a rate of at least three miles an hour. Casual strolling will not produce the same result.

JoAnn E. Manson, MD, DrPH, chief of preventive medicine, Brigham & Women's Hospital/Harvard Medical School, Boston.

Easy Exercises to Strengthen Your Back

American Journal of Nursing, New York City.

Strengthening the back and stomach muscles is the best protection against a back injury.

• **Flexed-knee sit-ups.** Lie on your back, with knees bent, feet flat on the floor and arms at your side. Sit up slowly by rolling forward, starting with your head.

• **Bent-knee leg lifts.** In the same position as the sit-ups, bring one knee as close as you can to your chest while extending the other leg. Alternate the legs.

• **Knee-chest leg lifts.** Work from the bent-knee sit-up position, but put a small pillow under your head. Use your hands to bring both knees up to your chest, then tighten your stomach muscles and hold that position for a count of 10.

• **Back flattening.** Lie on your back, flex your knees and put your arms above your head. Tighten your stomach and buttock muscles and press your lower back hard against the floor. Hold this position for a count of 10, relax and repeat.

Cautions: Don't overdo the exercises. Soreness is a sign that you should cut back. Never do these exercises with the legs straight. If you have back trouble, consult your doctor before starting this or any exercise program.

Walk for Good Health

Exercise doesn't have to be strenuous or punishing to be effective. Despite its economy of muscle use, walking is considered by most experts to be one of the best exercises. *Benefits...*

• **A preventive and a remedy for respiratory,** heart and circulation disorders.

• **Weight control.** Walking may take off pounds, or keep weight at a desirable level. (Particularly effective in keeping excess pounds from coming back once they have been dieted off.)

• **Aids digestion,** elimination and sleep.

• **Antidote to physical and psychological tensions.**

Walking works as a second heart. Expanding and contracting foot muscles, calves, thighs and buttocks help pump blood back to the heart. This aid is crucial. The heart can propel blood very well on its own, but the body's muscles are essential to the return flow from lower regions (legs, feet, stomach). When the blood transportation system becomes sluggish because of lack of exercise, the heart compensates by doing more work. Heart rate and blood pressure rise. (Elevated pressure can be helped to return to normal by a regimen of walking.)

Best daily routine...

• **Time.** Whenever it can be fitted into daily routine. (A mile takes only 15–20 minutes.) People who do sedentary office work usually average a mile and a half in a normal day. Stretch that by choosing to walk down the hall to a colleague instead of simply picking up the interoffice phone.

• **Place.** Wherever it's pleasant and convenient to your daily tasks. Walk to work at least partway. Or, if you're a daily commuter, walk to the train station. Walk not to the nearest but to the second or third bus or subway stop away from your house. Get off a stop or two earlier than the usual one. Park the car 10 blocks farther away. Walk 10 blocks to and from lunch. Walk after dinner, before sitting down to read a book, watch TV or do work.

• **Clothes.** Comfortable and seasonal, light rather than heavy. Avoid thin-soled shoes when walking city pavements. It may be desirable to use metatarsal pads or cushioned soles. (The impact on concrete weakens metatarsal arches and causes calluses.)

• **Length.** Walk modest distances at first. In the city the number of streets tells you how far you've gone. But in the country you can walk farther than you realize. *Consequences:* Fatigue on the return trip. *Instead:* Use a good pedometer.

• **Pace.** Walking for exercise should feel different from other kinds of walking. *Some suggestions...*

• Set out at a good pace. Use the longest possible stride that's comfortable. Let your arms swing and muscles stretch. Strike a rhythm and keep to it.

• Don't saunter. It's tiring. Walking at a good pace allows the momentum of each stride to carry over into the next.

• Lengthen the customary stride by swinging the foot a little farther ahead than usual. Lengthening the stride speeds the walking pace. It also loosens tense muscles, puts other neglected muscles to work and provides continual momentum that puts less weight on feet.

Most comfortable pace: Three miles per hour. It generally suits the average male and is the US Army pace for long hikes. With the right shoes and unconfining clothes, most women will be comfortable at that pace, too.

Exercise vs. Stroke

Exercise helps prevent stroke...and speeds rehabilitation of people who have already had a stroke.

In one recent study, men who exercised vigorously an hour a day, five days a week, cut their stroke risk in half.

In another study, stroke survivors who exercised regularly regained more of their strength and balance than those survivors who didn't exercise.

Pamela W. Duncan, PhD, former director, Brooks Center for Rehabilitation Studies, Gainesville, Florida, and professor and research fellow, Duke University Center for Clinical Health Policy Research, Durham, North Carolina.

Exercises for Desk-Bound Workers

Doug MacLennon, The Fitness Institute, Willowdale, Ontario, quoted in *Creative Selling*.

Exercises to do at your desk to stay mentally alert, tone sagging muscles and bring relief to strained muscles...

• **Tummy slimmer.** Sit erect, hands on knees. Exhale, pulling abdominal muscles in as far as possible. Relax. Inhale. Exhale as you draw in stomach again. Repeat 10 to 20 times.

• **Head circles.** Drop head forward, chin on chest, shoulders relaxed. Slowly move head in a semi-circle from one side to another, but not all the way around. Reverse direction. Do five to six times on each side.

• **Torso twist.** Raise elbows to shoulder level. Slowly twist around as far right as possible, then reverse. Do 10 to 12 turns each way.

• **Heel and toe lift.** Lean forward, hands on knees. Lift both heels off floor, strongly contracting calf muscles. Lower heels, lift toes high toward shins. Do 10 to 15 complete movements.

Cabbage Leaves for Arthritic Joints

Michael Van Straten, ND, DO, a naturopath and acupuncturist in private practice in London. He is the author of *Home Remedies: A Practical Guide to Common Ailments You Can Safely Treat at Home Using Conventional and Complementary Medicine* (McGraw-Hill).

Cabbage leaves contain powerful anti-inflammatory compounds. Applied to arthritic joints, these compounds are remarkably effective at relieving both pain and swelling.

Arthritis sufferers often rely on over-the-counter anti-inflammatory drugs like ibuprofen (Advil) for relief of their symptoms. But prolonged use of these drugs can cause stomach pain and even bleeding ulcers.

Using cabbage leaves instead helps reduce the amount of medication needed. And cabbage seems to work more effectively than topical creams marketed for arthritis relief.

What to do: Use a rolling pin or knife handle to bruise one or two large, outer, dark-green leaves from a head of a green cabbage.

Warm the leaves in a microwave, steamer or oven, then wrap them around the joint. Cover with a towel. Leave in place for 15 minutes.

The compress should be applied once daily for mild inflammation, two or three times a day for severe inflammation.

Warm cabbage leaves can also be used to curb inflammation resulting from tennis elbow, sprains or other minor injuries. Apply ice and elevate the injured limb to curb the initial swelling. Then apply the cabbage leaf compress two or three times daily until pain and swelling subside.

Odd as it sounds, women with painful breast cysts—as well as nursing mothers with inflamed, cracked nipples—can also get relief from cabbage leaves.

Line the cups of a bra with bruised cabbage leaves. Leave in place for an hour a day. It's not necessary to warm the leaves.

Jogging and Achilles Tendinitis

American Journal of Sports Medicine.

The repetitive impact of running frequently causes inflammation, degeneration and small tears in the heel tendons.

Orthopedists from Boston University Medical School suggest these preventive steps...

- **Decrease weekly mileage.**
- **Cut down on uphill workouts.**
- **Prepare for running by stretching the tendons.** With heels flat and knees straight, lean forward against a wall and hold for 30 seconds.
- **Warm heels and tendons with a heating pad before running.** After running, apply ice for 10 to 12 minutes.
- **Elevate heels by placing small felt pads inside running shoes.** They relieve tension on the Achilles tendon and contiguous structures.
- **Monitor wear on outer sides of shoes.** Tendons tend to become stressed when shoe sides give no support.
- **If these measures fail,** consult a physician about immobilization and anti-inflammatory drugs.

Breathing Your Way To Better Health

Robert Fried, PhD, director of the Stress and Biofeedback Clinic of the Albert Ellis Institute and senior professor of biopsychology at Hunter College, both in New York City. He is the author of several books, including *Breathe Well, Be Well* (John Wiley & Sons).

Everyone knows that taking a deep breath is a great way to cool off when you're getting angry.

And any woman who has used Lamaze breathing during childbirth is aware that the act of focusing on one's breath provides a welcome distraction from severe pain.

But few people realize that how you breathe day in and day out plays a key role in triggering—or preventing—chronic conditions. Among the conditions affected by breathing are high blood pressure...heart disease...migraines...and Raynaud's syndrome, a chronic circulatory disorder marked by uncomfortably cold hands and feet.

THE BREATH–BODY CONNECTION

The world is basically divided into two types of breathers...

- **Belly breathers** take slow, deep breaths, letting their abdomens rise with each inhalation and fall with each exhalation.

This form of breathing is ideal, but relatively few adults breathe this way.

- **Chest breathers** take rapid, shallow breaths. This form of breathing causes the body to expel too much carbon dioxide, adversely affecting how the blood carries oxygen to the organs and tissues.

To find out which kind of breather you are, sit comfortably and place your left hand on your chest, your right hand over your navel. Breathe normally for one minute. Note the movement of each of your hands as you inhale and exhale.

If your left hand is virtually motionless while your right hand moves out when you inhale and in when you exhale, you're a belly breather.

If your left hand rises noticeably—or if both hands move more or less simultaneously in a shallow motion—you're a chest breather.

Being a chest breather does not mean you're going to keel over anytime soon. But eventually, your health will suffer.

Reason: Chest breathing is less effective than belly breathing at introducing fresh, oxygenated air into the lower reaches of the lungs. That's where the tiny air sacs (alveoli) that absorb oxygen are most concentrated.

Less air reaching these alveoli means that less oxygen gets into the bloodstream with each breath. To get enough oxygen to meet all of the body's needs, these people must breathe rapidly.

Rapid breathing upsets the blood's normal acid-base balance (pH), which is measured on a scale that runs from zero to 14.

Ordinarily, blood has a pH of 7.38 (slightly alkaline). When blood pH climbs above that level, arteries constrict, impairing blood flow to all parts of the body.

Result: Increased susceptibility to high blood pressure...insomnia...anxiety...phobias ...Raynaud's syndrome...migraines...and, for heart patients, angina.

HOW TO BREATHE RIGHT

No matter how poor your current breathing habits may be, it's reassuring to know that each of us was born knowing how to breathe properly. And—it's surprisingly easy to relearn proper breathing habits. *The keys...*

•**Stop sucking in your gut.** A flat stomach may be attractive, but clenching the abdominal muscles inhibits proper movement of the diaphragm. That's the sheetlike muscle separating the abdomen from the chest cavity.

Since the movement of the diaphragm is what causes the lungs to fill and empty, proper breathing is possible only if it can move freely.

•**Avoid tight clothing.** Like clenching your abdominal muscles, wearing overly tight clothing can restrict movement of the diaphragm.

•**Breathe through your nose.** Doing so makes hyperventilation almost impossible. The only time you should breathe through your mouth is during vigorous exercise.

•**Practice belly breathing.** At least twice a day—for about four minutes each time—sit in a comfortable chair with your left hand on your chest, your right hand on your abdomen.

As you inhale, use your left hand to press lightly against your chest to help keep it from rising. Allow your right hand to move outward as air fills your belly.

With each exhalation, slowly pull your abdomen back in as far as it will go without raising your chest. With practice, your body will find its own natural rhythm.

Good idea: Practice belly breathing when you're stuck sitting in traffic, waiting in line at the store, etc.—whenever and wherever you can. It's a good use for time that would otherwise be wasted. Once you get the hang of it, practice belly breathing without using your hands.

You may want to augment the effects of these practice sessions by combining belly breathing with...

•**Classical music.** Stick with slow compositions, such as Pachelbel's *Canon* or Bach's *Jesu, Joy of Man's Desiring*. As you breathe, imagine that you are inhaling the music...and that it is filling every space in your body.

•**Muscle relaxation.** Imagine that the tension in the muscles in your forehead is flowing out of your body with each exhalation. Do the same thing, breath by breath, with your jaw, neck, shoulders, arms, hands, legs and feet.

•**Imagery.** Close your eyes, and imagine yourself standing on a sunny beach. Feel the warmth of the sun enveloping you. As you inhale, imagine the surf rolling toward your feet. As you exhale, picture the surf rolling back out to sea.

•**Do on-the-spot breathing therapy.** Once you've mastered belly breathing, you're ready to start using breathing as an instant feel-better tool.

A few deep belly breaths can dissipate anxiety...ward off an impending panic attack or migraine...restore circulation to cold, numb fingers and toes...and help ease you to sleep if you're experiencing insomnia.

If you're diligent about practicing belly breathing, there's a good chance it will become second nature. For most people, the change takes about six weeks.

Caution: Breathing exercises are safe for most people. But if you've recently suffered an injury or had surgery, check with a doctor.

Certain disorders, such as kidney disease, lead to rapid breathing to compensate for chemical changes in the body. If you suffer from one of these ailments, slow breathing may be unsafe.

Work Out With the Masters

Liz Neporent, regular health, fitness and medical correspondent for *The New York Daily News*. She is author of *Fitness Walking for Dummies* (IDG Books).

Get fit in the comfort of your living room. *To begin a home exercise program, try these DVDs...*

PILATES METHOD

•**Jennifer Kries.** *The Perfect Mix.* The DVD is based on the Pilates Method—a workout that emphasizes controlled movements and concentration to develop posture, abdominal strength and balance. 19-24 minutes per workout.

Collage Video, 800-819-7111; *www.collagevideo.com;* DVD only: $13.99.

STEP AEROBICS

•**Petra Kolber.** *PK Step.* Petra Kolber's workout includes leaps, power squats, straddle jumps and a toning section. 56 minutes.

Collage Video, 800-819-7111; *www.collagevideo.com,* DVD only: $13.99.

STRETCHING

•**Karen Voight.** *Pure & Simple Stretch.* Gentle, straightforward stretches for a full-body routine. Voight shows how to modify each move, depending on how limber you are. 38 minutes.

Collage Video, 800-819-7111; *www.collagevideo.com,* DVD only: $14.99.

WALKING

•**Leslie Sansone.** *One & Two Mile Walk.* Walking, low-impact aerobics workout. Simple moves. Not intimidating. 54 minutes.

Collage Video, 800-819-7111; *www.collagevideo.com;* DVD only: $11.99.

Stomach Muscles: The Key to Exercise

Pamela Francis, personal consultant and dance teacher, New York City.

The muscles of the mid-torso should be the focal point of any exercise program. Strong midsection or stomach muscles allow you to better control all your movements (to bend without flopping, for example) and increase your stretch. They also improve your posture and take strain off your lower back. *Problem:* Most people are hardly aware of these important muscles and must be taught to use them.

Good first exercise: Lie on your back on the floor. Bend your knees, keeping your feet flat on the floor. Clasp your hands behind your head. Slowly curl up (don't jerk up) from your head forward and see how far you can get. (Don't worry if it's only five or six inches.) Hold the position until you feel strain in the midriff. You have just found the muscles you need to strengthen. Repeat the exercise four times, doing so very slowly.

Note: Traditional sit-ups, with straight legs held down under the couch and arms raised overhead, are dangerous for beginners, who tend to use lower back muscles rather than stomach muscles. Putting hands behind the head keeps the novices from using the momentum of flailing arms to lift themselves.

Second exercise: Lie on your back on the floor. Raise your head and shoulders, put your elbows behind you and rest your upper body on your forearms. Keep your lower back (from just above the waist down) pressed against the floor. With feet together and knees bent, raise your legs four, five or six inches without raising your lower back off the floor. *Variations:* Raise bent legs, stretch them out, return them to bent position and lower them to the floor. Raise both legs and kick vertically, one leg at a time. Raise bent legs together, open and stretch, return to original position, and lower both. Raise bent legs, stretch them out and scissor-kick. Work up to 50 leg movements in four or five minutes.

Standing stomach exercise: This sexy workout uses a combination of leg and stomach muscles to improve lower-back flexibility. Stand with legs apart and slightly bent, and do rhythmic bumps (no grinds). With head and shoulders stationary, alternately arch and curl your back, throwing your pelvis back as you arch and forward as you curl. Use music with a strong beat. Start slowly and work up to double time.

Exercise regimen: Try to work out twice a day. Morning exercises loosen up your muscles and get you going. Later sessions accomplish more in building strength and flexibility because you are already warmed up.

Sauna, Steam Room And Hot Tub Hazards

US Centers for Disease Control and Prevention, Atlanta.

Use a sauna or steam room only about once a week, on a nonexercise day or after the week's final workout. Shower before entering, and go in wet. Your hair should also be wet or covered. Protect your nasal membranes by breathing through a cool, damp cloth. Drape a cool, wet towel over your neck and shoulders to help maintain normal blood temperature. Go in and out of the room frequently, showering between heat sessions to cool yourself down and build heat tolerance slowly. If you feel dizzy when leaving, shower right away with warm (not cold) water, wrap yourself in towels or get dressed, and lie down until you feel better.

Soaking in a communal hot tub contaminates the water with two to three pints of perspiration per hour per person. The salt, ammonia, etc., in perspiration must be neutralized after each use to keep the water clean and clear. *Required:* A sophisticated kit that tests pH, water hardness and chlorine levels.

New Shelter.

Infections from hot tubs are becoming more common because of a bacterium that thrives in the wood of which some are made. The germ causes skin rash and other infections that are painful but treatable. *Prevention:* Put larger-than-normal amounts of chlorine in the water. *Better:* Install a vinyl liner in the tub.

What Your Dreams Mean

Stephen Aizenstat, PhD, founding president of the Pacifica Graduate Institute in Carpenteria, California. Dr. Aizenstat is a licensed clinical psychologist and marriage and family therapist who teaches courses on "dreamtending."

Dreams provide us with a useful commentary from our inner selves. They put us in touch with an incredibly constructive and intricate source of intelligence that we have very little access to when we're awake.

Dreams don't draw conclusions or make assessments; they locate us, connecting us with our essential position in the world at any given moment. When we're faced with a decision or predicament, dreams can be a helpful resource, often shining a new light on old problems.

Dreams speak to us in the language of images and symbols. The psyche dreams in picture language because pictures tell stories that, if put into narrative form, would fill volumes. *Dreams can be interpreted on three different levels...*

• **The personal unconscious.** Dreams pick up the literal content of your day. We dream about incidents from the past or current problems, usually about incidents that caused some tension. Wish-fulfillment dreams fall into this category.

• **The collective unconscious.** There are patterns of behavior and experience that have been recounted in fairy tales and folklore throughout the ages. These universal patterns of human experience, known as archetypes, can be found in common dream themes that turn up throughout human history.

• **World unconscious.** This level includes a sense of connectedness to everything else in the world.

Recurring dreams signal that the psyche is trying to get a message across. Like someone tugging on a shirtsleeve, a recurring dream tries to get our attention by presenting us with the same theme over and over. If a dream repeats, there's bound to be something of tremendous value in it. *Helpful:* Look back to when you've had repetitive dreams. Did they signal something that was happening at that time?

Dreams speak indirectly in poetic metaphors and symbols. You need to think symbolically to figure out what the images mean. *Reassuring:* No expert knows better than you what your dreams mean. *Caution:* Don't be too literal about the translation. How do you know you've made the right interpretation? You get a tingle, a sense of perfect fit.

• **Losing teeth.** First check out the obvious. Are any of your teeth actually loose or decayed?

At the second level of meaning, losing teeth is connected to the loss of something valuable, often associated with appearance. *Metaphors:* Loss of face, of attractiveness, self-esteem or power. Also, a lost tooth could indicate the loss or death of a loved one.

- **Going back to school.** Usually people have this dream when they're frightened or unprepared. They feel under scrutiny—either at work or in a relationship—or they're being critical of themselves.

Look at where you landed in the dream. Was it in elementary school, high school or college? Explore that. When you were in that school, what were you afraid of? What did being unprepared mean then? How does that relate to what you're going through now?

- **Bathrooms and feces.** Personally, I believe that feces can be one of the most engaging images. Feces are manure, manure means seeds and seeds mean growth. When feces appear in dreams, I get hopeful. Right around the corner there's fertile ground for growth, new possibilities.

- **Nudity.** Usually embarrassment at finding yourself nude in public has to do with feeling vulnerable or exposed. In a second level of interpretation it's being without a persona, not having your clothes, your mask, that which mediates between you and the world.

This is a very important dream. The vulnerability of it signals openness, availability, willingness to drop defenses and take chances. It usually comes after a time of change in career or relationships. This type of dream may also be compensatory. If you're in a position that requires a rigid persona, such as politics or a conservative law firm, your dreams may be compensating by presenting you as a vulnerable human being.

- **Flying.** The flying motif has something to do with a discovery, a transcendent perspective. *Metaphors:* Flying high, flying off the handle. Sometimes when we're caught in a predicament, flying above it all gives us an overview that allows us to see something we just couldn't see before.

Downside: If we don't have our feet on the ground, we're somehow disconnected. Sometimes flying is a signal of inflation, being too carried

away with yourself or flying too high without a lifeline.

- **Falling.** Similar to flying dreams, falling dreams are especially terrifying for children. What catastrophic fear does the fall represent? What's the horrible consequence of falling? *Metaphors:* Falling in esteem, falling down on the job, falling from grace, a fear of dying.

How to deal with falling dreams: Tell yourself each night before going to sleep that when you have the dream you'll continue the fall and allow yourself to land safely. And that when you land you'll find something of value, put it in your dream pocket and take it back to your waking life. That's how primitive tribes worked with this dream.

- **Finding valuables.** Children often dream of finding money. This can be a wish-fulfillment dream or it can compensate for a fear of not having wealth. It can also be a reminder dream, reminding you that you're out of touch with what's valuable in your life. *Ask yourself:* What is there of value in me that I need to treasure even more? What is it I'm out of touch with in myself or am just beginning to value?

- **Sex.** Being sexual in a dream usually has little to do with actual sex. Flying dreams are probably more connected with libido than sex dreams are. Sex dreams can be a form of wish fulfillment; you can have lusty feelings for someone that can't be acted on in real life. The dream allows you to compensate. Like active sexual fantasies, these kinds of dreams are quite healthy.

Useful: What we do in dreams we can often do when we're awake. If you're a timid lover who becomes a magnificent lover in your dreams, you can translate this dream technique into real life.

A dream about intercourse is the most efficient way of suggesting intimate contact. It may have nothing to do with sex—it may be about wanting a relationship. Or if you find yourself having sex with someone you'd never be attracted to in real life, it may have to do with getting in touch with the aspects of yourself that person represents.

Sex is also a metaphor for creativity. There may be an aspect of your personality that's being repressed, causing you to be depressed or sad. Because the creative libido is yearning for expression, the sexual partner represents your hidden creativity.

Sleep Needs Differ

Requiring as much as eight or nine hours of sleep a night can be as normal as needing six or seven. According to one survey, more than 6% of American adults regularly sleep nine to 10 hours, with only about 1% sleeping more than 10 hours. Excessive sleeping can be a symptom of such disorders as narcolepsy, which causes people to become uncontrollably sleepy in the daytime.

Key to healthy sleep: The quality of the wakeful hours. If you're rested and energetic when you wake up, chances are that you needed all that sleep.

Merrill M. Mitler, PhD, one of the founders of the American Sleep Disorders Association (ASDA).

No More Panic Attacks

Elke Zuercher-White, PhD, a psychologist at Kaiser Permanente Medical Group in San Francisco and a psychotherapist in private practice in the San Francisco Bay area. She is the author of *An End to Panic: Breakthrough Techniques for Overcoming Panic Disorder* (MJF Books).

If you've ever suffered a panic attack, you're not alone. Researchers estimate that at least one-third of the population has experienced these frightening episodes, which are marked by intense psychological and physical symptoms.

Examples: Anxiety...a feeling of "unreality" or impending doom...a sense of going crazy or losing control...rapid heartbeat...shortness of breath...dizziness...tingling.

Panic attacks usually strike during times of stress—before giving a speech, for example, or taking a test. But sometimes they strike for no apparent reason.

For some individuals who have had one panic attack, the fear of having another leads to a cycle of further attacks and increased fear. This condition is known as panic disorder.

Left untreated, panic disorder can turn into agoraphobia. This debilitating disorder typically develops over a period of weeks, months or years, as an individual begins avoiding more and more situations in which a panic attack might occur—grocery shopping, riding in elevators, driving, etc.

Good news: Panic attacks can be overcome. *Several antipanic techniques have proven remarkably successful...*

BREATHE SLOWLY AND STEADILY

Diaphragmatic breathing—expanding the belly with each inhalation—stops the rapid breathing that commonly occurs with a panic attack. It also helps curb dizziness, rapid heart rate, light-headedness and tingling.

To learn diaphragmatic breathing: Lie on your back with a pillow or towel on your stomach. Time your breathing so that you're taking eight to 12 breaths a minute. The pillow should move up when you inhale, down when you exhale.

Once you've mastered this technique, put the pillow or towel aside. Place one hand on your belly, just over your navel. Feel your abdomen rise with each inhalation and fall with each exhalation.

Next, practice diaphragmatic breathing while lying down with your hands at your sides. Then try it while slouching on a sofa... then while sitting up straight...and then while standing.

Practice diaphragmatic breathing for five minutes, twice a day, until you master it. That may take one to three weeks.

Focus on your breathing a few times each day. Eventually, you'll be able to do diaphragmatic breathing even in the midst of a panic attack.

CHANGE THE WAY YOU THINK

Panic attack sufferers often worry that a racing heart means they're about to suffer a heart attack…or that irregular or labored breathing means they will suffocate. These catastrophic scenarios do not occur.

Such catastrophic thinking only intensifies the symptoms of panic, making the panic attack more unpleasant than it otherwise might be.

To combat catastrophic thinking, think rationally…

•**Identify the thought that arises automatically each time you panic.** If you fear losing control, ask yourself, "How would someone else be able to tell if I lost control? What exactly am I afraid would happen?"

•**Consider the evidence in support of your automatic thought.** You might think, "I fear I might lose control because I feel disoriented and can't concentrate."

•**Use your rational mind to refute this evidence.** You might say to yourself, "I've felt disoriented before—but I never became crazy or acted out of control." Consider more realistic explanations for your symptoms.

REVISIT THE SITE

People tend to avoid the site where their worst panic attack occurred—even if they don't have agoraphobia. But returning to that spot forces you to confront your fears…and gain confidence in your ability to cope with panic.

You'll probably have to return several times before you feel comfortable at the site. At first, you might ask a trusted friend or family member to accompany you. Keep going back until you can go all by yourself.

BECOME MORE ASSERTIVE

People who suffer from panic disorder often feel they have little control over personal relationships or their emotions. As a result, they direct all their energy into controlling harmless—although uncomfortable—anxiety symptoms.

Assertiveness skills can be learned from books, classes and self-help groups. Try a local bookstore or a nearby hospital.

CHALLENGING AGORAPHOBIA

The key to overcoming agoraphobia is to expose oneself to the dreaded places and/or situations.

These exposures must occur at least three times a week. Each exposure should eventually last from one to two hours.

Helpful: Break exposures into their component parts. If you fear driving, for example, you might start by riding in a car driven by someone you trust…then driving yourself as your friend sits beside you…then having your friend follow you in another car.

If you find that you're having trouble coping with panic on your own, seek professional help. Have a doctor check you for a mitral valve prolapse or another medical condition known to cause panic-like symptoms.

If no medical problem is found, consult a psychotherapist who has used cognitive-behavioral therapy to treat panic disorder.

Antidepressants and antianxiety drugs have been found helpful for panic disorder, but some drugs can lead to dependency. New research suggests they may not be needed.

More information: Contact the Anxiety Disorders Association of America at 240-485-1001, *www.adaa.org*.

Helping Yourself To Sleep Better

Charles P. Pollak, MD, director of the Center for Sleep Medicine at NewYork–Presbyterian/Weill Cornell Medical Center.

As the stress of doing business under unsettled conditions continues month after month, the sleeping patterns of executives with top responsibilities become more and more unraveled. Late meetings, travel and racing thoughts that produce late-night or morning insomnia result in irritability, poor work performance and lethargy at times when key decisions must be made.

IMPROVING SLEEP QUALITY

Researchers cannot easily determine how much sleep is optimum for each specific person. But they have determined that, on average, human beings need seven or eight hours of sleep a day.

The evidence is clear, however, that psychological and physical health improves as the quality of sleep is enhanced. *To sleep better, you should...*

• **Determine the right amount of sleep.** *How:* Keep a diary of sleeping patterns for at least 10 to 14 days. If you feel productive and alert, the average sleep time during that period is probably the amount you need.

• **Establish a regular bedtime and wake-up schedule,** then stick to it even on weekends and holidays.

• **Avoid trying to make up for loss of sleep one night by sleeping more the next.** Sleep deprivation of two to four hours does not severely affect performance. Having the normal amount of sleep the next night compensates for the loss without changing the regular sleep pattern. And that has long-term benefits.

• **Relax before bedtime.** *Good ways to unwind:* Take a bath, read, have a snack (milk is ideal for many people), engage in sex. Avoid late-night exercise, work, arguments and activities that cause tension.

FIGHTING INSOMNIA

Knowing the reason for insomnia is the only way to start overcoming it. If the cause is not quickly obvious, see a doctor. Many emotional and physical disorders express themselves as sleep disturbances.

Avoid sleeping pills. On a long-term basis, they are useless and sometimes dangerous. And when taken infrequently, they may produce a drug hangover the next day.

CATNAPS

Avoid naps in the middle of the day to compensate for lack of sleep the previous night. Take them only if you do so regularly and feel refreshed instead of groggy after a nap. *Test:* If you dream during a catnap, it is likely to delay sleep that evening or cause insomnia.

TAMPERING WITH NATURE

Deliberate attempts to reduce the total amount of sleep you need have a dangerous appeal to hard-pressed executives who think they never have enough time to work. *Fact:*

Evidence taken from monitoring subjects in sleep laboratories indicates that these schemes are not only ineffective but unhealthful. *Why:* The daily biological cycle cannot be changed by gradually cutting back sleep over a period of months. It's true that older persons seem to need slightly less sleep, but even here the exact difference is not yet known.

Hard-to-take but essential advice: Do not cut down on sleep in order to meet the clamoring and sometimes conflicting demands of a job, family and friends. You may pay a penalty of spending less time with family and friends or losing the edge at work that compulsive workaholism may provide. But the payoff is better health performance.

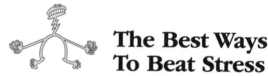

The Best Ways To Beat Stress

Carl Sherman, award-winning psychology writer. He is author of *Stress Remedies* (Rodale Press).

Stress comes at us from everywhere—the overbearing bureaucrat...the traffic that stops dead when we've got to get somewhere fast...the big bill we forget until the second notice arrives...and so on.

And—there are life-disrupting events, such as retirement, moving, divorce or the death of a loved one or friend, that are always ready to bombard us.

But actually, the feeling of stress doesn't come from the outside. It happens inside of us.

When we feel under pressure, our body releases chemicals, such as adrenaline, that ready us for action. We breathe faster, our pulse and blood pressure rise, our muscles tighten.

These physical symptoms comprise what is commonly known as the "fight-or-flight" response—a leftover from the days when most crises could be either fought or fled.

Today, however, we usually have to endure them. This endurance causes stress, which takes its toll on physical and mental health.

Some stress is unavoidable. But too much stress leads to troubles that range from upset stomachs to anxiety attacks to heart attacks.

Fact: As many as 90% of doctor visits are for stress-related symptoms.

What can you do to combat stress? There's a whole arsenal of stress remedies to help you change a difficult situation—or the way you interpret it—to reduce your body's response to stress and restore a calmer state.

The more you understand your stress, the better you can choose defenses that work for you. *Most effective...*

MEDITATION

Taking time every day to disengage from the demands of the world can ease your mind and your body into a deeply relaxed state—the opposite of the stress response.

Meditation fosters your ability to step back from life and observe the passing scene—and your own thoughts—in a detached way. Studies have linked the regular practice of meditation to reductions in anxiety, work-related stress...and blood pressure, too.

There are many meditation techniques, but I know of one that is simple—and the best that I have found...

• **Sit quietly and comfortably** in a place where you will not be disturbed.

• **Focus your attention on your breathing.** Feel the breath as it comes into your nose... and when it goes out.

• **Other thoughts will enter your mind.** Just observe them and let them go. Return your attention to your breath.

Start by practicing meditation for five to 10 minutes a day, gradually increasing it to 20 to 30 minutes.

Keep a clock nearby so you can keep track of the time. *Caution:* A clock alarm or kitchen timer is too jarring. Some people, though, set their wristwatch alarms.

EXERCISE

Physical activity neutralizes the fight-or-flight response, easing tension and anxiety and leaving you invigorated. Regular moderate exercise reverses much of the damage caused by stress, and it can also improve immune function, lower blood pressure and improve your mood.

Intense aerobic exercise—running or aerobics classes at a gym—is an effective stress-buster, but so is more relaxed walking.

Do what you want to do—any exercise that you find enjoyable—and do it for at least 20 minutes every day. More, though, isn't always better.

Trap: If you think of exercise as a burden, it will add to your stress.

BIOPHILIA

Human beings have an inborn affinity for nature. Scientists call it "biophilia." Contact with scenes of nature and living things has been shown to reverse the effects of stress. *Examples...*

• **Employees whose windows look out on trees and grass** report less work stress than those with views of parking lots.

• **An aquarium** in a dentist's waiting room lowers anxiety.

• **By eating lunch on a park bench,** your body will relax.

• **Spending a half hour in your garden** will make your work worries recede into the distance.

• **If you live in a city,** consider a back-to-nature vacation—a week in the mountains will recharge your batteries more deeply than a short stroll in the park.

• **Let a little piece of nature into your daily life**—get a pet. Persian cat or parakeet, goldfish, beagle or mouse—it doesn't really matter. Pet owners are healthier and respond better to stress than other folks.

HUMOR

The ability to take yourself—and your life—less seriously is the stress antidote *par excellence.* How tense can you be when you're laughing at yourself?

Try to look for the lighter side of every situation. Indulge your taste for entertaining books and movies.

Does a newspaper cartoon tickle your funny bone? Tape it to your bathroom mirror as a reminder to lighten up.

The next time your spouse acts up, ask yourself, *What would Groucho Marx have to say about this?*

Have funny props around. Keep a clown nose in your glove compartment to transform a traffic jam into circus time. Why should kids have all the fun?

FRIENDSHIP

Close ties to others make you feel warm inside...and they also temper your body's reaction to stress. The world feels safer when you know that other people are on your side. Expressing your worries and troubles to a sympathetic ear often makes them easier to bear.

The mere presence of a friend blunts the pulse and blood pressure rise that accompany stressful tasks. People with many friends have lower cholesterol and stronger immune systems. They live longer than loners, too.

Eat Right—and Live Longer

Brian Morgan, MD, PhD, clinical instructor at the University of California, San Francisco, Fresno, School of Medicine.

It's not too late to change the eating habits of a lifetime when you reach middle age. As a matter of fact, it's probably a necessity because of the changes the body undergoes at that time. *Most obvious change:* Slowing of the metabolic rate. Individuals who don't reduce their caloric intake after age 45 commonly gain 10 pounds a year regardless of the amount of exercise they get. It takes 12 hours of tennis to burn off 3,500 calories, which is roughly equivalent to one pound.

Unfortunately, a fine steak is often associated with success and reward. Steak, however, is highly caloric, and its fat content has been linked to coronary disease and colon cancer, two potentially fatal disorders that plague older people. Chicken and fish are more healthful alternative sources of protein.

Bones begin to grow progressively brittle after age 30. To counteract the condition, the body needs more calcium. But this important mineral can be absorbed effectively only by reducing the intake of protein (from meats) and phosphorous (from carbonated soft drinks). To prevent the brittle-bone problem, a calcium supplement of 1,000 to 1,500 milligrams per day is recommended by the National Institutes of Health.

Older people are vulnerable to anemia, one form of which is iron deficiency. The best source of iron is found in meat, especially liver. But to avoid eating too much meat, you should turn to iron-fortified foods, especially cereals. Absorption of iron is helped by intake of vitamin C, which is abundant in citrus fruits, broccoli, kale, red peppers and brussels sprouts. For some older people, taking an iron supplement may be necessary. If you have an iron deficiency, consult your doctor to be sure you don't have hidden causes of iron loss, such as undiagnosed intestinal bleeding.

Because many older people secrete less hydrochloric acid, they also have trouble absorbing vitamin B-12. A B-12 deficiency can lead to pernicious anemia, which can cause severe neurological problems. Strict vegetarians may be particularly at risk unless they take supplemental B-12 because the vitamin is found exclusively in animal products (especially liver) and shellfish. Multivitamin supplements may be needed to ensure that you get the right amount of each vitamin.

Caution: Although all the evidence is not yet in, most nutritionists advise against taking vitamin megadoses, which contain several hundred times the Recommended Daily Allowance. In the case of vitamins A and D, megadoses are highly dangerous.

Exception: Vitamin E, large doses of which may help to combat several disorders, including colon cancer and the painful blood vessel spasms in the legs that older people often experience. Even with this vitamin, however, you should consult a physician before considering taking megadoses.

Digestive problems associated with aging make fiber especially important to persons over 45. *Sources:* Whole grains, fruits, vegetables.

Older people generally use more drugs than others, but their doctors often overlook the interaction of medication and nutrition.

Some chronic aspirin users can suffer microscopic bleeding of the gastrointestinal tract, a condition that also causes loss of iron. Aspirin can also increase requirements for vitamin C and folic acid. Laxatives may deplete vitamin D, and antacids can lead to a phosphate deficiency. The diuretics prescribed for hypertension can promote the loss of potassium. In all these cases, vitamin and mineral supplements may be the solution.

Aging Bodies Need More Water

An aging body needs at least six glasses of water every day. *Reason:* A young adult's body is 60% water, but this amount decreases with age. *Result:* Skin dries out, and the kidneys do not flush wastes as well. Drinking more water means the skin has less chance of becoming dry. And the water dilutes the salts and minerals that pass through the kidneys, helping to prevent the formation of kidney stones. *Suggestion:* Have a glass of water with every meal and another before going to bed. Take the other two glasses during breaktime. Substitute water for that second and third cup of coffee.

Stay Healthy with Spices

Some common spices help to prevent food poisoning. Food microbiologists studied the effect of 23 different spices frequently used in cooking on food infected with *E. coli* bacteria, the most common villain in food poisoning. They found that five of the spices—garlic, cloves, cinnamon, oregano and sage—were particularly effective at killing bacteria in any food. While the experiment used very large amounts of the different spices, researchers report that the moderate amounts typically used are helpful in giving protection to home cooking—but do not kill all bacteria.

Daniel Y.C. Fung, PhD, professor of animal sciences and industry, and food science, Kansas State University, Manhattan.

Salt and High Blood Pressure

For about 30% of people who suffer from hypertension, cutting down on salt is a therapeutic necessity. For other victims of high blood pressure and for the general population, salt reduction may be an unnecessary hardship with possible risks. New research suggests that many factors other than salt are linked to hypertension. Obesity is one. Calcium deficiency is another. *Problem:* Reducing sodium in the diet may adversely affect the body's ability to absorb and use other necessary nutrients.

John Laragh, MD, director of the cardiovascular center, NewYork Presbyterian Hospital–Weill Cornell Medical Center, and David A. McCarron, MD, president of Academic Network LLC and visiting professor at the department of nutrition at University of California, Davis.

Beware the "Salt-Free" Label

Absence of the word "salt" on a list of ingredients does not necessarily guarantee that the product is salt-free. Other "salty" substances commonly used in food preparations include brine, disodium phosphate, sodium glutamate, baking powder and baking soda.

Almonds Cut Cholesterol

In one study, 45 people with high cholesterol levels were placed on a diet rich in almonds, olive oil or dairy products.

Result: After four weeks, the almond group had LDL (bad) cholesterol levels an average of 16 points lower than the olive oil group...and 33 points lower than the dairy group.

Almonds are rich sources of monounsaturated fats, fiber and the amino acid arginine. Each of these contributes to the cholesterol-lowering effect. Even if you are currently taking cholesterol-lowering medication, consider including almonds in your diet...along with lots of fruits, vegetables, beans, soy foods, whole grains and garlic.

Gene Spiller, PhD, director, Health Research and Studies Center, Los Altos, California.

How Much Caffeine Is Too Much?

American Council on Science and Health, New York City.

Americans are suddenly adding caffeine to their growing list of health worries. Decaffeinated colas now join decaffeinated coffees in luring the public away from the caffeine habit. *Some facts about caffeine...*

• **Low doses can increase alertness and motor ability,** reduce drowsiness and lessen fatigue. Small to moderate amounts of caffeine pose no health danger, according to the Clinical Nutrition Section of Boston's University Hospital. Heavy doses produce ill effects —nervousness, anxiety, irritability, headache, muscle twitch and insomnia.

• **Tolerance of caffeine varies widely from one person to another.** Two cups of caffeine-rich coffee make some people nervous. Others cannot survive the day without several cups. *Most sensitive to caffeine's effects:* Children and the elderly.

• **How much is too much:** Four cups of coffee a day (500 milligrams of caffeine) is a heavy dose for most people. *Note:* The caffeine quantity in coffee depends on how it is brewed. The drip method produces a higher caffeine content than does the percolator technique. Instant coffee contains much less caffeine than brewed coffee. Tea contains half as much caffeine as coffee, and cola drinks have even less.

Irony: Most of the caffeine taken from coffee in the decaffeinization process is bought by the soft-drink industry and added to soda.

While cola drinks have far less caffeine than coffee, they are still the best-selling drink among Americans. Americans consume an average of 54 gallons of soft drinks yearly. *Comparison:* 22 gallons of coffee.

Caffeine has been linked to many health problems, but there are questions about its adverse effects. *Examples...*

• **There is no evidence that caffeine is a causal factor** in either arteriosclerosis or heart attacks.

• **It does not increase the blood pressure** of regular users.

• **Caffeine does not seem to be a cancer hazard,** but other compounds (found in negligible amounts) in beverage coffee are known carcinogens in animals.

• **Caffeine is a much less important factor than cigarette smoking** in heart disease, hypertension, bladder cancer, peptic ulcers and cystic breast disease.

• **It does stimulate the central nervous system** and can help reduce boredom from repetitive tasks, increase the body's muscle strength and relieve certain types of headaches by dilating blood vessels and reducing muscle tension.

What Vitamin Manufacturers Don't Tell You

You should be careful when taking *any* supplement, but there are some specific dangers in taking vitamins. *Be aware of the following...*

• **Vitamin poisoning.** Certain high-dose B-6 tablets sold in health stores can be dangerous. The body needs only one or two milligrams of B-6 a day. Overdoses may lead to loss of sensory and motor control.

New England Journal of Medicine.

• **Vitamin E should be used with restraint.** High doses can cause blood clots, phlebitis, hypertension, severe fatigue, breast tumors and disturbances in the reproductive system. How much is too much? Dr. H. J. Roberts, MD, of Florida's Palm Beach Institute for Medical Research suggests that daily intake of more than 100 to 300 units of "active tocopherol" is excessive.

Journal of the American Medical Association.

• **Too much vitamin A and D.** Unlike some vitamins (the Bs and C) that are passed out of the body through the kidneys when taken in excess, vitamins A and D are stored in fat and the liver, where they can do damage. *Problems from overdoses:* Cirrhosis of the liver. Dry, itchy skin. Fatigue. Painful muscles. Loss of body hair. *Note:* A deficiency of vitamin A is believed to be related to the onset of cancer. But there is no evidence that increased amounts help prevent this disease. *Best:* Eat a balanced diet. Limit supplementary intake to the recommended daily dietary allowances.

The Health Letter.

• **Niacin is not a tranquilizer,** despite the stories about its calming effects. Taking niacin tablets in search of tranquility can cause niacin toxicity. *Symptoms:* Flushed face and blotchy skin on arms.

Cholesterol Fighter

Apple juice may be the best source of cholesterol-fighting phenols. Phenols are plant compounds that protect the arteries from the adverse effects of "bad" LDL cholesterol. A recent study showed that drinking apple juice daily may reduce LDL cholesterol damage by 34%.

Other good phenol sources: Cranberry juice…apples…red grapes or red grape juice …red wine.

Eric Gershwin, MD, distinguished professor of medicine and chief, division of rheumatology, allergy and clinical immunology, University of California at Davis.

Raisins and Cancer

Raisins may help prevent cancer. They contain a compound that helps the colon get rid of waste more efficiently…and this keeps the colon healthy. The compound—tartaric acid—is found mainly in raisins and grapes. Raisins are also high in potassium and protective antioxidants.

Gene Spiller, PhD, director, Health Research and Studies Center, Los Altos, California.

Microwave Oven Trap

Cooking chicken in microwave ovens won't kill harmful salmonella and other bacteria. *Reason:* Microwave ovens heat food through molecular friction, leaving surface temperatures too uneven to kill the contaminants.

Solution: Cook chicken in conventional ovens at 350°F until the meat thermometer registers 185°F in both the breast and thigh areas or until the juices run clear.

Ruth E. Lindsay, nutritionist, Georgia Southern College.

Minerals for Better Health

For the best absorption of iron supplements, take them with orange juice or with a meal containing meat or poultry…and avoid tea or coffee when taking iron. For the best absorption of calcium, take half in the morning and half in the evening. Take iron and calcium supplements at different times of the day—calcium can block the absorption of iron.

Not necessary: Chelated minerals, which are sold in health food stores. Chelation describes a type of chemical bond. It's no better for the body than standard mineral supplements.

James C. Fleet, PhD, professor, department of foods and nutrition, Purdue University, West Lafayette, Indiana.

Cleaning Up Your Drinking Water

Although public health systems must publish results of water safety tests, pure drinking water piped into the home must not be taken for granted.

Problems: Toxic chemicals such as nitrates, asbestos, arsenic, lead, trihalomethanes (THM). *Also:* High sodium levels are dangerous for people on sodium-restricted diets.

Statistic: Approximately 55% of the American population lives in areas with inadequate water-treatment plants.

Signs of possible contamination: Water has an odd taste, color or smell. *Possible problems:* Heavy construction or sewer installation in the area, a change in pesticide use, antiquated water-treatment facilities.

What to do: Get the most recent results of your town's water test as required by law. If you suspect the problem is with your home's pipes, consider testing the water yourself. Consult the *Yellow Pages* under "Laboratories—Testing" for a lab that handles water samples. *Cost:* From $15 to $200.

How to get cleaner drinking water…

• **Bottled water.** *Hitch:* There are no standards for purity. Some may contain traces of harmful substances. Of course, labels do not indicate this.

• **Water filters.** The only effective ones contain granules of activated carbon (GAC). *Useful:*

They are effective only against THM, not lead or arsenic. Never use filters that fit over the faucet. The water runs through too quickly to be properly filtered. *Note:* Filtered water is not necessary for such functions as dishwashing. The filter should have a bypass valve.

Visit the Environmental Protection Agency's Web site for water reports, *http://water.epa.gov/drink/emerprep/index.cfm.*

Fight Asthma with Better Breathing

Although it is unconventional, this non-drug asthma treatment teaches patients to breathe differently in an attempt to lower their medication needs.

Key: Take in small breaths through the nose to fill the lungs, hold for an extended period, and breathe out gently through a wide open mouth. Repeat as needed. Advocates say it can significantly reduce dependence on medicines. But before modifying medication, check with your physician.

Andrew L. Rubman, ND, founder and director, Southbury Clinic for Traditional Medicines, Southbury, Connecticut. *www.southburyclinic.com*

Diet Tips to Combat Stress

For short-term periods of stress, follow a high-carbohydrate, low-protein diet. The carbohydrates deliver energy to the body. *For longer stressful periods:* Reverse the diet—that is, consume more protein and fewer carbohydrates.

Example: Lean meats, eggs, fish, skinless poultry, low-fat milk and soy foods.

Other foods that fight stress: Those rich in vitamins C and A. Try raw carrots, peppers and broccoli. *Bonus:* Chewing crunchy foods helps dissipate the tension.

Sound Therapy Relieves Pain and More

Sound therapy is used to treat pain, Alzheimer's disease, attention deficit disorder, alcoholism, anxiety and some forms of depression.

To use sound: Listen carefully to various types of music and feel how each affects your mind and body. Then choose pieces to listen to on the basis of how you want to feel.

Examples: Bach's Goldberg Variations were commissioned to treat insomnia and are still effective in combating sleeplessness. Mozart's music lowers stress and increases concentration. New Age music can aid relaxation. Upbeat popular music can boost energy.

Kerri Bodmer, coauthor of *The Giant Book of Women's Health Secrets* (Soundview).

Be Savvy About Herbal Supplements

Be careful when taking herbal supplements. Scientists are not certain of how and why most herbs affect the body, and they sometimes cause serious side effects or even death.

Purity standards have been published for some popular herbs, but many supplements are complex mixtures of different herbs with poor quality control. Because they are classified as supplements rather than drugs, they are not strictly supervised by the US Food and Drug Administration (FDA).

Bottom line: Be as cautious in using supplements as you would be in taking prescription or over-the-counter drugs.

Norman R. Farnsworth, PhD, research professor of pharmacognosy—the study of the medicinal properties of plants—at the University of Illinois in Chicago.

New Approach to Chronic Disease

Writing has been shown to fight chronic disease. Patients who write about traumatic life experiences sometimes gain relief from such diseases as chronic asthma or rheumatoid arthritis.

Patients who wrote about the most stressful event in their lives for 20 minutes a day, three days in a row, were in better health four months later than those who didn't. Writing may help them make sense of bad experiences.

Study of 107 patients with chronic illnesses led by Joshua M. Smyth, PhD, Syracuse University, published in *The Journal of the American Medical Association*.

Oils That Improve Health

Eucalyptus is an antibacterial that soothes acne and relieves sinus congestion.

Geranium soaks up facial oiliness and also can tighten skin temporarily.

Lavender soothes tension headaches and migraines.

Rose hydrates and soothes sensitive, dry, itchy or inflamed skin.

Tea tree fights athlete's foot, dandruff, insect bites, cold sores and acne.

Caution: Except for lavender and tea tree, don't apply full-strength oils directly to skin. Dilute in a vegetable carrier oil such as almond oil or grape seed oil.

Victoria Edwards, founder, Aromatherapy Institute & Research, Fair Oaks, California, quoted in *Self,* 4 Times Square, New York City 10036.

The Secrets of Herbal Remedies

Ethan Russo, MD, clinical associate professor of medicine at the University of Washington School of Medicine in Seattle. He is author of *Handbook of Psychotropic Herbs* (Haworth Press).

People often assume that because herbs are "natural," they pose little risk. Not true. Some herbs are too toxic for medicinal use. Even some that are generally safe can cause liver or kidney damage. And like drugs, herbal remedies can react dangerously with certain drugs or foods.

How can you use herbal remedies for maximum safety and effectiveness? *It's important to follow these guidelines...*

•**Avoid herbs known to be dangerous.** Given their inherent dangers, it's best to avoid chaparral, comfrey, life root, germander, coltsfoot, sassafras and ephedra (ma huang).

•**Don't be misled by wild claims.** Federal law forbids herbal remedy manufacturers from saying their products offer outright cures.

But manufacturers often tout their products as providing relief from a ludicrously wide range of ailments.

Take manufacturers' claims with a grain of salt. The best manufacturers often make no health claims for their products.

•**Seek reliable information.** The average doctor knows little about herbs. The same is true for the average druggist.

Health food store clerks may sound knowledgeable, but their information often comes from herbal remedy manufacturers—hardly a source of unbiased information.

The most reliable source of information on herbs is *The Complete German Commission E Monographs: Therapeutic Guide to Herbal Medicines,* published by the American Botanical Council.*

•**Work with a knowledgeable practitioner.** For referral to an herb-savvy medical

*Your library may have this book. If not, it can be ordered from the American Botanical Council, *www.herbalgram.org*...or via an online bookseller.

doctor in your area, contact the American Botanical Council at 512-926-4900...or see its Web site at *www.herbalgram.org.*

Alternative: See a naturopathic physician. In addition to basic medical training, naturopaths have extensive instruction in the safe use of herbs.

For referral to a naturopath in your area, contact the American Association of Naturopathic Physicians at *www.naturopathic.org.*

•**Buy only standardized formulations.** Standardized herbal extracts have been formulated to provide the active ingredient or ingredients at a specific concentration. This increases the odds that the product is both potent and safe to use.

Look for the word "standardized" or the words "German standards" on the label.

•**Follow label directions carefully.** Like drugs, herbs work best at specific dosages. Take only the recommended dosage, and be sure to take the herb with or without meals, water, etc.—as indicated.

•**Don't mix herbs and drugs.** Herbs can boost the potency of certain medications. If you're taking a prescription drug, don't begin taking any herbal extract until you've checked with a physician or naturopath.

If a doctor has prescribed a drug for you, let the doctor know about any herbal remedies you're already taking. He or she may need to adjust the dosage.

Common herb–drug interactions include...

•**St. John's-wort and fluoxetine** (Prozac). The combination can raise brain levels of the neurotransmitter serotonin. "Serotonin syndrome" can cause delirium and other symptoms.

•**Ginkgo biloba and anticoagulants.** Like aspirin, *warfarin* (Coumadin) and other anticoagulants, ginkgo thins the blood. Taken along with an anticoagulant, ginkgo can cause internal bleeding.

•**Watch out for allergic reactions.** Introduce herbs one at a time. Don't add a second herb until you've taken the first for an entire week without experiencing any symptoms of an allergic reaction—rash, upset stomach, dizziness or headache.

If you experience any of these symptoms, stop taking the herb at once. Try taking it again one week later. If symptoms return, stop taking the herb for good.

Caution: If you become short of breath after taking an herb, you should call for an ambulance at once.

• **Don't take herbs during pregnancy.** Ginger, garlic and other herbs that are popular as foods are generally okay. But other herbs can cause serious problems for pregnant women.

It's also best to check with a doctor before giving any herbal remedy to a child under age 12.

Assertiveness Power Alleviates Stress

Sharon Anthony Bower, president of Confidence Training, Inc., an assertiveness and public speaking training company in Stanford, California. She is coauthor of *Asserting Yourself,* which details her DESC method (Da Capo Press).

We all know that psychological stress takes its toll on us physically as well as emotionally.

Stress has been linked to high blood pressure, increased susceptibility to colds and greater sensitivity to pain.

Stress also contributes to headache, backache, peptic ulcers, digestive problems and insomnia.

Meditation and other relaxation strategies help curb stress. So does regular aerobic exercise. But it's much better to prevent stress in the first place. One highly effective—and often overlooked—way to do this is simply to be more assertive.

WRITE YOUR OWN SCRIPT

Many intelligent people avoid speaking up for themselves because they fear they'll get flustered and be forced to back down.

It's helpful to have a "script" to follow. Committing your thoughts to paper forces you to clarify the stressful situation…figure out what you want…and then come up with the best way to get it.

You needn't memorize your script word for word. But by practicing your main points, you'll develop the confidence to stand up for yourself.

Helpful: As you rehearse your script, breathe slowly and deeply. Say to yourself, "I can meet this challenge." Visualize yourself speaking with confidence and power.

THE DESC METHOD

To write an effective script, use the "DESC" method…

• **Describe the behavior that bothers you.** Do not waste time trying to identify the other person's motives. Instead, focus on the specific behavior or behaviors that bother you.

Example: "Several times during the past few weeks, you asked me to baby-sit at the very last minute."

• **Express your feelings about the troublesome behavior.** Be calm but firm. Use "I messages" to avoid putting the other person on the defensive.

Example: "I'm inconvenienced when you ask me to baby-sit on short notice. I'm also frustrated because I then act tense with the kids."

• **Specify what you want the other person to do.** Make sure your request is reasonable.

Example: "I'd like you to give me at least two days' advance notice when you ask me to baby-sit. Will you do that?"

• **Consequences.** List all the benefits the person will reap if he or she agrees to your conditions.

Example: "Given two days' notice, I'll be happy to watch the kids two or even three times a month. Since I'll feel relaxed, the kids and I will be better able to enjoy our time together."

In some cases, you'll have to specify negative consequences that will come to pass if the other person doesn't cooperate. Negatives should be used only if the positive approach fails.

Example: "If you fail to give me advance notice, I'll say no next time you ask me to baby-sit."

Not every situation calls for a detailed four-step script. Often, you can get your point across in a single sentence, such as, "This radio has a defective speaker" or, "The line starts back there."

If you're caught off guard by someone's behavior and find it hard to be assertive right then and there, simply say, "Let me think about that. I'll get back to you in an hour." Use the time to write an assertiveness script.

Good news: Once you write a few DESC scripts, you'll find it easier to assert yourself on the spur of the moment.

DEALING WITH DETOURS

What if the other person keeps you from sticking to your script...or tries to "detour" the conversation? Imagine his reactions and objections—in advance—and prepare a detailed response.

Good ways to respond...

• **Persist.** Repeat your main point—the "specify" part of DESC—as many times as necessary.

• **Agree...but.** Acknowledge that the other person has a right to his feelings...but disagree with the notion that you must feel the same way.

• **Disagree.** Say something like, "I hold a different view" or "I see it another way."

• **Emphasize your feelings.** Give more details about your feelings or thoughts...or state them more firmly. *Common detours...*

Put-off detour: "Let's not go into that now"...or, "I'm too busy right now." *Reply:* "It's important to me that this be settled. If this isn't a good time, please name a time today when we can talk."

Reinterpreting detour: "I only meant that remark as a joke." *Reply:* "Perhaps so, but I didn't think it was appropriate. I felt hurt."

Blaming detour: "You're going through a tough stage now. You'll see things differently in a few weeks." *Reply:* "This is no stage. The problem isn't me, but the way you've been treating me."

HOW TO GET STARTED

Each day for the next few weeks, try one of the following exercises. *Each time you try*

one, pay attention to what happens—and how you feel...

• **Ask for clarification.** If someone criticizes you—or seems to be criticizing you—ask for more details.

Example: "I'm not sure what you mean when you say I've been defensive. In what ways have I been defensive?"

• **Ask for help.** When you feel overwhelmed, get help. Don't feel that you must be a superperson all the time.

Example: "I want to do a good job on this project, but I'm feeling overwhelmed. Could we hire an assistant?"

• **Fight the urge to justify yourself.** You have every right to your feelings. Devise simple statements that show you won't be drawn into an argument.

Example: "That's how I feel about the issue, and I don't have to supply you with more reasons. Let's get back to the issue at hand."

• **Use assertive body language.** Make eye contact, but shift your gaze every few seconds. Staring makes you seem aggressive.

Eliminate distracting gestures—covering your mouth, touching your hair, clearing your throat, shifting your weight back and forth, etc.

Practice your DESC message with a friend or in front of a mirror—or record yourself and play it back—until you can use it comfortably.

Control High Blood Pressure Without Medication

Sheldon G. Sheps, MD, emeritus professor of medicine at Mayo Medical School, Rochester, Minnesota. He was editor in chief of *Mayo Clinic on High Blood Pressure* (Mayo Foundation).

High blood pressure is a time bomb—but it's one that ticks very quietly. This "silent killer" causes no symptoms, but elevated pressure in the arteries eventually causes severe damage to several organs.*

This damage sets the stage for stroke, heart attack, kidney failure…and premature death.

Fifteen million Americans are unaware that they have high blood pressure (hypertension). Of the 35 million who know they have it, only two out of five are getting adequate treatment.

A generation ago, doctors tended to think of blood pressure as being "normal" or "high." Now the National Heart, Lung and Blood Institute (NHLBI) recognizes different levels of blood pressure. *Each succeeding level is associated with a higher degree of risk…*

- **Normal**…below 120/80

- **Prehypertension**…120/80 to 139/89.

- **Stage 1 hypertension**…140/90 to 159/99.

- **Stage 2 hypertension**…160/100 and above.

Cardiovascular disease risk doubles with each increment of 20/10.

If your pressure is elevated, here's how to get it down…

- **Follow the DASH diet.** In 1997, the Dietary Approaches to Stop Hypertension (DASH) study concluded that high-normal people and stage 1 hypertensives could achieve significant reductions in blood pressure simply by switching to a diet that stresses fruits, vegetables, grains and dairy products.

On average, study participants who followed the DASH diet lowered their blood pressure by 11 points systolic…and 5.5 points diastolic.

That was virtually the same level of reduction that is typically achieved with pressure-lowering medication—without the side effects associated with medication.

The daily DASH meal plan consists of…

- Seven or eight servings of grains, bread, cereal or pasta—preferably whole-grain varieties.

*Blood pressure readings are expressed as fractions —130/80, for example. The numerator (top number) represents *systolic* pressure—that existing in the arteries when the heart's main pumping chamber (left ventricle) contracts. The denominator (bottom number) represents *diastolic* pressure—that which exists between beats.

- Four to five servings of fruits and vegetables.

- Two or three servings of nonfat/low-fat dairy products.

- Two or fewer servings of meat, poultry or fish.

The DASH diet also calls for four or five servings per week of beans, peas, nuts or seeds.

- **Eat less salt.** Only about 40% of people with high blood pressure are salt-sensitive, but it's hard to know who falls into this category. *For this reason, everyone should limit sodium intake to 2,400 milligrams a day…*

- Read food labels and tally the sodium content of the foods you eat in a typical day.

- Cut out offending foods—such as fast food, cheese, bacon, pickles—as required.

- Avoid salt at the dining table…and in food preparation. Flavor foods instead with red pepper, cumin, onion, dill, lemon, etc.

It can take up to six weeks for your taste buds to adapt to less salt—so be patient. Once your taste buds adapt, you'll find you no longer crave salt.

- **Cut back on caffeine**—and nicotine. The caffeine that is in coffee, tea and soft drinks causes blood vessels to narrow for several hours. This then causes a transient rise in blood pressure. People who have hypertension should limit their daily caffeine intake to two cups of coffee, four cups of tea or four cans of caffeinated soda.

Like caffeine, nicotine causes a transient rise in blood pressure. Smoking just two cigarettes boosts systolic and diastolic pressure by up to 10 points. This increase persists for up to 90 minutes. Smoking can also interfere with the action of blood pressure medications.

- **Limit your drinking.** Excessive drinking—more than two drinks a day for men or one for women—is clearly a major contributor to hypertension.

If your drinking exceeds these levels, cut back. Do so gradually, over a few weeks. Going "cold turkey" can cause a rapid and potentially dangerous rise in blood pressure.

• **Lose weight.** The heavier you are, the larger the network of blood vessels your body must maintain. The larger this network, the more forcefully your heart must pump. This means higher blood pressure.

If you're overweight, losing as few as 10 pounds is often enough to lower your blood pressure significantly.

• **Alleviate psychological stress.** Stress causes the body to produce hormones that constrict blood vessels, thereby raising your blood pressure.

What to do: Get organized...make lists of tasks...set priorities...clean out clutter...say "no" to additional responsibilities...delegate work...and try meditation and other relaxation techniques.

• **Get more physical activity.** Walking, cycling, running and other forms of aerobic exercise boost your heart's pumping efficiency. The more efficient your heart, the wider the arteries open and the less forcefully the heart must contract.

Bonus: Regular exercise helps alleviate stress and promotes weight loss—thereby augmenting its pressure-lowering effect.

Aim for five to seven 30-minute workout sessions each week.

WHEN MEDICATION IS NECESSARY

If these lifestyle strategies are not enough to bring blood pressure to a healthy level, they may at least enable you to use a lower dosage of pressure-lowering medication. That's important, given the side effects associated with drug therapy.

How to Read Nutrition Labels

Men's Confidential.

Your local supermarket aisle now contains a lot more useful information than it used to. The Food and Drug Administration has decreed that all packaged food must have new, easier-to-understand labels.

"This is a step that could change the way America eats forever," declares the FDA's Edward Scarbrough, PhD. *Using a label from a bag of tortilla chips, we'll show you exactly what the new labels can do for you...*

• **The tip-off.** A "Nutrition Facts" label has replaced the old title "Nutrition Information per Serving."

• **Realistic serving size.** An old trick was to list calories and fat for an impossibly small serving size. No more playing the one chip game. The new serving size is more realistic and the same for all foods of a given type. A serving of tortilla chips, for example, is listed as one ounce, about 10 to 12 chips.

• **A simplified fat finder.** Calories derived from fat are listed so you can easily compare this number with the total calories. If it looks like the product gets half its calories from fat, beware. Fat should only comprise 30% of your total daily diet.

• **A way to keep track of the bad stuff.** Grams in each serving is pretty self-evident, but what's this "% Daily Value"? It has a confusing name, but a simple meaning. Just remember—for items that are potentially damaging to your health, you're aiming to stay below 100 percent each day for each of the items listed in this section of the label.

Let's take as an example one of the worst offenders—saturated fat. Percent daily value is listed here as 5 percent. That means you're spending five cents of your daily saturated fat dollar on this handful of tortilla chips. You've got 95 cents left for the rest of the day.

Zero in on what you're most worried about. If you're battling heart disease, try to spend less than your daily dollar on cholesterol, saturated fats and sodium.

For sugars and protein, there's a gram value listed, but no percentage. If you're diabetic or on a special high- or low-protein diet, check with your doctor about what daily totals are best for you.

AND THE GOOD STUFF

Your approach here is just like that to the undesirables, except here you'll want to celebrate if your percent daily values add up to 100 each day.

With dietary fiber, the key component in keeping you regular, you want to spend at least a dollar. These chips only used four cents —not too fiber-intensive. You'll need to spend 96 more during the course of the day.

All new labels also feature the big four nutrients…

• **Calcium.** Strengthens bones…may decrease risk of colon cancer and high blood pressure.

• **Vitamins A & C.** Antioxidants, possible cancer fighters, antiagers.

• **Iron.** Essential mineral, but men should stay below 100 percent.

Listing other information such as polyunsaturated and monounsaturated fat, potassium, other carbohydrates, vitamins and minerals is optional unless health claims are made, such as "rich in niacin."

• **Safety net.** If you don't like the percent daily values system, or if you tend to eat 2,500 calories a day instead of 2,000, then add up all the grams you've eaten on a given day of saturated fat, total fat or cholesterol and make sure they stay below the maximum value.

• **Proving an important point.** One gram of fat has more than twice the calories as a gram of carbohydrates or protein. The FDA thinks this is so important that they're including this reminder right on the label. Keep close tabs on your intake of fats.

NEW TRUTH IN ADVERTISING

The FDA is also cracking down on health claims made on food labels. In the past, some manufacturers have glibly used terms like "low fat" and "light" without a firm scientific basis. Now if they talk the talk, they've got to walk the walk.

• **"Free"**…means that a product has little or none of a particular nutrient.

Calorie-free = less than 5 calories

Fat-free = less than 0.5 grams (g)

Saturated fat-free = less than 0.5 g

Cholesterol-free = less than 2 milligrams (mg)

Sodium-free = less than 5 mg

Sugar-free = less than 0.5 g

• **"Lean"** and "extra lean," used to describe meats, poultry and seafood, has strict criteria to live up to. Here are some definitions for the most popular "eye-catchers."

Lean = Less than 10 g of fat, 4.5 g of saturated fat and 95 mg of cholesterol.

Extra lean = Less than 5 g of fat, 2 g of saturated fat and 95 mg of cholesterol.

• **"High"**…is now defined as an "excellent source of" by the FDA and will be used for products with 20% or more of the Daily Value.

• **"Light" or "lite"** products must contain at least one-third fewer calories, or no more than half the fat, of their reference food. Light cream cheese, for example, would need to be 5 g of fat or less than 67 calories per serving compared with regular cream cheese (100 calories, 10 g of fat per serving). Light can also apply to sodium if the product has at least 50% less sodium than a comparable food.

• **"Percent fat free"** refers to the actual amount of a food that is fat-free. A product could be 95% fat-free, but if it has a lot of calories, that 5% could pack a fatty punch. The new regulations limit the use of this phrase to products that are low calorie to begin with.

• **"More"** reveals that a food has at least 10 percent more of a nutrient's Daily Value, again compared with the standard product.

• **"Reduced,"** used for nutritionally altered foods, lets you know that a product has at least 25% less of a nutrient compared with the regular product. For example, reduced-cholesterol mayonnaise must contain less than 75% of the cholesterol of regular mayonnaise.

• **"Low"** can only be associated with foods that can be eaten frequently without exceeding dietary guidelines.

Low-calorie = less than 40 calories

Low-fat = less than 3 g

Low-saturated fat = less than 1 g

Low-cholesterol = less than 20 mg

Low-sodium = less than 140 mg

Very-low-sodium = less than 35 mg

• **"Good source,"** as in "a good source of protein, vitamin C, etc.," can only be used if a product has 10% to 19% of the Daily Value of a particular nutrient.

The FDA is also requiring that manufacturers back up claims that their products prevent health problems such as cancer, high blood pressure or heart disease. Take, for example, the link between dietary fat and certain forms of cancer. For a product to make a health claim, it has to meet the requirements of a low-fat food (3 g or less per serving) and restructure its claim ("a diet low in total fat may reduce the risk of some cancers").

These little labels are having big impact. According to a recent study in the *American Journal of Public Health,* these labels are expected to save more than 300,000 lives over the next two decades. Coronary heart disease and colon and prostate cancer are just a few health problems the FDA hopes to reduce. Taking advantage of this information will change the way you look at food forever, and it could just save your life.

The Value of Fiber

High-fiber diets fight heart disease. In a recent 10-year study, the risk of developing heart disease was twice as great among women who had the lowest intake of dietary fiber as among those who had the highest.

When researchers compared the types of fiber the women ate—from cereal, vegetables or fruit—they found that only fiber from cereal guarded against heart disease.

This finding presumably applies to men as well as to women.

Alicja Wolk, DMSc, professor of nutrition epidemiology, Karolinska Institute, Stockholm. Her study of 68,782 women 37 to 64 years of age was published in *The Journal of the American Medical Association,* 515 N. State St., Chicago 60610.

Dangerous Condiment

Wasabi, the green and fiery-hot horse-radish condiment that is typically served with sushi, should be eaten only a dab at a time—especially if you're not used to it. One man who gulped a large amount began sweating heavily, became confused and required a full day to recover. This reaction could be fatal in someone who has a heart condition or a tendency toward strokes.

Daniel Spitzer, MD, cited in *East West,* Box 13624, Scottsdale, Arizona 85260.

Milk Tip

Supermarket milk retains its nutrition better in fiberboard cartons than in clear plastic containers.

Reason: When exposed to fluorescent lights, low-fat or skim milk loses 90% of its vitamin A in 24 hours.

Research at Cornell University, Ithaca, New York.

Removing Pesticides From Produce

Pesticides cling to fruits and vegetables even after a water washing.

Best: Scrub the produce with a vegetable brush under running water. To be extra sure, use a mild detergent. Soak apples and pears in water containing one-fourth cup of vinegar before scrubbing.

The Practical Gourmet, Middle Island, New York.

Calcium vs. Memory

Memory impairment may be caused by too much calcium. Calcium is involved in the transmission of messages along brain neurons in the portion of the brain thought to direct memory functions. Studies have shown that as rats age, calcium flow into nerve cells increases, impairing the flow of messages.

Implications: If similar results occur in humans, calcium-blocking drugs might be used to prevent memory loss. Similarly, calcium supplements theoretically may contribute to memory loss though there is no evidence for this yet.

Philip Landfield, MD, professor and chair, molecular and biomedical pharmacology, University of Kentucky College of Medicine, Lexington.

Five Healing Foods for Your Regular Diet

Jamison Starbuck, ND, naturopathic physician in family practice and a lecturer at the University of Montana, both in Missoula. She is past president of the American Association of Naturopathic Physicians and a contributing editor of The Alternative Advisor: The Complete Guide to Natural Therapies & Alternative Treatments *(Time-Life).*

Of all the questions I get from my patients, none is more common than, "Doctor, what foods should I eat?" Here are my favorite foods. They're tasty, easy to prepare and available in grocery or health food stores. And unlike white flour products, luncheon meats, soft drinks and the other foods that many of us subsist on, these foods can help prevent—and even treat—certain illnesses.

• **Beets.** Both the red root—the part we ordinarily eat—and the green tops—the part we throw away—are full of magnesium and iron. These minerals are essential to good health.

But watch out. Like spinach, beet tops are rich in oxalic acid. This compound has been linked with formation of kidney stones. Beet tops are off-limits for anyone with stones or a history of stones. The red part is safe.

Beet tops can be torn like lettuce and added to salads. They can also be steamed and then added to soup—or served as you would serve spinach.

You can also eat beet roots raw. Grate directly into salad...or onto a sandwich made with lettuce, onion, tuna or fresh turkey and whole grain bread.

• **Kale.** I eat this dark, leafy green veggie at least twice a week during winter and early spring. At this time of year, the body's need for vitamins and minerals rises—the result of reduced exposure to sunlight and consumption of fresh food.

Kale is a fabulous source of calcium, iron, vitamins C and A, folic acid and chlorophyll. Unlike corn, beans and tomatoes, kale can be found fresh all year long.

Kale improves circulation and helps ward off colds. The compounds that give kale its bitter flavor help improve digestion and decrease the production of mucus.

Lightly steamed kale is delicious. It tastes a bit like spinach, though more flavorful. I eat the whole leaf, but you may want to avoid the stems. They can be tough.

• **Nuts.** Brazil nuts, almonds, filberts and walnuts are packed with minerals, folic acid, vitamins B and E and beneficial oils.

I recommend buying unshelled nuts—for two reasons. First, the shell keeps nut oil from going rancid. Second, the effort required to crack each nut by hand helps ensure that you won't eat too many of these nutritious—but calorie-dense—treats.

• **Parsley.** Though best known as a garnish, parsley has much more to offer. It improves digestion, freshens the breath and curbs breast tenderness associated with premenstrual syndrome. It's also a tonic for the adrenal glands, which can become "exhausted" as a result of hard work or stress.

I like to add abundant amounts of chopped raw parsley to salads or pasta, or simply eat sprigs as a snack. Ounce for ounce, parsley contains three times as much vitamin C as an orange.

Women who are pregnant or nursing should have no more than a sprig of parsley per day. More than that, and it can cause breast milk to dry up. It can even cause premature labor.

• **Sweet potatoes.** This starchy vegetable is rich in vitamin A and other carotenoids, which are necessary for healthy eyes, skin and lungs.

Bake them or combine with onions, garlic, tomatoes and chickpeas to make a hearty stew.

Perils of Crash Diets

Crash diets actually make people fatter in the long run. *Reason:* When dieters consume fewer than 1,200 calories a day, they lose muscle tissue as well as fat. If they go far enough below that level, their percentage of body fat will increase even though their weight may go down.

Berkeley Wellness Letter, Berkeley, CA.

• **Repeated crash dieting can increase the chance of heart disease.** The faster weight is lost from the body, the faster it tends to go back on. It is this rapid accumulation of weight that results in higher levels of blood cholesterol. Quick weight gain also accelerates the rate at which cholesterol is deposited in the blood vessels.

The 100% Natural, Purely Organic, Cholesterol-Free Megavitamin, Low-Carbohydrate Nutrition Hoax by Elizabeth Whalen (Simon Schuster).

• **Crash diets impair the immune system response** and make dieters more vulnerable to infection. *Special danger:* Surgery patients with poor nutrition have a much higher rate of contracting postoperative infections.

The late Peter Lindner, MD, director of continuing medical education, American Society of Bariatric Physicians, quoted in *Prevention,* Emmaus, Pennsylvania.

The "Don't Think" Diet

Robban Sica-Cohen, MD, holistic doctor in Orange, Connecticut. She specializes in environmental and nutritional medicine.

People do lose weight on trendy diets. But most of them gain back the pounds —and then some. Successful weight loss occurs only when you make a permanent commitment to replacing refined, calorie-dense foods with foods that are natural and unrefined. It's not that difficult.

Typical American dinner: A big piece of steak, a heap of fries and a tiny pile of vegetables. You can slash fat and calories simply by shifting the proportions. Eat one-half or one-third the portion of meat (or substitute fish) plus two big piles of veggies—and brown rice or another whole grain. You'll still feel satisfied.

To cut fat even more, replace the meat with lentils or beans. *Caution:* If you don't feel well on a vegetarian diet, do not force yourself. I'd estimate that one-third of the population has trouble metabolizing grains, fruits, vegetables and other carbohydrates. For these people, a carbohydrate-intensive diet can cause big trouble—including heart disease or a cholesterol or blood sugar problem.

The mineral chromium is a great weight-loss aid. It burns fat, builds muscle and helps reduce cravings for sweets. And chromium may lower levels of LDL (bad) cholesterol and raise levels of HDL (good) cholesterol.

It's hard to get enough chromium from food. Vegetables are poor sources—most are grown in chromium-depleted soil. Organ meats and dairy products contain chromium—but they're too fatty. Whole grains are chromium-rich, too, but they contain phytates, compounds that block the body's absorption of chromium and other trace elements.

Solution: Supplements of chromium picolinate. I recommend 200 micrograms (mcg)—three times a day, with meals—for any overweight adult, especially those who crave sweets or who have a blood sugar or cholesterol/triglyceride problem. *Caution:* Chromium can cause glucose levels to drop in diabetics, requiring a reduction in dosage of insulin. Even if you don't have diabetes, talk to your doctor before taking chromium.

To further boost your fat-burning power, team chromium with the amino acid L-carnitine. *Recommended:* 250 milligrams (mg) three times a day, with meals.

Garlic and Your Health

John Milner, PhD, chief, nutritional science research group, division of cancer prevention, National Cancer Institute, Bethesda, Maryland. Dr. Milner chaired a major conference on the health benefits of garlic.

Recent studies conducted in the US, Europe and China suggest that garlic can lower cholesterol levels...fight bacterial and viral infections...prevent cancer... and boost memory.

How strong is the evidence? Could you benefit by adding more garlic to your diet...or by taking garlic pills?

GARLIC VERSUS CHOLESTEROL

As proponents of garlic are quick to point out, numerous studies suggest that regular consumption of garlic—one clove a day or the equivalent in supplement form—cuts serum cholesterol by 7% to 15%. Garlic seems to be especially helpful at reducing LDL (bad) cholesterol.

Other studies suggest that garlic has little or no effect on cholesterol levels.

Example: A study conducted at the University of Bonn and published in *The Journal of the American Medical Association* showed that cholesterol levels remained unchanged even when garlic oil equivalent to four to five cloves of garlic was consumed on a daily basis for 12 weeks.

What explains the inconsistency of the studies? It may be that only some people respond to garlic. It's also possible that garlic interacts with the other foods in one's diet.

Another possible explanation for the inconsistency may be the fact that the studies have used various garlic preparations. Some have used unprocessed garlic. Others have used a garlic extract—which might or might not have the same biological activity as whole garlic.

GARLIC VERSUS CANCER

Research suggests that garlic can help prevent a variety of malignancies...

• **Stomach cancer.** In a 1984 study conducted in China, people who ate garlic regularly had an unusually low rate of this potentially deadly cancer.

• **Colon cancer.** A 1994 study of women in Iowa found that the incidence of colon cancer was 50% lower among those who consumed the most garlic.

• **Prostate cancer.** A 1997 study conducted in Oxford, England, found that men who consumed garlic two or more times per week were one-third less likely than other men to develop prostate cancer.

If garlic does protect against cancer, the explanation may lie in the sulfur compounds it contains.

Some laboratory studies have demonstrated that these compounds block the synthesis of carcinogens known as nitrosamines. In the absence of sulfur, the digestive process leads to the formation of nitrosamines each time nitrates and nitrites are consumed.

Nitrates and nitrites are both found in preservatives and also in beets, spinach and certain other foods.

Garlic also stimulates the body to synthesize glutathione. In addition to deactivating certain carcinogens, this natural antioxidant protects cell membranes against damage caused by renegade molecules known as free radicals.

Recent studies suggest that it might be possible to derive cancer chemotherapy drugs from garlic.

In one study, a garlic derivative called S-allylmercaptocysteine inhibited the growth of human prostate tumors that had been transplanted to mice.

In another study, a garlic extract called diallyldisulfide inhibited the growth of human breast cancer cells.

HOW TO EAT GARLIC

There is no proof that garlic can reduce cholesterol, lower cancer risk or do anything else to protect your health. But given the evidence in garlic's favor—plus the fact that the only downside to garlic consumption is bad breath—it makes sense to include some in your diet.

One to three grams of garlic per day—the equivalent of one clove—should be enough.

If you want to cook with garlic, be careful to preserve the potentially beneficial sulfur compounds. To do this, peel garlic, chop or crush it and then let it stand for 15 to 30 minutes before cooking. This "waiting period" facilitates chemical reactions that yield the biologically active compounds.

If you don't like the taste or smell of garlic, deodorized supplements are available. These products contain compounds similar to those found in raw garlic.

Foods That Fight Prostate Cancer

D. Duane Baldwin, MD, former chief resident urologist, Loma Linda University Health Care, Loma Linda, California.

It's now clear that a low-fat diet helps prevent prostate cancer. *In addition, certain foods are beneficial…*

•**Allicin.** This garlic compound has potent anticancer properties. Add minced garlic to pasta sauces and stir-frys…toss a peeled clove into the juicer when making fruit juice.

•**Citrus fruits.** Oranges, lemons, etc., are loaded with pectin, a fiber that fights cancer. Since most pectin is found in the peels of citrus fruits, try zesting small slices into salads and stir-frys.

•**Gluten.** In a recent study, men who ate gluten-based meat substitutes were two-thirds less likely to have an elevated level of PSA (prostate-specific antigen), a marker for prostate cancer. Try the meat substitute seitan. It's sold in health food stores.

•**Omega-3 fatty acids.** In recent studies, men who ate little omega-3 acids and lots of saturated fat were three times more likely to develop prostate cancer than other men. Omega-3 fatty acids are found in salmon, mackerel and other cold-water fish.

•**Selenium.** In a recent study, men who took selenium supplements had a lower risk for prostate cancer. *Good source of selenium:* Brazil nuts.

•**Soy.** Tofu, tempeh, miso and other soy foods contain genistein and other isoflavones, which are compounds that retard the growth of cancer cells. Eat two to three ounces of soy foods a day.

•**Tomatoes.** They're rich in lycopene, a pigment that develops anticancer properties once it's been cooked. Make homemade tomato sauce or grill fresh tomatoes.

Eat Tomatoes— Fight Cancer

Eating tomatoes cuts risk not only of prostate cancer, but also of cancers of the lung, stomach and cervix. Preliminary evidence suggests that eating tomatoes also helps prevent cancers of the pancreas, colon, rectum, esophagus, mouth and breast. In 57 of 72 studies, tomatoes and tomato-based products, such as pasta sauce, were found to have anticancer properties.

Theory: An antioxidant called lycopene in tomatoes protects cells from oxidants that have been linked to cancer.

Edward Giovannucci, MD, ScD, professor of medicine, Harvard Medical School, and epidemiologist, department of medicine, Brigham and Women's Hospital, both in Boston. His review of 72 studies of tomatoes and cancer was published in the *Journal of the National Cancer Institute,* Bethesda, Maryland.

Stroke-Reducing Nutrients

Eating bananas and other foods rich in potassium and/or magnesium can reduce the risk for stroke among people with high blood pressure.

Recent finding: Men with high potassium intake faced a stroke risk 36% lower than that of men with low potassium intake. Stroke risk was also lower among men using potassium supplements—but not magnesium supplements.

Fruits and vegetables—particularly oranges, cantaloupe and tomatoes—are good sources of potassium. Foods rich in magnesium include green vegetables, whole grains and beans and peas.

Alberto Ascherio, MD, MPH, DPH, associate professor of nutrition and epidemiology and researcher, department of nutrition, Harvard School of Public Health, Boston.

Lower Cholesterol With Peanuts

Peanuts may be heart-healthy after all. Health-conscious individuals have long shunned the nuts because of their high fat content. *New finding:* Levels of LDL (bad) cholesterol and triglycerides were lower among healthy men and women who regularly ate peanuts, peanut butter or peanut oil than among people who ate a low-fat diet but didn't eat peanut products.

Theory: Like olive oil, peanuts are a good source of heart-healthy monounsaturated fat.

Penny Kris-Etherton, PhD, RD, distinguished professor of nutrition, department of nutritional sciences, Pennsylvania State University, University Park. Her study of 22 men and women 21 to 54 years of age was presented at the Experimental Biology conference in San Francisco.

Spa Cuisine Every Day

Get recipes for high-nutrition, low-fat dishes made by spa chefs by visiting the Web site *www.spafinder.com/spalifestyle/spaathome/ cuisine/index.jsp*. The recipes show many creative ways of serving fruit, vegetables and whole grains.

What's Good for You Can Be Bad for You

Fruit juice can be hazardous to health. Six ounces of apple juice contain the equivalent of more than five teaspoonfuls of sugar—40% more sugar than a chocolate bar and more sugar per ounce than cola. Blood-sugar-sensitive types who experience a temporary lift from sugar followed by fatigue should be cautious about fruit juice intake. *Recommended:* Eat a whole apple or orange instead of drinking juice. The fiber dilutes the sugar impact. *Alternative:* Eat cheese, nuts or other protein with juice.

•**Nondairy cream substitutes,** often used by those on low-fat diets, usually contain coconut oil and have a higher fat content than the dairy product for which they're being substituted.

•**Decaffeinated coffee** leads to significant stomach-acid secretion, causing heartburn and indigestion in many people. Caffeine was assumed to be the culprit, but a new study shows that decaffeinated coffee is even worse. The effect is seen in doses as small as a half cup of decaffeinated coffee. People experiencing ulcer symptoms, heartburn and dyspepsia should avoid decaffeinated as well as regular coffee.

Journal of the American Medical Association, Chicago.

•**Most commercial products billed as alternatives to salt** are based on potassium chloride. *Problem:* Although potassium chloride does enhance flavor, it leaves a slightly bitter or metallic taste. And excessive potassium may be even worse for your health than too much salt. *Alternatives to the alternatives:* Mrs. Dash, a commercial blend of 14 herbs and spices…Lite Salt, a half-sodium, half-potassium blend…or try adding parsley, a delightful herb that enhances flavor all by itself.

•**One of the few proven substances** that can bring on flare-ups of acne is iodine. Excessive, long-term intake of iodine (a natural ingredient of many foods) can bring on acne in anyone, but for people who are already prone to the condition, iodine is especially damaging. Once iodine hits the bloodstream, any excess is excreted through the oil glands of the skin. This process irritates the pores and causes eruptions and inflammation. *Major sources of iodine in the diet:* Iodized table salt, kelp, beef liver, asparagus, turkey and vitamin and mineral supplements. For chronic acne sufferers, cutting down on these high-iodine foods and looking for vitamins without iodine may bring relief.

• **Chronic diarrhea, gas and other stomach complaints** are often linked to lactose intolerance, the inability to digest milk. One of every four adults suffers from this problem. *Reason:* Their bodies don't make enough lactase, the enzyme that breaks down milk sugar in the intestinal tract. *Among the offending foods:* Milk, ice cream, chocolate, soft cheese, some yogurts and sherbet. Lactose is also used as a filler in gum, candies and many canned goods.

• **People on low-sodium diets** should check out tap water as a source of salt intake. Some local water systems have eight times the amount of sodium (20 milligrams per quart) than people with heart problems or hypertension should use.

The Sodium Content of Your Food, Federal Citizen Information Center, Pueblo, CO.

• **Health-food candy** is really no better for you than traditional chocolates. *Comparison:* Health-food candy contains about the same number of calories. The fat content is as high or higher. Bars made of carob are caffeine-free, but the amount of caffeine in chocolate is negligible. And the natural sugars in health bars have no nutritional advantage over refined sugars.

What's Bad for You Can Be Good for You

Chocolate lovers will be pleased to know that chocolate is not as dangerous to teeth as other candies. Antidecay factors in cocoa counter the damaging action of the sugar. Cocoa tannins seem to inhibit plaque formation, and the fat in cocoa may protect teeth by forming an antibacterial coating.

National Institute for Dental Research.

• **Treat a cold with booze fumes.** Take a thick mug and fill it with boiling water. After about two minutes, throw the water away. Put in two ounces of brandy or bourbon, and then fill the mug almost to the top with boiling water. Cup your hands over the top of the mug to make a nose cone. Place your mouth and nose inside the cone. Blow on the surface and inhale the fumes for 15 minutes. You should feel the vapor penetrating your sinuses. Drink the mixture if you want to. Take a cold pill to keep your sinuses open overnight, and repeat the treatment in the morning. If you start this at the first signs of a cold (before nasal passages are blocked), your cold should vanish in 24 hours.

4

Medical Solutions

Health Secrets Only the Insurance Industry Knows

ctuarial tables prepared by the life insurance industry to predict mortality rates present some interesting facts. *For example…*

• **A larger abdomen than chest** (when expanded) is the most dangerous type of obesity.

• **Death rates at all ages are more than twice as high among smokers.**

• **The death of both parents before they reach age 60** increases the mortality risk in children up to one-third.

• **Overweight people have a markedly lower suicide rate.** Being underweight generally leads to a longer life.

• **It is much more dangerous to your health to live alone** than in a stable relationship.

• **The wealthy live longer,** in large part because they get the best medical care, hygiene and nutrition.

• **A stroke before age 60 becomes less and less of a mortality factor** the longer the person lives uneventfully after it. Getting insurance is virtually impossible for those who have a stroke after 60.

• **The nearsighted are unusually prone to anxiety.**

• **Obsessive personality types (compulsively neat and thorough)** are especially likely to become depressed and kill themselves in later life.

• **Severe drunkenness once a month doubles the risk of mortality.** So does getting boisterously drunk every weekend.

• **Those involved in kinky sex** are much more likely to die violently or to kill themselves.

The Invisible Bankers: Everything the Insurance Industry Never Wanted You to Know by Andrew Tobias, personal finance commentator (Pocket Books).

• **Susceptibility to fear** seems to correlate with blood coagulation associated with phlebitis.

• **About one insurance applicant in 10,000 is denied coverage** because of a hazardous occupation. About one in 250 has to pay a surcharge because of occupation.

• **Farmers,** college teachers and Anglican ministers are extremely good risks.

Beware of Online Medical Information

Online medical information can be hazardous to your health—and life. A review of information on the World Wide Web about childhood diarrhea—a potentially life-threatening condition—found that many recommendations were dangerous. And misinformation was found even on sites of major academic medical centers.

Important: Review all online medical information with a qualified professional before taking action.

The late H. Juhling McClung, MD, professor of pediatrics at Ohio State University and medical director of Children's Homecare Services at Children's Hospital, both in Columbus.

Most Dangerous Time of Year to Be in a Hospital

If you need competent care, put off nonemergency surgery and medical tests until late fall if you can. *Reason:* In the cycles of medical education, new residents—the least experienced doctors on a hospital staff—take up their duties on July 1. Senior staff physicians often take summer vacations. *Bottom line:* The hospital is more likely to run smoothly after the new residents have worked into the routine.

Jo-Ann Friedman, president, Health Marketing Systems, New York City.

Patients' Rights

Natalie J. Kaplan, former hospital legal consultant, now in private practice in New York City.

People who are asked to sign medical consent forms are often in the worst possible psychological shape to make a decision about anything. Serious illness is a terrible shock. It brings out the part of human nature that wants to abdicate responsibility and put fate in the hands of an omnipotent being—in this case, the doctor. It's important to understand before you get sick what your rights as a patient are and what medical consent actually means.

The law in this country guarantees the patient an informed consent. That means the patient must be thoroughly informed in advance about all significant aspects of the proposed treatment. Consent is necessary in all nonemergency situations in which there are invasive procedures or treatments involving risks. This includes not only surgery but also more minor procedures such as invasive diagnostic tests or injections of any substance that may have negative side effects.

Making a decision about treatment of a serious illness is traumatic. *Things you should do to be sure your decision is the right one...*

• **Some hospitals provide patient representatives.** Ask for one to sit in on the informed-consent procedure.

• **Write down all your questions in advance.** Take notes or use a tape recorder for the answers.

• **Ask the doctor for recommended reading** about your illness and its treatment.

• **Get second (or third) opinions.**

• **Take a friend or relative with you.** Someone who is uninvolved will be cool-headed enough to get more information.

• **Don't agree to anything just to get it over with.** Listen closely to the alternatives and also the risks.

The essence of informed consent is what takes place between the patient and the doctor. A consent form signed by the patient does not in itself constitute informed consent. The form is simply evidence collected by doctors and hospitals as protection in case of an eventual lawsuit. In all states the patient has the right to an explanation and must understand the procedure. And in some states the informed consent must be obtained by the doctor performing the procedure. *Example:* The risks of anesthesia must be explained by the anesthesiologist. The explanation must be in simple language the patient can understand. *Basics...*

- **Consent for a medical procedure on a child or an unconscious adult can be given over the telephone,** but hospitals and doctors will want it confirmed in writing.

- **Consent can be revoked at any time prior to the procedure.** Medical consents are not legally binding prior to the procedure, and you don't give up any rights when you sign a form and then change your mind.

- **Consent must be to a specific procedure.** A general consent form is not evidence of consent for those specific procedures that require that specific information be imparted to the patient to make him or her "informed." *Recommended:* Sign general consent forms for basic hospital care. After you're admitted, it's still the hospital's and doctor's responsibility to explain any specific procedures in order to obtain consent that's informed.

- **Consent is not necessary for an emergency procedure** where the patient is incompetent or unconscious and no authorized person can be located to consent. *Emergency:* This is any procedure that is medically necessary to treat a condition dangerous to life or health.

What Doctors and Hospitals Don't Tell You

Medical Economics

Always count the pills in the bottle you get, and check the total against the prescription. Discrepancies between the number of pills the doctor prescribes and the number the pharmacist gives you are quite common.

- **Physicians routinely neglect to inform their patients about the possible side effects of the drugs they prescribe.** About three-quarters of patients do not receive these briefings, according to the Food and Drug Administration. And 35% of all patients get no information at all about prescribed drugs. *Protection:* Question your doctor until you know all about the drug you are to take.

- **Diagnostic error.** Poor bite is often misdiagnosed as a migraine or pinched nerve. People with faulty bite often unconsciously grind their teeth to align them better. *Result:* Headaches, earaches and pains in the jaw, neck and shoulders. *Treatments:* Spot grinding by a dentist to even the bite. Exercises to relax the jaw muscles. A plastic device that fits over the upper and lower teeth to protect them from grinding, help readjust the bite and ease pressure on jaw muscles.

- **Doctors who operate frequently have better safety records because they maintain their skills.** *Guideline:* The doctor should have a minimum of 40 to 50 operations a year, even more for heart surgery. Aim for a hospital that does many similar operations. *Best bets:* Teaching and specialty hospitals. A good one substantially improves the chances of avoiding serious complications or death.

- **Postoperative delirium is a short-lived but frightening phenomenon** common to patients who have undergone serious surgery. Some become disoriented or lose touch. Others suffer hallucinations. Patients who are warned about this possibility before an operation are much less likely to experience it. If they do, the effects are much less severe.

Nursing Research

- **Keep your medical records private.** Never sign a blanket medical release form. The only medical release forms you sign should specifically identify the following: Information to be released, who is releasing the information and who is to receive it. Releases are not self-limiting as to time. A form you signed 10 years ago can still be used to obtain information, but a period of one year is suggested.

- **Many hospital procedures can be managed at home**—effectively and efficiently—which will spare the patient's pocketbook. A home chemotherapy program run by M.D. Anderson Cancer Center in Houston saved an average of $1,500 per patient. Home recipients of intravenous feedings through a Cleveland clinic reduced their bills by an estimated $100 a day. In Nashua, New Hampshire, patients who took intravenous antibiotic therapy at home instead of in the hospital saved $286 a day. *Bottom line:* Check with your doctor about local home-care programs the next time a loved one is hospitalized. Keep in mind that insurance companies may not pay for some home-care services.

• **Wrong pills in hospitals.** Since 1962, when a study of hospital medication practices uncovered an error in every six doses given to patients by nurses, the handling of drugs in US hospitals has upgraded appreciably. A majority now have central pharmacies that make up unit doses that are to be dispensed by nurses and/or technicians in most of their departments. Where unit dose systems are in place, errors average only three per 100. However, that 3% can be fatal, and the number of errors in departments and hospitals not served by the central pharmacy is still very high (8% to 20%). *The problem:* Overworked nurses, confusing and similar drug names and packaging and illegibly written prescriptions. *How to protect yourself:* Be sure you know exactly which drugs and what dosages your doctor has ordered for you. Never accept medication without knowing what it is and what it is for.

• **Blood pressure readings taken in a doctor's office may not be accurate** because of the anxiety of being there. *Better:* Using portable devices, patients can measure their own pressures during the day while continuing their normal activities. These measurements are particularly helpful in deciding whether to start medication in patients who have borderline hypertension. Be sure to check the accuracy of your device by bringing it with you to the doctor's office.

Journal of the American Medical Association

• **Doctors' handwriting.** When doctors write the names of drugs on prescription slips, a misreading by the pharmacist can be disastrous. A drug for arthritis, Tolectin, has been mistaken for Tolinase, which lowers blood sugar in diabetics. Coumadin, a drug that thins blood in heart-disease patients, was confused with Kemadrin, which is for Parkinson's disease. *Useful:* Tell the pharmacist the disease for which the medicine is being prescribed. The pharmacist can then check it.

Protect Yourself Against Hospital Billing Errors

Janice Spillane, RN, MS, former editorial director, NY/NJ division of *Nursing Spectrum*.

When the mechanic hands you a bill for $500, it's unlikely that you'd pay it without a glance at the charges. But when given a hospital bill for $5,000, most people tend to do just that.

As it turns out, hospitals and doctors are far from infallible when it comes to billing. According to the New York Life Insurance Company, which has been auditing hospital bills for several years, the average hospital bill contains hundreds of dollars worth of erroneous charges. This money comes not only out of the insurance company's pocket but also out of yours. You can save money by knowing how the system works and how to spot billing errors.

With the rising costs of health care, the current trend in the insurance industry is to have the insured employee share in the cost of health care. Under major medical plans, employees are usually responsible for a fixed dollar amount, termed out-of-pocket expenses, which includes deductibles and coinsurance. In addition, many employees pay a portion of their health-care premium, so it is to their advantage to keep health-care costs down to avoid unnecessary increases in premiums.

How it works: Let's say the out-of-pocket limit is $1,000. The insurance company usually pays 80% (and the patient 20%) of all non-room-and-board charges until the $1,000 out-of-pocket expense limit is reached. After that, insurance takes over 100%. However, most patients don't reach the out-of-pocket limit, since they'd have to run up at least $5,000 worth of non-room-and-board hospital expenses or other health-care costs to do so. Therefore, while your contribution to out-of-pocket is still adding up, it clearly pays to keep costs down.

There are many billing errors for the simple reason that many hospitals have inefficient billing systems. *Major problem:* Hospitals are geared toward making sure that patients are billed for services provided and not toward verifying charges.

Typical mistake: Because of a clerical error, a $50 electrocardiogram is entered on your bill at a $500 charge. Since you may not know the typical cost of an EKG, the error goes undetected.

Another example: A lab technician comes in to draw blood and finds that the patient is no longer there. However, he's still charged. *Reason:* Billing starts from the day the charges are entered in the book, and this person's charges are never canceled.

Similar mistakes occur with drug prescriptions. *Example:* The doctor might order 10 days of penicillin and then switch to tetracycline after seven days. If the unused three days' worth of penicillin is not returned, the patient is billed for it.

THE FOUR MAJOR MISTAKE AREAS

• **Respiratory therapy.** Equipment such as oxygen tanks and breathing masks isn't credited when it's discontinued. Sometimes it's not even removed from the room promptly.

• **Pharmacy charges.** Credit isn't given for drugs that were returned, or when unused drugs are not returned.

• **Lab tests.** Cancellations of tests aren't noted.

• **Central supply items.** Hospital staff or nurses may run out of something and borrow it from another patient. They intend to give credit or return the item, but often they don't get around to it.

WHAT YOU CAN DO

• **Keep track of the most basic things,** such as how many times your blood was drawn. *Suggestion:* If you're able, jot down what happens daily. *Note:* If the patient is too sick to keep track of services rendered, a family member should try to keep track of the charges. Although it may be difficult to know how many routine things such as blood counts or X-rays

were done, someone who visits regularly is likely to know about nonroutine services, such as barium enemas or cardiac catheterizations.

• **Ask questions.** Ask the doctor to be specific about tests. If X-rays are ordered, ask what type of X-rays. If the doctor doesn't answer the question to your satisfaction, ask the nurse. Always ask. It's the most important thing a health-care consumer can do. *Reassuring change:* The newer generation of doctors is more willing to involve patients in their own care.

• **Insist on an itemized bill,** not just a summary of charges.

• **Check room and board charges.** Count the days you were in the hospital and what kind of room you had. Are you being charged for a private room even though you were in a semiprivate one? Some hospitals have different semiprivate rates for two- and four-bed rooms. Check your rate.

• **Review the charges for TV rental and phone service.**

• **Be equally careful with doctor bills.** Often these bills are made out by the doctor's assistant, who may not be sure of what was done. *Most common errors:* Charges for services in the doctor's office, such as a chest X-ray or an injection, that weren't actually performed. Charges for routine hospital physician visits on days that the doctor was not in attendance.

High-Tech Medical Dangers

Charles B. Inlander, consumer advocate and health-care consultant based in Fogelsville, Pennsylvania. He was founding president of People's Medical Society, a consumer health advocacy group. He is author of more than 20 books, including Take This Book to the Hospital with You *(St. Martin's).*

The medical profession is growing more sophisticated and high-tech. There are now treatments and cures available that were considered miracles a few years ago.

But the health-care system is also more dangerous than ever.

With more diagnostic tools and surgical options available, many more opportunities exist for physicians to make mistakes or to act on incomplete knowledge. The wrong doctor—or the wrong lab test or the wrong surgery—is dangerous and even deadly. More than 200,000 Americans die each year, according to some estimates, because of their doctors' negligence.

To survive the modern health-care system, patients must be assertive, informed and ready to protect themselves from myriad hazards. *These include...*

• **Misdiagnosis.** It happens more than you think. A study of 1,800 autopsies from 32 hospitals found a diagnosis error rate of 20%. Half the errors—180 cases in all—led to the patients' deaths. *Most commonly overlooked:* Pulmonary embolisms, peritonitis and pulmonary abscesses, all of which are life-threatening conditions.

• **Laboratory errors.** More and more doctors do lab work at their offices these days. It's a big money-maker for them and it's also hazardous to your health. Doctor-operated labs have double the error rates of independent or hospital laboratories, which are monitored far more tightly by the state. And even these are not failsafe. As many as 35% of Pap smears produce false-positive or false-negative results. The former can lead to an unneeded hysterectomy, the latter to an untreated cancer.

• **Hospital infections and errors.** A hospital is the most dangerous place in the world for sick people. One out of every 10 patients gets a new infection inside the hospital. Many of these are fatal and 80% are preventable. In addition, even a good hospital may have a 2% to 3% error rate in medicating its patients. On average, every minute in this country one patient gets either the wrong medicine, too much or too little or is dosed at the wrong time. This problem has worsened with the recent nursing shortage, since more nurses come out of "pools" and there is less continuity of care.

• **Alcoholic, drug-addicted or incompetent doctors.** The local medical society might know who they are but they keep the information confidential. You'll know, too, if your doctor shows up bleary-eyed, mumbling or wobbly. The problem is that many impaired doctors—and particularly surgeons—are not so obvious.

Choosing the Right Anesthesiologist

Leonard H. Glantz, professor of health law, Boston University School of Public Health, Boston.

It is common knowledge that patients should consult more than one doctor before proceeding with any kind of surgery. But when it comes to the selection of an anesthesiologist, we tend to be much more passive. However, the quality of the care we receive from our anesthesiologist is as important—or more so—as the quality of surgical care. Anesthesiologists' work involves not only the administration of potentially lethal drugs but also the monitoring of the patient's vital signs during surgery.

Typically, the first contact with the anesthesiologist takes place in the hospital the night before the operation. *Better:* Ask your surgeon for the name of the anesthesiologist when the operation itself is discussed. Meet the proposed anesthesiologist well before the operation.

Ask your surgeon how often he has worked with this anesthesiologist. Ask anyone you know who works at the hospital—nurses, volunteers, etc.—for the hospital grapevine's assessment of the anesthesiologist.

Make sure the doctor is board-certified. Look up his/her credentials (in any medical-specialist book at a public library or on-line at the American Board of Medical Specialties Web site, *www.abms.org*) to find out where he trained and how long he has been practicing.

Interview the proposed anesthesiologist. Ask him or her to explain the options available to you and to tell you why a particular course is recommended. Feel free to discuss anything that bothers you.

If you are at all dissatisfied with the proposed anesthesiologist's qualifications or competence, request another one and check him out. If that can't be arranged, seriously consider changing to another surgeon and/or hospital. The choice is *always* the patient's.

Free Information About Medicare

Government agencies and private nonprofit organizations are trying to provide Medicare information as clearly and concisely as possible. To get information, contact the Social Security Administration at 800-772-1213 or visit *www.ssa.gov.*

You can also find information at the following Web sites...

• **Social Security Administration.** *www.ssa.gov/pubs/10043.html*

• **Official Medicare site.** *www.medicare.gov*

• **Centers for Medicare & Medicaid Services.** *www.cms.gov*

• **Center for Medicare Advocacy, Inc.** *www.medicareadvocacy.org*

• **National Senior Citizens Law Center.** *www.nsclc.org*

• **Medicare Rights Center.** *www.medicarerights.org*

New Way to Reach Your Doctor

Send E-mail to your doctor. It's a good way to handle routine matters such as referrals, billing questions, appointments, medication questions and prescription renewals. Many doctors are willing to communicate with patients through E-mail, if patients do not abuse the privilege by flooding the doctor with messages or using E-mail improperly. E-mail is not for diagnoses, complex questions or emergencies of any type. Ask your doctor if he or she uses E-mail or would be willing to try.

David Stern, MD, PhD, associate professor, department of internal medicine, University of Michigan, Ann Arbor, quoted in *Prevention*.

New Drug Theory— Less Is More

Seymour M. Antelman, PhD, professor of psychiatry at the University of Pittsburgh School of Medicine.

Virtually all drugs are administered with the common assumption that the higher the dose—and the more often the dose is repeated—the greater and longer-lasting the effect.

But it turns out that the opposite may be true —according to research done with animals. The drugs grow more potent as the intervals between doses are lengthened. In other words, weekly doses have more impact than daily doses. Monthly doses provoke an even greater response. The longer you wait between doses, the more quickly the medicine works.

In addition, we have found that a drug continues to exert effects long after all traces of it have disappeared from the body. This time-dependent sensitization theory, now being tested with humans, holds dramatic potential for patients now taking stimulants, antidepressants, antianxiety drugs and anti-psychotics.

It offers a possible solution to the common problem of tolerance—the body's tendency to respond less and less to a drug the more often it is taken. At the same time, greater intervals between doses would reduce—if not eliminate—undesirable side effects.

THE HOLDUP

Despite the publication of several papers in top scientific journals supporting these findings, there is little funding for further experiments. *Reason:* The theory may represent a radical change in the way drugs should be prescribed. It goes against the long-held views of both academia and the pharmaceutical industry.

HOW IT WORKS

The body is pushed to respond to a drug because of its foreignness. The body recognizes the medicine as an unfamiliar substance and therefore as a stressor and a potential threat. But if the drug is introduced repeatedly within a short period, and to no ill effect, the body begins to make peace with the intruder. The drug's potency is muted. This is the phenomenon of tolerance.

If, on the other hand, the drug is administered intermittently—with several weeks or months between doses—the body will still respond to each dose as if it were the first dose. The drug will still work with full force each time.

When a person begins to take antidepressants, weeks often go by before any benefit is observed. According to conventional wisdom, the drug must be given continually until it accumulates to a certain level in the body, at which point it begins to take effect.

Another possibility: The body may need several weeks after the first dose to "learn" to respond to a second dose. The intervening doses will not accelerate that process. They only decrease sensitivity and build tolerance.

Much more testing is, of course, necessary, and our findings may not be applicable in all cases. There is, however, strong reason to believe that the theory could lead to a reduction in expense and complications in many, many cases.

Arthritis Medication That Protects Your Stomach

Ibuprofen and other nonsteroidal anti-inflammatory drugs (NSAIDs) are often the first line of defense against arthritis pain and inflammation—but they can cause stomach problems, such as gastric ulcers and bleeding, in some patients.

Alternative: The prescription medication Arthrotec combines an NSAID (*diclofenac*) with *misoprostol,* which protects the stomach lining.

Arthrotec is good at relieving arthritis symptoms and its side effects include water retention and occasional stomach upset.

Vivian P. Bykerk, BSc, MD, FRCPC, assistant director, division of advanced therapeutics/early arthritis program, Mount Sinai Hospital, Toronto, and assistant professor of medicine, University of Toronto.

Herbs and Surgery

Herbal remedies should be stopped at least two weeks prior to any surgical procedure. St. John's wort, ginkgo biloba, feverfew, ginseng and other herbs can cause dangerous changes in heart rate and blood pressure when combined with anesthesia or other drugs.

John B. Neeld, Jr., MD, chair of the department of anesthesiology, Northside Hospital, Atlanta, and past president, American Society of Anesthesiologists, Park Ridge, Illinois. For more information, contact the ASA at 847-825-5586. *www.asahq.org*

Lifestyle Strategies To Prevent Colon Cancer

The late Samuel Meyers, MD, clinical professor of medicine at Mount Sinai School of Medicine in New York City. He is a coauthor of the medical textbook *Bockus Gastroenterology* (W.B. Saunders).

If you're concerned about colon malignancies and other intestinal cancers, chances are you already know to avoid the cancer-causing chemicals found in charred or charcoal-broiled meats. You also may know that cigarettes not only cause lung cancer, but also promote the growth of colon polyps and tumors.

Fortunately, researchers now have discovered seven additional lifestyle factors that can affect your risk even more...

• **Dietary fat.** It does more than promote weight gain. Dietary fat also increases colon cancer risk. Limit your daily intake to one-third of total calories. The saturated fats found in meat and whole-milk products are believed to be particularly harmful.

What to do: Eat fish that contains healthful omega-3 oils, such as salmon and tuna, three times a week. Omega-3s reduce levels of *prostaglandins,* body chemicals that promote cancer growth. Limit meat consumption to once or twice a week. Substitute skim milk for whole-milk products.

• **Fiber.** Although several recent studies suggest that fiber may be less important than once thought, most evidence still indicates that a diet rich in fiber-containing foods, such as fruits, vegetables and whole-grain products, lowers cancer risk. There is no question that it aids general bowel health, lessening the incidence of constipation, diverticulosis (small, balloon-like sacs in the digestive tract) and hemorrhoids.

What to do: Aim for 25 to 30 grams (g) of fiber daily. This can include fiber supplements, such as Metamucil or FiberCon. *Even better:* Get fiber from natural food sources, which also contain antioxidants and other cancer-fighting compounds.

Examples: Broccoli, cabbage or brussels sprouts.

•**Exercise.** Active people have a 30% lower rate of colon cancer (and some other types of cancer as well). The more exercise, the better.

What to do: Get one-half hour of activity, such as walking, cycling or swimming, vigorous enough to break a light sweat, at least three—preferably five—days a week.

•**Body weight.** Exercise and a low-fat, high-fiber diet will help prevent you from becoming overweight, which increases cancer risk in general.

What to do: Maintain a body mass index (BMI) of 19 to 25. BMI is a measure of body fat based on height and weight. It is calculated by multiplying your weight in pounds by 704.5, and dividing that number by your height in inches squared. *Example for a 180-pound, six-foot tall man:* (180 x 704.5) ÷ (72 x 72) = 24.5. For a BMI calculator, visit the National Heart, Lung and Blood Institute's Web site at *http://nhlbisupport.com/bmi.*

•**Calcium.** Some evidence suggests that calcium prevents the formation of polyps. This provides a reason beyond bone health to get at least the recommended daily intake of this mineral—1,200 milligrams (mg). Because the body cannot absorb this amount at one time, take 600 mg twice a day, with food.

What to do: Eat more calcium-rich foods, such as low-fat dairy products and calcium-enriched orange juice, and/or take a daily calcium supplement.

•**Folate.** This B vitamin appears to reduce colon cancer risk as well by decreasing the amount of damage done to the body's DNA.

What to do: Eat folate-rich foods, such as fortified cereals and leafy, green vegetables. Take a supplement with 400 micrograms (mcg) daily, or a multivitamin that includes this amount.

•**Aspirin.** Recent studies have shown that small doses of aspirin reduce recurrent colon polyps by about one-third in people who have already had them.

What to do: Take one low-dose aspirin daily (81 mg) if you've had colon polyps. Aspirin is thought to reduce colon malignancies by inhibiting cancer-promoting prostaglandins.

The FDA also has approved daily use of the nonsteroidal anti-inflammatory drug (NSAID) *celecoxib* (Celebrex*) to prevent polyps in people who have a condition called *familial adenomatous polyposis* (FAP), a genetic predisposition to develop polyps.

Other NSAIDs, such as *ibuprofen* (Advil) and *naproxen* (Aleve), are believed to have the same effect. However, there is less evidence to support their use for this purpose. They also are more likely to cause adverse side effects, such as stomach ulcers. If you don't have a personal or family history of polyps, the benefit of aspirin or NSAIDs is unclear.

Important: Check with your doctor before taking these drugs. If you are prone to gastrointestinal irritation or bleeding, the risk may outweigh the benefit.

*Celebrex can increase your risk of life-threatening heart or circulation problems, including heart attack or stroke that can lead to death. Please check with your doctor before taking this medicine.

Dangerous Mixes

Don't mix citrus fruits and juices (orange, grapefruit) and aluminum-containing medications or medications that contain aluminum and citrates. *Reason:* Too much aluminum in the system increases one's risk of brain damage, brittle bones and possibly senile dementia. Citrus increases aluminum absorption by as much as 50-fold.

Even safer precaution: Avoid ingesting aluminum in any form.

The Lancet

Medicines And Winter

The weather affects both the body and the mind. And winter, the most extreme season of all, elicits the most extreme effects. Drug potency changes in the winter. Digitalis, the heart drug, becomes more toxic as barometric pressure drops. And diabetics respond more slowly to insulin.

Important: Discuss dosage adjustment with your doctor.

The late Maria Simonson, PhD, ScD, director of the Health, Weight and Stress Clinic, Johns Hopkins Medical Institution, Baltimore.

Viruses Can Damage The Heart

Serious viral infections may cause coronary damage that facilitates a heart attack. The viral infections are those that commonly bring on bad colds. If they persist, they could inflame the heart muscle, making the patient susceptible to attacks.

The Harvard Medical School.

Time-Release Medication For Heart Problems

Skin patches are replacing tablets as a way for people with heart problems to take *nitroglycerin*. When placed on the skin, the patches gradually release the drug, creating a constant level for 24 hours. Though more expensive than tablets, the patches are safer and have fewer significant side effects. The patches are for people who have angina pectoris or congestive heart failure.

Therapaeia

Sunlight Helps High Blood Pressure

High blood pressure can be reduced by ultraviolet B light (UVB)—a component of sunlight. In a recent study, people with mild hypertension who were exposed to UVB had marked declines in blood pressure.

Theory: UVB promotes synthesis of vitamin D in the body. Vitamin D helps regulate calcium levels, and calcium is known to help regulate hormones that affect blood pressure.

Helpful: Get five to 10 minutes of exposure to sunlight—hands, face and arms—two or three times a week.

Michael F. Holick, MD, professor of medicine, physiology and biophysics and director of the General Clinical Research Center, Boston University School of Medicine.

Craving for Salt Can Signal Hypertension

Hypertensive craving for salt may be a symptom of the disease rather than a cause. *Reason:* Researchers speculate that hypertensives have a diminished taste for salt and thus use more of it.

Many Herbs and Drugs Don't Mix

Mark Blumenthal, founder and executive director of the American Botanical Council (ABC), *www.herbal gram.org*, an Austin, Texas–based nonprofit organization that disseminates information on herbs and medicinal plants. He is also senior editor of *The ABC Clinical Guide to Herbs* (American Botanical Council).

Most herbal remedies are safe. But some herbs can pose potential risks when mixed with prescription or over-the-counter (OTC) drugs.* That's because herbal

*Tell your doctor and pharmacist about all herbal supplements you are taking. Pregnant women should avoid most herbs.

formulas can have a physiological effect on the body, such as raising or lowering blood pressure, blood sugar levels or heart rate. *Note:* The culinary use of herbs usually has no effect on prescription and OTC drugs.

RISKY COMBINATIONS

Drugs that should not be combined with some herbs...

•**Antacids.** Medications that ease the discomforts of persistent heartburn, indigestion or peptic ulcer are among the most popular OTC and prescription drugs in the US. These drugs include substances that either neutralize gastric acid (antacids) or inhibit its secretion (proton pump inhibitors).

People who take antacids, such as Alka-Seltzer or Mylanta, or proton pump inhibitors, such as *omeprazole* (Prilosec) or *esomeprazole* (Nexium), should avoid herbal formulas that *enhance* stomach acid secretion. This includes cayenne fruit (red pepper), which is typically used to treat peptic ulcer.

•**Anticoagulants.** Millions of Americans use aspirin or prescription blood thinners, such as *warfarin* (Coumadin), to protect against heart attack and stroke.

What many people fail to realize is that some herbs can also have a blood-thinning effect. *These include...*

　•Feverfew, used for migraines.
　•Garlic, used for cardiovascular health.
　•Ginger, used to aid digestion.
　•Ginkgo, used for cognitive impairment in older adults.
　•Ginseng, used to boost physical endurance.

People who combine any of these herbs with an anticoagulant may experience excessive bleeding if they suffer a cut or a wound... as well as increased risk for internal bleeding or a stroke if they sustain an injury.

•**Antidepressants.** If you take a prescription antidepressant, you should avoid the herbal remedy St. John's wort. Although St. John's wort can be an effective treatment for mild to moderate depression, it can act in concert with the class of antidepressant drugs known as selective serotonin reuptake inhibitors (SSRIs) to produce "serotonin syndrome." The condition causes drowsiness, rapid eye movement, restlessness and confusion. Commonly used SSRIs include *fluoxetine* (Prozac), *paroxetine* (Paxil), *sertraline* (Zoloft) and *citalopram* (Celexa).

•**Anti-anxiety drugs.** Kava, an herbal supplement used to relieve anxiety and stress, should not be taken with prescription medication for anxiety, such as *chlordiazepoxide* (Librium), *diazepam* (Valium), *alprazolam* (Xanax) and *lorazepam* (Ativan). Combining kava with one of these drugs can result in a loss of motor skills.

Caution: The FDA has warned consumers that kava has been linked to severe liver damage. Regulatory agencies in some European countries have also issued warnings or banned the herb from the marketplace.

If you have a history of liver disease...drink moderate or large amounts of alcohol...or take *acetaminophen* (Tylenol) or other drugs with possible toxic effects on the liver, you should avoid kava unless your treatment is supervised by a physician.

•**Antihypertensives.** If your doctor has prescribed drugs, such as thiazide diuretics, to lower your blood pressure, don't eat licorice candy or use licorice supplements that contain true licorice extract. It can counteract the medication's ability to lower blood pressure. Check the ingredients listed on the licorice label.

Licorice candy flavored with anise—rather than true licorice extract—is considered safe if you're taking diuretics.

Licorice supplements that contain *deglycyrrhizinated licorice* (DGL), often used for gastric ulcers, can also be used safely.

•**Oral contraceptives.** Women who take oral contraceptives should avoid chastetree. Commonly used to ease premenstrual syndrome (PMS), this herb affects the regulation of hormones and may interfere with the effectiveness of oral contraceptives.

Oral contraceptive users should also consult a physician before taking St. John's wort. Recent reports from Scandinavia have found that St. John's wort lowers the effectiveness of birth control pills, which could result in unwanted pregnancy.

BUY WISELY

To help ensure the purity and integrity of an herbal product, check the label for a seal from one of the following...

• **ConsumerLab.com,** an independent testing organization that publishes on the Internet results for products that pass its tests.

• **NSF International,** a nonprofit organization that assesses factory procedures and product quality. *www.nsf.org.*

• **United States Pharmacopeia** (USP), a government commissioned organization that establishes standards for drugs and dietary supplements.

Any of these seals ensures that the product contains the ingredients and amounts that are listed on the label.

The nonprofit American Botanical Council also provides information about drug interactions and other safety guidelines on some product labels.

For professional advice about using herbal supplements, consult a naturopathic physician, a health-care practitioner who prescribes a variety of alternative therapies, including herbal remedies.

To find a naturopath in your area, contact the American Association of Naturopathic Physicians, 866-538-2267, *www.naturopathic.org.*

Blood-Pressure Drugs May Disturb Sleep

High-blood-pressure drugs can cause insomnia and nightmares as well as daytime drowsiness. For those who develop sleep disturbances, taking the medication in the morning may help. Others may do better taking the medication at bedtime. Consult your doctor before changing the schedule.

RN

Rapid Blood-Pressure Drop May Signal Danger

Low blood pressure, if it is your normal reading, is a healthy sign. Actuarial data show that people with low blood pressure tend to live longest. But any sudden drop in blood pressure may be dangerous, signaling rapid bleeding, fluid loss or possibly a heart attack or other serious illness. Prompt emergency treatment is imperative if blood pressure ever falls precipitously.

Best Cancer Fighters

Certain fruits, such as raspberries, strawberries and grapes, contain the highest levels of the cancer-preventing compound known as *ellagic acid.*

This compound—which is found in slightly lower concentrations in nuts and other fruits— helps protect DNA by binding to and thereby deactivating chemical carcinogens. Such damage raises the risk for cancer. Ellagic acid is also thought to reduce risk for stroke and heart attack.

Miriam Rossi, PhD, professor of chemistry, Vassar College, Poughkeepsie, New York.

Eye–Kidney Connection

Eye and kidney abnormalities that are associated with diabetes may be reversible by supplementing with vitamin E.

Recent study: Diabetics at risk for the potentially blinding eye disorder retinopathy and/or the kidney disorder nephropathy took 1,800 international units (IU) of vitamin E a day for four months.

Result: Blood tests revealed that their risk for the two conditions was diminished. The greater the risk for eye or kidney trouble, the greater the benefit.

Sven-Erik Bursell, PhD, investigator, eye research section, Joslin Diabetes Center, Boston. His eight-month study of 50 diabetics and 13 nondiabetics was presented at a meeting of the American Diabetes Association.

Avoid the "Big Three" Eye Diseases

Marc R. Rose, MD, ophthalmologist in private practice in Los Angeles. He and his brother, Michael Rose, MD, are coauthors of *Save Your Sight!* (Warner Books).

As we reach our sixties and beyond, our eyes become increasingly vulnerable to three vision-robbing disorders...

•**Macular degeneration.** The leading cause of blindness in older people, this disorder destroys cells in the retina.

•**Cataracts.** A gradual clouding over of the lenses within the eyes causes light sensitivity and blurry vision.

•**Glaucoma.** Rising pressure in the eye damages the optic nerves, causing tunnel vision.

Lifestyle plays a major role in determining who develops these problems...and who does not. *Here's how to minimize your risk...*

•**Eat at least five servings of fruits and vegetables a day.** Antioxidants found in plant foods help deactivate cell-damaging compounds known as *free radicals*. Free radicals are associated with every major eye disease.

Carrots, squash, broccoli and red onions contain the antioxidant *beta-carotene*. Spinach, collard greens, celery, corn, green beans, kiwi fruit and red grapes contain the antioxidants *lutein* and *zeaxanthin*.

Asparagus, garlic and onions are rich in sulfur, which the body uses to make a key antioxidant known as glutathione.

•**Eat less sugar.** Too much sugar leads to *hyperinsulinemia*, a condition in which the pancreas secretes abnormally high amounts of insulin. Hyperinsulinemia is associated with all three eye diseases, as well as diabetes, high blood pressure and cancer.

To keep insulin levels in check, you must limit your intake of sugary desserts and other sweets—but that's not all. Substitute brown rice for white rice, and eat sprouted grain breads instead of ordinary flour-containing bread.

Emphasize nutritious sources of protein, such as tofu...and salmon, cod, sardines and other deep-water fish.

•**Get enough essential fatty acids.** Cold-water fish are good sources of omega-3 fatty acids, which help curb the body's inflammatory response. Ordinarily, this process helps heal injured cells. But when it gets out of hand, pressure builds inside the eyes. This can lead to glaucoma.

For maximum benefit, eat cold-water fish three times a week. If you don't like fish, get fatty acids by eating ground flaxseed instead. One to three tablespoons a day—sprinkled on cereal or salads—is fine.

•**Take a daily vitamin supplement.** *It should include...*

•**B-complex.** Vitamins B-6, B-12 and folic acid help neutralize *homocysteine*, a toxic by-product of cellular metabolism.

•**Chromium.** This trace mineral helps stabilize blood sugar levels, preventing hyperinsulinemia.

•**Vanadyl sulfate.** Works like chromium to stabilize blood sugar.

•**Zinc.** Zinc deficiency is now thought to contribute to macular degeneration.

Supplements specially formulated for the eyes can also be helpful. Sold in health food stores, these usually contain lutein, zeaxanthin, bilberry extract (to strengthen capillaries in the eye) and vitamin C.

•**Drink at least six eight-ounce glasses of water a day.** Some researchers believe that chronic dehydration contributes to degenerative diseases, including those that affect the eyes.

•**Wear wraparound sunglasses.** If you're out in the sun for more than 10 minutes—or at midday for any length of time—wear wraparound sunglasses. These should block 100% of ultraviolet A and B light.

Too much sunlight contributes to macular degeneration and cataracts.

Trap: Not all sunglasses labeled "UV-blocking" really are. Play it safe by buying your sunglasses from an optometrist or ophthalmologist you trust.

If you wear prescription glasses, have wraparound sunglasses made up in your prescription...or wear plastic eye protectors over your regular glasses. These protectors are sold at drugstores for about $10.

• **Don't smoke.** Smoking is known to increase the risk for cataracts, macular degeneration and glaucoma.

• **Use medication with caution.** Some prescription drugs can cause eye damage. *Be especially careful about…*

• **Aspirin, ibuprofen and acetaminophen.** These drugs can cause dry eyes and corneal deposits. There's even evidence that they can cause delicate vessels in the eyes to hemorrhage.

• **Corticosteroids.** Use of *prednisone* (Deltasone) and similar drugs has been linked with cataracts and glaucoma.

• **Photosensitizing drugs.** Certain antibiotics, diuretics and antiarrhythmic drugs make eyes sensitive to sunlight, raising the risk for retinal damage.

If you take any of these drugs on a regular basis, ask your doctor about their possible effects on your eyes. There may be a safer alternative.

• **Get regular screenings.** Everyone age 40 or older should see an ophthalmologist or optometrist for an eye exam at least every two years (annually if you take drugs that can affect the eyes or if there is a family history of eye disease).

Important: Testing blood glucose levels is a standard part of a yearly physical. If you have a family history of diabetes or hypoglycemia, your glucose levels should be tested twice a year after the age of 40.

Ask your doctor for the fasting blood sugar and fasting insulin tests rather than a simple blood glucose test.

• **Always wear protective sports goggles or glasses** while playing racquetball, baseball, etc.…and using power tools.

Important Facts About Laser Eye Surgery

LASIK laser surgery to correct nearsightedness requires a highly experienced eye surgeon to minimize complications.

LASIK corrects nearsightedness by using a laser beam to remove a thin layer of tissue from the cornea to flatten it. A study of 574 patients who had LASIK found that complications occurred about 5% of the time, and serious vision loss in three cases. Complications were more frequent when the operation was performed by inexperienced surgeons.

R. Doyle Stulting, MD, PhD, professor of ophthalmology at Emory University, Atlanta.

Contact Lens Swimming Danger

Don't wear soft contact lenses in a pool, lake or hot tub. Soft-lens wearers are susceptible to corneal infection caused by acanthamoeba, a parasite found in water. Routine levels of chlorination do not kill this organism. It can cause a serious, extremely painful corneal infection resulting in partial or total blindness.

Rodale Press, 33 E. Minor St., Emmaus, Pennsylvania 18098.

Getting Rid of Bad Breath

Mouthwash does not kill the germs that cause bad breath, according to the Food and Drug Administration. *What does improve bad breath:* Form the habit of brushing your teeth and tongue often and using dental floss to clean between the teeth and under the gums. If halitosis persists, see a doctor.

E.L. Attia, MD, otolaryngologist, quoted in *American Health*.

How to Treat Cankers

Canker sores, those painful irritants that attack the lining of the mouth, are usually started by a scratch from a hard-bristled toothbrush, a sharp utensil or even sharp-cornered foods such as peanut brittle or nuts. However, recurring canker sores may be a reflection of an iron, vitamin B12 or folic acid deficiency. In that case, correcting the deficiency clears up the sores.

Abner L. Notkins, MD, and David Wray, MD, National Institute of Dental and Craniofacial Research, Bethesda, Maryland.

Brace Wearers Need Calcium

People who wear braces on their teeth may need more calcium. When teeth are moved, it creates gaps in the jawbone that must be filled. New bone requires calcium.

Sources: Green leafy vegetables such as asparagus, broccoli and turnip greens, milk, calcium supplements.

David Ostreicher, DDS and orthodontist, graduate of the School of Dental and Oral Surgery, Columbia University, New York City.

Herbs and Dental Care

Let your dentist know about any herbal remedies you take regularly so that he or she can consider possible side effects.

Example: Ginkgo biloba may cause bleeding gums or make existing gum disease worse.

Andrew Rubman, ND, founder and director, Southbury Clinic for Traditional Medicines, Southbury, Connecticut. *www.southburyclinic.com*

Saving a Knocked-Out Tooth

When a tooth has been knocked out, there is a 90% chance that it can be successfully replanted if you get the tooth and

the patient to a dentist within 30 minutes. *Procedure:* Wrap the tooth in a damp cloth without cleaning it and get to a dentist's office right away. After two hours, the odds of being able to save the tooth drop to only 10%.

J.O. Andreasen, DDS, University Hospital, Copenhagen, Denmark.

Another way: Replace the tooth in its socket and hurry to the dentist. *Next best:* Pop it into a glass of milk for the trip.

Frank Courts, DDS, PhD, associate professor and chairman of pediatric dentistry at the University of Florida, Gainesville.

Everything You Should Know About Dental Implants

Dental implants have become an increasingly popular form of tooth replacement. According to the American Academy of Implant Dentistry, some 500,000 implant procedures are performed each year. Their growing popularity is not surprising, as implants have a number of advantages over older, traditional methods of tooth replacement. Success rates have also increased and are well over 90 percent—the result of better implant materials and improved placement techniques developed over the last several years.

Dental implants offer a number of advantages over fixed bridges and partial and full dentures. Fixed bridges, for example, require the dentist to prepare adjacent teeth; whereas implants leave existing teeth intact. The primary benefits of implants, however, are that they feel more stable, comfortable and produce a more natural chewing ability than full and partial dentures. Implants can also provide relief from sores caused by dentures, are brushed and flossed like teeth and can often provide a near-natural esthetic appearance. Perhaps most importantly, implants make people feel secure, confident and able to maintain a positive self-image.

Still, not everyone is a candidate for implants. For example, implants are not for the impatient, says Arthur Brisman, DDS, a former professor of implantology at New York University College of Dentistry. He explained, "We can fit a patient with dentures in a couple of weeks. Implant therapy, on the other hand, is a sophisticated, three-step process that takes several months to complete."

First, there is the surgery to place the implants into the jaw bone. This usually takes about an hour and is performed in the dentist's office using local anesthesia, although patients who are anxious about the sounds and vibrations may request oral sedatives.

During the surgery, the dentist moves the gum away from the bone, drills a hole in the jaw bone and inserts the implant. The surgery itself is generally not painful, but patients may feel uncomfortable in the next few days as they recover.

Then the patient must wait a few months for the implants to integrate or fuse with their bone. When this has occurred, the gum tissue above the implants is removed, and the new teeth are attached.

One drawback to implants is the expense. Because of the technology, materials and time involved, dental implants are expensive. Although some medical insurance is beginning to cover the surgery and a few dental insurance policies partially pay for the prosthetics, implant patients are advised that the procedure can cost thousands of dollars.

Still, satisfied patients universally endorse the procedure. Amy Sheldon, a vegetarian, felt implants were her only choice after an accident knocked out several of her front teeth. Rhetorically, she asked, "How else could I eat apples, carrots and the other crunchy foods that I live on?"

Stockbroker Madeline Fazzallari traded in her dentures for implants. "I was constantly worrying about my dentures slipping while I was talking with clients—or worse, on the exchange floor," she explained.

Elliot Albright opted for implants when his 85-year-old teeth finally succumbed to advanced gum and bone disease. A recent widower re-entering the dating scene for the first time in decades, Mr. Albright candidly said that he wanted to feel comfortable and confident when eating and talking with his new female friends.

Early implant efforts were plagued by a high incidence of failure. But Dr. Brisman reports that a majority of the causes for this have been eliminated.

Most implants are now made of titanium or a metal coated with hydroxyappetite, both of which allow easy integration with the bone and have greatly reduced the number of implants rejected. In addition, dentists have identified the type of bone structure that is best suited for implants. And when patients seeking implants do not have enough bone, the dentist adds or grafts bone to the area before placing the implants—a process that greatly enhances the odds for success.

Finally, dentists know where to place implants in the bone for optimal functional and esthetic results.

Individuals considering dental implant therapy should consult their dentists for more information.

Irritable Bowel Relief

Irritable-bowel syndrome (IBS) patients often get marked relief simply by following a restricted diet.

IBS patients often complain that certain foods trigger stomach pain, fatigue, diarrhea and constipation.

Patients reported improvements in each symptom after two weeks on a diet that excluded beef and all cereals except rice... replaced dairy products with soy-based products...and reduced consumption of citrus fruits, caffeinated drinks, tap water and yeast.

Bonus: The patients produced less gas while on the diet.

Timothy King, MD, registrar, department of gastroenterology, Addenbrooke's Hospital, Cambridge, England. His study of 12 women, six with IBS, was published in *The Lancet*.

Drug-Free Solutions to Digestive Problems

Jamison Starbuck, ND, naturopathic physician in family practice and a lecturer at the University of Montana, both in Missoula. She is past president of the American Association of Naturopathic Physicians and a contributing editor of *The Alternative Advisor: The Complete Guide to Natural Therapies and Alternative Treatments* (Time Life).

Do you use Tums, Tagamet or another acid-reducing medication more than once a month?

Are you avoiding certain foods—even healthful foods like beans and vegetables—because they cause stomach upset?

Do you frequently experience belching, flatulence or a bloated feeling after meals?

Do your bowel movements tend to occur less frequently than once a day?

If you answered "yes" to any of these questions, your digestion may need improving.

The keys to proper digestion are a good supply of digestive juices...a healthy gut lining... and lots of beneficial bacteria in the stomach and intestines. Without these things, you're likely to develop a sour stomach, belching, flatulence, abdominal pain and/or constipation.

Digestive juice is made up of hydrochloric acid from the stomach lining, enzymes from the pancreas and bile from the gallbladder. When enough hydrochloric acid is present, digestive juice is highly acidic. Without enough acid, the stomach becomes distended and crampy. In many cases of low acidity, digestive juice and partially digested food are forced upward into the esophagus, resulting in the pain of heartburn.

Studies show that almost 50% of people over age 50 have too little acid. Yet many physicians continue to prescribe antacids for indigestion. Antacids often do curb the pain, and they may be fine for occasional use. But regular, long-term use of antacids is unwise. Antacid "abuse" can result in certain nutritional deficiencies, especially of calcium and magnesium. These minerals—essential for keeping bones strong—are properly absorbed only under conditions of high acidity.

Antacids can also cause a range of side effects, including headache, depression, insomnia, impotence and even liver damage.

A better approach is to improve your digestion naturally. Gobbling food under stressful conditions—while driving, during a meeting, etc.—lowers the production of stomach acid. On the other hand, 60 seconds of relaxation at the start of a meal—deep breathing, meditation or simply saying grace—brings a marked increase in secretions.

Since it gives food a "head start" on the digestive process, thorough chewing can be very helpful. So can the use of "bitters." Available at health-food stores, bitters is a tincture made of gentian, wormwood, white horehound, anise and/or other herbs. Ten to 15 drops on the tongue at the start of a meal stimulates the vagus nerve. That's the nerve responsible for telling the stomach to start digestion.

Good digestion also requires a large population of healthy bacteria. I often urge my patients to take a daily pill containing one billion live bacteria...or a daily cup of plain yogurt that contains "active cultures."

If digestive trouble has led to a peptic ulcer or gastritis, deglycyrrhizinated licorice (DGL) can be helpful. Studies have shown that DGL can be just as effective as Tagamet or Zantac in the treatment of these problems.

DGL is sold at health food stores. It can be safely used for up to six weeks. The typical dosage is two to four 400-mg tablets a day, taken between meals.

Aspirin Won't Help Your Cold

Taking aspirin or another medication to bring down a fever when you have a virus actually weakens your body's defenses. Interferon, a protein produced by the body to fight off the virus, works less effectively when the fever is brought down.

American Physical Fitness Research Institute.

Antihistamines Can Prolong A Cold

Discontinue antihistamines when a cold shifts to the chest. They help relieve upper respiratory conditions but can aggravate lower respiratory ones, such as bronchitis and asthma. By reducing mucus production, antihistamines make bronchial secretions stickier. This blocks the bronchial tubes and makes it harder to clear them with coughing.

John H. Dirckx, MD, writing in *Consultant*.

Cough Medicines That Don't Do What They Advertise

Sidney Wolfe, MD, director, Public Citizen's Health Research Group, Washington, DC, and others, quoted in *Executive Fitness*.

The Food and Drug Administration is beginning to agree with an increasing number of independent doctors who say commercial cough remedies are of little benefit. *Basic drawback:* Virtually all commercial medications interfere with the body's natural way of clearing the respiratory tract, which is coughing. *Doctors are especially concerned with...*

• **Antihistamines,** which they say work by thickening, not thinning, lung secretions. Good only for allergies.

• **Decongestants,** which might be good for extreme stuffiness but are otherwise of doubtful effectiveness.

• **Expectorants,** which drug companies say loosen mucus and phlegm, although the evidence is scant.

• **Suppressants,** which suppress the brain's cough reflex. They are especially hazardous for people with asthma or bronchitis who rely on coughing to ease breathing when their lungs are not clear.

Skeptics of cough medications say home remedies may be more effective and less risky. Chicken soup and fruit juices may work as well as an expectorant. Vaporizers and humidifiers offer relief, as does a drop of honey on the back of the tongue.

Wine as a Cold Remedy

It acts as a short-term antibiotic, particularly after the first signs of a cold. *Remedy recipe:* Pour a bottle of red wine into a double boiler and heat to 140°F. Add a slice of lemon or orange peel and a tablespoon of cinnamon. Simmer for three minutes. Drink one glassful twice a day for three days.

Measles Vaccine Alert

A measles vaccine should be given to any adult born after 1956 who has not had either a documented case of the disease or an injection with live virus vaccine. (A medical study of blood samples has shown that most people born before 1956 either have had the disease or are immune to it.)

Caution: The killed-virus vaccines that were available between 1963 and 1967 are now ineffective. If you're unsure whether or not you're protected, it is advisable to have a live-virus vaccine administered.

Steven Wassilak, MD, medical epidemiologist, division of immunization, Centers for Disease Control and Prevention, Atlanta.

Nosedrop Warning

Nasal decongestants can make your stuffy nose worse. They may give temporary relief—but when they wear off, the tissues become more congested. Continual use can cause formation of skin folds (polyps) or thickening of the nose lining. Both inhibit breathing. Cilia (the microscopic hairs lining the nose) need some mucus to lubricate them and to help them filter dust.

Constant drying up of the mucus by decongestants causes the cilia to become irritated and inflamed. *Other side effects:* The chemicals used in the drops can cause blood-pressure problems (especially under anesthesia) and reduction of the adrenaline needed to handle stress. Also, fluid can drip into the lungs from the nasal passages, causing pneumonia.

Prevention

Eating Smart to Beat a Virus

Bruce H. Yaffe, MD, internist and digestive disease specialist, New York City.

Your body has to fight viral infections by itself. Antibiotics won't do a thing for colds or stomach virus, or for the sore throats and diarrhea that often accompany them. You can help your system to recover by carefully watching what you eat and drink.

In general, when a virus strikes, you should eat simply. Avoid foods that are hard to digest, such as fried dishes, rich sauces, gravy and heavy desserts. Extra vitamins are not necessary during a short illness (four or five days). If you are not hungry, don't force yourself to eat. A day or two without food won't hurt you, but you do need liquids. As you recover, your appetite will pick up, and you can work back to your normal diet.

Specifically, how you should eat depends upon where the virus strikes and what your symptoms are. The same virus can cause different reactions in each of its victims.

- **Fever.** High fever makes you sweat. The dangers are dehydration and loss of salt. Make yourself drink liquids with a high salt content, such as Gatorade, tomato juice or lemonade with a pinch of salt. If you are hot, treat yourself to cool drinks. In the chills stage, drink hot soup or tea (although caffeinated tea alone can increase urine output and cause further dehydration). Fever burns up extra calories. But weight loss from a virus is usually due more to water loss than to fat loss. *Keep it plain:* Toast, soup, cottage cheese and yogurt.

- **Stuffy nose.** There's some evidence that chicken soup actually does help clear nasal passages.

- **Headache.** When headaches are brought on by fever and sinus congestion, caffeine can bring relief because it constricts blood vessels. Drink tea, coffee or colas, as well as aspirin preparations that include caffeine. It is important to treat sinus headaches with decongestants.

- **Upset stomach.** Nausea and vomiting can cause dehydration, as well as a lack of desire to eat or drink. You don't have to eat, but liquids are important. Chew on ice chips or sip water or soda. Milk is often hard for adults to digest. When the stomach is unsettled, milk should be avoided for several days. Coffee and alcohol also irritate the stomach. Some people cannot tolerate citrus juice, because of the acid. When the nausea is over, start eating light foods such as unbuttered toast, yogurt and cottage cheese. Avoid fats and spicy foods for several days.

- **Diarrhea.** Replacing lost fluids, potassium and sodium with juice or broth is necessary in the case of severe diarrhea. *Best:* Sweet lemonade or Gatorade. *When you are feeling better, you can begin eating simple foods with slightly constipating properties:* Rice, bananas and mild cheeses.

- **Preventive eating.** A healthy diet for keeping fit and staving off infections is high in fiber and complex carbohydrates (whole grains, fresh fruits and vegetables), with adequate protein (meat, fish and dairy products) and low in fats (particularly saturated ones like butter and cheese) and simple carbohydrates (sweets).

Hay Fever Remedies

For mild, occasional cases, over-the-counter antihistamines will give relief. If one kind doesn't work, another may. *Caution:* Some antihistamines tend to make you drowsy (don't drive), and all interact dangerously with alcohol (don't drink). For more severe and longer-lasting cases, professional help is needed. Steroid nasal sprays, available only by prescription, give quick relief with few side effects. *For seasonal sufferers:* Wash your hair before bed to keep pollen off your pillow. Keep the shoes you wear outdoors out of the bedroom. Keep windows closed until 9 pm. Use the car air conditioner while driving. Don't go outside in early morning or late evening, when cool air puts more pollen at nose level.

Stanley Wolf, MD, The Allergy Center, Silver Spring, Maryland.

Sinus Remedies That Backfire

The sinuses are four pairs of spaces in the human skull, each lined with mucous membranes. When these membranes swell, the drainage of mucus slows or stops, causing painful discomfort. *Causes:* Primarily viral infections, such as a cold or flu.

But sinus membranes also swell from pressure changes during air flights, from swimming or diving in chlorinated water or from sudden changes of temperature, such as going from the hot sun to an air-conditioned room.

Over-the-counter drug tablets and capsules work only temporarily. When this medicine wears off, it may leave the patient with more pain, which requires more medication. The same is true for decongestant nose drops and nasal sprays.

Best: Apply hot-water compresses to the affected areas. Drink extra fluids. Use a humidifier or vaporizer in your room. Be sure to sterilize it frequently. If bacteria are the cause of the problem, see your physician for a prescription for antibiotics.

Humor Helps

Humor boosts the immune system. A study of men found their antibody levels were elevated for two days after events such as entertaining friends, playing with kids and engaging in lighthearted conversation.

Other researchers found that antibodies and T-cells (part of the immune system that protects us from disease) are elevated after watching performances of a professional comedian.

Study conducted under Arthur Stone, PhD, professor and vice chair for research, department of psychiatry, School of Medicine, State University of New York at Stony Brook.

What Causes Choking?

An estimated 9,000 Americans choke to death every year, most frequently while dining out. Researchers at the Swallowing Center at Johns Hopkins Medical Institutions in Baltimore now suspect that muscle and nerve disorders of the throat are at fault in many cases. Swallowing problems can appear at any age, but stroke victims seem to be particularly susceptible. Symptoms include difficulty in swallowing, coughing, a lump-in-the-throat sensation, voice changes and occasional choking episodes. Treatment ranges from surgery to swallow-safe diets. People who suffer from swallowing disorders can choke in their sleep. But a restaurant seems to distract many sufferers from the normal swallowing process and to stimulate choking episodes.

Precaution: Always sit up straight while eating and keep your head erect. Never tilt your head back or eat while lying down.

Save Yourself from Choking

A choking person can save himself by falling so that a table or a chair hits his diaphragm, thrusting it up against the lungs. It is the forced expulsion of air from the lungs that blows out the obstruction.

Henry J. Heimlich, MD, president, Heimlich Institute at Deaconess Hospital, Cincinnati, and originator of the Heimlich maneuver (whereby a second person saves the choker).

Low Calcium and Hearing Loss

Hearing loss is associated with a diet that is low in calcium. Impaired hearing is the fourth-most-common chronic health problem suffered by older people. And a study of women age 60 to age 71 found that those who had suffered hearing loss had 25% to 30% lower calcium intake on average than those with normal hearing. The same women tended to have lower bone density of the spine, also associated with a low-calcium diet.

Study conducted by Mary Ann Johnson, PhD, professor of food and nutrition, University of Georgia, Athens.

How to Treat Fever

When you have a fever, take aspirin or acetaminophen only when your temperature is over 102°F and you're uncomfortable. Dress lightly enough so that body heat can escape. Sponge with tepid water, not alcohol (the vapors can be dangerous). Take a bath and wash your hair if you feel like it—the evaporating water may lower your temperature. Drink eight to 12 glasses of liquid a day to avoid dehydration.

Take your temperature first thing in the morning for the most accurate reading. Wait 30 minutes after eating, drinking, smoking or exercising so your mouth will be neither cooled down nor heated up.

Call the doctor for a fever when: (1) A child's temperature goes above 102°F or an adult's over 101°F…(2) The fever persists for more than 24 hours with no obvious cause… (3) The fever lasts for more than 72 hours even if there's an obvious cause…(4) An infant under three months old has any temperature elevation…(5) There is a serious disease involved. *Bottom line:* Call the doctor when you feel really sick, even if you don't have a fever.

Simple Causes Of Backache

Backache may be caused by discomfort and tension arising from poor everyday living habits. *Examples:* Gobbling food, sleeping on a sagging mattress, wearing uncomfortable clothing, using appliances in a restrictive way or simply sitting in the same position too long.

TIPS TO AVOID BACKACHES

• **Clothing should never be tight.** This applies to pajamas and nightgowns as well as to everyday dress.

• **Avoid narrow-toed shoes.** They tense the leg muscles, which in turn affect the back. Heels should not be too loose or too tight. Either extreme produces ankle sway, which works its way up to the back and neck. Women's high-heeled shoes shorten the hamstring and calf muscles, causing the tension that frequently leads to backache.

• **Toes of socks and stockings should not be tight.** You should be able to wiggle your toes freely.

• **Too high or too tight a collar** can cause a stiff neck. Wear collars half a size larger, and if your neck is short, stick to soft, narrow collars.

• **Narrow shoulder straps** of brassieres can cause shoulder and upper-back pain, especially if they are pulled too tight.

• **Wide shoulders require bigger pillows** for those who sleep on their sides.

• **Foam-rubber pillows force the neck into a rigid position.** Use a down-filled feather pillow.

• **Never sit in one position for more than an hour** or two. Get up and move around.

•**On car trips,** stop frequently to stretch and limber up.

•**While reading, avoid strain** by keeping the page at a comfortable distance. It's also important to have enough light.

•**To use muscles more evenly,** office workers should shift the telephone from one side of the desk to the other each day.

•**Instead of tensing when the phone rings,** make it a practice to shrug the shoulders before reaching out to pick up the receiver.

Antibiotics and Calcium Don't Mix

Taking *fluoroquinolone* antibiotics, such as Cipro, Levaquin or Tequin, with calcium-rich or -fortified foods, such as milk, orange juice and breakfast cereals, can reduce antibiotic absorption. This makes treatment less effective and may produce antibiotic-resistant bacteria.

Self-defense: Whenever possible, take these antibiotics with water—and either two hours before or after meals. Ask your doctor how to take other antibiotics, which also may need to be taken separately from meals.

Guy Amsden, PharmD, Bassett Healthcare Research, Cooperstown, New York, and leader of a study of antibiotic absorption, reported in *Journal of Clinical Pharmacology.*

Why You Have A Headache

Usually headaches aren't serious. *Tension headache:* Pressure is equal on both sides of the head but may come from front or back. Tight neck muscles or emotion could be the cause. *Migraine or vascular headache:* Throbbing is stronger on one side. The sides may alternate during an attack.

Warning symptoms (flashing lights, blind spots) occur for one-fifth of sufferers. Cigarette smoke, chocolate or cheese can trigger attacks. *Hangovers:* The throbbing on both sides of the head has several causes. Complex flavorings (i.e., brandies) are toxic, and dehydration interferes with the body's water levels. *Surprise:* Allergies and sinus congestion are rarely the cause of headaches.

Treating Pain with Ice

Ice rather than heat (the traditional method) may be the best long-term treatment for muscle and joint aches caused by overexercising. Apply the ice for 10 to 15 minutes before and after gently exercising the sore area. It has a mild anesthetic effect that minimizes exercising pain. Prolonged use of heat can actually increase swelling.

Rob Roy MacGregor, MD, Philadelphia.

Quick Fix for Leg Cramps

Leg cramps can usually be alleviated by firmly pinching your upper lip for 20 to 30 seconds.

Donald Cooper, MD, former US Olympics team doctor, and emeritus director of athletic medicine, Oklahoma State University, Stillwater.

Ease Those Aching Knees

Arthritic pains in the knees are effectively relieved with bags of ice water. This simple, drug-free treatment consists of application of the ice bags above and below the knee for 20 minutes three times daily. *Bonus:* The relief enables many sufferers of rheumatoid arthritis to cut back on doses of potentially harmful painkilling drugs. *To make an ice bag:* Put six cubes of ice in a plastic bag and add a quart of cold water.

Peter D. Utsinger, MD, Germantown Medical Center, Philadelphia, Pennsylvania.

Quick Fixes That Work

When you need fast relief of a health related concern, there are some things you can do that may help. *For example, try these solutions…*

• **Muscle trick to relieve cramps and spasms.** Contract the muscles in the muscle group opposite the one that is cramped. This causes the troubled muscle to relax. *Example:* If your calf cramps, tighten the muscles in the front of your lower leg to relieve the discomfort.

American Health

• **To cure hiccups,** swallow a teaspoon of granulated sugar or eat crackers. The slight irritation in the back of the throat interrupts the hiccup cycle.

Alternatives: Suck on a lemon wedge soaked in angostura bitters. Or induce sneezing by sniffing pepper. Or take a sniff of something with a strong aroma, such as vinegar.

• **Instant ice pack.** Try a bag of frozen vegetables (such as peas or corn niblets). The bag is clean, watertight and pliable enough to fit almost any part of the body.

Harvard Medical School Health Letter

• **Drugless headache cures.**
  • Eat a cheese sandwich.
  • Take a hot shower, followed by a cold one —until you shiver.
  • Place crushed ice in the mouth and throat (not for the elderly or ill).
  • Massage the lower part of the big toe and beneath all the toes.
  • Breathe into a paper bag (stops hyperventilation).
  • Ask a partner to press your "trigger" points (temples, back of the neck, under shoulder blades).
  • Rotate a hairbrush in small circles, starting above your temples and working it down over your ears to your neck.

Spring

• **Mosquito-bite relief.** Turn your hair dryer on the bite for a minute. The warm, dry air dulls the itch.

• **Bad-tasting medicine goes down more easily** when you rub an ice cube over a child's tongue first. This temporarily "freezes" the taste buds and makes the medication more palatable.

Practical Parenting Tips by Vicki Lansky. Meadowbrook.

• **Pills slide down the throat more easily** if the patient swallows some water before taking the medicine. The water moistens the mucous membranes, which facilitates the swallowing of pills with water. This works best for someone whose mouth is dry from sleeping and for those who may be dehydrated, such as the elderly.

Joan Durbak, RN, Newark, Ohio, writing in *RN*.

• **Avoid the natural inclination to bend your head back** when swallowing a capsule. It's better to tilt your head or upper body forward. Then the lighter-than-water capsule can float toward the throat.

Modern Maturity

• **To stop fingernail loss** that usually occurs after you hit your fingertip with a hammer or crush it in a door, squeeze the nail steadily for about five minutes. Start immediately after you hit it. Nail loss results because a bruise forms under the nail bed and displaces it. Squeezing prevents blood from leaking out to form the bruise.

Use Honey
On Wounds

Honey can be used as a salve for minor wounds. If no antibiotic ointment is available, a dab of honey spread on a cut or scrape will reduce the risk for infection—and speed healing. Wash the wound first…and be sure to use pasteurized honey. Unpasteurized honey can contain disease-causing microbes.

Manfred Kroger, PhD, professor emeritus of food science, Pennsylvania State University, University Park.

Eye Drops Can
Make Your Eyes
Redder

Overusing eye drops can trigger a rebound effect, causing your eyes to stay red with or without drops.

Best: Apply a saline solution known as artificial tears as often as you like. But avoid daily use of vasoconstrictors, which shrink surface blood vessels. Your pharmacist can help you distinguish between the two varieties.

Cosmopolitan

Skin Cancers Are
On the Rise

A contributing factor to the increase in cases of skin cancer is the thinning ozone layer. Without this natural shield around the earth, more ultraviolet radiation penetrates the atmosphere. These rays cause melanomas and other skin cancers. *Why the ozone layer is thinning:* Widespread use of chlorofluorocarbons (CFCs) in aerosol sprays, refrigeration and air-conditioning systems, insulation-blowing devices and liquid fast-freezing of food.

Prognosis: Today one in three melanomas is diagnosed too late to save the patient's life. *One reason:* Patients often do not disrobe completely during physical exams, leaving areas of skin unexamined.

RN

Malignant melanoma (skin cancer characterized by a black molelike growth) can now often be cured if caught early. *Finding:* Survival rate after eight years is about 99% when the lesion is cut out while still very thin. *Advice:* Ask your doctor to check for melanomas at every visit. The cancer appears to be related to sun exposure.

Medical World News

Dandruff Shampoos
That Don't Work

Antidandruff shampoos can actually cause the condition, a study shows. *Reason:* The harsh solutions irritate the scalp. Simply switching to a milder shampoo may control the problem. It's also a good idea to discontinue the use of hair oils.

Suggestion: Visit a dermatologist, who can prescribe a topical antibacterial agent.

International Journal of Dermatology

Excessive Sweating
May Signal a Problem

Unexplained sweating can be a symptom of serious disease. Exertion, excitement, anxiety and ingestion of spicy foods may all cause increased perspiration. But excessive sweating may also be symptomatic of hyperthyroidism, undiagnosed infections with chronic fever and rheumatoid arthritis. *Other causes:* Some painkillers (Demerol and Talwin) or heart drugs (Isordil).

RN

Preventing Smelly Feet

Smelly feet can be prevented quite easily by keeping the feet dry and cool to minimize bacterial growth. *Strategy:* Wear leather shoes (leather breathes), and alternate pairs so they can dry out. Avoid socks or stockings made of synthetic fibers. *Best:* Light cotton. Use ordinary talcum powder. *For special problems:* Prescription antiperspirants are available.

The Harvard Medical School Health Letter

How to Choose The Right Sun Lotion

You can determine which sunscreen is best for you, thanks to sophisticated tests that have established the degree of protection given by various sunscreen brands. The measure of protection a sunscreen affords is its sun protection factor (SPF). This number tells the length of time it takes the sun's rays to penetrate the sunscreen and burn your skin. The higher the SPF number, the longer you can stay in the sun without getting burned. *Example:* If you're going sailing for four hours, you'll want a sunscreen with a high SPF. The lowest SPF number is 2, which offers virtually no protection against the sun's rays.

In addition to giving protection against the sun, a sunscreen should be durable. It should not wash off as soon as you get wet or begin to perspire. *Also important:* It should not be toxic to your skin, smell bad, feel offensive or stain.

To find the best protection: Look for the Skin Cancer Foundation seal of recommendation when choosing a sunscreen. The foundation conducted tests of the leading sunscreens to determine their actual effectiveness outdoors and the degree to which they have all the other important properties (durability, lack of toxicity, etc.). Its seal of recommendation was assigned to the brands that met these standards. The seal appears on the container.

Brands that don't have the seal of recommendation aren't necessarily ineffective. They may simply not have been included in the tests.

So-called "alternate" sunscreens of aloe or coconut compounds are worthless as protection.

Tan gradually. Don't sit in the sun until you get red. Redness means it's too late—the sun's rays have already damaged your skin.

Perry Robins, MD, professor emeritus of dermatology, New York University Medical Center.

How the sunscreen number is determined: The time it takes the skin to arrive at the state of minimal redness, unprotected, is divided into the time it takes the skin to reach that condition with a sunscreen. This gives the sunscreen's SPF number. *Example:* If it takes 10 minutes under a bright sun to become slightly red, and it takes 90 minutes wearing a sunscreen to arrive at that same condition, the sunscreen had the SPF number of 9.

Sunscreen Danger

Discolored sunscreens are dangerous to your health. Old sunscreens separate and lose their effectiveness at screening out harmful ultraviolet rays. Discard sunscreens that have lost their creamy consistency…avoid buying sunscreens packaged in discolored, smudged or beaten-up bottles…and mark new sunscreens with the date of purchase.

The late Madhu Pathak, MD, PhD, senior associate, department of dermatology, Harvard Medical School, Boston.

Aspirin Can Relieve Sunburn

Minimize sunburn inflammation by taking two aspirin three to four times daily as soon as you notice you're turning red. Aspirin's main component, acetylsalicylic acid, cuts down on the inflammation caused by dilation of surface blood vessels (sunburn symptom).

The aspirin also relieves sunburn pain. *Caution:* Aspirin in these dosages also can cause stomach upset.

Harvey Blank, MD, dermatologist, quoted in *Self.*

Medications and Sun Don't Mix

Many common drugs can make your skin more susceptible to burning. *Major ones: Tetracyclines* (antibiotics), *sulfa* drugs (antibacterials), *phenothiazine* derivatives (major tranquilizers), *griseofulvins* (antifungals), *sulfonylureas* (antidiabetics) and *thiazides* (diuretics).

Maureen Poh-Fitzpatrick, MD, formerly of Columbia University College of Physicians and Surgeons, writing in *Self.*

Sun rash or a quick burn can result when people with sensitive skin put cologne or perfume on areas of the body that are exposed to the sun. (Some soaps and deodorants may also produce this effect.) *The ailment:* Photodermatitis. *Remedy:* Apply colognes and perfume to clothing, not to skin.

Smoking and Surgery Don't Mix

Smoking produces *carboxyhemoglobin* (nonoxygen carrier) in the blood, which takes space away from hemoglobin (an oxygen carrier). The reduced amount of oxygen carried to the tissues affects the body like anemia, greatly reducing the body's ability to withstand the trauma of surgery. *Helpful:* Stop smoking at least 12 hours before surgery to give your body time to get rid of the carboxyhemoglobin buildup.

Smoking May Cause Impotence

Even a single cigarette causes enough constriction of peripheral blood vessels that a thermographic camera shows a drop in hand temperature before and after the smoke. In men particularly sensitive to tobacco, an evening of smoking can so constrict the flow of blood to the penis that a full erection is impossible. Though this phenomenon is temporary, long-term smoking can have a permanent adverse effect on potency by inducing arteriosclerosis.

Arne M. Olsson, University of Lund, Sweden, writing in *Medical Aspects of Human Sexuality.*

Smoking and Alzheimer's

In a health study conducted by Harvard University, it was observed that individuals who smoked more than one pack of cigarettes a day were four times as likely to develop Alzheimer's disease as those who smoked less. *Reason:* Unknown.

Stuart L. Shalat, ScD, associate professor, Environmental and Occupational Health Sciences Institute, Piscataway, New Jersey.

Beer May Raise Psoriasis Risk

Women who drank five or more beers per week were 76% more likely to have psoriasis than ones who did not drink alcohol. Psoriasis is a chronic autoimmune disease characterized by scaly red patches on the skin. There was no increased psoriasis incidence in women who drank light beer, wine or liquor.

One possible explanation: The grain protein gluten is found in significant amounts only in regular beer—and gluten intake has previously been linked to psoriasis.

Abrar A. Qureshi, MD, MPH, assistant professor, department of dermatology, Harvard Medical School and Brigham and Women's Hospital, both in Boston, and coauthor of a study of 82,869 women, published in *Archives of Dermatology.*

 # Moderate Drinking Can Be Harmful

Even moderate drinking may be bad news for some people (susceptibility varies widely). Serious mental and physical disabilities can sometimes result from the intake of three to four drinks a day (or fewer if the alcohol content is high).

Sleep disorders—sleeplessness and awakening early—may also result. *Reason:* Alcohol depresses body functions for four to six hours. So an evening drinker may awaken at 4 or 5 am as the body begins to rebound. (Similarly, lunchtime drinkers may get nervous by late day and decide to have another drink.)

Robert Millman, MD, psychiatrist and director of drug and alcohol abuse treatment at NewYork-Presbyterian Hospital.

Alcohol Linked To Heart Disease

Researchers have discovered chemical compounds, called fatty-acid ethyl esters, in the hearts of people who died while intoxicated. These may explain the connection between alcohol intoxication and heart disease.

Potential effect: Discovery of the role these compounds play in heart disease could lead to the development of drugs to counteract them.

Study by Washington University School of Medicine.

Alcohol May Cause Vitamin Deficiency

Vitamin B-1 deficiency often leads to neurological ailments such as loss of memory or muscle coordination. *Background:* Vitamin B-1 (thiamine) helps the brain use glucose as a food. Without thiamine, the brain risks death by starvation.

Signs of vitamin B-1 deficiency: Behavior changes, depression, insomnia, chest pain and chronic fatigue. *Most common cause:* Excessive drinking.

Hangover Help

Study by Gaston Pawan, MD, Middlesex Hospital, London.

There is no cure for inebriation or any magic formula to prevent the headache and general malaise that follow an evening of drinking too much alcohol too quickly. However, some measures can keep a night on the town from being a total disaster.

• **Eat fatty or oily foods before you have the first drink.** That lines your stomach and slows the body's absorption of alcohol. (Cheese and nuts are good choices.)

• **Eat starches while you drink to soak up the alcohol.** (Bread or crackers work.)

• **Avoid spirits with high levels of cogeners** (additives that can cause toxic effects). Brandy, red wine, dark rum and sherry are the worst. Vodka and white wine are the least adulterated.

If you wake up with a hangover, you can only try to treat the symptoms and help bring back to normal all the bodily functions disrupted by alcohol. *Some suggestions...*

• **A dry mouth is a sign of dehydration.** Drink plenty of water to replace the lost fluid.

• **Alcohol depletes the system of many nutrients,** particularly the vitamins A, B, B6 and C, and such minerals as niacin, calcium, magnesium and potassium. Take a multivitamin that includes minerals.

• **Take charcoal tablets to speed up the removal of the cogeners** (four tablets if you are small and up to six for large people). Cabbage and vitamin C are reputed to help in this area as well.

• **To work the alcohol out of your system** (actually to metabolize it), a little exercise is useful. It increases your intake of oxygen, and oxygen speeds up this process. So does the fructose found in honey and fruit juices.

• **For pain or nausea,** over-the-counter analgesics or antacids are the antidote.

• **A little "hair of the dog that bit you" is an old cure that has some basis in reality.** The brain cells affected by alcohol can return to normal quite suddenly. This explains the supersensitivity to noise and smells associated with hangover. A small amount of alcohol (one to one and a half ounces) can ease your brain back into awareness. *Recommended:* If you try this panacea, mix the spirits with something nutritious. *Other possibilities:* A can of beer. Or try a Fernet Branca, a packaged alcoholic mixture that includes herbs and folk-medicine standbys such as camomile and aloe.

The highest rating for morning-after headaches goes to brandy, with red wine running a close second. *In descending order of toxicity:* Dark rum, sherry, scotch, whiskey, beer, white wine, gin and vodka.

Only Abstinence Helps Alcoholics

Controlled drinking for recovered alcoholics was the controversial goal of a recent, understandably well-publicized study of the problem. But follow-up analysis now indicates that alcoholics are better off when they remain abstemious. *Statistics:* Of the original 20 persons who tried the controlled-drinking experiment, only one remained a controlled drinker. Eight went on to drink excessively. Four died from alcohol-related causes. One

is missing after becoming disabled by drinking. Six abandoned the program to swear off completely.

UCLA research study reported in *Science.*

What Every Man Needs to Know About Testosterone

Stephen J. Winters, MD, professor of medicine and biochemistry/molecular biology, and chief, division of endocrinology and metabolism, University of Louisville Health Sciences Center.

For years, it's been known that testosterone levels start to decline as men advance toward middle age.

Lately, a growing number of doctors have begun prescribing testosterone supplements for their older male patients. The hope is that restoring testosterone to youthful levels will boost physical and mental function.

At the same time, many younger men with normal levels of testosterone have been taking supplemental testosterone to enhance athletic performance.

• **Who stands to benefit from testosterone supplements?** Men with chronically low testosterone levels clearly benefit. This condition—known as *hypogonadism*—is often caused by a disease process affecting the testicles, such as an injury, mumps during childhood or Klinefelter's syndrome. That's a hereditary disorder marked by an extra X chromosome.

Hypogonadism can also result from a pituitary tumor that shuts down testosterone production...or from AIDS or another disease involving poor nutrition and weight loss.

For men who fall into one of these categories, testosterone-replacement therapy brings increases in energy, muscle mass, strength, stamina, bone density, body hair, beard growth and sexual function.

Collectively, these changes bring heightened athletic prowess and self-confidence...and a significantly enhanced sense of well-being.

• **How can a man tell if his testosterone level is low?** Some men have clear symptoms of testosterone deficiency, such as a weak sex drive, erectile dysfunction, fatigue, depression and/or a loss of motivation.

Physical signs of testosterone deficiency include low muscle mass, sparse body hair and beard, abnormally small testicles, enlarged breasts and a boyish appearance.

But testosterone deficiency isn't always obvious. The only way a man can be sure of his testosterone level is to have a blood test.

• **Are testosterone levels tested as part of the standard physical exam?** No. The test is usually done only if the doctor—or patient—suspects hypogonadism.

By the way, if an older man shows no symptoms or signs of hypogonadism, I don't even think he should have his testosterone level tested. His level is likely to be naturally a little low—and this could trigger unnecessary concern.

• **What level of testosterone is considered normal?** Among young men, peak (morning) testosterone averages 700 to 800 nanograms per deciliter (ng/dL). Any young man whose morning value falls under 350 is likely to have hypogonadism.

The threshold value for hypogonadism is lower for older men. Doctors often recommend testosterone replacement if a 55-year-old man has a morning value of less than 300...or if a 65-year-old has a value under 250.

• **Might older men benefit from supplemental testosterone** if their testosterone level is only moderately depressed? We don't know. We do know that women experience an analogous decline in estrogen at menopause and after years of recommending estrogen replacement, doctors are now doubting the wisdom of earlier advice.

Many ongoing studies, including a large-scale National Institutes of Health study, are addressing the issue of age-related testosterone decline. But some doctors aren't waiting to learn the results of these studies. They are prescribing testosterone for healthy older men.

I consider this premature. Older men given testosterone tend to feel stronger and have a stronger sex drive. But testosterone supplemen-

tation may increase the risk for benign prostatic hyperplasia (BPH) and prostate cancer.

• **What if the test indicates hypogonadism?** If testosterone is found to be low on one test in the morning, a second blood test should be done to confirm the reading.

Tests should also be done to measure levels of the pituitary hormones LH and FSH. If these tests also show abnormally low values, the problem is likely to be in the pituitary gland. Magnetic resonance imaging (MRI) tests and additional blood tests should be done.

High levels of LH and FSH, on the other hand, suggest a testicular problem.

If no pituitary problem can be found, testosterone supplements are probably appropriate.

Because testosterone plays a role in BPH and prostate cancer, men who begin testosterone-replacement therapy should be sure to have a digital rectal exam and a blood test for prostate-specific antigen (PSA) each year.

• **What's the best type of testosterone supplement?** Some doctors prescribe self-injections of testosterone every two weeks. Others prescribe a transdermal patch, which is applied to the skin once a day, usually at night. Testosterone is also available in a gel, which is placed on the skin. Testosterone cannot be taken orally, because it breaks down in the digestive tract before it has any effect. Injections can be painful. Also, some men experience mood swings as their level of testosterone spikes and then gradually declines.

Because of these drawbacks, more men are opting for the testosterone patch or the gel.

• **How safe are over-the-counter testosterone precursors like androstenedione and DHEA?** We simply don't have enough data to know.

A recent study found that men who took 200 mg of "andro" each day for several months did not experience a rise in testosterone levels. They did, however, experience a slight rise in estrogen levels.

The implication of this research is that andro may not boost athletic performance—but might cause breast enlargement. It is better to steer clear of these supplements until more information is known.

You and Your Hormones

It's a common misconception that an under-active thyroid can cause obesity. This is virtually impossible.

Reason: The thyroid regulates the interaction of body metabolism and appetite. If the thyroid is underactive, appetite will not be great enough to create obesity. About 99% of people with an underactive thyroid are not overweight.

Dangerous: Thyroid hormone to treat obesity. An excessive amount can induce hyperthyroidism, causing such severe side effects as an overworked heart, muscle breakdown and psychological changes.

The late Norbert Freinkel, MD, Kettering professor of medicine and director of the Center for Endocrinology, Metabolism and Nutrition at Northwestern University Medical School.

•**Older men who have trouble attaining erections at night** can do better with morning sex. Testosterone levels are higher earlier in the day.

Medical Aspects of Human Sexuality

•**Alcohol affects a woman** most on the days just before and at the start of her period. *Why:* Hormones influence the way alcohol is metabolized and absorbed into the body.

Should Gallstones Be Removed?

Gallstones may best be left alone until they act up. *Current practice:* Removing them as soon as they are detected. A recent long-term study of 123 males with gallstones showed that over a 15-year period, only 16 developed problems and only 14 required surgery. About 15 million people have gallstones.

William A. Gracie, MD, reporting in *The New England Journal of Medicine.*

How to Treat Varicose Veins

Luis Navarro, MD, instructor of surgery at Mount Sinai School of Medicine, and medical director of The Vein Treatment Center, both in New York City. He is the coauthor of *No More Varicose Veins* (Bantam Books).

Just a few years ago, anyone who consulted a doctor about unsightly varicose veins would often have been advised to "live with it."

The only available treatment—surgery—involved large incisions, potentially risky anesthesia and a hospital stay. It was used only in extreme cases—leg ulcers, phlebitis, etc.

Today, 90% of unsightly blue, bulging varicose veins—as well as the tiny "spider veins" that pop up from toe to groin—can be easily removed without surgery.

Varicose veins and spider veins are extremely common, affecting 10% of men and 50% of women in the US. Often, they run in families. If one or both of your parents had varicose veins, the odds are you will, too.

CAUSES

What causes varicose veins? Researchers believe they develop in individuals whose leg veins have weak walls, weak valves or fewer than the normal number of valves. Fewer valves forces the existing valves to work harder, causing them to fail, resulting in visible veins.

Your leg veins help transport blood against the pull of gravity back to the heart—a long haul. When valves located along the length of the saphenous vein—the main vein running along the inside of the calf—fail to open and close properly, blood pools in the legs. The veins bulge under the pressure of the pooled blood and become permanently dilated (varicosed).

PREVENTING VARICOSE VEINS

Although little can be done to prevent varicose veins, certain tactics aimed at improving circulation in the legs can forestall their appearance...

•**Get plenty of exercise.**

•**Don't cross your legs.**

• **Don't sit or stand for long periods of time.** Vary your position.

• **Maintain an ideal weight.**

• **Elevate your legs when you sit or sleep.**

TREATMENT OPTIONS

The first step in treating varicose veins is to determine how many veins are affected, exactly where they're located and how big they are. To do this, doctors use ultrasound imaging, much like that used to view developing fetuses.

No single treatment is right for everyone. In fact, most people need several different forms of treatment, including:

• **Sclerotherapy.** A chemical solution injected into the vein closes it off, causing the vein to collapse and slowly disintegrate.

Each sclerotherapy session lasts about 15 to 30 minutes—time for up to 50 separate injections. All you feel is a slight pinprick.

Cost: $150 and up per session.

Following treatment, your leg will be wrapped in an elastic bandage. It must be left in place for several hours. As with the other two forms of therapy, it's important to walk as much as possible in the days following treatment. This helps get your blood circulation going again.

Occasionally, blood leaks into surrounding tissue, causing brown stains that may take several months to fade.

A sclerotherapy solution called *polidocanol* (Asclera) was approved by the FDA in 2010. Especially mild, it seems less likely to cause complications or pigmentation problems.

• **Laser therapy.** Spider veins are eliminated by short, intense bursts of laser light beamed onto the skin. Each 15- to 30-minute laser session—virtually painless—permits "zapping" of multiple spider veins.

Cost: $300 to $500 per session.

Freckle-like dark spots appear around the treated area, but these disappear within two weeks.

Also, a laserlike tool called the photoderm uses a broader light spectrum and emits light in longer pulses than a conventional laser. It permits treatment of larger blood vessels and is less likely to damage surrounding tissue.

• **Surgery.** This option is reserved only for the saphenous vein. Two incisions are required—a one-inch cut just under the pubic hair and a half-inch cut in the lower part of the ankle. Through these incisions, the surgeon removes the entire vein.

The surgery takes 30 to 60 minutes. The entire hospital stay is about four hours. The surgery is performed under local, spinal or general anesthesia.

Cost: More than $2,000 per leg.

Other than having to change the dressings, little aftercare is involved. Though tiny, the incisions may hurt for a while. Leg bruises and swelling sometimes occur. These last from a few days to a few weeks.

Mini-phlebectomy, a modified surgical technique, can be performed right in the doctor's office. It involves local anesthesia, smaller incisions and allows you to walk home two hours later. It's an "in-between" treatment—used when sclerotherapy is difficult to perform and surgery is inappropriate.

Alzheimer's Help

Rocking chairs help relieve symptoms of Alzheimer's disease.

Recent study: After rocking for at least 80 minutes a day for six weeks, many Alzheimer's patients felt less depressed and anxious. Those who rocked the most experienced the greatest improvement.

Theory: Rhythmic rocking triggers the release of endorphins, natural compounds that relieve pain and improve mood.

Nancy M. Watson, RN, PhD, director of the Center for Clinical Research on Aging, University of Rochester School of Nursing, Rochester, New York. Her two-year study of 25 nursing home residents aged 72 to 95 years was presented at a meeting of the Eastern Nursing Research Society.

How Safe Is Vitamin E?

Some studies in the 1990s suggested that high doses of vitamin E reduced the risk of heart disease and fatal heart attack and possibly protected against cancer and Alzheimer's disease. Millions of Americans started taking vitamin E, and even doctors who felt that it wouldn't help thought it certainly wouldn't harm anyone.

But one significant report found that high doses of vitamin E supplements may *shorten* your life. The study, led by researchers at Johns Hopkins University School of Medicine, concluded that supplementing with high doses of vitamin E increases the risk of dying from heart disease and other causes.

Edgar R. Miller III, MD, PhD, associate professor of medicine, Johns Hopkins University School of Medicine and Johns Hopkins Bloomberg School of Public Health, both in Baltimore. He was lead author of the report "High-Dosage Vitamin E Supplementation May Increase All-Causes Mortality," presented at a conference of the American Heart Association.

Senility May Be Curable

Medications can bring on reactions that resemble senility. *Drugs seniors should watch:* Sedatives, tranquilizers, even antihistamines.

Point: Senility is not an inevitable product of aging. Its symptoms are often induced by curable ailments. The cure might be as simple as a change of medication. *Best:* Consult a physician who is skilled in geriatrics.

National Institute of Aging, Bethesda, Maryland.

How to Age-Proof Your Body...Naturally

Norman D. Ford, writer, fitness enthusiast and anti-aging expert. Now in his 80s, he is a dedicated long-distance cyclist. He is author of many health books, including *18 Natural Ways to Look & Feel Half Your Age* (Keats Publishing).

Our bodies are designed by nature to age at a very slow pace. Ideally, we should stay strong and healthy well into our 80s and beyond. *But three aspects of our modern lifestyle speed up the process...*

- **Sedentary living.**
- **A high-fat, low-fiber diet.**
- **Worry, anxiety and stress.**

If you begin to address these three core areas, you can maintain a biological age that's many years younger than your chronological age. Scientists now believe that chronological age is actually irrelevant. An 80-year-old can have the body of a 40-year-old—and be virtually disease-proof—by adopting a healthy, active, stress-free lifestyle.

In fact, when researchers at the Human Nutrition Research Center (HNRC) at Tufts University established a number of "biomarkers" to measure aging, they concluded that declines in every biomarker were caused primarily by a high-fat diet and lack of aerobic and strength training exercise.

Fortunately, they also found these declines could be easily reversed in a fairly short time, simply by changing diet and lifestyle.

AEROBIC EXERCISE

Many people think it's "natural" to lose strength and fitness as they get older. But this decline has nothing to do with age...it starts the minute we put our feet up and start to take life easy.

Only about 10% of Americans exercise enough to improve their health. The rest have abandoned all strenuous exercise, and a slow, inexorable decline is under way.

But this decline isn't inevitable. At any age, a program of regular exercise will lower your biological age in a few short months—even if you haven't exercised for years.

Example: The human cardiovascular system has evolved to the point where it can function in top condition for at least 100 years. Studies have shown that a healthy 90-year-old heart can pump blood just as effectively as the heart of a 20-year-old. Yet without exercise, the average 65-year-old has lost 30% to 40% of his or her aerobic capacity.

To begin restoring the health of your heart, lungs and arteries—and maintaining it—I recommend doing some aerobic exercise every other day. This could be walking, swimming, bicycling or other brisk, rhythmic movement.

Start by doing 20 minutes, and build up until you're doing four to five miles of walking, or an hour of swimming or cycling. This will take a few weeks to a few months.

When you exercise, move briskly, but don't push yourself so hard that you feel fatigued.

You can begin this age-proofing technique—and start reaping benefits—immediately.

Hundreds of studies have shown that regular aerobic exercise reduces the risk of type II diabetes, raises your HDL ("good") cholesterol while lowering dangerous LDL cholesterol, reduces brain neuron loss, increases bone density and lowers the risk of breast or prostate cancer. It also creates tremendous increases in energy, stamina and endurance. And the more out of shape you are, the more rapid your progress.

STRENGTH TRAINING

Until the early 1990s, most exercise physiologists focused on aerobics as the principal antiaging exercise. But they now believe that strength training may be even more important than aerobics because strength training builds more muscle mass in a way that aerobics can't.

Above everything else, this muscle mass is the key to youthfulness. After scores of tests and surveys, the HNRC concluded that loss of muscle mass and strength is the underlying cause of almost every sign of aging. Muscle mass is also the key to shedding fat, since large, strong muscles burn more calories—24 hours a day, even when you're not exercising.

A thrice-weekly schedule of strength training —done on the days between your aerobic workouts—should be at the core of your anti-aging program.

Join a health club that has weight machines and instructors who can show you the right exercises.

I recommend doing nine exercises, focusing on these muscle groups—biceps, pectorals, triceps, abdominals, lower back, quadriceps, upper back, shoulders and hamstrings.

For each exercise, find the maximum amount you can lift one time, then use 80% of that weight and lift it smoothly, up to eight or nine times in a row. It's OK if you can only do three or four repetitions. Once you can easily lift a weight 10 times or more, you'll need to increase the weight.

Begin with one exercise per muscle group, then gradually add an additional set or two as you gain strength and stamina.

EAT A LOW-FAT DIET WITH LOTS OF FRUITS AND VEGETABLES

Scientists now believe that most premature aging is caused by disease, possibly related to free radicals—electrically charged particles that wreak havoc on our cells by causing toxic chain reactions. Wrinkled skin, clogged arteries and weak immune response have all been linked to free-radical damage.

One of the main causes of free-radical buildup is a high-fat diet. Fat molecules produce free radicals as they're oxidized. If you eat too many fat molecules, these free radicals cause plaque to build up in your arteries, and can lead to heart disease, cancer and other diseases.

Fortunately there's a natural antidote. Fruits and vegetables contain hundreds of compounds called phytochemicals, which work to prevent free-radical formation (which is why they're often called antioxidants).

The Framingham Heart Study found that increasing the amount of fruit and vegetables you eat greatly reduces your risk of heart attack.

These foods also tend to be high in dietary fiber, which speeds digestion and may have anti-cancer benefits.

On the other hand, animal products—beef, eggs, fish, poultry, dairy products, etc.—contain no antioxidants, no fiber and few cancer-preventing chemicals. To age-proof your body against disease, cut down on these foods and increase your intake of fruits and vegetables.

FREE YOUR MIND

Whatever you can do to eliminate stress will also help stop the aging process. One way is to practice forgiveness. Being unable to forgive is a major cause of stress. *Other stress-busters...*

•**Progressive muscle relaxation.** Lie on a rug in semidarkness with a pillow under your head. Tense each muscle group in turn for about six seconds, then relax. You can cover your whole body in about 90 seconds with this method. Next, concentrate on mentally warming your hands. With practice, you can increase the blood flow to your body in just a few minutes.

•**Watch TV as little as possible.** Television is the most passive, useless activity in which you can engage—yet half the US population sits hypnotized by the tube for four hours a day or more.

•**Use your mind actively and creatively.** The more you exercise your mind, the healthier and more alert you will be. Mental activity can even help speed up your physical reflexes!

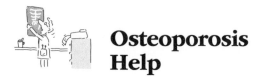

Osteoporosis Help

Harris McIlwain, MD, rheumatologist who specializes in the prevention and treatment of osteoporosis. He is coauthor of *The Osteoporosis Cure: Reverse the Crippling Effects with New Treatments* (Avon).

Age-related thinning of the bones—osteoporosis—is a major health problem. It vastly increases the risk of broken hips, ribs, pelvis and other weakened bones.

It is osteoporosis that leads to the stooped posture associated with advanced age. *Cause:* An accumulation of small fractures in the vertebrae. But there is new hope for aging bones.

A program of dietary supplements, exercise and bone-restoring medication makes it possible to minimize bone-density loss due to aging. It's even possible to increase your bone density. Best of all, these treatments are effective at any age and it's never too late to start.

CHECKING BONE DENSITY

Doctors used to wait until an actual bone fracture occurred in an elderly person before worrying about osteoporosis—but they now realize that the best approach is to address the problem of bone loss much earlier in life, by starting to check the bone density of people at risk for bone loss in middle age.

By detecting and treating bone loss when people are in their 40s and 50s, we can hopefully prevent age-related bone fractures from happening at all.

The first crucial step is to take a bone density test. This easy, inexpensive procedure can often be done right in your doctor's office (if not, you'll be referred to a lab).

The simplest test, used as a prescreen, measures the density of the wrist and/or heel using a technique called DXA, or dual-energy X-ray absorptiometry. If bone loss is indicated, the next step is to do a more definitive DXA test of your hip and lumbar spine.

WHO SHOULD GET A BONE DENSITY TEST?

Despite the increasing availability of bone density tests, only about 10% of Americans with osteoporosis ever have their bone density evaluated and treated.

You should have a bone density test done if two or more of the following risk factors are present...

•**You've had a bone fracture after age 40.**

•**You're a postmenopausal Caucasian woman** who isn't taking estrogen.

•**You smoke cigarettes.**

•**You are over 50 years of age.**

•**You have a relative,** such as a parent or grandparent, who had osteoporosis.

•**You're taking a bone-thinning medication** (cortisone-type drugs or antacids containing aluminum).

PREVENTION AND TREATMENT OF OSTEOPOROSIS

The key is to retain as much of your "peak bone mass" as possible, through a bone-building calcium-rich diet, exercise and—if necessary—medication. *Prevention strategies...*

•**Eat a diet high in calcium and vitamin D.** A sufficient daily intake of calcium is essential to help maintain bone density. Adult women should get at least 1,200 milligrams (mg) of calcium each day (men can get by with slightly less), but the daily requirement jumps back up to 1,500 mg when women reach menopause.

Healthy calcium sources: Skim or low-fat milk (300 mg of calcium per eight-ounce glass), nonfat yogurt, low-fat cheese, soy products, salmon (with bones), sardines, leafy green vegetables such as broccoli and kale, baked beans and calcium-enriched juices and breads.

• **Take a calcium supplement.** Since postmenopausal American women consume just 800 mg of calcium a day on average—700 mg below their daily requirement—calcium supplements are necessary to ensure strong bones.

The problem with antacids containing calcium carbonate or calcium phosphate, which many women use as calcium supplements, is that only two-fifths of this calcium is absorbed. (You'll get only 200 mg of calcium from each 500 mg antacid tablet.)

Calcium citrate tablets are more effective. Calcium citrate is 60% more "bioavailable" than calcium carbonate or phosphate.

Caution: Space your calcium tablets out during the day (high doses taken at one time aren't absorbed as well as smaller doses taken several hours apart). Always take them with meals or a snack (but not with whole-grain cereal or other high-fiber foods, since fiber blocks calcium absorption).

Also: Never take them at the same time as an iron supplement since the two minerals will bind together, limiting absorption of both.

• **Be sure you get enough vitamin D.** You need a certain amount of vitamin D a day to facilitate calcium absorption. Most people get this from sunlight (15 minutes a day is enough), but as people get older, the skin is less efficient at absorbing sunlight—and less efficient at converting it to vitamin D.

For this reason, doctors suggest people over age 65 take an 800 international unit (IU) daily supplement of vitamin D. Some experts recommend starting even earlier, at age 50.

• **Do weight-bearing exercise.** While calcium helps to build bone, several days a week of weight-bearing exercise is also needed to stimulate the bone-building cells to do their work. (This is why even young astronauts start to lose bone mass in space.)

Exercise could include walking, biking, low-impact aerobics, tennis, stair-climbing or rowing. Exercises to strengthen the back and legs are also recommended, since muscle strength has been linked to stronger bones.

• **Avoid cigarettes and moderate your alcohol intake.** For reasons not yet known, the chemicals in cigarette smoke hasten bone loss, making smokers two times more vulnerable to osteoporosis than the rest of the population.

Alcohol's effects are more mixed. Light consumption (one drink a day) appears to boost bone density slightly—but more than three drinks a day will lower your bone density and contribute to osteoporosis.

Although hormone-replacement therapy (HRT) may be effective in preventing osteoporosis, this treatment is falling out of favor due to the risk of heart disease, breast cancer and strokes. Alternative bone-building medications are now available, including Fosamax (effective in 86% of cases) and Evista.

Doses: If bone density is near normal—five mg of Fosamax or 60 mg of Evista a day to prevent bone loss. If bone density is low—10 mg of Fosamax a day to increase bone mass.

Surprising Paper-Cut Treatment

Use instant-bonding glue, such as Krazy Glue. It takes about one minute for the glue to set, and it stays on until it is worn off by time or removed with nail-polish remover. *Alternative:* Dermabond, a medical adhesive used by doctors. Unlike instant-bonding glue, it is approved by the FDA for use on skin. But it costs about $18 per application—more than 10 times as much as instant-bonding glue.

Stephen P. Stone, MD, dermatologist and professor of clinical medicine, Southern Illinois University School of Medicine, Springfield.

For Easier Pregnancy

If you're having trouble getting comfortable during your pregnancy, you may want to try these suggestions...

• **Wear supportive shoes that help to alleviate foot pain.** *Best:* Rubber soles, low heels, good arch support, wide toe and wide supporting heel.

• **Work out** to strengthen hip muscles...and to avoid the "pregnancy waddle."

Helpful exercise: Stand with your back against a wall. Slowly lower your buttocks until your thighs are parallel to the floor. Hold three seconds. Tighten thigh muscles as you return to the start position. Repeat five times.

• **Sleep on your side.** Place one pillow between your knees, another under your abdomen...and hug a third.

Aim: To keep your body aligned and promote a healthier pregnancy.

Cynthia Markel Feldt, MPT, ATC, director of Rehab Initiatives and former director of practice of the American Physical Therapy Association's women's health section.

5

Improving Your Appearance

How to Buy Clothes That Make You Look Good

It's a mistake to choose color to "go with" your hair and eyes. It's your skin tone that matters most crucially in your choice of color. That's what determines how a particular color looks on you. *More mistakes...*

Mistake: **The idea that black will make you look slimmer.** Black will make you stand out, particularly against any light background. (The walls of most rooms are light.) The more intense and dark your clothing, the larger you'll appear and the less likely to blend into the environment. *Another problem:* Black is usually draining, especially on men, who don't have the help of makeup to offset the pasty look that black gives. Most men should beware of very dark or black suits. *Similar problem color:* White, which tends to wash out the face and yellow the teeth. Soft ivory tones are somewhat better but look good on relatively few people.

Mistake: **Sticking to one or two color groups because you think they are good**

for you. Most people can wear many different color groups. It's the shade that's important. (There are some shades of your favorite color that can look deadly on you.) The point: Don't rule out entire color groups—all blues or all greens. Most people can wear certain shades of most color groups. *Exceptions:* There are a few color groups, such as orange and purple, that are really not good for many people in any shade.

Mistake: **Failing to pay attention to pattern or weave.** People who are short or small-boned should not wear big prints or checks. They can wear a small true tweed. Slender, small-ish men and women are overwhelmed by heavy fabrics. Light wools are better for them than heavy worsteds.

Mistake: **Not considering aging skin in choosing colors.** Wrinkled skin is minimized by softer shades. Hard, dark, intense colors maximize the evidence of aging.

Mistake: **Not allowing for the way environment affects your physical appearance.** The colors and textures of your office or living

Adrienne Gold and Anne Herman, partners in Color-conscious, Inc., Larchmont, NY.

room can affect your looks for better or worse especially in a small room. The colors surrounding you determine the way in which the eye perceives your skin and even your features. Some colors will produce deep shadows, enlarge certain features or produce deep facial lines because of the way they interact with your skin tone.

Women's mistake: Changing makeup to "go with" clothes. Makeup should be chosen according to skin tone only. Using the wrong color makeup is worse than wearing the wrong color clothing.

Men's mistake: Misplaced affection for plaid and madras in sports clothes. Men tend to think they look terrific in these patterns. *Fact:* Most men can't wear them. *Reason for the disastrous choices men make in their sports wardrobe:* They are restricted, or restrict themselves, to conservative business clothes. A man rarely lets himself wear, say, a green suit to the office. *Result:* When men choose sports clothes, they go wild in the other direction, having had little practice in choosing dramatic colors that are suitable.

Mistake: Ignoring the effect of graying hair on complexion. Few men have the sort of skin that takes graying hair well. Men whose skin looks sallow next to graying hair should consider covering the gray.

Mistake: Thinking you can wear colors you ordinarily don't look good in because you have a tan. A tan does make you look healthier, but it doesn't change the basic effect certain colors have on your skin. With a tan, wearing colors you normally look good in is important because that's when those colors look better than ever. *Point:* Neither season nor fashion should dictate the colors of your clothing.

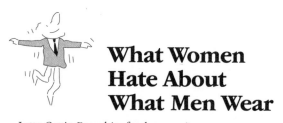

What Women Hate About What Men Wear

Letty Cottin Pogrebin, freelance writer.

No matter how differently women dress from one another, they are surprisingly unanimous about what looks good on men. To verify that hypothesis, an informal survey across the female stylistic spectrum was conducted. *The survey included all types of women:* Preppies in gray flannel Bermudas, ladies who wore gold lamé to lunch, dress-for-success executives in skirt suits, SoHo trend-setters flashing blue nail polish, dignified disciples of designer labels, overaged hippies with feathered headbands and no-nonsense types in polyester pantsuits with matching vinyl shoes and bags.

The result of this survey is a 10-point program:

•**Socks.** These were by far the most frequently mentioned item of annoyance. Socks, women say, must be long enough to cover the calf or "it's death to a woman's libido." Nothing is less titillating than a glimpse of hairy skin below the trouser cuff when a man wearing short socks crosses his legs (except maybe wearing socks to bed when otherwise naked). Also "out" are socks with clogs, black socks with tennis sneakers, white cotton socks with business shoes, and socks with holes in the heels.

•**Comb-overs.** Although not strictly a dress item, the habit of letting hair grow long at the side and combing it over a bald head was high on women's list of loathing. "Who does he think he's kidding?" they ask. "And when the wind blows, oh brother, if he could see himself!" Pulses may quicken over young men with full heads of hair, but women don't dislike baldness per se. They do dislike comb-overs and other compensatory acts of denial and bravado. They like men who like themselves.

•**Miami Beach macho.** Those who sold men on exposing five buttons' worth of chest and a medallion should be hanged at dawn by their own gold chains. Women hate that look. Even women who think men are nifty in manicures and pinky rings hate that look.

•**Misfits.** Women say clothes that don't fit advertise poor character traits. Either the guy doesn't really see himself, which means he is probably oblivious to all his other flaws, too, or he doesn't like himself enough to care how he looks, which means a woman will spend her life shoring up his self-image. Or he's got the Alexander Haig syndrome, choosing the pigeon-breasted tight-jacket look to give the impression that he's too big for clothing to contain him. Or he blames his buttons bursting in midair on shirt shrinkage (his wife's fault), not calories. Whatever the analysis, most women conclude that a man in poorly fitting clothes bodes ill for women.

• **Textures.** Passions run high. "Men shouldn't wear velour; it's like being with a stuffed animal." "Silk is arrogant. If a man has to wear a robe, only terry cloth is forgivable." Corduroy, yes! Rayon, no! Camel's hair, yes! Double knit, no! *Eventually, one rule emerges:* Men shouldn't shine. Anything synthetic that glistens is too glitzy and anything naturally shiny is "pseudo-regal." Or, as one woman put it, "Men need a matte finish."

• **Affectations.** Women opt for simplicity. They like their men unadorned, not gimmicky. "Playboy rabbit insignia drives me wiggo," said a normally subdued woman. "Full-dress fully grown cowboys look ludicrous on Lake Shore Drive," said another. *Also contemptible:* Men wearing one earring (not to mention two); initials on shirts; tie clips or lapel pins promoting a lodge, Lions Club, PT-109, the American flag or God; sweaters with reindeer ("I thought of establishing a moth colony to get rid of it"); leprechaun hats; and "anything Tyrolean."

• **Shoes.** This is an easy one. Whether women were partial to men in Guccis or Adidas, cordovans or bucks, glove-leather wing tips or crepe-sole Hush Puppies, none of them liked tassel loafers.

• **Color.** Anything goes—except the too-bright tones. For instance, heather green is great in a sport jacket, kelly green ghastly. For a sweater, buttercup yellow is warm and friendly, chartreuse off-putting. *General consensus:* If it stops traffic, stop wearing it.

• **Gestures.** If women understand the power of clothing better than men, it is because traditional female socialization teaches them to gain approval through their appearance. Women also know that clothing inspires attitudes in the wearer. An elegant gown can inspire even a child to act aristocratic. And women say certain items of clothing inspire annoying gestures in men. *The worst:* "Shooting cuffs"—the almost spastic movement with which a man pushes his arms out so that his sleeves show more of his shirt cuffs (usually monogrammed and affixed with ostentatious cuff links). "The mirror sneak" —checking and rearranging his tie in every looking glass. "The hoist"—the unceremonious, vaguely obscene lifting of the waistband of loose trousers. *Women's advice on the subject:* Stop posturing, sit still and pay more attention to us.

• **Underwear.** Questions about boxer shorts versus jockey shorts and T-shirts versus sleeveless undershirts produced another quick consensus. The issue is settled by body type. The man with a "good bottom" and tight belly should wear jockeys. The well-muscled-shoulder man should wear sleeveless undershirts. Everyone else shouldn't. And if boxer shorts are what a man wants, women prefer that the ones with pictures and slogans be left to the little boys.

Proper Pants Fit

It's not the waist size but the rise (the measurement from waistband to crotch) that determines the way a man's pants fit, according to the head tailor at Brooks Brothers. A man 5 feet 6 inches tall or shorter needs a short rise. *Regular:* 5 feet 6 inches up to 5 feet 9 inches. *Long:* 5 feet 9 inches to 6 feet 3 inches.

Accentuate the Positive, Eliminate the Negative

There are many strategies women can use to minimize figure flaws during the summer season.

Top-heavy: Wear tunics that glide over the problem areas, V-necked blouses to make shoulders and bosom appear smaller, a diagonal-wrap one-piece bathing suit in contrasting colors, blousy tops (gathered at the waist).

Chunky: To suggest curviness, wear nipped-in waists and eye-catching belts, a blouson dress or drop-waist dress, a one-piece bathing suit with vertical or diagonal stripes.

Bottom-heavy: Pants that end below the knees to show shapely calves, classic pantsuit that falls smoothly in a straight line without pleats or cuffs, vertically striped wraparound dress, one-piece bathing suit with a colorful bra top and darker color below.

The Best Perfumes

The best perfumes for women to wear in the office are the lighter scents. This is particularly true for those with dry skin. *Reason:* Dry skin makes any perfume more pungent.

Avoid Oriental scents such as musk and heavy jasmines. *Reason:* Too strong.

Best Time to Use An Antiperspirant

To stay dry all day, it helps to put on anti-perspirant at bedtime. The main ingredient (aluminum chlorohydrate) works by plugging sweat glands, and it does that best when they're dry for as long as possible. You're dry longest when you're asleep. To build up sweat protection, it's best to use antiperspirant every day. It takes up to eight days for an antiperspirant to reach a level of maximum effectiveness.

Kenneth Hiller, PhD, coordinator, Procter & Gamble Beauty Care Council.

The Best Soaps for Your Skin Type

Contrary to traditional wisdom, a soap with a high pH content, or high alkalinity, does not irritate normal skin. It does cause soap film, especially in hard-water areas. *Who should be cautious in choosing a soap:* The elderly if they have sun-damaged skin. Women who have

overused makeup and soaps. People with very dry skin.

Best for these skin types: A petroleum-based, synthetic imitation soap. This type has gentler ingredients as well as added moisturizers.

Dangers of "Unscented" Cosmetics

Cosmetics labeled "unscented" can still cause the itchy, swollen skin known as dermatitis because they contain masking perfumes.

Best bet: Look for "fragrance free" labels on makeup and creams. Dab perfume only on clothes or hair.

American Academy of Dermatology, cited in *Women's Health.*

A Better Way to Beat Baldness

Now there's a better way to treat baldness—tissue expanders, balloonlike rubber implants used to stretch the skin.

How they work: The bladder is implanted under the skin in the problem area, then injected with a saltwater solution. This produces a slight tension in the overlying skin. Once or twice a week more solution is added to maintain tension as the skin begins to stretch. After one to two months the bladder is removed and the skin is manipulated to cover the defect.

Tissue expanders have virtually limitless potential for reconstructive surgery. Essentially they give surgeons new skin to work with without the need for skin grafts.

Male pattern baldness: By removing a portion of hairless scalp and expanding hair-covered areas, doctors can redistribute hair to cover the entire head. Tissue expander treatment works better than hair plugs or skin grafts. *Drawback:* Patients undergoing tissue expansion of the scalp look odd during the two-month process. Privacy is essential.

Andrew Kleinman, MD, associate adjunct of plastic surgery at the New York Eye and Ear Infirmary in New York City.

Why Women Go Bald

Arthur Bertolino, MD, PhD, adjunct associate professor of dermatology and director of the Hair Consultation Unit at New York University School of Medicine, New York City.

About 30 million men and 30 million women in the United States go bald from natural causes. *Surprising:* Genetic malfunctions, illness, medication and stress can cause more women than men to go bald— sometimes irreversibly.

CAUSES OF HAIR LOSS

• **Temporary loss.** Women can suffer hair loss for weeks or months due to physiological stress and hormonal changes caused by any of these factors:

• Ingestion of particular prescription drugs, such as beta-blockers, vitamin A analogs (taken for acne) and thyroid supplements.

• Changes in hormonal levels—occurring, for instance, when a woman has a baby or stops taking birth-control pills.

• Overuse of cosmetic treatments such as dyes, permanents, etc.

• Severe illness and high fever.

• General anesthesia.

• Underactive thyroid.

• **Permanent loss.** This can be caused by the following conditions:

• Androgenetic alopecia, the most common cause of female balding, is thought to be a genetically predisposed oversensitivity to the male hormones active in every female. *Background:* The small amounts of male hormones can cause hair follicles to shrink, first making hairs grow finer and then preventing hair growth altogether. *Result:* Diffuse balding.

• Alopecia areata (a localized patch of hair loss) is an autoimmune disease in which antibodies damage hair cells. *Sometimes helpful:* Steroid treatments.

MAKING HAIR LOOK FULLER

• **Surgery.** Small sections of hair-bearing scalp can be transplanted to bald spots. *Caution:* These procedures are less effective for female balding than for the larger, unified patterns typical of male balding.

• **Minoxidil.** The lotion form of this drug is an effective treatment. The drug enlarges hair follicles so that thick instead of thin hair grows, a particularly effective approach for diffuse balding.

Drawbacks: Minoxidil works on only 25% of those who use it, and if treatment is halted gains are reversed.

• **Hairpieces and wigs.** These are still the safest and easiest way to cover baldness. Custom-made pieces of real hair are virtually undetectable.

The Secrets of a Great Shave

A good shave with a blade demands the best possible equipment and proper preparation of the beard. Blades and shaving creams are constantly being improved, so it pays to treat your face to the most up-to-date equipment available. *What to look for...*

Shaving cream: All types of cream (lather, brushless and aerosol in either lather or gel form) are equally efficient. Brushless shaving cream is recommended for dry skin.

If you like, buy three or four different kinds of shaving cream. Use different ones for different moods.

Blades: Modern technology makes the current stainless-steel blades a real pleasure to use. *The best type:* The triple blade.

Proper preparation: Wash your face with soap at least twice before shaving. This helps soften the skin, saturate the beard and remove facial oils. *Best:* Shave after a warm shower.

The secret of shaving cream is its ability to hold water on the hairs of the beard, which allows them to absorb the moisture. Thus any cream is more effective if left on the face for

129

a few minutes prior to actual shaving. This saturation causes the facial hairs to expand by about one-third, which enhances the cutting ability of the blade. *One routine:* With the lather on your face, brush your teeth and then set up your razor and other equipment. Do other minor tasks while allowing the lather to soak the beard.

Except on the warmest days, preheat shaving lather in the can or tube by immersing it in hot water.

The art of shaving: The manufacturing process leaves a slight oily residue on the edge of the new blade. This can catch and pull the tender facial skin during the first couple of strokes. So start by trimming the sideburns, a painless way of breaking in the new blade. Always shave the upper lip and chin last. *Why:* The coarsest hairs grow here. Your skin will benefit from the extra minutes of saturation and wetness.

When you have finished shaving, rinse the blade and shake the razor dry. Never wipe a blade dry; this dulls the edge. When rinsing the blade, hold it low in the water stream for quicker results.

After shaving: Save money by skipping the highly advertised aftershave lotions. Use witch hazel instead. It is odorless, less astringent, leaves no residue and is better for your skin than most of the aftershave lotions.

What Dry Cleaners Don't Tell You

Joseph Boms, former assistant manager, Kless dry cleaning chain, Brooklyn, NY.

The dry cleaning process is not mysterious, but it is highly technical. After marking and sorting your clothes on the basis of color and type of material, the cleaner puts them into a dry cleaning machine. This operates like a washing machine except that it uses special solvents instead of water. After the clothes have gone through the dryer, the operator removes stains from them.

A good dry cleaner will use just the right chemical to remove a stain without damaging the fabric. Pressing correctly is next—also a matter of skill. With some fabrics, the garment is put on a form and steamed from the inside to preserve the finish. After pressing, the clothing is bagged.

WHAT TO LOOK FOR

- **Suits** should be put on shoulder shapers.
- **Fancy dresses and gowns** should be on torso dummies.
- **Blouses and shirts** should be stuffed with tissue paper at the shoulders.
- **Except for pants and plain skirts,** each piece should be bagged separately.

TAKING PRECAUTIONS

- **Bring in together all parts of a suit to be cleaned.** Colors may undergo subtle change in the dry cleaning process.
- **Check all pockets before bringing in your clothing.** A pen left in a pocket can ruin the garment.
- **Read care labels carefully.** Many clothes cannot be dry-cleaned at all. Do not dry-clean clothing that has printed lettering or rubber, nylon or plastic parts. If you're not sure, ask your dry cleaner.
- **Make sure your dry cleaner is insured** if you intend to store a large amount of clothing during the winter or summer months.
- **Examine your clothes before leaving them with the cleaner.** Point out stains and ask whether or not you can expect them to be removed.

For best results, tell the cleaner what caused the stain.

GETTING YOUR MONEY'S WORTH

- **Don't wash clothes and then bring them to the cleaner's for pressing.** The savings are minimal.
- **Don't try to remove stains yourself.** You may only make them worse. Bring

stained clothing to the cleaner as soon as possible. Old stains are harder to remove.

• **Ask if the cleaner will make minor repairs as part of the cleaning cost.** Many cleaners offer such services free.

• **Don't request same-day service unless absolutely necessary.** Rushed cleaners often do a sloppy job.

DAMAGE OR LOSS

• **If your cleaner loses or ruins a garment,** you should be reimbursed or given a credit. Most dry cleaners are neighborhood businesses where reputation is vital. You can damage a cleaner's reputation by giving the cleaner bad word of mouth. You might remind the store of this fact if there is resistance to satisfying your complaint.

• **If your cleaner fails to remove a stain you were told could be removed,** you still have to pay for the cleaning job.

• **If your cleaner dry-cleans a garment with a "do not dry-clean" label,** the store is responsible for ruining the garment.

• **If your cleaner ruins a garment that should not be dry-cleaned** but lacks the "do not dry-clean" label, responsibility is a matter of opinion. The cleaner may reimburse you to keep your goodwill, or you may have to complain to an outside agency.

• **The amount you will be reimbursed is always up for bargaining.** You will have to consider original value and depreciation, and whether you have a receipt.

MAKING COMPLAINTS

If you cannot get satisfaction from your cleaner voluntarily, most states have dry cleaners associations to arbitrate complaints. These associations go under various names in different states, so check with your local Department of Consumer Affairs. Be sure to keep all dry cleaning receipts and other relevant information to substantiate your complaint.

Caring for Down

Down is almost spongelike in its ability to absorb moisture, oils and dirt, its worst enemies. But cleaning is hard on down and even harder on its owner. *Some maintenance tips for staving off cleanings…*

• **Sponge off the shell fabric as soon as possible after spotting.** Be sure to use mild soap and water.

• **Enclose comforters in removable sheet casings** that can be washed frequently. (These are available in most department stores.)

• **Let garments air-dry away from steam pipes,** sun or other heat sources before putting them in the closet. (Or put them in a large dryer at low heat with a clean sneaker.)

• **Patch tears, rips, or holes** in the shell with the pressure-sensitive tapes sold in sporting-goods stores until you can make a permanent repair with a fine needle and thread or have a professional make a "hot spot" repair.

• **Hang vertically channeled coats upside down** occasionally to redistribute the down.

• **Store clean down flat or loosely folded.** Wrap it in a breathable covering such as a sheet to protect it from dust, light and rodents.

WASHING DOWN

Care labels frequently recommend washing. (Gore-Tex® for example, is destroyed by dry cleaning.) Smaller items can be easily washed in a front-loading, tumble-type machine. Empty the pockets and close all the zippers, snaps and Velcro tabs.

Run the washer on medium cycle with warm water. Use half the amount of nonphosphorated soap or detergent recommended. Rinse twice to be sure the soap is all out.

Never use a top-loading agitator machine. It will take apart seams, fray internal edges and diminish the life of the garment by 75%.

For larger items, use the bathtub. Dissolve mild soap or detergent in warm water first. Then submerge the jacket or coat completely. Let it soak no more than 15 minutes. Let the water drain without disturbing the article, and rinse several times until the water runs clear. Don't twist or wring, but compress the excess water out before hanging the garment over a rack or several lines to dry. Be extra careful with comforters or you will tear the baffling, which is irreplaceable.

DRYING DOWN

Never a fast process, air-drying can take several days even in perfect weather. Be patient, and turn the article often. Home dryers are good only for small items such as vests and children's jackets. Larger items don't have room to fluff properly. Hot dryers can melt nylon zippers and even some fabrics. *Best:* Commercial dryer with a low heat cycle. Add a couple of clean sneakers (laces removed) or clean tennis balls and a large towel to break up the wet down clumps. Take plenty of change; the process requires several hours.

DRY-CLEANING DOWN

Professional dry cleaning may be the easiest way to restore good down clothing and bedding. However, there are traps in this. The best solvent for cleaning is a nonchlorinated petroleum product that is banned from most city cleaning establishments because of its flammability. Two companies* specialize in this preferred type of cleaning and take care of customers through United Parcel Service. Both also handle repairs and restylings.

Conventional dry cleaning, which is harder on the product, necessitates careful airing afterward to allow toxic fumes to evaporate.

Always spray clean garments with silicone water repellent yourself. Professional waterproofing is a dip that soaks the down. (Nylon shells will not take silicone spray or dip.)

*Down East, New York; Down Depot, San Francisco.

Cosmetic Surgery

Neal B. Schultz, MD, dermatologist with Park Avenue Skin Care, 1130 Park Ave., New York City 10128.

Every year thousands of Americans try the latest plastic surgery techniques designed to keep them looking younger longer. *Problem:* Each new procedure is only as good as the surgeon who administers it. And not being aware of the risks ahead of time could leave you emotionally as well as physically scarred.

How to decide whether you should have surgery: Consider your emotional need to have the procedure done, as well as the problems that may result from it. Then try to balance the two to determine what you should do.

•**Liposuction,** removing fat cells from the body to produce smoother contours, has been around for a few years. We're now discovering more of its many risks.

Problems: If too much fat and fluid are removed you can go into shock, bleed internally—or die. *Bottom line:* This is a cosmetic procedure that in the wrong hands could end in disaster. And even when it's performed correctly, it can cause dimpled or sagging skin.

CHOOSING A GOOD SURGEON

The success of any cosmetic procedure depends on the skill of the surgeon. *To find a good one...*

•**Call a teaching hospital in your area** and ask the staff for recommendations. *Reason:* Teaching hospitals offer much higher-quality control and peer review.

•**Talk to people who have had the type of surgery that you are considering.** See if they are happy with it and find out who their doctors are.

•**Choose a board-certified plastic surgeon.** *Note:* Although this is a form of quality control, it does not necessarily mean you will get the best surgeon. *Reason:* Plastic surgery is an art and to become board-certified, all you have to do is pass an exam. *Better:* Seek out a recommendation from someone who has had successful surgery.

•**Make sure the surgeon you choose has performed the procedure hundreds—** if not thousands—of times. And the surgeon should be able to give you the names of at least three satisfied patients. You should call them to verify the surgeon's results.

No More Facial Wrinkles

Neal B. Schultz, MD, dermatologist with Park Avenue Skin Care, 1130 Park Ave., New York City 10128.

Facial wrinkles are caused by a variety of factors, including heredity, excessive sun exposure and smoking. There are several different ways to have these wrinkles removed or minimized at a dermatologist's office.

LASER SKIN RESURFACING

This is suitable for treating lines and wrinkles of all depths. It is performed under local anesthesia.

How it works: A computer-controlled laser beam vaporizes the skin of the wrinkled area to a flat or almost flat surface. The surgeon using this technique halts the process when the lines disappear. Healing takes seven to 10 days. It is more rapid than dermabrasion and deep chemical peeling.

Follow-up: Usually there is no pain shortly after the procedure. During the first seven to 10 days of healing, the skin is bright red. After this period, the skin is pink—but the color fades over the ensuing weeks and months and is easily concealed with makeup.

While a significant part of the improvement in the wrinkles is visible one to two months after the procedure, improvement continues for six to 12 months after the procedure as new skin grows.

Important: During healing (until the pink color fades), it is essential to avoid the sun because sun exposure can cause the skin to heal with uneven color and cause serious damage.

SKIN PEELS

•**Dermabrasion.** The top layers of the skin are "sanded" off with a rapidly rotating wire brush. The treated area heals as new skin grows in.

This process removes wrinkles of all depths and can be done under local or general anesthesia. The procedure takes about one hour.

Results are less predictable than with laser resurfacing—except when performed by surgeons with exceptional experience. Some pain is experienced in the first few days after the procedure.

The skin that was removed grows back in one to two weeks, and your face's pinkness will disappear in about two to three months. The sun must be avoided during this time.

•**Deep peels are done with an acid.** The acid peels away the skin until the wrinkles flatten out. These peels are suitable for mild to moderately deep wrinkles. The skin that was removed grows back in seven to 10 days. Your skin's pinkness will fade over a period of two to three months. Here, too, avoid the sun.

Results of this type of peel are less predictable than with laser resurfacing because the depth of penetration of the acid solution is more difficult to control. There is also a greater risk of scarring and loss of color.

•**Glycolic and beta-peels.** The acid is painlessly applied for several minutes and then removed. These need to be repeated six to 10 times. The peels have little effect on wrinkles and are more suitable for treating uneven skin texture and skin tone.

•**Retin A is a wonderful drug that replaces a sallow color with some pinkness,** causes blood vessels beneath the surface to proliferate collagen formation (thereby plumping up the skin and filling out the fine wrinkles). It is used topically at bedtime in very small quantities. *Net results:* Removal of very fine crosshatch wrinkles, evening and removal of brown mottling that often results from prolonged skin exposure and refreshment of scaly dull skin while plumping it up and restoring some pinkness.

Problems: Treatment leaves you much more susceptible to sunburn. And too much Retin A can cause redness and peeling.

COLLAGEN INJECTIONS

Collagen injections fill out the wrinkles instead of burning or scraping them away. This is better for people with dark skin for whom the pinkness of raw skin would be more obvious and in whom there is a greater chance of discoloration from laser peels and dermabrasion. A six-week skin test is required to determine if there is an allergic reaction.

Drawback: The injected collagen lasts only a few months before wrinkles begin to re-emerge. As a result, injections need to be repeated on a regular basis.

Solution: Use a natural lip gloss. If you must have color, stain your lips with beet or berry juice and brush colored clays (available at most natural-food stores) on cheeks and eyelids. Buy unscented, hypoallergenic mascara.

Debra Lynn Dadd, author of *Nontoxic Home* (Penguin).

Liposuction Safety Net

Liposuction is safest when performed as an outpatient procedure under local anesthesia—in a doctor's office, not in a hospital. The doctor should be a board-certified dermatologic surgeon.

Avoid doctors who plan to extract large amounts of fat at one time...and those who perform multiple procedures at the same time.

Liposuction is usually safe, but serious complications do occur in rare cases—usually when general anesthesia is used. *These include:* Shock, blood clots, infection, bowel perforation in abdominal procedures.

William Coleman III, MD, clinical professor of dermatology, Tulane University Health Sciences Center, New Orleans, and leader of a study of 257 liposuction-related insurance claims, published in *Dermatalogic Surgery.*

Finger Beauty Danger

Nail-wrapping, glue-on false nails and nail augmentation can cause rashes, redness, scaling and swelling of the skin surrounding the nail or worse, infection of the nail bed (skin beneath the nail) and even permanent loss of nails.

Problems: Cyanoacrylates, an ingredient found in nail glues, trigger allergic reactions. Infection-causing bacteria, fungi and yeast get trapped in the nail bed by waterproof nail-wrappings. Longer nails increase the chance of tearing the nail plate from the nail bed.

Solution: Halt use of products. *Better:* Keep nails a reasonable length and if a problem develops, dispense with enhancement techniques.

Paul Kechijian, MD, chief of the nail section at New York University School of Medicine, New York City.

Dangers in Personal-Care Products

Many beauty and hygiene products contain chemicals that can make you sick—or even kill you.

Cosmetics are often made from harmful substances. Lipstick may contain PVP (polyvinylpyrrolidone plastic), saccharin and mineral oil, all of which have caused cancer in animals. Formaldehyde, alcohol and plastic resins in mascara can cause irritation and burning and swelling of the eyes.

Questions to Ask Your Plastic Surgeon

Neal B. Schultz, MD, dermatologist with Park Avenue Skin Care, 1130 Park Ave., New York City 10128.

Plastic surgery for cosmetic reasons is surrounded by a lot of hype. The fantasy that your life will be magically transformed by surgery can play into the hands of the unscrupulous. Although the overwhelming majority of plastic surgeons are competent and ethical, there are a few bad apples.

If you know which questions to ask both yourself and your doctor before you make a commitment to surgery, you'll save heartache —to say nothing of money.

WHAT TO ASK YOURSELF

Do I really need plastic surgery? You must be objective when you look in the mirror. Some people want surgery for a couple of wrinkles that are barely noticeable to anyone but themselves. Their vulnerability to the power of perfection may make them easy marks. *How it can happen:* Someone who thinks he or she needs a face-lift begs the surgeon to "just give me a little tuck." An unethical surgeon who is pushed, instead of refusing, may put the patient under general anesthesia, make a couple of incisions and sew him up. The patient then wakes up with two healing incision lines near his ears and thinks he looks great. In reality, he has paid up to $8,000 for virtually nothing. *Criteria to follow:* Would repair of an imperfection that bothers you enhance your well-being? Does that imperfection actually exist?

What do I want done and what will it accomplish for me? Although the psychological factor in cosmetic surgery cannot be overlooked, it must be approached realistically. Cosmetic surgery can improve your state of well-being—for some people, how they feel depends on how they look—but it usually does not change anyone's life. Many people blame all their difficulties on a particular physical defect. They delude themselves into believing that their difficulties will instantly be overcome if their physical defect is corrected.

How did you find your plastic surgeon? Did you fall prey to advertisements for low-cost surgery (with limousine service thrown in)? Like anything else, you get what you pay for. Stay away from high-pressure advertising. *Best:* Referral from other satisfied patients. If you don't know anyone who has had the type of surgery you want, ask your family doctor or internist for a recommendation. If you have a good relationship with your primary physician, there will be quality control. Your doctor can't afford to have his reputation damaged by recommending a bad doctor.

Have I asked for a second opinion? There's no other area where second opinions are more valuable. Only another doctor can confirm that you actually need the surgery and that the particular procedure your surgeon wants to do is reasonable for the result you seek.

WHAT TO ASK YOUR PLASTIC SURGEON

Realistically, what will be done? Not what can be done, or what you can hope for, but what you can expect. You'll also want to know what will happen if you don't get the result the doctor promises. How will he remedy that situation? Will you have to pay for the unsatisfactory job? Will he do a corrective procedure at no cost? Or will he say, "Sorry, I can't help you"? *Crucial:* Preoperative and postoperative pictures taken by the same photographer. Only with photos can you prove that you didn't get the promised result.

What is the chance of real damage, and if it happens, what might the extent of it be? Plastic surgeons aren't gods. They are physicians who have had extensive training in delicate repair of skin; but nobody can break the integrity of normal skin without leaving a mark. Plastic surgeons are only a bit like magicians. They leave marks in areas that are less conspicuous. But if you have a big growth in the middle of your cheek, you can't expect the doctor to cut it out without leaving a mark. *Other areas of concern:* The chances of infection and other complications.

Where will the surgery be done? Although many reputable plastic surgeons operate out of their own offices, surgery done in a hospital inevitably offers more quality control. There's much less room for nonprofessionalism in a hospital, where nurses and operating-room teams are provided by the institution and there is peer review of a surgeon's work. *Generally safest bet:* A doctor who is university-affiliated and teaches in a hospital or medical school.

May I see your book of before and after pictures? You may want to ask if you can contact a surgeon's other patients. But since this might violate confidentiality, he may only

135

be willing to show you his patients' before and after pictures. If he offers you a whole book of good results, you can certainly feel confident.

Can the surgery be done in stages? A male model had a bad result on facial moles that a plastic surgeon had treated with liquid nitrogen. His skin had darkened, and there were brown spots and scars. The surgeon hadn't done a trial on one mole but had treated them all at one session. *Suggestion:* If you have many of the same defects, have one corrected first to see if you like the result.

Is there a less serious procedure that will produce a similar result? Very effective collagen injections available today eliminate both wrinkles and acne scars. Suction lipectomy can remove fat pockets. You may want to look into such lesser procedures before under-going full-scale surgery.

How much will it cost? How much time will it take? How long will I be out of work or away from home? Ask whatever other questions concern you. Prepare a written list. No matter how many questions you have or how trivial you feel they are, ask!

Facts About Face-Lifts

Each year half a million Americans choose face-lift operations as a way to turn back the clock.

Factors that hasten this decline: Hereditary tendencies (some faces age faster than others)...cigarette smoking, which decreases blood flow to the skin...excessive use of alcohol...poor nutrition...lack of sleep and exercise. *Main culprit:* Sunlight. To keep skin smooth, stay out of the sun. When exposed, apply sunscreen lotion.

A face-lift is major surgery. *What is done:* The facial and neck skin are literally lifted from the underlying tissue and set back in place. This gives the face a smoothed-out appearance. *Possible complications:* Blood clots, hemorrhages under the skin, facial-nerve injuries, abnormal scarring.

Payoff: The operation removes wrinkles and restores firmness. But at best it makes the face look 10 years younger.

Avoid: A mini-lift in which the skin is pulled tight rather than lifted off the face.

Note: Most insurance policies do not cover elective cosmetic surgery.

6

Your Home

Save Money (Even Make Money) On Housing for Your College Student

If you're sending a child to college away from home, be prepared to pay big—and not just for tuition. For the 2012–2013 academic year, the average cost for room and board at public universities was approximately $9,200, the College Board reports. At private colleges, the average cost was approximately $10,500.

Bottom line: You can expect to spend $30,000 or more for room and board for each child who goes away to college for four years.

Strategy: *Buy* your child a place to live near the campus. In today's buyer's market for housing, you might find a very good deal.

If you sell the property a few years from now, you may get a better price. Even if you just break even on the real estate, you'll save by not paying for college housing.

REAL TAX BREAKS

In a simple example, you might buy an apartment where your daughter can live while she goes to school.

Tax benefits: If you itemize, and as long as you're not subject to the alternative minimum tax, you will be able to deduct the property tax you pay. If you use a mortgage to help finance the purchase, the interest you pay will be tax deductible, too. In essence, the apartment would be taxed as if you were using it as a second home.

Final accounting: When you sell the apartment, assuming that you've owned it for more than a year, any gain will be taxed at up to 23.8%.

Trap: A loss on your sale won't be treated as a capital loss because you can't take a capital loss on the sale of a residence, so you would get no tax benefit.

Strategy: Rather than take a loss, you may

Greg Weyandt, CPA, MPA, director of operations, Welch Group, 3940 Montclair Rd., Birmingham, Alabama 35213. A partner in a wealth-management firm, Mr. Weyandt profited from an investment in near-campus housing when two of his children went to Auburn University.

prefer to rent the apartment, perhaps to a different student, after your daughter moves on. You can receive rental income while you wait for your apartment's value to recover.

ALL IN THE FAMILY

A more ambitious venture is to buy a larger apartment than your child needs or a house near the campus.

Next step: Let your own child live in this residence *and* rent space in it to one or more other students. Because they'll pay rent to you, the residence will become income-producing property.

Tax treatment: Operating costs will become tax deductible. That could include everything from utility bills to insurance.

You also will be able to take depreciation deductions for the real estate, furnishings, fixtures, etc.

Management fees: Name your child as property manager. Your child's responsibilities could include screening tenants, getting leases signed, collecting rents, arranging for property maintenance, and so on.

For those services, you could pay your child a management fee. Approximately 10% to 12% of the rental income received from tenants might be reasonable, depending on other property management fees in the area.

Loophole: Such management fees will be deductible for you, the property owner. They can reduce taxable income from rents or contribute to a loss for tax purposes.

At the same time, income from these management fees probably will be tax free to your child. In 2013, because of the standard deduction, single taxpayers may have up to $6,100 in earned income and owe no tax.

Therefore, this arrangement can be a tax-efficient way to give your collegian spending money.

Travel smart: What's more, your trips to visit the college town may be deductible if your primary purpose is to check up on your investment property. *Note:* Be sure to document that you checked on the house's condition, spoke with the property manager (your child) about maintenance, met with student-tenants to see if they have concerns, researched nearby rents, etc.

LOSS LEADER

Deductions for management fees, depreciation, travel, and other expenses may generate a taxable loss from the property each year. This might be the case even if you have positive cash flow from rental income.

Tax treatment: Such a loss would be considered a *passive loss*. As long as your adjusted gross income (AGI) is less than $100,000, up to $25,000 worth of passive losses can be deducted each year.

As your AGI goes from $100,000 to $150,000, your maximum passive loss phases out, from $25,000 to zero.

End of the deal: When you ultimately sell the property, you can use any passive losses not previously deducted. Those losses can decrease a taxable gain or increase a capital loss from rental property.

PROCEED WITH CAUTION

Tax benefits will help a near-campus investment, but there is risk in any real estate venture. Some basic precautions can increase your chance of success.

Location: This is always crucial for real estate investing. Look for a place not far from the school in a neighborhood that's safe and doesn't seem intimidating in any way. A good location will help make student-tenants and their parents feel comfortable. Moreover, it will make it easier to eventually sell the property.

Tenant tactics: Be cautious about selecting tenants. Get references from employers to see if the students have been reliable. Have the students' parents sign 12-month leases and provide guarantees that they'll be responsible for the rent.

Documenting The Deed

Your house deed will be recorded among the land records in the jurisdiction where your house is located, so don't worry if you find you have lost it when it comes time to sell the house. The title attorney handling the sale of the house will be able to prepare a new deed from these records. *Alternative:* The attorney or title company that conducted your settlement. Either of these two parties might have the original recorded deed in their company files.

Important house documents to keep (in addition to the deed to the house): The settlement sheet (for future tax purposes), the deed of trust and the promissory note that you sign with your lender.

Evaluating a Condo... A Checklist

When you evaluate a condominium, consider first the physical appearance of the grounds and the units for sale. *Ask yourself these questions...*

- **Are the building exteriors and the common areas well-maintained?**
- **Does the development offer the amenities that you enjoy?**
- **Are there recreational facilities that you will not use but will pay for?**
- **Are the living units well-constructed,** with good quality materials and fixtures? Is there adequate soundproofing?
- **Does the floor plan suit your lifestyle?**
- **Is the location of the unit within the development a desirable one?**
- **Is the development itself well-situated,** with easy access to shops and community facilities?
- **Does it offer a safe, secure living environment?**
- **Will you and your family have sufficient privacy?**
- **Would you enjoy having the other residents as neighbors?**

H.L. Kibbey, author of a series of books for home buyers and sellers, including *The Growing Older Guide to Real Estate* (Panoply Press).

Self-Defense for Tenants

Tenants are rapidly becoming a beleaguered species as rents continue to increase and vacancies in desirable urban areas plummet. Faced with the high cost of home ownership, more individuals are renting, and demand is quickly outpacing supply. Landlords often become greedy in this kind of environment and take advantage of tenants' desperation. Most states with major populated areas now have some form of protection for tenants, however. Tenant remedies vary according to state or local laws. But there is one power that a tenant anywhere has and should use when circumstances warrant it—the power to withhold the rent. If you understand the basic concepts of tenant law, you will know when and how to use your ultimate weapon.

Your apartment must be suitable for habitation by a human being. If it's not, the law in most states requires the landlord to do whatever is necessary to make it habitable. *The following must be provided...*

- **Heat,** hot and cold water.
- **Electricity or a facility for it** if it's metered through a public utility.
- **Air-conditioning** if it's in your lease.
- **Absence of roaches and vermin.**
- **Clean public areas (lobbies, halls)** in the building.
- **No dangerous health conditions** in the apartment. *Examples:* Falling plaster, peeling lead-based paint.

The warranty of habitability deals mainly with health, not with cosmetics. If your bathtub is cracked, it isn't a violation of the warranty unless water is leaking. The crack might be a violation of the local tenant-protection act, however, which varies from state to state.

The question of unfair leases came up because landlords were taking advantage of the scarce housing situation to force tenants into signing leases with unconscionable provisions. *Examples:* Clauses saying the landlord doesn't have to provide heat and hot water; clauses waiving a tenant's right to trial by jury in a landlord/tenant conflict; clauses giving the landlord the right to change a tenant's locks

139

if the tenant doesn't pay the rent—all without going through the court system.

Recommended: Sign whatever lease the landlord offers. Then take him to court if some of the provisions prove unconscionable.

The best way to find out the law in your area is to call your local congressperson. Many local legislators have a hotline or an open evening for community residents to air their problems. At the very least, a local legislator can point you in the right direction—to a community group or a tenants' organization in your area.

Don't run to a lawyer immediately. Try a community group first. If you do decide to hire a lawyer, make sure he's a specialist in landlord/tenant law. This is a very specialized and volatile area. Laws change frequently, and an amateur can do you more harm than good.

The most effective method of confronting the landlord is through a tenants' organization. If you are having problems with your landlord, the same is probably true of the other tenants in your building. If you approach the problem as a group, your chances of success improve immeasurably.

HOW TO GO ABOUT IT

• **Talk to the other tenants in your building and distribute flyers calling an organizational meeting.** At the meeting, elect a committee of tenants to lead the group.

• **Pass out questionnaires to all tenants,** asking them to list needed repairs in their apartments.

• **When the questionnaires have been collected,** a member of the committee should call the landlord and suggest a meeting with him to negotiate complaints. Many landlords will comply with this request, since the spectre of all their tenants withholding rent can be a frightening prospect. Negotiation is always preferable to litigation. It is a very effective tool. *Also:* Negotiation can be desirable for a landlord who is not getting his rent on time. Tenants can emphasize that they are willing to improve the landlord's cash-flow problems by paying on the first of the month if he is willing to make repairs.

• **If negotiation fails,** organize a rent strike. That's a procedure whereby tenants withhold rent collectively, depositing the money each month in an escrow fund or with the court until repairs are made. If your tenant organization is forced to go this route, you will need a good lawyer. Be prepared for a long court battle.

If the other tenants won't cooperate, you can withhold your rent as an individual. *Reasonable grounds:* Lack of services (heat, hot water, garbage collection, elevator). Don't withhold rent unless you have a good reason. If you lose, you'll be liable for the landlord's attorney's fees plus court costs. *Advantage of withholding:* You'll get your day in court and the opportunity to explain to a judge what the problem is. Even if you lose, you will be allowed to pay rent up to date and not be evicted. The harassment value of forcing your landlord to take you to court will probably make him more compliant in the future. Get a lawyer to represent you if the problem is severe.

Tenant versus tenant. *If a tenant in your building is involved in crime or drugs or is excessively noisy, a number of possibilities are available to you...*

• **Take out a summons,** claiming harassment or assault. *Probable result:* The court will admonish the tenant to stop causing a disturbance (which may or may not have any effect).

• **Sue for damages in civil court.** You may win (although collecting the judgment is another story).

• **Try to persuade your landlord to evict the undesirable tenant.** *Best way:* Put pressure on him through your tenants' organization. A landlord can't be forced to evict anyone. He has the right to rent to whomever he chooses. But if your association has a decent relationship with the landlord, he might comply, especially if the tenant is causing a dangerous condition or destroying property.

• **You do have the right to break your lease** if you're being harassed by another tenant, but this may not be much comfort if apartments in your area are scarce.

Moving Fragile Objects

When moving valuables, consider carriers other than household movers. Special handling is important for irreplaceable and fragile objects as well as for jewelry, collections and currency. *Options:* Air freight, UPS, armored service, registered US mail, yourself.

Moving Does Not Have to Be Traumatic

Cathy Goodwin, PhD, author of *Making the Big Move: How to Transform Relocation into a Creative Life Transition* (New Harbinger Publications). She has moved more than 12 times in her life. Dr. Goodwin is a former professor of marketing at Nova Southeastern University in Fort Lauderdale, Florida.

Whether you are moving to a smaller space in the same city…to a retirement community in another state… or to an apartment across the country, there are steps you can take to minimize the disruption that relocation invariably causes.

First, make sure moving is something you want to do. People who feel forced to move often experience anger and resentment on top of all the normal relocation-induced feelings of loneliness, anxiety, excitement and expectation.

PSYCHOLOGICAL ISSUES

If moving is something you've decided is right for you, make it easier on yourself by working through some of the psychological issues ahead of time.

• **List the activities you most enjoy doing.** Think of the roles you play in life that define you. Ask yourself what it is about your home environment that energizes you.

It's often the seemingly trivial routines and comforts—like a morning cup of cappuccino at the local coffee shop—that we miss most in a new location. If you make careful note of these comforts, you'll be able to duplicate them in your new home.

• **Prepare for moving by deciding who you are.** Decide what you need around you in order to fully express your identity.

Exercise 1: Who are you? As quickly as you can, complete the sentence, "I am a _____" 10 times.

Examples: I am a mother, I am an artist, I am a gardener, etc.

Review what you've written and think about what it reveals about you. What, if anything, will change if you move to a new location?

Exercise 2: Which routines are most important to you? You will gain a better understanding of the importance of your daily routines by writing them down. *As thoroughly as possible, write down…*

• **What you do on weekday mornings.**

Example: Wake up without an alarm clock …walk the dogs…drive to the local newsstand for the paper…stop at the corner coffee shop.

• **What you do to relax in the evening.**

• **How you spend Saturday mornings.** When you've completed this exercise, ask yourself how you'd feel about interrupting these routines.

Though the details you record may seem trivial, it's often these little changes and losses that increase the psychological trauma of moving.

PRESERVING COMFORTS AND ROUTINES

By understanding which routines and comforts are important to you, you'll more easily develop replacements in your new community. *Do some homework before the move…*

• **Learn all you can about your prospective community.** Use the Internet to research the community and learn about its character/culture.

By typing in the city and state you're considering, you can learn about museums and theater programs…local businesses and restaurants…opportunities for continuing education …medical services…transportation, etc.

Use the library to research the archives of the local newspaper.

Better: Make a premove visit to the area you're considering and talk to people of all ages about what it's like to live in the area.

• **Visualize how you'll spend a day in the new location.** Begin by visualizing your new home for 15 to 20 minutes. Relax, close your eyes and get comfortable.

Ask yourself: What is my ideal home? Where does the sun rise and set? Are there skylight windows? Lamps? Overhead lighting?

What is the shape of each room, and what kind of furniture do I see in each? Who or what do I see in the home with me (spouse, dog, cat)?

After you've pictured your new home in your mind, visualize a day in your new community. See yourself waking up. What will you do next? What familiar roles might be useful in your new location? What new roles or activities might you engage in? What problems might you encounter (e.g., no coffee shop!) and how will you deal with these problems?

When you've completed this exercise, write down any insights you've gained, then compare your notes with your real life in the new location after you've moved.

FOR RENTERS

If you choose to rent, place a "Rental Wanted" classified ad in the local paper. I've done this twice. As a result, I've learned about really fine properties that are typically only rented by word-of-mouth.

And, contrary to what many people think, I didn't get any crank phone calls.

Sample ad: Model tenant with steady income seeks single-level, three-bedroom apartment. References provided.

PLANNING A NO-TEARS MOVE

• **Use the checklists provided by moving companies** as well as lists found in books. *For example…*

• *Smooth Moves* by Ellen Carlisle (Teacup Press).

• *Steiner's Complete How-to-Move Handbook* by Clyde L. Steiner and Shari Steiner (IIP Consumer).

• **Put together an emotional first-aid kit.** Your kit can include coping statements such as, "I will just let go and relax"…"I can deal with this"…or "I've survived this before—and I can do it again."

Add to the kit meditation and visualization books and tapes. Also include the phone numbers of old friends—at least one to laugh with, one to listen to you and one who moved recently and can give good advice. Pick up a journal in which you can record your thoughts, concerns and feelings.

Making the Most of Your House

Charles Jacob, Irving & Jacob Architects, Norwalk, Connecticut.

Many homeowners are taking a new look at their houses with an eye toward either extending and upgrading through additions and renovations or constricting living space for greater efficiency.

Procedure for additions or renovations: The architect compiles a set of preliminary drawings to obtain a rough idea of costs from contractors. Next, a complete set of drawings makes closer estimates possible. For small jobs, rely on the cost estimate of a reputable local contractor. For more complex work, get estimates from two or three contractors. No estimate is reliable unless it is based on a complete set of drawings.

Costs: Per square foot, a new bathroom is the most costly room in the house. *Next most expensive:* The kitchen. *Least expensive:* A bedroom.

Planning: Try to have all the outside work done during the fair-weather months and save the interior finishing for winter.

Problem: Kitchen renovation. No matter what time of the year this work is done, you end up with sawdust in the scrambled eggs. *Best:* Take a vacation while the kitchen is being rebuilt. *More realistically:* See that as much work as possible is done outside the kitchen. Then have the actual installation of items such as cabinets, counters and appliances concentrated in one burst of activity. This might take as little as one week.

In the search for more living space, many owners convert an attached garage into a family room. A new, level floor should be installed over the existing concrete slab, which is often pitched. *Important:* Insulate the space under this new floor. Slip new windows and doors into the old openings. *Convenience:* A new bathroom for this area. If the plumbing is prepared properly, a kitchenette can be added later. Thus the family room can be quickly converted into a rental apartment for added income when the kids have grown up and moved out, assuming local zoning allows for accessory apartments in residential neighborhoods.

Parents whose children no longer live at home often adopt a country-kitchen style of living. The couple centers its activities around the kitchen, even sleeping in a nearby room. *Aim:* To conserve heat by warming only the core of the house in winter.

Source of heat and comfort: An old-fashioned wood-burning stove. *Warning:* Charming as these stoves are, they can cause fires if they are not installed properly.

Other things to know…

• **Zoning and building permits are required** before the construction of most additions. *Key word:* Setbacks. These are the hypothetical lines on your property beyond which you are not allowed to build without a variance.

• **No addition may encroach on an existing water well,** septic tank or septic field. Find where these are located and plan accordingly.

• **Know the capacity of your present electrical service.** An older house may receive only 60 to 100 amps. You may have to push service to 200 amps to meet the demands of the newly finished space.

Choosing a Building Contractor

Before you hire a contractor, do some homework so you know what to expect. *For example…*

• **Get bids from three contractors** whom you have selected by looking at their work or through friends' recommendations.

• **Make sure your job specifications are the same** for each contractor so that all the bids will be for exactly the same requirements.

• **Watch out for low bids.** They may presage shoddy workmanship or inferior materials.

• **Run a thorough check on the contractor** you decide to use (credit, bonding references, insurance, etc.).

• **Be specific about every detail of the job,** leaving nothing in doubt when you draw up the final agreement.

• **Pay one-third up front,** one-third when the job is almost done and the balance at the conclusion of the job, if you are satisfied.

• **If you make changes during construction that are not in the contract,** get all the costs in writing before the alterations are made.

Getting Your Money's Worth from a Home-Improvement Contractor

Plunging ahead with major improvements or additions to your home without a carefully thought-out contract is asking for trouble. What to get in writing?

• **Material specifications,** including brand names and a work-completion schedule.

• **All details of the contractor's guarantees,** including the expiration dates. *Also:* Procedures to be followed if materials or workmanship should prove defective. *Trap:* Do not confuse manufacturers' guarantees with the contractor's guarantees of proper installation.

• **An automatic arbitration clause.** This provides that an impartial board will mediate if problems of excessive cost overruns arise.

• **A clause holding the contractor responsible** for negligence on the part of subcontractors. Check with your lawyer for specifics.

• **A cleanup provision** specifying that all debris be removed.

DOS AND DON'TS OF A CONTRACT JOB

• **Do consult a lawyer** before signing a complex contract.

• **Don't sign a contract with any blank spaces.** Write "void" across them.

• **Don't sign a work-completion certificate** without proof that the contractor has paid all subcontractors and suppliers of materials.

• **Don't pay in full until you are completely satisfied.**

• **Don't pay cash.**

Beware of Certain Home Improvements

Edith Lank, real-estate broker who writes a nationally syndicated column about real estate. She is also author of *The Home Seller's Kit, Fourth Edition* (Real Estate Primer Publishers) and *The Homebuyer's Kit* (Dearborn Trade Publishing).

A big problem for some home owners— the house you bought for $50,000 in the 1960s is now worth $500,000... and you'd like to put some of the profit into your pocket. There are effective steps you can take now to enhance the value of your house whether you decide to sell or to get cash from it by renting or mortgaging.

Most people are now aware that when they sell a house, they never recoup the value of swimming pools, finished basements and most other major improvements.

But what many people don't know is that these additions can actually decrease the value of the home.

Reason: Some prospective buyers don't like swimming pools, and others have their own ideas about finishing the basement. By making these improvements yourself, you simply lose these prospects.

Even if you are lucky enough to find a would-be buyer who wants a pool, you won't get your money back because the price of your house is largely determined by the average home price in your neighborhood. Prospective buyers looking for a more expensive house will look in a neighborhood that has many houses in that price range.

Exceptions: Good bathrooms and kitchens do help to sell a house. If yours are in bad shape, fix them up. It pays to consult an agent if you're in doubt about fixing up a room. Tell the agent you're selling in a year, making it in the agent's interest to give you free advice.

Ironically, the improvements that really help sell a house are basically cosmetic and inexpensive. In today's market, however, they can be very important. *Some of the easy and inexpensive improvements you can make...*

- **Trim the lawns and shrubs.**
- **Paint the front entrance,** and put a couple of pots of geraniums by the door.
- **Make sure the porch light and the bell** are in working order.
- **Clean the house thoroughly,** and keep the windows clean. If this isn't your forte, hire a cleaning service.
- **If rooms are even the slightest bit cluttered,** move out some of the furniture.
- **No matter what you have in your closets,** take at least half of it out. Remove at least half of what you have on your kitchen counter.
- **Tighten any loose knobs or faucets.**

And, before the agent shows the house, be sure you...

- **Close the garage door.**
- **Park the kids and the pets with a neighbor.**
- **Put away the kids' toys.**
- **Remove all conspicuous personal items** such as awards, souvenirs and religious items. (They might make you more interesting, but not the house.)
- **Turn on all the lights and open all the curtains.** *Exception:* Leave the curtains drawn if the window looks out on a used-car lot.
- **If there's a smoker in the house,** remove ashtrays and all other evidence of tobacco.
- **Use an air freshener if the house doesn't smell fresh.** But don't bother if there's a nice cooking aroma coming from the kitchen.
- **Turn off appliances.** It's okay, however, to have very soft music playing in the background.

How to Have a Successful Garage Sale

Monica Rix-Paxson, coauthor of *The Fabulous Money Making Garage Sale Kit* (Sourcebooks, Inc).

The most profitable garage sales are the ones with the most merchandise. Tables should be laden with goods. Lots of clothes should be hanging on racks. Boxes to rummage through should be everywhere.

Suggestion: Get your friends and neighbors to join in the fun and be cosellers—and coworkers. Tell them to bring over any and all of their recyclable household goods and turn the garage sale into a big event—so everyone makes money …and has a good time, too.

Once you've interested your friends and neighbors, the next step is to start planning and organizing. A garage sale requires preparation and creativity, but your efforts will pay big dividends.

Start by setting up a schedule of activities that begins at least two weeks before the first bargain hunter arrives—and preferably four weeks before—and ends the day after you make your final sale.

TWO TO FOUR WEEKS BEFORE

•**Select a date** (and rain date) for the sale. Do not schedule the sale on a holiday weekend.

•**Call Town Hall** and find out if you need a permit.

•**Warn your immediate neighbors** so they have time to put up "no parking" signs on their property if they want to or put their cars in their garages to provide more parking.

•**Invite cosellers and assign them their own specific price tag** (red, blue, green, etc.) to be hung on their merchandise for easy record-keeping.

ONE WEEK BEFORE THE SALE

•**Schedule friends and family to keep an eye on things.**

•**Write and submit classified ads to your local newspaper and radio station.** Don't forget to put notices up around town, too. Use index cards or flyers and post them in supermarkets, libraries, etc.

•**Design garage sale signs and decide what street corners they'll go on.** Use large construction paper. Tape signs to telephone poles and trees with arrows pointing people in the right direction. Put some signs on the main road and some at intersections.

•**Decide if unsold merchandise will be taken back** or find a charitable organization that will pick up unsold goods.

•**Plan lunch for helpers and cosellers.**

THREE DAYS BEFORE THE SALE

•**Arrange for cosellers to bring their own tables and racks,** as well as bags and boxes for buyers to use to take merchandise home.

•**Price items intended for sale,** clean them, make minor repairs and tag them.

•**Create colorful banners to hang over displays**—Toys! Kitchen! Bath!

•**Go to the stationery store and buy cashier-station materials,** like receipts, a cash box, a hand calculator, etc.

•**Make name tags for cosellers and helpers.**

•**Buy enough plastic cups,** coffee, cream and sugar to be able to hand a cup to browsers.

•**Rig a small dressing room in the garage** so people can try things on.

ONE DAY BEFORE THE SALE

•**Review cashier procedures** and give helpers their assignments and schedules.

•**Have $50 in change in a cash box:** 15 $1 bills, four $5 bills, one $10 bill and $5 in change.

•**Make an arrangement for your pets to be out of sight and sound.**

•**Put garage sale signs around the area.**

•**Arrange merchandise by hanging clothes on racks,** having $10, $5, $1 and $.50 tables and boxes for rummaging clearly marked in advance with what is contained inside of them.

•**Place a "sale begins at 9 o'clock" sign on your door to discourage early birds,** but expect an onslaught by 9.

DAY OF THE SALE

•**Put on the coffee at 8 am.**

•**Have cosellers and helpers take up their positions.**

•**Lock the house or rooms where the sale is not taking place.**

•**Open for business.**

•**Periodically remove extra cash from the cash box.**

AFTER THE SALE

•**Count the money!**

•**Distribute the proceeds to the various cosellers.**

- **Return anything borrowed.**
- **Box up goods for return.**
- **Remove garage sale signs.**
- **Thank everyone and congratulate yourself!**

A garage sale is a shared experience that is always a lot of work, but potentially also a great deal of fun and enjoyment.

Great Products to Combat Clutter

Debbie Gilster, president and organizing consultant, Center for Productivity, Laguna Niguel, California. *http://centerforproductivity.com*

I t's a cinch to organize your home and office when everything has a place. *Try these quick and easy organizing solutions…*

COMPUTER SOFTWARE

•**Kiplinger's Taming the Paper Tiger.** This program makes paper files easy to find. To use, number each file. Then enter their names, locations and identifying keywords into the database. An Internet-like search engine determines the location of any item in seconds. Also use it to organize CDs, wines, videos, etc. *Features:* Printable reports…"to do" lists…label printer. The Monticello Corporation, 866-701-1561. $50/yr. *www.thepapertiger.com*

UNDER-BED STORAGE

•**Bed riser.** Works with all angle-iron bed frames to raise the height of any box spring and mattress by up to 10 inches. *Result:* Plenty of under-bed storage space. Stacks & Stacks. 800-761-5222. $10.99–$79.99. *www.stacksandstacks.com*

GARAGE STORAGE

•**Interchange modular wall storage system.** Sturdy mounting on a wall to hold any of 11 interchangeable racks, hooks and hangers that lock securely in place. *Including:* Tool hanger, utility hooks, three-tier trays, vertical and horizontal bike hooks, cord wrap, hose rack, catch-all basket. Racor Home Stor-

age Products, 800-783-7725. $8 to $49.99 per piece. *www.racorstoragesolutions.com*

ADJUSTABLE DRAWER DIVIDERS

•**Drawer organizers.** Sturdy clear or white plastic tabs are easily cut to size to create drawer dividers in any configuration—just score with a knife and snap. Use for organizing kitchen utensils, clothing, jewelry, etc. Available in 1″, 2″, 3″ and 4″ heights. Lifestyle Systems, 800-955-3383. $10 to $24.95 per drawer, depending on height. *www.lifestylesystems.com*

Building A Tennis Court

Ray Babij, tennis-court builder, Remsenberg, New York.

T here are four types of tennis courts… clay, Har-Tru (pulverized green stone with a gypsum binder), asphalt and concrete. Clay and Har-Tru are soft and need daily maintenance. Asphalt and concrete are hard courts that require little upkeep.

•**Choosing the right court.** Soil and rock conditions can dictate the best type for your yard as much as your playing preference. Sandy soil with good drainage makes an ideal base for any kind of court. Heavy clay soil holds an all-weather court easily but requires additional excavation and filling for a soft court. Rocky areas may need blasting to create a proper base for any kind of court.

•**Construction time.** A tennis court needs time to settle, particularly the hard surfaces (asphalt and concrete) that might crack if the base were to heave. In the northern part of the country, where winters are severe, the ideal building schedule for hard courts is to excavate in the fall, let the base settle over the winter and finish the surfacing in the late spring or early summer. With soft courts, settling is less of a problem because cracks can be filled in with more clay or Har-Tru. A soft court can be built in six to eight weeks, with three weeks for settling.

• **Zoning and permits.** Property owners must provide an up-to-date survey of their property and be sure that the proposed court fits within the setback requirements—or get zoning variances if necessary. Contractors obtain the building permits. Many communities require fencing.

• **Costs.** Prices vary considerably from one part of the country to another. Special excavating problems create only one of the price variables. In general, however, a clay court with sprinkler system and fencing is less expensive than a similar Har-Tru court. All-weather courts (asphalt in the East, concrete in the West) are the least expensive of all.

• **Maintenance.** Soft courts must be swept and relined daily, sprinkled and rolled periodically and refurbished annually (or more often in climates where they get year-round use). Hard courts must be resurfaced every five to seven years. Many builders offer maintenance-service contracts.

Home tennis courts require much more space than is commonly believed. While the actual playing area of a court is relatively small (36 by 78 feet), adding the out-of-bounds areas pushes the total required to 60 by 120 feet, about one-sixth of an acre.

Safer Home Chemicals

Combustible liquids—gasoline, kerosene for backyard torches and charcoal lighter fluid—cause more deaths and injuries than all other summer chemicals combined. *Trap:* The combustible liquid could spill near someone who is smoking or near an open flame and ignite.

Another way people get hurt is by adding an extra dose of lighter fluid to boost an already lit fire. *Result:* The can may explode, scattering burning lighter fluid all over. *Recommended:* Put plenty of lighter fluid on the first time. If the fire doesn't catch, douse the whole thing with water and start over with fresh charcoal.

Or better yet, buy charcoal that doesn't require lighter fluid.

Paint. In the warm summer months, many people paint or varnish furniture, decks, etc. *Caution:* If the label says "use with adequate ventilation," do the project outdoors. Opening windows and doors in the house does not provide enough ventilation. If you can't take the project outdoors (you're painting a room, for instance), use water-based paint, which doesn't require as much ventilation during use.

Jay Young, chemical health and safety consultant in Silver Spring, Maryland.

Keeping Your Home Safe

A multipurpose dry chemical unit is the best home fire extinguisher. Check the label to see what kinds of fires it's effective against. It should cover Class A (ordinary combustibles like wood and cloth), Class B (gases, greases, flammable liquids) and Class C (electrical fires).

Smoke detectors work best in a two-unit system. Place an ionization detector in the hallway outside your bedroom for a quick alert on a racing fire. Then install a photoelectric model downstairs in the general living area or the main stairway that will detect smoke from smoldering upholstery or rugs.

Aluminum wiring, which was used in two million homes and apartments built between 1965 and 1973, has caused more than 500 home fires in the past 10 years. *To check:* Ask the original electrical contractor, or look for an "AL" stamp on exposed wires in your basement. If you do have aluminum wiring, a qualified electrician may be able to make your house safe at a moderate cost. Never attempt repairs (even simple ones) on your own.

Consumer Adviser, Reader's Digest Association Inc., Pleasantville, New York.

Oil- vs. Water-Based Paint

Neil Janovic, whose grandfather founded the paint and paper company Janovic Plaza Inc. in 1888 in New York City.

Water-based paint has many distinct advantages over oil-based paint. It dries in less than an hour, has no paintlike odor, doesn't show brush or roller lap marks as distinctly and makes for an easy soap-and-water cleanup. It also wears longer, is washable and holds color best. *Overwhelming choice:* Water-based paint (also known as latex or acrylic).

Stick with high-quality oil-based paint if the exterior surface is already painted with several coats of oil-based paint (alkyd resin). *Reason:* Latex expands and contracts more easily than oil does during the freeze-thaw weather cycle. This action may pull off any underlayers of oil-based paint that aren't locked onto the surface.

Latex exterior paints are ideal for exterior surfaces. *Why:* They allow the surface to breathe. And their flexibility during the freeze-thaw cycle enables them to adhere to the surface better. Latex house paint color has superior resistance to bleaching and fading. (If you have latex over an oil-based layer that is holding, continue with water-based paint.)

When painting over an already painted exterior surface, first rough up the gloss with sandpaper or a wire brush. This gives the smooth surface some tooth, on which the fresh paint can grip and bond. Make sure all chalking surfaces are clean and sound.

Before painting, scrub under the eaves and in protected spots with a solution of detergent and water. *Reason:* Salts from the air collect in these areas that are not washed clean by rain. Exterior paints won't hold.

Use latex paint for any interior jobs, even if it means covering existing oil-based layers. *Exception:* When there is a water-soluble substance underneath the oil. The water in latex softens these substances, which leads to peeling. Enough coats of oil-based paint usually shield the underlying calcimines or sizers from the water in the latex. *Test:* Paint a small area with latex. If there is no peeling within a couple of hours, continue with latex.

Painting Trouble Areas

Often, paint peels in one section of a wall or ceiling. *Causes...*

• **A leak making its way through the walls** from a plumbing break or an opening to the outside.

• **The plaster is giving out in that area** due to age or wear and tear.

• **The paint layers may be so thick** that the force of gravity plus vibrations from outside make the paint pop and peel in the weakest spot.

Fix: If it's a leak, find and correct it. Otherwise, remove as much of the existing paint as you can. Scrape away any loose, damp or crumbling plaster. Spackle and smooth the area. Prime and paint it.

For real problem areas: Spackle, then paste on a thin layer of canvas. Apply it as though it were wallpaper. Smooth it out so it becomes part of the surface. Then prime and paint it.

Best Color to Paint A House

Yellow houses have the most "curb appeal" and sell faster than those of any other color. Most people associate yellow with sunshine, optimism and warmth.

Leatrice Eiseman, color consultant and educator in Tarzana, California. *www.colorexpert.com.*

Painting Pads

Originally made for coating wood shingles, pads are coming into general use. They are now available in a number of sizes and shapes for jobs such as edges and window trim or entire walls, indoors and out. Once the basic stroke has been mastered, most home painters find pads faster and neater than either rollers or brushes. Made of nylon fiber pile, pads leave a smoother finish than other applicators with both oil- and water-based paints.

How to Avert Structural Damage

Repair cracks in concrete as soon as you spot them. Look for them in the warm months, before the troublesome weather hits. The action of water, especially as it freezes and thaws, can quickly turn a small crack into a major one, possibly even resulting in structural damage.

Essential: First investigate and correct the cause of the crack.

New Shelter

Protection from Storm Windows

See-through plastic windowpanes guard against breakage in hazardous locations such as storm and garage doors and basement windows. Use acrylic plastic one-eighth inch or one-quarter inch thick. Cut with a power saw fitted with a fine-toothed blade. Or cut by hand, using a scribing tool.

Roof Longevity

Slate or tiled roofs should last a human lifetime, as should terne (lead and tin) or copper sheeting. Asphalt shingles should hold out for 15 to 25 years.

Good precaution: After a roof is 15 years old, have a roofer inspect and repair it annually.

Modernize Your Home Heating

Heating systems that are more than a few years old need modernizing.

Gas: Install a stack damper and electric ignition to produce an average gas savings of 10%.

Oil: Older systems don't have a flame-retention head burner, which saves 15%.

Both systems pay for themselves in about three years.

Eleven Ways to Conserve Home Heating Fuel

Frank C. Capozza, former manager of Frank's Fuel.

There are certain things you can do to save money on heating. *Try these simple conservation ideas…*

1. Buy a new heating system. *Reason:* Systems more than 20 years old operate in the 65% efficiency range. New models average at least 80% efficiency. Increasing efficiency from 65% to 80% saves about $765 a year in a house that uses 1,700 gallons of heating fuel at $3 a gallon.

2. Service heating systems annually. *Point:* A 2% increase in efficiency will pay for tests and adjustments.

3. Reduce the hot-water heater setting to 120°F or lower. (Average settings range from 140° to 160°F.)

4. Minimize use of hot-water appliances.

5. Install automatic flue stack dampers on hot-water and steam-heating systems. They conserve heat by closing the flue pipe when the oil burner is off. *Potential savings:* 5% to 10%.

6. Install clock thermostats that automatically reduce heat at certain times during the day or night. *Potential savings:* If the clock thermostat is set to reduce the temperature from 70°F to 65°F for 16 hours a day, heating bills will drop 10%.

7. Use spot heating when needed.

8. Use draperies, shades and blinds to prevent heat from escaping. Minimize use of exhaust fans.

9. Insulate.

10. Use trees and shrubs as windbreakers.

11. Use humidifiers. *Reason:* Rooms with less than 30% humidity will feel chilly even when well-heated.

Heating and cooling use 70% of the energy. Water heating takes 20%. Cooking, refrigeration, lighting, etc., total only 10% of use.

Weather Stripping

To test the airtightness of a window or door, move a lighted candle along its frame. If there is enough draft to make the flame dance, then caulk or weather-strip it. For a door, add weather stripping if you can slip a quarter underneath it.

Is Home Siding Economical?

New home siding of vinyl, aluminum or steel beautifies but does not save energy. The FTC has warned about advertising that claims adding siding helps lower fuel bills. *Exception:* Some insulating effect occurs when the siding is installed over sheets of formed plastic.

Special Telephone Secret

Carl Oppedahl, New York City–based lawyer and author of *The Telephone Book* (Weber Systems).

A network interface is a special telephone jack that allows you to determine which wires are faulty when your phone goes dead—outside wires, which the phone company must repair at no cost to you, or inside, which the phone company may charge to repair.

Installation: If you want to install your own interface, buy the materials at a phone-supply store. If your phone repairman installs it, you must purchase the materials from him. *Tip:* To avoid charges for the visit, have the repairman install the interface when he is at your house doing other phone work.

How the interface works: When your wires go dead, simply plug a phone into the network interface. If you hear a dial tone, the problem is in the wiring on your premises. If there is no dial tone, something is wrong with the wires leading to your house. *Extra benefit:* If the problem is internal, the phone plugged into the interface will provide phone service until repairs are made.

Cost advantages: You are no longer susceptible to billing tricks of the phone company.

Example of such a trick: If you don't pay inside wire maintenance fees, phone repairmen often claim that the problem is in the wiring on your premises—when it's really in outside wiring. *Result:* The phone company charges you for the repairs and visit, which should be free.

Also: You can repair an internal problem yourself or have an electrician do the job, which is often cheaper than the phone company's work. And you no longer have to pay inside wire-maintenance fees, which cover the cost of any service call the phone company makes on the wires inside your house. Since these wires almost never break, you can save up to $50/year for maintenance you don't need.

Capping the Chimney Flue

Chimney problem—warm air leaks out, and birds nest in the flue. *Solution:* Install a chimney cap, which closes off the chimney flue at the roof. A long chain hangs down into the fireplace. To open the flue, pull the chain to release the spring-loaded cover. A tug on the chain closes the flue.

at a distance, and radiator covers should have ample holes at the top and bottom.

Home Energy Hints

Try these simple solutions to save money and energy…

• **Draft resistance.** Before winter sets in, trace drafts. A ¹⁄₁₆-inch crack beneath a door lets out as much warm air as a 4-inch-square hole in the wall. Check with your utility about local energy audit services to help find leaks and stop heat losses.

• **Cut kitchen heat loss by covering the range hood's vent** (when not in use, of course). Use a piece of ¾-inch Styrofoam encased in aluminum foil. Attach it to the hood with springs, or by fastening temporarily with duct tape.

• **Solar protection.** Keep insurance in mind when converting a home to even partial solar power. *Among the hazards:* Rooftop storage tanks that are too heavy for present structural supports…vulnerability of collection panels to hail, lightning, falling objects and vandalism …potential bursting of pipes if liquid freezes in heat-transfer systems.

Do-It-Yourself Heat Saver

Homemade reflectors placed behind your radiators provide more efficient heating.

Directions: Cut radiator-size sheets of quarter-inch-thick Styrofoam and cover one side with heavy-gauge aluminum foil. (Tape or staple it into place on the reverse side.) Slip the reflector behind the radiator, with the foil facing the room. The Styrofoam keeps the cold wall from absorbing heat, and the foil directs the heat out into the room.

For best circulation of radiator heat, keep the radiator fins well dusted and make sure that there is a free flow of air above and below the radiator. Drapes and furniture should be

Cooling the House Without Air-Conditioning

John A. Constance, licensed engineer specializing in industrial ventilation, Newtown, Pennsylvania.

Ventilating fans can cool an entire house—or a single room—at a fraction (about 10%) of the cost of air-conditioning. The trick is knowing how to use them.

Unlike oscillating fans, which simply move air around, ventilating fans exhaust hot air while pulling in cooler air. You control the source of the cooler air by manipulating windows. During the day, for example, downstairs windows on the shady northern or eastern side of the house are most likely to provide cool air. All other windows should be closed and shaded from direct sun with blinds and drapes.

At night, lower-floor windows can be shut for security while upstairs windows provide cool air. The very motion of air, like a light breeze, has a cooling effect.

TYPES OF VENTILATING FANS

• **Attic fans** are permanent installations above the upper floor. They are powerful enough to cool the entire house. The opening to the outside must be as large as the fan-blade frame in order to handle the air flow properly. Louvers, bird screening and (particularly) insect screening all reduce the exhaust capacity of a fan. A doorway or other opening must allow the fan to pull cool air directly up from the rest of the house. Direct-connected fans are quieter than belt-driven fans. Some attic fans have thermometers that automatically turn them off and on when the attic temperature reaches a certain degree of heat.

• **Window fans** have adjustable screw-on panels to fit different window sizes. Less powerful than attic fans, they serve more limited spaces.

• **Box fans** are portable and can be moved from room to room to cool smaller areas.

PICKING THE RIGHT-SIZE FAN

Ventilating fans are rated by the cubic feet per minute (CFM) of air that they can exhaust. For effective cooling, engineers recommend an air-change rate of 20 per hour (the entire volume of air in the area to be cooled is changed 20 times every 60 minutes). To determine the required CFM rating for a particular room, calculate its volume in cubic feet. Then multiply this figure by 20/60 (⅓). *Example:* A room 20 feet by 15 feet with an eight-foot ceiling contains 2,400 cubic feet of air. This multiplied by ⅓ gives a CFM rating of 800 for a proper-size fan.

The CFM rating of an attic fan is determined in the same way. Total the cubic feet of the rooms and hallways you want cooled before multiplying by ⅓.

Air-Conditioning Secrets

John A. Constance, licensed engineer specializing in industrial ventilation, Newtown, Pennsylvania.

Room air conditioners mounted in a window or through the wall are ideal for keeping small, comfortable havens cool against the worst of summer's hot spells. They can be more economical than central air conditioning because they are flexible—you cool only the rooms you are using. But even a single unit can be expensive.

Buy for economy. Tailor the size of the unit to the room. Oversize air conditioners cool a room so fast that they don't have time to dehumidify the air properly. Slightly undersize units are more efficient (and cost less to begin with). Check the energy-efficiency tags on different models for lowest operating costs.

To keep a room cool with minimum use of the air conditioner…

• **Limit the use of the air conditioner in the "open vent" setting**—it brings in hot outside air that the machine must work hard to keep cooling.

• **Protect the room from the direct heat of the sun** with awnings, drapes or blinds.

• **Close off air-conditioned rooms.**

• **Turn off unnecessary lights**—they add extra heat (fluorescent lights are coolest).

• **Turn off the unit if you will be out of the room** for more than 30 minutes.

• **Service room air conditioners annually to keep them efficient.** Replace filters, keep condensers clean and lubricate the moving parts.

Buying an air conditioner that is too large is uneconomical. *To find the most efficient machine:* Divide the BTU rating by the watts rating (also on the label). If the resulting number (the energy-efficiency rating) is eight or more, it won't run up your electric bill unduly.

Compare prices. Energy-efficient air conditioners cost more initially. Where use is heavy (the South) or electric rates are high (the Northeast), the price difference is probably worth the investment. *Bonus:* Energy-efficient air conditioners cool rooms faster.

Supplement central air-conditioning with a room air conditioner in the most-used room. Greatest saving is when only one person is home and the excess cooling isn't needed.

Home Emergency Checklist

Vital information about the house should be known by everyone in the family in case of emergency.

Key items: The location of the fuse box or circuit-breaker panel, placement of the main shutoff valves for the water and gas lines and the location of the septic tank or the line to the main sewer.

Also keep easily accessible: Records of the brands, ages and model numbers of the stove, refrigerator, freezer, dishwasher, furnace, washer and dryer.

Woman's Day

Visible Address May Save Your Life

A clear address outside your house helps emergency vehicles (and visitors) locate you easily. *Complaint of firefighters and ambulance drivers:* Most street addresses are difficult to find and hard to read.

Solution: Put large figures where they are easily read from the center of the street at night during poor visibility.

Buying a Burglar Alarm

Home alarm systems, once mainly for the rich, are coming into widespread use. *Reason:* Locks aren't deterring burglars. Recent FBI figures show that 82% of the time, illegal entrance is gained through home doors, most often the front door.

Burglars just break open the door with their shoulders. Faced with a deadbolt or double lock, the burglar will use a heavy tool to take out the frame.

Best type of alarm: One that sounds off (not a silent alarm), so that the burglar is aware of it and alarm central (a security-company office or the local police) is alerted. This makes sense, since most burglars are youngsters ages 12 to 24 who live within an eight-block radius of the target.

Select a system with sensors on vulnerable doors and windows. The inexpensive alarm promoted at many electronics stores is not worthwhile. Good systems need a complex electrical tie-in in the basement as well as a control panel installed away from prying eyes and little children. Good systems can also switch on lights and TV sets and alert alarm central by automatic telephone dialing or a radio signal.

Have a secondary line of defense. This can be a few thin electronic pressure pads under rugs in high-traffic areas, or strategically placed photoelectric cells.

Choose a reputable, well-tested system. Two brand names are ADT and Honeywell.

Drawbacks: The greatest is the danger of continual false alarms. The police may ticket you if the family is to blame. Also, an alarm system needs regular testing and a routine for setting at night or when you're away.

Alarm systems can provide a false sense of security. The homeowner may not take all necessary precautions with locks or may leave the garage door partially open.

Secrets of a Professional Burglar

From my own experience as a successful burglar, and also from talking with hundreds of fellow inmates in prison for burglary, I've concluded that burglary is a psychological game. The only real deterrent is the realization that there is immediate danger to him, the burglar. Locks don't do this. Alarms don't do it. Hardcore doors don't do it. Only mind games really work. I'm not against good locks, sturdy doors and alarm systems. But if you rely 70% on mind games and 30% on hardware, you'll do much better in the end.

If a burglar sees warning signs, no matter how outlandish, on your house, he will think twice before breaking in. These signs should be handwritten, in large, clear print, on six-inch by eight-inch cards posted above each doorknob. Don't put them on the street or in your yard where passersby can see them. You don't want to give a burglar a reason to case your place and find out they are not true. You can make up your own wording. Just be sure the signs look fresh and new. *Some suggestions...*

• **"Danger: Extremely vicious,** barkless German Doberman." In his nervous frame of mind, a burglar probably isn't going to wonder if there is such a thing. He won't want to take the chance.

• **"Knock all you want. We don't answer the door."** Most burglars check to see if anyone's home before breaking in. About 95% of those questioned said they'd pass up a house with that sign.

• **"Carpenter: Please do not enter through this door.** My son's three rattlesnakes have gotten out of the cage and we've closed them off in this room until he returns, hopefully in a few days. We're sorry for this inconvenience, but we don't want anyone else to get bitten. The first is still in the hospital."

• **"Please stop!** We've already been forced to kill one burglar who was trying to get in while we weren't home. Please don't become the second." Like the barkless dog sign, this one seems outlandish. But a jittery burglar isn't going to stick around thinking up ways you could kill him while you're not home.

• **"Attack dogs trained and sold here."** Again, 95% said they'd be gone like a shot if they saw this sign. *Suggestion:* Have one engraved, and post it on your front door (so it can't be seen from the street).

Leave extremely large bones and two-foot-wide dog dishes near all entrances. Someone who's up to no good will think a very large dog lives there.

Paste stickers on the windows indicating that you have an alarm system. *Try motion-detector alarms:* "This building is equipped with laser-type motion-detector devices. Bodily movement inside will set off audible or silent alarm." Some 85% of inmates questioned said they'd pass up a house with this notice. *Also:* Paste alarm foil along windows. Put suction cups on the inside of windows and alarm-type bells on the outside walls.

Put fine gravel in your driveway or in gardens surrounding the house. This makes a lot of noise that burglars won't want to chance.

When you go away on vacation, don't tell anybody except the local police. Ask a neighbor to pick up your mail and newspapers and occasionally empty a small can of junk into your trash can. Close all shades, blinds or curtains. Leave one or two radios on. Have your outside lights on a light-sensitive switch and inside ones on an alternating timer. Put up your deterrent signs.

Buy an air horn (the kind small-boat owners use). If someone breaks in while you're at home, go to the opposite window and squeeze the horn. These horns can be heard for a mile over water. Everyone said this tactic would scare them off.

COMMON LOCK AND ALARM MISTAKES

• **Putting a deadbolt or other expensive lock** on a flimsy door that can be kicked in. *Also:* Thinking that this lock will do the trick. The burglar simply uses a bigger crowbar.

• **Not locking the door when you're home.**

• **Positioning a lock on a door with a glass window** in such a way that if the window is broken, the burglar can reach in and unlock the door.

• **Installing the burglar alarm on/off switch outside the house,** not inside it.

• **Forgetting to turn on your alarm.**

SOME BURGLAR-SURVEY RESULTS

• **85% were deterred by hearing a TV or radio in the house.**

• **75% were more likely to go through windows than doors.** (Sliding glass doors are easier to open than wooden ones.) *Remedy:* Storm windows. None of the burglars surveyed would bother with these at all.

• **85% cased out a house before hitting it.** *Recommended:* If you see a stranger hanging around, call the police.

• **Only 20% picked locks or tried to pick them.** *Why:* It takes too much skill. There are so many faster ways into a house.

• **63% cut the phone lines before entering.** *Remedy:* Put up a sign that says the police will be notified automatically if the phone lines are cut.

• **65% said that a large,** unfriendly dog would scare them away. *Most frightening:* Dobermans.

• **80% looked in garage windows to see if a homeowner's car was there.** *Remedy:* Cover your garage windows.

• **50% said that neighborhood security guards didn't deter them.**

• **72% made their entrance from the back.**

• **56% continued to burglarize if they were already inside** when they realized that people were at home but asleep.

Recommendations of A Master Locksmith

Menasche Sofer, All-Over Locksmith, Inc., New York City.

Traditional wisdom says there's no point in putting a good lock on a flimsy door. This is not true. In most cases you must prove forcible entry to collect insurance. If you have a poor lock, your cylinder can be picked in seconds. You're inviting your insurance company to give you a hard time.

THE BEST STRATEGIES

• **If you have a wooden door, get what the industry calls a police lock.** This is a brace lock with a bar that goes from the lock into the floor about 30 inches away from the base of the door. It can be locked from the inside, but you can get out easily in an emergency. *Also:* Get a police lock if your door frame is weak. It keeps the door from giving because of the brace in the floor. Even the best regular locks won't protect you if the whole frame gives.

• **If you're buying a door,** buy a metal flush door without panels and get an equally strong frame to match it. *What makes a good frame:* A hollow metal construction, same as the door.

• **On a metal door,** I like a Segal lock on the inside and a Medeco on the outside with a Medeco BodyGuard cylinder guard plate. If it's a tubular lock, get Medeco's Maxum. It gives you the option of a key on the inside, and you don't need a guard plate.

• **If your door opens out instead of in,** get a double-bar lock—one that extends horizontally on each side. With a door that opens out, the hinges are often exposed on the outside, allowing a burglar to remove the door from its hinges. With a double-bar lock he can't pull the door out.

OTHER IMPORTANT DEVICES

• **Plates.** Pulling out the lock cylinder is the burglar's easiest and most effective way of getting in. Most people put a plate over their lock and think that will take care of it. But most plates have bolts that are exposed on the outside. With a hollow metal door, the burglar can pull that plate away from the door with a wedge and simply cut the bolts. If the head of the bolt is exposed, he can pull it out slightly with pliers and snap it right off. *Remedy:* Medeco's BodyGuard. A cylinder and plate combination, it's a drill-resistant, one-piece unit with no exposed bolts a sleeve to prevent burglars from chiseling the bolts and a hardened plate to protect the keyhole.

• **Jimmy bars.** Don't bother with them. They're psychological protection only. If you have a metal door, a good lock is sufficient protection. With a metal door, we recommend a jimmy bar only if the door has been damaged through a forcible break-in and is separated from the frame. In this case, the bar will straighten out the door and hide some of the light shining through. If you have a wooden door, a jimmy bar can actually help a burglar by giving him leverage. He can put a crowbar up against it, dig into the wood and break through the door.

• **Peepholes.** Get one that's as small as possible. Large peepholes use a one-way mirror that doesn't permit you to see around corners. And if someone hits that mirror while you're looking through, it could damage your eye. Small peepholes use a double lens, making it possible to see around corners. And if the small peephole is knocked off the door, it won't benefit the burglar. If a big one is knocked off, it creates a weakness in your security. *Recommended:* If you already have a large peephole, remove it. Have the locksmith bolt two plates on the door, with a smaller hole in the center to accommodate a small peephole.

• **Closets.** Let's say you want to protect a closet—not necessarily against burglars but against someone who might have a key to your house or apartment. Locking the closet isn't sufficient because most closets open out and have hinges on the outside, making it easy to remove the door. *Remedy:* A door pin. This involves putting the pin on the hinge side of the door and through a receiving hole in the frame. Anyone who cut the hinges off or removed the pins couldn't lift the door out.

• **Window locks.** The best window locks use a key, which makes them difficult to manipulate from the outside. Without a key, almost any window lock is vulnerable. *Best:* Try one with a heavy pin, which allows you to drill holes for either complete locking or three- or six-inch ventilation.

• **Window gates.** In New York and other cities, the fire laws prohibit window gates that lock with a key. *Remedy:* Gates with keyless locks. They allow you to get out easily, but a burglar can't put his hand through the gate to open it.

CHOOSING A LOCKSMITH

Go to locksmiths' shops to size them up. Make sure the store is devoted exclusively to the locksmith business and isn't just doing locksmithing on the side. Ask to see the locksmith's license if it's not displayed. There are a lot of unlicensed people doing business illegally. *Best:* Locksmiths who belong to an association—they keep up with the latest developments. Look for a sticker in the window indicating membership in a local or national locksmiths' association.

Best Place in Your House To Hide Valuables

John Littlejohn, manager of Abbey Locksmith, Inc., New York City.

Even if you have a safe, you still need a good place to hide for the safe key or combination. Obviously, it should not be hidden anywhere near the safe. And if you don't have a safe, you should hide your jewelry and other valuables where they won't be found.

RECOMMENDATIONS

• **Don't hide things in any piece of furniture that has drawers.** Drawers are the first place burglars will ransack.

• **Don't hide anything in the bedroom.** Thieves tend to be most thorough in checking out bedrooms. Find hiding places in the attic, basement or other out-of-the-way areas. *Best:* The kitchen. In 90% of burglaries the kitchen is untouched.

• **Don't be paranoid.** If you have thought up a good location, relax. A burglar can't read your mind.

GOOD HIDING PLACES

• **Inside the phony wall switches** and generic label cans sold by mail-order houses.

• **In a book, if you have a large book collection.** So you don't forget which book you chose, use the title to remind you (for example, *The Golden Treasury of Science Fiction*). Or buy a hollowed-out book for this purpose.

• **Inside zippered couch cushions.**

• **In the back of a console TV or stereo speakers** (thieves usually steal only receivers, not speakers) or in the type of speakers that look like books.

• **Under the dirt in a plant.** Put nonpaper valuables in a plastic bag and bury them.

• **Under the carpet.**

• **In between stacks of pots in the kitchen** or wrapped up and labeled as food in the refrigerator or freezer.

The best hiding places for household valuables are those that look completely innocent and, preferably, would be inconvenient to take apart. *Examples:* Inside an old, out-of-order TV or vacuum cleaner in the basement. In a pile of scrap wood beneath the workbench. In the middle of a sack of grass seed.

How to Hide Your Valuables by Linda C. Cain (Beehive Communications). Limited availability.

Remember it's a crime!

Biggest House-Fire Danger Spot

Not the kitchen, as commonly believed, but the living room. Fires there account for the largest number of deaths year after year. *Safety measure:* Install a smoke detector in the living room.

Journal of American Insurance

One smoke alarm isn't enough. *Recommended:* An alarm on each level of your home and in each bedroom.

International Association of Fire Chiefs, Fairfax, Virginia.

Easy Ways to Do Hard Things

Keep aluminum windows and doors in working order with simple maintenance procedures when you switch from screens to storm panels. *You should:* (1) Clean the channels where window panels slide up and down with the crevice nozzle of the vacuum cleaner or a tiny stiff brush. Spray with silicone lubricant. (2) Spray stiff spring locks with a moisture-displacing penetrating lubricant (WD-40, for example). (3) To prevent oxidation and pitting on frames, scrub with a detergent solution, rinse and coat with a good grade of automobile wax.

•**To unclog a sink drain,** first place a basin below the trap (the U-shaped drainpipe beneath the sink); the basin will catch water that runs from the trap. Then use a wrench to unscrew the plug at the bottom of the trap. Slip on a rubber glove and move a finger into the open trap to loosen any blockages. To complete the job, run a stiff wire into either side of the trap. Screw in the plug and tighten it with the wrench.

•**Sluggish sink drains respond to one of these treatments:** Remove the strainer. Pour several pots of boiling-hot water down the drain. Then run hot tap water down the drain for a couple of minutes. If this does not bring results, pour one cup of baking soda into the drain. Follow this with one cup of vinegar.

Cover the drain opening tightly for 20 minutes. Then run hot tap water down the drain. *Last resort:* A commercial preparation.

•**Prevent clogged drains by replacing the S-trap** in the drainpipe with a squeezable trap. One hard squeeze sends a drain block on its way. Available from hardware and plumbing-supply stores. Easily connected with a screwdriver.

•**To clean a burned pot,** first dampen it. Sprinkle baking soda on the charred area, and add a little vinegar. Let it stand for 20 minutes. The pot should then wash clean.

•**Alcohol stains on tabletops.** To remove white rings, rub gently in one direction with moistened cigar ash or superfine steel wool dipped in mineral oil.

•**Furniture scratches.** *For small blemishes:* Try toothpaste—its mild abrasive action is effective on minor scratches. *Deeper scratches or wide areas:* Use a blend stick, crayon, liquid shoe polish or paste boot polish. Apply toothpaste to even out the finish after coloring. Then wax with furniture polish and buff with a clean cloth.

•**Sticky drawers.** Rub the bottom rails with soap. If the rails are rough or worn, rub chalk on the drawer runners or sides or on the chest's rails or guides. Put the drawer back in and move it until it sticks. That spot will be marked by chalk. Sand or plane the sticky spot and then rub the area with soap.

•**Cutting down on dust.** Spray your home furnace filter with a no-wax dusting product that attracts and holds circulating particles. Then clean the filter regularly. Do the same with the air-conditioner filter.

•**Contact lenses lost in a carpet.** Place a nylon stocking over the nozzle of a vacuum cleaner and carefully vacuum the area. The lens will be pulled up onto the stocking.

Best Toilet Bowl Cleaner

In-tank toilet bowl cleaners containing calcium hypochlorite corrode the flushing mechanism. Moreover, these cleaners are of little use. All toilet bowls get dirty, and the best way to clean them is with a sponge or brush and a liquid cleaner.

Try a nonhypochlorite cleaner: Ty-D-Bol Blue is a good one.

How to Noiseproof Your Home

Noise intrusion is a constant and nagging problem in many buildings because of thin walls and badly insulated floors and ceilings. *Some solutions...*

• **Walls.** Hang sound-absorbing materials such as quilts, decorative rugs or blankets. *Note:* Cork board and heavy window draperies absorb sound within a room but do not help much with noise from outside. *Unique step:* Carpeted walls provide excellent sound-proofing. Some brands of carpet can be attached to the wall with adhesive. *Alternative:* Try a frame that can be attached to the wall. Insulation goes on the wall within the frame, and then a fabric is affixed to the frame.

• **Ceilings.** Acoustical tile may be applied directly to the ceiling with adhesive. *Best:* A dropped ceiling of acoustical tile with about six inches of insulation between the new and existing ceiling is a good bet.

• **Floors.** A thick plush carpet that is laid over a dense sponge-rubber padding works well. *Key:* The padding must be dense, at least three-eighths of an inch thick. Your foot should not press down to the floor when you step on the padding.

Versatile Vinegar

This safe, natural and inexpensive product is a handy thing to have around the house, aside from its obvious usefulness in the kitchen. It can be used as a cleanser and a deoxidizer, an antiseptic for minor first-aid needs or a fluid (three parts vinegar and one part water) that keeps windshields both ice- and frost-free.

Antique Furniture Care

Use a room humidifier when central heating is on. (Dryness causes cracks and splits.) Keep furniture away from heat sources such as radiators, working fireplaces and direct sunlight. (Excessive heat will make it warp.) Use a clear, hard wax once a year, but avoid liquid or spray waxes containing silicon, which damages wood. Don't worry about any tiny bumps or scratches; they're signs of authenticity.

Diversion

Top-Notch Home-Cleaning Secrets

Cheryl Mendelson, Esq., graduate of Harvard Law School and author of *Home Comforts: The Art & Science of Keeping House* (Scribner).

When my home was undergoing major renovations, I found myself with some knotty cleaning questions. I couldn't find effective information for removing many stains or getting all the different surfaces of my home as clean as I wanted.

For answers, I consulted manufacturers, private businesses and craftsmen around the country. *Here is what I learned...*

KITCHENS

- **Sweeping.** Use a broom with even nylon or synthetic bristles. It collects dirt better than corn brooms.

Start sweeping at the walls, and move dirt toward the center so you push it the shortest distance. Don't lift the broom high off the floor after a stroke—this flings dirt into the air.

Store brooms with the bristles up. Otherwise bristles break or bend.

- **Coffee or tea stains on china,** plastic and glassware. Mix one-eighth cup of regular chlorine bleach with one cup of water. Pour into the bottom of your dishwasher before starting the wash cycle.

Important: Make sure nothing aluminum or silver is in the machine—it can become discolored.

BATHROOMS

- **Hardened soap scum on tiles.** Coat the entire surface with undiluted liquid detergent, and allow it to dry overnight. Wet the surface and scrub with a stiff brush and scouring powder. Rinse and buff with a bath towel.

- **Nonslip treads on bathtub floor.** Try Naval Jelly or KRC-7, a porcelain and tile cleaner (both available at plumbing supply stores). These cleaners may remove mineral stains without eating away at the treads.

- **Rust around faucets and fixtures.** Use a powder containing oxalic acid, such as Bar Keeper's Friend or Zud (both available at hardware stores).

Important: Never mix these rust removers with chlorine bleach. The fumes are toxic.

- **Concentrate on the spots where fingerprints accumulate**—if you want to disinfect your bathroom in addition to just cleaning it.

Examples: Toilet handles, light switches and knobs on the shower door, medicine cabinet and door.

FURNITURE

- **Water rings on hardwood surfaces.** Try mildly abrasive substances, such as mayonnaise mixed with a bit of ashes or toothpaste. The secret is to rub gently for a long time—as long as 45 minutes—so you remove the stain without scratching the finish.

Afterward, wax the whole surface to even the finish. Use paste wax (sold at home centers and hardware stores). It is more protective than oils or liquid waxes.

- **Minor scratches on wood.** I use Old English Scratch Cover (sold at hardware stores). If in doubt about which color to use, start with a lighter color. Apply the product to your wiping cloth, not directly on the furniture.

- **Use the right dust rag.** Soft white flannel or cheesecloth is best because dust adheres to it so well. Dampen the cloth very slightly with water. For heirlooms and valuable antique woods, use distilled water to dampen rags. For carved furniture, china, ceramics, chandeliers and vases, use a small artist's paintbrush made from natural- or hog's-hair bristles.

UPHOLSTERY

- **Stains from eggs,** milk, chocolate. Rub with a solution of one tablespoon household ammonia and one-half cup of water.

- **Coffee, cola and beer stains.** Rub with a solution of one-third cup of white vinegar mixed with two-thirds cup of water. Avoid soap, which can set the stain permanently.

- **Ink stains.** Sponge with rubbing alcohol.

WALLS

- **Nonwashable wallpaper.** For grease stains, place an absorbent towel over the stain and cover it with an iron set at low for several seconds. For ink or pencil marks, try rubbing the wall with cleaning putty such as Absorene (available at home centers) or a wadded-up piece of fresh, soft, white bread.

- **Washable vinyl wallpaper.** For stubborn stains, such as crayon, tar or adhesives, use WD-40 (available in hardware stores).

- **Painted walls.** Mix a thick paste of baking soda and water. Dip your cloth in it, and rub marks very gently to remove fingerprints, crayon, etc.

CARPETS

- **Spills.** Use as little water as possible. Blot as much of the spill as possible with paper towels. Then, in a bowl, whip up a sudsy foam using water and mild detergent. For delicate carpets, I use Orvus WA Paste from Procter &

Gamble (available at veterinary stores or feed stores and on-line).

Dip your brush into the foam, not the water. Brush stain lightly, then wipe off excess foam with a clean cloth. Rinse with a 50/50 solution of white vinegar and water. Then rinse with plain warm water. Blot thoroughly.

• **Use a vacuum with low dust emissions.** If you have asthma or other allergies, consider investing in a vacuum with a HEPA filter. Miele vacuum cleaners, 800-843-7231, *www.miele usa.com.*

WOOD FLOORS

• **Scuffs and heel marks on hard-finish or urethane-type floors.** Dampen a cloth with a small amount of mineral spirits (available at hardware stores). Rub gently in the direction of the grain.

• **Oil or grease stains on natural-finish floors.** Saturate a cotton ball with hydrogen peroxide, and place over the stain for several minutes. Saturate a second cotton ball with ammonia, and place over the stain for several minutes. Repeat until the stain is removed. Let the area dry, then buff with a soft cloth.

COMPUTERS

• **Keyboards.** Try rubbing alcohol or degreaser sprays (available at electronics stores) to clean off the grime.

• **Computer screens.** Make sure screen is off. Use a slightly damp cloth. Avoid those special-purpose towelettes sold in office-supply stores. They leave a soapy residue.

When You Need An Exterminator And When You Don't

Tom Heffernan, president of the Ozane Exterminating Co., Brooklyn, New York.

Clifton Meloan, professor emeritus, Kansas State University, writing in *Science.*

Bug problems can usually be solved without an exterminator. *Keys:* Careful prevention techniques, basic supermarket products and apartment-building cooperation.

Roaches are persistent pests that are the bane of apartment dwellers. The problem is not that roaches are so difficult to kill but that the effort has to be made collectively, by every tenant in a particular building. Roaches cannot be exterminated effectively from an individual apartment. If one apartment has them, they'll quickly spread throughout the building.

Most landlords hire exterminating services that visit during daytime hours when most tenants are at work. They wind up spraying just a few apartments, which is totally ineffective. *Recommended...*

• **Apartment dwellers have to get together,** contact their landlord and arrange for all apartments to be exterminated at the same time. If the landlord is uncooperative, the Board of Health should be notified. If you live in a co-op, the co-op board should make arrangements for building extermination. *Best:* A superintendent or member of the building staff should perform the regular exterminations, since he can get into apartments at odd hours when the tenants are not at home. A professional exterminator should be called only as a backup, in case of a severe problem in a particular apartment.

• **Incinerators that no longer burn garbage are a major source of infestation in large buildings.** In an attempt to cut down on air pollution, many cities have ordered the compacting rather than the burning of garbage. Garbage is still thrown down the old brick chutes, which have been cracked from heat, to be compacted in the basement. Roaches breed in these cracks, fed by the wet garbage that comes down the chute, and travel to tenants' apartments. *Remedy:* Brick chutes should be replaced with smooth metal chutes, which don't provide breeding places. *Also:* Compactors must be cleaned at least once a week.

• **Homeowners do not need regular extermination for roaches.** Since a house is an individual unit, a onetime extermination should do the job. Food stores are the major source of roach infestation in private homes. People bring roaches home with the groceries. Check your paper grocery bags for roaches before you store them.

• **Ants and silverfish can be brought under control** without professional help unless there is a major infestation. Don't call the exterminator for a half-dozen ants or silverfish. Try a store-bought spray first. *Exception:* Carpenter ants and grease-eating ants must be exterminated professionally.

• **Clover mites come from cutting the grass.** They look like little red dots. The mites land on windowsills after the lawn has been mowed and then travel into the house. *Remedy:* Spray your grass with miticide before cutting.

• **Spiders don't require an exterminator.** Any aerosol will get rid of them.

• **Termite control is a major job** that needs specialized chemicals and equipment. Call an exterminator.

• **Bees, wasps and hornets should be dealt with professionally.** Their nests must be located and attacked after dusk, when the insects have returned to them. If the nest is not destroyed properly, damage to your home could result. *Also:* Many people are allergic to stings and don't know it until they are stung.

• **Clothes moths can be eliminated** by hanging a no-pest strip in your closet and keeping the door closed tightly.

• **Flies can be minimized with an aerosol or sticky strip.** An exterminator is of no help in getting rid of flies. *Best:* Install screens on all the windows and doors.

• **Weevils and meal moths can be prevented by storing cereals,** rice and grains in sealed containers. *Also:* Cereals are treated with bromides to repel infestation, but the bromides break down eventually. Throw out old cereals.

There is no 100% effective solution to exterminating mice. *Try these alternatives...*

• **Trapping is effective unless you have small children or pets.**

• **Poison should be placed behind the stove or refrigerator,** where children and pets can't get at it.

• **Glue boards** (available in supermarkets) placed along the walls can be very effective. Mice tend to run along the walls because they have poor eyesight.

Many of the residual (long-lasting) sprays have been outlawed because they don't break down and disappear in the environment. The old favorites, DDT and Chlordane, are no longer permitted except for particular problems such as termite control. *What to use...*

• **Baygon and Diazanon are general-purpose,** toxic organophosphates meant for residual use in wet areas. They're recommended for all indoor insects, including roaches.

• **Drione is a nontoxic silica gel that dries up the membranes in insects.** Recommended for indoor use in dry areas only, it is especially effective against roaches.

• **Malathion is helpful in gardens,** but it should not be used indoors.

• **Pyrethrin is highly recommended,** since it is made from flowers and is nontoxic. It has no residual effect but is good for on-contact spraying of roaches and other insects. If there is a baby in the house, Pyrethrin is especially useful, since children under three months should never be exposed to toxic chemicals. Don't use it around hay-fever or asthma sufferers.

When buying products in the store, look at the label to determine the percentage of active ingredients. Solutions vary from 5% to 15%. The stronger the solution, the better the results.

Prevention is synonymous with sanitation. If you are not scrupulous about cleanliness, you will be wasting your money on sprays or exterminators. Moisture is the main attractor of insects. If you live in a moist climate, you must be especially vigilant. Coffee spills, plumbing leaks, fish tanks, pet litter and pet food all attract bugs. Clean up after your pets, and take care of leaks and spills immediately. If puddles tend to collect around your house after it rains, improve the drainage.

• **Word of mouth is the best way to choose a good exterminator.** Don't rely on the *Yellow Pages*.

• **Contracts for regular service,** which many exterminators try to promote, are not recommended for private homes. A onetime extermination should do the trick, but apartment dwellers must exterminate building-wide on a regular basis.

• **Rout roaches without poisoning your kitchen.** Boric acid or crumbled bay leaves will keep your cupboards pest-free. *Another benign repellent:* Chopped cucumbers.

• **Wood storage and insects.** Firewood kept in the house becomes a refuge and breeding ground for insects. *Risky solution:* Spraying the logs with insecticides. (When the sprayed wood burns, dangerous fumes could be emitted.) *Better:* Stack the wood (under plastic) outside and carry in only the amount needed.

• **To remove a bat from your house at night, confine it to a single room,** open the window and leave the bat alone. Chances are it will fly right out. Otherwise, during the day when the bat is torpid, flick it into a coffee can or other container. (Use gloves if you are squeamish.) Release it outdoors. Bats are really very valuable. A single brown bat can eat 3,000 mosquitoes a night. *Note:* Bats, like other mammals, can carry rabies. If you find a downed bat or you are scratched or bitten by one, call your local animal-control agency and keep the animal for testing. However, very few people have contracted rabies directly from bats. *More likely source:* Skunks.

Plant Poisoning

Plant poisoning among adults has increased alarmingly in the past decade. For children who are under the age of five, plants are second only to medicines as a cause of poisoning. *Prime sources:* Common houseplants, garden flowers and shrubs, as well as wild mushrooms, weeds and berries.

Most important rule: Never eat anything that you are not absolutely sure is safe. More than 700 US plants have been identified as poisonous when eaten, causing violent illness and sometimes death. *If you suspect someone has eaten a poisonous plant:* Call the nearest poison-control center and your doctor. Try to collect samples of the plant for identification.

Among the most common poisonous plants:

• **Garden flowers.** Bleeding heart, daffodil, delphinium, foxglove, hen-and-chickens, lantana, lily of the valley, lupine, sweet pea.

• **Houseplants.** Caladium, dieffenbachia, philodendron.

• **Garden shrubs.** Azalea, mountain laurel, oleander, privet, rhododendron, yew.

• **Wildflowers.** Autumn crocus, buttercup, jimsonweed, mayapple, moonseed berry, poison hemlock, water hemlock, wild mushrooms.

Indoor Plant Care

Spider plants are the champion indoor plant for fast growing, catchy looks and long life with little care. The leaf colors range from solid deep green to green-and-white stripes. *Fastest growers:* Plants with all-green leaves. A small plant fills out in four months. Hang it in a north window (flowers form faster in low light). Keep the soil damp and fertilize once a month.

Self-watering planters can tend your indoor garden while you are on vacation or simply save you time in regular maintenance. Based on the principle of capillary action, these non-mechanical pots come in a variety of sizes, shapes and finishes. They can be bought at garden centers or florist shops. Foliage plants with modest demands will stay sufficiently moist for as long as three months. *Names to look for:* Grosfillex and Natural Spring.

Home Remedies for Houseplant Pests

Use simple, natural solutions to eliminate common household insects. *For example…*

• **Red spider mites.** Four tablespoons of dishwashing liquid or one-half cake of yellow soap dissolved in one gallon of water. Spray weekly until mites are gone, then do so monthly.

• **Hardshell scale.** One-fourth teaspoon olive oil, two tablespoons baking soda, one teaspoon Dove liquid soap in two gallons of water. Spray or wipe on once a week for three weeks; repeat if necessary.

• **Mold on soil.** One tablespoon of vinegar in two quarts of water. Water weekly with solution until mold disappears.

• **Mealybugs.** Wipe with cotton swabs dipped in alcohol. Spray larger plants weekly with a solution of one part alcohol to three parts water until bugs no longer hatch.

Decora Interior Plantscapes, Greenwich, Connecticut.

Ten Foolproof Houseplants

Edmond O. Moulin, former director of horticulture, Brooklyn Botanic Garden, New York.

These hardy species will survive almost anywhere and are a good choice for timid beginners who don't have a lot of sunny windows.

• **Aspidistra (cast-iron plant).** This Victorian favorite, known as "The Spittoon Plant," survived the implied indignity in many a tavern.

• **Rubber plant.** Likes a dim, cool interior (like a hallway). If given sun, it grows like crazy.

• **Century (Kentia) palm.** A long-lived, slow-growing plant that needs uniform moisture. Give it an occasional shower to dust it.

• **Philodendrons.** They like medium to low light and even moisture but will tolerate dryness and poor light.

• **Dumb cane.** Tolerates a dry interior and low light but responds to better conditions. Be careful not to chew the foliage or your tongue will swell.

• **Bromeliads.** Exotic and slow-growing, they like frequent misting but are practically immune to neglect and will flower even in subdued light.

• **Corn plant (dracaena).** Good for hot, dry apartments.

• **Snake plant.** Will survive almost anything.

• **Spider plant.** A tough, low-light plant that makes a great trailer and endures neglect.

• **Nephthytis.** Will flourish in poor light and survive the forgetful waterer.

Secrets of a Great Lawn

Less work makes a grassier lawn. *Mowing:* Set the blades to a height of two to two-and-a-half inches, and cut the grass only once a week. When the weather gets really hot, every other week is fine. *Benefits of taller grass:* Less mowing, stronger and healthier plants that spread faster, more shade to discourage weeds. *Bonus:* Let the clippings lie. They will return nutrients to the soil.

Other work- and lawn-saving tips…

• **Water only when there has been no significant rain for three or four weeks.** Then give a one-inch soak. (Use a cup under the sprinkler pattern to measure—it takes longer than you think.) Frequent shallow watering keeps roots close to the surface, where they are vulnerable to drought and fungus disease.

• **Use herbicides and insecticides only for specific problems.** Routine use weakens the grass and kills earthworms.

• **Sow bare spots with rye grass for a quick fix.** Proper reseeding should be done in late August or early September, when the ground is cooler and moister.

• **Apply fertilizer twice a year,** but not in the spring. September and November are the right months.

Gardening for Fun and Food

Sally Sherwin, former editor of *Investment Cooking*.

Growing your own produce can save money. But even when it doesn't, you still get exercise, fresh air, tension release and vitamin-packed harvests.

Home gardeners feel deep satisfaction in making the salad or seasoning the casserole with freshly picked plants. The taste is incomparable. It also works more fresh vegetables into meals. The surplus can be frozen or given as gifts. *Here's how anyone can benefit from home-grown produce…*

• **Where space is limited, grow a mini-garden, indoors or out.** Windowsills, balconies and doorstep areas can be used, as well as milk cartons, pails, plastic buckets and cans.

• **Gear planting to local weather conditions.** Summer planting can still be done in June in most regions. Planning for fall crops can be started in early summer.

• **Proper spacing is very important.** One sturdy plant is better than several weak ones. Crowding chokes root systems, causing spindly growth and poor production. Save packet directions for referral.

• **Look for hybrid bush seeds** rather than vining ones to save space.

• **Seeds do not always have to be bought.** Reasonably fresh dill, anise, fennel, coriander and other seeds already on the spice rack should grow. If not, they are too old to add much to food anyway and should be replaced. Plant sprouting garlic cloves, ginger eyes, onions and potato eyes.

• **Scoop out seeds from vegetables you've bought.** Dry them a week or so before planting. Zucchini, summer squash, beans and peas are among the easiest. Or try tomato seeds, especially cherry tomatoes.

• **Buy seeds for growing vegetables that don't contain seeds**—beets, radishes, carrots, swiss chard, mustard greens, scallions, celery, shallots, endive, brussels sprouts, kale.

• **Consider grapes and berries.** Though some take a while to get established, they bear more each year.

• **Gardening offers a change from the monotony of the supermarket.** You can grow yellow tomatoes, ornamental purple kale, scalloped squash—all interesting variations.

Ruffled-leaf lettuces grow more easily and are much more nutritious than iceberg. Sprouting (stalk) broccoli is easier than head broccoli.

Planting suggestions:

• **Soil preparation is crucial for good results.** Have the soil tested annually. Every state has a land-grant college that will test soil for a small fee. It will give abundant basic gardening advice, largely free, through its Cooperative Extension arm. Check state or federal government listings under Agriculture. There are even offices in some large urban centers. Many have helpful USDA Home and Garden Bulletins available. No. 202, *Growing Vegetables in the Home Garden,* and No. 163, *Minigardens for Vegetables,* are good starters. Some offices publish newsletters that give local planting suggestions plus listings of courses or talks about gardening. Get on mailing lists. Always be guided by local experts on the specifics, since weather can vary greatly even within a few miles.

• **Minimize weeding with mulch** (hay or black plastic surrounding plants). It also helps retain soil moisture.

• **Companion planting can help insect control.** *Example:* Basil with tomatoes. (See organic gardening publications.)

• **Look into raised-bed or hill planting when space or soil is limited.**

• **Where light is limited,** put the smallest plants in front of the sun's arc, larger ones behind it.

• **Harvest often.** Many vegetables stop producing if allowed to mature fully.

• **Don't expect instant results.**

• **Vegetable seeds' life span.** *One to three years:* Hybrid tomatoes, leeks, onions, corn. *Three years:* Beans, carrots, peas. *Four years:* Chard, fennel, beets, standard tomatoes. *Five years:* Brussels sprouts, broccoli, cantaloupe, radishes. *To store seeds:* Seal packet with freezer tape. Mark with date and freeze in container.

7

Your Car

Fixing Your Present Car Vs. Buying a New One

More and more people are faced with the decision of whether to junk the old car or keep it and fix it up. Statistics show more people are choosing to do the latter. Remanufactured engines offer a "new lease on life" for older cars. Many people have found that "it's cheaper to keep 'er." *There are a number of reasons to fix up an older car…*

• **You already know what your older car needs.** If you have kept it up all along, you have already invested a considerable sum of money in it. Cars like this are good candidates for "keepers."

• **An older car is less expensive to insure.**

• **An older car is less likely to be stolen.**

• **Parts are less expensive.** Many parts are available at a fraction of their original cost from junkyards.

• **Many older cars were made of better materials** than modern cars.

• **The cost of operation, mile for mile, is much less** for an older vehicle.

• **Operating an older vehicle reduces the amount of waste** and environmental damage from the junking of that car and the manufacturing of the new replacement cars.

Reasons to get rid of an older car…

• **If you haven't kept up the car** and it needs a considerable amount of body work or is in bad mechanical condition.

• **It is a gas guzzler** and/or contributes a great deal of pollution.

• **Parts are becoming harder to find.**

• **It has an inherent safety flaw.**

• **It doesn't have shoulder belts.**

• **It has a driveline that is known to be problematic.**

David Solomon, certified master auto technician and chairman, MotorWatch, Box 123, Butler, Maryland 21023.

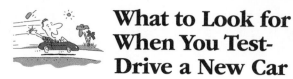

What to Look for When You Test-Drive a New Car

David Solomon, certified master auto technician and chairman, MotorWatch, Box 123, Butler, Maryland 21023.

Before buying a new car, take full advantage of your test-drive. Make sure the dealer lets you drive the vehicle where you can give it a thorough workout—like on bumpy roads, in stop-and-go traffic and on the highway.

Pay special attention to how the car matches up to your expectations for comfort, drivability, interior layout and power.

COMFORT

• **Clearance.** Can you get in and out without hitting your head?

• **Headroom.** Your hair shouldn't touch the ceiling. A sunroof will give you another inch of space when it's open, but it decreases overall headroom by about two inches.

• **Seat height.** Does it give you good visibility of the road?

• **Headrest.** Will your head, neck and back be comfortable after driving for a while?

• **Leg room.** Does the seat move far enough forward and back?

DRIVABILITY

Test-drive the car at night to make sure that the headlights are powerful enough for your overall comfort.

• **Power.** Does the car run smoothly and accelerate adequately? Make sure the car you test-drive has the engine size, transmission type or gear ratios that you want.

• **Rear visibility.** Is your visibility adequate with the exterior rear-view mirrors? If you think they are too small, be aware that replacements do not exist.

• **Noise.** Does engine exhaust, tire noise or wind noise bother you?

• **Fuel type.** Does the car require expensive premium gas? High-performance, multivalve, super-and turbo-charged models all do.

INTERIOR

• **Instrumentation.** Can you read the gauges easily?

• **Controls.** Do you hit the wiper switch and put the radio on? Are the controls lit well at night?

• **Door handles.** Can you find them easily in the dark?

EXTERIOR

Check out the finish of the car to make sure you haven't been sold a vehicle that already has been driven or damaged in transit.

Look for tell-tale signs that the car has been repainted. *Examples:* Paint traces on the rubber stripping or trim, mismatched colors and misfit panels. Also look at the undercoating. It should look slightly weathered—not sparkling clean and still soft.

Luxury Car Opportunity

When there is a glut of expiring luxury-car leases, it means these "preowned" vehicles are now selling for as much as 40% less than new cars of the same model. The dealers keep the best cars, including those with manufacturer-subsidized warranties.

Guidelines: Consider newer cars within three years and less than 12,000 miles per year… look for a pampered auto with complete service records…examine three or four cars at different dealers for value…go to an independent specialist mechanic for inspection…don't accept the first price—on most luxury cars you can save an additional 3% to 6% so it pays to bargain.

Ashly Knapp, founder of AutoAdvisor.com, the nation's oldest buyer's service, Seattle. 800-326-1976.

How to Buy a Car Without Getting Taken for a Ride

Two veteran car salesmen who asked to remain anonymous.

There's more to buying a car than price. Where you buy it counts, too. Take the time to evaluate different dealerships.

Go to a few and walk around. When a salesperson comes up to you—and one will—say, "I'm just looking around. I'll come to you when I'm ready." Don't let any of them intimidate you.

Walk through the service area and sit down. Stay for about a half-hour. *Observe...*

- **Is it orderly and run efficiently?**
- **Is the manager there and working?**
- **Are the customers treated with respect?**

Proceed into the service lot and look at the license plate frames. In a good dealership you'll see frames from competing dealerships, too.

Don't choose a dealership that's out of the way. The salespeople know that they have just one chance to make a sale, and they lean hard on you. Also avoid multifranchise dealerships. Too many people run different parts of the operation, causing confusion in service.

Choose your salespeople—don't let them choose you. Speak with several. *Ask...*

- **How long have you been at this dealership?** (The longer, the better.)
- **Where else have you worked?** And for how long?
- **May I get the name and number of a recent customer?** (Follow up with a phone call to him/her.)

If there's a lot of turnover, leave—the dealership is unstable.

Trap: **Looking for a salesperson who's a member of your ethnic group because you think you'll get special treatment.** You won't, and you'll be letting your guard down.

Educate yourself. Get as much information as possible about a car before you sit down with the salesperson. Collect brochures (dealers don't usually keep them on display, because they want you to approach the salespeople) and read consumer magazines that rate autos.

Don't let salespeople woo you into trusting them with their "impressive" knowledge of a car. That's how they try to establish authority and take control of the sale.

Know the competition, too. If you say that you're considering a competing brand, the salesperson will knock it and be very convincing if you're uninformed.

If you're not firm about what you want, you could easily end up with what the salesperson wants to sell you—the most expensive model, with the most extravagant options, at the highest price.

Once you show serious intentions of buying, the salesperson will offer you a test drive, during which he will talk glowingly about the car to get you to take mental ownership of it. He is seducing you. Resist.

Trap: **Negotiating to buy when you're tired of shopping.** Salespeople are attracted to this kind of customer like bees to honey. They know that if they promise you what you've been looking for—whether they have it or not—you'll probably buy on the spot. Buy only in an energetic mood.

Few salespeople ask idle questions. Seemingly irrelevant questions are actually attempts to find out about your lifestyle, income, driving habits, etc. Avoid answering these questions.

Options are where dealers make their money. *Common tactic:* The dealer says, "Sorry, but all the cars arrive with power windows. If you don't want them, I'll have to make a special order. It could take several months." *Result:* You end up paying for an option that you don't want. But if you stand firm, he'll work something out—he wants the sale.

Also make sure every option has the car's name on it: That means the dealership is responsible for it if it breaks. For example, Honda uses Alpine brand radios, but Honda's name is on the faceplate—which means Honda is responsible.

To get the best price, get a range of prices from several dealerships and write them down. When you're at the first one, don't let the salesperson know it. When he asks what other dealers have quoted, say, "Why don't you give me your best deal and we'll take it from there."

Read this sticker carefully: "DAP" stands for Dealer Added Profit. "Locator Cost" means the dealer located the car. These charges are negotiable.

Take particular note of a common price-padding tactic: A prep fee of $100 or more (whatever the dealership thinks it can get away with). The cost of preparing your car for delivery is already included in the manufacturer's sticker price.

Salespeople's trick: They'll consult with the manager constantly and pretend that they're on your side. They aren't—they work on commission.

Don't shop for price by phone because salespeople will quote anything just to get you into the dealership. Shop for financing in advance so you'll know a good deal when you hear one. Don't believe salespeople who claim that they can get you good insurance rates—they can't.

Trap: **Accepting a trade-in price for your old car that you know is too high.** The dealership will make up the difference on the price of the new car or on the options.

Don't let yourself get "turned over." If a salesperson feels that he's not in control of the sale, he'll say that he's going on a coffee break and will "turn you over" to another salesperson. In a high-pressure operation, this could happen three or four times, until they wear you down. *How to resist:* Go out for a walk, have a cup of coffee at a nearby diner, say that you need to think about it. Get away from the salespeople so you can think clearly.

When the deed is done, inspect your new car thoroughly before you leave the dealership. Make sure everything is working correctly.

Final dirty trick: The car was dented in transport, so the dealer parks it close to a wall to hide the damage—which greets you when you arrive home.

Best Time of Year to Get A Good Deal on a Car

The best car-buying time is shortly before Christmas, when business tends to be slow and dealers are willing to take smaller profits.

Also good: The postholiday period into February, especially in cold-winter climates. *Best day:* A rainy Monday.

Consumer Adviser, Reader's Digest Association, Inc., Pleasantville, New York.

Leasing vs. Buying

Leasing a car costs an average 15% more than buying, but it pays off in some situations.

Lease if you: Keep a car for only two or three years, don't like to deal with auto maintenance, want to use the auto down-payment money for other investments, drive your car for business purposes, prefer a medium- or high-priced vehicle.

Be careful: Leases have mileage limits, so make sure to stay under your allowed amount. Each mile over can be very expensive.

How to Buy a Hard-to-Get Car

When a car is in high demand, dealers can charge a premium over the sticker prices.

To get the car you want at the price you want to pay…

• **Survey Internet pricing services** such as *www.autobytel.com* and *http://autos.msn. com.* You can learn what the model you want to buy is selling for and get a price quote.

• **Check** ***www.edmunds.com*** **and** ***www. kbb.com*** to find out the dealer invoice on the car, including options.

• **Contact several local dealers,** and offer about $500 more than the invoice price for the car you want. Listen to their counteroffers— and then wait a week or so before making a counteroffer to the dealers who offer the lowest prices.

• **Negotiate the best possible deal,** and put down a deposit on the car.

• **Contact the other dealers**—since it may be several weeks before the car arrives—and tell them you're willing to buy and happily wait if they can do better.

Expect to save about $1,000 by following this strategy, compared with what you would have paid otherwise.

Ashly Knapp, founder of AutoAdvisor.com, the nation's oldest buyer's service, Seattle. 800-326-1976.

Use the Internet to Save Money on a New Car

Ashly Knapp, founder of AutoAdvisor.com, the nation's oldest buyer's service, Seattle. 800-326-1976.

The Internet is a convenient, free resource for people who are looking to save money on a new car. But some sites are better than others.

RESEARCHING CARS

•**Visit automakers' sites.** Almost every carmaker has a Web site to promote its models. Most sites can be found by typing the company's name—or some form of it—in the address bar of your Web browser.

Examples: Typing in *www.gm.com* or *www.toyota.com* will access the General Motors or Toyota site.

Company sites display color photos of cars and list available options and color choices. They also include dealer listings, manufacturer prices and sometimes finance options.

•**Compare features** by accessing sites that provide direct feature comparisons of makes and models.

Example: http://autos.excite.com/home.html

•**Use a search engine** when you have narrowed your choices to a particular model. Internet search engines such as Google or Yahoo! allow you to access newspaper and magazine reviews.

Example: Detroit Free Press (*www.freep. com*) and *www.thecarconnection.com* have especially sharp car reviews.

CHECKING DEALER COSTS

There are several sites that provide price information for specific makes and models. These Web sites will give you suggested retail prices...and the amount that the cars cost the dealers. Try to get as close as you can to cost, but remember dealers often get lower prices after discounts from automakers. *To find dealer costs...*

•**Edmunds** (*www.edmunds.com*), which prints the most thorough reports.

•**Kelley Blue Book** (*www.kbb.com*) makes a great double check.

Both are based on their print price guides. Armed with this information, you should be able to bargain more effectively with a dealer. While the dealer invoice price is a good place to start, buyers need to understand that dealers also have costs that are not reflected in the invoice price.

Example: Different dealers have different costs of operation...and receive different compensation after the vehicles are sold. So, while all dealers pay the same to buy a car, they have different costs to sell the car.

No Web site tracks these cost differences. So buyers need to exercise caution when bargaining with dealers.

STRATEGY

To achieve the best price you can find, go to Web sites like...

•*www.autobytel.com*

•*www.autovantage.com*

•*http://autos.msn.com*

Then use the quotes/prices from these sites as your starting point with your neighborhood dealers.

BUYING CARS

You can rarely buy a new car directly over the Internet, but you can initiate the transaction, then meet face-to-face with the dealer to complete the purchase.

Colors That Increase A Car's Resale Value And Safety

All other things being equal, a car's color can be a deciding factor that affects its safety and resale value.

Safety: White is the most visible color in most situations. Yellow and orange are best when driving in heavy snow or on white sand. Under adverse conditions, the most difficult colors to detect are gray, red, blue, brown or black. The least visible color in general is dark green.

Resale value: Red and beige are the most popular colors. Blue cars also sell well (unless they're a very light shade of blue). But yellow, white and metallics are not much in demand.

National Association of Fleet Administrators.

Taking Delivery

Before accepting your car from the dealer, allow him enough time to "prepare" the car. Before you buy, find out what the dealer's preparation includes. Engine tune-up? Emission checks? Installation of optional equipment and a test drive? Some automobile dealers charge extra for every step of the preparation.

Inspect the car yourself. Check paint and body moldings. Examine the car in daylight. Look for imperfections and mismatched colors. The car may have been damaged in transit and repainted.

Compare the list of options on your bill of sale with those that are actually on the car. Be sure they are the options you ordered and not inferior substitutes.

Examine doors, latches and windows to see whether they are operating properly. Inspect tires for cuts and bulges. Look at the interior finish. Test the heater, the radio and the air conditioner.

During the first week of ownership, test-drive the car under as many conditions as possible. If the car does not perform satisfactorily, you will have a better chance of getting the dealer to make adjustments than you would if you wait a month or two before complaining.

What You Must Know to Buy A Used Car

Burke Leon, owner of BL Auto Enterprises, a used-car broker in Placentia, California. He is coauthor of *The Insider's Guide to Buying a New or Used Car* (Betterway Publications).

Don't let your words or actions indicate what car you really want. If you say you want a Chevy, a Chevy will suddenly cost more than any Ford on the lot.

Browse around at the dealership. Make the salesperson spend time with you—and use this as leverage to pay less. Only when the salesperson is nearly exasperated should you zero in on the car you really want and begin your serious negotiating.

• **Negotiate a price first,** then have your mechanic evaluate the car. If possible, drive the car to your mechanic. Otherwise, bring your mechanic to the dealer's lot. If there's a problem with the car, you're in a good position because the dealer is anticipating the sale. Ask to have any problems corrected at no cost to you.

• **Negotiate a warranty.** Some used-car dealers don't offer warranties, but you should have one. Ask for a 100% 30-day warranty to cover all parts and labor, but be willing to accept a 50/50 warranty (under which you'll pay 50% of costs). Demand that labor costs be based on a mechanic's estimate. Request the right to buy parts yourself and supply them to the dealership. Many dealers mark up parts by 100%.

• **Don't forget to nibble.** Ask for the little extras that can add up, such as an oil or filter change or new tires. If the car doesn't turn over on the first key turn, ask for a new battery ($100 or more).

• You can save a lot by buying directly from an owner instead of a dealership. *To get negotiating leverage over the phone, ask the following questions...*

• Is there a defect in the title? (Is this a recovered stolen car or a rebuilt car with a salvaged title?)

• What concerns do you have about the car?

• What's your bottom line price? Then, offer $100 less.

How to Sell Your Car

Sal Nuccio, president of the Nuccio Organization, financial consultants, Yonkers, New York.

When you're ready to sell your car, there are things you must examine before you set a selling price. *Be sure to consider...*

Body: Wash and wax your car, and touch up small nicks and scratches. If major bodywork or repainting is required, determine whether you would do better by making the investment or by selling the car as is.

Interior: Vacuum and dust, cover worn carpeting with mats, oil squeaky hinges. If necessary, replace pedal pads.

Engine: Remove oil and grease with products made for that purpose. Use a baking-soda solution to clean battery terminals. If it's needed, get a tune-up.

What price? Look up your car's value in the *NADA Official Used-Car Guide* (*www.nada guides.com*) or the *Red Book* (*www.redbook. com.au*) at your library, bank, auto club or auto dealership. Both books will give you guidance in allowing for accessories, condition and mileage. You will arrive at the wholesale (trade-in or loan) value and the retail value (normally charged by dealers).

Ask a couple of dealers what they would offer you for the car. Compare that with your wholesale value. Look at the prices of comparable cars advertised in your newspaper.

By now, you should have a good idea of the price you can expect. It will be somewhere between wholesale and retail. Determine your asking price and the minimum amount you would accept. Now you're all ready to go to market.

Your best bet is to advertise in your local newspaper on Friday, Saturday and Sunday, when most people are looking to buy. Use positive phrases like "one owner," "low mileage" and "excellent condition" if they truly apply. There is debate about the wisdom of stating a price, but if you do, you will eliminate shoppers looking for giveaways. Suggest negotiability. *Example:* Asking $2,000.

Precautions: Most people will want to road-test the car they are considering buying and perhaps have a mechanic inspect it. However, be wary of car thieves and irresponsible drivers. Join the prospective buyer on the test drive. If that's not possible, protect yourself by asking to see his/her driver's license and other identification. Record the information. Agree to a reasonable amount of time for the excursion, but no more than an hour. It is reassuring if the person arrives by car and leaves that vehicle while testing yours.

Payment: Accept only cash or a certified check. If it is a personal check, go with the buyer to the bank to have it cashed. Do not transfer title until you have been fully paid.

Notifications: Let your state's motor vehicles department know of the sale so that you won't be held responsible for the new owner's traffic violations. Also notify your insurance company.

Get the Right Headrest

Check the built-in head restraints before buying a new car. The higher they are, the more protection they provide in a crash. When you drive, the headrest should reach as close to the top of your head as possible and touch the back of your head.

Best system available: Active head restraint/seat systems on some new Volvos and

Saabs, which move to protect your head and neck in the event of a crash.

To protect yourself in your current car: Adjust the headrest to make it high enough to touch the back of your head, but not your neck. Keep the seat back as close to vertical as possible.

Most at risk: Tall people, whose heads roll back over the top of the restraints in a crash.

David Solomon, certified master auto technician and chairman, MotorWatch, Box 123, Butler, Maryland 21023.

Air Bags

Air bags save lives but leave you vulnerable to other injuries.

Reason: Even when an air bag deploys during a crash, the driver's lower extremities can be injured by the instrument panel or floor.

Possible results: Ankle fractures...crushed feet...broken legs and hips. *However:* While such injuries can be serious, victims may have died without the air bags.

Study of victims of automobile crashes by Jeffrey S. Augenstein, MD, PhD, chief, division of trauma and surgical critical care, and co-director of the Ryder Trauma Center, University of Miami.

Car Leases and Lemon Laws

Lemon laws are designed to protect car owners who buy unfixable vehicles. But when you lease a car, you are not the owner, and about one-third of the states either exclude leased cars from lemon-law coverage or cover lessees only under certain circumstances.

Bottom line: Before signing any leasing contract, contact your state attorney general's office and find out if lemon laws apply. If they do not, make sure you get a manufacturer's warranty when you lease—not a leasing-company warranty.

Philip Nowicki, automotive division director, Governor's office of consumer affairs, Atlanta.

Extended Car Warranties

Extended car warranties make sense for those who don't intend to trade in their cars after a few years. Today's cars are loaded with technology that could break down after 36,000 miles. While the price of most factory-backed warranties is $800 to $1,200, they are negotiable. Offer half the asking price, and don't pay more than two-thirds. Only buy a warranty that is backed by the manufacturer.

W. James Bragg, coauthor of *Car Buyer's and Leaser's Negotiating Bible* (Random House).

Car Air-Conditioning Service Danger

Some replacement refrigerants can contain isobutane, which is highly flammable. The refrigerants were developed to replace the commonly used Freon, which is being phased out by the Environmental Protection Agency.

Self-defense: If you suspect a problem, take your car to a shop that can put the refrigerant into a special storage container and replace it with the new, safer form of Freon—R-134A.

Important: Your car's cooling system would have to be converted to accommodate R-134A. Most new cars are being manufactured with this new air-conditioning system.

David Solomon, certified master auto technician and chairman, MotorWatch, Box 123, Butler, Maryland 21023.

Car Bumper Safety

Add-on bumper and grille guards are available for some large cars—but they do not provide any extra safety in a car accident... not even in the slightest fender bender. Don't be deceived if you see these guards attached to the front ends of taxis and police cars. Here, they are used to prevent the front and rear fenders of two cars from getting locked —for example, when taxis are in bumper-to-bumper traffic...or when police officers must push another vehicle out of the way.

David Solomon, certified master auto technician and chairman, MotorWatch, Box 123, Butler, Maryland 21023.

Most Dangerous Time of Day to Drive

The worst time to drive is between midnight and 3 am. You're 13 times more likely to have a fatal car accident than between 6 am and 6 pm. *Most dangerous hour:* From 2 am to 3 am on Sunday morning (after many bars close)—your chance of a fatal accident then is 22 times higher.

Study by Sherman Stein, retired professor of mathematics, University of California at Davis.

Car-Safety Secrets

Don't pump the brakes, especially if your car has an antilock brake system (ABS). *The danger:* ABS is designed to pump the brakes for you...if you pump the brakes, you aren't using ABS to its full potential. *If your car doesn't have ABS:* Apply slow, steady pressure when braking and don't pump.

- **Front-wheel-drive vehicles.** (1) Don't take your foot off the gas too suddenly when going into a skid. *Better:* Step lightly on the gas pedal. If the road is too narrow for that, shift into neutral and continue to steer. (2) Never put extra weight in the rear trunk compartment. It reduces traction rather than improves it.

- **Driving on ice.** The warmer the temperature, the more hazardous the driving on icy surfaces. Ice at 30°F is twice as slippery as ice at 0°F.

- **Skidding.** *For front-wheel-drive cars:* If rear wheels lose traction, step lightly on the gas. (The front wheels pull the car forward, and the rear wheels follow.) Don't do this when front wheels lose traction. That could make matters worse.

- **Stuck in snow.** Turn the auto's wheels from side to side to clear snow away. Then gently ease forward with wheels kept as straight as possible. Rocking back and forth can be helpful as long as you swing higher in each move.

- **Windshield freeze-up.** The washer fluid must be correct for the outdoor temperature. Before using the fluid, prepare the windshield by heating it with a full blast from the defroster.

- **Fog and mist.** Use all lights, including four-way flashers.

- **Braking distance.** For rear-wheel-drive vehicles moving at 20 mph, use of snow tires will not necessarily result in any improvement over regular all-season tires. Snow tires help most when driving on loosely packed snow. *Estimated improvement:* 13%. Snow tires are now designed to handle ice and snow better than all-season tires in the winter.

National Association of Fleet Administrators (NAFA) Bulletin. *www.nafa.org*

Winterizing Checklist

Before the cold weather sets in, it's a good idea to make sure your car can handle extremely severe elements. *Some things to check...*

- **Radiator coolant.** Read the label on your antifreeze to be sure you make the right blend of water and antifreeze. The antifreeze keeps your radiator from freezing and cracking; the water, even in winter, keeps your car from overheating.

- **Battery condition.** Your car needs three to four times more starting power in winter than in summer. Have a mechanic do a complete battery draw and load test. If your battery fails, a recharge may save it for another year. Otherwise, invest in a new one.

• **Windshield-washer fluid.** Frozen fluid in the washer tank is dangerous. Use a premixed commercial fluid. Check that the hoses are clear, and clean the washer nozzles out with a thin piece of wire.

• **Electrical system.** Make sure the distributor cap, points, condenser, ignition coil, spark plugs and spark-plug cables are in good shape. Borderline components that still function in summer may break in cold weather.

• **Hoses and belts.** If they are cracking or fraying, replace them.

• **Tires.** If you have all-season tires, be sure the tread is still good enough to give you traction on slippery roads. Otherwise, you should put on snow tires. *Important:* Be sure to use four snow tires or four all-seasons—never mix tires. Also, store summer tires on their sides, not on the tread. (Storing on the tread creates a flat spot and leads to an unbalanced tire.) Inflate stored tires to only 50% of their operating pressure.

• **Windshield.** Apply antifogging compound to the inside.

• **Cleaning.** Clear dead bugs off the radiator by hosing it from the inside of the engine compartment. Pick out dead leaves and debris from the fresh-air intake box of the ventilation system.

• **Stock up.** Buy emergency flares, an aerosol wire-drying agent, a scraper and brush, chains and a military-style collapsible trench tool. Keep a lock deicer at home and/or at the office for opening up frozen car doors in extremely cold conditions.

Winter Windshield Wipers

Snow Belt drivers may want to shift to windshield-wiper blades specially designed to handle snow and ice. A rubber boot completely covers the blade, preventing ice buildup on the connectors. This maintains the flexing action needed when the wiper moves over the curved surface of the windshield.

All About Speeding Tickets

The best way to avoid speeding tickets is, of course, to avoid speeding. But all of us drive over the limit occasionally.

Here are some suggestions to help you avoid tickets…

• **Know the limits.** It's no illusion that police officers generally ignore cars driving just slightly over the posted speed. In fact, many departments set threshold speeds (for example, six miles an hour above the limit) at which officers are to take no action. You might be able to slip by at 65 mph in a 55 mph zone, but you're unlikely to do the same at 70 mph.

• **Be selective.** Most speeding tickets are written during the morning and evening rush hours, when there are more motorists and more police officers on the road. Late-night and very early-morning traffic are not likely to be watched as carefully.

• **Drive unobtrusively.** Flashy cars attract attention, something to keep in mind if you drive a red Ferrari. The same applies to flashy driving styles. Don't tailgate slower cars to force them aside. Don't weave in and out of traffic.

• **Be vigilant.** The likeliest spot to get nabbed on the highway is just beyond a blind curve or the crest of a hill, the best hiding places for patrol cars. Learn to recognize probable traps, and reduce your speed whenever appropriate.

• **Remember that police officers can nab speeders from virtually any position**—the rear, the front, the side, or even from aircraft. Be on the lookout at all times. An unmarked car with its trunk open on the side of the road is especially suspect. (A radar device may be inside.)

• **Fight back.** Radar guns can be foiled occasionally. *What to do:* Position your car close to other cars whenever possible. Police officers generally cannot match your speed with the speed indicated on their guns unless they have an unobstructed view of your car. In most states, motorists also can make use of radar detectors, devices designed to alert drivers to radar early enough for them to slow down before police officers can get a good reading. If you do a lot of driving, a detector is a sensible investment if it is legal in your area.

• **Use psychology.** All is not lost even if you are pulled over. Police officers feel vulnerable when stopping speeders. You could be speeding away from a murder for all they know, and consequently they are usually nervous. Put them at ease. Sit still, keep your hands in plain view (on the steering wheel is a good place). Be courteous and respectful. Above all, be honest. If you have a good excuse for going over the limit, state it. Otherwise, admit guilt and apologize. Police officers can be surprisingly lenient if you're cordial.

Automatic Transmissions Smarts

Keep automatic transmissions cool by removing leaves and debris from the cooling grid, located at the front of the car. *Also:* Replace transmission oil at regular intervals—every 25,000 to 35,000 miles, as recommended by your car's manufacturer.

Brian Workman, manager/technical information specialist, Aamco Transmissions, Inc., transmission repair shops, Bala Cynwyd, Pennsylvania.

Simple Car Care

Half the cars checked in a recent survey had dirty air filters. One-third of the cars had more than one underinflated tire and were more than one quart low on oil. Almost half had corroded batteries, were low on coolant and lacked windshield-wiper fluid.

Survey by Car Care Council. *www.carcare.org*

Weather Checklist

Automobile Association of America. *www.aaa.com*

The last thing you want is to have car trouble when the weather is bad. *Use these precautions...*

• **Inspect the radiator for leaks** and check the fluid level.

• **Check all hoses** for possible cracks or sponginess. Make sure all connections are tight and leak-free.

• **Test the thermostat** for proper operation. If it does not operate at the proper temperature, overheating could occur.

• **Inspect the fan belt** for cracks and proper tension. Belt slippage is a common cause of boilovers. It also drains electrical power.

• **If loss of coolant has been a problem,** check for water seepage on the water pump around the engine block.

EMERGENCY ROAD ACTION

• **Don't turn off the engine when the temperature warning light goes on.** If stuck in traffic, shift to neutral and race the engine moderately for 30 seconds at two-minute intervals.

• **Shut off the air conditioner** to avoid further overtaxing of the cooling system.

• **Turn on the heater for a few minutes** —it may help.

• **If the radiator continues to overheat,** drive the car off the road, turn off the engine and raise the hood.

• **Wait at least a half-hour before removing the radiator cap.** Then do it very slowly and carefully, with the help of a towel or thick rag. Keep your face turned away from the radiator.

• **If your car has a see-through overflow catch tank,** replace any loss of coolant. Don't touch the radiator.

• **If the fluid level is low,** restart the car and add cool or warm water as the engine idles.

Car-Maintenance Secrets

You don't have to be a professional mechanic to take care of your car. *Basic maintenance is simple...*

• **Replace the brake fluid at least once a year.** This isn't a common practice, and few owners' manuals mention it, but brake fluid attracts water (from condensation and humidity in the air), often causing corrosion in the master and wheel cylinders and shortening their lives. Replacing your car's brake fluid regularly saves the more costly replacement of cylinders.

The Durability Factor, edited by Roger B. Yepsen, Jr. Rodale Press.

• **Cold weather means your tires need more air.** A tire that may have lost a few pounds of pressure during the summer and fall driving season could easily become eight to 10 pounds underinflated on a freezing day. This is enough to cut tire life by 25%. *Rule of thumb:* For every 10-degree drop in the ambient temperature, the air pressure in a tire decreases by one-half to one pound.

• **Average life expectancy for some vital parts of your car.** *Suspension system:* 15,000 miles. *Ignition wires:* 25,000 miles. *Water pump:* 30,000 miles. *Starter:* 40,000 miles. *Brake master cylinder, carburetor and steering mechanism (ball joints):* 50,000 miles. *Fuel pump:* 75,000 miles. *Clutch, timing gear chain/belt, universal joints:* Up to 100,000 miles.

• **The oil-pressure warning light on the dashboard is not a foolproof system.** By the time the light flashes, the engine has been without oil long enough to harm the machinery.

• **Car-scratch repair.** *When a scratch hasn't penetrated to the metal:* Sand with fine sandpaper (400 to 600 grit) until it disappears. Wipe the area clean with a soft cloth. Paint it carefully and let the paint dry for a few days. Then apply rubbing compound according to the directions on the package. *When the scratch has penetrated to the metal:* After sanding with fine paper, apply a primer. Then, after the primer dries, sand again with 300- to 400-grit sandpaper. Paint and let dry.

Apply rubbing compound. Materials are available at most auto-supplies stores.

• **Use vinegar to clean dirt from chipped exterior car surfaces.** Then when the spot is dry, restore with touch-up paint.

• **Idling the car doesn't warm up all the car's systems,** such as lubricants, steering fluid or even all the drive train. *Better:* Keep speeds under 30 mph for the first quarter mile and not much over that for the next several miles.

National Association of Fleet Administrators (NAFA) Bulletin. *www.nafa.org*

• **Replace radials whenever the tread is worn down** to $\frac{1}{16}$ inch from the bottom of the tire groove. At that point, the grooves are too shallow to take water away, and hydroplaning may occur at higher speeds.

National Association of Fleet Administrators (NAFA) Bulletin. *www.nafa.org*

• **Do not "cross-switch" radials.** Always exchange the left front with the left rear and the right front with the right rear. Radials should never be remounted in a manner that will change the direction of rotation.

• **If your car is shaking and vibrating,** wheels may need aligning. Improper alignment causes excessive tire wear and increases fuel consumption.

• **Wax your car at least twice a year,** more often if it is exposed to salt air, road salt or industrial air, or if it's parked outside. *Clue:* If water doesn't bead up on the car's surface after rain, waxing is needed.

• **Car washing damages the luster and finish if laundry detergents are used.** *Best:* Stay with products designed to clean auto finishes. *Brand names:* DuPont Teflon Car Wash, Meguiar's NXT Generation Car Wash, Simoniz Car Wash Concentrate, Star Brite Car Polish. *Next best:* Mild liquid dishwashing detergents.

A car cannot be washed too often if you use the proper cleansers. *Procedure:* Work in the shade. Flood the car's surface with a hose before applying suds. Rinse before drying. When washing the outside, spray the wheel wells and also the underside of the car to clean out corrosive agents.

Car Smarts

In a collision, the single most important safety feature in a car is its size. All other things being equal, a heavier car is safer than a lighter one. But—taller vehicles, such as sport-utility vehicles, may be more prone to rolling over, decreasing their safety.

Other important safety features: Air bags that protect the head against front and side impacts…comfortable, well-fitting safety belts. And, before you choose a car, check the crash-test results, available from the National Highway Traffic Safety Administration (*www.nhtsa.gov*) and the Insurance Institute for Highway Safety (*www.iihs.org*).

Brian O'Neill, former president, Insurance Institute for Highway Safety, 1005 N. Glebe Rd., Arlington, VA 22201.

•**After a windshield replacement,** leave your car at the shop long enough for the adhesive to dry. Afterwards, limit driving for 24 hours. Do not slam doors with all the windows closed. Do not put the car through a car wash for 24 hours. Wait at least 48 hours before using glass cleaners containing ammonia or alcohol.

David Solomon, certified master auto technician and chairman, MotorWatch, Box 123, Butler, MD 21023.

•**Pothole damage to your car isn't covered** unless you can prove the city knew about the pothole and did nothing to fix it. Proving this is almost impossible.

Also: In many states, immunity is granted to city government for failure to fix a road hazard, when the failure can be traced to how it allocates available funds. So you will probably have to pay for the repairs yourself or through your insurance.

Best Car Battery For Cold Climates

When buying a car battery, get a cold-cranking amperage (CCA) that is at least equal to the engine size in cubic inches.

Choose a CCA of at least 250 no matter how small the engine.

The Family Handyman

Engine Oil Alert

For long auto life, the single most important maintenance procedure is to change your oil and filter every 3,000 to 4,000 miles regardless of operating-manual instructions. *Reason:* The acids caused by combustion break down the additives now found in all modern lubricating oils. These acids can begin to corrode engine parts.

The Durability Factor, edited by Roger B. Yepsen, Jr. Rodale Press.

Change the oil filter with each oil change. Synthetic oil, although far more expensive than petroleum, lasts longer and may in some instances increase gas mileage.

When Your Warranty Expires

Auto repairs are sometimes covered by the manufacturer even after the car is off warranty, especially for problems that began before the warranty expired.

Essential: The original receipts of the paid invoices for all previous repairs must be presented. This means getting originals (not copies) for all repairs, even those that were done after the warranty period expired.

The Road Ahead

Key to Unlocking Doors

When the car-door key can't be inserted, try flushing the lock with a spray lubricant. Dirt usually causes the jam-up. Don't use oil. It will mix with the dirt and worsen the clog.

Best Auto Mechanics

Find one who's been certified in your area of concern (front end, brakes, etc.) by the National Institute for Automotive Service Excellence. Certified mechanics wear a gear-shaped shoulder patch on their workshirts. Bar-shaped patches underneath list their specialties.

Best: A Master Auto Technician gold patch indicates that the mechanic has passed all eight certification tests.

Popular Mechanics

Flat Tire Dos And Don'ts

Repair a tire only when the puncture in the tread area is ¼ inch in diameter or smaller. This puncture must be at least 15 inches away from a prior one, and tread depth must be more than ¹⁄₁₆ inch.

• **It's important for the mechanic to remove the tire from the wheel.** A permanent repair can be made only from inside the tire. *Another reason:* An internal inspection is a "must," because driving on a flat (even a short distance at low speeds) can damage the crucial inner surface.

• **After repair, have the tire and wheel assembly rebalanced.** This will more than pay for itself in a smoother ride and longer tire life.

• **Avoid the use of instant tire sealants.** They camouflage the slow loss of air that signals a punctured tire.

Tire Pressure Is Important

Test your car's tires weekly with a dial-type gauge (gauges without dials are often inaccurate). Studies show that most cars have two or more tires that have low air pressure, causing poor fuel mileage, unsafe handling, excessive wear and heat buildup. All these problems can cause early tire failure.

The Durability Factor, edited by Roger B. Yepsen, Jr. Rodale Press.

Correcting tire pressure before taking off on that long summer trip can knock as much as 3% off fuel bills.

Best Car Burglar Alarms

Like your other valuables, you want to make sure your car is protected—especially when left out in a public space. A car alarm provides security and peace of mind. *The features of a good alarm...*

• **Passively armed system.** That means it should require nothing more of the driver than shutting off the motor and removing the ignition key. There should not be complicated setup procedures.

• **Instant "on" at all openings.** That means the alarm should activate as soon as any door, the hood or the trunk is opened.

• **Remotely disarmed by a code instead of by means of a switch or a key.** A lock can be picked, a code is impossible to break.

• **Hood lock.** Denying a thief access to your engine, battery and siren is a major deterrent.

• **Backup battery to prevent a thief from crawling under your car,** cutting the car's main battery and destroying the entire electrical system and therefore the alarm system.

• **Motion detector.** The best kind are the electronic motion detectors that sense a car's spatial attitude at the time the alarm is armed whether it's on a hill, on uneven ground, etc. (Also, least prone to false alarms.)

Beyond these essentials, such extras as pressure-sensitive pads in the seats and under carpeting, glass-breakage detectors, paging systems and air horns are available and can be added to all systems. Wheel locks are a good item to have on your car if you own expensive optional wheels.

Most insurance companies will give you a discount if your car is so equipped. Generally it's 10% off the premium—each year.

Don't put stickers in the window announcing to the world what type of burglar-alarm system you have. Most experts feel that this removes the element of surprise and can even help the thief.

Cheap alarms provide little more than a false sense of security for a car owner. A good thief can foil them easily. A completely unprotected car can be stolen in less than 30 seconds.

Car-Theft Patterns

An auto is most likely to be stolen on a Monday or Friday night when it's parked on the street at home. Most thieves enter through an unlocked door and pull out the ignition-lock cylinder. *What makes the job even easier:* Alarm systems that aren't in use or don't function 25% of the time.

Survey by General Motors and auto insurers, reported in *Journal of American Insurance.*

Outthinking Car Thieves

There are some smart ways you can protect your car from thieves in a variety of situations. *For example...*

To prevent being towed away: Put the car in "park" or "gear," depending upon whether it is an automatic or a standard. Then apply the emergency brake.

To prevent theft at airports and other long-term parking lots: Remove the distributor cap or the coil wire from under the hood. It is impossible to start the car without this connecting wire unless your thief is particularly knowledgeable and has brought an extra coil wire with him. *Extra precaution:* Replace the coil wire with a broken one. This

way, the thief will not know why the car isn't starting up.

To prevent theft in your driveway: Back in rather than driving straight in. The thief will then be forced to do his suspicious tinkering in full view of neighbors.

National Association of Fleet Administrators (NAFA) Bulletin. *www.nafa.org*

How to Have a Good-Looking Finish

Park in the shade instead of direct sunlight whenever possible. Never wipe off dust with a dry cloth—that may scratch the paint. If buying a new car, consider a light-colored one—light finishes last longer and stay shinier than dark ones.

Bob Sikorsky, author of *Drive It Forever* (ATG Media), and syndicated automotive columnist.

How to Get Better Fuel Economy

Replacing a car's dirty air filter can improve fuel economy by up to 10%.

Carmakers' recommendation: Change the filter annually or every 12,000 miles if you tend to drive over dusty roads...every two years or 24,000 miles for normal conditions.

Car & Travel, 1415 Kellum Place, Garden City, New York 11530. 11 issues. Free to members of Automobile Club of America.

Safer Driving

For greatest control, inflate tires to the recommended tire pressure found on the stickers or plates inside the door. It is the correct pressure for that model.

Trade-off: Higher pressure will give you maximum control—but a bumpier ride. *One reason you never want to underinflate tires:* Reducing pressure by one psi reduces tires' life by 600 miles…and increases gas consumption.

Anthony Ricci, president, Advanced Driving & Security Inc., North Kingstown, Rhode Island. *www.1adsi.com*

Auto-Accident Checklist

Move all involved cars safely off the main roadway. Many injuries can occur after an accident as people mill around on a busy road.

• **Call for medical help for the injured people.** If someone appears to be injured but says he or she is OK, call for help anyway.

• **Call the police and stay put until they arrive.** *Important:* Never admit your guilt or negligence. Just relay the facts and let the police determine who—if anyone—was at fault.

• **Get data from each driver involved—** no matter how minor the accident. *Important…*

• **Name**

• **Address**

• **Phone number**

• **Driver's license number**

• **Insurance information**

Also: Get names, addresses and phone numbers of the witnesses, including passengers in the cars that were involved.

• **Write down the details of the accident while they're still fresh in your mind.** *Describe:* Car directions, speed, whether signal and brake lights were functioning and used, etc.

• **Draw a map of the accident.** Note the location of any stop signs, traffic lights, objects in the road, etc.

• **If you carry a camera in the car,** photograph the accident from all angles and get good shots of any damage to each car.

• **Remain calm and follow all police instructions.**

8

Travel and Vacations

Secrets of Flying Safely In Unsafe Times

Despite new technology, there's no evidence that airlines are appreciably safer than they were a decade ago. Part of the problem is an unintentional consequence of deregulation. During the era of federal control, many airlines exceeded minimum safety requirements. But today fewer airlines exceed the standards because deregulation has intensified competition, thereby creating financial problems that have forced some airlines to divert resources away from safety.

But, more information about airline performance is now available, and it gives passengers new ways to choose safer airlines and increase their chances of surviving a crash. *How to choose safer airlines…*

•**Rule #1.** If possible, don't fly an airline that's in financial difficulty. There's no certainty that a money-troubled airline will be less safe. But the FAA itself increases safety surveillance of such airlines on the assumption that they're under pressure to cut corners on safety and maintenance.

For similar reasons, think twice about flying an airline that's having severe labor problems, especially those that may disrupt maintenance operations.

•**Rule #2.** Avoid small regional airlines whenever possible. Although some regionals have good safety records, statistics show that you're three times more likely to die in a crash on a plane with 30 or fewer seats than on a larger craft. Among other problems, regionals often use small airports that aren't as well equipped to guide planes in at night and in bad weather as larger airports are. Also, small

Paul Hudson, executive director, Aviation Consumer Action Project, an advocacy group for airline safety and passenger rights, 529 14th Street, NW, Suite 923, Washington, DC 20045. The organization also publishes *Facts and Advice for Airline Passengers,* a booklet that gives more information on safety and consumer rights.

airplanes often lack the more sophisticated instrumentation for bad-weather flying, and regional pilots are generally not as experienced as those who fly for major carriers.

Trap: Airlines don't always tell passengers that they're routed on a regional carrier for a particular leg of their trip. For that reason, always ask which airline you'll be flying on each leg. You may find that another major airline will fly directly to your destination or that you can rent a car and drive from a nearby major city.

SAFEST PLANES

The National Transportation Safety Board (*www.ntsb.gov*) keeps records on accidents of specific planes, and these are available to the public. *Challenge:* The accident data are difficult to interpret because problems may originate with the different kinds of engines that a single type of aircraft may use. And some aircraft that are flown over more dangerous routes may appear statistically less safe than others when they're really not.

Nevertheless, if for no other reason than peace of mind, travelers can avoid specific types of planes, particularly the DC-10 that's been involved in several disasters. And avoiding a certain type of plane is easier than most passengers realize.

When you make reservations, ask the ticket or travel agents what kind of plane is scheduled on your flight. If they balk, be insistent—agents virtually always have that information. If you have qualms about the type of plane being flown, ask for another flight or make reservations with another airline.

Before you leave for the airport, check again with the airline to see if there's been a change in planes. If there has been, and if you don't want to fly on the craft, you again have the option of making other travel arrangements (unless you have a nonrefundable ticket).

Even with a nonrefundable ticket, don't give up. Go to the airport and use persuasion on the ticket agent. Unfortunately, you have no other power to ask that your flight be switched. Agents are under no obligation to help travelers in that situation. But if you make it clear that the only reason you want to switch is to fly on another type of aircraft, then the agent may accommodate you to earn goodwill for the airline.

CHOOSING THE SAFEST SEATS

Myth: That the safest seats on all commercial aircraft are the ones that are located next to the plane's emergency exits.

Reality: Aisle seats close to the over-wing emergency exits are safer. These seats are commonly in the mid-front section of the plane. If you sit in the window seat next to an emergency exit, you may be worse off in the event of a crash that jams the exit. Aisle seats near several exits give you more escape options in a crash.

Lifesaving precaution: When you take your seat in the plane, count and memorize the number of rows to the nearest exits. *Reason:* If smoke fills the cabin after a crash, you may have to feel your way in the dark to an exit. This precaution is based on the tactics that crash survivors have actually used to get out of a plane.

• **For some protection against fire,** wear full-length clothing (long sleeves and pants), suits or dresses made of wool or cotton, sturdy shoes and eyeglasses with an attachable lanyard. Avoid wearing shorts or clothing that is made with synthetics, such as polyester, which can melt to your skin in a fire.

• **Women should not wear high-heeled shoes on a plane.** They can cause you to trip, and they can snag on the emergency-exit slide.

• **If the plane fills with smoke,** stay low, even if you have to crawl. Two or three breaths of toxic smoke can kill you. If there's enough warning before a crash, place a damp cloth over your mouth in order to breathe through smoke.

• **Get as far away from the plane as possible** if you're lucky enough to escape it after a crash.

• **Learn how to open the exits near your seat by reading the emergency instructions** soon after you get on the plane. That's something you don't want to try to learn as the aircraft bursts into flames.

Flying Smarter And Safer

Michael Goldfarb, former FAA Chief of Staff. He currently runs MGA, a management-consulting business specializing in transportation and information technology, based in Washington, DC.

***

Air travel is by far the safest form of transportation. In fact, you would need to spend 2,500 years flying every day before it became statistically likely that you would be involved in a crash. Yet some crashes do happen.

Travelers can make this already safe form of travel even safer.

FLYING SMARTER

When a plane crashes, the intense media coverage often scares the flying public. Statistically, plane crashes are so rare and their causes so unique that there is little one can do to avoid them.

To lessen passenger fear and "white-knuckle flying," travelers can check the safety records of each airline through the Federal Aviation Administration (FAA) Web site, *www.faa.gov.* Click on "Data & Research."

A history of repeated fines suggests systemic problems with a particular airline.

THE RIGHT PLANE

Boarding a plane that was manufactured between 30 and 40 years ago concerns some fliers. Many planes from the 1960s are still in the air, but these "old" planes aren't really old.

So even a 40-year-old plane will have components that are much younger than the manufacture date suggests.

Safety concerns: Problems arise when older aircraft are not aggressively maintained under an airline's aging-aircraft maintenance program. Problems also arise when older aircraft, such as DC-9s, are not properly cared for or are not continuously upgraded by the airline to carry the latest safety equipment in the cockpit.

FLIGHT LENGTH

Airline passengers tend to be more concerned about long flights. But, in fact, shorter flights pose the greater risk per mile.

If I have a choice between a nonstop flight and a flight involving a transfer, I will take the nonstop—and not only because it saves time.

Of the few accidents that occur, most are the result of pilot error. And pilot error is most common on takeoffs and landings—so more takeoffs and landings mean greater risk.

AIRLINE SIZE

Looking at aviation safety statistics, it appears that small commuter planes are riskier than large commercial planes.

But these statistics are deceptive. Recently, the FAA adopted the same set of safety rules for small planes—fewer than 30 seats—that are in place for larger ones. You're just as safe on a commuter plane in the US as you are on a wide-body jet.

Exception: Alaska. The state is so big that commuter-type planes are among the most common forms of transportation, despite the fact that flying a small plane in Alaska's difficult climate is inherently dangerous.

FOREIGN CARRIERS

Airline passengers often hesitate to book a flight on a foreign-based carrier, assuming that safety regulations are less strict in foreign countries. These fears are unwarranted—unless your flight includes a foreign stopover.

All planes flying into and out of the US must comply with US safety guidelines, whether the airline is based here or abroad.

However, flying internationally does raise some fears. Safety regulations in some countries are not always as tough as in the US.

Additionally, some areas of the world do not have the radar and ground navigational aids that are needed for safe navigation. Most modern aircraft have avionics that allow pilots to compensate for the lack of ground radar.

Danger: If your flight includes a transfer once you're overseas, you may end up on a plane that is not up to US safety standards. Since most major US carriers have alliances with foreign carriers, this might be true even if you book your flight with a well-known US airline.

Problems with airlines and airports are most common in Africa…South America…and some parts of the former Soviet Union.

Self-defense: Check the International Aviation Safety Assessment's Web page for concerns about particular countries *(www.faa.gov/about/initiatives/iasa)*. When you book a flight with a US carrier that involves a transfer, ask if other carriers will be involved.

How to Get a Passport Faster

Go to the passport office in person. *Bring:* Your airline ticket, two passport pictures, proof of citizenship (an old passport, voter registration or birth certificate), a piece of identification with your photo on it and the $100 fee ($75 for a renewal). Give the passport office a good reason why you are rushed. *Result:* A few days' versus several weeks' wait.

If your passport is lost or stolen when you're traveling abroad, notify the local police and the US embassy or consulate immediately. *Good news:* An overnight replacement is sometimes possible in an emergency. *To hasten the process:* Know your passport number. This speeds up verification of the original application. *Next best:* Have a valid identification document with you. *Shrewd:* Take a photocopy of your passport on the trip.

Nancy Dunnan, publisher, *TravelSmart*, Box 397, Dobbs Ferry, New York 10522, 800-FARE-OFF (800-327-3633). *www.travelsmartnewsletter.com*

Overlooked Airfare Saver

Many airlines will reimburse you for the amount of any drop in the price of an airline ticket that occurs after you buy it but before you use it. But you won't get a reimbursement if you don't ask. *Advice:* Before getting on your flight, ask the ticket agent to check his computer for the current price of your ticket, and see if you are entitled to a refund.

The Wall Street Journal

Cheaper Airfares

Airfares are usually cheapest on Tuesdays, Wednesdays and Saturday mornings, highest on Mondays and Fridays. Rates are discounted most often on midday and late-night flights, rarely during morning and evening business commuting hours.

Travel & Leisure

Secrets of Safer International Travel

John Healy, coauthor of *Do's and Taboos of Preparing for Your Trip Abroad* (John Wiley & Sons).

Start preparing for your trip by doing some homework on your destination. Read newspapers to keep abreast of current events. Do research at your library.

Extreme: If there's a war or revolution brewing you might want to put off your visit for a safer time.

•**For the latest information.** The US Department of State offers a recording of travel advisories for dangerous areas around the world. Contact the Department of State's Office of American Citizens' Services hotline at 202-647-5225 *http://travel.state.gov/travel.* In addition, don't hesitate to ask your travel agent about safety measures to take for the country or countries you're planning to visit.

- **Before leaving home.** Make sure all your documents are in order and make copies of everything—passport, visa, plane tickets, driver's license, credit cards—to leave at home with a friend or relative. Also, when you arrive at your destination, keep extra copies of your valuable documents separate from where you're holding the originals.

- **Bring extra passport photos.** Should your passport be lost or stolen, they'll make replacement less of a headache. If you have an expired passport, bring it along, for the same reason.

- **Use common sense when in a strange land.** Avoid flashy jewelry, maintain a low-key appearance. A hotel concierge can be an excellent source of information about a city. Don't be afraid to ask what areas may be safe or unsafe.

- **Know where the closest US embassy, consulate or mission is.** Keep their phone numbers handy in case of an emergency.

- **Observe local customs and laws.** Stay away from black market currency exchanges. The rates may be better than the official exchange rates—but they are illegal.

More Overseas Precautions

John P. Caulfield, former consul general, US Embassy, London.

On a trip abroad you can encounter problems you might never have thought of. It's important to make adequate preparation and to be aware of how American embassies abroad operate.

BEFORE YOU LEAVE

- **Check your health and accident insurance** to see if you're covered for illness or injury abroad. *Also:* Will your policy pay for transportation home if you're on a litter and need more than one airplane seat? Although a number of companies will pay for treatment, transportation is rarely covered. *Recommended:* Fill in the section provided in your

passport for a contact in case of emergency. Keep it accurate and up-to-date for each trip. Don't list your spouse if he or she is going with you. It can delay notification of your next of kin by the Department of State.

- **Take a copy of the prescriptions for any medications** you're carrying.

IF SOMETHING HAPPENS

US embassies or consulates all have consular sections to assist American travelers who encounter emergencies abroad. If you're in any trouble, don't hesitate to use their services. Call or visit the embassy. Consuls are responsive to the needs of Americans traveling or residing abroad. However, they must devote the majority of their priority time and energy to those Americans who are in serious trouble (legal, medical, etc.).

LOST PASSPORTS AND CREDIT CARDS

If your passport is lost or stolen, contact the nearest embassy or consulate immediately. A consul will interview you, and if he or she is satisfied with your US citizenship and identity, a new passport can be quickly issued. Will he believe you? Most Americans are able to satisfy the consular officer on the basis of a personal interview and presentation of identification that was not stolen or lost with the passport. In some cases, however, the consul may find it necessary to wire the Department of State to verify that you had been issued a previous passport.

The consul will be able to refer you to any local offices of the major credit cards and traveler's checks for reporting loss of credit cards or travelers checks. If you lose all your money, the embassy will assist you in having funds transferred from a friend or relative in the US through State Department channels. *What it won't do:* Lend you money.

MISSING PERSONS

The State Department often receives emergency requests to locate a friend or relative who has disappeared abroad. If you're worried about someone who's abroad, call the Department of State. It maintains a hotline at 202-647-5225, *http://travel.state.gov/travel.* The center will provide a liaison between the concerned person in the States and the appropriate embassy, which will try to locate the missing traveler. If you contact the Department of State for assistance in locating someone abroad, provide as much information as possible about the itinerary of the person you wish to locate. (This is one reason travelers should leave a detailed itinerary with a relative. *Note:* Under the Privacy Act of 1974, the consul cannot provide information about a US citizen without the authorization of that person.)

MEDICAL CARE

The embassy or consulate has lists of local English-speaking doctors, some of whom were trained in the US, and lists of the better local hospitals.

International Travel Know-How

Stuart R. Rose, MD, director, International Travel Clinic at Noble Hospital, Westfield, Massachusetts, and president, Travel Medicine, a travel-oriented publishing and mail-order company, Northampton, Massachusetts. He is coauthor of *International Travel Health Guide* (Elsevier Health Sciences).

These days, travelers are vulnerable to everything from infectious diseases to terrorism, as demonstrated by the recent SARS scare.

Here are the most significant threats travelers now face—and how to guard against them on your next trip abroad…

MOTOR VEHICLE ACCIDENTS

You may be surprised to learn that infectious diseases, such as malaria, account for only 1% of deaths among international travelers. Nowadays, the biggest danger to Americans abroad is accidental injury, especially from motor vehicle accidents.

You already know how important it is to wear seat belts. *Here are some other ways to minimize your risk of being injured or killed in an accident…*

• **Don't drive at night in rural areas.**

• **Don't ride a motorcycle, moped or bicycle**—even if you feel comfortable riding one at home.

• **Don't accept a ride in an overcrowded bus** or other vehicle.

• **Bring a car seat for any infant traveling with you.**

If you hire a guide or driver, don't hesitate to tell him or her to slow down—and drive cautiously.

If you plan to rent a car, go for the biggest car you can afford. The bigger the car, the greater the protection it affords occupants in case of a collision.

Make sure you can decipher road signs and traffic patterns in the country you'll be visiting.

Helpful resource: The Association for Safe International Road Travel in Potomac, Maryland, 240-249-0100, *www.asirt.org*. This not-for-profit organization will send you a report on road safety and driving conditions in over 150 foreign countries.

FIRES AND VIOLENT CRIME

Aircraft crashes, homicides and fires—along with drownings—account for most of the other deaths among Americans abroad. One way to protect yourself from these threats is to avoid regions in which drug trafficking is a problem. *Other ways…*

• **Avoid small airlines or charter flights in undeveloped nations.**

• **Don't travel alone or outside urban areas at night.**

• **Don't hitchhike**—or pick up hitchhikers.

• **Don't sleep in a vehicle that is parked along the road.**

• **If possible, book your hotel room between the second and seventh floors.** That's high enough to prevent easy access by intruders…yet low enough for fire equipment to reach you.

If you're planning a trip to a region troubled by violence or political instability, contact the US State Department before your departure. Experts at the Department's Bureau of Consular Affairs can alert you to crime, terrorism or other concerns in more than 200 countries. The Department can be reached at *http://travel. state.gov*…via telephone at 202-647-5225.

If terrorism is a concern, do not wear expensive clothing...and don't wear or carry any item with a corporate logo or another detail that marks you as an American.

LYME DISEASE

This tick-borne illness occurs throughout Canada, Europe, Asia and the US.

It's a good idea to avoid ticks if possible. This means wearing long-sleeved shirts and long pants tucked into socks whenever you venture outdoors in an area where Lyme is a problem. Light-colored clothes make it easier to spot the ticks, which are dark.

Spray clothes with the insecticide *permethrin* (Duranon). Treat exposed skin with a bug repellent containing at least 20% DEET.

Caution: If you develop symptoms of Lyme, see a doctor, who should prescribe the appropriate antibiotics right away.

Lyme symptoms include fever, headache, muscle and joint aches, swollen glands, fatigue, nausea, loss of appetite and a circular, bull's-eye shaped, pink rash at the site of the tick bite.

Good news: The same precautions used to prevent Lyme disease also reduce your risk for malaria, dengue fever and other diseases transmitted by insects.

DIARRHEA AND HEPATITIS

Traveler's diarrhea and hepatitis A—a liver disorder that causes fever, fatigue and jaundice—are common diseases in countries that have poor sanitation.

To cut your risk for both diseases: When traveling in a region where sanitation conditions are questionable, drink only commercially bottled or packaged beverages...or water that's been boiled or chemically treated. Ice cubes are usually made from tap water, so it's best to avoid them.

Eat only well-cooked foods served hot. Avoid salads. Fruits and vegetables are okay only if you can peel them yourself. Don't eat food from street vendors.

If diarrhea strikes: Begin a three-day course of *ofloxacin* (Floxin) right away. It's best to get a supply of this prescription drug before departure and take it along.

For fastest relief of diarrhea, take two tablets of *loperamide* (Imodium) along with the first dose of ofloxacin.

For total protection against hepatitis A, you should ask your doctor about getting the Havrix or VAQTA vaccine at least three weeks before your departure. This is generally a good idea for all international travelers over age two who are headed to any foreign country outside Canada, Western Europe, Australia, New Zealand or Japan.

EMERGENCY EVACUATION

If you need sophisticated medical treatment in a hurry, a travel health insurance policy that arranges and pays for an air ambulance can save your life. *Two reputable companies:* International SOS Assistance—800-523-8662, *www.internationalsos.com*...and Europ Assistance USA—800-777-8710, *www.europassistance-usa.com*.

Vital Travel Web Site

A good site to check before you travel is the US Department of State Bureau of Consular Affairs. Travel warnings for areas of instability or high crime...passport and visa information...links to foreign embassies in Washington, DC...emergency telephone numbers...and more. *http://travel.state.gov.*

Clearing Customs

The US Customs agents you may encounter have very specific requirements on goods they will allow. *For example...*

Personal exemption: $800 ($600 from 24 Caribbean Basin countries). *The next $1,000:* A flat rate of 3% duty. *Above this:* Individual assessments are made on goods.

Sending gifts: Such gifts are duty-free if marked unsolicited gift, value under $100.

Gifts cannot be sent to yourself or to a traveling companion.

• **Sending goods home.** Duty must be paid on major items. They do not count as part of a personal exemption.

• **Liquor and tobacco.** You are allowed one liter of alcohol, 100 cigars and 200 cigarettes.

• **Drugs.** Medications obtained abroad could be seized.

Know Before You Go, free from US Customs, 202-325-8000. *www.cbp.gov*

If You Are Arrested Overseas

John P. Caulfield, former consul general, US Embassy, London.

In a sample year, 3,000 Americans were arrested in 97 foreign countries for offenses ranging from narcotics and disorderly conduct to murder. If arrested, you should ask to contact your embassy. Be polite but persistent in making this request. American embassies are usually informed when Americans are arrested in foreign countries. A consular officer will visit an American in prison as soon as possible and provide him or her with a list of local attorneys, including their specialties and qualifications. The consul can also call an attorney for the American if he isn't able to make a call, notify friends or relatives at home, help wire for funds, make sure basic health and safety needs are being met and make sure he's not being discriminated against because he's an American. *What the embassy can't do:* Get someone out of jail. Americans are subject to the laws of the country in which they are residing or visiting.

DANGERS

• **Auto accidents.** In many foreign countries, you can be arrested or imprisoned for driving while intoxicated or held criminally liable for an accident in which someone is injured. Drive carefully!

• **Narcotics.** Those convicted of possession or trafficking in drugs usually spend from two to 10 years in jail, often with long waits in jail for a trial. Bail is generally not possible for narcotics offenses or other serious offenses in most foreign countries. *Important:* If you get a call from abroad saying your youngster has been arrested, confirm the arrest with the Overseas Citizens Services, 202-501-4444 (regular business hours) or 202-647-4000 (after hours and weekends) before sending money. The call might be an extortion attempt.

• **Black marketeering.** This is a very serious offense in many countries and is often punished by a prison term. *Also:* Beware of blackmarket currency transactions. You could be robbed or wind up with counterfeit currency.

How to Fly On Commuter Airlines

Privileged information from pilots, air-traffic controllers, consumer protectionists and government officials.

Most of the big catastrophes involving major airlines have been attributed to either poor weather conditions or air-traffic controller errors. But most commuter airline crashes stem from pilot error. According to the watchdogs at the Aviation Consumer Action Project, you are three times more likely to be in a fatal accident on a commuter airline than on a large trunk carrier.

Scary reasons: Many commuter pilots are inexperienced, hired fresh out of flight school with very little—and sometimes no—bad-weather or emergency training. For economic reasons, these pilots get most of their hands-on training late at night or on weekends, after they've already put in a full day of flying. Most of them are never trained in simulators—standard for the big airlines—because the commuter lines operate on a shoestring budget.

WHAT'S IN YOUR CONTROL

Even seasoned travelers often don't realize that commuter airline passengers have much more control over flight operations than do passengers on the big trunk carriers. *Strategy:* Assume that you and the pilot are the only ones on the plane, even if you're surrounded by other passengers. Commuter pilots have more leeway than you'd think and, according to our sources, are often willing to act on passenger suggestions, as long as they're reasonable and don't jeopardize safety.

Whether you're flying in a 20-seat jet or a two-seat air taxi, there are a few things you can do to increase your personal safety. Some of these steps might cost you time or money, but they could save your life.

• **Make sure the pilot checks the plane thoroughly before takeoff.** For example, does the pilot take fuel samples?

• **Ask about weather conditions.** If the skies are cloudy, ask whether the pilot is instrument-rated, whether he or she is up-to-date on the navigation equipment and whether a flight plan has been filed to allow the plane to be navigated based on instrument readings rather than on visual information. If the answer to any of these questions is "no," you are in great peril, especially at night. If at all possible, skip this flight.

• **If every seat is full,** ask if the plane is too heavy for takeoff, especially on a warm day or when you're taking off from a short runway. Many small planes are dangerous if every seat is full.

• **Once in the plane,** watch the pilot get ready for departure. He should be using a checklist and checking everything methodically. Don't trust anything to his memory.

• **Once aloft, watch weather.** If you hear the pilot talking about thunderstorms with an air-traffic controller and the plane's not equipped with radar or a Stormscope, tell the pilot that you're in no hurry. He can take a longer—and safer—route.

• **If you see ice forming on the plane,** suggest that the pilot take a rest-room stop. (It sounds odd, but it's more common than most people think.)

• **If the pilot is flying visually (by sight, not instruments),** and it appears that he can't see a good distance, tell the pilot that you'd prefer to discontinue this flight.

• **If the pilot tries to entertain you by flying low,** making steep bank turns or pulling the plane in for a closer look at something on the ground, calmly insist that he take you back to the airport.

• **If an approach and landing are being tried in bad weather,** tell the pilot that it's okay with you to land at another airport.

• **If fuel gauges appear low or the pilot says he's stretching it,** suggest a refueling stop sooner, not later.

Warning: Commuter airlines are not governed by the same stringent rules as the large trunk carriers. If your trip requires a change of plane, the second leg of your journey could be on a commuter plane. *Option:* Consider renting a car or taking a train or bus.

Reduce Airline Luggage Losses

Buy extra baggage insurance when you check in at the airport. It's called excess valuation. Estimate the value of your bags and their contents. You must provide receipts of the contents in order to collect on a loss. However, the chances of loss are reduced because airlines take extra care in handling bags covered by excess valuation.

Nancy Dunnan, publisher, *TravelSmart*, Box 397, Dobbs Ferry, New York 10522, 800-FARE-OFF (800-327-3633). *www.travelsmartnewsletter.com*

Airline Trap to Avoid

Many airlines are canceling prebooked seat assignments if you do not check in at least 15 minutes before flight time. Some close the doors to their skybridges as much as nine minutes before flight time—since, technically, passengers must be at the gate 10 minutes before flight time to board.

Bottom line: If you often cut it close when flying, change your habits so you can avoid missing flights.

Nancy Dunnan, publisher, *TravelSmart*, Box 397, Dobbs Ferry, New York 10522, 800-FARE-OFF (800-327-3633). *www.travelsmartnewsletter.com*

Better Food

Airlines are serving better food now that they are charging passengers for it. *American Airlines* is working with well-known chefs, such as Marcus Samuelsson, to provide better meals. *Alaska Airlines* offers a healthful snack pack. *Air Canada* has introduced vegetarian sandwiches and yogurt parfaits. Other airlines also are trying to improve the quality of their food.

The New York Times

How to Get the Best Foreign-Exchange Rates

To get the most for your dollar while traveling, change your money in commercial banks, not in hotels and restaurants. Make sure you take some local currency in case you reach a country after banking hours. Find out the banks' closing times and holidays when you arrive so you won't be caught short.

Travelers' Health Secrets

Being sick is uncomfortable—and it's tougher to deal with when you're traveling. *Try these aids for relief…*

•**Motion-sickness cure.** By taking your mind off the motion, you can help your body restore equilibrium without drugs. *How to do it:* Close your eyes, or concentrate on a spot in front of you, and hold your head as steady as possible. Then focus your attention on your breathing or on alternately tensing and relaxing your muscles. Continue to concentrate until the nausea has vanished.

•**Traveler's diarrhea aid.** Get a prescription for the antibiotic doxycycline. One tablet a day generally prevents the problem. *Limitation:* It is not recommended for pregnant women or children because it can discolor developing teeth.

Healthwise

•**Congested sinuses and airplanes don't mix.** *Reason:* Aircraft cabins are pressurized below atmospheric pressure. If a sinus is blocked, the trapped air inside expands and can lead to serious infection, including brain infections. *Advice:* Don't fly with a serious sinus problem. Improve drainage prior to ascent and descent with decongestants.

How to Avoid Travel Anxiety

Pretrip jitters hit many travelers, even veterans. *Remedies:* Since the cause of jitters is often anxiety over things left undone, pack a few days early and make checklists.

When you travel, avoid putting pressure on yourself: Don't rush to the boarding gate the moment your flight is announced. Relax in the waiting room until the rush is over—your seat is reserved. Similarly, wait in your seat after the plane lands. Those who push for the exits end up standing for long periods. Unless absolutely necessary, don't run to catch a bus, cab or subway. When commuting by car, occasionally take the less-traveled routes.

Ross A. Webber, author, *Time Is Money!* (Simon & Schuster).

Midday Hotels

If your schedule permits, nap for several hours between connecting flights when traveling out of town. There are some hotels that rent rooms for day use at only about half the regular rate.

OAG/Frequent Flyer

Lower Hotel Rates

When visiting a company in another city, ask whether that company has a special deal with one of the hotels in town. Most hotels offer a rate to local companies that's even lower than the corporate rate for other firms. If that's the case, ask the local company to make the reservation.

Nancy Dunnan, publisher, *TravelSmart*, Box 397, Dobbs Ferry, New York 10522, 800-FARE-OFF (800-327-3633). *www.travel smartnewsletter.com*

How to Cancel Noncancelable Tickets

Some discount tickets cost as little as 30% of regular airfares, but airlines say you can't get a refund if you change travel plans. *Solution:* A cooperative travel agent.

When you buy a ticket from an agent, the agent makes your reservation immediately. But he/she doesn't forward your money to the airline for a few days—in some cases not until a week later. That's because agents pay airlines only once a week. During the time gap, a friendly travel agent will allow you to cancel the reservation and get your money back.

Credit card purchases do not apply because the Airlines Reporting Corporation requires travel agencies to report their charge card sales on a daily basis.

Caution: Travel agents don't have to accommodate you. But if you're a good customer and the agent wants to keep your business, chances are good that you can get a refund.

Helpful: Check with your agent to see if two round-trip, noncancelable discount fares cost less than one full round-trip ticket. Even if you use only half of each of the discount tickets, the cost for both may be less than a full-fare ticket.

Harold Seligman, president, Management Alternatives, travel management consultants, Stamford, Connecticut.

Traveling with Teens Can Be Fun—Yes, Fun!

Susan Farewell, founder and CEO of FarewellTravels. com, an online travel news and information site that draws upon the insights and expertise of passionate travelers all over the world, including Susan's daughter, Justine, who accompanies her on many trips. *http://farewelltravels.com*

When kids are young, basically the only requirement for a fun vacation is choosing a hotel that has a pool. But it can be a lot more challenging keeping teenagers happy on a family vacation. *Here are vacation ideas that will please both you and your teen...*

• **Outdoor activities**. Staying active can be the key to a successful family vacation with teens. Some tour companies offer travel packages that help you do exactly that.

Example: Row Adventures offers a family trip in northern Idaho and Montana that includes three-and-a-half days of bicycling (a van follows along if you need to take a break)...a half-day of lake kayaking...and a day of moderate whitewater rafting. *www.rowadventures.com/idaho-bike-tour.html*

Cost: $1,595 per person.*

• **Learn a sport.** If your kids were busy with, say, soccer growing up and missed out on learning the basics of tennis, the last thing they want to do is be a beginner in front of their classmates.

Solution: Take them for a family vacation at a tennis camp. A good resource about the various tennis programs (for adults as well as kids)

*Prices and specific tours are subject to change.

is *www.tennisresortsonline.com. Other sports vacation options:* Learn to play golf (check out *www.usgolfschoolguide.com*)…ride horses (*http://duderanch.org*)…and ski (most ski resorts have ski schools for all levels and ages). Of course, focusing on one sport doesn't have to take over the entire vacation. For example, in Hawaii, sign your child up for a two-hour surfing lesson. That will magically turn the vacation into the trip of a lifetime.

• *Scuba diving/snorkeling.* You'll find top-notch snorkeling and scuba courses at many tropical resorts, including in the Caribbean. Before committing to plans, make sure that the dive operation is affiliated with a certifying agency, such as the Professional Association of Dive Instructors (*www.padi.com/scuba*) or National Association of Underwater Instructors (*http://naui.org*).

• *Seaside towns and islands.* Small resort towns are ideal for teens. One example is Cape May, New Jersey. Pick a hotel near the boardwalk, and let the kids come and go to the beach and arcades as they please. There's plenty of history in this Victorian town, as well as a variety of restaurants and shops to keep everyone in the family satisfied.

Other seaside towns for family getaways: Provincetown on Cape Cod in Massachusetts… Venice Beach or Carmel, California…Seaside, Oregon…and Port Townsend, Washington.

As for islands: Nantucket and Martha's Vineyard, off the New England coast…San Juan Island, off the Washington coast.

• *Big, famous cities.* You can't go wrong by visiting New York or San Francisco. There are so many distractions in these cities that your kids will be too preoccupied to complain. At hotels in both places, you can find reasonably priced family suites.

Examples: In midtown Manhattan, try the superhip Pod Hotel (230 East 51 St., New York City 10022, 800-742-5945, *www.thepodhotel.com*). Family suites—called Townhouse Studio pods— start as low as $209 (depending on availability) and include one queen-size bed and two singles. In San Francisco, try the Sheraton Fisherman's Wharf Hotel (2500 Mason St., 415-362-5500, *www. sheratonatthewharf.com*).

Hotel Robbery Prevention

Hotel thieves have a favorite technique. They strike up a conversation with their victim on the hotel elevator. They step off at the same floor and pretend to be otherwise occupied. Then, when the victim has opened his or her door, the robbers push in and go to work.

Andrea Forrest, president, Preventive Security Services, New York City.

Hotel Bargains Via the Internet

Major hotel chains use the Internet to offer last-minute bargains on rooms that otherwise would go unsold.

And—there are also many bargains on advance reservations. *Hotel Web sites…*

• **Quikbook,** *www.quikbook.com.*

• **hoteldiscount!com,** *www.hoteldiscounts. com.*

• **Hilton,** *www.hilton.com.*

• **Radisson,** *www.radisson.com.*

• **Priceline.com,** *www.priceline.com.*

When subscribing to some of these sites, you can be automatically notified by E-mail of new bargain offerings.

Resolving Taxi-Driver Quarrels

To settle a dispute with a taxi driver when traveling abroad, ask the driver to take you to your hotel, where the bell captain can straighten it out. You are unlikely to succeed arguing the issue alone with the driver.

Luggage-Identification Warning

Luggage-identification tags properly filled out will return that lost bag to you. However, your name and office address, not home address, should be on the tag. With the crime rate increasing, don't advertise that you will be out of town. When you make your travel reservations, a phone contact is always requested. Leave your office number (or a friend's), not your home number.

Judith Preston, travel consultant, Park Ridge, Illinois.

Motel Liability

A motel clerk handed out a room key to the wrong person, who used it to rob a guest of a large sum of money. The motel claimed that its posted notice of a safe available for guests' property limited its liability to $100 by state law. The Louisiana Supreme Court held that the $100 limit referred only to contractual liability as a depository. There was no limitation when the loss was caused by the negligence of the motel or its employees.

Kraaz v. LaQuinta Motor Inns, Inc., 410 So. 1048.

A motel's liability for guests' property applies to a guest's vehicle and its contents while in a parking lot provided for guests and under the care of motel keepers.

Vilella v. Sabine, Inc., Okla. S. Ct., 5-27-82.

What the Airlines Don't Tell You

Never accept the first fare quoted. Half the time, some other airline has a special, less expensive deal available within hours of the flight you booked.

• **Take advantage of "illegal" connections.** These are connecting flights usually less than 45 minutes apart—too close for airlines to feel safe in making them connect. *Result:* These flights usually do not even show up on the computer when your trip is being routed. *Solution:* Have your agent write up your flight on two separate tickets. The second is for the illegal connection that originates at your transfer point.

Example: You arrive at O'Hare in Chicago on the way to San Francisco. Instead of waiting three hours for the safe connecting flight, you have a separate ticket from O'Hare to San Francisco on an illegal connection. If you miss the connection, you turn that ticket in for the next available flight. *Cost for two separate tickets:* No more than for one through ticket. *Baggage:* Waiting for it to be unloaded can cost you valuable time on this tight schedule. *Best:* Travel with carry-on luggage.

Martin G. Blinder, MD, San Francisco.

• **Use online do-it-yourself searches.** Plug into the *Official Airlines Guide* database (*www.oag.com*) and retrieve all information needed on alternative flights and fares. *How the electronic database works:* First, search the flights available at the desired time. Using another code, find out what fares are available on each airline for the time period. At this point if no asterisk is shown, it's possible to book the flight right up to the last minute. If there is an asterisk next to the airline flight number, ask the system what the restrictions are.

Harold Seligman, president, Management Alternatives, travel management consultants, Stamford, Connecticut.

• **Be imaginative, and do a little calculating.** Some discount fares are so low that even if you can't stay as long as their requirements (usually seven days) you will save by buying two round-trip tickets—one from your home to your destination for the day you want to leave and one from your destination to your home for the day you want to return. The total may be less than the regular round-trip fare.

Robert Z. Aliber, author, Your Money and Your Life (Stanford Economics and Finance).

• **If you miss your flight and there's just time to catch another one,** go right to the other airline's departure gate instead of to its ticket counter. If it has an empty seat, the second airline will usually honor the ticket for the flight you missed.

Barbara Pletcher, PhD, former president, National Association for Professional Saleswomen.

• **Best seat in the plane.** After first class, the choices center on your priorities. For comfort and a smooth ride, pick a seat over the wings. For silence, sit as far forward as possible, but avoid the galley and rest rooms. For legroom, try the first row or seats beside the emergency exits.

• **Jet-engine noise warning.** Jet-engine noise can harm hearing, especially if you're sitting in economy class. Many people whose ears feel stuffy after a flight think pressure problems are the cause. But cabin noise alone can cause the problem. Any temporary hearing loss usually corrects itself quickly. To avoid it in the first place, sit in front of the engines and wear ear plugs.

Rebecca Johnson, San Francisco attorney and co-author of *Travel Fitness* (Human Kinetics).

• **Airport duty-free shops are not always bargains.** Know prices before you buy. Even without state and local taxes and import duties, prices can be high. *Trap:* The owners of such shops pay high rents for the privilege of being monopoly sellers and pass these costs on.

Robert Z. Aliber, author, *Your Money and Your Life* (Stanford Economics and Finance).

E-Ticket Danger

Electronic airline tickets can cause problems when your flight is canceled and you have to switch to another airline to get to your destination.

Since airline computer systems are not linked, the second carrier will not have any record of your reservation.

Helpful: Have the original airline print you a paper ticket, which will be accepted for travel by the second airline.

Joe Brancatelli, creator of *www.joesentme.com*, a Web site for business travelers.

Confirming Reservations

Confirm airline reservations on international flights at least 72 hours prior to departure. *For the return flight:* Confirm on arrival at your destination. Do it at the airport. Or consult your airline ticket envelope for the local phone number. *Backup:* Note the date and time of your confirmation call and the name of the airline person with whom you speak.

Know Your Rights When You Travel

The Airline Passengers' Bill of Rights states that domestic carriers must allow passengers to disembark if a plane has been sitting on the tarmac for three hours. US airlines operating domestic flights must provide food and water within two hours of the delay, as well as working toilets. The Bill of Rights went into effect on April 29, 2010. Airlines that don't adhere to it face fines of $27,500 per passenger.

TravelSmart. www.travelsmartnewsletter.com

Flight Plan

Carry an airline guide (or photocopies of specific pages) on trips so you can look up schedules if you need to change reservations. Don't rely on the airlines to tell you the next flight out on any airline. They will usually tell you when their next flight is.

Execu-Time

What Car-Rental Agencies Don't Tell You

Nancy Dunnan, publisher, *TravelSmart*, Box 397, Dobbs Ferry, New York 10522, 800-FARE-OFF (800-327-3633). *www.travelsmartnewsletter.com*

There are so many details to consider when traveling, make sure you don't get ripped off when renting a car. *Tricks of the trade...*

• **Give a rented car the once-over before driving away in it.** Check the headlights, turn signals and brakes. Squirt the windshield washer to be sure there is fluid. Check the oil level. Drive it around the lot before leaving.

• **Don't pay for more insurance than you need on a rented car.** Rental agents routinely encourage customers to pay around $5 a day for optional collision coverage. Chances are, however, that your own personal-car policy may extend coverage to a rented car. Check the insurance policy before signing up for unnecessary coverage.

• **Automatic drop-off can be a rip-off on late-night rental-car returns.** Unlike normal rental-car check-in, where the clerk totals up the costs and gives you a copy of the bill, automatic drop-offs require you to return all copies. You often don't get a copy until your credit card company has billed you. *Protection alternatives:* Return your rental car during business hours. Make a copy of the rental form before returning it, noting your entry of the final mileage. Don't pay your credit card bill until you get the rental-car bill, and make sure their figures agree with yours. If they have overcharged you, dispute the bill and let the credit card company know about the problem.

Save on Car Rentals In Europe

Renting a car in Europe costs much more if you want an automatic transmission (or air conditioning). Most Europeans drive stick shifts, and European car rental companies have a difficult time selling cars with automatic transmissions, so they get their profits by charging more for renting them. *Result:* You may save a lot by renting a car with a manual transmission in Europe.

Brent Rolfe, former vice president of operations, Auto Europe, quoted in *Travel Holiday.*

Long-Distance Driving

For a safe, healthy trip when you're driving long-distance, do most of your driving during daytime hours. Visual acuity is reduced at night. Be particularly careful to check your car's exhaust system before leaving—a leak can emit odorless but deadly gases. To ensure sufficient fresh air inside the car, leave both a front and a back window open, and keep the tailgate window (if you have one) closed. Your air conditioner provides fresh air and quiet inside the car. Although it reduces gas mileage, the loss is not much more than the loss from the open windows' drag.

Use seat belts and shoulder harnesses to relieve fatigue as well as to boost safety. Take 20- to 30-minute rest breaks after every one-and-a-half or two hours of driving. Exercise during your breaks. Have frequent high-protein snacks for improved driving performance. Don't stare straight ahead even if you're the only car on the road. Keep your eyes moving.

Car Games

To make the ride less tedious, here are some fun games the whole family can play on the road...

EDUCATIONAL GAMES

• **Spelling Bee.** Take along a dictionary.

•**Discover America.** As someone keeps score, riders name the states of the Union and their capitals.

•**Add a Letter.** Start with a single letter and form a word with each new letter as you go from one player to the next.

•**I'm a Famous Person.** Pretend to be a celebrity—living or dead. Give clues to your personality as others try to guess who you are.

•**Quiz Kids.** Before the trip, collect an assortment of difficult questions and answers.

•**Words.** Select a long word, such as *separation,* and then see how many other words can be made from the same letters. Have pencil and paper handy.

SILLY GAMES

•**Famous Pairs.** Within a given period of time, perhaps half an hour, reel off the names of famous couples. *Examples:* George and Martha, Ron and Nancy, Bill and Hillary, G.W and Laura.

•**Don't Say That Word.** Prohibit certain words—such as *it, no, yes.* Try to maintain a conversation without using them.

•**What Time Do We Arrive?** Each person guesses the time of arrival at various places along the route—the next big city on the map, when you stop for lunch or gasoline.

•**Animals.** See who can spot the most cows, horses, etc., in the fields by the side of the road.

•**Name That License Plate.** Look for funny personal license plates that have names, initials or unusual numerical combinations.

•**Sign Games.** Think up lines to rhyme with interesting billboards or signs.

•**Let's Find It.** Agree to look for one special thing—a covered bridge, a bright red automobile. The first one to spot it wins and then selects the next thing to look for.

•**If I Were a Millionaire.** Ask what people would want if they were millionaires. Then ask them for second wishes.

•**Favorite Books and Movies.** Review the books and movies you have liked best. Tell what makes them enjoyable.

•**Sports Favorites.** Prepare a series of questions about sports events and stars before you depart. Then quiz sports fans while on the trip.

•**Where Am I Going?** Mentally select a place that you are headed for. Give hints about your imaginary destination, and let the other passengers guess where you are going.

SONG GAMES

•**Sing-Along.** See how many songs you can sing by different composers—Cole Porter, Irving Berlin, Billy Joel, The Beatles.

•**Sing Along with Me.** Bring a book of popular songs and lead the car in an old-fashioned sing-along.

•**Tap-a-Song.** Tap out the rhythm of a famous song. Give each person three guesses.

SEMISERIOUS GAMES

•**Personal History.** Spin tales of family remembrances—a special time spent with grandparents, a favorite birthday, a lovely trip taken in the past. Give each person a chance to share an experience.

•**Play Psychiatrist.** Ask everyone what bothers them most about their lives. Try to help them resolve their problems.

Best Places to Eat On the Road

Don't simply follow the truck drivers. Their first priority is a huge parking lot, not the best food.

•**Avoid restaurants on or very near major highways and in shopping centers.** You'll do better downtown. *Good bets:* College or university towns.

•**Best authorities.** Probably bookstore managers, fancy kitchenware and gourmet food store's personnel. *Worst:* Tollbooth or gas-station attendants.

•**Check out the parking lot.** Too many out-of-state license plates suggests a tourist trap. *Good sign:* A high proportion of foreign cars (especially European models).

Travel & Leisure.

Transporting Your Car

Drive-away services drive your car to a destination if you don't want to do it yourself. It takes about seven to 10 days to go cross-country. *Drawbacks:* Insurance, gas and maintenance for the trip are usually extra. Your car also suffers the strains of a long trip. *Alternative:* Send your car by truck or train. Although the price is higher, it includes insurance.

International Driving Permits

US residents may drive in most foreign countries with a valid driver's license from their home state. However, an American International Driving Permit is required in some countries. Ask your travel agent where you can buy one. In Italy and Germany, you need a translation of your American license or an American International Driving Permit. Drive on the left in Great Britain, Ireland, Cyprus, Australia and several other countries.

American Society of Travel Agents, Alexandria, Virginia, 703-739-2782. *www.asta.org*

Unique Ways to Plan Your Trip

Letty Cottin Pogrebin, freelance writer.

If you're the type who finds the sameness of Holiday Inns comforting or prefers to have dinner at McDonald's—in Paris—this advice isn't for you. But if you love country inns, a pot of coffee brewing in your room, four-poster beds, claw-legged bathtubs, lunch beside a swan pond, discovering the best wine cellar in Vermont, or the trail that isn't on a map, then you might want to plan your vacations differently.

Consult the guidebooks and travel agents last. Before that, in fact year-round, collect information on all kinds of interesting vacation possibilities. Then, whether the trip is for summer or winter, a weekend or longer, a family vacation or a getaway for two, the research accumulated over the months will allow you to make a choice based on a highly personalized and selective array of options. *Here is how you can do it...*

• **Keep files.** Keep geographic files with such labels as Caribbean, West Coast, the South, New England, Europe, Israel, Japan and Exotic Places. You can make your own headings and add new folders when the catchall category gets too full to be manageable. Subdivide your files into subject files labeled Ski Vacations, Tennis Vacations, Club Med Locations, Charming Inns/Elegant Small Hotels, Houses for Rent or Exchange and Great Restaurants in Other Places (to distinguish it from your hometown restaurant file).

It doesn't matter what categories head each folder as long as you remember what you meant. To start planning, decide on a location or a specific type of vacation, reach into the appropriate folder for articles and tips on things to do and see in that place, and then choose just the right lodging. Finally, make a list of restaurants you mustn't miss while you're there. Voila! A retrieval system without computer assistance. But how do you fill the files in the first place?

Articles that are taken from airline magazines, newsletters and the travel section of your newspaper are the obvious resources. *Some less obvious resources...*

• **Interview friends.** When you agree with your friends' taste in food, furnishings, theater or artwork, chances are you can trust their vacation advice, too. Don't wait for them to show their home movies. Ask where they have been lately that they've loved and why, what it looked like, what's to do there, and whether it's a good place for kids, a lovers' retreat, a flake-out resort, or a center for sports and nightlife. Jot it all down and put it in the files.

Go beyond your closest circle. Talk with neighbors, clients, tradespeople, friends at work. The more people you talk with, the more information you'll gather.

Friends you meet on one vacation can become hosts on another.

People who really "know how to live" can become splendid sources of vacation ideas because you can save the picture postcards they send you from wherever they travel.

• **Eavesdrop.** This quirky information source is surprisingly fertile for first leads. In an airport or restaurant, on the bus or train to work, if you hear a total stranger describe a perfect meal she had in Kansas City, or a rustic lodge in the Adirondacks with a gorgeous view of the sunset, jot it down. *You can check out the details later.* That's where guidebooks and travel agents come in handy.

If you tune in on the middle of a conversation and missed the name of the place being discussed, interrupt the stranger and ask for it. People are flattered to be seen as authorities in wining, dining or travel.

• **Books, movies, magazines.** In vacation terms, life can imitate art. You'll want to visit Big Sur if you've read Henry Miller or seen where Elizabeth Taylor's breathtaking house is set in the movie *The Sandpiper.* Hemingway and Gertrude Stein make you eager to retrace their steps all over Paris. If you're an antique-car buff and you've seen the British movie *Genevieve,* why not meander around the same English countryside where the automobiles rally?

In a *Fortune* profile of a business tycoon, he mentions his favorite beachfront refuge in Antigua; clip the page and file it. A fashion layout is photographed on a verdant Scottish golf course surrounded by charming cottages; you can track its identity through the ad agency. You can even dope out the names of the resort where Richard Burton and Ava Gardner carried on in the film *Night of the Iguana,* or the one in which Dudley Moore and Bo Derek made a mockery of the libido in *10.*

It's not hard to notice beautiful or intriguing locations that are featured in books, magazines, television shows or movies. What's hard is to realize that they're not always the most expensive vacation spots. Harder still is recording the information and putting it where you can find it when you're ready to act on it.

• **Business trips as fieldwork.** When traveling for business, ask the people you meet where you should stay if you ever come back to their city for pure fun. If you're meeting over lunch or dinner, ask them to pick a restaurant they love instead of going to your hotel's dining room. That's how you can discover the best hush puppies in Atlanta, the best Tex-Mex restaurant in Dallas and the best ice cream in Vancouver—and that's how the list of "bests" gets into your files for your next pleasure trip to those territories.

If you're invited someplace to lecture, ask to be put up not in a motel with a pool overlooking the interstate but at a guest house, inn or bed-and-breakfast on the chance that it will turn out to be special enough to return to with your family.

How to Get The Best Tables In Restaurants

You can get better restaurant tables by making reservations through a hotel concierge. *Reason:* The restaurant wants the hotel to continue to recommend it to customers, so it keeps the hotel guests happy by giving them the best seats.

Great Places in the Great Capitals of Europe

Mike Michaelson, award-winning travel writer and author of the *Best-Kept Secrets* guidebook series for Chicago, London, New York and Toronto (NTC Publishing).

More Americans are traveling to Europe each year, making it a very popular area to visit. *My favorite hotels, restaurants and stores in the top European destinations...*

LONDON

• **Dorchester Hotel.** Imagine an antique-filled English country house that is equipped with state-of-the-art amenities. Royals, presidents and movie stars enjoy a luxurious spa, sumptuous afternoon tea and two excellent restaurants—The Grill and China Tang.

45 Park Lane, 800-727-9820. *www.thedorchester.com*

• **Blakes Hotel.** Occupying four Victorian town houses on a leafy street, this hideaway is very popular with music stars and fashion-conscious travelers. Unconventional luxury that is worthy of a Hollywood set designer… no two rooms are alike.

33 Roland Gardens, 800-926-3173. *www.blakeshotels.com*

• **Bibendum.** An Anglo-French restaurant in the refurbished 1911 headquarters of the Michelin Tyre Co. London's best roast beef coexists with the likes of curried apple soup, mussels and grilled rabbit.

81 Fulham Rd., 011-44-20-7581-5817. *www.bibendum.co.uk*

• **Geale's.** Traditional fish and chips in an upscale setting. Actors and soccer stars are among patrons who enjoy wonderfully fresh fish at this painted-brick, corner storefront.

2 Farmer St., 011-44-20-7727-7528. *www.geales.com*

• **Anderson & Sheppard.** A fixture on London's famous Savile Row since 1906. Dignified tailors measure you top to bottom for custom-made suits.

32 Old Burlington Street, 011-44-20-7734-1420. *www.anderson-sheppard.co.uk*

MADRID

• **Hotel Ritz.** Aristocratic and luxurious, with tapestries, terraces, landscaped gardens and music concerts. Rooms decorated with expensive art and antiques, fitted with marble baths…no two rooms are alike.

5 Plaza de la Lealtad, 800-237-1236. *www.ritzmadrid.com*

• **Reina Victoria Hotel.** Old Madrid hotel that has ornate spire, landmark facade. Once favored by bullfighters and aficionado Ernest Hemingway, the 1920s makeover has modern amenities, bullfight memorabilia and spacious rooms with great views.

14 Plaza de Santa Ana, 011-34-91-701-6000. *http://memadridreinavictoria.madridhotels.it*

• **Horcher.** Housed in a mansion, this elegant, indulgent German-owned restaurant has Austro-Hungarian flair. Wild boar, roast wild duck, baby lamb chops, stroganoff and goulash, plus flambéed desserts.

6 Alfonso XII, 011-34-91-522-0731. *www.restauranteborcher.com*

• **Casa Botìn.** Castillian restaurant was another Hemingway hangout and setting for *The Sun Also Rises.* Decorated with ceramics and posters, visited by minstrels in medieval costumes. Suckling pig, lamb roasted in circa 1725 ovens.

17 Calle de los Cuchilleros, 011-34-91-366-4217. *www.botin.es*

• **Casa de Diego.** Exquisitely crafted fans—plus canes and umbrellas—at a shop where they've been made since 1858.

12 Puerta del Sol, 011-34-91-522-6643. *www.casadediego.net*

PARIS

• **Hotel Montalembert.** Choose between high-tech contemporary and traditional French Empire rooms—both stylishly executed in this boutique beaux arts hotel that is designers' textbook.

3 rue de Montalembert, 011-33-1-45-49-68-68. *www.hotel-montalembert.fr*

• **Hôtel Balzac.** Opulent belle epoch mansion beautifully made over with subtle Eastern motif. Efficient business center, close to Champs-Elysées, fine restaurant on the premises.

6 rue Balzac, 011-33-1-44-35-18-00. *www.hotelbalzac.com*

• **Le Grand Véfour.** Innovative food featuring the freshest ingredients. Gilt, frescoes, mirrored ceilings, Napoleonic murals and the one-time presence of Napoleon himself give a sense of history.

17 rue de Beaujolais, 011-33-1-42-96-56-27, *www.grand-vefour.com*

• **Guy Savoy.** The eponymous M. Savoy owns several bistros along with this luxury restaurant. The Euro superstar chef produces exquisite sea bass, red snapper, duck and venison dishes and delights in mushrooms.

18 rue Troyon, 011-33-1-43-80-40-61. *www.guysavoy.com*

• **Elle Boutique.** The famous magazine of cutting-edge fashion runs this boutique. Featured are stylish clothing and home furnishings from the pages of *Elle.*

30 rue St-Sulpice, 011-33-1-43-26-46-10.

ROME

•**The Hassler.** Luxury hotel in the former Hassler Villa Medici at the top of the Spanish Steps. Murals in many rooms, elegant glass-enclosed rooftop restaurant with incomparable views.

Piazza Trinita dei Monti 6, 011-39-06-699-340. *www.hotelhasslerroma.com*

•**Hotel Eden.** Visiting celebrities have enjoyed views from the penthouse bar as well as first-class Roman cuisine in the stunning restaurant. Some rooms have balconies... many overlook soothing gardens.

Via Ludovisi 49, 011-39-06-478-121. *www.edenroma.com*

•**La Pergola.** Views from hilltop location make it worthwhile to shuttle to the outlying Cavalieri Hilton to visit this 3-Michelin-star rooftop restaurant. Elegant ambiance, excellent antipasto, scampi.

Via Alberto Cadlolo 101, 011-39-06-350-91. *www.romecavalieri.com*

•**El Toulà.** Sophisticated 19th-century country house setting, impeccable service, acclaimed Venetian cuisine. Don't miss the classic pasta-and-bean soup.

Via della Lupa 29B, 011-39-06-687-3750. *www.toula.it*

VIENNA

•**Hotel Bristol.** On Ringstrasse across from State Opera House, blends traditional Viennese charm with modern amenities. Antiques, black marble fireplaces, comfortable bars, top-rated Korso restaurant. Was a US military headquarters following World War II.

1 Kaerntner Ring, 011-43-1-515-160. *www.bristolvienna.com*

•**Steirereck.** Rustic eatery features trappings from a castle and cuisine from the province of Styria—hare, venison, schnitzel, rack of boar. Celebrity/business clientele.

Am Heumarkt 2A, 011-43-1-713-3168. *http://steirereck.at*

•**Café Sacher Wein.** Sample traditional Viennese café life and signature Sacher-Torte dessert as well as ambrosial crêpes. Famed restaurant and hotel was a favorite of Emperor Franz Josef.

4 Philharmonikerstrasse, 011-43-1-51-456-0. *www.sacher.com/en-cafe-vienna.htm*

•**Loden-Plankl.** Find loden coats, leder-hosen, dirndl and other items of local dress at this long-established shop.

6 Michaelerplatz, 011-43-1-533-8032. *www.loden-plankl.at*

To Save on Travel

Diane Warner, author of *How to Have a Great Retirement on a Limited Budget* (F&W Publications).

Take full advantage of senior-citizen discount airfares. Remember, if you are retired you have more free time to make phone calls and find the best deal for you. Advance-purchase fares could save you even more than senior discounts.

•**Other travel discounts.** It pays to be a senior in other areas of travel as well. Amtrak takes 15% off its fares for passengers over 62. And—bus companies, auto rental agencies and hotels all have senior discounts. But you have to ask.

•**Bed and breakfasts** are often excellent values, especially if you want a breakfast bigger than tea and toast.

•**College campuses** have lots of empty dorm rooms during the summer. You can rent some of them for as little as $15 a night.

•**You can trade your home for someone else's home** in a far-flung location. That way, you save plenty and get someone to keep an eye on things at home while you're away.

•**Take a cruise**—at the very last minute. Most cruise lines have "unbooked space" bargains that sell as sailing time gets closer.

•**Arrange to give lectures on a cruise.** Simply send out queries to various cruise lines detailing your qualifications. Using your expertise can be gratifying and gratis.

•**Arrange a group tour** for at least 10 people. Tell your travel agent or tour operator you've got a group ready to go to a certain destination and you can get free passage for your trouble.

•**Get a job with a travel agency,** even part time, and get the travel perks that go along with it.

How to Pack Clothes So They Won't Wrinkle

Judith Gilford, packing specialist. She is author of *The Packing Book: Secrets of the Carry-on Traveler* (Ten Speed Press).

Learn these valuable tips from a packing expert, and you'll always look neatly pressed.

•**Lay your suitcase on the bed and open it wide so that it lies flat.** Start by packing your largest, heaviest and longest item of clothing—excluding slacks.

•**Then lay slacks lengthwise on top,** with the waistband touching the side of the suitcase. Drape the bottom of the slacks over the other side of the suitcase.

•**For straight skirts,** lay the waistband along the handle edge of the suitcase, with the hem draped over the hinged end.

•**Add long-sleeved shirts or blouses.** Lay shirts or blouses face-down, starting with the collar centered at the hinge end. Drape the sleeves and bottoms over the sides of the bag or cross down the back.

•**Short-sleeved shirts are next.** Place in the same way you placed long-sleeved shirts.

•**Pack sweaters over the short-sleeved shirts.** Drape the sleeves and bottoms over the sides.

•**Pack shorts.** Long shorts can be packed vertically with bottoms draped over one end of the suitcase. Shorter shorts can be packed horizontally and added last.

•**Create a core "pouch" in the center for your swimsuit and undergarments.** The "pouch" should take up an 11" x 16" space, with about two inches of space left all around it. The fuller the edges of the core, the less wrinkling.

Folding it all up…

•**Place the core pouch in the center of the draped clothing.** Take the last item packed and fold over the core and so on until all are folded.

•**Pack remaining items such as toiletries in plastic bags,** and shoes, belts, etc. around the edges or in the bag's other compartments.

Best of the Best Restaurants in the US

Tim Zagat, publisher of *Zagat Survey,* the best-selling restaurant guides that annually survey thousands of regular restaurant-goers all over the country. 4 Columbus Circle, New York City 10019, 800-333-3421. *www.zagat.com*

Here are our favorite elegant restaurants in America when the price of dinner is not a concern…

NEW YORK CITY

•**Daniel.** Featuring the celebrated chef Daniel Boulud, known for his contemporary French cuisine prepared with the finest American ingredients. *Favorite entrée:* Black angus short ribs with cauliflower mousseline.

60 E. 65th St. (bet. Madison & Park Aves.). 212-288-0033. *www.danielnyc.com*

PHILADELPHIA

•**Le Bec-Fin.** Classic French–Louis XIV setting. *Favorite entrée:* Verbena-infused guinea hen served with chanterelle mushrooms and fava beans.

1523 Walnut St. 215-567-1000. *www.lebecfin.com*

SAN FRANCISCO

•**Masa's.** Romantic French restaurant. *Favorite entrée:* Sonoma duck breast with seared foie gras, chive-scented spaetzle and glazed baby onions.

648 Bush St. 415-989-7154. *www.masasrestaurant.com*

ST. LOUIS

•**Tony's.** Traditional Italian cuisine. Located in the heart of the city, just five blocks from the city's famous Arch. *Favorite entrée:* Fresh lobster meat with wild mushrooms in a white brandy and cream sauce that is served with seasonal vegetables or a rice ball filled with chopped veal.

410 Market St. 314-231-7007. *http://tonysstlouis.com*

WAIKIKI

•**La Mer Restaurant.** Large French restaurant with a view of the Pacific from every table. *Favorite entrée:* Hawaiian salt-crusted baked red snapper filled with fresh thyme, rosemary and tomatoes placed over a bed of spinach and tea leaves.

2199 Kalia Rd. 808-923-2311. *www.halekulani.com*

doons, wild rice and grapefruit brown butter jus. *For dessert:* Chocolate tart souffle with gianduja ice cream.

135 West 42nd St. 212-319-1660.

America's Lively Restaurants

Tim Zagat, publisher of *Zagat Survey,* the best-selling restaurant guides that annually survey thousands of regular restaurant-goers all over the country. 4 Columbus Circle, New York City 10019. 800-333-3421. *www.zagat.com*

Make a good restaurant part of your travel plans, and you will have a memorable trip. *Try these...*

DALLAS

• **Amici Signature Italian.** Serves both Italian and French foods. *Best:* Specials are frequently changed, but try the rack of lamb in a cabernet-shallot sauce or beef medallions in a peppercorn brandy cream sauce.

1022 S. Broadway, Carrollton. 972-245-3191. *www.amici signature.com*

HOUSTON

• **Artista.** A fine-dining restaurant that offers creative contemporary American cuisine, top-notch service and a location convenient to downtown entertainment. *Best:* Veal Chateaubriand with mascarpone mashed potatoes and rosemary-cremini sauce...crisp-roasted salmon with habanero-citrus sauce.

800 Bagby St., Suite 400. 713-278-4782.

NEW YORK CITY

• **Aureole.** New American culinary delights. *Best:* Roasted venison loin, parsnip purée, car-

Best Restaurants in Washington, DC

In a city full of politics, certain eateries are always in the know. *Some to try...*

• **Marcel's.** 2401 Pennsylvania Ave. NW, 202-296-1166. *www.marcelsdc.com.* Hearty and adventurous French-Belgian cuisine.

• **Makoto,** 4822 MacArthur Blvd. NW, 202-298-6866. Authentic Japanese cuisine.

• **The Palm,** 1225 19th St. NW, 202-293-9091. A sturdy steak house. *www.thepalm.com*

Best Restaurants in Philadelphia

No other city has experienced the spectacular change in fine dining that Philadelphia boasts. *Among the top restaurants...*

• **Le Bec-Fin,** 1523 Walnut St., 215-567-1000. *www.lebecfin.com.* Among the best dining in Philadelphia. Owner George Perrier features the freshest foie gras and truffles anywhere, and quenelles as light as a feather. Try the Bec-Fin cake.

• **Fountain Restaurant,** Four Seasons Hotel, 1 Logan Square, 215-963-1500. Glorious restaurant in a lavish new hotel. Here you will find old favorites cooked to perfection.

Best Restaurants In Chicago

Chicago has long been known for it's fine cuisine. *These restaurants add to the city's reputation…*

• **Berghoff,** 17 W. Adams, 312-427-3170. *www.theberghoff.com.* A big, friendly German restaurant with huge portions of excellent, hearty food.

• **The Signature Room,** John Hancock Center, 875 N. Michigan Ave., 312-787-9596. *www.signatureroom.com* For the best views in Chicago, try this 95th-floor restaurant. The food is American contemporary.

Favorite Restaurants In New York City's Theater District

Tim Zagat, publisher of *Zagat Survey,* the best-selling restaurant guides that annually survey thousands of regular restaurant-goers all over the country. 4 Columbus Circle, New York City 10019, 800-333-3421. *www.zagat.com*

Like the city itself, Manhattan restaurants can satisfy a variety of tastes. *Some good pre- or post-theater eateries…*

CHINESE

• **Ollie's Noodle Shop and Grille** serves satisfying food at reasonable prices. Entrées range from $10 to $14. While Ollie's has an extensive menu, its specialty is oversized bowls of soup made with combinations of meat, fish, vegetables and noodles.

Wonderful: Pickled cabbage and pork with cellophane noodles.

160 Freedom Place, 212-595-8181.

• **Shun Lee Cafe** is across from Lincoln Center, home of the Metropolitan Opera and the New York City Ballet. The dim sum is served in a black-and-white Art Deco room.

Especially wonderful: Hot and sour soup.

43 W. 65th St., 212-595-8895. *www.shunleewest.com*

CONTINENTAL

• **Brasserie 44 is in The Hotel Royalton,** where many film and rock celebrities stay when they're in New York. The restaurant is the perfect place to get you in the mood for the theater. Two or three appetizers are sufficient for an exciting meal.

Wonderful: The Caesar salad and all of the fish dishes.

44 W. 44th St., 212-944-8844. *www.brasseriefortyfour.com*

ITALIAN

• **Lattanzi** is an earthy, traditional restaurant. Nearly all of the dishes are hearty and full-flavored. Along with the menus comes a basket of wafer-thin, crispy bread brushed with garlic and oil and served warm (served after 8 pm).

Wonderful: Start with the cold or hot antipasto, followed by any of the pasta dishes.

361 W. 46th St., 212-315-0980. *www.lattanzinyc.com*

• **Orso** is decorated with clay pitchers and interesting photography. An appetizer and a pizza or pasta will hold you through the theater.

Wonderful: The margarita pizza—mozzarella, tomato and fresh basil leaves.

322 W. 46th St., 212-489-7212. *www.orsorestaurant.com*

Best Breakfast Spots In the Big Apple

Business meetings over bacon and eggs or croissants and espresso give New Yorkers a head start. *Favorite rooms for mixing work with the most important meal of the day…*

• **Carlyle Hotel** (The Carlyle Restaurant). Fresh brioche and croissant served elegantly in a quiet Continental atmosphere. 35 E. 76th St., 212-744-1600; opens at 7. *www.thecarlyle.com.*

• **Hotel InterContinental.** (The Barclay). A popular spot for diplomats. Good food. Good service. 111 E. 48th St., 212-755-5900; opens at 7.

- **The Pierre, a Taj Hotel.** (Café Pierre). Elegant decor, perfect service and fine food. 2 E. 61st St., 212-838-8000; opens at 7.

- **Loews Regency Hotel** (540 Park). First-rate food and service for a power-broker clientele. 540 Park Ave., 212-759-4100; opens at 7.

- **One UN New York** (Ambassador Grill). Modern, mirrored elegance with an international flavor. 1 United Nations Plaza at 44th St., 212-758-1234; opens at 7. *www.millenniumhotels.com.*

Best New York City Bars

There's a watering hole on practically every corner of the Big Apple, but some have unique character and charm. *Such as…*

- **The Four Seasons,** 99 E. 52nd St., 212-754-9494. Manhattan's most beautiful bar and probably the best place to capture the feeling of the city. *www.fourseasonsrestaurant.com.*

- **PJ Clarke's,** 915 Third Ave., 212-317-1616. Recently refurbished, this classic NYC hangout retains the atmosphere of a neighborhood saloon—Sinatra on the jukebox, a bar that's open until 4:00 am. *www.pjclarkes.com.*

HOTEL BARS

- **Ambassador Grill,** One UN New York, 1 United Nations Plaza at 44th St., 212-702-5014. Right across from the United Nations building, and filled with the diplomatic crowd.

- **Bemelmans Bar,** Hotel Carlyle, Madison Ave. at 76th St., 212-744-1600. Lovely bar with good background music.

- **Café Pierre,** The Pierre, Fifth Ave. at 61st St., 212-838-8000. Loved by the international set.

- **The Fireside Restaurant and Bar,** Omni Berkshire Place Hotel, Madison Ave. at 52nd St., 212-754-5011. Excellent midtown location. A crowded, handsome bar with wonderful drinks and atmosphere.

How to Get a Great Meal at a Great Restaurant

Restaurateurs, like other business people, are dependent on their regular customers and give them special attention. However, few people can afford to be regulars at very expensive establishments. Most save their visits for special events or, if they live out of town, for infrequent trips to that city. Such celebratory meals can be doubly disappointing if the service is poor or the choice of food is not what the kitchen does best.

Mimi Sheraton's practical suggestions for making a rare visit to a special restaurant the event you had hoped for…

- **Avoid Friday and (particularly) Saturday nights.** That's when restaurants are at their busiest and have the least time to give you the special attention you want.

- **Do your homework.** Read up on the restaurant to find out its strengths and weaknesses so you can order the best it has to offer.

- **Make a reservation well in advance.** Explain how much you have looked forward to coming and ask for some help in choosing your menu.

- **Confirm your reservation by telephone that day.** Even the best-run places have an occasional slip-up. (If the number of people in your party changes, be sure to notify the restaurant.)

- **Check out ahead of time what credit cards the restaurant takes and any dress requirements** so there will be no embarrassment at the door.

 # Best Shopping Bargains in New York

Ellen Telzer and Sharon Dunn Greene, authors of *The Lower East Side Shopping Guide.* The Shopping Experience, New York City.

Tucked away in a corner of lower Manhattan is a shoppers' paradise, the Lower East Side. Historically the area was a way station for the immigrants who came to America in the late 19th and early 20th centuries. It's not history, though, that brings people to the Lower East Side these days. It is bargains on some of the finest merchandise available anywhere!

Sunday is the busiest shopping day. If it's the only day you can get there, go early in the morning. *Best:* Shop early on a weekday. Business hours are generally 9 to 5, but many stores close early on Friday. For more details, visit *www.lowereastsideny.com.*

The stores listed here carry only top-quality merchandise. Discounts are at least 20%.

• **Dolce & Dolce,** 136 Orchard, 646-654-0505. This is the place for better men's shoes and clothing. They also carry big and tall sizes.

At the corner of Orchard and Grand is the beginning of the domestic dry-goods center of the Lower East Side. Turn left on Grand Street to find store after store of designer sheets, towels and bedspreads, always at great prices.

• **A.W. Kaufman,** 73 Orchard, 212-226-1629. Specializing in the finest European and designer lingerie, all at discount prices.

• **Giselle,** 143 Orchard, 212-673-1900; toll-free 877-447-3553. Four floors of women's designer clothing. Lots of variety. Wonderful buys, especially toward the end of a season.

You've come to the end of Orchard Street, at the corner of E. Houston, which is the food street of the Lower East Side.

If you like to sit down and be served, walk left three blocks to Yonah Schimmel's Knish Bakery. This Lower East Side landmark has homemade apple strudel, knishes of every variety and yogurt made on the premises. Or walk one block to the right to Katz's Delicatessen (corner Houston and Ludlow) for the ultimate hot dog, french fries and a soft drink. Enjoy!

New York City Off the Beaten Path

Allan Ishac, author of *New York's 50 Best Places to Find Peace and Quiet* (Universe).

It is hard to imagine that a place as busy as New York City really has any hidden spots—areas that are truly off the beaten path. Yet, amazingly, this city of millions has plenty of hidden gems where people can go to explore or just relax. *My favorites…*

• **Mount Vernon Hotel Museum & Garden.** Nothing in New York seems quite as out of place as Mount Vernon Hotel Museum & Garden. Located on E. 61st St., surrounded by garages and warehouses and just off the hustle and bustle of First Avenue, this is one of eight remaining 18th-century buildings left in New York. Inside, the house has been faithfully restored and is filled with a wide array of antiques. *Bonus:* There is a front lawn and a lovely garden and terrace out back that's perfect for relaxing.

421 E. 61st St. between First and York Aves. 212-838-6878. *www.mvhm.org*

• **The Bell Tower at Riverside Church** is a wonderful place to steal away for some quiet reflection—and some great views of Manhattan. The Riverside Church tower is almost 400 feet tall. Most of the journey to the top can be made by elevator. An observation platform stands at the top of this Gothic belfry. It is rarely, if ever, crowded and provides a magnificent view of the city and surrounding area. If the view isn't enough, make sure to check out the 74 carillon bells, which range in weight from 20 tons to 10 pounds.

490 Riverside Dr. at 120th St. 212-870-6700.

• **The Ford Foundation Building** isn't exactly off the beaten path. But that doesn't mean it isn't overlooked. This building contains one of the city's true, little-used treasures, a lush third-of-an-acre terrace garden that is filled with more than a dozen full-grown trees, about 1,000 shrubs, 150 vines and more than 20,000 plants. Not only is this rain forest-like setting rarely crowded, it is green all year.

320 E. 43rd St. between First and Second Aves. 212-573-5000.

• **The General Theological Seminary** has pristine grounds and red brick buildings that are open to the public. It all seems too perfect to be exposed to the hustle and bustle of the city. Yet visitors are not only allowed in, they are welcome, often being warmly greeted by the seminarians who study at the Episcopal Church in this Chelsea neighborhood. At the heart of the grounds is the Chapel of the Good Shepherd, a country-like chapel that is marked by stained glass and dark wood carvings.

175 Ninth Ave. between 20th and 21st Sts. 212-243-5150. *www.gts.edu*

• **The Nicholas Roerich Museum** is a treasure not only because it contains 200 paintings of the Russian-born artist who specialized in intense landscapes of tempera blues, whites, violets and reds, but because it is set in a charming town house that's incredibly inviting. Guests are welcome to sit in any of the parlor-like rooms for hours to gaze at Roerich's work or just relax.

319 W. 107th St. between Broadway and Riverside Dr. 212-864-7752. *www.roerich.org*

• **Greenacre Park** and **Paley Park** are two little-used havens that seem to have been slipped undetected into the folds of midtown. Aptly called vest-pocket parks, they are largely ignored or unknown. Yet, they both provide a chance to escape the pressures of the city. Greenacre Park contains a two-story waterfall, a babbling brook and a small pool. Nearby Paley Park is smaller, but it also provides a tranquil setting, complete with its own waterfall.

Greenacre Park is at 217 E. 51st St. between Second and Third Avenues, Paley Park is at 53rd St. between Fifth and Madison Avenues.

• **The Russian & Turkish Baths** will take you back in time. It is an authentic Old World bathhouse that has occupied the same Lower East Side brownstone since 1892. Don't expect to be pampered. Rather, relax and enjoy the baths' offbeat charm. Visitors can choose the Russian room (dry heat), the Turkish room (wet heat), a cold plunge and a Swedish shower.

268 E. 10th St. between First Ave. and Ave. A. 212-674-9250. *www.russianturkishbaths.com*

There Are a Variety of Exciting Ways to See This Wonderful World

Robert William Kirk, college professor in Northern California who has logged more than 250,000 miles of free travel during the past two decades.

Too many people think that foreign travel is an expensive option open only to the well-to-do. They may long to see other parts of the world and meet people from other cultures, but they can't seem to put aside enough money for the big trip.

Fact: You don't need a lot of money to go abroad if you really want to do it. You can use your own enthusiasm and interests to pay for part of your trip—and you can custom-design the itinerary to your own specifications. Or you can—with even less effort—cut your costs to a minimum by getting free transportation or lodging.

PUTTING A GROUP TOGETHER

There are several ways to get free trips by organizing your own travel group…

• **Tour-company representative.** Several tour groups, for example, will give you a complimentary package tour (including transportation and lodging) if you act as their representative (part-time)—and sell their packages. When you meet their quota of five or six paid-up travelers, they'll award you a free package trip. If you double the quota, you can get a free package trip for your spouse as well.

• **Tour organizer.** You can get a free trip by becoming the designated organizer for a tour put together by many of the national travel companies, such as American Express or Thomas Cook. Your obligation is to bring in 10 or more paying customers for one of their nationally advertised travel packages. Look at affinity groups you belong to. An art-history lecturer, for example, put together her quota from students who valued her judgment in choosing an art tour. A minister attracted participants for a trip to the Holy Land from his congregation.

• **Chaperone students.** If you work with young people—as a teacher, coach or Scout leader, for example—you can get a free trip by recruiting and chaperoning a group of paying students to almost anywhere in the world.

Not everyone enjoys such a "busman's holiday" but my wife and I have found sharing young people's delight in discovering another culture to be quite rewarding in itself.

• **Lead a special-interest tour.** A lawyer we know planned a two-week legal-eagle tour of London with his travel agent—and recruited enough colleagues and spouses to pay for his and his wife's fares and lodgings. He made arrangements for the group to hear trials at Old Bailey and at the Royal Courts of Justice. They visited the Inns of Court and met with solicitors and barristers.

If you have a passion for art, theater, photography, wine, food or architecture, you can use your knowledge to design a trip that will be special to you and your friends.

• **Design your own adventure vacation.** If you are an experienced outdoors person, you can put together the challenge trip of your dreams with a travel agent and attract your own group of adventurers. You can organize a camelback trek with the Tuaregs out of Timbuktu, climb the Himalayas or balloon over French vineyards and châteaus.

FREE LODGING

• **If you don't have the time or inclination to package your entire trip,** you can still cut down on your travel expenses appreciably by joining a home or hospitality exchange.

Best Months at the Top Tourist Spots On Six Continents

Before you plan a trip abroad, consider the best time to travel to your destination. *A few guidelines…*

EUROPE

• **Greece.** March–May, October and November.
• **London.** April–June, October and November.

• **Paris.** April–June, October and November.
• **Riviera** (Monaco, France, Italy). Christmas, New Year's and Easter holidays. *Also:* June-August.
• **Rome.** March–May, October–December.
• **Scandinavia.** May–September. *Winter sports:* February and March.
• **Switzerland.** *Winter sports:* December–April. *Summer activities:* May–August.
• **Russia.** April–June, September and October. Summers are torrid, with no air conditioning. Winters are harsh.
• **Venice.** March–June.

AFRICA

• **Egypt**. Always hot and humid. *Best:* March–May, October–December.
• **Kenya.** Seasons are reversed. June, July and August are coolest. December, January, February and March are hot and dry.
• **Morocco.** The sun shines 300 days a year. *In the south around Agadir and in the town of Marrakesh:* December–March. Avoid visiting in August or September.
• **South Africa.** There are no extremes of climate. *Cape Town:* January–March. *Kruger National Park:* June–September. *Johannesburg:* May–August.

MIDDLE EAST

• **Israel.** *Tel Aviv:* April–June, October–December. *Jerusalem:* January–June, October and November.
• **Jordan.** Hot and dry all year. *Best:* March–May, November and December.
• **Saudi Arabia.** December–March.

FAR EAST

• **China.** The country is vast, with a wide-ranging climate. The most visited cities are Beijing, Tientsin, Nankin, Hangchow, Shanghai and Canton, where summers are hot and humid and winters are relatively mild. *Best:* April–June and October.
• **Japan.** April–June, October and November.

ASIA AND THE PACIFIC

• **Australia.** Seasons are reversed. *Melbourne, Sydney, Canberra:* October–February. *Darwin:* June–August.

•**India.** The climate varies greatly. *Best:* November, December, February and March. *Monsoons:* June–September.

•**Malaysia.** March–July and September.

•**Nepal** (Himalayas). September–November.

•**New Zealand.** The weather is always cool and temperate.

•**Philippines.** November–March.

•**Singapore.** Always hot, with little variation in rainfall.

•**South Korea.** March–May, October and November.

•**Tahiti.** May–October.

•**Thailand.** November–April.

SOUTH AMERICA

•**Argentina.** October–March.

•**Brazil.** March–October.

•**Chile.** October–February.

•**Peru.** *Lima:* January–March. *Mountains:* June–September.

•**Venezuela.** December–March.

CLOSER TO HOME

•**Bermuda.** May–October. *Also:* Easter week.

•**Canada.** *Winter sports:* November–April. *Summer sports and city vacations:* May–September.

•**Caribbean.** November–April.

•**Florida.** December–April.

•**Hawaii.** Ideal all year.

•**Mexico.** October–April.

•**Puerto Rico.** November–April.

Tropical Travel Concern

Dengue fever is a serious health concern for travelers to tropical areas, such as Central America, the north of South America, India, Southeast Asia and parts of coastal Africa. There is no treatment or vaccine for this severe, flu-like illness, which lasts for one to two weeks. A second dengue infection may result in dengue hemorrhagic fever, a potentially fatal disease. The mosquitoes that carry dengue fever are widespread in warm regions, especially in cities, and are most active at dawn and dusk.

Self-defense: Wear protective clothing on which you have sprayed the insecticide *permethrin,* and use mosquito repellent that has a DEET content of 30% to 35%. Consult a travel-medicine specialist before your trip.

Mayo Clinic Health Letter

Great Deals at Resorts And Spas

Travelzoo.com lists deeply discounted resort and spa stays in its "Travel Deals" section. Discounts change regularly and are for stays within the next few weeks.

Travel & Leisure

Costs Are Dropping

The cost of a luxury suite is going down at many hotels. To fill these higher-priced rooms, hotel operators are reducing the cost of upgrading to a suite or executive floor and training clerks to get customers to upgrade at check-in.

Example: In Atlanta, club-level rooms cost 25% to 30% more than standard ones—down from 50% to 60% more.

What to do: Ask how much an upgrade will cost and what other amenities the hotel is offering—some include vouchers and other inducements to take the costlier rooms.

USA Today

Private Sales of Hotel Rooms

Private sales of hotel rooms can save travelers hundreds of dollars. Several Web sites give their registered members information on these private sales—which hotels use to fill rooms that would otherwise go empty without needing to cut prices for the general public. Site registration usually is free.

What to do: Visit *www.jetsetter.com...www.sniqueaway.com...www.tablethotels.com...*and *www.bonvoyou.com* and join any that appeal to you.

Kiplinger's Personal Finance. www.kiplinger.com

Choosing a Caribbean Hotel

The windward side of the island is best—the breeze will cool you at night and keep the bugs away. Caribbean-side beaches are less dramatic than those on the Atlantic but safer for swimming and superior for snorkeling or sailing. Upstairs rooms get better views and breezes. *Best of all:* A corner room. Be sure your room has air-conditioning.

Travel & Leisure, 1120 Avenue of the Americas, New York City 10036.

Advice for Solo Travelers

Natalie Windsor, author of *How to Fly: Relaxed & Happy From Takeoff to Touchdown* (CorkScrew Press).

Traveling alone by air can have its advantages. You don't have to think about anyone but yourself, you can relax, watch a movie, read a book or work in peace. Or can you? What if the traveler next to you won't stop talking? What if your wallet or purse disappears? *For trouble-free trips...*

- **Don't travel without telling someone.** Contact a friend or family member. Give him/her your itinerary so that someone knows how to find you.

- **Streamline your wallet or purse.** Avoid having to replace everything—if it's lost or stolen—by only carrying identification and those cards that you may actually use.

- **Don't wear fine jewelry.** It's dangerous to put it in your luggage so leave it home.

- **Travel light.** An overloaded traveler is a vulnerable traveler. Ship bulky items in advance.

- **Keep an inventory of items**—and put a copy of it and your personal identification inside your suitcase, and keep a copy, too. You'll know by checking the inventory if something's missing and you will increase the odds that you'll see it again if it's lost.

- **Wear a wedding ring.** You'll discourage unwanted advances.

- **Wear headphones.** You don't even have to plug them in, but you'll politely tune out chatterers.

- **Avoid the bulkhead**—the area that separates first class from coach. If there's an unescorted child on board, that's where he or she is most likely to be.

- **Have single bills handy.** You won't have to get change and attract the wrong kind of attention, and you'll speed your progress through the airport if you need to give a tip.

Online Park Reservations

National park reservations can be made over the Internet. The National Parks Service Web site (*www.nps.gov*) now provides full information on most national parks and historic sites, including maps, descriptions of facilities, lodging rates and directions.

You can make reservations online under "Plan Your Visit."

Health Spas...The Best Places in the US

Bernard Burt, original author of *Fodor's Healthy Escapes* (Fodor's), and publisher of *Bernard Burt's Spa-Goer,* 2400 Virginia Ave., Washington, DC 20037. *www. spagoer.com*

Today's spas are about wellness, maintaining a healthy appearance, fitness and, of course, having fun. And—more and more of America's hundreds of spas are offering weekend or even one-day packages at reduced rates.*

Here are some of the best health spas in the country...

WEST COAST

• **The Golden Door** is one of the nation's premier spas. Situated on 177 acres of canyon, orchard and Oriental gardens, it accommodates only 40 guests.

Guests begin each day with a brisk, pre-breakfast mountain hike. Later, they're presented with the day's schedule. Fifty-minute exercise periods fill the morning. Afternoons are reserved for spa treatments, private workouts, additional hikes, etc.

Services: Massage, aromatherapy, herbal wraps, body scrubs, facials, manicures/pedicures, hair salon. Training sessions in meditation, problem-solving, yoga and movement. Two outdoor pools and two tennis courts.

The Golden Door, Box 463077, Escondido, California 92046. 800-424-0777. *www.goldendoor.com*

SOUTHWEST

• **Canyon Ranch** is set on 70 acres in the foothills of the Santa Catalina Mountains. Each day begins with a pre-breakfast walk at dawn.

Services: Exercise equipment, nine types of massage, aromatherapy, body scrub with crushed pearls, nutritional consultations, fitness evaluations. Training in biofeedback and smoking cessation. One indoor and three outdoor pools, racquetball, squash, tennis courts, biking, hiking. Golf and horseback riding nearby.

Canyon Ranch, 8600 E. Rockcliff Rd., Tucson, Arizona 85750. 800-742-9000. *www.canyonranch.com*

*Prices vary based on number of people, season, special mini-getaways, etc. Call ahead for up-to-date rates and package deals.

• **The Centre for Well-Being Phoenician** is nestled at the base of Camelback Mountain on 130 acres of manicured lawn and desert terrain. It combines elegant accommodations, sports and a wide range of spa services.

Services: Exercise equipment, aerobics classes, 27-hole championship golf course, nine outdoor pools, 12 tennis courts, croquet, lawn bowling and volleyball...plus massage, seaweed and desert clay body wraps, fitness consultations, body composition analysis, cholesterol testing, herbology, yoga and tai chi.

The Centre for Well-Being at the Phoenician, 6000 E. Camelback Rd., Scottsdale, Arizona 85251. 800-888-8234. *www.thephoenician.com*

CENTRAL STATES

• **Lake Austin Spa Resort** features water aerobics, gym workouts and 7 am walks in the beautiful Hill Country of Texas. Guests stay in lakeside cottages.

Services: Exercise equipment, sculling, paddle boats, Jacuzzi, tennis, massage, reflexology, herbal wraps and personal consultations on fitness and nutrition. Golf and horseback riding nearby.

Lake Austin Spa Resort, 1705 S. Quinlan Park Rd., Austin, Texas 78732. 800-847-5637. *www.lakeaustin.com*

MIDWEST

• **Birdwing Spa**—with just nine guest rooms in a Tudor mansion set on a lakeside estate— is geared toward outdoor activities, including skiing, canoeing and bicycling.

Services: Exercise equipment, outdoor pool, men's and women's saunas, coed whirlpool, Swedish and Esalen massage, hair and nail care, aromatherapy, paraffin therapy, nutritional counseling, fitness evaluations.

Birdwing Spa, 21398 575 Ave., Litchfield, MN 55355. 320-693-6064. *www.birdwingspa.com*

• **The Heartland Spa** is located on a 30-acre converted dairy farm (with weight machines and an aerobics studio in a barn). Days can be as structured or unstructured as you please.

Services: Exercise equipment, massage, facials, hair/skin care, personal fitness assessment, nutrition evaluation, indoor pool, three-acre lake, two lighted outdoor tennis courts, parcourse, hiking, cross-country skiing, fishing.

The Heartland Spa, Kam Lake Estate, 1237 E. 1600 North Rd., Gilman, IL 60938. 800-545-4853. *www.heartlandspa.com*

MID-ATLANTIC STATES

• **The Greenbrier** blends old-world resort with high-tech spa treatments. While the hotel may be crowded with conference-goers, the spa itself is serene and small. The Greenbrier Clinic occupies a separate building completely equipped for diagnostic and preventive medicine.

Services: Hydrotherapy, massage, body treatments, two pools, 15 outdoor and five indoor tennis courts, three golf courses, fishing, skeet- and trapshooting, horseback riding, carriage rides, jogging, hiking.

The Greenbrier, 300 W. Main St., White Sulphur Springs, West Virginia 24986. 800-453-4858. *www.greenbrier.com*

SOUTH

• **Doral Golf Resort & Spa** is like a vision of Tuscany, with formal gardens, statuary, cascading fountains and a red-tile roof. Staffers at this spa compare your health profile with a computerized model and plan your workout regimen. Seven-day stress-management programs are held at various times throughout the year.

Services: Exercise equipment, body and facial treatments, aerobics, yoga, three pools, five golf courses, 15 tennis courts.

Doral Golf Resort and Spa, 4400 N.W. 87th Ave., Miami 33178. 800-713-6725. *www.doralresort.com*

• **Château Élan Winery & Resort** is situated on the grounds of a working winery, complete with vineyards and a reproduction 16th-century French chateau. Guests come to this spa because they prefer personalized rather than group activities. The staff includes nutritionists and experts in smoking cessation and behavior modification.

Services: Exercise equipment, massage, reflexology, collagen masques, seaweed wraps, sauna, steam bath, whirlpool, three pools, biking, three golf courses and a tennis center.

Château Élan Inn, 100 Rue Charlemagne, Braselton, Georgia 30517. 800-233-9463. *www.chateauelanatlanta.com*

NORTHEAST

• **Canyon Ranch in the Berkshires** has a mind–body approach to fitness and healthy living. Skiers can get in shape before tackling nearby cross-country trails, and stressed-out executives can use the latest biofeedback equipment to learn to relax. Jacob's Pillow, the well-known dance venue, and the Tanglewood music festival are within easy driving distance.

Services: Exercise equipment, herbal wraps, aromatherapy, acupuncture, holistic health counseling, indoor and outdoor pools, cross-country skiing, hiking, indoor and outdoor tennis courts, two racquetball courts, squash court, indoor track, canoeing.

Canyon Ranch in the Berkshires, 165 Kemble St., Lenox, Massachusetts 01240. 800-742-9000. *www.canyonranch.com*

• **New Age Health Spa**—a favorite of harried New Yorkers—is committed to a holistic lifestyle. Guests set their own pace. Before breakfast, opt for Zen meditation, a tai chi class or a three- to five-mile aerobic walk. Move on to a weight-management lecture, followed by a series of low-impact aerobics classes.

Services: Exercise equipment, massage, body treatments, indoor and outdoor pools, cross-country skiing, snowshoeing.

New Age Health Spa, Box 658, Rte. 55, Neversink, New York 12765. 800-682-4348. *www.newagehealthspa.com*

Best Dude Ranches

Ranches offer attractive, offbeat vacations. They're particularly appropriate for families with children and those interested in the outdoors (especially horseback riding and fishing). Our list includes some of the best in the country. They are, understandably, all in the West.

CALIFORNIA

• **Rankin Ranch,** Box 36-HP, Caliente 93518, 661-867-2511. *www.rankinranch.com.* Rate includes meals and horses. April through first week of October.

COLORADO

• **Vista Verde Ranch,** Box 770465, Steamboat Springs 80477, 800-526-7433. *www.vistaverde.com.* Rate includes everything. Summer for horses, river rafting, rock climbing and fly fishing...winter for skiing.

TEXAS

• **Rancho Encantado,** 9239 FM 133, Cotulla, 78014, 830-676-3573. *www.ranchoencantado. com.* Guest ranch, year-round.

WYOMING

• **Eatons' Ranch,** Wolf 82844, 800-210-1049. *www.eatonsranch.com.* Rate includes meals and horses. Lodging. June 1 to September 30.

Great Golf Vacations

The late Stephen Birnbaum, editorial director, *Diversion.*

A superior golf resort provides comfortable accommodations and special courses that offer unusual scenery, challenges and/or history. *The following ones are exceptional...*

• **Casa de Campo,** La Romana, Dominican Republic. 800-877-3643, *www.casadecampo. com.do.* One of the best of the tropical golf resorts. Contact your travel agent for information and reservations.

• **Doral Golf Resort & Spa,** 4400 NW 87th Ave., Miami, FL 33178, 800-713-6725, *www. doralresort.com.* Features five 18-hole courses. The Blue Monster Course is the home of the Ford Championship at Doral PGA tour event.

• **Gleneagles Hotel,** Perthshire, Scotland. 866-881-9525, *www.gleneagles.com.* One of the great manor houses of the United Kingdom. There are three 18-hole championship courses, and one nine-hole course. Open all year. Call your travel agent for information.

• **The Greenbrier,** 300 W. Main St., White Sulphur Springs, WV 24986, 800-453-4858, *www.greenbrier.com.* Has three golf courses, one of them designed by Jack Nicklaus.

• **Pebble Beach Golf Links,** 17 Mile Dr., Pebble Beach, CA 93953, 800-654-9300, *www.pebblebeach.com.* Home of the annual AT&T Pebble Beach National Pro-Am, the 1977 PGA Championship and the 1972, '82 and '92 U.S. Open Championships. Pebble Beach also features two famous golf holes (the 19th hole and Best Finishing Hole).

• **Marriott Sawgrass Resort & Spa,** 1000 PGA Tour Blvd., Ponte Vedra Beach, FL 32082, 904-285-7777, *www.sawgrassmarriott.com.* This resort is home to the Player's Championship, the richest purse on the PGA tour.

• **The Sea Pines Resort,** 32 Greenwood Drive, Hilton Head Island, SC 29928, 866-561-8802, *www.seapines.com.* Three courses are available. One, the Harbour Town Golf Links, is world-class and is the site of the Heritage Classic PGA golf tournament.

Getting VIP Treatment On a Cruise Ship

First, get the word to the shipping line that you rate A-1 treatment. This can be done by your travel agent writing the shipping line. Or you might have the public relations director of your firm write with the same message. This one-two attack is bound to get your name starred for VIP treatment when you come aboard. That could include dinner at the captain's table, an invitation to the captain's special cocktail party or perhaps flowers and assorted gifts in your cabin. Also, of course, the more expensive your cabin accommodations are, the better the treatment you will generally get.

Make sure you get a good seat in the dining room. Usually that means in the center, close to the captain's table. Go over the dining-room plan in advance of your trip with your travel agent and pick out the two or three tables you want. Then ask your travel agent to reserve the table for you in advance. If that can't be done, make sure that as soon as you go aboard ship, you visit the maitre d' and tell him what you want—with a tip.

It's desirable to have an early talk with your dining-room captain and waiter. Ask them what the chef's specialties are. Order those far in advance for your dinners later on the cruise. See if you can order such items as chateaubriand, crepes suzette, special soufflés, scampi, lobster, Caesar salad. These items can usually be ordered on most cruise ships. The trick is to know what specialties the kitchen is good at, and give the chef time to prepare them.

Tip the dining-room captain and let him know there's more for him if the service is excellent. Also give the dining-room waiter, in advance, half the amount you would normally tip him at the end of the cruise and indicate that he'll get at least as much more for top-notch service.

Your room steward can get you all sorts of snacks, such as fruit, cheeses, sandwiches, iced tea and ice cream—almost any time of day or night. Ask him what is available and if there is a best time to order these items for your cabin. If you want ice cream at 11 pm every night, tell him in advance so he can plan accordingly. Give him half the tip in advance and let him know that good service will bring a reward.

If you want to impress your friends, invite them to the ship for a bon voyage party. It can be quite elegant but remain inexpensive. Make all the arrangements through the shipping company. The ship will usually supply setups, soda and hors d'oeuvres at a very modest price. Expect to bring your own liquor when the ship is in port, but you can easily buy a few bottles from a local liquor store and bring them aboard.

The steward can serve drinks and other items to your guests in your cabin. If your crowd is large enough, ask for a section of one of the public rooms.

You can play expansive host by holding nightly parties while cruising, and it won't be too costly. The ship's staff will help you plan parties in your room or in a public room at a fraction of the cost of a party in a hotel ashore. The liquor costs are minimal. Setups and other items often come free, as do canapés and other party snacks. You also usually get the service of waiters and bartenders at no cost (but you provide the tips).

Book the second sitting for meals when on a cruise. That leaves you more time to get ready for dinner after a day of touring, a longer cocktail hour and less time to kill until the evening activities begin.

How to Get a Cruise Ship's Best Price

Don't rely solely on travel agents. Not all of them are knowledgeable about cruises, and some promote only one or two lines. *Better:* Read the latest issues of *Travel Weekly,* especially the issues with a cruise guide.

After choosing several possible cruises, go to a few travel agents to see which can get you the best price. Surprisingly, these often vary because of the many promotional gimmicks of the cruise lines. Ask about cash rebates, free airfare to the port of departure, flat rates for inside and outside cabins, free passage for third and fourth persons. Frequently the steamship company itself can get you an even better deal.

Daniel A. Nesbett, travel marketing consultant, Darien, Connecticut.

What You Should Know Before Taking a Cruise

Marylyn Springer, authority on passenger ships. Ms. Springer writes about the cruise industry for newspapers and magazines, and authored numerous editions of Frommer's Guide to Cruises *(Macmillan).*

Virtually all cruise fares are termed "all-inclusive prices." This means they cover accommodations, meals and entertainment, transfers and use of facilities.

Not included: Liquor, personalized spa or beauty treatments and some shore excursions.

•**The only real "wild card" in the price of a cruise** is whether it includes airfare to and from the ship's port of departure and return. Many prices do. However, if you don't want or need it, make sure you receive an "allowance" that translates into a price cut.

•**Almost all ships have doctors,** although the level of treatment varies from ship to ship. The *Queen Elizabeth 2,* for example, has its own operating room. Many ships, particularly older ships, are limited in the type of service they can provide.

213

• **Cruise lines have improved their facilities to accommodate disabled individuals,**
providing such things as larger rooms and
bathrooms. Nonetheless, older ships—those
five to 10 years old or older—tend to be less
accessible. These ships may not provide elevator access to all floors.

PROBLEMS

• **Not all ships are well-equipped to
handle children.** Yet some offer wonderful programs designed for kids of all ages.
Beyond programs and events, these ships also
tend to have baby-sitting services, children's
dining rooms, special kids' newspapers and,
of course, several playrooms.

• **The destination of your cruise** determines how far in advance you need to book.
Cruises to the Mediterranean, Europe, Bermuda, Asia, Alaska and Canada all have limited seasons, which means space fills up fast.
These cruises should be booked six months
in advance. Caribbean cruises are generally
more available. Bookings need to be made
no more than 30 to 60 days in advance.

• **Rarely is crime a problem** while on
ship. However, passengers always have the
option of placing valuables in a safe. Unfortunately, crime can surface at ports of call.

• **Cancellation policies are available**
through travel agents at relatively low fees.
They guarantee refunds should you need to
cancel your trip. Most passengers can probably skip them unless they're involved in a
business where schedules change rapidly.

• **Unlike airlines, which require advance
notice for special meals,** cruise ships can
accommodate virtually any dietary need on
demand.

Freighter and
Cargo Cruises

These cruises are becoming increasingly
popular, but they can be taken only by
people who can be away from business
for long periods of time and have flexible
schedules. They're very good for retirees.

There is no assurance that a ship scheduled
to depart on a particular day will indeed
leave that day. The first consideration of such
ships is their cargo, and they will stay in port
until they are completely loaded, even if that
means waiting for weeks. The same holds
true all along the route. You are protected on
price, however. The longer the voyage, the
lower the per diem costs.

Some advantages of these cruises...

• **The costs are considerably lower than
for other types of cruises.** Everything is
included in the price.

• **Most ships carry only eight to 12 passengers,** so you have an excellent opportunity to get to know your fellow cruisers.
(However, you might travel with people you
don't care for.)

• **You get more port time** than with regular ships.

• **The quarters are usually first-rate.** The
food is simple and good. Larger ships sometimes have their own swimming pools.

There are certain restrictions on age and
health on the smaller ships. On those with 12
or more passengers, a doctor is required, so
they are more lenient about health restrictions.

When you make your reservation, you pay
a deposit. The balance of the cost must be
paid a month before scheduled sailing time.
Cancellations are refundable if the ship company is able to resell your space.

Although all the freighter lines do have
individuals who book trips directly, it is recommended that you work through a travel
agency familiar with this type of ship. A travel
agency can help you with the many documents to be filed. It often will charter an
entire ship and hold all the bookable space. It
can assist you in the event a refund is necessary. Travel agencies that specialize in freighter
and cargo cruises are also well aware of the
conditions on the various ships and can direct
you to the one best suited to your own needs.

Popular freight and cargo lines...

•**Hurtigruten Pluss AS,** Box 451209, Sunrise, FL 33345. 866-552-0371. *www.hurtigruten. us/norway*

•**Hapag-Lloyd,** 877-445-7447. *www. hapag-lloyd.com*

Wintertime Adventures

Joan Rattner Heilman, author of *Unbelievably Good Deals & Great Adventures that You Absolutely Can't Get Unless You're Over 50* (McGraw-Hill).

Winter does not have to be a time to sit back and wait for springtime. There are increasing numbers of snow-covered adventure vacations specifically geared for people over 50. And they are not limited to skiing—or to the US—for that matter.

As a bonus, there are often substantial travel savings—such as airline coupons and hotel discounts—for older vacationers that aren't available to younger people, making the journey not only fun but relatively cost-efficient. *Some of my favorite winter adventures…*

•**The Over The Hill Gang International** was started in Colorado many years ago as a ski club for people over 50 who wanted companionship on the slopes. Since then, it has grown to include many other activities. It organizes senior ski weeks—both downhill and cross-country—at ski areas all over the world with packages that include transportation, lodging, lift tickets and social activities. Its local "gangs" or chapters also run their own ski trips and all members are invited.

2121 North Weber Street, Colorado Springs, Colorado 80907. 719-389-0022. *www.othgi.com*

•**Silver Streaks of Waterville Valley** is a club for skiers who have reached their 50th birthday. What you get Mondays through Thursdays for a fee of $80 for the season is reserved parking, coffee and pastries every morning, a different ski school clinic periodically and guided ski runs. Additional happenings include après-ski parties and banquets.

Single-day guest passes are also available.

1 Ski Area Rd., Box 540, Waterville Valley, New Hampshire 03215. 800-468-2553. *www.waterville.com*

•**Road Scholar/Elderhostel** is the world's leading specialist in low-cost learning vacations for people older than 55 (travel companions may be younger). Its packages worldwide include many winter tours that offer cross-country and downhill skiing, snowshoeing, animal tracking, dogsledding, survival strategies and winter nature explorations. The list of programs changes constantly, so send for the voluminous Elderhostel catalogs.

11 Avenue de Lafayette, Boston 02111. 800-454-5768. *www.roadscholar.org*

WINTER GAMES

•**Senior Winter Games at the Summit** are open to anyone who is over 50 and looking for winter sports, competition and a good time. Held in the quaint Victorian town of Breckenridge, Colorado, early in February, the games include downhill and cross-country skiing, speed skating, figure skating, snowshoe races, among other wintry activities. There is a small entry fee.

Summit County Community and Senior Center.

•**Connecticut Winter Games for Seniors.** In late February, these senior winter games, featuring downhill, giant slalom and snowshoe races, take place at Ski Sundown in New Hartford, Connecticut. Open to anyone from anywhere who is 50 and an amateur, the games currently require a $35 entry fee to cover costs. Preregistration is recommended.

Connecticut Ski Council and Ski Sundown. *www. skisundown.com*

•**Green Mountain Senior Winter Games.** Vermont hosts one set of winter games each year for any amateur athlete over 55. On a wintry day every March, the Cross-Country Senior Games features ski and snowshoe competitions at Blueberry Lake, Sugarbush Ski Resort, Warren, Vermont. The entry fee of $25 covers everything.

131 Holden Hill Rd., Weston, Vermont 05161. 802-824-6521.

Off-Beat Vacations

Jennifer Cecil, author of *Traveling Solo* (HarperCollins).

Some of the best vacation destinations in the world are actually the least known. If you're looking for a trip that offers adventure, comradery, hospitality, unique accommodations and good food, read on.

FOR THE OUTDOOR LOVER

• **The Complete Fly Fisher** does everything for you. The lodge specializes in beginners, and the guides are patient and knowledgeable. Guests fish on the Big Hole River, a trout-filled, 127-mile-long stream. Some menu specialities are tabbouleh, tarragon chicken salad sandwiches, home-baked cookies, and tea and wine. The cabins are knotty-pine, and there are lots of cottonwoods.

The Complete Fly Fisher, 66771 Hwy 43, Box 127, Wise River, Montana 59762. 406-832-3175 or 866-832-3175. *www.completeflyfisher.com*

• **Nantahala Outdoor Center** has all kinds of paddling trips, including two- to seven-day beginner courses in kayaking and a Grand Canyon whitewater rafting trip. They take trips to Chile and Mexico and also offer sea kayaking. The food is very good and elegantly served, even when dining beside a river. You don't have to be a paddler to enjoy these truly spectacular trips.

Nantahala Outdoor Center, 13077 Highway 19 W., Bryson City, North Carolina 28713. 888-905-7238. *www.noc.com*

• **Wilderness Southeast** offers nature-oriented camping trips to the islands along the coast of Georgia…through the Florida Everglades…up into the Great Smoky Mountains in North Carolina…and over to the Big Bend area of Texas.

The guides are well-versed on ecology and the ecosystem and manage to present information in an interesting manner—rather than continuous lectures. These trips are really for those who like to camp and do not demand fancy accommodations.

Wilderness Southeast, 3025 Bull St., #302, Savannah, Georgia 31405. 912-236-8115. *www.wilderness-southeast.org*

FOR THE DOWNHILL SKIER

• **Alta Lodge** has been family-run since 1939. Despite its exclusiveness, this wood and glass lodge in the beautiful Wasatch Range is not overly expensive. It attracts an enthusiastic and interesting group of middle-aged intermediate and advanced skiers.

Lift tickets and skiing lessons cost about half that of other prime ski areas, and you can ski from the front door to the Wildcat and Collins lifts in about 20 seconds. At the end of the day, you can enjoy a hot whirlpool bath…complimentary confections and tea…a roaring fire in the lobby or lounge…and lively dinner conversation accompanied by a delicious meal.

Alta Lodge, PO Box 8040, Alta, Utah 84092. 800-707-2582. *www.altalodge.com*

• **Hotel St. Bernard** sits 9,400 feet up in New Mexico's Sangre de Cristo Mountains and has a little more of a party atmosphere than the Alta Lodge. Meals are accompanied by a country music trio that inspires most to get up and hit the dance floor. Lifts are right outside the door and are best for intermediate and advanced skiers. You must book way in advance at this zesty place, which attracts mostly 35- to 65-year-old professionals from all over the world.

Hotel St. Bernard, PO Box 88, Taos Ski Valley, New Mexico 87525. 575-776-2251. *www.stbernardtaos.com*

FOR THE EQUESTRIAN

• **Circle Z Ranch** is tucked between rocky Sanford Butte and Sonoita Creek outside of Patagonia, Arizona, at an altitude of 4,000 feet. One of the oldest dude ranches in the state, it has horseback riding, tennis, a solar-heated pool, trap shooting and shuffleboard for its 40 guests. The mission-style buildings are decorated with Mexican furnishings. The horses at this 6,500-acre ranch are top-notch. And the food is excellent. The atmosphere is casual and the hospitality is unmatched. The ranch is open from late October to mid-May. The town of Patagonia is interesting to explore.

Circle Z Ranch, PO Box 194, Patagonia, Arizona 85624. 888-854-2525. *www.circlez.com*

FOR SUN AND SEA LOVERS

• **Trimarine.** Fabulous scuba diving trips in the British Virgin Islands on the largest trimaran in the world—the 105-foot *Cuan Law.*

The crew is very professional and friendly… the food is outstanding…and the diving is some of the best you'll ever find.

It's a perfect vacation for anyone looking for a good diving trip with all the amenities to make it a comfortable sailing trip as well. The boat itself houses 20, and all of the cabins have private baths and showers.

Trimarine Boat Co., Box 8309, PMB 613, Cruz Bay, Virgin Islands 00831. 284-494-2490. *www.bvidiving.com*

FOR THE SPA-LOVER

•**The Spa at Norwich Inn** offers a two-day (or more) personally tailored program selected from various services, treatments and classes. Accommodations and meals at the inn are included. You can dine on lighter spa cuisine, or on heartier classic American fare at the Norwich Inn's Prince of Wales restaurant. The meticulously renovated Georgian-style inn was built in 1929 and has 65 rooms. There are 43 acres, including 74 mini-condominium units with small kitchens and fireplaces.

The Spa at Norwich Inn, 607 W. Thames St., Norwich, Connecticut 06360. 800-275-4772. *www.thespaatnorwich inn.com*

Best Family Camping Tents

A tent for camping should allow about 25 square feet of floor space for each adult and half that for each child. *For a family of four:* At least 80 square feet.

Best: An umbrella tent. It folds up neatly to fit into a car trunk. And it weighs only 24 to 40 pounds. *Best material:* Nylon. *Features to look for:* Good cross-ventilation…openings with sturdy mesh to keep out insects…windows that close during a storm…seams double-stitched with eight to 10 stitches per inch. *Also:* Seams should be lap-felled (the material folded back on itself for extra strength and waterproofing).

Good tents have extra stitching at points of stress. Before taking the tent on a trip, set it up in the yard and douse it with a hose. Check for leaks (particularly at the seams).

Travel Accessories

Convenient containers for travel and backpacking are empty *Squeeze Parkay* holders. They nest together, have pour spouts and can be made watertight. *How:* Place a double piece of foil over the opening before replacing the top. Liquids such as syrup, honey and cooking oil can be kept without leaking. Or the containers can be used for nonliquids like dry milk or sugar.

America's Best Museums

Some of the finest museums in the world are right here in the US. *Make a cultural stop at these…*

CALIFORNIA

•**J. Paul Getty Museum,** 1200 Getty Center Dr., Los Angeles. Extraordinary private art collection from antiquity to 20th century. *www.getty.edu/museum*

•**The Huntington Library, Art Collections and Botanical Gardens,** 1151 Oxford Rd., San Marino. Gainsborough's Blue Boy, 18th-century British and European art. *www.huntington.org*

•**Los Angeles County Museum of Art,** 5905 Wilshire Blvd., Los Angeles. Outstanding collection from antiquities to 20th-century art. *www.lacma.org*

•**Asian Art Museum of San Francisco,** 200 Larkin St., San Francisco. Finest collection of Oriental art in the Western world. *www.asianart.org*

COLORADO

•**Denver Art Museum,** 100 W. 14th Ave. Pkwy., Denver. North and South American Indian collections. *www.denverartmuseum.org*

CONNECTICUT

•**Wadsworth Atheneum,** 600 Main St., Hartford. The oldest art museum in the United States and one of the best. *www.wadsworth atheneum.org*

• **Yale University Art Gallery,** 1111 Chapel St., New Haven. Recently renovated to three buildings and includes 1,100 new acquisitions. John Trumbull's paintings of the American Revolution and much more. *http://artgallery. yale.edu*

DISTRICT OF COLUMBIA

• **Corcoran Gallery of Art,** 500 17th St. NW. Historic American paintings, European art. *www.corcoran.org*

• **Freer Gallery of Art,** 1050 Independence Ave. SW, Far and Near Eastern art... Whistler's works. *www.asia.si.edu*

• **Hirshhorn Museum and Sculpture Garden,** Independence Ave. at 7th St. SW. The entire collection—sculpture and modern art—of millionaire Joseph Hirshhorn. *www.hirshhorn.si.edu*

• **National Gallery of Art,** 6th and Constitution Ave. NW between 3rd and 7th Sts. A jewel of a museum with a brilliant wing by I. M. Pei. General European and American art collection. *www.nga.gov*

• **National Portrait Gallery,** 8th St. at F St. Portraits of all the American presidents displayed in an 1840 Greek Revival building, the former US Patent Office. *www.npg.si.edu*

GEORGIA

• **High Museum of Art,** 1280 Peachtree St., NE, Atlanta. Renaissance of 20th-century American and European paintings, sculpture and decorative arts. *www.high.org*

ILLINOIS

• **The Art Institute,** 111 S. Michigan Ave., Chicago. Outstanding Impressionists and post-Impressionists in a first-rate collection. *www. artic.edu*

MARYLAND

• **The Baltimore Museum of Art,** 10 Art Museum Dr. (near N. Charles and 31st St.), Baltimore. Fine French post-Impressionist works... mosaics from Antioch. *www.artbma.org*

MASSACHUSETTS

• **Museum of Fine Arts, Boston,** 465 Huntington Ave., Boston. The I. M. Pei wing is impressive. *www.mfa.org*

MICHIGAN

• **The Detroit Institute of Arts,** 5200 Woodward Ave., Detroit. Great masters and moderns. *www.dia.org*

MINNESOTA

• **Walker Art Center,** 1750 Hennepin Ave., Minneapolis. Post-Impressionist and contemporary art. *www.walkerart.org*

NEW YORK

• **Albright-Knox Art Gallery,** 1285 Elmwood Ave., Buffalo. Splendid modern collection, as well as general collection. *www. albrightknox.org*

• **Brooklyn Museum,** 200 Eastern Parkway, Brooklyn. Fine general collection with strong Egyptian art and American paintings. *www. brooklynmuseum.org*

• **The Frick Collection,** Fifth Ave. at 70th St., New York City. One of the best private collections. *www.frick.org*

• **Solomon R. Guggenheim Museum,** 1071 Fifth Ave. at 89th St., New York City. Modern art and sculpture in a circular building designed by Frank Lloyd Wright. *www.guggen heim.org*

• **The Metropolitan Museum of Art,** Fifth Ave. at 82nd St., New York City. Probably the finest general collection in the US. *www. metmuseum.org*

• **The Museum of Modern Art (MOMA),** 11 W. 53rd St., New York City. First US museum devoted to contemporary art—paintings and sculpture, design and film. *www.moma.org*

• **The Morgan Library & Museum,** 225 Madison Ave., New York City. Illuminated Bibles and other superb art. *www.themorgan.org*

• **Whitney Museum of American Art,** 945 Madison Ave. at 75th St., New York City. 20th-century US art. *http://whitney.org*

OHIO

• **The Cleveland Museum of Art,** 11150 East Blvd. at University Circle, Cleveland. Focus on all cultures. Strong on medieval and Oriental art. *www.clevelandart.org*

OREGON

• **Portland Art Museum,** 1219 SW Park Ave., Portland. Appealing outdoor sculpture, mall, general collection. *www.portlandartmuseum.org*

PENNSYLVANIA

• **The Frick Art Museum,** 7227 Reynolds St., Pittsburgh. Eclectic collection of Russian, Chinese, Flemish and French art and artifacts. *www.thefrickpittsburgh.org*

• **Philadelphia Museum of Art,** 26th St. and Benjamin Franklin Parkway, Philadelphia. Magnificent general collection. *www.philamuseum.org*

• **Rodin Museum,** 22nd St. and Benjamin Franklin Parkway, Philadelphia. Sculpture, sketches and drawings by this famous French artist. *www.rodinmuseum.org*

TEXAS

• **Amon Carter Museum,** 3501 Camp Bowie Blvd., Fort Worth. Extensive collection of Frederic Remington's and Charles Russell's works. *www.cartermuseum.org*

• **The Museum of Fine Arts, Houston,** 1001 Bissonnet St., Houston. Fine general collection. *www.mfah.org*

Renting a Summer Place

Jacqueline Kyle Kall, City Island, New York, realtor specializing in resort properties in the US and worldwide.

If you rent a place for the summer, you'll make a substantial investment of time and money. With some planning, you can avoid disappointments.

DRAW UP A LEASE

If you don't go through a real-estate broker, draw up a complete contract with the owner of the home. Do not make a friendly verbal agreement or scribble your contract on a paper napkin. You can locate a standard lease form online (*www.scribd.com/doc/24019116/vacation-rental-agreement-sample*) that covers summer rentals. Have the lease witnessed and notarized, preferably by a lawyer or a real-estate agent. Go through the lease form to make sure all clauses in it are acceptable to you.

• **Most important lease item.** A list of all household property and the specific condition of each. *Specify items such as:* "Pale green carpet in fine condition."

• **A normal-wear-and-tear clause is reasonable.** The lessee won't be held responsible for each minor thing—sand in the rug, for example.

• **Improvements.** If you plan to make any improvements on the house or property, these must be noted in the lease, along with the owner's approval and any reimbursement agreement.

EXPENSES AND RESPONSIBILITIES

• **The renter should expect to pay for heat, hot water, electricity and telephone** for the rental period. You may be asked to install a phone in your own name.

• **The renter is generally responsible for the care and watering of the plants and lawn,** raking the beach, keeping the place reasonably clean and other standard household maintenance. Responsibility for expensive or highly technical maintenance, such as pool cleaning or skilled gardening, should be discussed and outlined in the lease. Owners often include items such as pool maintenance as part of the rental price.

• **The owner must tell the renter about climatic changes** (such as summer floods), insect or rodent infestation or anything else that affects the house's habitability. Failure to do so is grounds for breaking the lease and getting your money back.

• **The owner must repair any essential items** that break down in midseason (such as the refrigerator or the plumbing). If the owner is unavailable, you can pay for repairs and bill him.

• **The owner must return your remaining rent,** plus security, if an act of God makes the house uninhabitable during the season.

DAMAGES

The house must be left in the same condition in which you found it. If you damage something, you must replace it with a similar item. *Recommended:* Attempt to work things out amicably with the owner. Offer to pay for anything you have broken before the owner discovers the problem.

RENT AND SECURITY

• **Expect to pay all the rent plus the security** (which is as much as half the rent) in advance. Installment payments are generally unacceptable.

• **Your security will be returned when the outstanding bills have been paid.** The best way to ensure that you will get your security back in full is to check the house thoroughly before the lease is signed. Make sure everything is listed so you can't be accused of taking something that wasn't there.

WHAT TO LOOK FOR

When you're inspecting a summer house, check out the plumbing, kitchen equipment, water pressure, availability of heat and climate problems. Ask the owner what the neighborhood is like.

INSURANCE

• **Your summer house should be covered by your landlord's homeowner's policy** for burglary, accident, damage to the house and grounds, fire and flood. However, if you caused the damage, you can be held responsible.

Example: If the house is burglarized and the police find that the door was left unlocked, you can be held liable. Get a rider on your own homeowner's policy to cover the rental.

• **Insure your own property.** Your jewelry and other valuables will not be covered by your landlord's homeowner's policy.

REFERENCES

Be prepared to give both business and personal references when you rent a summer place. As more owners have harrowing experiences, they are becoming more careful about whom they rent to. *Example:* An elderly European man rented his apartment for the summer without asking for references from the two "nice-looking young men wearing suits and ties" who said they were schoolteachers. At the end of the summer, he discovered that they had fled, after leaving a sacrificial altar in the middle of the living-room floor. It had burned right through the floorboards to the apartment below.

References commonly requested: Your place of business and length of time employed. A current or former landlord as a personal reference. Your phone and utility account numbers (to check your payment record). A credit reference (some owners are now subscribing to services that check the credit rating of prospective tenants).

Better Summer Weekends

The most desirable thing to look for in a weekend house is ease of maintenance. Get rid of rugs in the summer. Ask the landlord to remove accumulations of dust-catching decorator touches. And keep your own importations to a minimum. In a summer house, bare is beautiful.

• **Cut down on weekend cleaning chores** and outdoor work with hired help. In some communities this is relatively simple, especially with the guidance of a neighbor who is a year-round resident. Or the rental agent may have a network of people who are willing to help out.

• **Expand your leisure time by commuting with the laundry.** That's cumbersome but better than hours in a laundromat on a sunny afternoon.

• **Learn the fine art of list making.** Shopping and menu planning can be almost painless if the list is done right. One couple owns an island where everything, including drinking water, has to be brought in. And they haven't run out of anything in years.

• **Bring the specialties with you.** If you're planning a Saturday dinner party, don't rely on the local supermarket for the perfect roast unless you've ordered (and confirmed) in advance. It's far safer to bring the main course with you and shop locally for the fresh produce. The accompanying wines might be better purchased at home, too, unless you're sure of your local supplier.

• **Double up on medical supplies.** It's a good idea to take the same precautions you would for a trip—extra reading glasses and copies of prescriptions might save you an unwanted journey home.

Buying a Time-Share In a Vacation Condo

Watch out for abuses. Time-sharing (purchasing rights to a hotel or apartment unit at a resort for a specific week or two each year) has been subject to incidents of fraud and deception. *Example:* 2,100 people bought time-shares in Colorado resort condominiums before the developers went bankrupt.

Two men were jailed in South Carolina for selling shares in a nonexistent resort. *Protection:* Consult a lawyer before buying. Study all documents carefully. Call the Better Business Bureau or Department of Consumer Affairs for information about the project and developer. Go to inspect the resort. Resist high-pressure sales techniques.

Vacation time-shares can be more of a burden than a bargain. *Problems:* Time-share vacations are very expensive. The same place every year is boring. The money invested does not earn interest. Resale of used time-shares can be very difficult. The real cost of a time-share is much higher than its selling price. Financing involves payment of 16% to 17% interest. Few banks give loans for time-sharing.

If you buy a time-share vacation home: (1) Pick a place you are sure to love year after year. (2) Don't pay more than 10 times the going rate for comparable time in a rental unit in the same area. (3) Buy early—prices are lower. (4) Buy where geography and/or zoning prevent overbuilding. (5) Buy from an experienced builder. *To enhance your selling/swapping prospects:* Buy a one- or two-bedroom unit in a place that's easy to reach during the peak season.

Vacation Like a Multimillionaire For a Week

If you want to experience a magic vacation week—seven days to match your wildest fantasies—try any of these ideas. Like the super-rich you will be emulating, you should let your travel agent take care of the details.

• **Travel first-class by present standards and those of another age.** Whip to London then settle into the Venice-Simplon *Orient Express* for a leisurely trip to Venice. The legendary train (with its 1920s cars completely restored to their former polished-brass-and-crystal glory) makes the London-Paris-Venice run twice a week, March through November. Base your Venetian sightseeing at the Hotel Cipriani before returning to London and flying home.

• **Lose weight in luxury with the comprehensive program at Brenner's Park Hotel and Spa** in Baden-Baden, Germany. (The main building was a residence of Napoleon III.) Do water exercises in a Pompeiian pool. Have a daily massage, facial, body wrap and sumptuous low-calorie meals. Makeup, manicures and pedicures are part of the program. Baden-Baden has colonnaded shops and a famous casino.

• **See Burgundy by balloon. View the châteaus and vineyards of southeastern France** from the gondola of a flowered hot-air balloon (between terrestrial tours of the region by car). Stay in the Hotels de la Poste in Beaune and Vezelay, sampling the local wines. The great French Balloon Adventure leaves every Sunday from Paris starting in May and is organized by the Bombard Society in San Francisco. 800-862-8537. *www.buddybombard.com*

• **Charter a yacht—with crew—and cruise the Caribbean.** Captain, cook, hands and provisions are included.

• **Try a villa or a castle for a week.** With airfare, ground transportation, staff and food, two can enjoy Dromoland Castle in Ireland.

221

• **Entertain like a king** (or a Comstock Lode heiress) in San Francisco by renting the penthouse suite of the Fairmont Hotel. Designed in the 1920s for Maude Flood, a gold and silver baroness, the suite has a walnut-paneled living room, a dining room that seats 50, a domed library, a mosaic-walled game room complete with pool table, three bedrooms and baths with gold fixtures. The kitchen is fully equipped. The bar is stocked. Dinnerware, silver and linens are included, as well as a vault, a baby-grand piano, books, artwork, a butler and a maid.

• **Great hotels.** Pick a city you want to explore and put yourself in the hands of a master innkeeper for a week. *Some suggestions…*

• **California wine country,** Sonoma Mission Inn.

• **Colorado Springs,** The Broadmoor Hotel.

• **Paris,** The Plaza Athénée.

• **Palm Beach,** The Colony Hotel.

• **Beverly Hills,** The Beverly Hills Hotel.

• **New York,** The Peninsula.

• **London,** The Savoy.

• **Dallas,** The Mansion on Turtle Creek.

• **Rio de Janeiro,** The Meridien Hotel.

Royal Vacation At a European Castle

Pamela Barrus, Laguna Beach, CA–based travel writer who has visited more than 150 countries. She is author of *Dream Sleeps: Castle & Palace Hotels of Europe* (Carousel Press).

Royalty used to reside in them…celebrities, such as Sir Paul McCartney and Madonna, have held their wedding celebrations in them…and you can sleep in many of them.

Faced with astronomical taxes and upkeep costs, some European castles and palaces now operate as hotels. Virtually all of them have been modernized to include private bathrooms and central heating and air conditioning.

My favorites…

ENGLAND

• **Langley Castle, Hexham,** Northumberland. Ten acres of peaceful woodlands surround this 14th-century castle situated in the forests of northern England. All the rooms have four-poster beds and window seats set into seven-foot-thick walls. The castle features a stunning grand hall and a stone-walled drawing room with an open fireplace. Nearby attractions include Hadrian's Wall and Northumberland National Park. You also can get married in the castle.

Double-occupancy rooms in the castle are $200 to $300 per night.* Also available are "castle-view" rooms—they offer views of the castle from across the grounds. These rooms start at $175.

011-44-1434-688-888…*www.langleycastle.com.*

FRANCE

• **Château de la Treyne, Lot.** This 14th-century castle is built on a cliff above the Dordogne River. It is surrounded by 300 acres of beautiful parkland. Double-occupancy rooms range from $160 to $440, depending on size.

011-33-5-65-27-60-60…*www.chateaudelatreyne.com.*

IRELAND

• **Markree Castle, Collooney,** County Sligo. This 17th-century castle in northwest Ireland is more child-friendly than most castle hotels. The castle houses the famed Knockmuldowney Restaurant. Explore the countryside on horseback, or take a drive through "Yeats country." You also can fish and play golf.

Double-occupancy rooms are $185 to $260. Children under 12 can share parents' room for $25 extra.

011-353-71-9167800…*www.markreecastle.ie.*

PORTUGAL

• **Hotel Palace do Buçaco, Buçaco Forest.** This 19th-century palace is located in the stunning national park of Buçaco in central Portugal. It originally was built as an extravagant hunting lodge for Portuguese royalty. Enjoy romantic dining on the terrace, forest walks and tennis. Double-occupancy rooms range from $124 to $217, which includes breakfast and all taxes.

www.manorhouses.com/hotels/bussaco.html.

*All prices converted into US dollars. Prices are subject to change.

SPAIN

• **Parador de Alarcón, Cuenca.** This well-preserved medieval fortress sits atop a rocky crag 100 miles across the plains of La Mancha, west of Valencia. Sections of the castle date to the Moors of the eighth century. Double-occupancy rooms are about $300.

011-34-969-33-03-03...*www.parador.es.*

How to Enjoy a Day At the Races Without Going Broke

The late Peter Shaw, cultural critic, historian, college professor and occasional bettor.

The aim of a day at the track should be to enjoy every race while controlling your losses. Fifty dollars lost out of a hundred dollars played with could be considered a highly satisfactory day.

STRATEGY FOR BETTING

• **Begin with the choices of the handicappers.** Handicapping—the prediction of likely winners—is done by a track official who assigns odds to the horses in the morning races. Handicapping is also done by bettors in the course of the day (which causes the odds to change). Both kinds of handicappers represent a well-informed consensus of serious students of racing. One-third of the favorites chosen by handicappers win their races.

• **Decide on the amount of money you are willing to lose.** Set aside one-fifth of it for entertainment betting. The rest should be spent on serious betting. For about $20 you can bet on every race plus the daily double. Then you have continual action. Avoid the tendency of most bettors to increase bets when losing in order to catch up. Also avoid the trap of betting more when winning to try to make a killing. *To control spending:* Bet just 20% of your remaining capital each time you bet, whether your capital goes up or down.

To pick horses for fun betting: Choose horses by name, jockey, appearance or any means you wish. You may get lucky and win one out of 10 bets this way. Plan to make four serious bets in the course of a day.

Most important requirements...

• **Pick the appropriate races to bet on.** *Always eliminate the following races for serious betting:* Maiden races (the horse's first year of racing), two-year-old races and races where it's indicated that the horses chosen won no race but their maiden race. These are all races in which handicapping is not effective, and there is too much uncertainty. Use these for fun bets and to hone your skills.

• **Picking the two or three likeliest winners in the race.** To do this, see handicappers' choices in local newspapers, racing forms and tip sheets sold at the track. Look especially for handicappers who predict in great detail how the race will be run (in addition to giving their pick). Look for the handicapper who tells you the front runners, the come-from-behind horse and the outcome. On the basis of the predictions of several of these tipping sources (they tend to agree), choose the likeliest horses.

• **Combine this intelligence with local conditions,** easily observable changing factors that can influence the outcome of a race. (This is one advantage of actually being at the track.) Be alert to late scratches (the elimination of contenders), which can very much change the projected script of a race. If one of the two predicted front-runners is scratched, the remaining front-runner's chance is increased. That makes a good bet.

Also pay attention to the weather conditions, especially rain. In the racing form, mudders (horses that have a history of doing well in the rain) are indicated with an asterisk. As the track is progressively softened by rain, the chances of mudders improve. Most adversely affected by rain-softened tracks are the horses closest to the rail at the outset (post-position horses 1, 2 and 3). *Reason:* Those positions are where most of the running takes place, so the track gets especially muddy there. The horse in the most adverse position on a rain-sodden track is a speed horse—a front-runner in the post position.

Another local condition to watch for: Shifts in odds. Lengthening (higher) odds on a horse increase your chance of a good return. Watch for obvious reasons for a drop in popularity in the course of a day. The physical condition of the horse can be observed during the viewing ritual, when the horses are paraded at the rear of the track before each race. This is one of the best parts of the event. *But it's important to watch for negative signs so that you can eliminate horses...*

• **Front-leg bandages.**

• **A prolonged struggle as the jockey attempts to mount.** A bit of liveliness and fight against the jockey is a good sign, but a prolonged struggle can exhaust a horse.

• **Sweats and tremors.** Sweat shows as a yellow lather around the haunches, rectum and genitals.

Kinds of bets you can place: There are win bets (they pay only if the horse wins), place bets (they pay if the horse comes in first or second) and show bets (paying if the horse comes in first, second or third). If you choose win bets alone, you can usually hope for at least one win out of four. A combination of bets, such as a win and place or a win and a show, increases your chances of a payoff. But the return will be smaller.

Shortcut method of choosing horses: Gather all the racing forms and tip sheets. Look at all the choices in a given race. Then bet on a horse mentioned by at least one handicapper on which the odds offered are greater than the number of horses in the field. (However, don't pick any horse going at odds greater than 50 to one.)

The point: To bet a long shot in each race, hoping to win once in the day at a very large payoff. The horse you're choosing is assured of having some kind of chance if it is mentioned by at least one handicapper.

Secrets of Picking Harness Winners

Don Valliere, former track manager and author of *Betting Winners: A Guide for the Harness Fan* (Gambling Book Club Press).

Harness racing is far easier to handicap than Thoroughbred ("flat") racing. *Reason:* The bettor has fewer variables to take into consideration.

Harness races are almost always at a mile and on the dirt. The fields are more manageable, with rarely more than nine entries. And since the horses carry no weight on their backs, there are no weight differences to compensate for. (Thanks to some complex law of physics, the sulky pulled by the horse actually adds momentum rather than drag.)

Standardbred harness horses are calmer, tougher and more dependable than Thoroughbreds. The favorites win more often than Thoroughbred favorites. Still, most bettors are chronic losers, in part because they ignore the most important betting factors.

Most decisive of all is post position, especially on short half-mile or five-eighths-mile tracks. The nearer the rail, the less distance the horse must travel, both at the start and around a turn. The horse in the number-one post (at the far inside) has a tremendous advantage. Since he's already at the rail, he doesn't need to spend energy to get there. So even if he doesn't make the lead, he will probably be close enough to make a move in the stretch.

Conversely, if a horse draws an outside post (six or higher), the driver will either have to "park" outside other horses while contending for the lead or take back to the rear. Later on, he may be boxed in with no racing room. To mount a stretch drive, he will have to return outside, losing at least one and a half lengths around the final turn. And given the width of the other sulkies, there may be no convenient holes to burst through. All in all, it's tough to catch the leader.

Post positions are also a key to interpreting past performances. *Example:* A horse named Armbro Gold once raced from the eight post and finished a distant sixth. But in the race before that, starting from the one post, he led the way and won handily. If he's returning to an inside post, you can expect Armbro Gold to improve, perhaps at good odds.

The other underrated factor: The driver's ability. Every track has a few leading drivers—check their names in your program and try to remember them. Steer clear of any driver who fails to win at least 10% of his starts. And you should never place a bet on a novice or provisional driver.

Positive sign: A switch from a trainer-driver to a leading full-time driver. This often means the trainer believes the horse is now at his best, ready to win.

But even the best driver can't help a slow starter from an outside post. *Good advice:* Check each race (consult the track program) for horses with good early speed. There are no Silky Sullivans in harness racing—no champions who consistently come from last place to take the purse. You'll find that the winner is usually among the first four horses at the half mile.

In weighing past performances, the horse's time in the final quarter mile is more revealing than his overall time. *Most promising:* A fast final quarter (under 31 seconds) following a fast first half mile.

It's also positive if the horse…

•**Won his last race** (unless he won by a small margin that was less than the last time).

•**Is going off at lower odds than in his last race.**

•**Raced steadily last time while parked** (indicated by a small o in the program) for one or more calls. ("Parked" means outside one or more other horses.)

But don't bet heavily if the horse…

•**Is moving up steeply in class** (signified by purse money or claiming price).

•**Hasn't been in a race for more than two weeks.**

•**Seems clearly superior in the program but is going off at odds of five to two or greater.** (The horse's handlers don't think he can win.)

•**Broke stride in his last race** (check in your track program).

•**Has pinned ears** (ears are back flat against his head) or is nervous or sweating in prerace warm-ups.

State Lottery Winning Strategy

When playing a state lottery, it's a good idea to choose at least one number higher than 31. *Reason:* Many lottery players use number combinations based on birthdays, anniversaries and other dates. Since this group concentrates on numbers of 31 or lower, a winning combination with one or more higher numbers will probably be shared by fewer people.

Dr. Jim Maxwell, American Mathematics Society.

How to Win in Vegas

To win in Las Vegas, play bingo. Since 1989, casinos have lost an average of 2.44% per year on bingo. *However:* Visitors rarely play bingo—it is the locals who are winning.

Donald Currier, editor, *Las Vegas Insider,* Box 1185, Chino Valley, Arizona 86323.

How to Win at Poker

Mike Caro, gambling teacher and theorist, and former columnist for *Gambling Times.* He is author of *Caro on Gambling* (Gambling Times) and *Caro's Book of Poker Tells* (Cardoza Publishing).

Not so many years ago, every poker book told you the same thing: Play tight (fold bad hands). This is still good advice as far as it goes. In a typical home game, the players who win the most pots wind up as losers because they throw too much money away on all the pots they play—but don't win. You can beat these games to death simply by contesting 20% fewer hands than anyone else. Be selective but aggressive. Ideally you should end a hand by either folding or raising. Avoid calling bets with vulnerable hands, such as two pairs.

Your goal: To own the table psychologically so that the other players are glancing at you every time they make a bet. Be friendly, but at the same time be confusing and unpredictable. Never gloat. You want your opponents to enjoy trying to beat you.

In a low-to-moderate-limit game, you can win without mathematical genius or brilliant originality. In fact, most of your profit will come from your opponents' mistakes. *Their chief error:* Calling for too many pots with mediocre hands.

This makes bluffing a poor strategy. First of all, unsophisticated opponents won't even understand your intended deception. Second, they're likely to call you anyway, a habit you want to encourage.

Exception: You might try a strategic bluff just once, early in the session, as an "advertisement."

Example: You can even advertise without bluffing. In a five-card draw, you call the opener and then rap pat (taking no cards) with absolute garbage, such as 10-7-6-3-2 of different suits. After the other players draw and check to you, you check as well as show your pathetic cards. You'll lose, of course, but your opponents will feel forced to call your good hands later on.

The only other time to bluff is when your legitimate hand fizzles at the end. If you calculate that pot odds (the money already in the pot versus the amount it would cost to bluff) are favorable, bluff on.

Discipline is especially crucial in a low-limit game, when you need more hands to make up losses.

You must decide in advance how you will react in each of various situations. Never play a hand out of impatience or on a "hunch." Play it for a good reason. Monitor yourself carefully. If you make a mistake, admit it to

yourself and get back on track. Don't let one bad play erode your entire system.

Also avoid: Looking for immediate revenge after an opponent burns you on a big pot. If you force the action, you're apt to get burned again.

Refusing to quit after you've already taken a beating. In fact, you should stay later when you're ahead and leave early when behind. When you're losing, you have no psychological control of the game. Opponents try to bluff you out of pots and are less likely to call your good hands. (When you're on a hot streak, they are more likely to call. If they lose, they can always console themselves by blaming it on your luck.)

Complaining about bad luck. The cards don't owe you a fair shake every session.

Of course, one of your goals will be to try to avoid getting behind in the first place.

Regardless of how your cards are running, you can gain a heavy advantage by watching for and learning to read opponents' "tells"—the mannerisms they fall into that tend to give away whether their hands are good or bad.

In general, follow the rule of opposites: Players usually act weak when their hands are strong, and they commonly act strong when their hands are weak.

Recognize the body language and involuntary signs that are trademarks of bluffers…

• **Breathing shallowly or holding their breath.**

• **Staring at their hands—or at you as you prepare to bet.**

• **Reaching for chips out of turn.**

• **Making a bet with an authoritative pronouncement.**

• **Flinging chips into the pot with an outstretched forearm.**

• **Showing unusual friendliness toward opponents.**

Players with powerful hands have their own set of tells…

• **Sharing a hand with a bystander** (especially a spouse).

• **Shaking noticeably while making a bet.** (This reflects a release of tension. Most players show obvious outward nervousness only when they feel they're in little danger.)

- **Talking easily and naturally.**

- **Behaving in an unusually gruff manner** toward opponents.

- **Leaning forward in a seat.**

- **Betting with a sigh, shrug or negative tone of voice.**

- **Asking, "How much is it to me?" or requesting another clarification.**

- **Glancing quickly at the player's chips after receiving a (good) card.**

"Tells" can be extremely helpful, but they can also induce a player to call too many pots.

Bottom line: Look for reasons to fold just as eagerly as you look for reasons to call.

Insider's Guide to Casino Gambling

Jerry L. Patterson, professional gambler who once had a 10-year winning streak. He is also coauthor of Casino Gambling: A Winner's Guide to Blackjack, Craps, Roulette, Baccarat, and Casino Poker *(Penguin).*

As a weekend gambler, you're basically out for a good time. The odds are you won't break the bank. But you can enhance your enjoyment—and maybe even take home some house money—if you follow a few general rules.

- **Go in with a game plan and stick to it.** Decide in advance how much money you're going to take, how much you can afford to lose and at what point you will quit.

- **Limit each bet to 1% of your original stake.** That may be as little as $2 to $5 (the weekday minimum in Atlantic City). Up your bets only when you are ahead. Never bet more than 10% of the stake. If you start chasing money you have lost, the odds of going broke are much higher.

- **Don't push your luck.** If you have won $100 with a given dealer and then lose $20 of your profits, back off. Take a deep breath or break for dinner. In any case, find a new table.

- **Pass up the free drinks.** Casinos offer them for a reason. If you drink too much alcohol and lose your inhibitions, you may desert your strategy and change your betting patterns. You want to keep a clear head.

Blackjack is the best casino game—the only one in which a skilled player can beat the house over time. Overall, of course, the casinos make a nice profit because their edge against the average "hunch" player runs from 6% to 15%.

However, with an advanced card-counting system, the odds are turned around. The experienced player has a 2% advantage. Mastery of the counting system takes time and practice. A simplified version gives the player a 1.5% edge, but it still requires instruction and some dedicated use.

For the recreational gambler, a basic blackjack strategy—with no counting—can cut the house edge to only .4%. Given those odds, you'd lose about $2 in an average hour if you bet $5 per hand—not a bad entertainment value.

RULES FOR THE NO-COUNT SYSTEM

- **Never split pairs of 4s, 5s or 10s.** Always split aces and 8s. Split other pairs if the dealer's up card is 2 through 6.

- **Double your bet on 11 unless the dealer's hand shows an ace.** Double on 10 unless the dealer shows an ace or 10. Double on 9 if the dealer shows 3 through 6 and on soft hands (hands with an ace that can be counted as 11 without going over 21) of 13 through 18 if the dealer shows 4 through 6.

- **Always stand on hard hands** (hands with no ace or an ace that must be counted as 1) of 17 and up. Stand on hands of 12 through 16 if the dealer shows 2 through 6. (Otherwise, hit.) Always stand on soft hands of 18 and up. Always hit on soft hands of 17 or less if it is too late to double.

These rules will keep you out of serious trouble. But human nature being what it is, you will naturally want to play an occasional hunch against the odds. *Best hunch bet:* An "insurance" bet on the dealer's hand when you have been dealt a blackjack. *Reason:* When you have a blackjack, the only thing that can keep you from winning is the dealer also having a blackjack. An insurance bet on his cards assures you of getting at least something on the hand.

Craps: This is the most emotional casino game. Fast and noisy, it can sweep you into making more bets per hour than other games —as many as 150. *Result:* The money turns over faster and you can lose more. However, if you stick to the most favorable bets, you concede an edge of only .8% to the house.

Bets to make: Pass line. Don't pass. Come. Don't come. In each case, always make the maximum accompanying "odds" bets (these offer the best percentage of all). The only other acceptable wagers are "place" bets on 6 or 8 (the house edge is 1.4% on these).

Avoid all long-shot and one-roll bets like "hardway 4." The stickman will encourage this action because it makes money for the casino. The odds against you are enormous because the house advantage runs from 10% to 16%.

Under the laws of probability, there is no true number system to help the craps gambler. Each roll of the dice is independent. But there are useful betting strategies. *A good one:* After the roller has thrown two passes (winning rolls), up your bet 50% every other pass thereafter.

ROULETTE

Number systems will do you no good in roulette. *The general house edge is high: 5.3%. To halve your disadvantage, stick to "outside" even-money bets:* Red-black, odd-even, high-low. If 0 or 00 comes up, you lose only half of these wagers. Other bets are lost in full.

BACCARAT

Although the house edge is only 1.1%, this "upper crust" game gives the player no control. *You make only two decisions:* How much you want to put down and whether you choose the banker or the player.

Baccarat players tend to be superstitious, and they are notorious for being streak players.

Warning: The baccarat minimum is generally pretty high—$20 to $25. This makes it an expensive game to play.

SLOT MACHINES

Casinos make more than half their profit on slot machines. The house edge is 17%. If you must play, find a "progressive" machine that increases its jackpot as money is pumped through it. Some $1 machines pay as high as $250,000.

The ultimate sucker bet is the big wheel, a giant circle where numbered sections pay various odds. The house take approaches 25%.

FINAL SHOT

Don't be greedy. Just as you set a strict loss limit (say, 20% of your stake) and stop at it, you should quit while you are ahead, too. Enjoy the sights and the shows, and go home with your profit. If everyone did that, the casinos would be in trouble.

Pauline Frommer's Favorite Travel Web Sites

Pauline Frommer is creator of the *Pauline Frommer Guidebooks* (Wiley) and cohost of *The Travel Show*, a nationally syndicated radio show. She is a two-time winner of the North American Travel Journalists Association's "Guidebook of the Year" award. The daughter of Arthur Frommer (founder of the famed Frommer's travel guides), she has been traveling extensively since she was four months old. Her free site, *www.frommers. com/pauline*, offers up-to-date information on tourist locations around the globe.

When it comes to travel Web sites, there are a few big names that dominate the market—but I don't regularly use any of them. Instead, as a professional travel writer, editor and travel talk-show host, I tend to turn to the following smaller and/or lesser-known sites because I have found, time and again, that they save me money and offer the most useful information…

AIRFARES

• **Momondo.com.** When it comes to finding the lowest airfare, Momondo's no-stone-unturned, cutting-edge technology comes out on top. And unlike most of its competitors, it covers all the airlines, even those that don't offer companies a commission for referrals (such as Southwest, Ryannair and EasyJet, airlines you generally won't find on the major search engines). Once you find a fare, you click a link to purchase the ticket at a site such as Priceline.com or Travelocity.com.

Worthy competitors: Dohop.com also offers a broad, impartial search. For multistop itineraries (Momondo and DoHop can do only one-way and round-trip flights), Kayak.com is the place to turn, though it doesn't cover every airline out there.

CAR RENTALS

• **AutoSlash.com.** This nifty new site offers two waysp2ve lower rates.

Another smart option for low-cost car rental—the blind bidding sites mentioned below under "Hotels."

HOTELS

• **HotelsCombined.com.** Ever heard of HotelClub.com, Travel Worm.com or HRS.com? HotelsCombined.com has, and it searches the listings of all of these relatively obscure discounters (many of which buy blocks of rooms and then sell them at a steep markdown), along with the hotel chain sites and such major travel Web sites as Hotels.com and Travelocity.com. The breadth of its results page is awesome, with rates that often are 50% lower than the published rates.

Worthy competitors: Travelers who just want a bed for the night and don't really care which hotel they stay at pay even less by bidding blindly at such Web sites as Priceline.com, Hotwire.com and the new GetARoom.com.

But what if you want a clue first as to where you might be sleeping? You can never guarantee where you'll be staying when you "bid blind," but such Web sites as BetterBidding.com and BiddingForTravel.com eliminate some of the guesswork. Both offer impartial reports from travelers who have recently bid for travel on these sites, spilling the beans on which hotels they got and for how much money. It's valuable information because the bidding sites tend to use the same hotels over and over in many areas.

HOME RENTALS

• **HomeAway.com.** The latest Web site to join Google, this claims to be the largest home-rental site on the Web. And it might well be, with more than 230,000 rentals. Instead of cramming your family into a small hotel room, you can rent a condo or complete house. Users contact owners directly and negotiate prices. A key perk of rentals is that they come with kitchens, which is great when you are traveling with picky eaters or don't want to spend too much on restaurant meals. Many rentals require a minimum stay of four nights or more. Be sure to thoroughly research your rental before you put down a deposit—there usually are few ways to get your money back if you're disappointed.

Worthy competitors: VRBO.com, Zonder.com, Rentalo.com and a number of others work in just the way HomeAway.com does, serving as forums for property owners to connect with would-be renters.

Another good alternative for budget-minded travelers is renting a room in a local's house for very little money. The premier site for this type of accommodation is AirBNB.com.

CRUISES

• **VacationsToGo.com.** Those travel agencies that sell the most cruises are rewarded by the cruise lines with perks for customers, such as free upgrades, shipboard credits (typically $100 to $300), a bottle of wine in the room and more. VacationsToGo.com, as one of the biggest sellers of cruises, consistently offers these types of money-saving extras, items you simply won't get if you book directly with a cruise line or with an agency that doesn't do much cruise business.

Worthy competitors: Before booking with VacationsToGo, also check CruisesOnly.com…CruiseStar.com…CruiseBrothers.com…Cruise.com…and OnlineVacationCenter.com—these agencies also move a lot of cabins and thus have the same types of perks and discounts to offer.

CruiseCritic.com is a fine source for reviews of cruise ships and also has a section on current discounts.

For shore excursions, check out PortCompass.com and ShoreTrips.com. Both companies vet local operators of shore excursions that typically are less crowded and less costly than the cruise lines' excursions.

OTHER TOP-NOTCH SITES
FOR TRAVELERS

• **Zicasso.com.** Connects specialty travel companies with vacationers who don't want to plan all aspects of their trips.

• **Translate.Google.com.** A tool to use on your Web-enabled cell phone when you don't speak the local language.

• **XE.com.** A lickety-split, accurate curency-exchange calculator.

• **MapQuest.com** beats Google maps by a hair, thanks to its new functionality, which allows you to add helpful resources, such as gas stations and restaurants, to your maps.

• **Maps.Google.com/streetview** gives you a quick look at where you're going before you get there.

• **HopStop.com.** Easy-to-follow, logical directions for using public transportation in 20 major tourist areas around the globe.

• **WebFlyer.com.** For those who want to maximize frequent-flier miles. News, tips, mileage calculators and more.

9

Sports and Recreation

The Best Fly-Fishing Equipment and Where To Fish with It

Fly-fishing offers a rare opportunity to connect with creatures of beauty and power in extraordinary settings. Timing, patience and good companions all add to the joy of fishing.

Over the past eight years, as the number of fly fishermen in this country tripled to more than three million, we have entered a golden age of fly-fishing equipment. *How to get started...*

BUYING THE RIGHT ROD

A quality fishing rod is important. *Helpful:* Beginners should invest most of their start-up money in a good rod. A first-class rod costs $325 to $400. Most veteran fly fishermen own several different rods.

A good all-purpose rod is a "9-for-7"—a nine-foot rod with a seven-weight line. This rod will work for brook trout, steelhead, Canadian bass and pike, as well as larger trout in the Rockies. As long as you stick with a reputable rod maker—Fisher, L.L. Bean, Loomis, Orvis and Sage, among others—it is difficult to go wrong. *Other considerations about your rod...*

- **Material.** Bamboo rods are wonderful to look at but require considerable expertise to be wielded effectively.

Graphite rods have higher strength-to-weight ratios. A typical graphite rod might weigh only three ounces, compared to between four and five ounces for a bamboo or fiberglass rod. *Result:* Superior "feel" and responsiveness.

- **Style.** "Eastern" rods are more flexible and have slower casting action than other types of rods. This makes them ideal for beginners. They're best suited for catching smaller fish in smaller streams.

In windy conditions and bigger streams—such as those found in the Rocky Mountains

---

Howell Raines, Pulitzer Prize–winning journalist and former executive editor of *The New York Times*. He is author of *Fly Fishing Through the Midlife Crisis* (Harper-Collins).

or Pacific Northwest—stiffer "Western" rods can shoot out longer casts.

• **Portability.** With a total length of eight to nine feet, a two-piece rod is fine if you are driving to a stream. It will fit easily in the trunk of your car. But a three-piece rod is more convenient for air travel, since it can fit in a carry-on bag.

• **Line weight.** Rods are designated by the weight of the line they cast. Line weights range from Number 1, for tiny trout and panfish, to Number 15, for tarpon and marlin.

• **Economy.** G. Loomis, Orvis and Sage sell budget versions of their high-quality graphite rods with less expensive fittings. The reel seats and handles aren't as aesthetically fine as those of top-of-the-line models, but the rod functions almost as well.

OTHER EQUIPMENT

• **Reels.** An excellent reel is the Orvis CFO ($179 to $198), which is spool-milled from a block of solid aluminum and lasts indefinitely. Comparable reels are made by Abel and Lamsom.

For approximately $100, you can purchase good—but heavier—models by Cortland, Orvis Battenkill and Scientific Anglers.

• **Flies.** Excellent ready-tied trout flies are made by Orvis and L.L. Bean and cost less than $2 each. You'll want a combination of "dry" flies—for when fish are dimpling the surface for bugs…and "wet" flies—for when fish are feeding below the surface.

Basic assortment: Dry flies—Adams, Elk Hair Caddis, Light Cahill, Royal Wulff. Wet flies—Wooly Bugger, Hare's Ear Nymph, Pheasant Tail Nymph. *Better:* The Clouser Minnow that, in various sizes and colors, works for trout, bass, pike and saltwater fish.

GREAT FISHING SPOTS

• **Delaware Water Gap, Pennsylvania.** Water gaps—the places where big rivers come through big mountains—are ideal for their panoramic settings. Only two hours from New York City, the Delaware Water Gap offers some of the best trout fishing in the country.

More information: Aquatic Resources Program Specialist, 717-626-9081.

• **Leeville, LaFourche Parish, Louisiana.** Atmospheric marshlands and a great spot for catching redfish (also known as channel bass)—a shallow-water ocean fish.

More information: LaFourche Welcome Center, 985-537-5800.

• **Rapidan River, Virginia.** Like the Big Sur coast or the Grand Tetons above Jackson Hole, Wyoming, the Rapidan River is an ideal expression of its kind. It is an Eastern mountain stream plunging through hemlock forest. Since the Rapidan flows within the Shenandoah National Park, it is protected from development.

More information: Department of Game and Inland Fisheries, 804-367-1000.

• **Snake River, near Jackson Hole, Wyoming.** Overwhelmingly beautiful scenery, lots of fish and a variety of conditions, from fast and deep channels to shallow flats.

More information: Wyoming Game and Fish Department, 307-777-4600.

• **Yellowstone River, Yellowstone Park, Wyoming.** Even beginning fly fishermen may catch big fish at this premier protected cutthroat trout fishery.

More information: Yellowstone Park Information, 307-344-7381.

WILD FISH

Many experienced fly fishermen prefer streams with wild—not stocked—fish. Stocked fish are those added to streams by park rangers for ecological and sporting purposes. Wild fish offer more fight and are harder to deceive.

In any waters, wild fish can flourish only if fly fishermen release every fish they catch. After 40 years of fishing, I do not own a single mounted fish. My photographs and memories are trophies enough.

Fishing Demystified

R ivers, lakes or open sea—if you know where to start looking, you can catch any fish successfully. *For example, bass tend to congregate…*

•**Near trees that have recently fallen into the water.**

•**In hot weather.** Under lily pads, especially in the only shallow spots around.

•**In consistently mild weather.** In backwater ponds and coves off the main lake. *Best:* Good weed or brush cover, with a creek running in.

•**Anytime at all.** In sunken moss beds near the shore.

Outdoor Life

For fishing around a fallen tree, start at the top, using deep-running lures. Along the sides, use medium-running lures. Toward the base of the tree, change to shallow and surface lures.

Sports Afield

For good year-round fishing, try Florida's east coast from Melbourne Beach to Fort Pierce. *Fall and spring:* Runs of snook, the delicious saltwater gamefish that weighs up to 30 pounds. *Winter:* Surf fishing for blues, big whiting and pompano, which many think is the best-tasting of all the saltwater fish. The nearby Indian River also provides good year-round fishing with light tackle.

Best Offshore Fishing

Barry Gibson, former editor, *Salt Water Sportsman*, and John F. Klein, a charter captain out of Sarasota, Florida.

Face it. You've always wanted to play Ernest Hemingway for a day, your muscles straining, your face stinging from salt and sun, hair lashed by the wind, hooting and hollering in pain, exultation and glory as you engage in mortal combat with a colossus of the deep—man versus marlin.

Fact: Offshore fishing for big game fish requires the least amount of previous experience of any type of sportfishing. You don't have to rig your tackle, bait a hook, cast a line, or navigate. All you need is a good boat, a good captain, a competent crew and a strong back!

Once known as "deep-sea fishing" (a term now seen only in the brochures of tropical resorts), offshore fishing refers to sportfishing for larger species—billfish (marlin, sailfish and swordfish), tuna, tarpon, cobia and shark. The US offers excellent fishing off all three coasts.

Chartering a boat: The procedure is similar everywhere. If time permits, visit the boat docks at sunset when charters return. See what kinds of fish are being brought in. Talk with the passengers. Were their previous fishing experiences and their expectations similar to yours? Did they have fun? Are they satisfied with their day's trip? Would they do it again?

Talk to the mates. Are they pleasant? Enthusiastic about the captain?

Next, inspect the boat. Is it clean and well maintained? Does it appear to have proper radio and safety equipment? Naturally, a boat will not look its best on its return from a day's fishing—but are the running gear and fishing tackle well kept? Or has tackle been stowed randomly, paint chipped, hardware corroded?

Many fishermen prefer an owner-operated boat to a vessel run by a salaried captain. In either case, check to see if the captain has been licensed by the Coast Guard.

Boats that carry six passengers or fewer are not required to pass an annual Coast Guard inspection, but they must carry mandatory safety equipment. Boats that have undergone a voluntary inspection will display a Coast Guard sticker. If you're planning to bring a child along, ask if junior-size life preservers are available.

If you expect to be able to keep your catch, check with the captain beforehand to avoid a dispute at the end of the day.

Expect to pay $300 to $400 a day for a private charter. In some areas, $600 to $800 is not uncommon.

Variations in costs depend largely on how far the boat must travel to reach prime fishing waters. In Boothbay, Maine, for example, you may have to travel only three to 10 miles offshore, while from Montauk, New York, 60 or 70 miles is not unusual.

Although some areas may offer half-day charters if the travel distance is not too great, it is more common for a good fishing trip to take a whole day.

Regardless of whether or not fish are caught, it is customary to tip the mate at the end of the day (and also the captain, especially if he is salaried and not the owner of the boat). The going rate is about 10% of the cost of the trip. Of course, as in any service business, a good catch and/or good service may inspire a more generous tip.

Party boats: For a less costly trip, though not necessarily a less enjoyable one, try a "party boat" or "head boat." These big, stable boats, equipped for a large number of passengers, range in cost from $15 or so for half a day to $20 to $30 and up for a longer trip. These boats are a great introduction for a beginning angler or for a fisherman who is new to an area. They offer wide variety and often concentrate on "good-eating" fish. *Disadvantages:* The equipment may be worn from continual use. (Don't hesitate to request another pole if you don't think yours is working right.) And you can't ask to go home if you're not having a good time.

On the Pacific Coast, some boats offer three-day to three-week trips for about $100 a day. They fish for numerous species along the Mexican coast. Passengers may keep their catch.

Most boats let you keep most or all of what you catch. The mate is usually happy to clean and fillet your fish for a small fee. But it is in very poor taste to ask the captain or the mate to clean your fish and then try to sell it on the dock. Take what you plan to eat and offer the rest to the boat. Keep your fish on ice in a cooler, being careful not to let your fillets come into contact with fresh water or ice.

ETIQUETTE

• **Dress appropriately.** Bring extra layers of clothing even if you are in the Florida Keys. It can be a lot cooler on the water than on land, and mornings are often chilly. Wear soft-soled boat shoes, polarized sunglasses and a hat, and bring a sunscreen.

• **Take precautions against seasickness.** Ask your doctor for medication ahead of time if you think you'll need it and begin to take it at least 24 hours before your departure. (This allows you to sleep off the early, drowsy part and be fully alert for your trip.) Medications for seasickness do not help if you wait until you are already queasy to take them.

• **Bring plenty of nonalcoholic beverages.** It is easy to get dehydrated while you are on the water. Also, bring any food you may want (it's a good idea to include a salty snack). Most charter boats do not supply food or drink, although many party boats have snack bars. *Note:* Although it is not in poor taste to enjoy a few beers over the course of a day's fishing, it is downright boorish, and frequently dangerous, to become drunk while on the water.

• **Limit the number of passengers.** Many people make the mistake of overloading a boat, hoping to split the cost. But on a charter boat with only one or two "fighting chairs," passengers take turns fishing. The more people on board, the fewer your turns to fish actively. As a general rule, a 28- to 30-foot boat accommodates four passengers comfortably. A 35-foot or larger boat can handle six.

• **Listen to the instructions of your captain and mate.** They have spent years studying an area, and they want you to catch fish. There are many differences in tackle, bait and techniques, and your favorite walleye lure may not be appetizing to a yellowfin tuna.

• **If you are a novice, say so.** Not only will the captain and mate appreciate your honesty, but they will best be able to help you if they have some idea of your previous experience.

• **Fish with an open mind.** The vacation day you have allocated for fishing may turn out to be a day fish are not feeding. Your guide isn't holding out on you.

Long-distance chartering: Many people don't have time to explore the docks of an area before they choose a boat. For recommendations by telephone, try calling a local tackle shop or the editors of a major outdoor magazine. (Resort hotels usually limit their referrals to the guides who service the hotel.)

Several travel agencies specialize (at no cost) in arranging fishing trips. *One good one:* Fishing International, Santa Rosa, California, 800-950-4242.

A few other pointers: Many captains will take "split charters." If you are traveling in a small group and would like to divide the cost of a charter, inquire at the dock for similar parties.

It is not polite, however, to ask a captain to find five other people to share your trip.

If you plan to take children, choose a charter that is geared toward variety fishing. Try a half-day charter first, and stay away from hard-core game fishing—it is boring just to watch Daddy fish all day!

Many of the favorite captains are booked solid a year in advance. Scout around early if you plan to fish in a new area.

SEASONAL SUGGESTIONS

• **April and May.** It's long-range party-boat season in Southern California. San Diego is the biggest port. Party boats in New York and New Jersey venture out for flounder, cod and other bottom fishing. Party boats and skiff guides are active in the Florida Keys.

• **June.** Head for the Gulf Stream from the Outer Banks of North Carolina to catch tuna and white marlin. It's big game billfish season offshore in the Gulf of Mexico from Louisiana to Texas.

• **July, August, early September.** In New York through New England, fish for giant tuna (up to 1,000 pounds!). It's peak season for white and blue marlin in North Carolina. There's excellent fishing in the Florida Keys (not crowded) for sailfish, bonefish and permit. Party and charter boats fish for salmon in the Pacific Northwest through Alaska.

• **September and October.** Catch bluefin tuna off Prince Edward Island before they migrate south.

• **October and November.** Big game fishing is winding down in the North and in the Gulf. But it's great for bluefish from Massachusetts through Chesapeake Bay.

• **September through November.** For a more glamorous trip, black marlin fishing is tremendous off the Great Barrier Reef in Australia or New Zealand.

• **December and January.** Winter is winter, even in the Florida Keys, but sailfish like the cold, rough seas. (Dress warmly.)

• **February and March.** The weather is very changeable in southern waters, so allow at least three to five days for a fishing trip. You may thus get one or two good days of fishing.

There is still plenty of good fishing in the Caribbean even though it is not peak season. Try for marlin and billfish in the Bahamas.

• **November through March.** Cabo San Lucas, Mexico, is prime for marlin, sails, dolphin (the fish, not the mammal) and roosterfish.

Good fishing! Once you try it, I bet you'll be hooked!

Great Wildlife Watching

Santa Cruz, California, Natural Bridge State Beach, 831-423-4609, where hundreds of thousands of monarch butterflies make their home from October through February…Sullivan County, New York, Eagle Institute, 845-583-1010, where more than 100 bald eagles winter from mid-December to mid-March…Florence, Oregon, Sea Lion Caves, 541-547-3111, where sea lions frolic year-round…Grand Island, Nebraska, Crane Meadows Nature Center, 308-382-1820, where hundreds of thousands of sandhill cranes and other waterfowl can be seen March to mid-April.

Diane Bair and Pamela Wright, coauthors, *Wild Encounters* (Willow Creek Press), writing in *Family Fun*.

Outdoor Programs For Young and Old

Great Camp Sagamore, a national historic site in New York's Adirondack mountains, offers a wide range of recreational and nature activities, 20 miles of hiking trails and a clear view of the Milky Way. Weekend and week-long programs include canoeing, history activities and llama trekking. Costs start at $299 per person.

Contact: Sagamore Historic Adirondack Great Camp, Box 40, Raquette Lake, NY 13436, 315-354-5311 or *http://greatcampsagamore.org.*

Mature Outlook

How to Get Into Shape For Skiing

Being physically fit makes skiing more fun and helps prevent soreness and injuries. Getting ready for the slopes can be like your regular exercise regimen.

Muscle tone and flexibility: Stretching exercises keep your muscles long and pliable. They also warm muscles up for strenuous sports and help relax them afterward. Always stretch slowly. Hold the extended position for 20 to 30 seconds. Don't bounce. Do simple stretches. Rotate your head. Bend from side to side. Touch your toes. Lunge forward while keeping the back foot flat on the floor. Do sit-ups with your knees bent to strengthen abdominal muscles (they can take stress off the back).

Endurance and strength: Practicing any active sport, from swimming to tennis, for three one-hour sessions a week will get you into shape. Jogging builds up the muscles of the lower torso and legs. Running downhill strengthens the front thigh muscles, essential to skiing. Running on uneven terrain promotes strong and flexible ankles. Biking builds strong legs and improves balance.

Top 10 Skiing Resorts

An industry insider who has visited more than 120 North American ski centers during the past 22 years.

What makes one ski resort more exciting than all the rest? *According to our insider, it's the destination's diversity:* thrilling trails, cushy lodges and lots of after-ski activities. *The following are his North American favorites...*

- **Lake Louise, Alberta.** Probably the most outstanding scenery in North America. Canada's largest ski area with thousands of acres of bowl skiing, long tree-lined runs and high-speed lifts. Many enchanting and affordable ski lodges, including the spectacular Fairmont Chateau Lake Louise. 866-540-4413.
- **Snowbird, Utah.** One hour from Salt Lake City. Forty feet of snow each winter, plenty of difficult trails and a first-class spa. 800-232-9542.
- **Snowmass, Colorado.** Wide-open cruising terrain. Twenty-two lifts (seven of them high speed), 88 trails. Lodge lets you ski from your room to the lift. 800-923-8920.

   Bonus: Trendy Aspen is only 10 minutes away by frequent, free shuttle bus.
- **Steamboat, Colorado.** Located above a quaint Western town, great mix of tree skiing and wide-open cruising trails. Has 142 trails and 25 lifts. Hot-springs-fed pools for bathing, horse-drawn sleigh rides. 877-237-2628.
- **Stowe, Vermont.** New England's tallest peak. 48 trails, modern lifts, improved snowmaking, great food and views. Cross-country skiing and night skiing. Twelve lifts (two high speed). 800-253-4754.
- **Sunday River, Maine.** Super-efficient lifts, snowmaking and grooming, plus all-ability terrain and lodging that allows you to ski to and from your door. Has grown to encompass 128 trails and three high-speed lifts. 207-824-3500.
- **Taos Ski Valley, New Mexico.** One of the finest ski schools. More than 100 trails, 12 lifts, abundant powder and sun 300 days a year. 866-968-7386.
- **Telluride, Colorado.** An expert's paradise, located above an old mining town nestled in a spectacular canyon. A modern ski-lodging development. 888-253-1080.
- **Vail, Colorado.** Largest single ski mountain in the US. Thirty-four lifts (many of them high speed), 5,289 acres of terrain, 193 trails and lots of powder, thanks to the high altitude. And, there are horse-drawn sleigh rides—including evening trips to local restaurants. 877-204-7881.
- **Whistler/Blackcomb, British Columbia.** Two mountains, 33 lifts, 8,100 acres of terrain, a mile of vertical descent that allows skiers to take their time winding down their choice of more than 200 trails. Has an enchanting base village with more than 100 shops. 877-932-0606.

When Sharpening Is Bad for Skis

Sharpening skis frequently to remove nicks and restore the edges can change their performance. Flat-filing the bottom reduces the thickness of the plastic base and makes skis more flexible. Side-filing can narrow skis and change the turning radius. For experts, this may be a problem, but most recreational skiers won't notice a difference.

Skiing

How to Buy Ski Boots

The first rule in buying ski boots is, if a boot is not comfortable in the store, it will be worse on the slopes. *Proper fit:* Toes should be able to wiggle while the heel, instep and ball of the foot are effectively but not painfully immobilized. An experienced shop technician can expand the shell and modify the footbed and heel wedge. *Forward flex:* When you bend your foot, you should feel no pressure points on your shin or upper ankle. *Boot height:* A high boot spreads flexing loads across a wider shin area than low boots do. Most recreational skiers are at ease in a high boot with a soft forward flex. Low, stiff boots concentrate loads just above the ankle, which can be painful for the occasional skier.

Ski

Golf Smarts

One way to improve your golf game while waiting your turn at the tee is to take some practice swings from the opposite side—if you are right-handed, take swings left-handed. Start slowly, and do not go more than 70% of your normal swing speed. Do the swings a few times on the first three or four holes of every round. Also do a few opposite-side swings at the driving range. They will help strengthen and balance your muscles, making it easier to hit longer drives.

Gregory Florez, golf trainer, Salt Lake City, quoted in *Men's Health*.

How to Play Better Golf

John Youngblood, author of *How I Went from 28 to Scratch in One Year Playing Once a Week at the Age of 70* (Price Stern Sloan).

I studied every prominent golfer who ever played the game and listed the techniques they shared. From this, I distilled my system, *Ultimate Golf Swing Fundamentals*. Within nine months, at the age of 70, I reduced my handicap from 28 to scratch.

How it works: The backbone of this system is a *stairstep* program. The principle is simple. I believe that the foundation of every sound golf game resides in putting.

The fundamentals for every succeeding swing—from the chip and pitch, through the irons, to the woods and driver—are the same. The only difference is that the golfer's stroke becomes successively longer.

According to the *stairstep* principle, the golfer must perfect every shot possible with a particular club before moving on to the next club, up the *stairstep*.

MORE ADVICE

In addition to practicing on the course's practice area (and doing it right), *I recommend the following steps for any golfers intent on sharpening their game:*

• **Play regularly.** In my turn-around year, I increased my frequency of play from once a month to once a week. I finally got to know my golf course, and could begin to aim my shots to areas where the following shots would be easier.

- **Do your golf exercises in front of a mirror.** I achieved a major breakthrough while swinging a 5-iron before a full-length mirror. *Don't be modest:* Dressed only in my shorts, I soon isolated my problem—a quivering of my right knee during my backswing, the source of my frequently errant iron shots. With proper exercise I developed control of my knee—and with it my iron game.

- **Never rush on the golf course.** Allow time upon arrival for your practice shots and putts. Once on the tee, visualize the shot to be made and the spot where you expect it to land. Concentrate on this spot—and not on anyone who may be watching you—as you stroke the ball.

- **Skip the practice swings before you hit.** Most people tend to tighten up with extra swings. It's better to relax and fire away.

- **Don't overswing.** Use a three-quarter backswing with your irons—and only a one-half backswing for your chips and pitches. You'll more than gain in control and accuracy anything you might lose in distance.

All About In-line Skates

Joel Rappelfeld, in-line-skating instructor in New York City and author of *The Complete In-Line Skater* (St. Martin's Press).

In-line skates—skates with their wheels all in a row—have become very popular. More than a million pairs have been sold in the US, and sales are increasing each year.

Often called rollerblades, after the manufacturer Rollerblade, Inc., these skates…

- **Ride faster and more smoothly than conventional roller skates.** Because the wheels are in a straight line, the rubber makes less contact with the ground—avoiding more surface bumps and other obstructions. And because the wheels are under each boot, rather than at the four corners, they can't hit each other if your feet come close together.

- **Provide better ankle support than most conventional roller skates.** In-line skates have a polyurethane boot with an inner liner—much like a ski boot.

- **Provide excellent exercise.** Skaters burn up to 450 calories in 30 minutes.

In-line skates cost $100 to $500 a pair—about the same as conventional skates. Plan to spend at least $200. Cheaper models are less comfortable and have inferior wheels and bearings, which can slow down your progress in learning. *Learning how…*

The biggest risk is falling, usually from not knowing how to stop, or because of surface hazards—gravel, oil, etc. *Self-defense:* Wear knee and elbow pads, wrist guards and a lightweight bicycle helmet.

I also advise people to take a lesson or two before trying to skate on their own. Find an instructor through the shop where you buy your skates.

Protection: Find out how qualified the instructor is. *Ask questions:* How long have you been in-line skating? What type of training have you received from other in-line skating instructors? Do you have any related training and background in similar sports, such as ice skating, skiing or roller skating?

Tennis Pro Secrets

Psyching yourself up for a big point on the tennis court means employing a normal physiological mechanism—the adrenaline response. When adrenaline is pumped into our systems, we are stronger, faster and quicker for a brief period. *How to trigger the response:* Open your eyes wide and fix them on a nearby object. Breathe deeply and forcefully. Think of yourself as a powerful, aggressive individual. Exhort yourself with phrases like "Fight!" Try to raise goose bumps on your skin—they signal a high point. *Note:* Save this response for a key moment toward the end of the match. Psyching yourself up too often will leave you drained.

Tennis

Tennis players often have trouble switching from one type of playing surface to another. Ease transitions by preparing. If you're moving to fast cement from slow clay, for example, practice charging the net before the switch. If it's the other way around, spend extra time on your ground strokes. Tactical adjustments should also be made in advance.

World Tennis

WHEN YOU'RE FACING A SUPERIOR TENNIS PLAYER

• **Suspend all expectations.** Avoid thinking about the situation. Watch the ball, not the opponent.

• **Play your game.** Don't try to impress your opponent with difficult shots you normally never try.

• **Hit the ball deep and down the middle.** The more chances there are for your opponent to return your shot, the more chances there are for him/her to err.

• **Concentrate on your serve.** No matter how outgunned you may be, you can stay in the match if you hold your serve.

Choosing the Right Tennis Ball

Tennis balls come in four varieties. Heavy-duty, regular, high-altitude and pressureless. *Difference between heavy-duty and regular:* The felt cover. Heavy-duty balls have additional nylon to resist wear on hard courts. Regulars have more wool in the covering for play on clay courts. *Note:* Do not use heavy-duty balls on clay. They become slower as the nylon in the cover picks up dirt. High-altitude balls are for courts that are more than 5,000 feet above sea level. Pressureless balls are long-lasting, but they are heavier than most American players are accustomed to.

Save the slightly fluffier tennis ball for your second serve. The fluff lets the ball take the spin more easily than would a fresh, new ball or an old, bare one. Until the nap is fluffed, a new ball flies faster, skids farther and has less bounce.

Tennis

How to Play Good Tennis After 40

Older tennis players can win and avoid injuries by using the right strategies and techniques. The late Pancho Gonzales, a former champion, advised playing a "thinking man's" game.

PANCHO'S PRACTICAL POINTERS

With age, it becomes harder to concentrate on the ball. *Recommended:* When hitting, watch the ball right up to the point where it hits the strings of the racket.

Aim for consistency rather than winners. *Common error made by older players:* Hitting too hard. For power and pace, shift your body weight forward on every stroke. At impact, the weight should be completely on the front foot.

Anticipate your opponent. *Example:* If you have hit a shot to your right, it will probably be returned to your left. Be ready to move left, but don't commit yourself until the ball has been hit.

Back swing: The "how" (straight back or a looping motion) doesn't matter as much as getting the racket back quickly and all the way.

BETTER STRATEGY

Try to swing the same way on every shot—both for consistency and deception. Your opponent shouldn't be able to tell from the swing whether the shot is hard or soft. *Not recommended:* The underspin slice. *Reason:* The ball travels more slowly, giving older players a better chance to reach it. *Better:* Flat shots deep to the corners.

• **Always change a losing game.** Try to lob frequently against opponents who are dominating plays, especially if they have a winning net game. Against winning baseline players, hit drop shots to force them to come in and play the net.

• **Save energy.** Take plenty of time between points and before serving. Don't go all out in a game that you are losing by a score of 0-40.

THE SERVE! THE SERVE!!

Work on a consistent second serve. The resulting gain of confidence will lead to improvement of the first serve.

When practicing the serve, spend time on the toss. *Suggestion:* Practice with a bucket placed where a perfect toss should fall.

Beware of the topspin serve. Though effective, it is hard on the back muscles.

Return serves as early as possible, and keep them low.

HEALTH AND CONDITIONING

Playing tennis twice a week or so isn't enough to keep in shape. Weekly running and other cross-training exercises are a must. Squeezing an old tennis ball a few minutes a day builds up arm muscles, and rope jumping improves footwork.

Rest before and after playing. Use a warmup jacket to speed the loosening of the muscles before play. During play, run with bent knees to reduce shock to knees. After play, apply lotion to the palm of your racket hand to keep it from scaling and blistering.

EQUIPMENT

Both the beginner and intermediate player would choose a graphite with fiber racket for its flexibility. The advanced player would choose a 100% graphite racket, which is more durable and stiffer. Older players will probably be more comfortable playing with lighter-weight rackets, and they also may improve their game by using a racket that has been strung loosely.

DOUBLES STRATEGY

A doubles team should agree on strategy and signals before playing. *Most important signal:* Net players must let their partners know when they plan to cross over to intercept the return of a serve. (A clenched fist behind the back is often used.) During this move and all other moves, both partners should be in motion, one to make the shot and the other to cover the exposed part of the court.

The weaker player should take the forehand court. This player should be assigned to serve when the wind and sun are behind the server. The weaker player should play closer to the net. *Reason:* It is easier to volley in this position.

In doubles, one player normally concentrates on setting up shots. The job is to hit the ball low in order to force the opponents at the net to hit up on the ball. The second player has the job of making the put-aways.

Picking the Right Running Shoes

Gary Muhrcke, proprietor of the Super Runners Shop, 337 Lexington Ave., New York City 10001.

You walk into a store, and the choices seem endless. Where do your feet fit in the race for the perfect pair?

There are five important things to look for in running shoes...

• **A heel counter stiff enough to hold your heel in place** and keep it from rolling in and out.

• **Flexibility in the forefoot area** so the shoe bends easily with your foot. (If the shoe is stiff, your leg and foot muscles will have to work too hard.)

• **An arch support** to keep the foot stable and minimize rolling inside.

• **A fairly wide base for stability and balance.** The bottom of the heel, for example, should be as wide as the top of the shoe.

• **Cushioning that compresses easily.** (Several different materials are used now.) The mid-sole area absorbs the most shock and should have the greatest amount of padding. However, the heel (which particularly for women should be three-quarters of an inch higher than the sole) needs padding, too. Too much padding causes fatigue, and too little causes bruising.

Running shoes do not need to be broken in. They should feel good the moment you try them on.

FITTING

• **Start with manufacturers' least costly shoes** and keep trying until you find the one that feels best.

• **Try on running shoes** with the same kind of socks you wear when you run. If you don't wear socks, try on shoes using pantyhose or ultra-thin socks.

• **Light people need less cushioning** than heavier people do.

• **If you have a low arch or tend toward flat feet,** pick a more stable shoe with more rear-foot control, called a "cement"-lasted or boarded shoe. ("Last" is the foot shape that the shoe is built around.)

• **For a high arch,** try a softer, more curved last (called a "slip" last).

• **Be sure you have adequate toe room** (at least one-half inch of clearance). Running shoes, particularly in women's sizes, run small, and women often need a half-size or even a full-size-larger running shoe than street shoe.

How to Buy the Right Bike

Commuters have special biking requirements. If you're in the suit-and-tie crowd, you'll want fenders to keep yourself clean. You may want a rack on the back for a newspaper or side racks for your briefcase. Bicycle sacks (panniers) are made of heavier nylon, with stiffeners to retain their briefcase shape. Although rubber pedals are less durable than steel, they'll help preserve your leather soles. And every city rider needs a topnotch lock. The U-bolt models by Kryptonite and Citadel are among the best.

WHAT KIND TO BUY

Touring bikes are right for most people. They have a longer wheelbase for a "Cadillac" ride. Racing bikes offer a "Fiat" ride. With their shorter wheelbase, you feel the road more, but you get better handling and efficiency.

The Japanese have learned how to make bikes better and more cheaply. A European bike of equivalent quality will cost at least 20% more. Although there are many different Japanese makes, they're all produced by one of two corporate families, so they're all about the same.

The best American bikes offer better frames, with superior materials and hand-craftsmanship. But you sacrifice quality on components.

CHOOSING PARTS

A good frame design for women is the mixte (pronounced *mix-tay*). Two parts run from the head tube to the rear axle for added stability. With longer skirts, many women can use a man's 10-speed, and they do. The men's models are lighter and stronger.

For those riders who find bicycles uncomfortable, an anatomically designed saddle may be the answer. These seats, made of leather with foam padding, feature two ridges to support the pelvic bones, with a valley in between to avoid pinching the sciatic nerve.

Mixte handlebars, which project almost perpendicularly to the frame, are good for all-around cycling, as are racing (or drop) bars. The traditional curved bars are not recommended for city riding. They keep you sitting erect, so your spine is jolted by each bump. And foam grips will absorb more road shock than standard cloth tape grips.

In buying a helmet, look for a low-impact plastic shell. In a typical biking accident, this will protect the head best. Some states require by law that cyclists wear helmets.

Padded bike gloves make good shock absorbers. Sheepskin bike shorts provide added comfort. Bike jerseys with rear pockets will keep your keys from digging into your leg with each push of the pedal.

Charles McCorkell, owner, Bicycle Habitat, 244 Lafayette St., New York City.

Female bike riders should point the seat slightly downward to avoid irritating the genital area. Men should point the seat upward to avoid problems such as irritation of the urinary tract and injury to the testes.

The Physician and Sportsmedicine

• **Sizing up a new bike.** Straddle the frame with your feet flat on the floor. There should be an inch of clearance between your crotch and the top tube. *If you can't find* *an exact fit:* Buy the next smaller size, then adjust seat and handlebar height. A frame that's too big can't be adjusted.

Best Ski Pants

Stretch ski pants look great, but not all models are warm enough—especially for the novice or intermediate, who burns fewer calories and generates less heat.

What to look for: High wool content (preferably with the wool floated to the inside, nearest your body)...terry lining (traps insulating dead air). *For those who get cold easily:* Highly insulated stretch pants, which have a three-layer sandwich construction, should do the job.

Ski

Volunteering Opportunities

Web site for Action Without Borders includes a directory of more than 59,883 nonprofit and volunteer organizations in 165 countries, as well as postings of nonprofit jobs and internships. *www.idealist.org*

Gourmet Cooking

Designed and managed by *Bon Appétit* and *Gourmet* magazines, Epicurious attractively features thousands of recipes, cooking suggestions, etc. *www.epicurious.com*

Butterfly Watching

The web site for the North American Butterfly Association provides links to publications, information about local chapters, butterfly gardening...and more. *www.naba.org*

How to Buy Sports Goggles

Some types of swimming goggles apply pressure in the wrong places. *Best:* Buy the kind with soft rubber rims around the eyes.

Racquet sports, particularly squash and racquetball, can and do cause serious eye injuries if players don't wear protective goggles of some sort. *Least effective:* Open goggles without lenses. *Best:* Polycarbonate lenses that have been tested to stop a .22 bullet at 20 feet in a lab test.

How to Choose Ice Skates

The most important feature in choosing skates is a stiff boot with a snug fit. Toes should reach the tip of the boot but lie flat. Lace the boot tightly through the toe area, very tightly through the instep and comfortably at the top. *To check the fit:* Walk. If your ankles wiggle even though the lacing is correct, ask for smaller or stiffer skates.

How to Choose a Canoe

Before buying a canoe consider what you're going to use it for, where you'll use it and how many people you'll be carrying. *For rocky rivers:* Get an aluminum or plastic hull. Rocks destroy fiberglass hulls. Royalex ABS plastic hulls (made by Old Town) are the most popular. *Disadvantages:* ABS canoes are more expensive than aluminum and are vulnerable to wear and tear on bow and stern. One remedy is optional skid plates. *Good starter boat:* The Coleman polyethylene plastic canoe, which you can assemble yourself.

Canoe

Buying an Inflatable Boat

Inflatable boats are no longer considered toys. They are now reputable crafts with a variety of functions. Inflatables perform well with much less horsepower than that required by rigid-hulled boats.

They can be stored at home, saving winter storage costs and mooring fees. They're easier to transport. *What to look for:* A design with several airtight compartments, an inflatable keel, self-bailers, bow handles and fitted D-rings, lifelines, heavy-duty fitted oarlocks, wooden or antislip aluminum floorboards and bow-dodgers with windshields for added spray protection.

Public Land Recreation

More than 2,500 federal recreation areas are listed at *www.recreation.gov*. The site offers a searchable map and links to national reservation systems. In addition to sites run by the National Park Service and Bureau of Land Management, it includes recreation sites of the Tennessee Valley Authority, National Wildlife Refuges and more.

Camping Life

For Digital-Music Lovers

Easy to download to your computer, there are hundreds of thousands of CD-quality digitized songs available. Search online music sites, download the songs, play them on your computer and load them onto your iPod or any solid-state portable music player designed for MP3. You can even record CDs. Check out *www.mp3.com* and *www.emusic.com*.

Bingo Never Was a Game Of Chance

John "Dee" Wyrick, the author of *Complete Authoritative Guide to Bingo* (Gambler's Book Club).

Most people play bingo as if it were a game of sheer chance—as if any set of cards had just as good a chance of winning as any other. They are mistaken. If you choose the cards you play correctly, you can significantly improve your odds of winning any bingo game.

My system works with straight bingo (where you must cover five squares in a row—vertically, horizontally or diagonally), coverall (a jackpot game, in which you must cover every square on your card) or any other variation.

Key strategy: To get as many of the 75 numbers as possible on a given set of cards. There are 24 numbers printed on every bingo card. (There are 25 squares, but the center square is a nonnumbered free space.) If you chose three cards at random, their 72 numbered spaces would represent only 49 different numbers—the other 23 spaces would have duplicate numbers.

It is possible, however, to find sets of three cards with no duplicates—with 72 different numbers. (Time permitting, players can choose their cards freely at the beginning of any session.) If you were to play such a set, you would be 25% more likely to win a given game than a player with a random set. Depending on the size of the prizes, that edge can translate into hundreds—or even thousands—of dollars of winnings within a few weeks.

Ironically, most players choose sets that are worse than random. They look for cards with one or two "lucky" numbers—7 or 11, for example. And they are especially drawn to cards where those lucky numbers are at the corners.

The results are devastating. In an average straight game with 1,000 cards in play, a bingo will occur after 15 numbers are called. That means that any given number—regardless of whether it is "lucky" or not—will be called in only one of five games. In those other four games, any set of cards with an uncalled "lucky" number is 25% less likely to win. (When a number is at a corner, it affects three lines—one vertical, one horizontal and one diagonal.)

Another advantage of choosing nonduplicating cards is that it makes it easier to keep track of the numbers you're covering—and harder to miss one by accident.

Example: If you are playing three cards on which there are no duplicate numbers, every time a number is called, you know you will cover a space. *Exception:* If the number is called on the N line, you will cover a space only 80% of the time because the center square, which contains the free space, is in the N line.

There are countless statistical systems favored by bingo players, but this is the only one I've found that generates consistent profits.

The only other live variable in bingo is the proportion of money collected that is returned to the players. Most operators hold back at least 50% for overhead and revenue. (The percentage is usually posted on the bingo sheets or somewhere in the hall.)

Other games, however, return as much as 75% to the players. The more money that comes back, of course, the better are your chances of coming out ahead.

10

Consumer Guide

Best Bargain Buying On the Internet

The Internet is chock full of bargains for consumers—with more appearing every day. You may have to hunt and search a little bit, but your efforts will generally result in big savings.

To get started, here are a few of the "best bargain" sites on the Web today.

And if these don't work for you, there are thousands of other Web sites that offer bargains...

AIRFARES

Airlines now offer unsold seats at steep discounts through their own Web sites and weekly E-mail "alerts" sent to subscribers.

Snag: The average consumer can't watch all these sites and E-mail lists. But the WebFlyer site will do it for you.

WebFlyer surveys the airlines' Web sites and E-mail lists and organizes the "best bargain" information from them in one place.

Tell WebFlyer the city you want to travel from, and it will list the best deals available—and give you discount prices for hotels and car rentals, too.

The WebFlyer site is run by Randy Petersen, the publisher of *Inside Flyer* magazine. The site also presents a wealth of other free travel information. *www.webflyer.com.*

AUTOMOBILES

Find a deal on a new or used car at Autoweb, the leading Internet car-selling service. It uses a network of dealers in the US. Enter the make and description of the car you're looking for along with your zip code, and you'll be offered a price from a dealer near you within 24 hours.

If you're not ready to buy yet, you can research different models at the site's "showroom,"

Patricia Robison, president, Computing Independence in New York City.

245

read product reviews and examine technical specifications. *www.autobytel.com.*

BOOKS, MUSIC AND MORE

You can order almost any book, CD, DVD or video in the world from Amazon.com, including very hard to find titles rarely found in conventional bookstores or "superstores."

You can also search for books of interest, get publishing details and read customer reviews. In addition, Amazon offers multiple ways to personalize the site using your preferences—for example, it will search for your favorite titles and get specific product information. *www.amazon.com.*

Alternative: The giant Barnes & Noble bookstore chain has its own Web site at *www. barnesandnoble.com.* It offers current bestsellers as well as thousands of used books, text books, CDs, DVDs and more.

COLLECTIBLES

If you want to buy or sell coins, stamps, antiques, jewelry, pottery and glass, dolls, sports memorabilia or any other collectible you have gathering dust, visit the eBay electronic flea market. It runs 24 hours a day, seven days a week.

At any given time there are more than *78 million* items available in more than 50,000 different categories. New categories are being added all the time. Items range from home-run baseballs to classic designer clothing. *www.ebay.com.*

INSURANCE

The InsWeb site can help you find the best price for life, health, auto, homeowner's and renter's insurance. Describe the coverage you want and the information will be submitted to a range of leading insurers. You'll receive quotes tailored to your needs, and you select the best.

The InsWeb site also gives a range of educational information, including auto and life insurance needs analyzers—work sheets to fill out that help you determine how much coverage you should buy. *www.insweb.com.*

INVESTMENT RESEARCH

Do you use a discount broker to save fees, but miss the research that full-service brokers provide?

You may be able to find the best of both worlds. Morningstar, for instance offers extensive investment research on its Web sites, with a free 14-day trial.

For premium services: www.morning star.com.

In addition, you can always obtain free investment information from Yahoo! Finance (*http://finance.yahoo.com*) or The Motley Fool (*www.fool.com*).

INVESTMENT TRADING

You can trade stocks and mutual funds in all American markets from your personal computer through the E*TRADE Web site, for as little as $9.99 per trade. Stock or fund shares can be paid for through electronic fund transfer.

E*TRADE offers margin accounts and lets you place market, limit, stop and stop limit orders, just as you would at a full-service broker. E*TRADE also provides market data, corporate data and other "intelligence" needed by investors. *www.etrade.com.*

TRAVEL

A unique "reverse auction" buying technique is offered by Priceline.com for travel items like airline tickets, hotel rooms, rental cars and more.

Key: Other Web sites search out the best prices offered by many different sellers (such as auto dealers or insurance companies). At Price-line.com, you set the price that you want to pay, and the sellers come to you—accepting or rejecting your price.

If an airline has an empty seat or a hotel has an empty room when you want it, you may get it at a price much lower than the airline or hotel would ever publicly offer it.

Priceline.com also offers tours, cruises and more. Check it out at *www.priceline.com.*

More Bargain Internet Shopping Sites

John Edwards, technology writer based near Phoenix.

The World Wide Web has become the world's largest—and most diverse—shopping mall. Web merchants are selling products that range from pet food to diamonds, many—but not all—at prices that can't be matched by traditional retailers.

Here's a closer look at bargain shopping available on the Internet...

AIRLINE TICKETS

A variety of airline Web sites offer special deals to Internet shoppers, including...

• **American Airlines' "Fare Sales & Special Offers,"** *www.aa.com.*

• **Southwest Airlines' "Special Offers,"** *www.southwest.com.*

• **United Airlines' "Special Deals,"** *www.united.com.*

• **U.S. Airways'"Specials,"** *www.usairways.com.*

Before you buy a ticket: Check Priceline.com (*www.priceline.com*), an Internet-based buying service that lets users name their price for airline tickets.

Shoppers simply post their request and guarantee the offer with a major credit card. Priceline.com then tries to find a seller who can fulfill the request—at no extra charge to the customer. *Note:* You have to commit to buying the ticket if they find it for you. It is not refundable.

Priceline.com also operates similar services for people who want to book a hotel room or rent a car.

CDs

• **Amazon** stocks more than one million books but also offers discounts on CDs, DVDs and videos. *www.amazon.com.*

CARS

• **Autobytel.com** helps Web surfers buy a new or used car or truck at the best possible price.

Shoppers specify the make, model and other relevant information for the vehicle they wish to purchase.

The information is then submitted to an Autobytel.com manager at a nearby dealership. Within 24 hours, the manager supplies the closest match and suggests a price. The shopper can then purchase the vehicle or look elsewhere for a better deal. *www.autobytel.com.*

• **MSN Autos,** has a nationwide network of dealers to help shoppers find the new or used car or truck they want at the lowest possible price. *http://autos.msn.com.*

HOTELS AND MOTELS

Many hospitality chains use their Web sites to promote weekend and other special rates...

• **Best Western's "Special Offers,"** *www.bestwestern.com.*

• **Embassy Suites' "Specials & Packages,"** *www.embassysuites.com.*

• **Hilton's "Specials & Packages,"** *www.hilton.com.*

• **Hyatt's "Special Offers,"** *www.hyatt.com.*

• **Radisson's "Hotel Deals,"** *www.radisson.com.*

• **Ramada's "Deals & Discounts,"** *www.ramada.com.*

• **Ritz Carlton's "Offers,"** *www.ritzcarlton.com.*

• **Wyndham's "Deals & Discounts,"** *www.wyndham.com.*

HOME ENTERTAINMENT

• **Crutchfield** features a vast array of TVs, DVD and MP3 players, car stereos and other entertainment systems at prices that are generally competitive with those at leading superstores. Check out the "specials" area for impressive discounts on selected products. *www.crutchfield.com.*

APPAREL

• **Burlington Coat Factory** offers savings of up to 60% off department and other specialty store prices on a large selection of designer and brand-name fashions, as well as linens and jewelry. *www.burlingtoncoatfactory.com.*

OTHER APPAREL SPECIALS

- **Eddie Bauer,** *www.eddiebauer.com.*
- **J.Crew,** *www.jcrew.com.*
- **Lands' End,** *www.landsend.com.*
- **L.L. Bean,** *www.llbean.com.*

BEST DEALS ON WEB PURCHASES

Comparison-pricing sites let you choose among retailers throughout the US. The sites are especially useful when shopping for computers and computer products. *Sites worth visiting...*

- **"CNET Shopper.com,"** *http://shopper.cnet.com.*
- **"Bottom Dollar,"** *www1.bottomdollar.com.*
- **"PriceGrabber.com,"** *www.pricegrabber.com.*

How to Avoid the Pitfalls Of Shopping Online

Preston Gralla, computer and Internet technology writer based in Cambridge, Massachusetts. He is author of *The Complete Idiot's Guide to Online Shopping* (Alpha Books).

The Internet is the ultimate shopper's paradise. Anything you could ever want to buy—from an abacus to a zither—is just a few mouse clicks away.

Shopping online is convenient and simple and you can save a lot of money, but...

Trap: Scams and con artists are everywhere on the Internet. Even savvy online consumers are vulnerable.

To avoid being ripped off on the Internet...

- **Never buy from a site that does not list its mailing address or phone number.** It's harder online than in the mall to know whether a store is reputable. A mailing address and phone number are important if you have problems with the merchandise you buy. You'll be able to complain and send it back.

- **Never shop a site that is not secure.** A secure site uses encryption technology to ensure that personal information—such as your credit card number and your address—is kept confidential.

Secure sites generally carry an icon that pops up when you log on. The icon looks like a lock. If no icon shows up, go to "Frequently Asked Questions" or "Help." Typically, secure sites explain their meaning of security.

- **Be especially careful when buying directly from individuals.** Most online shopping problems occur at auction sites where you are not buying from an established merchant, but from an individual you don't know.

Self-defense: Before sending money to an individual, check the background of that person—or the company he or she says he represents. Even the most reputable sites take very little, if any, action against problem sellers. Buyers' complaints, however, may be listed for you to read and come to your own conclusions. If you're dissatisfied with a seller, you must take your own action against him. Some sites have an ombudsman who tries to sort out problems.

Strategy: For big-ticket items, use an Internet escrow service. This is an independent third party that acts as a conduit between the buyer and the seller. There are benefits to both buyer and seller. On eBay, for example, you would use Escrow.com, which charges a fee that varies according to the amount of the purchase and the method of payment.

Alternative: Ask the seller to send the item COD (and to pay the extra mailing cost if it's the first time you've dealt with him/her). Most sellers wait until the check clears before they ship the goods.

- **Don't give your credit card numbers** unless you're using a secure Web site. Check the Web address—a secure site will show "https" (the "s" at the end for "secure") rather than "http".

- **Don't give personal information,** such as a Social Security number, PIN number, etc., to anyone online. There's no reason a legitimate seller needs this information. Con artists who, in the past, used telemarketing and the mail, have now turned their sights to the Internet.

- **Read the fine print before signing up for a "free trial."** You usually have to give your credit card number in order to receive the offer.

And usually you'll be billed for the item or service unless you cancel before a certain time.

There are many con artists playing the "free trial" game on the Internet. They will continue to bill you each month even though you've told them you don't want the product.

•**Watch for hidden costs on sales.** What appears to be a good buy may not be so good when sales tax and shipping costs are added in.

Example: A $25 book with a 20% online discount sounds great. But if shipping and handling add more than $5 to the cost, you'd be better off picking it up for full cost at your neighborhood bookstore. *Hidden costs include...*

•**Sales tax.** The sales tax moratorium imposed by the federal *Internet Tax Freedom Act* was signed into law in 1998 and has been extended until November 2014. Some states may tax online sales, so be sure to check the amount being charged on the purchase page.

•**Shipping and handling charges.** The majority of online merchants add on these charges. But costs vary widely. Be clear about how the items are being sent—first-class mail, overnight express delivery, etc.

•**Know your rights if something goes wrong.** *Always check the site's policies concerning...*

•Warranties. Does the warranty come from the site or the manufacturer?

•Return policies. Can you return the goods for cash or just for credit or exchange?

Caution: In most cases, merchandise bought online from retailers can't be returned to their retail stores. It must be returned online to the warehouse it was shipped from.

Recent development: Some retailers, such as the Gap and Macy's, will allow returns of Internet purchases at their retail stores.

•**Don't buy goods, stocks or services solely on advice from discussion boards or chat rooms.** It's too easy for con artists to self-promote on these sites by forging names and logging on multiple times.

•**Always thoroughly tour the site where you're planning on making a purchase.**

See if the site offers product reviews that are honest and unbiased instead of merely sales pitches.

•**Protect yourself against Internet scammers.** Check out any seller with the Better Business Bureau (*www.bbb.org*) before you make a purchase.

Check with government agencies, such as the Federal Trade Commission (*www.ftc.gov*), and private agencies, such as the National Fraud Information Center (*www.fraud.org*), about any complaints against particular sites.

These sites are also good places to file complaints against Internet scammers (if you keep careful records of online purchases).

•**Stay away from too-good-to-be-true offers.** While scams aren't limited to cyberspace, they seem to be abundant there. *It's generally a good idea to steer clear of the following...*

•Work-at-home offers that promise instant wealth and success. You'll wind up paying for fees and materials. The people making money from these offers are the con artists who push them.

•Credit-repair services. They can't do anything you can't do yourself—free. If they offer you a second credit file (using a second Social Security number), don't deal with them. This practice is illegal.

Web Savvy

Beware—offers on Web sites are not considered to be offers in writing...and are not binding. Web sites can be easily changed, and you cannot prove what an offer was when you first saw it.

Bottom line: If you see a good offer on the Web, get a letter confirming it.

The late John Awerdick, attorney who specialized in direct marketing, Hall Dickler Kent Friedman & Wood, New York City.

How to Buy Shoes That Really Fit

John F. Waller, Jr., MD, foot and ankle surgeon in private practice in New York City.

Shoes should provide a lot of cushioning to match the type of surface that the bare foot needs.

Poor: A rigid, so-called supportive shoe. Shoes should be loose and giving.

Good: The running shoe, the most physiological shoe made. Soft and malleable, it provides cushioning and a little bit of support.

Women: If you wear a high-heeled, thin-soled shoe, have a thin rubber sole cemented onto the bottom to cushion the ball of the foot.

• **Fit shoes with your hands, not with your feet.** There should be an index finger's breadth between the tip of the toes and the front of the shoe. Tell the salesperson to start with a half size larger than you usually wear and work down. The shoe shouldn't be pushed out of shape when you stand. The leather should not be drawn taut.

• **An ideal heel height for a woman is 1½–2 inches.** This is not a magic number, simply the most comfortable. If a man wore a 1½-inch heel, he'd be more comfortable than in the traditional ¾-inch heel.

• **Flat feet are not bad feet.** A flat, flexible foot is very functional. Most great athletes have them.

Problem: The shoe industry does not make shoes to fit flat feet. Look for low-heeled shoes that feel balanced. They should not throw your weight forward on the balls of your feet or gap at the arches.

• **Buy shoes in the late afternoon when your feet have had a full day's workout and are slightly spread.** Shoes that you try on first thing in the morning may be too tight by evening and generally uncomfortable for all-day wear.

How to Recognize Quality Clothes in Off-Price Stores

To take advantage of sales, discount designer stores or consignment shops, learn the details that signal first-class workmanship, label or no label. *Look for...*

• **Stripes and plaids that are carefully matched** at the seams.

• **Finished seam edges** on fabrics that fray easily (linen, loose woolens, etc.).

• **Generous seams** of one-half inch or more.

• **Buttons made of mother-of-pearl,** wood or brass.

• **Neat, well-spaced buttonholes** that fit the buttons tightly.

• **Felt backing on woolen collars** to retain the shape.

• **Ample, even hems.**

• **Straight, even stitching** in colors that match the fabric.

• **Good-quality linings** that are not attached all around. (Loose linings wear better.)

Designer Bargains For Women in Boys' Department

Not all the smart women shopping in the boys' department have sons. Many are just looking for bargains in shirts, sweaters, pants, jackets, robes and belts for themselves. Even designer boys' clothes may cost 20% to 50% less than similar items in the women's department. *How to size up boys' wear...*

Women's size	Boys' size
5/6	14 top, 29/30 pants
7/8	16 top, 30/31 pants
9/10	18 top, 31/32 pants
11/12	20 top, 32/33 pants

How to Buy Sunglasses

Be sure they are large enough. Light should not enter around the edges. *Best:* Try frames that curve back toward the temple. *Lenses:* Plastic is less heavy than glass. *Drawback:* It scratches easily. Clean with a soft cloth, not a silicone tissue.

To prevent glare: Greenish grays, neutral grays and browns are best. Other colors absorb wavelengths and upset color balance. *Test:* Try on the glasses. The world should appear in true color, but not as bright.

Good all-around choice: Sun-sensor lenses, which adjust from dark to light. For use near water, polarized lenses block reflected glare. An old pair of prescription lenses can be tinted to a desired density.

Best Eyeglass Cleaner

Use a piece of damp newspaper. There is less chance that it will scratch the lenses than cloth or facial tissue.

How to Choose the Right Hairbrush

The best hairbrush bristles come from boars. Their uneven surface cleans better than smooth nylon. *Stiffest:* Black bristles from the back of the boar's neck. Good for thick, heavy hair, these are the rarest and most expensive bristles. White bristles are better for fine and/or thinning hair.

Jan Hansum, Kent of London, quoted in *The Best Report,* New York City.

Best Mouthwash

Bad breath is cured best by mouthwashes that contain zinc. This is because the source of most mouth odor is sulfur compounds. The zinc mouthwashes negate these compounds for at least three hours. *Contrast:* Non-zinc mouthwashes attack bacteria. *Point:* Check the labels of mouthwashes for zinc.

Joseph Tonzetich, PhD, the late professor of oral biology, University of British Columbia, Vancouver.

Best Insect Repellents

Insect repellents vary in the amounts of active ingredients they contain and their effectiveness. *Active ingredients:* N, N-diethyl-m-toluamide (DEET) and ethyl hexanediol. *Most effective:* DEET. *Spray with high DEET level:* Off! Deep Woods (25%). *Lotion with high DEET level:* 3M Ultrathon (31%).

Best Sleeping Bags

Waterfowl down still offers the best warmth-to-weight performance as padding (or fill). But now the newer, lightweight, polyester-filled sleeping bags (in most above-freezing conditions) are preferred by campers on practical grounds. *Polyester's virtues...*

• **It keeps two-thirds of its insulating capacity when wet** (it absorbs very little moisture), and it dries much faster. Down is worthless when wet. It takes hours to dry and must be refluffed before the bag can be used again.

• **It's washable, even by machine.** Down bags are best dry-cleaned.

• **It's nonallergenic because it doesn't collect dust.** Down is a magnet for dust, the real cause of suffering for those who think they are allergic to it.

• **It's much cheaper than down.** Most polyester-filled sleeping bags cost about 50% less than comparable down-filled ones.

How to Buy a Mattress

The quality of sleep makes the quantity less important. To enable you to relax, your mattress must provide proper support for your body yet be resilient enough for comfort. The old-fashioned double bed gives each sleeper only 26 inches of space, about the same width as a baby's crib. The most popular size—queen—is seven inches wider and five inches longer than the old double bed. King size is an additional 16 inches wider.

Mattress prices depend on the materials, quality of construction, size, number of layers of upholstery and the store's markup. (Prices may be lower in small, neighborhood stores with low overhead.)

Standard mattresses have two different kinds of construction, innerspring or foam rubber. Top-quality innerspring mattresses have covered metal coils, cushioning material and an insulator between the coils to prevent them from protruding.

Foam mattresses are made of a solid block of urethane, high-resiliency foam or laminated layers of varying density sandwiched together. A good foam mattress is at least five to six inches high and feels heavy when lifted. A high-density foam mattress should last 10 to 15 years. Foam mattresses can be used on a wooden platform for extra firmness or with a conventional boxspring.

When shopping for a mattress...

• **Sit on the edge of the bed.** The mattress should support you without feeling flimsy, and it should spring back into shape when you get up. A reinforced border increases durability.

• **Lie down.** (If the bed is to be used by a couple, both partners should test it by lying down.) Check several different firmnesses in order to choose the one you're most comfortable with. Next, roll from side to side and then to the center. The mattress should not sway, jiggle or sag in the middle. If you hear creaking springs, don't buy it.

• **Examine the covering.** *Best:* Sturdy ticking with a pattern that's woven, not printed on.

• **Check for handles on the sides for easy turning,** small metal vents to disperse heat and allow air to circulate inside and plastic corner guards.

• **Up to 80% of the sleeper's weight is borne by the boxspring.** The finest mattress won't be effective unless it's accompanied by a boxspring of equal quality. When a new mattress is needed, both the mattress and the boxspring should be replaced to ensure that the support system is designed specifically for the mattress.

Queen-sized innerspring sets should be used in a sturdy bed frame with a footboard or in a six-leg heavy steel support. Twin and double sized can use a four-leg metal frame. A good innerspring sleep set should last 15 to 20 years.

There is no proven medical advantage to sleeping on a hard surface, so consider comfort as the key factor. According to Dr. Hamilton Hall, an orthopedic surgeon who specializes in techniques to relieve back pain, there is no single perfect mattress. "What's perfect for one person may be uncomfortable for another," he says.

Best advice: Buy only sleep sets made by a manufacturer with a good reputation and sold by a reputable dealer. Be very wary of advertised bargains.

Test of Well-Made Wooden Furniture

Is the piece stable when you gently push down on a top corner or press against the side? Is the back panel inset and attached with screws (not nails)? Do drawers and doors fit well and move smoothly? Are corners of drawers joined with dovetail joints? Do long shelves have center braces? Are table leaves well supported? Are hinges strong and well secured?

Better Homes & Gardens

Test of Good Carpeting

Insist on density. Closely packed surface yarns and tightly woven backing make for carpets that wear and look good longer. Bend a piece of the carpet backward. If a lot of backing is visible through the pile, go for a higher quality.

•**Avoid soft plush textures** when covering moderate-to-heavy traffic areas.

•**Invest in good padding.** It absorbs shocks, lengthens carpet life and creates a more comfortable surface.

•**If cost is a factor,** compromise on the amount or size of carpet, not on the quality. Or choose lesser qualities for low-traffic areas.

Better Homes & Gardens

Oriental Rug Test

Spread the pile apart. If you see knots at the bottom, the rug was made by hand. But sewn-on fringes are a clear machine-made giveaway.

Pasargad Carpets Inc., rug importers and manufacturers, Washington, DC.

Buying a Piano

The best sound comes from a grand piano, but new ones can cost a bundle. A smaller spinet, console or studio upright will provide satisfactory sound for most people and costs much less.

How to test a piano before purchase: Play it by running up and down the scales. High notes should be clean and crisp; low notes should resonate. If you are considering the purchase of a used piano, look for one that's 10 years old or less. Don't buy one that's more than 20 years old. Have a piano tuner check out a used piano.

Best Pots for Pot Roast

Pot roasts cook best in heavy-cast ironware. That's one tale that happens to be true, though it is mysterious. *Other iron-pot pluses:* They're energy savers, since they hold heat longer. And traces of iron released chemically into food (unlike nonferrous metals) are good for you, especially for those who suffer from iron-deficiency anemia. People with rare hemochromatosis (too much iron in the system) should avoid all food contact with ironware.

Beatrice Trum Hunter, *How Safe Is Food in Your Kitchen?* (MacMillan).

Best Toilet Seat

The standard toilet seat was the most uncomfortable of all those tested in a university's contest of designs. *A winner:* An elongated seat contoured to support the thighs and buttocks.

Report on tests made at Loughborough University, Loughborough, Leiceistershire, England, in *New Scientist.*

Buying Kitchen Knives

The best steel for knives is high-carbon stainless steel. It takes and holds a sharp edge well and resists discoloration. *Also good:* Carbon steel. And it is relatively inexpensive. *Drawback:* Carbon steel must be kept dry or it will deteriorate. *Worst:* Stainless steel. It is very difficult to sharpen. *Top brands:* Wusthof, Forschner/Victorinox, Henckels and Sabatier.

Appliances That Pay for Themselves

Jennifer Thorne Amann, buildings program director, American Council for an Energy-Efficient Economy, a nonprofit organization founded in 1980 to encourage energy efficiency. *www.aceee.org*. She is coauthor of *Consumer Guide to Home Energy Savings* (New Society).

The latest energy-efficient appliances can cost up to hundreds of dollars more than standard models. But many pay for themselves over their 12- to 20-year life spans. Virtually all major appliance manufacturers —even some smaller ones—offer energy-efficient models. Visit *www.energystar.gov* or *www.aceee.org* for details.

Important: Look for the blue "Energy Star" label when you shop for appliances. To earn this label, appliances must exceed government efficiency guidelines. Also keep an eye out for the Federal Trade Commission's yellow "EnergyGuide" label. This provides estimated annual energy consumption for an appliance based on typical usage.

REFRIGERATORS

The greatest progress in energy-efficient appliances has been made in refrigerators. Many models built before 1988 consume more than $100 worth of electricity a year. Those made in the 1970s can use as much as $200.

Current standard refrigerators save an average of $50 a year in electricity. Since many new refrigerators retail in the $500 range, a new unit will pay for itself in about 10 years. High-efficiency units can run on less than $40 a year.

Caution: The Energy Star and EnergyGuide labels can be somewhat deceiving with refrigerators. The units are compared only between similar models. Thus a 22-cubic-foot side-by-side refrigerator might earn the Energy Star label, while an 18-cubic-foot freezer-on-top unit might not, even though it uses far less energy.

Refrigerators with freezers on top or bottom tend to be about 7% to 13% more efficient than side-by-side models. An automatic ice maker installed in the door can reduce efficiency by up to 20%.

Small units are more efficient than larger ones—but one large fridge is more efficient than two small ones. Don't buy something so small that you have to put the old unit in the basement for extra storage. If you do need an extra refrigerator, buy a new one.

Helpful: Consumers often feel that throwing out a working refrigerator is wasteful. But virtually every part of an old refrigerator is likely to be recycled. It is more wasteful to continue using an energy hog.

WASHING MACHINES

The typical washing machine lasts 12 years or more and consumes about $800 worth of electricity during that time.

Some new machines consume less than half as much power, principally by using less hot water. Ninety percent of the energy used to wash clothes is to heat the water.

Buying an energy-efficient washer makes good financial sense. High-efficiency machines cost as little as $600—about $200 more than typical washers. They also deliver as much as $60 in annual energy savings, so they can pay for themselves over their lifetimes.

In addition to the energy savings, a high-efficiency machine should save 6,000 to 8,000 gallons of water per year, based on annual average family use of around 400 loads.

Front-loading machines typically are much more efficient than top loaders. They use less water, and their higher spin speeds remove more moisture, reducing the energy used.

Energy saver: Wash clothes in cold water whenever appropriate.

CLOTHES DRYERS

Many new dryer models have temperature or moisture gauges that automatically turn off the unit when clothes are dry. Moisture sensors located inside the drum tend to be more accurate than temperature sensors. These can reduce your energy costs by up to 15%.

A typical new dryer will consume $85 worth of power a year, creating an annual savings of perhaps $10. Over the expected 11-year life of a dryer, that is a total of $110.

Sensor models cost $150 to $250 more than base models. But given the energy savings, they come close to paying for the extra cost— and often do in areas where electricity is expensive.

Ask retailers which dryer models contain in-drum moisture or temperature sensors, or check for them yourself. They usually look like small, black patches located either in the back of the drum or near the lint filter.

Helpful: Replacing an electric dryer with a gas-powered model can reduce your energy bills to about 13 cents per load from about 35 cents, based on current average electricity.

DISHWASHERS

There is a debate regarding dishwasher energy efficiency. A number of models include a "soil sensor," which detects how dirty the dishes are and adjusts wash time and water usage. The potential energy advantage of this is obvious.

Manufacturers, however, can't agree on how much energy a soil sensor saves. The current Department of Energy tests are of little use because they test only with clean plates.

For the time being, it is difficult to say which models are best. A knowledgeable salesperson might offer some guidance. But if you need a dishwasher, check the Energy Guide and Energy Star labels. Even without soil sensors, new models tend to be much more efficient.

Helpful: Don't prerinse dishes. Newer, more efficient dishwashers let you save time, water, electricity and elbow grease.

Where to Buy Hard-to-Find Recordings By Mail

TimeLife.com, PO Box 8988, Pueblo, CO 81008. *www.timelife.com.* Selected masters as well as a large selection of country, rock, pop, R&B and soul, jazz, gospel and other music CDs.

Best Chocolates In the World

The finest chocolates in the world need be no farther than your mailbox. However, some chocolatiers ship throughout the US only from October through May. (High temperatures are too hard on good chocolates to risk summer shipment.)

• **Bissinger's Handcrafted Chocolates,** 3983 Gratiot St., St. Louis, MO 63110, 800-325-8881. *www.bissingers.com.* Chocolate-covered mints, malted milk balls and other specialities. Free catalog.

• **Martine's Chocolates** at 400 East 82nd St., New York City 10028, 212-744-6289. *www.martineschocolates.com. Noteworthy selections include:* Assorted truffles of caramel with praline crunch, orange peel and coffee, among others. "Oysters," an exquisite blend of five Belgian chocolates—their secret recipe. No catalog.

• **André's Confiserie Suisse,** 5018 Main St., Kansas City, MO 64112, 800-892-1234. *www.andreschocolates.com.* Bold and rich Swiss-type chocolates. Call directly to be sent a free catalog.

• **Dilettante Chocolates,** 538 Broadway Ave. East, Seattle 98102, 800-800-9490. Hand-dipped light or dark chocolates, truffles, marzipan and French butter creams. Catalog online at *www.dilettante.com.*

• **Dan's Chocolates,** 800-800-DANS. *www.danschocolates.com.* Dan's chocolates are hand-made in small batches in their Rhode Island factory. Because they are shipped directly to you, they are incredibly fresh.

• **Edelweiss Chocolates,** 444 North Canon Dr., Beverly Hills, CA 90210, 888-615-8800. *www.edelweisschocolates.com.* Liquored truffles and brandied cherries. Free catalog.

• **See's Candies,** 754 Clement St., San Francisco 94118, 800-347-7337. *www.sees.com.* Old-fashioned fudge.

• **Teuscher Chocolates of Switzerland,** 620 Fifth Ave., New York City 10020, 800-554-0924 *www.teuscher.com.* They have chocolates called rusty tools (for their shapes) which are dusted with cocoa. The champagne truffles are justly popular. Free brochure.

Best Time to Drink Champagne

Vintage champagne should be drunk shortly after purchase. Sparkling wine does not improve with age, and it will deteriorate with prolonged refrigeration. *For proper chilling:* Use an ice bucket with ice and a little bit of water.

The Wine Spectator

Easy-Opening Champagne

Opening champagne is easier if the bottle is chilled in a bucket of ice rather than in a refrigerator. If the neck of the bottle gets too cold, the cork won't come out. Then you lose the satisfying, dramatic effect of a forceful cork-popping.

Successful Meetings

The Six Best Champagnes

Drinking a fine sparkling wine is one of life's truest pleasures. *Six of the best…*

• **Taittinger Comtes de Champagne**—vintage only. An exceptionally good rosé champagne. Taittinger also makes a fine blanc de blancs and a nonvintage brut.

• **Dom Perignon**—vintage only. This is probably the most widely acclaimed champagne, and deservedly so. Elegant and light, with delicate bubbles. The producer also makes, under its Moet et Chandon name, a vintage rosé champagne, a vintage champagne, a nonvintage champagne and a nonvintage brut.

• **Perrier-Jouët Fleur de Champagne**—vintage only. This house produces champagne of the highest quality in a particularly popular style. The wine is austere yet tasteful. It is also extremely dry without being harsh or acidic. Perrier-Jouët also produces a rosé champagne.

• **Louis Roederer Cristal**—vintage only. *Cristal's magic lies in its plays with opposites:* Elegant yet robust, rich taste without weightiness. Roederer also produces a sparkling rosé, a vintage champagne and a nonvintage brut.

• **Bollinger Vieilles Vignes Françaises**—vintage only. This is the rarest of all fancy champagnes. Its vines have existed since before phylloxera (a plant louse) killed most French grapevines in the mid-1800s. The wine is robust and rich-flavored. Bollinger also makes a vintage champagne and a nonvintage brut.

• **Dom Ruinart Blanc de Blancs**—vintage only. Produced by Dom Perignon in Reims rather than in Epernay, it is held in low profile so as not to compete strongly with its illustrious coproduct but is every bit as good. The wine is light (not thin), complex, very alive, yet velvety.

Grace M. Scotto, veteran of the wine business and former owner, Scotto Wine Cellar, Brooklyn.

Best American Beers

The Gourmet Guide to Beer by Howard Hillman. Facts on File.

The quality of beers varies almost as widely as the quality of wine…but the difference in price between the worst and the best is far narrower. Unlike wine, beer can be judged visually. Like wine, taste is the ultimate test.

How to tell a fine beer by sight: Use a tulip-shaped glass or a large brandy snifter. The beer should be at about 50° (a bit warmer than refrigerator temperature). Pour it straight down the center of the glass. Side pouring is necessary only if the beer has been jostled or insufficiently chilled. *Now look for the three visual signs of excellence…*

1. Small bubbles that continue to rise for several minutes.

2. A dense head, one-and-one-half to two-inches high, that lasts.

3. No trace of cloudiness.

After drinking, look for the clear "Brussels lace" tracery that should remain on the inside of the glass.

- **Best American regular beers.**
  - Sierra Nevada Pale Ale
  - Yeungling Traditional Lager
  - Samual Adams Boston Lager
- **Best American dark beers.**
  - Rogue Chocolate Stout
  - Dogfish Head Indian Brown Ale
  - Old Rasputin Russian Imperial Stout
- **Best beers to go with meals.**
  - Kronenbourg (from France)
  - Kirin (from Japan)
- **To buy and store beer…**
  - Be sure the bottles are filled to within one-and-one-half inches of the top.
  - Buy bottles instead of cans. Avoid twist-cap bottles if possible.
  - Try to buy refrigerated beer that has not been exposed to fluorescent light.
  - Store bottles upright at 40° to 50°. Avoid agitating the bottles in transit or in storage. (For example, do not put them on the door shelves of a refrigerator.)
  - Do not store beer for long periods.
  - Do not quick-chill beer in the freezer.

Best Corkscrew

Waiter's corkscrew is 25% longer than the traditional model, resulting in greater leverage. This device is usually much more durable and also has a handy knife for careful removal of the capsule on bottles.

Grace M. Scotto, veteran of the wine business and former owner, Scotto Wine Cellar, Brooklyn.

Greatest White Wine

Alsatian white wines are among the greatest in the world, yet strangely go underappreciated, says *The Wine Advocate* former editor Robert M. Parker, Jr. Dry, rich and full-bodied, they are closer to white Burgundies than to German Reislings. Great bargains include the Domaine Weinbach Reserve Pinot Blanc and the F.E. Trimbach Pinot Gris.

Connoisseur

Best Sparkling Water

Time

Connoisseurship apparently knows no limits. Many people who used to ask for whiskey by the brand do the same with sparkling water. Some may even distinguish among flavors, but not if ice cubes and limes are used. Differences are hard to spot, even when the waters are downed neat. But they do exist, as the following list indicates. *Brands of club soda and carbonated mineral water are ranked by preference and rated as follows:* Four boxes, excellent; three, very good; two, good; one, fair; zero, must suit tastes other than mine.

□□□□*San Pellegrino, Italy:* A real charmer with a lively, gentle fizz. Clear, springlike flavor is balanced and sprightly.

□□□*Saratoga, US:* There's a bracing lilt to the soft fizz. The clear, neutral flavor has a slightly dry, citric pungency.

□□□*Perrier, France:* Dependably neutral when cold, but a mineral taste develops. Overly strong fizz softens quickly.

□□*Poland Spring, US:* Fizz is a bit overpowering. Generally acceptable flavor with some citric-sodium aftertaste.

□*Canada Dry, US:* Despite an overly strong fizz, this has a fairly neutral flavor with mild saline-citric accents.

□*Apollinaris, Germany:* Strong, needling fizz and a warm, heavy mineral flavor that suggests bicarbonate of soda.

□*Calistoga, US:* After the gently soft fizz, it's all downhill. Musty, earthy flavor has salt-sodium overtones.

Seagram's, US: Sugar-water sweetness is a real shocker. Citric bitterness develops later. Moderate fizz.

Schweppes, US: A prevailing citric-saline bitterness makes this dry in the mouth. Fizz is extremely strong.

How to Select a Cigar

Fondle a fine cigar from tip to tip. It should feel supple and soft, never hard. *Avoid:* Cigars that have wrapper leaves with lumps or veins. Shop only at a tobacconist's store. *Favored:* Unwrapped cigars that have been kept under perfect storage conditions. They have better flavor than cigars sold in metal or plastic tubes.

Cable-TV for Less

Pay less for cable-TV by simply asking. Research the plans that your cable company and its competitors are offering. Then call your company and get through to a person, not a recording. Explain that your bill is higher than you wish, and ask the company to match one of the plans you have found. Some customer-service reps, but not all, will agree—but you can call again if the first one refuses. Of course, you also may cut costs by checking your service contract carefully and dropping items you do not need… or buying a package that includes phone and Internet service as well as cable.

The Motley Fool, multimedia financial-services company. *www.fool.com*

Put Your Computer on TV

John Falcone, executive editor with CNET, a technology and consumer electronics news and review Web site owned by CBS Interactive. He manages CNET's New York City review team and specializes in home theater products. CNET reviews more than 1,000 products a year. *www.cnet.com*

More and more TV shows, movies and live sporting events are available for you to view on the Internet. But the stumbling block has been how best to get those images from the computer to your TV so that you can watch them on a big screen in the comfort of your living room.

That's where a growing assortment of affordable, easy-to-use gadgets known as *streaming media devices* come in. Typically, you connect one of these boxes to your TV and link it to the programming from the Internet via a wireless or wired router, such as those available from Netgear or Linksys.

What you get: These devices can give you anytime access to a wide array of on-demand programming, often for free or at lower cost than on cable-TV or satellite-TV, and they can allow some cable and satellite customers to cut back to less expensive packages…or even stop subscribing to cable or satellite entirely.

What you need to know first: Even though online programming tends to be cheaper than cable- or satellite-TV, it often isn't free. You may have to subscribe to a service such as Netflix, which offers more than 20,000 TV and movie titles for instant streaming but tends not to stream the most recent films ($7.99 per month, *www.netflix.com*) and/or Hulu Plus, which offers many recent TV shows ($7.99 per month, *www.hulu.com*). Or you can rent movies à la carte from Amazon.com (*www.amazon.com*) or Apple (*www.apple.com/itunes*) for between 99 cents and $4.99 apiece. Also, Amazon offers unlimited streaming of 40,000 mostly older films and TV shows to subscribers of Amazon Prime, which provides free two-day shipping on merchandise bought from Amazon ($79/yr.). And subscriptions to sports packages from various services can cost $100 per season, even though the local teams' games are likely to be blacked out.

But if you are a film, TV and/or sports fan, the convenient access provided by these services may be worth the price.

The leading devices all deliver picture and sound quality about as good as the standard- or high-definition programming offered by cable or satellite providers if you have a fast, strong Internet connection.

But there are important differences among these devices. Some are easier to set up and use than others, and they don't all offer access to the same online content. *Among the options...*

BEST ALL AROUND

•Roku XDS (*www.roku.com*)

Advantages: Roku offers access to a wide range of content, including Netflix, Hulu Plus, Amazon Instant Video, the free Internet music service Pandora and live Major League Baseball and National Hockey League games, as well as news programming from a variety of TV networks.

Roku is easy to set up—on-screen directions guide you through the process. You then use a Roku remote control to browse among and select movies, programs or sporting events.

Disadvantage: You can't access content from most free Web sites, such as free TV shows on the basic Hulu site and on TV network sites.

Price: $99 for Roku's top-of-the-line XDS model or $79 for the mid-range XD. The Roku HD model costs $59, but the ability of the XD and XDS to stream the highest-resolution HD pictures (1080p) and avoid WiFi signal interference is worth the cost.

BEST FOR FREE CONTENT

•Veebeam (*www.veebeam.com*)

Advantages: The Veebeam lets you transfer any online content to your TV screen. That includes content you have paid for from services, such as Hulu Plus and Netflix, as well as free content that other streaming media devices cannot deliver, such as TV shows from basic Hulu and the TV networks' own Web sites.

Some similar devices, such as the $199 Boxee Box, have promised to provide free Web sites on TVs, but popular free content sites, such as Hulu basic and TV networks, end

up blocking access on those devices. By not signaling that programs are being transferred to a TV, Veebeam sidesteps attempts by networks and other sites to block such transfers.

The Veebeam is very easy to set up—just download its software to your computer, attach the computer to your TV, then push a small antenna into one of the computer's USB ports. You don't even need to add the Veebeam to your home WiFi network.

Disadvantages: Veebeam will not give you the classic couch-potato experience. While the other devices listed here provide easy-to-use remote controls and on-screen guides, the Veebeam requires that you use your computer to locate and control programming. That makes it a better choice for people who have a computer that can be positioned close to the TV—especially one that won't be needed for other purposes while someone is using the Veebeam—rather than a computer in a less convenient location. Your computer must be relatively modern and powerful, or your picture and sound could be choppy. Use the compatibility tool on the Veebeam Web site (click "Downloads" under "Support") to test your computer before buying Veebeam.

Price: $149 for the HD model, which works with standard-definition TV sets as well.

BEST FOR APPLE FANS

•Apple TV (*www.apple.com*)

Advantages: Apple TV can stream content from your iTunes library and other Apple devices, including iPads and recent-model iPhones and iPod Touches, in addition to video from Netflix, Hulu Plus and YouTube. It's very easy to set up and use on Macs and PCs. Available in up to 1080p.

Price: $99.

BEST IF YOU ALSO WANT A BLU-RAY DISC PLAYER

•Top Blu-ray players

Sony BDP-S5100 3D Blu-ray Disc Player (*www.sonystyle.com*)...Samsung BD-D6500 Blu-ray Disc Player (*www.samsung.com*)...and LG BD550 Network Blu-ray Disc Player (*www.lg.com*).

Advantage: Buying a Blu-ray disc player with built-in streaming media capabilities is cheaper than buying these devices separately. Sony, Samsung and LG Blu-ray players in particular tend to offer a reasonable range of online content and are easy to use.

Price: As of early 2013, the models listed here could be found for between $150 and $200. They're likely to be replaced by newer models, but any Sony, Samsung or LG Wi-Fi Blu-ray player in the $150-to-$180 range that has "built-in WiFi" is likely to be a solid choice.

Warning: "WiFi Ready" is not the same as "built-in WiFi," though an electronics-store salesperson might imply that it is. If you purchase a "WiFi Ready" Blu-ray player, you'll need to purchase an additional piece of equipment to connect it to your WiFi network, and that can cost up to $80.

IF YOU HAVE A GAMING DEVICE...

Some people already have a streaming media device at home but don't realize it. The gaming devices Play-Station 3, Xbox 360 and Wii can serve as streaming media devices. High-end HDTVs that have built-in WiFi capabilities can do this, too.

Advantage: There's no need to purchase additional hardware.

Disadvantage: The gaming devices offer more limited programming options, and the reception quality varies. PlayStation 3 offers better resolution than other gaming devices.

Price: Free, if you already own these devices—though the Xbox 360 offers Netflix streaming only if you subscribe to Xbox Live Gold ($60/yr.). If you don't own one, the gaming devices generally cost between $199 and $299.

THE BEST CONNECTION

Some devices in this article work best with an HDMI cable.

Helpful: Very good HDMI cables are available for $10 or less on Amazon.com and other Web sites. Do not pay the inflated HDMI cable prices charged by most electronics stores—$30, $40 or even $100.

Satellite Television Systems

Margaret J. Parone, former senior vice president of communications, Satellite Broadcasting & Communications Association.

More than 27 million American households now own home satellite television systems. Today's DBS or C-band satellite television system owner enjoys the widest variety of entertainment programming available with access to over 250 channels of video programming and CD-quality picture and audio reproduction.

Satellite system owners can also receive an additional 100 services from around the world. These systems utilize satellites that transmit programming signals with 5- to 17-watt transponders and require an average receiver antenna size of seven feet.

DIRECTV

Through the DIRECTV-brand DSS satellite system featuring an 18-inch satellite dish, consumers have access to over 285 channels of entertainment and informational programming, as well as digital audio services.

DIRECTV is sold at popular consumer electronics stores and satellite dealerships across the country for around $69 to $250, plus installation and an additional monthly programming fee, which ranges from $29.99 to $83.99. There are a variety of sports and movie packages available as well. *www.directv.com.*

DISH NETWORK

DISH Network offers consumers monthly satellite packages that range from $24.99 to $84.99, and offers as well a number of premium packages for sports and movies. A receiver and 20-inch satellite dish start at around $200, and you can buy additional receivers on which you can view different stations with their DISH 500 system (unlike earlier dishes, the DISH 500 can receive two separate feeds).

Like DIRECTV, DISH Network can be purchased at electronics stores and satellite dealerships. *www.dish.com.*

What makes satellite television such an attractive alternative to other multichannel video providers?

• **Satellite television** delivers unparalleled studio-quality picture performance.

• **Satellite-delivered digital stereo** is considered to be the highest fidelity of any broadcasting transmission.

• **Compact state-of-the-art components** are highly user-friendly and easily operated by all members of the household.

• **Parental programming lockout** features allow parents to guide child viewing to preselected channels only.

When the industry was born in the late 1970s, the typical satellite system was manufactured in the basement of some enterprising entrepreneur or small manufacturing shop, and had an average retail price tag of around $35,000, if and when you could find them. Since that time, the satellite industry has seen increasing unit sales.

Over 5,000 professional satellite television retailers are located across the United States. Consult the local *Yellow Pages* for the names of area retailers. As with any large purchase, ask for a listing of references and shop around. There are about 20 different brands of receivers and dishes being manufactured today.

Certainly, the satellite receiving system is the most sophisticated video gear in the consumer's home today. No other component combination could come close to the technology needed to capture a microwave signal from over 23,000 miles in space, focus it, amplify, process and convert that energy to a flawless, ghost-free picture perfect for presentation on today's high-tech television.

How to Buy a Used Camera Without Getting Stung

Ask for a 90-day repair warranty (never less than 30 days) and a 10-day, no-risk trial period. Use the 10 days to shoot several rolls of slide film at different combinations of shutter speeds, f-stops and lighting conditions. The enlarged, projected slides will reveal whether any features are defective.

Unneeded camera attachments: A motor drive is usually a waste of money unless you take a lot of sports or fashion pictures. Zoom lenses are good only for sports events. Their many glass elements tend to produce glare and internal reflections. *Good substitute:* A 250-mm telephoto that does not zoom.

Best Binoculars

The key to enjoying birding is a great pair of binoculars. Prices for good models start at around $150, and excellent models can cost as much as a few thousand dollars.

Considerations beyond just the price: Weight…magnification…and lens size.

Example: Binoculars labeled "7 x 35" create an image that appears seven times closer to you. The 35 refers to the size of the objective lenses, which are on the far side of the binoculars.

All else being equal, a pair of binoculars that is lighter and smaller is better for the beginner.

Budget-minded birders can buy a good, lightweight 7 x 35 pair for between $150 and $300. *My favorites…*

• **Nikon Monarch ATB 10 x 42.** *Weight:* 24 oz. *Price:* $319.95.*

• **Canon 10 x 30.** *Weight:* 25 oz. *Price:* $359.00.

Before going out into the field, practice

*All prices are manufacturers' suggested list.

locating objects. Spot a target with your eye, then zero in with your binoculars. For comfort, you may wish to replace the binoculars' neck strap with a wider one.

Barry Kent MacKay, avid birder in Markham, Ontario, who has written and illustrated numerous books on the subject. He is author of *The Birdwatcher's Companion* (Key Porter Books).

Best Fire Extinguishers

Look for an extinguisher rated ABC to fight the three most common household fires. Class A fires involve paper, wood and cloth. Class B, flammable liquids and gases. Class C, electrical equipment. Choose the most powerful unit you can easily carry and use. Power categories range from 1 (low) to 10, indicating what size fire the unit can fight. *Recommended:* An all-purpose ABC unit having a minimum power rating of 2-A:10-B:C.

Be a Smart Shopper

Buyer beware—the biggest bargains may not be uncovered by Web sites that compare online prices for books, CDs and other merchandise (sites such as PriceGrabber.com, BizRate.com and FatWallet.com). Often listings are restricted to merchants who pay for these services. *However:* Local stores may offer even lower prices. Shipping costs are added to online orders...while sales tax is collected on in-store purchases.

Bottom line: Use Web sites as a tool to comparison shop—but not the only tool. When comparing prices, always make sure that the model number, size, etc. are the same. Buy only from reputable merchants.

Diane Rosener, former editor and publisher, *A Penny Saved,* Box 3471, Omaha, Nebraska 68103.

Your Rights When You Buy "As Is"

Buying "as is" doesn't mean the buyer has no rights at all. "As is" clauses relate to quality, not to general class or description

Example: If the buyer contracts to buy boxes of bolts as is, sight unseen, he or she won't be obligated if the boxes turn out to contain screws, not bolts.

Also, "as is" clauses don't override express warranties. They don't bar claims of fraud or misrepresentation. And they don't stop tort claims (personal injury actions if someone is injured by a defective product).

The late Dr. Russell Decker, professor emeritus of legal studies, Bowling Green State University, Bowling Green, Ohio.

How to Complain Effectively

Americans are not great defenders of their consumer rights. Two-thirds of the respondents in a major survey admitted to living with shoddy goods, incompetent services and broken promises. Only one-third of them had asked for redress.

People *should* complain. More than half of all consumer complaints result in some sort of satisfaction. (The psychological lift that comes with filing a protest is an added bonus.)

People don't complain because they think it won't do any good. *But there are effective ways to complain and get results...*

•**Have your facts straight before you act.** Be clear about dates, prices, payments and the exact nature of the problem.

•**Be specific about what you want done** —repair, replacement or refund.

•**Give reasonable deadlines for action you expect to be taken,** such as a week for store personnel to look into a problem. Deadlines move the action along.

- **Send copies of receipts.** Keep the originals for your records. File copies of all correspondence and notes (with dates) on any telephone dealings. Those records may be the pivotal factor if negotiations are prolonged or you must take your complaint elsewhere.

- **Be businesslike in your attitude** and project an expectation of a businesslike response.

- **Find out where you can go if the seller fails to make good,** and indicate your intention to follow through. Government agencies, such as a state attorney general's office, may need the very kind of evidence that your case provides to move against chronic offenders. Licensing boards or regulatory bodies are good bets for complaints against banks, insurance companies or professionals.

Additional recourse...

- **Consumer-action centers** sponsored by local newspapers and radio and television stations often get swift results.

- **Small-claims court.** If you can put a monetary value on your loss, you may get a judgment by suing in small-claims court. Collecting can be a problem (you must take the initiative yourself), but the law is on your side and the psychological benefits are enormous.

- **Trade associations** can be effective with their member organizations but not with outside companies.

Protect yourself before making large purchases or contracting for expensive services by dealing with reputable sellers. Companies that have been in business a long time have a vested interest in keeping their customers happy. Think about what recourse you will have if something does go wrong. A company with only a post office address, for example, will be impossible to trace.

What Goes On Sale When

If you're a serious shopper, you want to know when all the sales happen. *Here's a month-by-month schedule for dedicated bargain hunters...*

January:
  Appliances
  Baby carriages
  Books
  Carpets and rugs
  China and glassware
  Christmas cards
  Costume jewelry
  Furniture
  Furs
  Lingerie
  Men's overcoats
  Pocketbooks
  Preinventory sales
  Shoes
  Toys
  White goods (sheets, towels, etc.)

February:
  Air conditioners
  Art supplies
  Bedding
  Cars (used)
  Curtains
  Furniture
  Glassware and china
  Housewares
  Lamps
  Men's apparel
  Consumer electronics
  Silverware
  Sportswear and equipment
  Storm windows
  Toys

March:
  Boys' and girls' shoes
  Garden supplies
  Housewares
  Ice skates
  Infants' clothing
  Laundry equipment
  Luggage
  Ski equipment

April:
  Fabrics
  Hosiery
  Lingerie
  Painting supplies
  Women's shoes

May:
  Handbags
  Housecoats

Household linens
Jewelry
Luggage
Outdoor furniture
Rugs
Shoes
Sportswear
Tires and auto accessories
TV sets

June:

Bedding
Boys' clothing
Fabrics
Floor coverings
Lingerie, sleepwear and hosiery
Men's clothing
Women's shoes

July:

Air conditioners and other appliances
Bathing suits
Children's clothes
Electronic equipment
Furniture
Handbags
Lingerie and sleepwear
Luggage
Men's shirts
Men's shoes
Rugs
Sportswear
Summer clothes
Summer sports equipment

August:

Back-to-school specials
Bathing suits
Carpeting
Cosmetics
Curtains and drapes
Electric fans and air conditioners
Furniture
Furs
Men's coats
Tires
White goods
Women's coats

September:

Bicycles
Cars (outgoing models)
China and glassware
Fabrics
Fall fashions
Garden equipment

Hardware
Lamps
Paints

October:

Cars (outgoing models)
China and glassware
Fall/winter clothing
Fishing equipment
Furniture
Lingerie and hosiery
Major appliances
School supplies
Silver
Storewide clearances
Women's coats

November:

Blankets and quilts
Boys' suits and coats
Cars (used)
Lingerie
Major appliances
Men's suits and coats
Shoes
White goods
Winter clothing

December:

Blankets and quilts
Cars (used)
Children's clothes
Coats and hats
Men's furnishings
Resort and cruise wear
Shoes

A Shopper's Guide To Bargaining

Sharon Dunn Greene, coauthor of *The Lower East Side Shopping Guide,* Brooklyn.

The biggest problem most shoppers have with bargaining is a feeling that nice people don't do it. Before you can negotiate, you have to get over this attitude. Some ammunition…

•**Bargaining will not turn you into a social outcast.** All a shopkeeper sees when you walk in is dollar signs. If you are willing to spend, he or she will probably be willing to make a deal. He knows that everybody is trying to save money these days.

•**Bargaining is a business transaction.** You are not trying to cheat the merchant or get something for nothing. You are trying to agree on a fair price. You expect to negotiate for a house or a car—why not for a refrigerator or a winter coat?

•**You have a right to bargain,** particularly in small stores that don't discount. *Reasoning:* Department stores, which won't bargain as a rule, mark up prices 100% to 150% to cover high overhead costs. Small stores should charge lower prices because their costs are less.

The savvy approach: Set yourself a price limit for a particular item before you approach the storekeeper. Be prepared to walk out if he/she doesn't meet your limit. (You can always change your mind later.) Make him believe you really won't buy unless he comes down.

Be discreet in your negotiations. If other customers can overhear your dickering, the shop owner will feel obliged to remain firm. Be respectful of the merchandise and the storekeeper. Don't manhandle the goods that you inspect. Address the salesperson in a polite, friendly manner. Assume that he will want to do his best for you because he is such a nice, helpful person.

Shop during off hours. You will have more luck if business is slow.

Look for unmarked merchandise. If there is no price tag, you are invited to bargain.

Tactics that work…

•**Negotiate with cash.** In a store that takes credit cards, request a discount for paying in cash. (Charging entails overhead costs that the store must absorb.)

•**Buy in quantity.** A customer who is committed to a number of purchases has more bargaining power. When everything is picked out, approach the owner and suggest a total price about 20% less than the actual total. *Variation:* If you are buying more than one of an item, offer to pay full price on the first one

if the owner will give you a break on the others. *Storekeeper's alternative:* You spent $500 on clothing and asked for a better price. The owner said he couldn't charge you less, but he threw in a belt priced at $35 as a bonus.

•**Look for flawed merchandise.** This is the only acceptable bargaining point in department stores, but it can also save you money in small shops. If there's a spot, a split seam or a missing button, estimate what it would cost to have the garment fixed commercially and ask for a discount based on that figure. *Variations:* You find a chipped hairdryer. When you ask for a discount, the manager says he will return it to the manufacturer and find an undamaged one for you. *Your reply:* "Sell it to me for a little less and save yourself the trouble."

•**Adapt your haggling to the realities of the situation.** A true discount house has a low profit margin and depends on volume to make its money. Don't ask for more than 5% off in such a store. A boutique that charges what the traffic will bear has more leeway. Start by asking for 25% off, and dicker from there.

•**Buy at the end of the season,** when new stock is being put out. Offer to buy older goods—at a discount.

•**Neighborhood stores.** Push the local television or appliance dealer to give you a break so you can keep your service business in the community.

Hate Shopping?

Most big stores have employees who'll do your shopping for you. You don't even have to be there. Call the store and ask for the personal shopper. *Stores that specialize in personal shopping:* Bloomingdale's and Saks Fifth Avenue in New York City, and Nordstrom in Seattle.

Buying from Door-to-Door Salespeople

Impulse buys made from door-to-door salespeople or houseware parties need not be binding. Under Federal Trade Commission rules, you have three business days to reconsider at-home purchases of $25 or more.

Recommended procedure: At the time of purchase, always ask for two copies of a dated cancellation form that shows date of sale and a dated contract with the seller's name and address. The contract should specify your right to cancel. *Note:* If you have received no forms, contact the nearest office for advice within three business days.

To cancel: Sign and date one copy of the cancellation form, and keep the second copy. *Hint:* As insurance, send the cancellation by registered mail (return receipt requested).

Sellers have 10 days to act. *Their obligations:* To return any signed papers, down payment and trade-in. To arrange for pickup or shipping of any goods. (Sellers pay shipping.) Pickup must be made within 20 days of your dated cancellation notice.

Reminder about picking up merchandise: You must make it available. If no pickup is made within the 20 days, the goods are yours. If you agree to ship the goods back and then fail to do so, or if you fail to make the goods available for pickup, you may be held to the original contract.

Note: The same rules apply at a hotel, restaurant or any other location off the seller's normal business premises. They do not apply to sales made by mail or phone, or to sales of real estate, insurance, securities or emergency home repairs.

Bargaining with a Mail-Order Firm

Discounts from mail-order firms are often possible. *How:* Wait for the catalog to be out for three months or so. Then phone and ask if the company will give you a 25% discount off the item you want. Many won't, but some that are trying to get rid of unsold merchandise will welcome the opportunity.

Sue Goldstein, author of *The Underground Shopper* (Great Buy Press).

How to Avoid Junk Mail

To avoid much of today's advertising mail, get in touch with the Direct Marketing Association. DMA's Mail Preference Service (including more than 500 major national mailing houses) can get your name off many computerized mailing lists. They also handle the telemarketing Do Not Call list. *www.the-dma.org.*

Hidden Treasures at Yard Sales

Cari Cucksey, an antiques dealer and liquidator who owns RePurpose Estate Services in Northville, Michigan. She is host of Cash & Cari, a program about vintage merchandise appraisals and estate sales that airs on HGTV Saturday nights at 8:30. *www.hgtv.com*

A team of photography experts and investigators announced recently that a set of glass negatives purchased at a California yard sale for $45 likely were the work of Ansel Adams and potentially worth $200 million. Others have since disputed that conclusion, but if it turns out to be true, it wouldn't be the first million-dollar yard sale find.

A Pennsylvania man found an early copy of the Declaration of Independence behind a framed picture he purchased for $4 at a flea market in 1989. It sold at auction in 1991 for $2.42 million. A painting purchased at a Wisconsin rummage sale in the late 1990s for around $20 turned out to be by 19th-century artist Martin Johnson Heade. It sold at auction for $1.35 million.

Very few yard sale shoppers will stumble across a million-dollar discovery, of course. But you can make yard sale shopping profitable by learning which common items still have value to collectors or others. Such things might cost a few dollars apiece, so there's no huge financial risk, even if some of your finds turn out to be worthless.

Web sites such as eBay (*www.eBay.com*), eBay Classifieds (*www.eBayClassifieds.com*) and Craigslist (*www.Craigslist.org*) make it relatively easy to resell yard sale purchases. If you have questions about an item you have purchased, there are chat rooms and fan pages on the Internet for virtually every type of collectible. Type the name of the collectible into a search engine to find these.

Among the products that often are worth considerably more than they sell for at yard sales…

FISHER-PRICE TOYS FROM THE 1980S OR EARLIER

Kids who grew up in the 1970s and 1980s now are old enough to collect the toys that they once played with. Fisher-Price toys in good condition are particularly desirable.

Example: A vintage Fisher-Price Little People Castle from the 1970s in excellent condition with all of its accessories could be worth $150 or more. Even castles in lesser condition or the reissued castle from the 1980s can bring significant amounts. (The pennant on the side of the 1970s version says "Play Family Castle"…the one on the reissue has a sleeping dragon.)

MARANTZ STEREO EQUIPMENT

Decades-old electronics tend to be very inexpensive at yard sales, and some audiophiles prefer the sound from the elite stereo equipment of the past to today's audio electronics. If you come across an amplifier, receiver or speakers made by a company called Marantz in reasonable condition for a small sum at a yard sale, buy it, even if it looks out of date. It could be worth hundreds of dollars or more.

Example: A Marantz Model 2385 receiver in excellent condition from the late 1970s recently sold for close to $2,000 on eBay.

Some vintage Pioneer receivers are valuable as well. And any old amplifier or radio that contains vacuum tubes rather than transistors could be worth a gamble of a few dollars. Audiophiles sometimes buy old vacuum tubes to keep their own vintage stereos running. It's not uncommon for old tubes to sell for $10 to $20 or more apiece.

OLD HARDWARE

Doorknobs, doorknob plates, hinges, locking mechanisms, doorstops, drawer pulls and other hardware from the 1950s or earlier frequently turn up at yard sales for a few dollars apiece. These can be highly valued by designers and home remodelers.

Hardware that has an Arts & Crafts, Art Nouveau or Art Deco look is particularly likely to be valuable—but as long as a piece of hardware is old, attractive and in decent condition, it's likely that someone will pay more than yard sale prices for it. You typically can tell the difference between reproduction hardware and the real thing by the patina and construction. Older pieces tend to be heavier and show significant wear.

Example: A single chrome drawer pull from the 1950s can bring $10 to $20. Matching sets are particularly likely to get a good price.

OLD PAPER ITEMS

Sometimes you can buy a stack of old magazines, pamphlets or other printed items at a yard sale for just a few dollars, yet many printed materials from the 1950s or earlier are worth at least several dollars to collectors, if not more. As a rule of thumb, if it's pre-1960, made of paper and features eye-catching graphics or a picture of an iconic product or person, there probably is a collector out there who is willing to pay for it. Among the pre-1960 magazines that typically bring a good price are *Popular Mechanics, Life, Mad* and *Jet,* as well as almost any well-illustrated train magazine, World War II–focused magazine or women's magazine.

Examples: Issues of *Ladies' Home Journal* from the 1920s or earlier with appealing cover art in good condition often sell for $20 or more apiece on eBay. Issues of the World War II publication *Signal* magazine often sell for $50 to $75 or more.

Even paper items from the 1960s and 1970s can have some value if they are related to a highly collectible topic. It often is worth paying a dollar or two for an obscure car magazine from the 1960s or 1970s if it features eye-catching pictures of classic muscle cars…or a music magazine if it contains attractive full-page ads for famous rock acts or a cover story on a music icon, such as Michael Jackson.

VINTAGE NEEDLECRAFT ITEMS

Sewing and knitting are experiencing a major revival among young people, boosting the resale market for vintage sewing and knitting goods. Vintage knitting needles and crochet hooks often are worth $1 or more apiece, sometimes considerably more. Old spools of thread and knitting yarn can have value, too. That can really add up if you come across a sewing kit containing dozens of these things.

A sewing pattern from the 1980s and earlier can be worth some money, particularly if the garment still is considered fashionable. Patterns for iconic or attractive dresses from decades past tend to be worth the most.

Example: A 1960s Vogue Paris Original dress pattern brought $73. A vintage 1930s Simplicity dress pattern recently sold on eBay for about $50.

BARBIE'S OLD CLOTHES

If you come across a bin of doll clothes at a yard sale, search through it for any with styles that suggest the 1950s, 1960s or 1970s. If you find these, check inside for a Mattel Barbie tag (or the tag of one of the other Mattel dolls in the Barbie collection, such as Francie, Ken or Skipper). Old Barbie clothes sometimes are more valuable than the dolls themselves.

Example: I recently sold a 1960s Barbie raincoat, rain boots and umbrella set for $150.

MUSICAL INSTRUMENTS

Yard sale instruments often can be resold for much more than yard sale prices, either through one of the Web sites listed earlier or through a local music shop. High school–band–quality woodwind or brass instruments in good condition often bring $100

or more. String instruments in good shape usually bring at least $50 and potentially significantly more. Antique instruments can fetch thousands.

Example: My old high school clarinet is nothing special, yet it has a resale value of around $250.

VINTAGE PICTURE FRAMES

It might be worth paying a few dollars for an old painting even if the picture is unappealing—if it is in an old hand-carved wood frame. Such frames can be worth $50 or more.

Pick up the frame—a vintage hand-carved wood frame should be heavier than you expect. The more ornate the frame, the more it is likely to bring.

Example: Ornate gold-colored frames in good shape often are worth $50 to $100 and up.

DESIGNER CLOTHING FROM THE 1980s

Many young people are wearing retro styles—and they consider the 1980s retro. Garments from the 1980s that have famous designer labels are the best bets. High-end designers such as Dior and Gucci generally are most valuable, but even mass-market Izod clothes from the 1980s can have resale value if their look is iconic to that decade.

Example: Izod sweaters from the 1980s can bring $25 to $40 on eBay.

How to Bid and Win @ Online Auctions

Reyne Haines, antique-glass specialist, columnist for *AntiqueWeek* and a regular antique-glass appraiser on PBS *Antiques Roadshow*.

The Internet has produced hundreds of auction sites. Despite the growing popularity of these online sites, buyers and sellers need to take steps to protect themselves.

Reason: The sites only serve as the middlemen. They say up front that they don't guarantee the items offered at auctions are as described. They also don't ensure that winning buyers will pay the amount they bid.

HOW ONLINE AUCTIONS WORK

People who want to sell something through an online auction must first register with the auction site. Sellers provide the starting price and sometimes a "reserve price"—the dollar amount below which they can refuse to sell. And they list how long they want the auction to last, usually seven to 14 days.

An electronic photo of the item can be uploaded to accompany the item's description.

Buyers must also register and, on some sites, provide a driver's license number, Social Security number and date of birth to prove they are indeed who they say they are. Once the auction is over, the item is shipped, usually at the winner's expense, either immediately if the buyer pays by credit card or after a personal check to the seller has cleared.

DOING IT RIGHT

•**Watch out for skimpy descriptions.** Merchandise offered for auction will carry a description listing the history, condition, flaws, repairs and other important details.

If any part of the description seems to be missing—such as the date that the antique furniture was made—E-mail the seller requesting more information.

Once an item is sold, most auction sites will purge the description from the site.

Self-defense: Always save a copy of the description on your computer. When the item arrives, if it doesn't fit the description, you have recourse to return it to the seller and get your money refunded.

Some auction sites offer free insurance policies with up to $2,000 in coverage in case there is a problem.

Other than that, the auction sites do not guarantee an item's quality—or the reputations of either the buyer or the seller.

•**Read the feedback from previous buyers.** On most sites, buyers who have previously purchased items from a seller can report their experiences to the auction site feedback form. These "reviews" are available for all to read.

Better auction sites prevent shady sellers from having friends load up the board with positive comments by limiting access only to people who have bought or sold merchandise. Check to see if the auction site has such a policy.

•**Ask about the site's return policy.** While some sites require sellers to accept returns for any reason, others leave it up to the individual.

Legitimate sellers will give you at least three days after receipt of an item to notify them that you're returning it for a refund.

•**Stick to sellers who accept payment by credit card or check.** Beware of those who insist on money orders only.

By law, credit card companies must stand behind faulty merchandise or transactions paid for with their cards. Also, you can stop payment on a check.

•**Beware of snipers.** A sniper is someone who bids on an item moments before the bidding session closes.

Snipers might outbid you by as little as $1. Even if you're online at the time, there may not be enough time to submit a higher bid.

To prevent this problem, better sites have instituted a five-minute delay.

How it works: If a bid comes in within five minutes of the close, the deadline is extended an additional five minutes to give other potential buyers the chance to raise their own bids. This extension continues, five minutes at a time, until no more bids are received for one full five-minute period.

Caution: At sites that do not have a five-minute delay, never assume you're the only one bidding for an item—even if your bid is the only one listed on your computer screen.

•**Use automated bidding to stay in the action.** Better sites allow you to make an initial bid and then indicate privately a maximum bid. Then, if someone outbids your initial offer, the system automatically raises your offer in predetermined increments until it reaches your limit.

In the end, you may lose out on the item. But you won't spend more than you initially planned. You can always raise your bid higher than your set maximum if you want to.

FAVORITE AUCTION SITES

•**eBay.** The world's largest and most popular online auction site adds hundreds of thousands of new items daily. It sells more than half of everything offered for sale. Antiques, books, collectibles, memorabilia, stamps, trading cards. *www.ebay.com.*

• **uBid.com.** Brand-name, new and used computer and office equipment as well as jewelry and gifts, collectibles, apparel and more. *www.ubid.com.*

who won't provide them. Ask about warranties and return policies.

Be wary of hard-to-verify claims, such as stories about antiques.

Be careful when buying from an individual —consumer protection laws that apply to businesses won't apply.

Holly Anderson, Communications Director, Internet Fraud Watch of the National Consumers League. www.fraud.org.

Gearing Up for Auctions

Depending on the kind of auction (country, indoor) and the type of merchandise sought (bric-a-brac, tools, furniture), assemble the appropriate gear. *Suggestions...*

• **Cash, credit cards or checkbook.** (Some auctions accept only cash.)

• **Pens, pencils and notebook.**

• **Pocket calculator.**

• **Rope for tying items to car roof.**

• **Old blankets for cushioning.**

• **Tape measure.**

• **Magnet** (for detecting iron and steel under paint or plating).

• **Folding chair and umbrella** (if auction is outdoors).

• **Picnic lunch.**

Internet Auction Fraud Protection

When buying at an Internet auction, protect yourself against fraud. Internet auction firms like eBay and uBid are perfectly legitimate, but some of the thousands and thousands of people who use them are not.

Safety: Use the "escrow payment" option that most auction firms offer to hold your payment until satisfactory delivery of the item occurs. Obtain and verify the name and physical address of the seller—don't deal with those

How to Avoid Lines and Beat Crowds

Marilyn Machlowitz, PhD, New York City–based organizational psychologist and consultant, and the author of Workaholics: Living with Them, Working with Them *(Addison–Wesley).*

If time is scarcer than money for you, you might be willing to pay to add the equivalent of a twenty-fifth hour to your day.

Suppose your local museum offers free admission from, say, 6 pm to 8 pm one evening a week. I can guarantee that you'll have the museum to yourself if you go from 5 pm to 6 pm that night. Everyone else will be waiting for the stroke of 6.

Similarly, if your watering hole reduces the price of drinks during its happy hour from 5 pm to 7 pm, go after 7. (Unless, of course, you hope to meet someone, in which case you'll want to be there when it's most crowded.)

If you hate waiting in line, simply learn when places are least crowded and go then.

Some suggestions...

• **Movies are semi-deserted on Mondays,** since most people go out over the weekend. If it's a really hot film, the showing immediately after work is less likely to be crowded than the 8 pm or 10 pm show.

• **Bakeries are also almost empty on Mondays.** People start their diets promptly on Monday morning and forget them by Tuesday morning.

• **Banks are least busy before payday.** So go Thursdays if Fridays are payday where you live or on the 14th and 29th if paydays fall on the 15th and 30th.

• **Post offices aren't crowded on Thursday afternoons.**

• **Supermarkets have long lines 15 minutes before closing time** but no lines 15 minutes after opening.

If you're unsure about when your health club, swimming pool, Laundromat or barber shop is least crowded, just ask the manager.

Learn which days you have two opportunities to do something rather than one. *Example:* If your favorite restaurant offers two dinner seatings some evenings and only one on others, your best bet is to aim for a two-seating night. Similarly, you're more likely to get into an evening theater performance on a day when there's also a matinee.

Another trick is to reverse the logical sequence of things. Almost everyone buys tokens or commuter passes before boarding the train. If, instead, you line up as you exit, you'll be on your way in no time. Also, take forms with you when you leave the bank or airport. Fill them out at your convenience instead of struggling to complete them as you stand in line.

To minimize wasted telephone time, make your next appointment as you leave your dentist's or doctor's office. Make your next reservation as you leave a restaurant. You can do the same thing with your lunch companion or golf cronies as well.

If you hate being placed on hold, call before 9 or after 5. This is an old journalist's trick that almost guarantees that you won't be intercepted by a protective assistant. Learn the numbers of people's private lines. You can quietly copy these down when you're in the office, or you can ask. Most travel agents, for instance, know special numbers for reaching airlines and hotels. If all else fails, invest in a speaker phone. That way, at least, you can continue working while you hang on hold.

Slash Your Cell-Phone Bill

Peter Pham, former CEO, BillShrink.com, Redwood City, California, which helps consumers compare cell-phone options and find ways to save on their bills. www.billshrink.com

Cell-phone plans have become more and more complicated and a major expense for many households, sometimes running up hundreds of dollars in extra charges that result in "bill shock." But there is an array of tricks that you can use to shrink the bills. *How to beat the cell-phone companies at their own game…*

PRICE WAR? THANK YOU!

Price wars among cell-phone service providers have been raging. Rates for unlimited-usage plans have fallen by as much as $20 to $30 per month, with smaller decreases on lower-end calling plans. *Examples…*

• **Verizon Wireless** has the Share Everything plan, which provides unlimited calling within the US, unlimited text and shareable data from $150 per month. (800-922-0204, *www.verizonwireless.com*)

• **AT&T** cut the price of its unlimited voice and data plan for basic phones, which includes both unlimited calling within the US and unlimited data for $84.99 per month. (800-331-0500, *www.wireless.att.com*).

• **Sprint's** "Any Mobile, Anytime" program includes unlimited calling to all mobile phones—not just to other Sprint phones—and unlimited data transmission, including Internet access and text messaging. The program is included with select Sprint plans starting with the 450-minute plan, which costs $79.99 per month. (866-866-7509, *www.sprint.com*).

• **T-Mobile's** Monthly 4G plans feature attractive rates, starting at $50, without a contract, so you can switch to a different T-Mobile plan if prices continue to fall…or if you later decide another carrier would be better. (800-866-2453, *www.t-mobile.com*).

SHOP AROUND

• **If you are locked into a cellular service contract, check the latest offers available**

from your current provider. If you signed your contract two years ago, odds are that this provider now offers plans with more attractive terms than you originally received—and all major carriers now allow existing customers to switch among their offerings midcontract without paying an early termination fee or agreeing to a contract extension.

• **Seek unadvertised bargains.** Call your provider when your contract is nearing its end or already ended and say that you intend to change to a different carrier unless your current provider can do better than the rates it advertises. Phone reps sometimes have leeway to offer special deals, such as a "loyalty plan," to avoid losing existing customers.

• **If your provider does not offer a plan you like, check the terms offered by other carriers.** If you find a rate substantially lower than your current one, it might be worth paying an early termination fee to make the switch. These fees can range from less than $100 to more than $300.

IDENTIFY YOUR NEEDS

For savings no matter which carrier you use, consider these strategies…

• **Buy a plan with fewer minutes than you think you need.** Cell-phone users often are so anxious to avoid 40-to-50-cent-per-minute overage charges that they sign up for plans with more minutes than they really need. Paying them might be painful, but unless the overages average more than $20 per month, you're usually better off with the smaller plan.

Best: Adjust your plan on the go. Each month, consider how much you're likely to use your cell phone in the following month, then call your service provider's customer service department before that billing cycle begins and switch to the most appropriate plan. The major providers all allow this, though some restrictions may apply. *Warning:* Remember to switch back to your usual plan when months of exceptionally high or low calling conclude.

If you do exceed your plan's limits by a great amount, try asking your carrier to retroactively shift your account to a plan with higher limits on data and/or minutes and to drop the overage charges that you have run up.

• **Get a family plan.** Families almost always save when they sign up for one plan with shared minutes. Calls between family members don't count against those minutes. Most family plans include two initial lines, with lines three to five typically costing an extra $10 to $20 a month each. T-Mobile's Classic Unlimited family plans charge $10 for each additional line. *Warning:* Families with limited plans are more likely to accidentally overrun their minutes if they all do a lot of calling in a particular month.

• **Get a prepaid plan if you use less than 200 minutes per month.** Even the cheapest traditional calling plans cost at least $30 per month—$360 a year. If you use your cell phone only occasionally, it's cheaper to choose a prepaid plan that doesn't have a set monthly fee.

Top choice: TracFone, available at Walmart or online (800-867-7183, *www.tracfone.com*). It offers access to the excellent Verizon cellular network. For $119.99 to $139.99—depending on the current promotion—you can purchase a card that provides 800 minutes and that won't expire for one year. This card also automatically doubles the number of minutes you receive when you purchase additional calling time. TracFone cell phones cost as little as $9.99.

CUT BACK SERVICE CHARGES

How you use the plan that you pick affects your bills as well…

• **If you are subject to roaming charges** for making calls outside a certain area, find out how you can tell when your cell phone is roaming and what the extra charge would be. Also, check details of what extra charges you face for service outside the US.

• **Cancel unwanted services.** Many cell-phone users pay monthly fees for services they don't realize they have. Scan your bill for charges you can't identify, call your provider to ask what they are, and cancel any services that you don't want. *Example:* Emergency roadside assistance is tacked onto many bills, often for $3 to $5 per month.

• **If you don't use your cell phone to access the Internet, have that access disabled.** Almost all of today's cell phones are capable of Internet access. If you fail to disable that access, tapping the wrong button on your phone could trigger extra charges.

- **Check your voicemail from a landline if you are near your monthly minutes limit.** Checking voicemail from your cell phone counts against your plan minutes. Better to retrieve messages from a landline than to pay overage rates. Using a regular touchtone phone, dial your cell number, hit * or # (depending on your provider) during your outgoing message, then enter your pass code.

- **Drop your landline, and instead combine your cell phone with Skype or magicJack.** Doing without a landline can cut your overall telecom costs by $20 or more per month—but those savings might evaporate if eliminating the landline greatly increases your cell-phone usage. If you have Internet access, you can reduce your cell-phone usage by placing ultracheap calls through the Internet at home.

Options: Skype offers unlimited calls to phones in the US and Canada for $2.99 per month. Calls are placed through your computer, but the software is free and easy to use. All you need is a PC or Mac, an Internet connection—broadband is best—a Web cam (built-in or external) to make video calls and a built-in microphone or plug-in headset. *www.skype.com*

MagicJack requires the purchase of a $39.95 adapter, which includes one year of unlimited calling in the US and Canada. Additional years of service cost $19.95. Unlike Skype, magicJack lets you place and receive calls through a regular phone rather than a computer. *www.magicjack.com*

What You Need to Know About Cell Phones

R. Michael Feazel, executive editor, *Communications Daily,* a magazine for the telecommunications industry.

Here is what to do if you're in the market for a cellular phone or service provider...

- **Pick a service plan before you pick a phone.** New cell-phone designs are so seductive that many people sign up with providers only if they carry the phones they want. That can leave you with excessive calling charges.

Consider before signing up...

- **The number of minutes you'll likely be on the phone** each billing cycle.

- **How often you'll use your phone outside your local region.** Long-distance "roaming" charges are expensive.

- **Phone size and options you prefer.**

Also, most people are unaware that if they decide to switch service providers, they will have to buy new phones.

Reason: While service providers sell identical-looking phones built by the same manufacturers, each phone is designed to access the network of one carrier—and one carrier only.

- **Don't sign a service contract that lasts longer than one year.** Some firms offer two- and three-year deals with what appear to be attractive rates. But considering how far prices have fallen and how much cell-phone technology has improved in recent years, any contract today will be a terrible deal three years from now. Also, any phone will be obsolete in three years.

Hiring a Private Detective

James Casey, private investigator and former New York City police detective, East Northport, New York.

Times have changed for private detectives. They're no longer breaking down hotel doors to snap incriminating photos for divorce cases. The modern private eye's bread and butter lies in serving the business world, in both security and personnel matters.

Private detectives are often effective in tracking down runaway children. A missing-persons bureau may have to worry about 30 cases at a time; a private eye can focus and coordinate the leads for a single client, giving the matter undivided attention. *Caution:* If the detective can't find a hard lead within three days but is eager to continue, he or she may be milking the client.

For three hours' work, a detective can devise a home security plan that will satisfy any insurance company, including itemized lists, photographs, locks and alarms.

How to choose one: Before hiring a detective, interview the person for at least 20 minutes to discuss your needs and how they'd be met. Be sure that the detective is licensed and bonded. A bond larger than the minimum bond might be advisable for a broad investigation covering several states or even a foreign country. To make certain the private eye's record is clean, check with the appropriate state division on licensing (usually the Department of State). And ask the detective for a résumé. The best detectives usually have ample experience. The best gauge is frequently word of mouth. Reputations are hard-won in this business.

Get Rid of Pain Cheaply

Inexpensive aspirin works as well as the most expensive brand. So always buy the least expensive. This is heard so often that it is a cliché. *Surprise:* It happens to be true. *Findings of a new study:* All brands contain the same amount of aspirin in each tablet. All dissolve at approximately the same rate. Each is absorbed into the bloodstream to start relieving pain in about the same length of time.

Herbal Teas Can Be Dangerous

Herbal teas sometimes counter the effects of prescription drugs or cause serious side effects. *Severe diarrhea:* Senna (leaves, flowers and bark), buckthorn bark, dock roots and aloe leaves. *Allergic reactions:* Chamomile, goldenrod, marigold and yarrow. *Cancer:* Sassafras. *Toxic (possibly fatal) reactions:* Shave grass, Indian tobacco and mistletoe leaves. *Hallucinations:* Catnip, juniper, hydrangea, jimsonweed, lobelia, nutmeg and wormwood. Be sure to read ingredient lists.

Coffee-Lover's Guide

Lyn Stallworth, culinary-arts teacher, writer and author of *The Woman's Day Snack Cookbook* (Collier).

Which fruit product is most consumed by Americans? If you answered coffee, you were correct. The coffee bean is actually the pit of the round fruit of the coffee tree. (It's called a cherry by growers.)

Varieties: Two species account for most of the coffee we drink. Arabica, grown at high altitude and rich in flavor, is the larger crop. Robusta, mostly from Africa, is hardier but thinner in flavor.

IMPORTANT PRODUCERS

- **Brazil.** The quality ranges from indifferent to good. *Best:* Bourbon Santos.
- **Colombia.** Good to superlative coffees.
- **Costa Rica.** Arabicas, ranging from poor to great. Costa Rican coffees are rated by the hardness of the bean. Trust your coffee merchant or specialty store to provide strictly hard bean (SHB) or good hard bean (GHB), the mountain-grown best.
- **Jamaica.** Look for mellow, aromatic Blue Mountain.
- **Java.** The word *java* was once the slang for coffee. However, the finest trees were destroyed in World War II and replaced by robusta. Sturdy, rich, heady Indonesian arabica is now very scarce.
- **Kenya.** All of Kenya's crop is arabica—mild, smooth and round.

Roasting: Slightly roasted beans have little taste. Overroasted ones taste burned. Variations in roasting time affect flavor, but there is no right or wrong, just personal preference. Darker roasts are not stronger. The strength of the brew depends on the amount of coffee used.

SOME ROASTING TERMS

- **Light city roast.** Often called cinnamon. Can be thin.
- **City roast.** The most popular. Makes a tasty brew.
- **Full city roast.** Beans are dark brown, with no show of oil. Preferred by coffee-specialty shops.

- **Viennese roast.** Somewhere between full city and French roast.

- **French roast.** The beans are oily, and the color is that of semisweet chocolate. Approximates espresso but smoother.

- **Italian/espresso roast.** The beans are oily and almost black. Serious coffee, drunk in small amounts.

- **French/Italian roast.** Dark and full-flavored but not as bitter as espresso.

CHOOSING COFFEE

Most coffees are a blend of two or more varieties. A skillful blender balances the components.

Suggestion: Start with a coffee merchant's house blend. Like house wine, it must please a broad range of tastes and demonstrate the quality of the merchant's offerings. Go on to try many blends. Most merchants sell their coffees in half-pound or even quarter-pound amounts.

Best Place to Store Coffee

For fresher coffee, store it in the freezer. Frozen beans stay fresh longer than frozen ground.

The Washingtonian

How to Roast Beans In Your Own Oven

Coffee beans can be roasted in any ordinary oven. Place the green beans in a perforated pan under the broiler (set at 350°F). Toss them every two minutes. For a light American roast, go for 10 minutes. For a dark Italian roast, figure 20 minutes.

The Washingtonian

End-of-Season Barbecue Care

Soak grill in a plastic wastebasket with hot water, dishwasher detergent and a small amount of white vinegar to cut the grease. After about an hour of soaking, grease will almost rinse away—only a little scrubbing is needed. *For even easier cleaning:* Soak the grill after every use.

Gene Gary, syndicated home columnist, Copley News Service.

Buying and Storing Cheese

Neil Hearn, former proprietor of The Cheese Shop, Greenwich, Connecticut.

Believe it or not, it *does* matter where you buy cheese. You should go to an experienced cheesemonger because you should buy only cheese that is fully or almost fully ripened. Getting cheese to this prime state is a specialist's job. For example, our store buys Brie and Camembert 85% ripened. Then it takes us 10 days of expert care to bring it to eating condition. Supermarkets sell potentially good cheeses, but because they can't take the time to age them properly, the shopper is often disappointed. Any cheese is at its best when it is bought from a good cheese store in a perfectly ripened state and is eaten within hours.

How can you be sure all the different cheeses you might want for a party are at their best?

Visit your cheese shop a week or more in advance to make your choices. The proprietor can then have each variety ready at its optimal state—even pinpointed to a particular hour for serving it—on the day of the party.

What about the leftovers? Can they be kept successfully?

We find that cheese, if kept cool and well wrapped, doesn't really need that much care once it is ripened. We have mailed more than 5,000 packages of cheese and had only five complaints—and two of those were sent to the wrong addresses.

How do you store leftover cheese?

Wrap cheese "like a Christmas present" in plastic wrap or aluminum foil. Be generous with the wrapping, and tuck in the sides. A chunk of well-wrapped hard cheese will keep for more than a month in the refrigerator without losing much weight or moisture. If it develops surface mold, you can just brush that off.

Can you freeze cheese?

In most cases, yes, and the quicker you freeze it, the better. If you receive a gift wheel of Cheddar, Swiss, Muenster or Parmesan, for example, cut it into half-pound or one-pound portions. Make individual slabs, not wedges, so it will freeze evenly. Put the unwrapped slabs in the back of the freezer overnight. Take them out the next day, wrap them immediately and put them back into the freezer. The cheese should be good for six months. Let it defrost overnight in the refrigerator before you use it.

If you want blue cheese for crumbling over salads, we recommend refrigerating it unwrapped so it dries out a little. (Wrapped blues—Stilton, Roquefort and Danish blue—will keep for several weeks refrigerated.)

Which cheeses are poor keepers?

The triple cremes, such as St. Andre and Explorateur. The higher the cream content, the greater the risk of change. When creamy cheese is frozen, crystals form.

What about the glass cheese keepers sold in many gourmet shops?

You put vinegar and water in the bottom, supposedly to preserve the cheese. We find that it gives the cheese an unpleasant vinegar odor.

Food-Storage Secrets

For many people, how long to store and keep foods is a guessing game. *If you've ever had to throw away food that's gone bad, these guidelines will help...*

• **Banana bulletin.** For many years now it has been okay to put bananas in the refrigerator, contrary to the still-popular 1940s Chiquita Banana jingle. (More sophisticated picking and shipping have speeded the ripening process.) Yellow bananas can be held at the just-ripe stage in the refrigerator for up to six days. Although the peel might become slightly discolored, the fruit retains both its flavor and its nutritional content. Green bananas should ripen at room temperature first. Mashed banana pulp can be frozen.

• **Nuts in the shell keep at room temperature for only short periods of time.** Put them in a cool, dry place for prolonged storage. Shelled nuts remain fresh for several months when sealed in containers and refrigerated. For storage of up to a year, place either shelled or unshelled nuts in a tightly closed container in the freezer.

The Household Handbook by Tom Grady and Amy Rood. Meadowbrook Press.

• **Storage times for frozen meats vary significantly.** *Recommended holding time, in months*:* Beef roast or steak, 12. Ground beef, 6. Lamb, 12. Pork roasts and chops, 8 to 12. Bacon and ham, 1 to 2. Veal cutlets and chops, 6. Veal roasts, 8 to 10. Chicken and turkey, 12. Duck and goose, 6. Shellfish, not over 6. Cooked meat and poultry, 1.

• **Keep an accurate thermometer in your refrigerator or freezer.** *Optimal refrigerator temperature:* 40°F for food to be kept more than three or four days. *For the freezer:* 0°F is necessary for long-term storage. *Note:* Some parts of the freezer may be colder than others. Use the thermometer to determine which areas are safe for keeping foods long-term.

• **Freezing leftovers.** *Raw egg whites:* Freeze them in ice-cube trays. *Hard cheeses:* Grate them first. *Soup stock:* Divide it into portions. *Stale bread:* Turn it into crumbs in the blender. *Pancakes, French toast and waffles:* Freeze and reheat in the toaster oven at 375°F. *Whipped cream:* Drop into small mounds on a cookie sheet to freeze and then store the mounds in a plastic bag. *Citrus juices:* Freeze in an ice-cube tray.

*Based on a freezer kept at 0°F or lower.

•**Freezing fish.** Make a protective dip by stirring 1 tablespoonful of unflavored gelatin into ¼ cup lemon juice and 1¾ cups cold water. Heat over a low flame, stirring constantly, until gelatin dissolves and mixture is clear. Cool to room temperature. Dip the fish into this solution and drain. Wrap individual pieces of fish in heavy-duty freezer wrap. Then place them in heavy-duty freezer bags. Use within two months.

•**If you do your own food canning, preserve only enough food to eat within one year.** After that time, its quality deteriorates.

Freezing Vegetables From Your Garden

Some vegetables can be frozen and enjoyed any time. *A few that freeze well…*

Tomatoes: Cut out the stems and rotten spots. Squish each tomato as you put it into a big cooking pot. Boil the tomatoes down to about half their original volume. Then put them through an old-fashioned food mill, catching the purée and discarding the skins and seeds. Pour the purée into a large, deep metal baking pan and leave the uncovered pan in the freezer overnight. The next day, run some hot water on the bottom of the pan to remove the purée, place the block of purée on a chopping board and icepick it into small pieces. Bag and freeze the chunks (a few to each bag).

Zucchini: Peel and split it and scrape out the seeds. Grate coarsely. Stir-fry in butter or oil until half cooked. Follow the same freezing procedure as for tomatoes.

Greens: Boil, drain, squeeze the water out, chop to desired consistency and follow the same freezing process.

How to Become a Game Show Contestant…and How to Win, Too

Greg Muntean, former game show contestant coordinator. He is coauthor of *How to Become a Game Show Contestant* (Random House).

Some people think that all they have to do to become a game show contestant is write to the address they see on TV.

When I was the contestant coordinator for *Jeopardy!,* we used to test 200 people a day who hoped to be on the show—and maybe we accepted two.

The odds were just as daunting when I worked on *Wheel of Fortune.* The other 99% of applicants never got a chance to be on the program, but many of them could have avoided rejection.

Here are a few ways to improve your odds of becoming a game show contestant during the interview process…

•**Be realistic about your talents.** Choose your game show according to your skills. At every game show I've worked, people would come to auditions even though it was obvious this was not their show.

At *Jeopardy!,* we had people come in and score a zero on the written test. They couldn't answer a single question.

Sitting on the couch at home, all game shows seem easy. That's the illusion. If people couldn't play along at home, they wouldn't watch.

But with five cameras, a studio audience and other competitors, it's not quite as simple. You need to be very good to hold up under that pressure. So on *Jeopardy!,* we made the written test to qualify as a contestant a bit harder than the actual questions in order to select only the best contestants.

If you're only competitive and not superior to the players you see on TV, you might not pass the test.

Strategy: Don't pick your show because it offers the most valuable prizes or even because it's the most fun to watch. There are word games such as *Wheel of Fortune*…trivia games such as *Jeopardy!*, and *The Price Is Right*...and a wide variety of puzzle word games. Spend some time determining which category—and which game—caters to your strengths.

Note: The best-known shows are going to be the hardest to get on as a contestant.

●**Know your show.** Once you've selected a game show that's appropriate for your skills, watch it on TV for a while. Don't just try to answer the questions. Look for details, such as the jargon the contestants use.

Examples: If your show is *Jeopardy!*, practice putting your answers in question form and pay attention to the betting strategies. For *Wheel of Fortune*, the jargon is "I'd like to buy a vowel"—and "Come on, $5,000."

These are the details to which the people playing at home tend to pay less attention than the games themselves. But if you don't know them, they can hurt how you do at the audition.

●**Be personable.** Once you're in the audition, few things matter as much as your personality. A *Jeopardy!* contestant is very different from a *The Price Is Right* contestant, but the basic element of pleasantness is always there.

●**Be as upbeat as possible.** Game show executives look for contestants who will make their programs seem exciting. Again, you need to know the show. If you're auditioning for *Jeopardy!*, you don't have to jump up and down...but if you're aiming for *The Price Is Right*, you should jump.

●**Don't take anything for granted.** Even if you've already passed the written test and the audition and have been called to the studio, you can still be cut from the show—for just about any reason.

Example: On one program, a contestant's contact lens was causing him to blink too much during the rehearsal. The producer insisted we cut him to avoid the possibility it would happen during the show.

The studio is really the final interview. And even if you're simply phoning the show to confirm your rehearsal, be upbeat and energetic. Game shows have more than enough qualified potential contestants. Don't give them a reason to reject you.

While you can be rejected for any number of problems, game shows try to find a diverse group of contestants. You are not likely to be turned down on the basis of race, gender, age or occupation.

●**Take the process seriously.** Game shows seem lighthearted on television. That's the idea—they're supposed to be fun to watch. But game show producers take these shows very seriously.

Treat the show's application process as you would an interview for a job. Dress nicely for tests and the interview...be ready to display a knowledge of the show...and consider your responses to potential questions before you arrive.

Example: On many shows, the host asks the contestants about their occupations or families...or to relate an amusing anecdote. Those questions come from interviews the contestant coordinators conducted earlier in the process.

Have an interesting story or two prepared, but try to tell them with a degree of spontaneity, just as you would answer questions about yourself during a job interview. If you manage to survive the show's selection process, you earn the right to join the real competition—the game itself.

How to win at least something...

The skills and knowledge you'll need vary from show to show, but there are some strategies that will improve your odds of bringing home a prize.

●**Study the system of prize distribution for the show in which you are interested.** These distribution systems can be as different as the games themselves.

Examples: On *Jeopardy!*, only the winner keeps his or her cash. The other contestants receive parting gifts. But on *Wheel of Fortune*, all the contestants keep what they've won.

Consider the prize system when you're planning your strategy. If coming away with something is more important to you than actually winning the grand prize, you can improve your odds by selecting a game show that has more than one winner.

●**Consider your prize goals.** Are you happy with any award...or are you in it for cash only?

Many shows offer only merchandise—not cash—while nearly all shows give the losing contestants parting gifts. On some game shows, those gifts can be significant. So if you see victory slipping away, it might be worth angling for the second-place.

All prizes, whether they are cash or merchandise, are considered earned income by the IRS—so they are taxed at the fair market value (the lowest price you may find in an ad or a store). If you win a $30,000 boat, your tax bill could reach five figures. Of course, you can choose to turn down a prize after the game, but that's probably not what you had in mind.

• Be better prepared than your competitors. If possible, familiarize yourself with the mechanical aspects of the game.

Example: One of our first $100,000 winners on *Jeopardy!* practiced at home with an improvised buzzer to improve his timing. When he was on the game show, he was able to buzz in before the other contestants and that was a big part of his success.

Also, if there's a home version of the show available—either a board game or a computer game—buy it and play it often.

Secrets of Contest Winners

Rich Henderson and Ann Faith, coeditors of *Contest Newsletter,* PO Box 536, Bethel, Connecticut 06801. *www.contestnewsletter.com*

Cash, vacations, houses, cars, electronic equipment, cameras and much, much more are the dream prizes that keep millions of Americans doggedly filling out entry blanks and helping to lower the post-office deficit. More than $100 million worth of prize money and goods are dispensed annually through an estimated 500 promotional competitions and drawings.

Some dedicated hobbyists have been able to win as many as 50 prizes in a single year. *Lesson:* There is an advantage to a planned approach to overcome the heavy odds against each entrant.

Winning strategies…

• Use your talents. If you can write, cook or take photographs, put your energy into entering contests rather than sweepstakes. Since contests take skill, fewer people are likely to compete…improving your chances. Photography contests have the fewest average entries.

• Follow the rules precisely. If the instructions say to print your name, don't write it in script. If a three-by-five-inch piece of paper is called for, measure your entry exactly. The slightest variation can disqualify you.

• Enter often. Always be on the lookout for new sweepstakes and contests to enter. *Sources:* Magazines, newspapers, radio, television, store shelves and bulletin boards, product packaging.

• Make multiple entries, if they are permitted. The more entries you send in, the more you tip the odds in your favor. *A scheme for large sweepstakes:* Spread out your entries over the length of the contest—one a week for five weeks, for example. When the volume of entries is big enough, they will be delivered to the judges in a number of different sacks. The theory is that judges will pick from each sack, and your chances go up if you have an entry in each of several different mailbags. *Simple logic:* A second entry doubles your chances of winning.

• Keep informed. Join a local contest club or subscribe to a contest newsletter. Either source will help you to learn contest traps and problems—and solutions. They'll alert you, too, to new competitions.

• Be selective. You must pay taxes on items that you win, so be sure the prizes are appropriate for you. If you don't live near the water, winning an expensive boat could be a headache. (Some contests offer cash equivalents.)

If you do win, check with your CPA or tax lawyer immediately. You must report the fair market value of items that you win, whether you keep them, sell them or give them away. This can be tricky.

Some contests and sweepstakes ask you to enclose some proof of purchase or a plain piece of paper with a product name or number written on it. Obviously, since these competitions are designed to promote a product, the sponsors have a vested interest in your buying what they are selling. And many people assume that a real proof of purchase will improve their chances of winning. *Fact:* In a recent survey, more than half the winners of major prizes reported that they had not bought the sponsor's product.

Radio Contests: More Than Luck

Bob Gross, who has won more than $10,500 in cash and prizes in radio contests.

Almost every popular radio station uses giveaways. Rewards include cash, cars, vacations and other prizes, ranging from record albums to TV sets. Playing the contests won't make you rich, but there's nothing like the thrill of hearing your name announced over the radio—as a winner.

Although chance plays the major role, you can greatly increase your odds of winning by understanding how call-in contests are run.

To begin: Pick a few stations that have entertaining contests and good prizes. Listen to each closely for a few hours, and phone in several times to get a feel for how the game is played.

The more contests you enter, the greater your chance of winning. The trick is to do this without spending your life on the phone. *The key:* Each program's disk jockey has a format that he or she follows closely.

Example: My prime listening time is from 11 pm to 1 am. By monitoring the same four stations, I have found that one station holds its regular contests at 42 minutes after the hour, another at either 15 or 45 minutes after the hour, another at either 5 or 35 minutes after the hour and another at 5 minutes of the hour.

After the contest has been announced, several factors determine how quickly you should place your call...

- **The winning number.** The number of the winning call often corresponds to the station's location on the dial. For example, one station, at 95.5 FM, always rewards the ninety-fifth caller. If you dial right away, you'll be about number 20 (stations generally tell you your number when your call is answered). So wait 35 seconds before dialing. By the time the call goes through and the phone rings a few times (at least five seconds per ring), you'll be pretty close to call number 95. It usually takes the station 70 to 75 seconds to reach that call.
- **The number of lines at the station.** This helps determine how quickly they get to the winning number. A station with only two phone lines moves more slowly than one with 22. If you ask, most stations will tell you how many lines they use for contests.
- **The number of people answering the phones.** Stations that have two or more people handling the calls move more quickly than those where it's left up to the DJ. After you've played the contests a few times, you'll get to know the voices—and the number of phone answerers at each station.
- **Individual speeds.** Some DJs get the contest rolling quickly; others are slower.

There's always an element of chance. The difference between being caller number 94 and caller number 95 is a split second, and there's no way you can control that. But you can greatly increase the odds of winning.

Don't give up. If you get a call through and you're five or more numbers away from winning, hang up and try again. And don't let a busy signal discourage you. *Hint:* Many stations have a recording that says "Please try again later" if all the lines are busy. Stay on the line. Your call will be answered...sometimes in the middle of the recording.

Some DJs award the prize at random rather than counting through the calls to, say, number 95. Others announce that caller number two will win, so they don't have to answer 95 calls (and with such a low number, it's really no contest at all). Your only recourse in such a situation is to complain to the station's management.

11

Party and Entertainment Guide

How to Enjoy Holiday Entertaining

Although everyone is supposed to look forward to the holidays, it can be a season filled with stress and strain, especially for those who are hosting guests.

Everyone is likely to be overtired, overstimulated and overfed. Children come home from college, accustomed to being on their own. Parents arrive as houseguests. Divorcées/divorcés bring new partners. Patterns are changed and roles are shifted, and the results can be shattering.

If you are the host or hostess there are things you can do (aside from leaving town) to minimize the strain...

• **Include nonfamily in your invitations.** *Reason:* Everyone is then on "party manners," and the snide comments, teasing and rivalries are held back. This is not the time for letting it all hang out.

• **Accept help.** Encourage your family and friends not only to make their favorite or best dish but to be totally responsible for it—heating or freezing or unmolding and serving. *Reason:* It makes everyone feel better. The afternoon or evening becomes a participatory event rather than one where one or two people do all the work and the rest feel guilty or, worse still, awkwardly attempt to help. (The quality of the meal, by the way, improves enormously.) The one who hates to cook can supply the wine or champagne.

The best baker can be responsible for dessert. A favorite pudding, a special way to prepare vegetables, a conserve—all are welcome. Even the most unaccomplished cook can wash, peel and slice a colorful assortment of raw vegetables.

• **Let the table itself set a mood of fun,** and banish the usual air of formality. Use place cards wisely, and make them with amusing motifs that are appropriate for each

---

Florence Janovic, writer and marketing consultant.

guest instead of using names. Or let one of the younger children make them with a sketch of each guest or hand lettering. Set them out with forethought. Make sure a particularly squirmy youngster is nowhere near an aunt who is known for her fussy table manners. If there are to be helpers, seat them so they can get up and down with ease. Put the famous spiller where the disaster can be readily cleaned up. If the light is uneven, seat the older people in the brightest section.

• **Put everyone around a table.** It creates a warmer, more shared meal than does a buffet, and it's amazing how tables can expand. *Hint:* Use desk or rental chairs, which are much slimmer than dining chairs. (Avoid benches for older folks.)

• **Borrowing and lending furniture,** such as tables, can help you to find room for everyone. It doesn't matter if the setup is not symmetrical or everything doesn't match. A Ping-Pong table covered with pretty new sheets can provide plenty of room, or you can have tables jutting into hallways or living rooms. Using oversize cloths from bolts of attractive cotton can be an inexpensive way to cover your tables.

• **Have some after-dinner games ready.** Ping-pong, backgammon, chess and cards are among the favorites. You may want to buy the latest "in" game or a new word game. Often the games are never opened, but it is comforting to know that they are there, just in case. Bringing out old family albums can be fun, too.

• **Gift exchanging is really a potential hazard.** Children, especially, can grump all day if something they expected hasn't been forthcoming. Grandparents often ask what is wanted, but they may be unable to do the actual buying. Do it for them. A check is not a fun package to open. If you want to be sure no one overspends, set a limit. Or set a theme. Or rule out gifts altogether, except for the children.

Overcoming the Anxiety Of Giving a Dinner Party

Herbert J. Freudenberger and Gail North, *Situational Anxiety* (Avalon Publishing).

Hosts who constantly worry about whether everyone is "comfortable" or fear that their guests are not eating enough are suffering from the situational anxiety of a dinner party. Making the right preparations for the party will relieve these and similar anxieties.

Helpful: Define the goals of the dinner party. The main purpose may be to establish a professional connection or to bring together two people who may be attracted to each other romantically.

Eliminate anxieties by verbalizing them. *Example:* Fear that the guests will not get along. Ask your spouse or a close friend to listen while you describe your worst fears. Once verbalized, the actual possibilities will appear less of a problem than when they were vague apprehensions.

Specify that the invitation is for dinner. It's not enough to say that you are having a get-together at 7:30. Let people know about dress —casual, nice but not formal, formal but not black tie. While phoning, mention one or two of the other guests, what they do and, if possible, what they are interested in. If a guest is bringing a friend, don't hesitate to ask something about the friend. Is there anything special you should mention or avoid mentioning to this person?

Do not serve a dish you have never prepared before. Guests will enjoy what you prepare best, even if it is just plain steak and potatoes or a simple fish casserole.

Have everything ready at least an hour before the party. Take a relaxing warm bath or shower. Allow extra time to dress and make up, and give yourself an additional 20 minutes to sit quietly.

Suggestion: Arrange to be free from the kitchen when the first two or three guests arrive. They need the host's help to get the conversation going.

For the single host: Reduce last-minute anxieties by inviting a close friend to come over early, test the food and look over the arrangements.

Surviving the Cocktail Party Game

Letty Cottin Pogrebin, freelance writer.

In America, it's old news that everyone worships success, everyone litters and everyone lusts. But the deep, dark, dirty little secret that remains unspoken is that everyone hates cocktail parties.

Even people who give cocktail parties hate cocktail parties. They give them because it's the most efficient way to discharge a great number of social obligations in the shortest time at a cost ranging from modest to obscene. Trouble is, after you give a cocktail party your guests owe you a reciprocal treat and you have to go to their cocktail parties. And so it goes, year after year.

Here is a very simple plan to end the canapé competition: Fight back.

You can confess that you hate standing around like an asparagus stalk, watching the waiters' trays stripped bare by the guests clustered near the kitchen door while you chew ice cubes or OD on martini olives.

You can ask the American Medical Association to issue a warning against drinking while upright and shifting weight from one foot to the other and getting a chill from the condensation dripping from your glass into your sleeve and down your arm.

You can stand up in church, synagogue or group therapy and tell the truth about cocktail-party conversation (which is to human discourse what paint by numbers is to fine art). And the truth is that cocktail party conversation only suits people who have three sentences to offer on any given subject and

prefer their listener's eyes to be sweeping the room as they speak.

You can send in your check without making an appearance at the next charity cocktail party. Better still, start a trend. Ask potential donors, "How much will you pay not to have to go to a cocktail party?"

Seasoned political activists can boycott cocktail parties and petition the great hosts and hostesses of the world to give, instead, a sit-down dinner for 10, a round-robin Scrabble tournament, an intimate tea dance, a computer gamefest, a book circle or a quilting bee—anything but the dehumanizing ritual of the cocktail party.

Admit it. Cocktail parties are like sex. Everyone believes everyone else is doing it better and having more fun. Cocktail parties are like medicine. They may be good for your career, but often the cure is worse than the illness. Cocktail parties are poor indicators of interpersonal success. People who are good at glib smiles and small talk are often lousy at life.

But suppose you can't avoid cocktail parties? How can you survive them? *Five tips…*

• **If possible,** attend with someone sociable and loquacious who will stand at your side and banter with passersby as you think about tomorrow's headlines.

• **Pick one interesting person,** someone who seems to be eyeing the clock as longingly as you, and spend the next half hour getting to know that person as though the two of you were alone in the world. Cultivate your savior with as much energy as you would a sex partner. If you choose well, time will fly.

• **Act as you would if the party were in your honor.** Introduce yourself to everyone and ask them about themselves head-on. People will be profoundly grateful for your initiative. They don't call you overbearing—they call you charming.

• **Tell the host you have an injured leg.** Then commandeer a comfortable chair and let people come to you. (They'll be glad for an excuse to sit down.) If no one does, find an oversize art book to browse through or indulge in a few fantasies.

• **Help the host.** You'd be amazed at how overwhelmed a party giver can be and how many small tasks need doing—even with hired help. You can pass the hors d'oeuvres, hang up coats, refresh the ice buckets, and generally free the host for socializing. What's in it for you? A chance to move around (some call it "working the room"), the gratitude of your host and a nice feeling of usefulness.

Secrets of Successful Party Givers

Mary Risley, director of Tante Marie's Cooking School, San Francisco. *www.tantemarie.com*

The kind of entertaining you do depends on the length of your guest list and the dimensions of your house. For 10 or fewer people, a sit-down dinner is appropriate. For 25, a buffet is usually better. As the numbers grow, open houses and cocktail parties become the options. Limits are set by the size of your living space and the hours of the party. A cocktail party is traditionally scheduled for the two hours before dinner. An open house—usually 1 pm to 4 pm or 3 pm to 6 pm—can accommodate more people. If your rooms for entertaining hold 90 to 100 people for a party, you can invite as many as 250 to an open house. *Trick:* Stagger the hours you put on the invitations.

If you want to entertain several disparate groups—family, business associates and/or social friends—consider giving separate parties on succeeding nights. It takes stamina, but it does save effort and expense in the long run. *How:* You buy one order of flowers and greens for decorating the house. You assemble serving dishes and extra glasses (borrowed or rented) just once. You arrange furniture one time only. And you can consolidate food, ice and liquor orders, which, in bulk, can save money.

You want people at a cocktail party to stay on their feet and circulate, so your living area probably holds more people than you think. Removing some furniture—occasional chairs

and large tables—gives you space and keeps guests moving. Clear out a den or downstairs bedroom, and set up a food table or bar to attract guests to that room, too. If you have a pair of sofas facing each other in front of a fireplace, open them out so guests can easily walk around them. Use a bedroom or other out-of-the-way place for coats. (You can rent collapsible coatracks, hangers included.)

FOOD FOR ALL TASTES

Set up different foods in different parts of the party area. If you have open bars, put different drink mixes at each setup. A group drinking a variety of cocktails will not be able to congregate for refills in the same place. *Avoid bottlenecks:* Don't put a bar or buffet table in a narrow hall, for example, or at the back of a tiny room. To make the most of a small space, have waiters to take drink orders and a bartender to fill the orders in the kitchen or pantry. Waiters can also pass the hors d'oeuvres in tight quarters, avoiding the clustering at a food table.

Count on seven hors d'oeuvres or canapés per person. Some will eat less, but it will equal out between the dieters and the hungry folks who make a meal of the party. Stick to finger foods. You'll want a variety of eight to 10 canapés, but pass each separately, starting with the cold foods and bringing out the hot dishes later. Trays with a single selection look prettier and avoid the congestion that develops when each guest has to make a choice. For long parties where a turnover of guests is likely, arrange two cycles of passing food, so the later guests get the same fresh selection as the earlier guests.

LAY IN SOME LIQUOR

You know better than anyone what your guests like to drink. Chilled white wine is popular, as are mimosas (champagne and orange juice) for brunches and afternoon parties. Discuss amounts with your liquor dealer, and ask if you can return any unopened bottles and extras. It is often cheaper to buy mixers by the case. *A good nonalcoholic drink:* Half cranberry juice and half ginger ale over ice, garnished with a sprig of fresh mint and a slice of orange.

Ice: For a large party, you can get ice from an ice company. A 40-pound bag will be enough for 50 people. Get more if you are also chilling wine. Use a bathtub to keep the ice in. A bathtub full of ice and chilling champagne can in itself be a festive sight. Or you can decant from the tub to smaller ice chests for each bar. If the nearest bathtub is too far from the party area, buy a plastic garbage bin to hold the major supply.

ADVICE FROM OTHER EXPERTS

You cannot be a good host without hired hands to take care of the food and drinks. Your job is to keep the guests happy, meeting one another and circulating from group to group. At a minimum, you need a bartender to be in charge of drinks and someone else to be in charge of the food. The larger the party, the more help you will need. *Helpful:* A bartender at each setup, someone in charge of the kitchen, and one or more waiters to pass food and replace dirty ashtrays.

The late John Clancy, chef, teacher, restaurateur and author of several cookbooks.

• **For clear ice cubes,** boil the water first. Cool and then freeze it. (Clear ice cubes last longer because they have fewer air bubbles.) *To keep ice cubes separate:* Store them in a dry, chilled metal container in the freezer.

• **Separate the ice cubes for mixed drinks from the ice being used to cool the beer and soft drinks.** For the average cocktail party, figure on two-thirds of a pound of ice per guest; for a dinner party, one pound per guest. Ice for the cooling of mixers and soft drinks should be figured separately. For cooling large quantities, a combination of block ice and cubes is best.

Emily Post on Entertaining by Elizabeth L. Post. Harper-Collins.

• **For the best beer service,** use a spotlessly clean glass or mug (soap, grease or lint can ruin the taste). Just before pouring, rinse the glass in cold water and shake it dry, or put it into the freezer for a few minutes to frost it. Open the beer bottle or can carefully, without shaking its contents. Tilt the glass and pour the beer down the side to start. Then straighten the glass and pour into the center. How much foam is enough? It's a matter of taste, but you control the amount by the distance you hold the beer container from the glass as you pour. The greater the distance, the thicker the head.

• **The fastest way to cool off a bottle of soda, beer or anything else** is to hold it under running cold water. It's faster than putting it into the freezer.

• **Pile the food high when laying out a party buffet.** Avoid perfect rows of food. After the first attack, the rows look depleted, but piles of food retain some form. Place all the main-course food on one table. Don't allow empty spots, even if it means adding extra dishes. Put the food as high as possible, with platters or baskets on top of sturdy overturned bowls to add elevation.

Planning a Big Family Party

Unplug the Christmas Machine: A Complete Guide to Putting Love and Joy Back into the Season by Jo Robinson and Jean Staeheli. HarperCollins.

Are you hosting a large family gathering? Because a reunion brings together people of all ages, it presents special challenges. *Ideas to make your party more enjoyable for everyone...*

• **Infants and toddlers.** Parents will appreciate a place to change diapers and a quiet room for naps and nursing. Let them know if you can provide high chairs, cribs, safety gates or playpens. *Toys:* A box of safe kitchen equipment. *Food suggestions:* Mild cheese, bananas, crackers, fresh bread or rolls.

• **Preschool children.** Set aside a playroom. *Best toys:* Balloons, bubbles and crayons. Pay an older cousin or a neighborhood teen to baby-sit.

• **School-aged children.** A den or basement room and board games, felt pens and coloring books will keep them happy. Put them in charge of setting and decorating a children's dining table.

• **Teenagers.** Most teenagers find family reunions boring. For those who have to come, provide a room with a television, VCR/DVD player and a CD player. Teenagers may be shy around relatives they don't know. When they come out of hiding, give them tasks that encourage their involvement with others, such as helping out grandparents.

• **Older folks.** They need comfortable chairs where they can hear and see what's going on without being in the way. Some may also need easy access to a bathroom and a place to rest or to go to bed early. *Food considerations:* Ask if anyone needs a low-salt, low-cholesterol or special diabetic diet. Spicy foods are probably out. Make travel arrangements for those who can't drive so they don't have to worry about inconveniencing others.

Now that you've seen to individual needs, how do you bring everyone together? *Common denominator:* Family ties. Make an updated family tree and display it in a prominent place. If you have an instant camera, take pictures as people arrive and mount them on the appropriate branch of the tree.

Special: Ask everyone to bring contributions to a family museum. *Suitable objects:* Old photographs, family letters, heirlooms, written family histories, old family recipes. After dinner, gather around the fire and exchange family anecdotes. You may wish to record them.

Hiring Party Help

Whether you call them butlers or waiters/waitresses, they help you with the fundamental chores of your cocktail or dinner party.

Duties: Take coats, tend bar, prepare snacks or meals, serve and clean up.

How many are needed: One helper serves a seated dinner party for 10 guests or a cocktail buffet for 20, if the host prepares the food. Hire two for groups of 30. For 40 or more, use four helpers.

How to find them: Word of mouth is your best bet. Contact a local college or bartenders' school for willing students.

Payment: At the end of the party.

Rates: Experienced workers earn more, and often charge higher rates for late-night and holiday work.

Caviar Secrets

Keep the tin of caviar in the refrigerator until 15 minutes before serving. Then open the lid and place the tin in a serving bowl of crushed ice. Spoon helpings carefully, since caviar takes on an oily quality if the eggs are broken. Eat with a fork. Accompany with lightly toasted triangles of thinly buttered bread.

Caution: Never serve caviar with onion, sour cream or chopped egg, or squeeze lemon over it. These detract from the pure flavor. *Best:* Burst the eggs between the tongue and upper palate. This releases the full taste properly.

Christian Petrossian, caviar importer, quoted in *Harper's Bazaar.*

Creative Summer Drinks

With only a bit more effort than it takes to make a vodka and tonic or to pour a soft drink over ice, you can create impressive summer drinks.

Single alcoholic drinks…

• **Wine cooler.** Put 2 teaspoons of sugar and 1-teaspoon of cold water into a 10- to 12-ounce highball glass. Stir until sugar dissolves. Add 1 tablespoon of orange juice and 4 or 5 ice cubes. Fill with chilled red or white wine.

Garnish red-wine cooler with a lemon slice and white with an orange slice.

•Bullfrog. Mix 4 tablespoons of lime juice with 1 teaspoon of sugar in a highball glass. Add 2 ounces of vodka and 3 or 4 ice cubes. Fill with club soda and stir. Garnish with a lime slice.

•Floradora. Put 1 cup of crushed ice into a highball glass. Add ½ teaspoon of sugar, 3 tablespoons of lime juice, 2 ounces of gin, and 1 tablespoon of grenadine or raspberry syrup. Pour in 2 ounces of club soda or ginger ale. Stir gently.

•Iced Irish coffee. Combine 1 cup of strong chilled coffee and 1 teaspoon of sugar. Stir. Put 2 tablespoons of whipped cream in the bottom of a glass. Pour in coffee mixture. Stir. Add 3 or 4 ice cubes and 2 ounces of Irish whiskey. Top with 2 tablespoons of whipped cream. (*Regular iced coffee:* Omit the whiskey.)

SINGLE NONALCOHOLIC DRINKS

•Summer delight. Put 3 or 4 ice cubes into a 10- to 12-ounce glass. Add 3 tablespoons of lime juice and ¾ ounce of raspberry syrup. Fill with club soda and stir. Garnish with fruit.

•Saratoga. Combine 2 tablespoons of lemon juice, ½ teaspoon of sugar, and 2 dashes of Angostura bitters in a glass. Add 3 or 4 ice cubes. Fill with ginger ale.

PUNCHES

•Fish-house punch. In a punch bowl, dissolve 2 cups of sugar in 3 cups of lemon juice. Add a large block of ice. Add 1½ quarts of brandy, 1 pint of peach brandy, 1 pint of rum, and 1 quart of club soda. Stir well. Decorate with fruit. Serve in 4-ounce punch glasses. Makes about 32 servings.

•White-wine punch. Pour a 25-ounce bottle of white wine over a block of ice in a punch bowl. Add the juice of 1 lemon and the peel cut into strips. Sprinkle in 1 tablespoon of sugar. Stir. Add 2 ounces of brandy and 1 quart of club soda. Garnish each glass with a stick of cucumber. Makes about 15 four-ounce servings.

NONALCOHOLIC PUNCHES

•Strawberry cooler. Blend 1 pint of fresh strawberries with ½ cup of sugar in an electric blender. Add 2 cups of vanilla ice cream and 1 cup of milk. Blend again. Pour over a block of ice in a punch bowl and combine with 1¾-quarts of milk. Makes about 15 four-ounce servings.

•Pensacola punch. Combine 2 cups of sugar and 6 cups of water in a saucepan. Cook over low heat, stirring until sugar dissolves. Cool. Pour one 46-ounce can of grapefruit juice and 3½ cups of lime juice over crushed ice in a punch bowl. Add the sugar syrup and 1 pound of grapefruit sections. Garnish with maraschino cherries and mint sprigs. Serve in 8-ounce goblets. Makes about 18 servings.

BARTENDING TIPS

•Measure accurately. Use a double-ended measuring cup for pouring. One end is a jigger (1½ ounces) and the other is a pony (1-ounce). A dash is 3 drops.

•Use superfine sugar. The finest granulated sugar, superfine, dissolves quickly and easily. Confectioners' powdered sugar is not as good.

•Develop your own specialty. Experiment with recipes to create your own drinks. *Important:* With alcoholic drinks, don't be heavy-handed with the liquor—you'll spoil the taste and the effect of the drink.

Throwing Guests Out Gracefully

Close the bar. Glance at your watch occasionally. Stifle a yawn or two. Start emptying ashtrays and cleaning up. If subtle hints have no effect—tell the truth. Say you're exhausted…that you have to get up early the next morning…or simply that the party's over.

Emily Post on Entertaining by Elizabeth L. Post. Harper-Collins.

Putting Off Unwanted Guests

Favorite ploys of city dwellers who don't want to put up all the out-of-town relatives and friends who invite themselves— "We'd love to have you, but...The apartment is being painted...We will be out of town ourselves...The house is full of flu...My mother-in-law is visiting...The elevator is out of order... The furnace is broken and we have no heat or hot water [winter version]...The air-conditioning is out, and you know how hot and humid it gets here [summer version]."

Surviving Weekend Guests

Weekend guests can be a drag. They leave the lights on, show up late for breakfast and expect to be waited on. But the clever host or hostess graciously but firmly takes charge and doesn't allow guests to become a nuisance.

• **Be a benevolent dictator.** You can't run a house as a democracy. The host or hostess has the right not to be put upon. If someone is cadging an invitation when you'd rather be alone, suggest another time. You don't have to take a vote to decide on the dinner hour if there's a time that's most convenient for you. Some hosts post written house rules. For most households, though, verbal instructions are adequate.

If you live without servants, tell guests what you want them to do—pack the picnic lunch, bring in firewood. You'll resent them if they're having fun and you're not.

• **Don't let food preparation become a chore.** Plan sufficiently ahead to have options if you decide to spend the afternoon on the boat instead of in the kitchen. Have on hand a dish you can pull out of the freezer, or a fish or chicken that will cook by itself in the oven or crockpot and maybe yield leftovers for another meal.

• **Involve guests in preparation and cleanup.** If they volunteer to bring a house gift, ask for food. If guests have special diets that vary radically from your own, try to give them the responsibility for supplying and preparing their own food.

Breakfast can be a frustrating meal to coordinate. Even if you eat all other meals together, it's a good idea to give guests a kitchen tour and coffee-making instructions so they can fend for themselves when they wake up.

• **Lay out plans and options early.** *First:* Present your own fixed responsibilities and activities. Don't be embarrassed to do something without your guests. *Next:* Present optional activities for everyone. Mention anything you expect them to participate in. Discuss availability of transportation, facilities and other amenities.

Finally a pattern for the weekend will begin to emerge. Keep it flexible. Suggest ways to communicate changes and important information (a corkboard for messages, an answering machine, etc.).

• **Encourage independence.** Supply maps, guidebooks, extra keys. And provide alarm clocks, local newspapers, extra bicycles.

Even dictators can reward good behavior. Warm thanks, praise and other signs of appreciation go a long way toward encouraging more of the same. After all, a host or hostess can't punish bad guests...except by not inviting them back.

How to Throw a Very Successful Party

Penny Warner, author of *The Best Party Book—1001 Creative Ideas for Fun Parties* (Meadowbrook).

A successful party isn't hard to put together once you get the formula down. *Unforgettable parties are the result of the clever mix of...*

- **A legitimate reason** (or plausible excuse!) for a get-together.

- **A carefully orchestrated plan.**

- **Creativity.**

BE A DIRECTOR

Your party will be different if you direct it, rather than just invite folks and hope for the best. *Examples...*

- **If you host a baby shower,** make it a toys-only or baby's-bath-only shower, and your guests will head eagerly to the stores now that you've eliminated guesswork.

- **Center a retirement party on the retiree's hobby,** say golf, and have guests wear golf clothes.

- **Turn a going-away party into a movable feast where friends pick up and travel together from house to house for each course.** Meet at the first house for drinks and hors d'oeuvres. Move on to the second for soup and salad. Travel to the third for the main course. Wind up at the fourth house for dessert and coffee...and a fond farewell.

PARTY CHECKLIST

Once you have chosen the reason for a party, you must get yourself organized.

You don't want to be expecting your first guest to come through the door, only suddenly to remember you forgot to buy ice. To avoid that kind of catastrophe, develop a "things to do and things to buy" checklist that is divided into four sections that help you organize your time and effort as the day of the party approaches.

Section 1: Three weeks before the party. Develop a guest list, create the invitations (and mail them), decide the menu, write a grocery list and hire any serving help you might need.

Section 2: A week before the party. Call guests who didn't RSVP, purchase the food and drinks, prepare food and decide what you're wearing.

Section 3: One day before the party. Clean the house, arrange and decorate the party room, pull out the serving dishes and confirm deliveries and caterers.

Section 4: The day of the party. Finish decorating and cooking, then set up everything, mentally "travel through" the party and get dressed.

INVITATIONS

Make your invitation a show stopper. *Best:* Homemade invitations. *Examples...*

- **For a birthday party,** go to your library and get a photocopy of the front page of a newspaper from the day and year your birthday guest was born. Design your invitation to the size of a column in the paper, paste your column over an old column and photocopy as many invitations as you need.

- **For a baby shower,** cut out small footprints on which you've written party details.

- **For a Christmas party,** make gingerbread people, each one decorated with edible glitter. Tie a card with details around the neck.

THEME FOOD

Offer theme food—and serve it with flair. *Examples...*

- **For a graduation party,** serve high-quality food cafeteria style...on trays.

- **For dessert at a family reunion,** have each family contribute an eight-inch-square cake decorated with the contributor's name on it, and place the squares together to form a show-stopping pièce de résistance.

- **Break out the wicker baskets,** old-fashioned tins and large seashells to serve food, rather than use ordinary or dull serving dishes. Food looks and tastes better when it is served creatively.

ACTIVITIES

Plan unusual activities. No charades. No board games. Sustain the mood of the party. *Examples...*

- **For a baby shower,** buy eight jars of baby food, remove the labels and have each guest taste and write down the flavors she thinks she has just tasted. The guest with the most correct answers wins a prize—perhaps a home pregnancy kit or a stuffed toy.

- **Create a great birthday videotape by having guests relate funny anecdotes**

about the honoree. Play the tape during the party, and give the tape to the birthday boy or girl as a souvenir.

• **For a family reunion have the oldest relatives tell their life stories.**

DECORATIONS

A party without decorations is like a movie without a musical score—something is missing. Done well, decorations add immeasurably to the atmosphere and to the enjoyment of the people at the party.

And here's where the kids, a spouse and friends come in. Pass out assignments...to cut out legs and boots from felt and hang Santa's legs in the fireplace at Christmas...to create a basket of honeymoon items (cologne, mints, body paint, silk panties, videos) as a centerpiece at a bachelorette party...to collect and hang photos of the guest of honor from past to present (complete with captions) at a birthday party.

UNUSUAL THEMES

Every month of the year, there is a ready-made excuse to throw a party...

• **January 6,** Sherlock Holmes' Birthday.
• **March 24,** Harry Houdini's Birthday.

• **June 7,** Day of the Rice God.
• **July 14,** Bastille Day.
• **September 26,** Johnny Appleseed's Birthday.

Any excuse can be the perfect excuse for a party. *Examples...*

• An international evening where the guests bring dishes from the old country.

• A fashion-victim party where guests wear the unwearable.

• A ski party far from the slopes where the guests dress in snow bunny or ski bum apparel.

• An invite-a-friend party where each guest brings someone new to the group.

Put your imagination to work.

Parties don't have to be held in someone's house or in a rented hall. You can also create your own car road rally or biking party by designing your own map and clues along the way with a favorite restaurant as the ultimate destination.

You might also consider having everyone meet at a bowling alley, espresso bar or at a nearby dance studio.

12

Collecting and Hobbies

Secrets of a Famous Collector

Over the past 60 years, the late Roy Neuberger, founder and senior partner of the highly respected investment management house Neuberger Berman, amassed a collection of outstanding American art of the 19th and (primarily) 20th centuries. Much of it is now in the Neuberger Museum of the State University at Purchase, New York. *Here are some of Mr. Neuberger's secrets of successful collecting...*

TRAIN YOUR EYE

• **Pursue formal study.** This is one way, but it's not the only one.

• **Look at art.** This is the best way to develop your taste. Go to galleries. Look in museums, but be selective. There are too many museums today. Their experts who select what's to hang aren't infallible. Visit New York City, the current art capital of the world.

• **Never stop learning.** There is always more to know.

WHAT TO BUY

• **Unknown artists.** Buy someone you have never heard of before. This is especially good if you don't have much money. Names that are unfamiliar could turn out to be popular after a while.

• **Noninvestments.** I don't think of art as an investment. People should buy art because it's good for them and fulfills them. If art is meaningful to people, their judgment is likely to be sound, and then art could turn out to be a good investment.

• **Individuals, not schools.** Artists are individuals.

• **Be skeptical.** A lot of expensive, phony non-art masquerades as art.

WHERE TO BUY FINDS

• **Consultants.** Banks are charging 2% for their services as investment counselors on art.

The late Roy Neuberger, Neuberger Berman, New York City.

It's better to pay attention to an art critic whom you trust.

• **Dealers.** No matter how informed you become, a smart, honest dealer is important.

• **Local exhibitions.** There are good artists everywhere in the country.

Important: You can collect better if you're a good walker. Stay in top physical condition and get around.

Art as an Investment

Quality is the main factor at every level of the art market. It determines both purchase price and liquidity. The best items appreciate most when the economy is flush and maintain their value best in a recession.

The key to success is knowledge about art and the market. Knowledgeable collectors who follow their own intuition and buy what they like usually do better than investors who follow elaborate strategies.

Most experts agree that investors should never invest more than 10% of their assets in the art market. And art should be a long-term investment. Plan to keep an item for at least five years to get the best return. *To learn the market…*

• **Visit dealers.** Prices of comparable items can vary.

• **Attend auctions.** Dealers usually set their prices according to current auction prices.

• **Subscribe to auction catalogs.** Auction houses such as Sotheby's (*www.sothebys.com*) and Christie's (*www.christies.com*) annually publish prices brought by major items sold during the year.

• **Consult with experts.** Museum curators, dealers and art scholars can be very helpful, especially in assessing the work of lesser-known artists. Most will give free advice about a specific work. Never make a major purchase without consulting an expert.

Most works of art are bought and sold at private galleries and auction houses. A good dealer has a large selection of works pre-selected for their quality, whereas auction houses sometimes have to dispose of less worthy items. With a dealer, there is no waiting for a purchase time as there is for an auction, but a purchaser can still take time to reflect. A good dealer is willing to share knowledge, stands behind what is sold and often has an exchange policy. Ask a museum curator for the name of a reputable dealer.

For a knowledgeable collector, auctions present an advantage—comparable items can often be bought for less than from a dealer. *Primary advice:* Buy what you like, but buy quality—the best examples that you can find and afford.

BUYING GUIDELINES

• **When there is a preference for oil paintings in the art market,** drawings and sculpture will be better buys.

• **Less popular subjects**—some portraits, animals, religious paintings, violent subjects—are often less expensive.

• **Paintings that are under or over the most popular size** (two feet by three feet to three feet by four feet) tend to cost less.

• **Works that are not in an artist's most typical or mature style are usually less expensive.**

• **Avoid what's currently stylish.** Investigate the soon-to-be stylish.

• **Works of Western art that are not attributed or authenticated can be inexpensive,** but they are bad investments. A work with an authentic signature and date is always worth more than one without them.

COLLECTING CONTEMPORARY ART

At least 120,000 people in this country think of themselves as serious artists. Among them, fewer than 500 will ever see their works appreciate in value. Most of these artists are either very well known and very expensive or reasonably well known and reasonably expensive.

Works by artists who have not yet received the recognition they merit are affordable now and might appreciate in value. These artists are likely to be included in group exhibitions but may not have been shown alone. In private galleries, their paintings may sell for $5,000 to $20,000 and their drawings for $250 to $1,500. If the artist does not have a dealer, as the more famous artists do, you might be able to save 50%—the dealer's commission— by buying directly.

Large quality paintings by relatively unknown artists can be found for as little as $800. If you choose well, you can get a significant work of art, help support a deserving artist and, if you are very lucky, watch your work's value escalate.

Great Antiques Are Cheaper Than Good Modern Furniture

Judith H. McQuown, author of many investment books. She also writes about shopping, antiques and travel.

Antique furniture is a better buy than modern reproductions. For example, a modern reproduction of a Georgian mahogany bowfront chest can cost over $5,000, yet the originals frequently sell at auction for $800 to $1,000.

Antique furniture also "stores" value better than modern reproductions do. Like a new car driven out of a showroom, even expensive modern reproduction furniture becomes "used" as soon as it's delivered. Offered for resale, it generally brings one-third or less of its original cost. *Other ways antique furniture is the better investment and what to look for...*

• **In contrast to reproductions, antique furniture retains its value.** If you buy a Georgian mahogany chest at auction for $1,000, change your mind and consign it to the next auction, it will probably fetch around $1,000 again. Allowing for commissions at both ends, you'll have lost $200. But if you hold on to that chest for two or three years, you may see an increase in value. And the longer you keep an antique piece—barring your buying at

the top of a vogue and selling at its bottom— the more valuable it will become. It's a much better investment than its modern reproduction, which can cost you $3,000 to $4,000 and bring you only $1,000 to $1,200 if you should decide to resell it.

• **Furniture buyers should look for simple lines and consider their space limitations.** Buy basic shapes. You won't get tired of looking at the pieces, and they'll be easy to sell if you move or redecorate. Some antiques are especially suitable for small apartments—for example, drop leaf tables (often with a drawer underneath for silver and linens) and nests of tables. Very large pieces are often sold at low prices because most people don't have enough room to accommodate them. Similarly, tall chests sell for less than low chests because people can't hang pictures above them.

• **When buying antique furniture at auction, look closely at the catalog's glossary** and definition of terms. Christie's, for example, distinguishes among "A George II mahogany chest of drawers, mid-18th century" ("the piece is essentially of the period and has not been significantly altered or restored"), "A George II mahogany chest of drawers" (*no date:* "the piece is essentially of the period and has been significantly restored or altered") and "A George II-style mahogany chest of drawers" ("the piece is an intentional copy of an earlier design").

• **Antique furniture should be examined carefully before purchase.** For chests and desks, check the drawers to make sure they move properly, and check the alignment of the runners. Check tables for structural stability. Federal and Empire tables on a central pedestal are frequently top-heavy and wobbly. Open a drop leaf table to see whether its leaves lie flat or are warped. Are the leaves the same color? Or has the table been sitting in the sun so that one or more leaves have faded?

• **Inspect upholstered furniture very carefully.** If the upholstery is in good shape, the rest of the piece is probably sound or has only minor damage that can be repaired easily. Keep in mind that professional reupholstering adds at least $500 to $600 to the cost of a chair and $800 to $1,200 to the cost of a couch.

Other repairs: Any reputable auction house or antique dealer can recommend a good cabinetmaker and tell you what should be repaired and approximately how many hours it should take.

Even first-timers can learn a lot by asking auction-house personnel a few questions…

•**Has this piece been repaired or altered in any way?**

•**Were the repairs done well or badly?**

•**Will it need work? If so, what should be done?**

What kind of antique furniture comes up at auction? Just about everything that was made after 1650 in the US, England, Europe and the Orient. This furniture is less than museum quality, and there is a lot of it around.

Antiques: Spotting The Real Thing

Here are helpful guidelines to ensure you get the antique you think you're paying for…

•**Wedgwood.** The only way to determine if a piece of Wedgwood is old or recent (assuming it bears the impressed mark of "Wedgwood") is by close examination of the raised relief molding. The earlier works have greater depth and more delicacy.

•**Porcelain.** The Chinese made porcelains a thousand years before anyone else did. Pieces that were copied at a later date may also have had the original identifying marks copied. (The Chinese didn't do this to deceive but rather to pay their respects to the skill of their ancestors.) Only a real expert can distinguish between the old and the very old.

•**Pewter.** The alloy of tin and other metals is easily identified by its color and appearance, which are more mellow and subtle than silver or silver plate. If a piece called pewter is marked Dixon or Sheffield, with a number on its underside, it is not pewter at all but Britannia metal, a substitute.

•**Ironstone.** Mason's ironstone, found largely in jugs made for the home and in dinner services, is the original only if the words "Mason's Patent Ironstone China" appear in capital letters on the bottom.

•**Enamels.** A dealer offering Battersea enamel does not necessarily mean a snuffbox or needle-and-thread case made at the small factory at York House, Battersea, between 1753 and 1756. The term has come to be used for old enamels made mostly in other English towns in the 18th century. However, the piece could also have been produced within recent years in a factory in Birmingham, or even in Czechoslovakia. The originals are of copper, surfaced with an opaque glass that was then hand-decorated with inked paper transfers taken from copper plates.

•**Silver.** An old Sheffield plate will show the copper where the silver plating has worn off. This generally means that the piece was made before 1850. Once a piece has been resilvered by modern electroplating methods, it is just about impossible to differentiate it from other kinds of silver.

•**China.** The patterns are not always an indication of age since copyright is a relatively new idea. In years gone by, one porcelain maker cheerfully borrowed the pattern of a predecessor. The only way to cope with the resultant identification problem, say the experts, is to look carefully until you become savvy enough to recognize a Staffordshire printed earthenware plate by the flowers of its border.

•**Collecting in general.** When looking around, always be on the alert for items whose design is basically sound. In this way you have the best chance of picking up the so-called antiques of tomorrow. Meanwhile, since more and more Americans have become collectors, and the supply of items made before 1830 (an arbitrary cutoff date between antiques and nonantiques) is limited, the value of any *good* old piece increases.

Best Antique Shops In NYC

Depending on your taste, there's something for every antique shopper in Manhattan. *Some great shops to visit...*

ART DECO

• **Dalva Brothers,** 53 E. 77th St., 212-717-6600. *www.dalvabrothers.com.* Mainly 18th-century French antiques, including porcelain sculptures, but you can also find a few fine Italian and English pieces here.

• **Howard Kaplan Designs,** 240 E. 60th St., 646-443-7170. *www.howardkaplandesigns.com.* A treasure trove of French, English and American pieces. They also feature his original pieces.

• **Kentshire Galleries,** 37 E. 12th St., 212-673-6644. *www.kentshire.com.* The place for formal English antiques. Eight floors of first-quality English, ranging from Queen Anne through the Edwardian periods. Extensive collection of antique accessories and jewelry plus estate jewelry.

• **Newel Art Galleries,** 425 E. 53rd St., 212-758-1970. *www.newel.com.* An eclectic collection of formal furniture and a diverse collection of Decorative Art and Art Moderne.

• **Florian Papp,** 962 Madison Ave., 212-288-6770. *www.florianpapp.com.* In business since the turn of the century, with three floors of fine 19th-century furniture.

19TH-CENTURY AMERICAN FURNITURE

• **Didier Aaron, Inc.,** 32 E. 67th St., 212-988-5248. *www.didieraaron-cie.com.* English, French and Italian furniture.

OTHER SPECIALTY SHOPS

• **Leo Kaplan Antiques,** 114 E. 57th St., 212-355-7212. *www.leokaplan.com.* Eighteenth-century English pottery and porcelain. Large selection of antique and contemporary paperweights, English and French cameo glass and Russian enamel and porcelain.

• **Lillian Nassau,** 220 E. 57th St., 212-759-6062. *www.lilliannassau.com.* The best place in the US to buy Tiffany glass. Also has a fine collection of Art Nouveau and Art Deco glass and accessories.

• **James Robinson Inc.,** 480 Park Ave., 212-752-6166. *www.jrobinson.com.* Antique silver, china and glass, and a fine collection of antique jewelry.

• **A La Vieille Russie,** 781 Fifth Ave., 212-752-1727. *www.alvr.com.* Specializes in Imperial Russian Fabergé accessories and jewelry.

Collecting American Folk Art

The late Robert Bishop, founding director of the Museum of American Folk Art, New York City.

American folk art was discovered in the 1920s. Although there were a few pioneer museum exhibits, and a group of collectors founded the museum that was to become the Museum of American Folk Art in 1961, it didn't take off until recent years. Folk art has become increasingly popular for many reasons, including the country-furniture boom, its compatibility with modern design and the recent rise in Americans' appreciation of things American.

WHAT IS FOLK ART?

Folk art is difficult to define. It ranges from three-dimensional objects, such as copper weather vanes and carved wooden decoys, to native oil portraits and fanciful quilts. Traditionally it was created by immigrants who continued to use inherited design motifs—the Germans in Pennsylvania, the English in New England. But artisans outside of immigrant communities produced work that falls into this category, too. *Common denominators:* It is created by and for common folk, and it is utilitarian but has an aesthetic quality that elevates it beyond mere functionality.

Although country furniture is often classified as folk art, it really isn't. The country wood-worker is a professional.

THERE ARE THREE KINDS OF COLLECTORS

• **Antique collectors** who use folk art as decoration.

• **Fine-art collectors** who also collect folk art.

• **Those who collect folk art** as an investment.

HOW TO BEGIN

• **Visit galleries and museum exhibits that feature your special interest.**

• **Go to antique shows.**

• **Talk with antique dealers.** They are better informed than anyone in the field and are willing to share their information.

WHAT TO BUY

Acquire quality. It's better to buy one good thing than a lot of inferior pieces that will never be aesthetically pleasing and won't appreciate.

Specialize. Become knowledgeable in one particular area in order to be an effective competitor in the marketplace. But be flexible. It's shortsighted to say, "I don't collect that," and pass up something you really love.

Prices have skyrocketed in the past several years and are still high. But most folk art is still accessible to collectors who are just starting out. *Helpful:* Lots of 20th-century folk art is worth looking into. Ceramics, sculpture, quilts, textiles, paintings and other crafts are being produced all over the country. The problem is sorting out the quality. *The trick:* Look at enough good things to develop your eye.

CAVEAT EMPTOR

Anyone who is making a major purchase should ask for a written guarantee. It should include a description of the piece, the name of the maker, the period and disclosure of all restoration. The guarantee should specify that if any of the information proves to be incorrect, the piece can be returned for full refund.

Collecting Bronze Sculpture

Alice Levi-Duncan, Jody Greene and Christopher Burge, Christie's, New York City.

In the world of our grandparents and great-grandparents, no home was without its bronzes. J.P. Morgan and Henry Clay Frick collected them, and even families with modest incomes could afford these commercially produced pieces.

A recent revival of interest in sculpture of all kinds has created a lively market in old bronzes as well. They are plentiful, decorative and easy to take care of with a feather duster.

COLLECTING CATEGORIES

• **Academic or salon sculpture.** These realistic 19th-century bronzes from Europe and America were cast in a variety of subjects—portrait busts, prancing putti of India, laboring peasants and nudes. They provide a good starting point for beginners. *Important sculptors:* Jean Baptiste Carpeaus, Jules Dalou, Achille d'Orsi.

• **Animal sculpture.** A school of French artists led by Antoine-Louis Bayre produced sculptures of horses, dogs, lions and hunting scenes that are prized for their fine modeling and realistic movement. *Important artists:* Pierre-Jules Mene, Georges Gardet, Emanuel Fremiet, Alfred Dubucand. Attractive pieces are available starting at about $100, though name artists command more. *Examples:* A Mene bronze of two pointers sold for $1,100. A gilt-bronze, *Ostrich Hunting in the Sahara* by Dubucand, brought $4,620.

• **Art Nouveau and Art Deco.** Popular with collectors who specialize in all designs of these periods, these styles are subject to current fashion. Art Nouveau prices have leveled off after a period of inflation. Art Deco is still in and expensive. Bronze and ivory figures of exotic dancers by Demetre Chiparis recently brought $30,000. More modest Art Nouveau and Art Deco pieces, particularly by American designers, can be found for $500 to $5,000.

Many Deco bronzes are of athletes. "Pushing men" bookends are typical and popular.

• **American West sculpture.** The peak of this craze has passed, but prices are still high for this area of Americana. Frederic Remington's *The Norther* sold for $715,000. But this was the last available cast of a rare edition, and Remington is considered to be a major artist. Western sculpture by other artists is a less secure investment, but of course it is also less expensive.

• **Impressionist and Early Modern.** Bronzes by established artists of this era are considered to be fine art rather than decorative objects and are available only through auctions and galleries. Works by Rodin, Daumier, Degas, Maillol, Picasso, Henry Moore, Brancusi, etc., have proved to be sound investments, but they are extremely expensive—from $100,000 to millions of dollars.

• **Museum specialties.** Medieval, Renaissance, Baroque, Oriental and African bronzes require study and connoisseurship and attract only a few independent collectors. Expert advice is essential if you consider buying one of these pieces.

WHAT AFFECTS VALUE?

• **Fame of artist or founder.** Signatures or foundry marks should be crisp and clear. (Fakes abound.)

• **Edition.** A rare and limited edition is more valuable than a common one. *Problem:* Records of most 19th-century bronzes are sketchy. Many pieces were cast literally in thousands. And the records vary for established artists. Remingtons are carefully documented, including casts made by his family after the artist's death (called estate editions). Rodins, on the other hand, were made in several different foundries, and few records exist, providing a ripe market for forgeries or pirated editions. Estate editions, though authentic, are not as valuable as those supervised by the artist.

• **Condition.** Original condition is preferable. However, it is acceptable to have 19th-century bronzes repatinated or repaired in a reputable foundry if necessary.

• **Size.** This is a matter of fashion. Generally, the demand (and prices) are greatest for very large pieces appropriate for outdoor settings.

SPOTTING FAKES

Valuable bronzes, even those of contemporary artists like Henry Moore, have frequently been forged. The most common method is to make a "surmoulage" casting from the original. The fake will be slightly smaller than the original, since bronze shrinks as it cools, but the differences are minuscule. Fakes may also vary in color, weight and clarity of detail.

Danger signals: Bronzes that have been epoxied to a marble base so you can't check the hollow interior. An unnaturally even "Hershey-bar brown" color. Color that can be removed with nail-polish remover or scratched with a fingernail. A ghost impression around the signature or foundry mark. Air bubbles, bumps and craters around the base (good 19th-century craftsmen would have hand-finished such imperfections).

Seek expert advice as you learn the field. Stick to dealers and auction houses that guarantee the authenticity of the works they sell. *Make sure your receipt is specific:* "One bronze signed Henry Moore" says just that. It does not say the piece was made by Henry Moore.

BOOKS ON BRONZES

• *Bronzes* by Jennifer Montagu, Octopus Books Ltd., New York, 1972, out of print.

• *A Concise History of Bronzes* by George Savage, International Thomson Publishing, New York, 1969, out of print.

Collecting Art Deco

J. Alastair Duncan, formerly of Christie's; Herve Aaron, Didier Aaron, Inc.; Nicholas Dawes, antiques dealer; and Fred Silberman, Fred Silberman Gallery, all of New York City.

Art Deco is a design style that burst onto the international scene in the 1920s. (Its name comes from the 1925 Paris *Exposition International des Arts Decoratifs et Industriels*.) The sleek modern lines of the style appeared in architecture, furniture design, fabrics, posters, book covers, silver, glass, ceramics, clocks, boxes, cases, enamelware, jewelry and even clothing. Flamboyant and optimistic in the prewar years, it came out of Art Nouveau and melded into Art Moderne, a more industrial, machine-age fascination with technology and new materials, such as plastics and chrome, in the 1930s. Art Deco motifs were Egyptian, Mayan, cubistic and futuristic. The craftsmanship was superb.

Art Deco was rediscovered by collectors in the late 1960s, and prices escalated in the 1970s. Then, as with many other antiques and collectibles, the market softened in the 1980s, particularly for mass-produced items in good supply. When collectors and dealers sensed that Lalique was becoming cheap again, they started a new wave of buying, and the price roller coaster started up again.

Furniture by an Art Deco master like Emile Jacques Ruhlmann or lacquerwork by Jean Dunand (most famous for furnishings on the liner *Normandie*) has not weakened in price. The workmanship and rarity of such attributed pieces keep them at a premium. A record was set at a Christie's auction in 1997—the item was a 1916 Ruhlmann cupboard marqueted with ivory and ebony, which sold for over $650,000. You may still find chairs (and sometimes tables) for under $10,000 by Louis Sue and Andre Mare, Jules Leleu and Dominique. American names to look for are Donald Deskey (responsible for much of the Radio City Music Hall decor) and Paul Frankel.

For the beginning collector: Look for well-built wooden furniture. It was properly dried and crafted in the 1920s, using such rare woods as amboyna and black macasser ebony, which won't be seen again.

For the serious investor-collector, only signed, handmade pieces of great quality are safe buys for the future.

Mass-produced 20th-century decorative arts may not be an investment, but they are great fun to have. Charming design and good quality control make Art Deco household and personal items competitive with contemporary merchandise. Art Deco table silver, cigarette holders, ladies' compacts, perfume bottles, jewelry, boxes, lighters and other small items have great flair and affordable price tags. Some consider Art Deco low-quality art, but it has a sense of humor and great style.

Collecting Color Posters

Robert Brown, co-owner of the Reinhold-Brown Gallery, New York City.

Posters caught the public's fancy in the 1880s and have retained a fascination for collectors ever since. The development of cheap color lithography led to that first wave of artistic posters, most of which were designed for advertising. From 1880 to 1900, French, Belgian, English and American artists left their mark on the medium. *Best known:* The French Art Nouveau artists Toulouse-Lautrec, Mucha, Cheret and Steinlen.

German artists turned out the finest posters from 1900 to World War I. *Leading light:* Ludwig Hohlwein, who did posters for clothing stores and theatrical events and a famous series for the Munich zoo.

American posters came to prominence during World War I. *Uncle Sam Wants You*, the recruiting poster showing a determined Uncle Sam pointing toward the viewer, is an unforgettable image. *The artist:* James Montgomery Flagg. He and Howard Chandler Christy produced many of the most famous posters of their day. Today an Uncle Sam poster can sell for hundreds of dollars.

The work of French artist A.M. Cassandre stood out during the period between the two world wars. *His most popular contributions: The Nord Express* and other train posters done between 1925 and 1932. His widely reproduced and imposing *Normandie* was completed in 1936.

Posters of note since World War II include those of Ben Shahn and the San Francisco rock posters of the 1960s.

The categories for collectors encompass various subjects, such as circus, theater, ballet, movies, music halls and both World Wars. *Best buys:* Automobile posters (except those for American cars, which are not of very good quality). *Star:* The Peugeot poster by French artist Charles Loupot.

Posters in constant demand: Those connected to avant-garde art that combine strong typographic design with photomontage. *Rare finds:* Work from the 1920s associated with the Bauhaus, the Dada movement and Russian Constructivism. Constructivist film posters made between 1925 and 1931 usually measure about 40 inches by 28 inches. *Classic example:* Any of the few advertising the film *The Battleship Potemkin.*

Beginners should look at Japanese posters made from the mid-1970s to the present. *Also recommended:* Post-World War II Swiss posters for concerts and art exhibits.

Best: Stick to recent foreign posters made in limited editions and not distributed beyond their place of origin.

Poster condition: Creases and small tears in the margin are acceptable. Faded posters are undesirable. (The quality standards are not quite as stringent for posters as they are for prints.)

Collecting American Quilts

Barbara Doherty, co-owner of Pineapple Primitives, Brooklyn, New York.

Appreciation of American-made quilts has grown greatly in recent years. *Most sought after:* Amish or Mennonite quilts. Prices start at $1,000. Many are made in somber colors (black, purple, dark blue) with a geometric design. They look striking in modern interiors. The quilters were forbidden by their religion to use flowers or other frivolous designs or decoration. However, they often tricked sterner members of the sect by backing their quilts with patterned fabrics.

Does this patterned fabric add to the overall value? No. The fine stitching and the sophisticated color schemes are the spectacular features of an Amish quilt. Incidentally, you will find a deliberate mistake, such as one square in a color that clashes with the rest of the scheme, in every quilt. This symbolizes that only God is perfect.

Are most Amish quilts old? Actually, most of them were made in the 1920s and early 1930s. Quilts older than that will have worn out from use.

Are they entirely handmade? No. Most borders were put on by machine. (Sewing machines were in use as early as 1840.)

Are the Amish and Mennonites still making quilts? Yes, but unfortunately they now use a combination of cotton and polyester fabrics. Even the cottons aren't the same. The old ones were vegetable-dyed, which gave special richness to the colors.

What other kinds of quilts are desirable? White brides' quilts, which are very rare. Fine patchwork with tiny pieces. (Tiny pieces, if expertly sewn, add to the value of a quilt.) Appliqué, in which a tulip, a basket or some other motif is cut out and sewn on separately. Trapunto, quilting with a raised effect made by outlining the design with running stitches and then filling it with cotton.

How do you judge a quilt? By design, color harmony and needlecraft. However, mediocre design with wonderful stitching can be outstanding. So can a quilt with less fine needlework but marvelous pattern or colors. The ideal is to find great taste and great workmanship together.

Is it possible to find large quilts? Once in a while you'll see one that's 100-inches wide, but most are in the 72- to 78-inch range, and often square. Quilts are rarely a standard size. If you have a very fine quilt, don't use it on a bed. There's too much risk of wear.

Where are quilts found now? The best buys are in the Midwest, particularly in Ohio and Missouri, but also in upstate New York and other more remote rural communities. Search at auctions and antique fairs.

How are quilts displayed? They are used as wall hangings, which is what most dealers advise. Dramatic colors and designs are the qualities that you should look for in a quilt you would like to use as a wall hanging.

How do you care for a quilt? If you hang it behind glass, it must never touch the glass. To frame a quilt, treat it like a fine print, and back it with acid-free paper. Never display a quilt in direct sunlight—colors fade, especially the reds. To store, roll it (don't fold) to prevent wear cracks. Wrap it in acid-free paper. Avoid old quilts with brown materials. Something in the mordant (the dye-setter) or the dyes themselves causes the brown to disintegrate.

How do you clean a quilt? No dry cleaning, ever. The solvents are too strong. If you must wash the quilt, do it in the bathtub with a dishwashing detergent such as Joy. Then rinse the quilt many, many times with distilled water. But sometimes you may have to leave it dirty. Don't tamper with rust stains or with blood stains (made by pricked fingers) that were not washed out right away.

Collecting Coins

The late Dr. Martin Groder, business consultant to a coin dealership in Chapel Hill, North Carolina.

Coin collections fall into two categories—those done for the fun of it and those undertaken by collector-investors who mix value with the fun.

Collectors who are only looking for a pleasant hobby usually restrict themselves to inexpensive coins. *Basic procedure:* Obtain the standard books and buy albums in which to mount the coin purchases. Join clubs and attend shows to build up expertise at your leisure.

Collector-investors approach their coins with a higher level of commitment. *Main difference:* They spend significant amounts of money in the hope of reaping financial rewards.

SALIENT FACTS

• **The market for US Treasury-minted coins was once fairly steady since only collectors bought and sold.** But starting in the mid-1960s, noncollecting investors began to move cash in and out of the market, buying and selling coins as speculative investments much as they might stocks and bonds. This injection of volatile money transformed a relatively steady market into one of cycles, with booms and busts. Speculation increases demand for investment-grade coins, which makes those that are extant more and more valuable.

• **Experienced collector-investors and dealers often use their expertise to take advantage of the novice investor.** *Result:* Thousands of new collectors find that they are stuck with inexpensive junk when it is time to sell.

HOW TO AVOID BEING SKINNED

• **Study well before making major money investments.** There are a number of books about each major US coin series. These volumes discuss the historical background of the coins. *Examples:* How well the coins were struck and the condition of the dyes when the coins were made. The rare and common years for the coins and dozens of variations that make each coin distinct from others. The books often give values for the coins, but these are usually out of date. For the latest figures, consult the coin collectors' newsletters. *Point:* Learn all you can about a coin before investing. This background knowledge helps keep you from being cheated by a fast-talking dealer.

• **Learn from dealers.** Get acquainted with several to gain a sense of them as people. Be alert to their willingness to protect beginners from their own errors.

• **Do not depend on the advice of dealers for long.** To wean yourself away, spend lots of time at coin shows and auctions. Learn to identify and grade individual coins and note their sale prices. Subscribe to and study the literature read by professionals.

Crucial advice: Sell part of your collection every year. This shows you whether or not you knew what you were doing when you bought.

What to sell: Duplicates for which you have better samples. Coins from periods that no longer interest you. Samples that have lost their fascination.

Why should you start or rebuild a collection now? In the late 1970s and into 1980, a major speculative boom shot prices far beyond sustainable levels. After some panic selling, many paper profits disappeared. Now the market is pretty well cleared of all excess pricing. The boom drove away many novice and casual collectors as prices soared. But these people started drifting back into the marketplace as coins became more affordable.

Preservation: The value of a coin does not depend entirely on the market cycle. It can drop rapidly from poor handling or cleaning, or even from coughing on the coin. *Best:* Check with dealers and consult literature on the best methods of preservation. *Avoid:* Plastic holders made from polyvinyl chloride (PVC). This material breaks down with time and releases an oil that oxidizes the copper in coins, turning them green and oily. *Note:* Although damaged coins can be cleaned, they never look the same to an experienced eye.

Collecting Chinese Porcelain

Andrew Kahane, Andrew Kahane Ltd., New York City.

There have been times when fine Chinese porcelain has outpaced stocks, bonds and the money market, with an annual appreciation of 15% or more. A 14th-century pilgrim flask sold at a Doyle auction in 2003 for $5.8 million. This was the highest price ever paid for a Ming dynasty Chinese porcelain.

Chinese porcelain is pottery that contains the mineral products kaolin and feldspar (for translucency) and is fired at very high temperatures. Manufacture began in the late 10th century.

Why are dynasty names, such as Ming, used? Porcelain study is organized historically, and these names place an object in time. *The dynasties:* Northern Sung (960–1127), Southern Sung (1127–1279), Yuan (1280–1368), Ming (1368–1643), and Ch'ing (1644–1912). Also, names of certain rulers within dynasties are used, especially for the 17th and 18th centuries. *Example:* K'ang-hsi (1662–1722). K'ang-hsi blue-and-white ware is highly prized.

Are there ways for a beginner to identify a period by the shape or color of an object? It is a complicated subject that demands a lot of looking. However, there are a few broad generalizations. The earliest porcelains are the white wares of the Northern Sung dynasty, termed Ting. The first blue-and-whites appear in the Yuan period. They are called Mohammedan blue, because both cobalt and the techniques used to fashion the wares were imported from Persia. The floral and figural decorations on porcelain with a predominant background color (Famille Rose, Famille Noire, Famille Verte, etc.) are 17th and 18th century. The monochromes (pure yellows, celadons, oxbloods, peach blooms, etc.) are basically developments of the 18th century. They were extremely popular with collectors in the early part of this century.

What is most sought after now? The highest prices are for early Ming (15th century) blue-and-white pieces bearing a reign mark. In recent years, a very strong interest for reign marks has developed. The reign mark or seal was placed on the object as a sign of deference or goodwill. In Ming pieces, they are crucial. *Example:* A hypothetical good early Ming blue-and-white vase will bring $100,000 if marked. Unmarked, it will go for around $30,000.

How much do chips or cracks affect value? Very much, in today's market. Steer clear of anything that's the slightest bit damaged, underfired or overfired.

Is it possible to begin collecting without paying a great deal of money? Yes, indeed. For the new collector, transitional blue-and-white ware, which was made in the 17th century, between the end of the Ming and the beginning of the Ch'ing dynasties, is still reasonable. A hypothetical sleeve vase (flaring and cylindrical) made between 1640 and 1650, with some nice incised decorations, should cost $2,500 or more in perfect condition. That is not very much to pay when you consider the price of other antiques of equal artistry.

Another relatively modest way to start: Export wares made for European and American markets, especially those bearing family arms or marks. They were made from the 18th into the 19th century, often as tea or dinner services. Prices could run from about $200 for a small plate up to $5,000 to $8,000 for a fine tureen. It is fun to do research on the family arms and to track them down to the year the porcelain was commissioned.

Is it difficult to care for porcelain? As long as you don't drop it, porcelain is very durable. Use reasonable caution, and wash it in soapy water.

What is the state of the market? Strong. *Example:* In a recent Christie's auction, a blue-and-white moon flask from the Ming dynasty (Yongle period) sold for $1.1 million—double its low estimate.

What are the best reference works on Chinese porcelain? There are hundreds of books on the subject, but the following are unequaled for anyone who is seriously interested in the field. They can be found on-line and in good libraries.

• ***Chinese Ceramics, A New Comprehensive Survey from the Asian Art Museum of San Francisco*** by He Li (New York, 1996).

• ***Chinese Pottery and Porcelain*** by S.J. Vainker.

• ***A Handbook of Chinese Ceramics*** by Suzanne G. Valenstein.

• ***Underglaze Blue and Red: Elegant Decoration of Porcelain from Yuan, Ming and Qing*** by Wang Qingzheng.

• ***The Chinese Potter*** by Margaret Medley (London, 1976).

• ***Chinese Blue and White Porcelain*** by Duncan Macintosh (London, 1994).

Collecting Pewter

Price Glover, antiques dealer and specialist in pewter, New York City. *www.pricegloverinc.com*

Pewter appeals to collectors for both its handsomeness and its history. Because of their classic styles and satiny, silver-gray finish, pewter pieces also lend themselves well to decorative display.

Although pewter has sometimes been called the poor man's silver, fine pewter has always been esteemed. Basically, pewter is tin alloyed with lead, copper, bismuth and sometimes antimony. The proportions of metals vary according to the maker, but generally a lower proportion of lead (and subsequently lightness) means higher quality.

The most sought-after pewter in the US is American pre-19th century, both for its scarcity and the general fever to collect Americana. American craftspeople melted down damaged or badly worn pewter for recasting into new pieces. Constant remelting, heavy use and eventual discarding left little to survive. Since so few 17th- and early-18th-century American pieces are available, most collectors concentrate on post-Revolutionary War pewter.

The great scarcity has caused prices to escalate. A rare 1740 tankard sold for $15,000 at a recent auction. (Auctions with sizable collections of 18th-century pewter are also infrequent.) A late-18th-century plate or a small liquid tavern measure, however, might be found for $300 to $500.

Pewter was still made in the early 19th century, but in order to compete with the growing popularity of pottery and glass, some makers began adding antimony to their alloy. The result was a harder metal, adaptable to the refined patterns of silver. Called Britannia metal, this pewter was extremely popular until the mid-19th century. To a purist collector of pewter, though, it lacks the attraction of the traditional pewter.

By the mid-19th century, mass-production methods and the process of electroplating made silverplate more affordable, and pewter production died out. A collector might find pewter that was once silverplated with the plate later removed, but it is not as desirable as the original pewter.

Twentieth-century pewter pieces are not valued by collectors.

Beyond American shores, pewter has a truly ancient history that goes back to the Bronze Age. Pewter production has thrived in England since the Middle Ages. An astute collector may manage to find English pewter from as early as the 16th century. Imported by American dealers, 17th- and 18th-century English pewter is far more available than its American counterpart. It also commands about half the price of comparable American pieces, even when the English piece is as much as 75 years older. As American pewter becomes rarer, the urge for collecting English pewter seems likely to increase. Off-the-beaten-path antique stores in England are a source of bargains for the knowledgeable collector. So far, most European pewter is valued at only a fraction of English pewter's worth.

Design, good condition and an absence of discoloration are important considerations in evaluating pewter. The most important factors are age and origin. Touch marks imprinted on pewter are highly prized. Such symbols make it possible to date pieces and to determine if they are American (sometimes even the region is identified), English or Continental. However, Early American craftspeople often copied British symbols or stamped "London" on their wares to mislead the public. And some early pewter was not marked at all. The multitude of signs, hallmarks and makers' signatures makes reference-book research a necessity for the serious collector. Since fakes and forgeries are common, experts advise buying only from a very reputable dealer.

Early pewter was cast in heavy molds and then finished on a lathe. The finishing left shallow grooves called skimming marks on the pewter. When a handle was attached, the linen support placed under the handle left the impression of its weave. Hammer marks on the underside of a plate rim also indicate early craftsmanship. *Learning:* Most museums with Early American collections have displays of pewter that can be very informative for a beginner.

Collecting Antique American Clocks

Chris Bailey, former curator of the American Clock & Watch Museum, Bristol, Connecticut.

Clock collecting goes all the way back to 15th-century Europe, a time when royal patrons commissioned ornately jeweled timepieces. In America, quality clock making began in colonial times, and collecting by the affluent got an early start. A major display at the Columbian Exposition of 1893 was of colonial clocks.

MAJOR COLLECTING CATEGORIES

• **Tall-case clocks.** The earliest American-made clocks are over seven feet high and are popularly known as grandfather clocks. (Collectors call them tall-case clocks.) The earliest had square dials. Later versions have arched dials, often with pictures or moving figures that show the phases of the moon. Late-18th-century clocks may have wooden works. *Names to look for:* William Claggart, Peter Stretch and Simon & Aaron Willard. Prices for tall clocks range from the low thousands to several hundred thousands.

• **Banjo clocks.** In the late 18th century, banjo-shaped wall clocks were created. The earliest ones are now as valuable as tall-case clocks made in the same years. At one auction, an elaborate early-19th-century banjo clock by Lemuel Curtis sold for $15,000. One of uncertifiable make sold for $2,000.

• **Shelf clocks.** In the early 19th century, these more affordable clocks appeared. About two feet high, they fit comfortably on the mantel. Their mass-production methods, devised by Eli Terry and Seth Thomas, were America's main contribution to the clock industry. A good shelf clock can cost from $200 to thousands of dollars.

WHAT MAKES CLOCKS VALUABLE?

• **The best clocks have,** besides age and beauty, all their original parts in good working order. Cases must also be in good condition.

• **Replacements or repairs should have been expertly performed** using methods and materials of the clock's period. With proper restoration, a clock maintains its quality.

• **Signatures and labels** of esteemed clockmakers enhance value. But fine unsigned clocks also command good prices.

• **Embellishments to conform to a current fashion** detract from a clock's worth.

• **Scarcity is not synonymous with value.** Some fine clockmakers made many clocks, all of which command high prices because of quality, not rarity.

STARTING OUT

Veteran clock collectors have been described as one of the most canny groups of collectors. Fortunately, the novice can acquire information easily. Many good books are available in public libraries. Museum collections are a useful guide to variety and high quality. The National Association of Watch & Clock Collectors (*www.nawcc.org*) is a resource that has chapters nationwide, a bimonthly journal and research services.

For serious beginners, the best way to buy is through a reliable dealer who will give a written guarantee that the clock can be returned.

Clocks are no longer a good high-return, short-term investment. But quality clocks, especially tall-case clocks, will retain their value and grow with inflation. Even some pre-World War II clocks may be of collecting value. Two contemporary American clock companies, Chelsea and Howard, are still making limited quantities of high-quality clocks that may turn out to be the desirable antiques of the future.

For Big Band Enthusiasts

There is an Internet site that features recordings of big bands and jazz from the 1920s, 1930s and 1940s—plus biographies of many musicians of that era. The Past Perfect site is at *www.pastperfect.com.*

Michael Daly, cofounder and managing director, Past Perfect, Grange Mews, Station Rd., Launton, Oxfordshire OX26 5EE, United Kingdom.

Collecting Old Watches

Dr. Walter D. Bundens, former president of the National Association of Watch and Clock Collectors, and William Scolnik, dealer in antique watches, New York City.

Clocks were reduced to portable size in the early 1500s, when the first watches, highly decorated pendants, were proudly worn as fine jewelry. Technical advances in the 1870s, coupled with the newly chic long waistcoat (watches were slipped into convenient pockets), led to more practical timepieces. Two hundred years of innovations and refinements culminated in the precision instruments beloved by collectors today— primarily European, handcrafted mechanical watches made between 1700 and 1900.

EUROPEAN WATCHES

• **Decorative watches** have decorative cases with lids that close (called hunting cases) or unusual shapes and scenes or designs in engraved or repoussé gold, enamel or jewels.

• **Complicated watches** have intricate technical mechanisms for functions other than telling time. Some watches tell the month, day, year, phase of the moon, international times or even sidereal time. Others have alarms, timers or musical chimes. Watches were made with chronographs, thermometers and compasses—and one, sold for $1,350, had a built-in roulette wheel. A most popular type of watch, called a repeater, strikes on the hour, quarter hour or even minute, when a button is activated. Automata have moving figures that perform on the hour or quarter hour on demand. An erotic version was offered for almost $8,000. Always popular are skeletonized watches, whose movements are visible through clear cases. Some of these may sell for under $1,000.

• **The rarest of the rare.** It is the dream of every serious collector to own a watch by Abraham-Louis Breguet, an innovative French watchmaker of the late 18th to mid-19th centuries. Every watch he made is unique and distinctive. Only a small percentage of his known output has been accounted for. In 1895, a Breguet watch cost the equivalent of about 20 houses. Generally, one would sell for $20,000 to $150,000, and many fakes are around.

• **Other names to look for.** Patek-Philippe ("the Rolls-Royce of watches"), Frodsham, Rolex and Audemars Piguet.

AMERICAN WATCHES

• **Railroad watches.** Conductors and engineers of the late 19th century were dependent on their watches to keep to their timetables. These are the most popular collectible type in America. Often large and plain, and always accurate, they were expensive a century ago. *Names:* Waltham, Elgin, Howard, Illinois "Bunn Special," Hamilton and Ball.

• **Dollar watches.** Inexpensive, mass-produced pocket watches from the 1920s and 1930s are still cheap and easy to find. With few exceptions, dollar watches will probably never be highly valued, but they can be lots of fun for the beginning collector. *Exceptions:* Watches made for the World's Fairs (Chicago 1893, New York 1939 and others) or novelty watches like Mickey Mouse or Buck Rogers, currently selling for hundreds of dollars.

• **Top of the line.** Before 1915, many American watch companies made a "top of the line" model in limited quantities, numbered and inscribed that rivaled or even outshone contemporary European models. Collectors can learn to recognize these through reading and research.

• **Recent watches.** While the quartz watches hold little interest (so far) for collectors, early electric watches—the first Hamilton electric, for example—are sought, as are watches from Cartier or Tiffany made through the 1940s.

WHAT ADDS VALUE?

A famous maker or model. Degree of complication. Amount of purity of gold (or silver). Number of jewels. A low serial number (look inside). The beauty of case and movement. Condition. (Watches should be in working condition or repairable. Repairs must be done in the style of the original.)

WATCHES AS AN INVESTMENT

Prices of fine antique watches are soaring. At Christie's spring 2005 auction, an 18-karat gold, 1961 Patek-Philippe wristwatch with perpetual calendar and moon phases sold for more than $1 million, and an 18-karat pink gold, 1948 Patek-Philippe chronograph wristwatch with perpetual calendar and moon phases sold for $336,000.

Inexpensive watches are available wherever old jewelry is sold. When you consider purchasing an expensive watch, however, be sure to consult an expert. Estate auctions are generally good sources.

FOR THE BEGINNER

Membership in the National Association of Watch and Clock Collectors includes two publications: *The Bulletin* and *The Mart* (in which members buy, sell and trade watches —a wonderful source). The association also maintains a museum, a lending library and a new computerized "horological data bank." For more information, visit *www.nawcc.org.*

Collecting Native American Silver Jewelry

The late Teal McKibben, collector and owner of La Bodega de Rael, Santa Fe, NM, and Carl Druckman, researcher and consultant in Indian jewelry, Santa Fe, New Mexico.

In the late 1960s and early 1970s, Native American Indian silver jewelry, previously collected by a small coterie, began to capture the interest of the general public. Count on a 10% to 15% annual appreciation on the value of fine old and contemporary pieces.

Learning the ropes: Look at photographs, go to museums, read. Expect to make a few mistakes. You have to do some impulse buying, then go home, study what you bought and profit from the experience.

305

Background: Indians of the Southwest are the major producers of silver jewelry. *Most talented and prolific:* Navaho and Zuni. *Also on the market:* Limited amounts of Hopi (known for overlay work) and Santo Domingo (turquoise and shell, sometimes combined with silver or gold).

• **Navaho first-phase jewelry.** The Navaho were the first Indians in the Southwest to work with silver. They learned the craft from the Spanish-Mexicans in the mid-1860s. *Ornaments made for their own use or for trading with other Indians:* Concha belts, najas (bridal decorations), bracelets, squash-blossom necklaces. *Characteristics:* Primitive, simple design with Spanish influence. The quality of silver is often not good, and hairline cracks may be visible. *Cost:* Very expensive.

• **Navaho second phase.** Starting in about 1890 to 1900, they began to use ingots. They embellished traditional designs and used more turquoise. Coral from Europe was introduced around 1910 to 1920.

• **Early tourist jewelry.** This covers 1910 to 1940. Produced for barter with white traders, it included belts, bracelets, boxes, lipstick cases, ashtrays and cigarette holders.

• **Zuni.** After the 1920s, the Zuni began to make silver inlaid with coral, turquoise, mother-of-pearl and jet. They developed the cluster style (clusters of symmetrically shaped stones). They also devised channel work, which is silver strips, typically with beading, outlining shapes in which turquoises are inserted. Generally, Zuni jewelry is more delicate than Navaho.

Since there is very little jewelry on the market from the 1800s, start by buying early tourist jewelry. *Secret:* Buy what can be worn by you or someone close to you unselfconsciously. *Reason to choose:* Because you love the piece.

What to look for: Quality of stones, weight of silver, stamping, craftsmanship and soul. *Problem:* It is difficult to find outstanding examples of all these elements in one piece.

• **Contemporary silver.** If the artist is well known, you often pay more for a new piece than for an old one.

• **Sources.** Flea markets, antique shows, local arts-and-crafts galleries. *Best possibilities:* Indian sidewalk markets on the plazas in Santa Fe and Albuquerque…shops in pueblos and trading posts on reservations.

Collecting Antique Jewelry

Rose Leiman Goldemberg, author of *Antique Jewelry: A Practical and Passionate Guide* (Crown Publishers) and *All About Jewelry* (HarperCollins).

Antique jewelry satisfies a love of the past and the appreciation of fine craftsmanship. It fulfills the expectation that quality jewelry should give pleasure for a long time. In addition, some of the most beautiful and unusual gems and designs can be found in antique pieces.

INVESTMENT: NEW vs. OLD

Despite the fact that the markup on new jewelry is as much as 100%, resale value declines the minute a piece is purchased. Unless a new piece has gemstones that will at least double in value, its worth will decrease drastically in a short time.

Antique jewelry is, of course, also marked up for retail. However, other factors besides gemstones help stabilize and increase its value. Setting, workmanship, style, rarity and history all determine price. Time enhances rather than diminishes value. Excellent antique jewelry nearly always rises in value.

BUYING

Knowledge is essential. Many antique dealers are not well informed about jewelry. Look for a dealer who is long established, and seek personal recommendations from other jewelry collectors.

Browsing to compare prices and learning what you can from books are basic. Auctions can be instructive, but novices are better off out of the bidding until they have some expertise.

PERIODS OF DESIGN

Jewelry styles may overlap decades or be so classic that they are repeated from one era to another. However, one of the most important things to learn is the dominant periods of design. Pieces made before the 18th century are extremely scarce, very expensive and usually impractical to wear. *The following historical periods are the major sources of available antiques...*

Georgian: Jewelry from the early 1700s to approximately 1830 looks different from any other style in history. Its characteristics are well worth studying. Comparative rarity and aesthetic appeal keep its prices high.

Although Georgian gold jewelry appears to be substantial, it is light in weight. Stones were often foiled (backed with colored metal) to enhance their hue. Glass gems, cut and polished as carefully as real ones, were often set in silver. The brilliant-cut diamond was new to the era and popular, but all precious and semiprecious stones were used, as well as natural Oriental pearls, coral and ivory.

Victorian: From 1830 to the turn of the century, a great deal of jewelry was made, and much of it still survives. Victorian jewelry is characterized by massive pieces of heavy gold and silver. Colorful stones and impressive parures (matched sets) were common. Jewelry with sentimental messages was highly popular.

Most available Victorian jewelry is English-made. American-made jewelry, though simpler in design, is scarce and apt to be higher in price.

Art Nouveau: At the end of the Victorian era, the flowing, sensuous lines of Art Nouveau emerged to dominate design. Jewelry became graceful, slender and feminine. Sterling silver was often used, and popular stones were muted in color or even colorless.

Many odd stones were also used, and iridescence was highly regarded. Opals, mother-of-pearl, horn and shell were common. Craftspeople aimed for unique designs. Fakes and reproductions are common.

Art Deco: From World War I to about 1940, the angular, shiny designs of Art Deco came into vogue. Its clean geometric lines and contrasts of black and white are still appealing and very wearable. Onyx, enamel, white gold, crystal, diamonds and jade are characteristic. Although such jewelry is not old enough to qualify as truly antique, the continuing popularity of Art Deco has caused prices to escalate.

CONDITION

Never buy a piece solely because it is old. Antique jewelry should be in good or perfect condition. Damaged jewelry has little resale value.

A 10X jeweler's loupe is essential for the serious collector. Check for glued-in stones, thin ring shanks, and poorly mended or broken parts. Signs of repair or alteration are drawbacks. The jewelry should be very close to its original state. Avoid jewelry that has been put together from various pieces, such as earrings from bits of a necklace.

CARING FOR JEWELRY

If a piece breaks or wears out, it should be repaired by a jeweler who is an expert on antiques. Generally, the less repair the better.

When cleaning, be gentle. When in doubt, do nothing. Avoid overzealous polishing or electronic cleaning. It can be damaging, and it destroys the wonderful patina of age. Soapy water will do for most pieces, but read up on the care and composition of a piece before trying anything.

REAL OR REPRODUCTION?

Honest reproductions are acceptable—but be alert for deception. A reproduction is apt to show signs of haste in its construction. Modern touches such as safety catches are often giveaways. If more than one sample of a certain piece is on display, be leery—few identical pieces survive.

How to Buy Jewelry at Auction And Save

Judith H. McQuown, author of many investment books. She also writes about shopping, antiques and travel.

Clearly, "cutting out the middleman" can save jewelry shoppers thousands of dollars on just one purchase. This is especially true of single diamonds. D color,* the marker of internally flawless stones, sell at auction for much less per karat than the high figures reported in newspapers and magazines. Furthermore, many auction diamonds come with Gemological Institute of America (GIA) certificates that show the weight, color and clarity of the stone.

Expert advice on how to buy at auction depends in part on what you're interested in. If you're buying contemporary jewelry, where the value of the piece lies almost 100% in the gemstones, it's most important to do a little arithmetic to calculate the value of the stones. Divide the presale estimate by the total weight of the stones.

The size of the stone—separate from its weight—affects prices as well. *Example:* Two diamond bracelets may have equal total weights, but the bracelet that has fewer and larger stones will be worth more and will sell for more.

For antique jewelry, where condition can count far more than design, workmanship or the intrinsic value of the gold and gemstones, the rules differ. Reading the description of the piece in the auction catalog and seeing it are far more important. Such words as *repaired, altered, cracked* or *later additions* can lower the value of the piece drastically. Joyce Jonas, former director of the jewelry department of Phillips, New York City, recommends careful examination of the piece before purchasing. According to Jonas, "The most important investment you can make is a 10X jeweler's loupe, which costs less than $25. Carry it with you whenever you're examining jewelry. Look at the front. Look for alterations—the front of a brooch may be pink gold, but the pin in

*D is the highest rating.

back, added later, may be yellow gold. That reduces the value. Look for marks of soldering repair. Gold solder, if used carefully, will not alter the value of the piece. Lead solder, which leaves gray marks, can reduce the price by 50%. Condition is crucial."

Auction houses are legally bound by their catalog descriptions. Look for listed imperfections (often printed in italics), such as *stone missing, stone cracked, lead solder marks, repaired, enamel worn, later additions,* etc. More pleasantly, catalogs also note the shape and weight of large stones (sometimes with GIA diamond ratings), karat of gold (if not listed, it's 14K) and whether a piece is signed. Descriptions are often so detailed that collectors who become familiar with catalogs can visualize the pieces.

If you're planning to buy frequently, make friends with the auction-house jewelry curators. They will often point out the merits or flaws of a piece and can advise you on the maximum reasonable bid. Subscribe to and keep catalogs and lists of prices paid at auctions. They are excellent reference tools in helping you decide how much to bid at future auctions.

When it comes to bidding itself, there are pros and cons to attending the auction in person versus leaving a written bid. Many people, realizing their susceptibility to auction-fever overbidding, find that it's wiser to have a written bid. Others, including many dealers, prefer to attend in person so that they can better control their bidding. Delaying a bid until just before the hammer comes down can get you a piece for a lower price. *Strategy:* If you sit in the rear of the room, you'll be able to see who's bidding against you.

Auctions are generally advertised in the weekend "Arts and Leisure" or "Style" section of major newspapers: *The New York Times, The Boston Globe, The San Francisco Examiner, The Washington Post,* etc. The ads list viewing dates and times (usually three or four days before the auction), as well as the date and time of the auction itself.

Says one collector of antique jewelry, fingering her diamond bracelet, "I could never afford jewelry unless I bought at auction. And I get such a wonderful feeling when I see jewelry in stores that's vastly inferior to mine for thousands of dollars more."

Collecting Carved Chinese Jade

Simone Hartman, collector and co-owner of Rare Art galleries, New York City, Dallas and Palm Beach.

For centuries, jade was the precious gem of the Chinese nobility, and carved jade pieces have long been one of the most important facets of Chinese art and antiques.

Collecting jade is almost as venerable an activity as the art of carving it. Today the center of collecting is the West, where most of the finest antique jade carvings are now found.

Both for aesthetic satisfaction and the potential appreciation in value, jade collecting is attracting wider attention in the US. Good antique jade is still available.

TRUE JADE

Only two minerals, nephrite and jadeite, can truly be called jade. They are very similar but have slightly different compositions. Jadeite was virtually unknown to the Chinese before the 18th century.

Although jade is tough (difficult to shatter), it is not as hard as such gemstones as rubies and emeralds. It can scratch more easily. (Jadeite is the preferred form of jewelry because it is beautifully colored and harder than nephrite.) It is the toughness of jade that lends itself so well to precision carving and accounts for the survivability of antique jade.

To most people, jade means green. However, a great variety of colors are available. Jade is found in natural shades of blue, lavender, white, red and brown as well as green. One of the most prized types of nephrite is called mutton fat for its lustrous grayish-white color with tinges of pale green.

Small jades that are old, historically important, unusually colored and beautifully carved can command steep prices. However, a collector who begins with an investment of several hundred to $1,000 can find a valuable, small jade carving that is 100 to 300 years old. Besides being a fascinating work of art (owners seem to develop an intimate relationship with their small jades), a fine piece is likely to increase in value (with reservations due to uncertain economics).

A good recommendation often followed by new collectors is to specialize. The collector might narrow a collection to only zodiac animals or flowered snuff bottles.

Best: Simple and handmade.

A good carver has made use of the different patterns and textures of the raw material. Even imperfections become part of the design. Much of the carving done in Hong Kong today is machine-powered. Experts feel that something is lost in the process and that the result is often too elaborate. However, Hong Kong is still a source of fine, hand-carved contemporary pieces.

Much of modern jade has been dyed to alter or enhance its natural color. And much "jade" is not jade at all. The commonest substitute is serpentine.

A buyer should beware of both intentional deception and honest mistakes. In addition, jade is very hard to date. Even museum experts can find dating a piece problematical. A trustworthy dealer offers on the bill of sale a description confirming that the item is what it is presented to be.

Attending auctions of Chinese art is one way to learn possibilities and prices. Museum collections also offer a way to survey some of the finest examples of jade workmanship. The Metropolitan Museum of Art in New York City has on permanent display the most impressive pieces from the Bishop Collection, one of the best jade collections in the world.

Collecting Stamps

Bruce Stone, president of Stamp Portfolios, Inc., Stamford, Connecticut.

How much of an initial investment is required if you just want to collect for fun? Not much for starters, and that's one attraction of the hobby. Unlike coins, which are fairly expensive individual items, you can get started in stamps for about $20.

How does one start? By going through a learning curve. Consult the *Yellow Pages* for stamp shops in your area. Meet the owners. Find out about the weekend shows, called *bourses*. Subscribe to philatelic publications.

What are some collecting areas? Topicals are an excellent way to begin. If you have an interest in aviation, for instance, zero in on stamps depicting airplanes. Space stamps are a hot topical. Tropical fish are also popular.

First-day covers are another way to collect. Covers (envelopes) have the stamp canceled at first date of issue, from the town that is issuing for that particular stamp. (*Example:* The cover for the 75th anniversary of flight was issued at Kitty Hawk on December 17, 1978.) Covers bear a cachet (engraving) related to the subject. They are pretty and inexpensive, but they really have no long-term investment value.

Will they appreciate quickly? Slowly, because modern covers are issued in such quantity. Scarcity and historical importance are the key factors in philatelic value. Of course, if you could find a cover dated September 9, 1850, mailed from California, it would bring over $100,000. That's the date California became a state, and such a cover is prized.

How high do prices go? A collector paid $1 million for The Blue Boy, issued at Alexandria, VA, in 1846. This is actually a stampless cover. The postage stamp was invented in England in 1840 but not established in the US until 1847. Before that, letters were either franked (passed by official signature) or paid for on the receiving end.

What about stamps as an investment? Stamps seem to be recession-proof. Between January 2, 1978, and December 31, 1980, the Dow rose 2%. A cross section of 86 classic US stamps rose 85% in value during that same period. Demand for the supply of quality US stamps is great. The number is finite. There are more than 20 million collectors in the US. (Incidentally, over 95% are males. No one has explained that.)

How do you care for stamps? Investment stamps should be kept in a vault and not handled. Hobby stamps are slipped into glassine mounts for safety and arranged in albums.

What's the difference between a stamp collector and a philatelist? In a word, knowledge. A philatelist reads and has an eye toward a specific goal. The choice is limited only by imagination.

Collecting Autographs For Profit

The late Charles Hamilton, founder of Charles Hamilton Galleries, Inc., New York City, the first auction house in the US devoted exclusively to autograph material.

Autograph collecting is not limited to signatures. Collectors look for letters, manuscripts, documents and checks—anything signed or written by someone of interest. Most popular are presidents, composers, authors, scientists, black and feminist leaders and movie stars.

A doctor who is a music lover, for example, may concentrate on the correspondence of famous composers regarding their health. Many collectors strive to complete a "set," such as Pulitzer Prize winners or Mexican War generals.

The classic set of autographs to collect, the signers of the Declaration of Independence (known simply as "Signers"), also contains the most famous of rarities—the signature of Button Gwinnett, a Georgia pig farmer who perished in a duel less than a year after the signing. Genuine examples of Gwinnett's signature (he is frequently forged) have been auctioned for $150,000. A brief receipt signed by Gwinnett brought $100,000 at auction in 1979, the record price paid to date for a single signature.

Inexpensive and easy to find are signatures and signed promotional photographs of many entertainers and athletes, and signatures that have been clipped from the letters or documents they were once part of (a common practice in the 19th century). Complete letters or documents are much more desirable. A handwritten letter, manuscript or diary with historical interest is most valued of all.

WHAT AFFECTS VALUE

• **Content or context.** This extremely important factor brings history alive, thus ensuring enduring worth. A letter or journal by an unknown person describing field conditions during the Civil War is of far greater interest than a note from a famous person saying "Sorry, I can't make it on Tuesday," or "Here's the autograph you requested." Many collectors, especially youngsters, begin by writing to living noteworthies for their autographs. It is preferable to ask an original, thought-provoking question that will elicit a written reply instead of a form letter or a glossy photograph. Even a short response that reveals something of the personality of the writer will be of greater value later on.

Collectors of presidential signatures often prefer examples that date from the term of office. Ironically, it can be harder to find a signed, handwritten letter from a modern president (starting with Theodore Roosevelt) than from one of our "forefathers."

Reason: The advent of the proxy signature, the typewriter and the autopen. A signed, handwritten letter from President Ronald Reagan (during his administration or after) sells for $15,000. But signed typewritten letters from Ronald Reagan before he became president sell for $50 to $500, depending on their content.

• **Rarity.** The collector must learn what is scarce or common in his or her own field. Abraham Lincoln signed thousands of military appointments during the Civil War, but complete letters and signed photographs are rare. Charles Dickens seems to have written letters

daily throughout his long life, while Edgar Allan Poe's signature tempts the finest forgers.

• **Demand.** This has more to do with fashion than with fame. Even a figure as revered as Sir Winston Churchill could easily follow his predecessor, David Lloyd George, into relative obscurity as public attention shifts. A rare contract signed by ragtime composer Scott Joplin was sold for $5,000, outpricing a comparable piece by Beethoven.

As a general rule, villains outsell good guys. A John Wilkes Booth signature outprices Lincoln's, while Lee Harvey Oswald's is worth more than JFK's. Murderers' and Nazis' signatures are likely to remain popular.

• **Condition.** The strength and clarity of a signature, size and length of the material, condition of the paper and postal markings, among other variables, all affect the value of a piece. *Important:* Do not attempt repairs yourself. Never use cellophane tape on old papers.

• **Display.** The value of any collection can be enhanced by creative, attractive framing. Even inexpensive signatures take on new life when mounted with a portrait of the subject. Contemporary newspaper clippings, program covers or tickets, reproductions of documents and artwork can make exciting companion pieces of autograph material, as can early daguerreotypes, engravings, posters or other historical ephemera. Striking graphic design adds to the fun, and for this, a skilled professional framer is necessary. *Examples:* Irving Berlin's autograph, mounted on a background of red, white and blue stripes with his photograph and the original sheet music to *This Is the Army.* A check signed by Orville Wright, mounted next to an early photograph of his airplane. A Bela Lugosi autograph, set against a black cutout of a bat, beneath an early still from *Dracula.*

INVESTING AND THE MARKET

Unlike other collecting areas, there has been no slump in the market for autographs. Record prices continue to be set. This seems to be due to our increasing awareness of the importance of our cultural heritage, along with the desire to preserve as much as possible in this age of the telephone.

For investment purposes: Specialize in several areas at once. Perhaps interest in the American West will decline, while the astronauts hold their value—or vice versa. Select your purchases for the interest of their content or their relevance to a historical event. Don't be afraid to pay healthy prices for important material.

Private dealers and auction houses who will vouch for the authenticity of their material are the best sources for important pieces. A thorough knowledge of one's field is necessary to be able to recognize chance finds should they occur. Be careful of inscriptions in the flyleaves of old books, a favorite ground for the forger. Check the drawers in antique furniture, and don't throw out old family papers before consulting an expert.

For further reading: *Collecting Autographs and Manuscripts* by Charles Hamilton (Modoc Press).

Collectors' organization: Universal Autograph Collectors Club (UACC), 9669 Whirlaway St., Rancho Cucamonga, California 91737. Publishes the bimonthly journal *The Pen & Quill. www.uacc.org*

Collecting Maps

Ruth Shevin, late map specialist at the Argosy Gallery, New York City.

Mapmaking goes back to at least 2300 BC, which is the date of the earliest known clay picture of how to get from one place to another—found in Iraq. We know that the ancient Chinese made sophisticated silk maps, Eskimos carved maps in ivory, the Incas etched them in stone and prehistoric Europeans drew them on cave walls.

Collectors revere maps for a number of reasons. Many old maps are beautiful (all early world maps are fanciful as well) and very decorative. Historians look for changing political boundaries, documents of military campaigns or journeys of early explorers. Homebodies like to trace changes in their country or city layout over the years.

• **Early maps.** Maps from the Middle Ages—now seen in museums and libraries—were more symbolic and religious than realistic. World views included imaginary places or vast expanses of terra incognita, often with remarkable creatures to match. These delusions and distortions are the delight of collectors, but their rarity makes them irreplaceable treasures.

Maps for practical purposes began to proliferate in the 15th century with the establishment of printing. Explorers needed up-to-date guides to the oceans and lands of the world. They helped to chart new areas and revise old standards. Although it is possible for a collector to find a 16th-century map, it will cost in the thousands. Prices for 17th- and 18th-century maps—most are pages from bound atlases—will vary according to scarcity and demand. Good reproductions of such maps, while handsome and interesting, are of no investment value, so collectors must be careful of their sources.

• **19th-century maps.** Fine examples of these more recent world or local maps can be bought for less than $100. Some come from atlases. Others are official maps used to define states or territories. US Geological Survey maps, published since 1879, indicate elevation, roads, swamps, railway stations and churches. Many early city maps show landmark buildings in addition to the streets. Particularly popular at the moment are maps of the American West.

• **20th-century maps.** Even early 1900s maps are of little value so far. Dealers do not yet carry them, so the interested collector must cull flea markets and garage sales.

DETERMINING VALUE

Rarity, authenticity, beauty and condition make a map valuable. Even maps that were run off on printing presses in great numbers can become quite scarce over time. The paper they are printed on is fragile, for they were never meant to endure. When a map gets out of date, for whatever reason, it faces what one expert calls "a dangerous interval of vulnerability" during which it has no value in contemporary, practical terms and yet arouses little interest in the scholar or historian. Not many maps survive that interval.

Determining the authenticity of old maps is difficult. The best protection is knowledgeable dealers who stand behind what they sell. (A good dealer will also search for specific maps for you.) Although beauty is in the eye of the beholder, condition is an obvious asset to an old map. Creases hurt a map, so potential collectibles should be stored flat.

LEARNING THE ROPES

A beginning collector must start by browsing and reading. Most major libraries have cartography sections with a variety of maps and books on mapmaking that can help you zero in on the types that most interest you. A good general book on the subject is *The Mapmakers* by John Noble Wilford (Knopf). Many libraries also have dealers' catalogs that can give you a sense of what is available and the going prices.

Great Britain is the world center for map collecting. In the US, a few major dealers specialize in maps, and interest here is picking up rapidly. A directory of antique-map dealers is available on-line at *www.cosmography.com*.

Collecting Firearms

R.L. Wilson, historical consultant for Colt Firearms Division.

Firearms are among the oldest and most distinguished collectibles. (Henry VIII was a keen collector, as were George Washington and Thomas Jefferson.) And because firearms have been made since the 14th century, the field is vast. No individual can be expert in every aspect.

Most US collectors concentrate on Americana. For the past 40 years, they have tended to specialize—even down to a single gun series. A collector might choose the Colt Single Action Army group, the guns you see in Western movies, for example. They were called "the peacemakers" and "the thumb busters." The US Army adopted this series as a standard sidearm in 1873.

What are the criteria for collecting? Aesthetics play a great role. The finer guns are exquisite. The engraving can be compared with the work of Fabergé. Historical relevance is important, and so is condition. But quality and maker count more. Even excellent condition cannot make an ugly gun desirable. Add the allure of fine mechanics and also romance. Can you imagine Buffalo Bill without his six-shooters and Winchester rifles?

Who were the leading makers? The big four are Colt, founded in 1836; Remington, founded in 1816; Winchester, founded in 1866 but really dating from 1852, the same year as Smith & Wesson. (The last two companies trace their origin to the same firm.)

What about guns not from those firms? Many are very desirable. Tiffany was big in the gun business until 1911. And the Kentucky rifle (in excellent condition) is a classic collectible. These date from the early 18th century and continued to be made for about 100 years. They were made in small workshops, often by wonderful craftsmen. Kentucky rifles sell for $5,000 and up. One of them, circa 1810, sold for $103,500 in November 2004.

Are pairs more valuable than singles? Yes, indeed. *Also triplets:* A rifle, a revolver and a knife made as a set, for example.

Some collectors specialize in miniatures. These tiny weapons were a test of the gunsmith's art, and they were made for fun. (You can fire the little guns, though it's not advisable.) A society of miniature collectors exists.

Modern engraved guns are also very collectible. In the past few years, they've become a $25-million-per-year business. Colt, Remington and Winchester (among others) make these specialty firearms. The craftsmanship is magnificent. Some are the equal of anything done in the past. These are not replicas, and owners do not discharge them. One reason for collecting modern firearms is assurance of authenticity. However, after 1840 most US firearms were given serial numbers. If you own a weapon made after that date, a factory may have it on record.

How do you care for a collection? Rust is the great enemy. Try a light film of oil. Put on a pair of white cotton gloves, spray oil on the palm of one glove and rub the gun with it. If you use a rag, sweat from your hand will eventually mingle with the oil.

Should fine weapons ever be fired? Never! Well, hardly ever—only if the antique arm is not of much value. Black powder, outdated in the 1890s, is still available for shooting today. It is corrosive to metal and scars wood. If you do wish to shoot antique-type guns, you should buy replicas. About $100 million is spent on them annually. Even if black powder isn't used, wear and tear on the firearm lowers its value. Excessive refinishing or polishing is also not recommended.

Do you need a license for antique guns? Generally not, if they were made before 1898, the federal cutoff. But check with local authorities.

Gun collecting is expensive. How much should you spend? A few hundred dollars at the least—you can find very good sidearms from the 19th century for that price. However, before you invest any money, spend several hundred hours studying. There are over 12,000 books on the subject, but you should begin with the basic *Flayderman's Guide to Antique American Firearms and Their Values* by Norm Flayderman (Krause Publications).

Collecting Old Trains

Alan Spitz, owner of The Red Caboose, New York City, and the late Bruce Manson, editor emeritus of *Train Collectors Quarterly.*

Many children remember the thrill of receiving their first model train set. Some people like to recapture the excitement as adults, by collecting model trains as either a hobby or an investment or both. Certain old model railroad cars and sets have become so expensive that counterfeiters are making forgeries. Although most collectors are train buffs who belong to model railroad societies throughout the country and often attend "train swaps," the collectors also include some famous names. The late former newscaster Tom Snyder is a collector, as was the late Graham Claytor, former secretary of the Navy. Mick Jagger occasionally buys Lionel.

Finding bargains is difficult. Don't expect to discover valuable old train sets at garage sales or country auctions. Train collecting is a well-explored area. A price guide to all old Lionel cars is available, *Greenberg's Guide to Lionel Trains: Pocket Price Guide 1901-2010,* by Bruce C. Greenberg (Kalmbach Publishing).

Top collectors' items in the US consist primarily of pre-World War II standard-gauge Lionel cars. (Standard gauge refers to the 2⅛-inch width popular before the war.) Lionel stopped making the large-size sets in 1939 because the metals were needed for the war. Afterward, all trains were smaller. Other makes collected include American Flyer and Ives. (Both of these firms eventually merged with Lionel, so there is not such a large pool of items.) Marx was the manufacturer of smaller, cheaper trains that were sold through Woolworth's and other variety stores. They were eventually bought by Quaker Oats, and the line was discontinued. Marklin, a German manufacturer that began making trains in 1856, is the most prominent European producer.

[The highest price on record for a model train is $110,000, paid for a Marklin brass gauge I "circus train," which was sold at auction in 2004.] More expensive purchases may have been made privately, but there is no record of them.

The age of trains does not necessarily determine their price. Scarcity and demand are more important factors. *Example:* Any Lionel train with a Disney motif is likely to be very valuable. Lionel made an entire Disney circus train. In this case, the market is not limited to train buffs. Circus memorabilia collectors and Disney collectors also covet these trains.

Another rarity: Lionel made a special train for girls in the 1950s. The locomotive was pink and the caboose was blue. It sold poorly, and Lionel did not produce very many. Some dealers painted the trains black to get rid of them.

Those that are still pink and blue are therefore very valuable.

Reproductions: There are counterfeiters who may also call themselves restorers because they rebuild damaged trains. These trains are not very valuable. Some may be as much as 75% restored, in which case they are, for all intents and purposes, counterfeit. The most valuable trains are "in the box" or in mint condition. Since many trains were made of a zinc alloy called Zamac, which frequently became contaminated with other substances and disintegrated, many cars are partially original and partially restored.

How to tell: Lettering on counterfeit and restored pieces is usually stamped instead of using the old decal lettering. *Another tell-tale sign:* Original Lionel trains were dipped in paint. People should look for marks and imperfections in the paint job. Today, people spray-paint the cars, so it is easy to tell the difference. Other differences are more subtle, and it takes a great amount of expertise to distinguish a reproduction from an original.

Modern pieces: Manufacturing for the collector has become an important part of Lionel's business now. *Example:* The GG1 was first put on sale in 1956 for $49.95. When Lionel remade it in the 1970s, the list price was approximately $320. Not many parents spend that much on children's toys, but an investor might be interested.

Specializing: Many serious train buffs specialize in a single item, such as Number 8 locomotives or a certain kind of boxcar. There is a broad spectrum.

Displaying trains: While many collectors like setups (tracks on which the trains run), collector's items should be kept on display shelves.

Collecting Seashells

Jerome M. Eisenberg, director, Royal-Athena Galleries, and the late William Gera, The Collector's Cabinet, both in New York City.

She sells seashells by the seashore—and in cities, museum shops and through the mail. You can buy your shells or you can have the pleasure of finding them yourself. You needn't worry about investment, auctions or authenticity. Shell collecting is a just-for-the-fun-of-it hobby.

Begin by collecting as many types of shells as appeal to you. This way you can learn their names and become familiar with the distinctive qualities of each type. Most collectors are eventually drawn to one or two species and narrow their scope.

Prices within every species can range from 25¢ to several thousand dollars. But it is easy to put together a very broad collection of several thousand shells for $1 to $10 apiece, with an occasional splurge into the $20 to $25 range.

MOST POPULAR SPECIES

• **Cones (Conus).** Cone-shaped shells that exhibit an astonishing variety in pattern and color. One, *Conus bengalensis*, brought the record price ($2,510) for a shell sold at auction. At the time, it was only the fourth specimen known. However, several more were found shortly thereafter. It may now sell for $400 to $750, which is a warning to would-be investors. *C. textile:* Named for its wonderful repeating pattern, which resembles a Diane von Furstenberg knit. *C. marmoreus:* The model for a well-known Rembrandt etching.

• **Cowries (Cypraea).** Very rounded shells, with lips rolled inward to reveal regularly spaced teeth. Naturally so smooth, hard and glossy that they appear to have been lacquered, they are often considered the most pleasurable shells to handle. *Cypraea aurantium:* Deep orange—a classic rarity. The famous tiger cowrie, *C. tigris*, is speckled brown and white. *C. mappa:* Striking pattern resembles an antique map.

315

• **Murexes.** Swirling shells favored for their pointy spines, though many are delicate and hard to store. *Murex pecten (Venus comb):* Spectacular curving spires. *M. palmarosae:* Rose-branched murex, has floriate tips. *M. erythrostomus:* Has ladylike white ruffles and a luscious pink mouth.

• **Scallops (Pectens).** Shaped like ribbed fans in surprisingly intense reds, oranges, yellows and purples.

• **Volutes (Voluta) and Olives (Oliva).** Equally popular species. Best-loved classics are the triton *(Charonia tritonis)* and the chambered *Nautilus pompilus.*

Choose live-collected specimen shells in perfect or near-perfect condition, without natural flaws or broken spines or tips. Avoid lacquered shells and ground lips (an edge that has been filed will feel blunt rather than sharp). A label should accompany each shell, with its scientific name and location information.

Dealers have a worldwide selection of shells, access to professionally collected deep-sea varieties and experience in identifying tricky species. Dealers advertise in shell-collecting periodicals, and most sell through the mail or online.

Clubs provide contacts to trade with, up-to-date information on species, travel opportunities and techniques for cleaning and storage. Check the Internet or contact the nearest natural-history museum to find a local club.

The most colorful shells are found near coral reefs in tropical waters. Many areas offer special arrangements for shell collectors, from boat trips to uncombed beaches to guided snorkeling or scuba diving. Much of Southern California and Australia's Great Barrier Reef are closed or limited for environmental reasons.

Sanibel Island, Florida, is the best-known shelling spot in the US. It is especially well geared to the collector. Contact the Chamber of Commerce for online information, *www.sanibel-captiva.org.* Costa Rica offers both Atlantic and Pacific varieties, with pre-Colombian ruins as an added attraction. The Philippine Islands are known for their many local dealers and good values, as well as for fine beachcombing, snorkeling and diving. Cabo San Lucas, Mexico, on the southern tip of the Baja Peninsula, and the Portuguese Cape Verde Islands off Senegal offer great shelling.

Of course, you need never go near an ocean to start a fine collection of seashells. If camping in the mountains or dining in Paris is more to your taste, just bring along your copy of *Hawaiian Shell News.*

Great Web Sites For Train Lovers

The Web site Trains.com, *http://trc.trains.com,* offers links to sites for train lines in the US and overseas plus train organizations and railroad museums. Railpace, *www.railpace.com,* is the Web site for *Railpace Newsmagazine*—which focuses on the northeastern US. Railserve, *www.railserve.com,* has links to everything from model railroading to rail passenger lines worldwide. *Railway Preservation News, www.rypn.org,* is an online magazine about railway history and preservation.

Nancy Dunnan, publisher, *TravelSmart,* Box 397, Dobbs Ferry, New York 10522. 800-FARE-OFF (800-327-3633), *www.travelsmartnewsletter.com.*

Collecting Dolls

Collectors of fine art and antiques have discovered dolls in recent years. Dolls have surpassed coins in popularity and are now the world's second-largest collectible. (Stamps are number one.) The attractions are not only the investment potential of dolls but also their aesthetic appeal and cultural and historical significance.

Most collectors concentrate their attention on the "golden age of doll making" from 1840 to 1920, on modern dolls from 1920 to 1950, on artists' dolls from 1910 to the present or on such contemporary dolls as Shirley Temple and Barbie.

The doll market does not suffer from recession as do coins and stamps. *Reason:* Doll collectors are accumulators. Coin collectors don't buy multiples of the same thing, except for examples in better condition or for trading, but doll collectors do. One collector with 50 Brus (valuable French dolls) has 12 of the same size and mold number, yet each one is different because they are handmade and hand-decorated.

Dolls have "presence"—recognizable characteristics and humanlike personalities. As collectors grow more sophisticated, they become more aware of these distinctive characteristics and can recognize dolls they have seen before.

GOOD BUYS IN OLD DOLLS

• **German character dolls made between 1900 and 1917** by Simon & Halbig or Kammer and Reinhardt.

• **All dolls made by American artists.** The Georgene Averill baby has doubled in value in recent years.

• **Kamkins dolls made by Louise Kampus.** Buy any that is reasonably clean.

• **Kewpie dolls** (not figurines) are all good investments.

NEW DOLLS WITH POTENTIAL

• **Original creations** of members of the National Institute of American Doll Artists.

• **German dolls by Kathe Kruse.**

• **Steiff stuffed animals** (keep the tag and pin that come with them).

ADVICE TO NEW COLLECTORS

• **Educate yourself.** People who are in a hurry make mistakes. Become familiar with dolls. There are several excellent museums. *Leading ones:* The Strong Museum in Rochester, New York, and the doll collections at the Smithsonian Institution in Washington, DC.

A better way to learn about dolls: Visit stores and antique shows where you can touch and handle the dolls.

Guidelines: Many dolls are easy to identify because most manufacturers of bisque dolls numbered them. (Bisque is a form of china introduced in 1870 and used extensively until 1940.) But get a guarantee when you buy. Anyone who purchases a valuable object should be able to sell it back at any time. However, a guarantee is only as good as the dealer.

Dangerous buy: A damaged doll. You can't go wrong paying $500 for a damaged Bru doll worth $8,000—the parts alone are worth that. But don't pay $5,000. A damaged doll will always be a damaged doll.

Many people have dolls stored in attics, basements or closets. One woman heard a description of a rare doll on television. She realized she had just thrown away a similar doll. She retrieved it from the trash can and sold it for $16,500, an American record for a doll sold at auction.

George and Florence Theriault, Dollmasters, Annapolis, MD.

• **The 1959 Barbie doll that cost $3 may now bring up to $10,000**—but only if it's in mint condition, with original striped bathing suit and gold earrings. And if you've lost the box, you've lost half the value. *Rule of thumb:* The more common the doll, the better shape it must be in.

Collecting Comic Books

Michael Feuerstein, owner of M&M Comics, Nyack, New York.

Comic books sell for as little as 15¢ each and for as much as $75,000. It is estimated that there are over 100,000 collectors in the US.

When did comic books begin? There were comics in the 1920s, but they were reprints of newspaper strips. The first "superhero" comic book, *Action Comics No. 1*, was issued in 1938. The early books had 64 pages, with five or six stories featuring different heroes, and sold for 10¢.

What are the criteria for establishing worth? The first issue of anything is going to be the most valuable. The spread in price between the first issue and the second one is always great. A first issue may be worth $100 and the next only $35.

Condition is extremely important. Ten years or so ago, you'd have paid twice as much for a comic book in mint condition (practically untouched) as for a well-read one. Now if a mint book is worth $1,000, the same in well-read condition brings only $200. Mint condition is particularly important for books from the 1960s.

Scarcity also determines value. Books from the 1930s and early 1940s are rarest. Fewer were issued, and wartime paper drives prompted patriots to donate their collections.

How do you define scarce? Scarce is under a hundred known copies. Under 25 is considered rare.

How is a collection built? Usually collectors will try to get every issue of a particular title. It isn't easy, but the chase is part of the fun.

How do you decide on a title? Often nostalgia. Older collectors want comics from the Golden Age, from 1938 to 1956. After that, it's the Silver Age, starting with *The Flash*, a new character, in 1956.

How should one buy contemporary comics with an eye to future collectibility? Look for a good story line, superior artwork and popularity with fans. But what ultimately will determine a comic book's collectibility is its physical condition, scarcity and desirability. These factors are impossible to predict. So collect comics that you like, and keep them in great condition.

What about cartoon animals and other categories? The Walt Disney characters, especially those drawn by Carl Barks, appeal to specialists. A few of the scarcest sell for thousands of dollars. *Big Little Books*, small, thick and hardbound, may range from $3 to $350. *Classic Comics* appeal to some older collectors. There's a trap in the *Classics*. They were used in schools and reprinted every six months from the original plates. The dates were not changed. Many people who think they have originals actually have valueless reprints.

How should comic books be stored? Upright, in a box of some sort. Never store them flat—the spines of the bottom books

will become crushed. Also, you must handle them all to get at the lower ones. For valuable books, use inert plastic mylar cases.

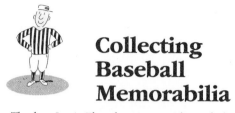

Collecting Baseball Memorabilia

The late Louis Ehrenkrantz, president of Ehrenkrantz King Nussbaum Inc., New York City.

When most people think of collecting baseball memorabilia, they think first of cards. Cards with players' pictures have been issued since the early days of the game, first by tobacco companies and more recently by chewing gum companies.

It's too late, from the viewpoint of investment, to collect cards. Recent cards will probably not be a collectible in the future.

Look back to the last era when people identified with baseball as the true national game, the late 1950s. Collect game programs, autographs and *Baseball Registers* from that time. For example, if you were a Dodger fan as a kid, you might like to have a number of old Ebbets Field programs.

An item that has gone up in value every year for the past 25 years is a publication called *The Baseball Register*. It's put out by *The Sporting News* and is a record of everything that happens in the major and minor leagues in a single year, including the results of every game played. Like any good investable book, it's rare. There's only one first edition. [The 1981 *Baseball Register* is bound to be worth something—a game-by-game record of the craziest season that ever was, and a whole history of the seven-week strike.]

Autographs from 1930 to 1950 are desirable, especially from good players who didn't give them out too freely. That said, Jackie Robinson and Babe Ruth both gave away a lot of autographs, but their signatures can still fetch thousands of dollars.

Buy autographs only from authorized dealers so you'll know they're not fakes. But you can buy game programs, *Baseball Register*s and old baseball magazines from anyone. They're self-explanatory.

Cards are not the repositories of our memories anymore. What is? Television. For earlier fans, radio. Old audiotapes by announcers Red Barber and Mel Allen would be worth a fortune.

Collecting Antique Playing Cards

Antique playing cards are amusing, interesting, inexpensive and, possibly, undervalued (worthwhile ones may start as low as $50). But collect them only for sheer pleasure…a buyer might be hard to find.

Popular Sheet Music

David A. Jasen, former vice president of the New York Sheet Music Society and author of *Rags and Ragtime* (Dover Publishing).

The mass production of sheet music of popular songs is a uniquely American commercial phenomenon that started in the early 19th century and began to wane only with the popularity of the phonograph record at the time of World War I.

Few titles or editions of the 2 million songs published in the past 150 years are of investment value. An early printing of *The Star-Spangled Banner* (1814) is worth about $35,000. Civil War songs are valuable because of their scarcity.

And original printings of Scott Joplin rags can bring as much as $2,000 at auction because jazz buffs have recognized the musical importance of 1890s ragtime tunes.

But most sheet music is collected for fun— by era, by subject, by composer or by the artwork on the cover. At one time the staple of home entertainment, sheet music was popular music that could be easily played on the piano and sung in groups, and it reflected the popular culture of its time.

Early-19th-century songs told stories of romantic love, tragic death, home and mother. Minstrel-show music was catchy and sentimental (like Stephen Foster's songs).

After the Civil War, songs were topical: *The Price of Meat Is Going Up Again* is just one example. Typical lyrics discussed the stock market, sports fads, inventions and social scandals. Sheet music became big business in the 1890s with *After the Ball* by Charles K. Harris, a best-seller that earned up to $25,000 a week.

The sheet-music industry was concentrated on New York City's 28th Street, dubbed Tin Pan Alley. Songs at the turn of the 20th century could sell a million copies or more, and these songs are the ones that are now most frequently collected.

Where to find sheet music: There are few dealers who specialize in it. Flea markets, thrift shops and even garage sales are good places to start. Be prepared to plow through dusty cartons. Ephemera shops usually carry some sheet music.

Offers are made in the newsletter of a national collectors' group. For more information, contact the New York Sheet Music Society at *www.nysms.org*.

Collecting Stock Certificates

Edward Mendlowitz, CPA, partner, WithumSmith+ Brown, 1 Spring St., New Brunswick, New Jersey 08901. *www.withum.com*

One type of certificate is "live" certificates, representing ownership in a company. These have wonderful engraved designs, called vignettes. (The New York and American Stock Exchanges require that all certificates carry a genuine engraving and a design with tones. This makes counterfeiting more difficult.) There are advantages to owning a single share in a company. You are on the company's mailing list and receive all financial information, including the annual report, which can be a collectible.

For someone starting a current collection, the following is recommended: One share each of Playboy Enterprises, Wells Fargo, Lion Country Safari, International Bank Note and Toro. These beautifully engraved stock certificates represent the New York and American Stock Exchanges as well as over-the-counter trading. Also, International Bank Note's annual report is quite a work of art.

Another collection you might want to start is of used, canceled stock certificates. Certain certificates are part of American financial history. For example, you might find an American Express certificate that was issued in the 1860s and signed by Mr. Wells and Mr. Fargo, then president and secretary of the company, respectively. (Many people's major interest in certificates is the autograph.) Millard Fillmore, John D. Rockefeller and Jay Gould once signed stock certificates.

One valuable certificate: Standard Oil, signed by John D. Rockefeller, which is worth approximately $4,500.

Old certificates needn't cost a lot of money. You can buy 20 to 30 for around $50. Some collectors specialize. They'll collect only oil companies or railroads, or only New York railroads, but you don't have to specialize. You should collect certificates for the fun of it as well as for the investment value.

Collecting Celebrity Memorabilia

Pamela Brown Sherer, Sotheby's York Avenue Galleries, and Julie Collier, Christie's, both in New York City.

Do you remember Rosebud, the sled that meant so much to Orson Welles' character in the 1941 film *Citizen Kane?* Rosebud means a lot to well-heeled movie buffs, too—the sled fetched $60,500 (including the buyer's fee) at Sotheby's New York.

Collectors have long cherished relics of the famous, and a market in celebrities' artifacts is well established. It was sparked by auction houses that found a willing market for television and movie memorabilia.

EXAMPLES

Christie's East, New York, sold a pair of ruby slippers worn by Judy Garland in the 1939 film *The Wizard of Oz* for $165,000 in June 1988—and sold again in May 2000 for $666,000. Few movies are strong enough in themselves to draw high prices for props or clothing. What could vie with the ruby slippers? Probably only a very recognizable item, such as a gown (in good condition) worn by Vivien Leigh in *Gone With the Wind.*

A Walter Plunkett costume sketch of Vivian Leigh in *Gone With the Wind* sold for $35,000 in April 2005. At a Profiles in History auction, Margaret Hamilton's Wicked Witch of the West hat from *The Wizard of Oz* sold for $54,625.

Who collects: A mixed group—friends of the famous as well as fans. Investment is always a consideration, but it takes a backseat to nostalgia.

The future: Hollywood memorabilia and collectibles will continue to be a hot market.

Collecting Butterflies

Michael Berman, The Butterfly Company, New York.

Papillon, *Schmetterling, farfalla,* mariposa —in almost any language, the word for butterfly trips across the tongue like the flitting, colorful creature it describes. Butterflies were held in lofty esteem by the ancient Greeks and by the early Christians, who saw in them symbols of the human soul.

The common names for some favorite butterflies range from painted ladies, jezebels, and jungle queens to emperors, rajas and Apollos. Ironically, these short-lived symbols of transient beauty, once captured and carefully mounted in a collector's cabinet, retain their shimmering colors for centuries, like frozen rainbows.

The lover of lepidoptera (butterflies and moths) must also be a lover of labels. There are 140,000 species of lepidoptera, about

20,000 of them butterflies. If the prospect of learning 20,000 scientific names is enough to give you butterflies in your stomach, you will understand why most collectors specialize in one family of butterflies (lepidopterists generally agree on 15 basic families) or further limit themselves to one genus or even to one species. Within any family, the price for a single specimen can range from less than $1 to several hundred dollars. Only extreme rarities sell for $1,000 or above. Females may be more costly than males because they are often left in the field to breed.

MAJOR COLLECTING CATEGORIES

• **Morphiodae** (Morphos) are the most popular (and flashy) butterflies to collect. The Morpho genus is conveniently small, about 80 species. What attracts collectors is their intense color—a dazzling, metallic blue that reflects light like satin, changing from deepest navy to royal blue to icy turquoise as one moves past them. Other morphos, patterned like watered silk, appear to be translucent white until, as one moves closer, they show subtle, opalescent colors, such as mother-of-pearl.

Examples: The large Peruvian morpho didius, an iridescent blue outlined in black, is extremely popular. A female, in softer pastels, sells for more.

• **Papilionidae is a family of about 700 species.** Particularly sought are the various swallowtails and the *Ornithoptera,* or "birdwings," including the largest-known butterfly, *Ornithoptera alexandrae.*

• **Nymphalidae contains several thousand species.** *Some of the subgroups most favored by collectors: Vanessidi* (vanessas), *Charaxes* (rajas), *Argrias* (a rare and expensive genus) and many others equally showy and varied, with colors, patterns and wing shapes resembling laces, leaves, Rorschach tests, stars in a night sky, maps, Dubuffet designs in magic marker, animals' eyes and Florentine bargello. An extreme rarity is the African species *Charaxes fournierae,* which may be worth more than $1,000 per pair.

Butterfly values are determined almost exclusively by their rarity. In this era of ecological abuse and species protection, this can be a tricky business, however, and it doesn't always work the way one might expect. For example, the *O. rothschildi,* for years worth $150 per pair, may only sell for $20.

Reason: A few years ago, it was bred in captivity and then released by the government, so it has become fairly common. Of course, the inverse is more often true. Fire or construction can wipe out a habitat in a short time. [The top price ever paid for a single butterfly was $2,436 brought by an *O. allotei* from the Solomon Islands at the 1966 sale of the Rousseau Decelle collection.]

Sets of 10 or so different butterflies are available for very little from hobby shops and on-line or mail-order dealers. The new collector must learn to mount specimens in open-wing position. Mounting equipment and instructions are available from the same sources.

Butterflies are usually kept in flat cases with glass or Plexiglas dustcovers that can be stored away from the light. A small container of mothballs in the storage area prevents other insects from attacking the collection. Some species, including many morphos, have greasy bodies that can harm the delicate wings. After the butterfly is mounted, the body can then be replaced with a dab of glue.

Buy only perfect specimens. Be sure each comes with its identification and date and location of capture for your labels.

The International Butterfly Book by Paul Smart is a good source of information. It's out of print but is available in many libraries.

Appraising Your Valuables

Valuable items worth over $100 should have written appraisals every two years. Replacement values change with current-day economics.

American Society of Appraisers, New York City. *www.appraisers.org*

Buying and Selling Collectibles on the Internet

Malcolm Katt, Millwood, New York–based antique dealer, also owner of Millwood Gallery, which specializes in militaria.

The volume of business on the Internet's collectible auction markets has exploded, and for very good reasons. *Collectible trading on the Internet gives you...*

• **Secure, anonymous, cheap and effortless access** to collectors all over the world.

• **The chance to view pictures of the thousands of items that are for sale** in your special field of collecting—no matter how quirky it is.

• **The opportunity to make a few extra dollars**—or a few thousand.

• **A fascinating entrance to the information superhighway**—if you're not there yet.

• **The possibility of developing friendships** through E-mail exchanges with other collectors.

If you're a serious collector, you may have to go online. [It has been estimated that within the next five years, 50% of all collectible sales will take place over the Internet.]

Fact: The world's largest Internet trading service, eBay, was started in September 1995 as a way to help its founder's girlfriend sell her collection of Pez dispensers. (The company went public in September 1998. The founder became a billionaire in only three years!)

BUYING AND SELLING ONLINE

Popular Internet auction sites are...

• *www.ebay.com*

• *www.amazon.com*

eBay is the biggest by far. Millions of people have used eBay to buy and sell merchandise in thousands of categories—from Beanie Babies to books. Every day there are millions of "page views," that is, viewings by potential buyers checking out wares.

What does it cost? Online auction companies typically charge an "insertion fee" for listing an item and a commission based on the selling price, plus other fees.

There are several software programs available to help sellers manage online selling. Check at a computer- or office-supplies store.

To be a buyer online: Register at one of the auction sites. Fill out an online application that includes your name and mailing address. You should never have to reveal your Social Security or credit card number. *Details...*

• **You are described online** only by a code name you have selected.

• **The highest bidder is notified by E-mail** and contacted by the seller to arrange payment.

• **Payment is made directly to the seller** by check or money order.

SAFEGUARDS

The buyer has the ability to verify the seller's honesty by checking a "feedback" rating. So, you can avoid dealing with individuals whose ratings raise questions.

Sellers receive positive, negative or neutral comments from previous buyers.

On eBay, if a seller has too many negative comments, he or she can be terminated from using the service.

Keep in mind that reputable sellers give the buyer the opportunity to return the item if unsatisfied for a valid reason.

Online escrow services for expensive items are also available.

There is no fee to view, bid and buy online. The seller pays the insertion fee and commission. Buyers typically pay for postage and insurance.

BUYER, BEWARE

Just like written descriptions, a photo seen on a small screen does not always reveal damage or problems that the seller has overlooked.

Remember that buying online is no different from buying in person. Often the seller is ignorant of what he is offering or is purposely deceitful. As always, *buyer beware.*

Portrait Photography Secrets

People are the most popular subject for photography. People pictures are our most treasured keepsakes. There are ways to turn snapshots of family and friends into memorable portraits.

TECHNIQUES

• **Get close.** Too much landscape overwhelms the subject.

• **Keep the head high in the frame as you compose the shot.** Particularly from a distance, centering the head leaves too much blank background and cuts off the body arbitrarily.

• **Avoid straight rows of heads in group shots.** It's better to have some subjects stand and others sit in a two-level setting.

• **Pose subjects in natural situations,** doing what they like to do—petting the cat, playing the piano and the like.

• **Simplify backgrounds.** Clutter is distracting. *Trick:* Use a large aperture (small f-stop number) to throw the background out of focus and highlight the subject.

• **Beware of harsh shadows.** The human eye accommodates greater contrast of light to dark than does a photographic system. Either shadows or highlights will be lost in the picture, usually the shadowed area.

FOR OUTDOOR PORTRAITS

• **Avoid the midday sun.** This light produces harsh shadows and makes people squint. Hazy sun, often found in the morning, is good. Cloudy days give a lovely, soft effect.

• **Use fill light to cut shadows.** A flash can be used outdoors, but it is hard to compute correctly. *Best fill-light method:* Ask someone to hold a large white card or white cloth near the subject to bounce the natural light into the shadowed area.

• **Use backlight.** When the sun is behind the subject (but out of the picture), the face receives a soft light. With a simple camera, the cloudy setting is correct. If your camera has a light meter, take a reading close to the subject or, from a distance, increase the exposure one or two stops from what the meter indicates.

• **Beware of dappled shade.** The effect created in the photograph will be disturbing.

FOR INDOOR PORTRAITS

• **Use window light.** A bright window out of direct sun is a good choice. However, if there is high contrast between the window light and the rest of the room, use filter-light techniques to diminish the shadow.

• **Use a flash.** A unit with a tilting head allows you to light the subject by bouncing the flash off the ceiling, creating a wonderful diffuse top lighting. (This won't work with high, dark or colored ceilings.)

• **Mix direct light and bounce flash.** An easy way to put twinkle in the eyes and lighten shadows when using bounce light is to add a little direct light. With the flash head pointed up, a small white card attached to the back of the flash will send light straight onto the subject.

• **Keep a group an even distance from the flash.** Otherwise the people in the back row will be dim, while those in front may even be overexposed.

Hot-Weather Hazards To Camera Gear

Humidity is the summer photographer's nemesis. *Here are some defensive maneuvers…*

• **Don't open new film until you are ready to load and shoot.** (It is packed in low-humidity conditions in sealed packets.)

• **Have exposed film processed as soon as possible.** Don't leave it in the camera for long periods—it may stick.

• **Use slow advance and rewind to avoid moisture static.**

•**Keep equipment dry with towels or warm (not hot) air from a hair dryer.** Store film and gear with silica gel to absorb excess moisture. (Cans of silica gel have an indicator that turns pink when the gel is damp. They can be reused after drying in the oven until the indicator is blue.)

Modern Photography

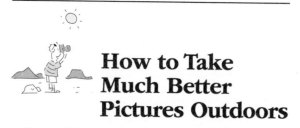

How to Take Much Better Pictures Outdoors

Susan McCartney, international freelance photographer who conducts workshops at the School of Visual Arts in New York City. She is author of *How to Shoot Great Travel Photos* and *Nature and Wildlife Photography: A Practical Guide to How to Shoot and Sell* (Allworth Press).

You don't need magical skills to be a nature photographer. Even without sophisticated equipment, you can come away with wonderful pictures of landscapes, plants or animals. *What you need to take great photos...*

PATIENCE

Nature photography is a contemplative activity. You cannot rush nature. You cannot make animals or a landscape do anything. For the best pictures, you must settle in and observe.

Types of questions to ask yourself: How is a flower affected by the play of sun and clouds or by passing breezes? How does a landscape change with the light from dawn to dusk?

Example: When I recently visited the Grand Canyon, I watched one person after another march up to the rim, stand with their backs to this marvel, have a friend take their picture and then move on. I sat on the rim of the canyon for the entire day, photographing at intervals and watching the play of light and clouds. I took the best pictures at sunset.

LOVE OF THE SUBJECT

The first challenge is to become familiar with your subject through repeated exposure.

African safaris and trips to Yellowstone National Park are wonderful opportunities, but you can also profit from less-expensive trips.

Where to start: A local park, zoo or woodland. For plants and flowers, a nearby botanical garden will do fine. Choose the subjects that most fascinate you, and "stalk" them like a hunter.

Caution: Avoid the woods during deer-hunting season. My own career was almost ended by a potshot in the Allegheny National Forest.

AWARENESS OF LIGHT

The best time to take photographs of nature is during the early or late day hours, when the low sun enhances the subject. *How to take advantage of the low-angle light...*

•**To produce dramatic pictures from even the simplest camera**—position yourself so that the light is coming diagonally over your shoulder onto the subject.

•**When shooting a landscape or the texture of animal fur,** bird feathers, fish scales or flower petals—position yourself so that the light is hitting the subject from the side. Side lighting reveals texture.

•**When you want to create a halo of light around animals or flowers or show the translucency of insects and plants**—position yourself so that the low sun is behind the subject. Be careful that the sun doesn't hit the camera lens directly.

Useful for all nature photos: Soft light that is diffused by thin clouds or light mist any time of day.

To be avoided: "Top" light from overhead summer sun, which casts shadows that record almost black on film. As a rule, I will not shoot if my shadow is shorter than I am.

EQUIPMENT

You can take good nature pictures with virtually any camera as long as you know its limitations. In fact, I have seen very good shots from point-and-shoot and even disposable cameras.

For serious nature photographers, a good tripod is an important accessory. It is absolutely essential for use in low light with long exposures or for close-ups made with slow small apertures and shutter speeds for maximum depth of field. It will minimize blur caused by camera shake when shooting with telephotos and zoom lenses.

OVERCOME YOUR LIMITATIONS

It is valuable to look at nature photographs taken by the masters to see the elements that make up great pictures.

Even more important is experience. Like driving a car or playing the piano, nature photography requires specific physical skills and quick reflexes. As you practice and experiment, those skills will become second nature—allowing you to seize those magical photographic moments.

Most common error: Viewing a subject—such as a landscape—through your eyes, and then barely glancing through your viewfinder before taking the picture. The camera's translation from three to two dimensions will change the view.

Exercise: Train yourself to look at everything through your viewfinder, closing your other eye if necessary.

Which eReader Is Right for You?

David Carnoy, executive editor with CNET (a division of CBS), the leading technology news Web site. He is CNET's lead editor for home and entertainment product reviews and has been reviewing consumer electronics for more than 15 years. *www.cnet.com*

More and more products are joining the increasingly crowded eReader market. Most feature easy-to-read screens and long-lasting batteries. These devices can be money savers for those who read a lot—digital books typically sell for $10 to $15, compared with $25 or more for a hardcover.

Which eReader is right for you depends in part on your priorities…

•**For versatility, buy the iPad.** Most eReaders just display books, magazines and other text files. The iPad is not only an eReader—it can browse the Internet, access e-mail, display photos, play videos, serve as a digital organizer and more. *Price:* From $499 for a model with a 16-gigabyte (GB) flash drive and Wi-Fi compatibility to $829 for a model with a 64-GB flash drive and Wi-Fi and 3G compatibility. (If you buy a 3G model, a wireless access plan costs $14.99 to $29 per month to access the Internet outside Wi-Fi range.) 800-692-7753, *www.apple.com.*

•**For affordability, buy the Amazon Kindle.** The basic Kindle model sells for $69. That's a lot less than an iPad and on par with other, less impressive eReaders. Amazon is making the Kindle seem like a bargain to win buyers away from the trendier iPad. *www.amazon.com*

The Nook ($269) is the second-best choice if affordability is key. Barnes & Noble has eliminated the Nook's initial kinks, and along with Wi-Fi and 3G wireless connectivity, it has an expansion port for more memory and a color screen that allows you to browse through books and view covers in full color. 800-843-2665, *www.barnesandnoble.com.*

•**For portability, buy the Sony Reader Pocket Edition.** At 6⅞ inches by 4⅜ inches and less than one-half-inch thick, it can fit in a small purse or large jacket pocket. On the downside, Sony's screen is smaller than screens of other eReaders, which makes it harder to read. *Price:* $129. 877-865-7669, *www.sonystyle.com.*

Alternatives: The iPhone and iPod touch can serve as very portable mini-eReaders. Both have access to books through Amazon, Barnes & Noble and other apps.

•**For ease of use, buy the Amazon Kindle or the iPad.** The Kindle is arguably the most convenient for finding and downloading books…but the iPad features Apple's famously intuitive controls.

Helpful: Many public libraries now lend digital versions of their books to members. Check with your library by phone, in person or through its Web site to find out whether the eReader you plan to purchase is compatible.

Yes, You Can Be an Artist!

Amy Cohen, an artist and art teacher based in New York City. She has more than 30 years of experience as a private art instructor and portfolio consultant for aspiring art school students. *www.amyartcohen.com*

Some people avoid artistic endeavors because they don't consider themselves skilled at drawing or painting. But even people who lack technical artistic skills can create works of art.

Bonus: Engaging in the artistic process can relieve stress, spur creative thinking and boost self-esteem.

Three fun art projects...

COLLAGE

Collages are artistic compositions created by combining things such as photographs, scraps of paper featuring distinctive graphics or drawings and small swatches of fabric.

First, collect materials that appeal to you. You can do this by buying old books containing evocative photos or drawings in thrift stores or at library book sales...saving small pieces of wrapping paper or cloth...and/or saving product packaging that includes distinctive graphics. I don't recommend saving images from modern magazines—they're not particularly intriguing.

Next, cut out elements from the materials you have collected, and glue them to a paper backing in combinations or patterns that you find compelling. Use heavy-weight drawing paper—look for "Bristol" paper—and an acid-free glue stick. These are available in art-supply stores, craft stores and even some office-supply stores. Don't use standard Elmer's glue or a child's glue stick—these could discolor or otherwise damage the materials.

If you are not sure how to start, just pick an image that you find compelling, cut it out, glue it to a page, then find another image that you think looks good when paired with it and repeat the process. Keep doing this, and see where it leads.

Helpful: The book *Cut & Paste: 21st Century Collage* by Richard Brereton and Caroline Roberts (Laurence King) is full of interesting collage ideas. Or search the Web for the word "collage" together with the names of artists Hannah Höch and/or Max Ernst to find collage examples to use as inspiration.

SODA CAN ART

Use tin snips or a strong pair of scissors to cut off the tops and bottoms of saved soda or beer cans, then cut open the cylinders. Unroll the cylinders, and press them flat under something heavy, such as a stack of books.

Warning: Wear sturdy work gloves while cutting aluminum to avoid getting cut by the metal's sharp edges.

Next, use small nails to affix a piece of aluminum flashing onto a rectangular piece of wood. Rolls of silver aluminum flashing can be purchased in home stores, often for less than $1 per square foot. Cut this aluminum so that it completely covers one side of the wood.

Once your cans have been pressed flat, cut shapes or patterns out of them, then use small nails to attach these pieces of colored aluminum onto the aluminum flashing to create distinctive metallic art. You can use the colored aluminum to create patterns or even to construct pictures.

Search on the Web for "soda can art" to view examples of projects.

DUCT TAPE ART

Duct tape might seem utilitarian and prosaic, but this well-known adhesive product now is available in a wide range of colors and patterns in art-supply stores and crafts stores.

If you purchase a selection of duct tape in different colors, you can combine them to create eye-catching artwork and crafts without ever touching a paintbrush or pen. My students, ages six to 90, love it!

Duck brand duct tape lists some of these arts and crafts projects on the company's Web site. (On *www.DuckBrand.com*, select "Ducktivities" from the "Duck Tape Club" pull-down menu.) Or search the Web for "duct tape crafts" and/or "duct tape art" to find potential projects.

You can create duct tape pictures with strips of duct tape on a piece of plywood or heavy cardboard. Or you can layer different colors. Then use a sharp craft knife to cut out sections of the top layer(s) and peel them away to expose the colors below.

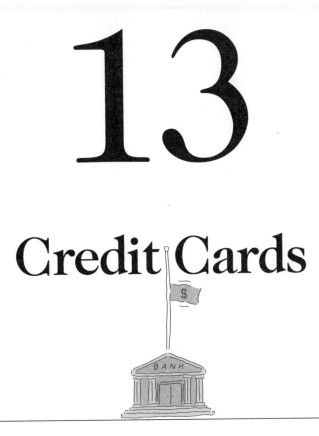

13

Credit Cards

You Can Outwit Credit Card Companies

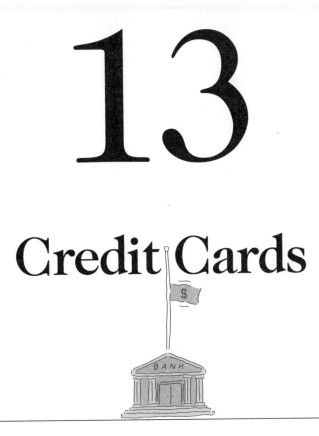

Hidden fees, high interest rates and penalties can make credit cards extremely expensive. *Tricks to help you cut costs and even come out ahead…*

SEEK 0% RATES

Credit card companies aggressively market introductory rates as low as 0% for the first six or 12 months. The interest rates then increase, sometimes dramatically. To win this game, shift your balance away from one introductory-rate card and onto another shortly before the low-rate period ends. Jumping from card to card can keep your rates low forever.

Watch for these low-intro-rate offers in the mail, or find them online at Bankrate.com or on my own site, CardRatings.com.

Caution: Don't enter any personal information online unless you are filling out an application on the card issuer's own site—and

you see "https" in the Web browser address line, which indicates that the site is "secure."

To make intro-rate flipping work…

• **Choose cards with introductory periods of at least 12 months.** Switching cards more often is a headache. It could also hurt your credit rating because each time you apply for a new credit card, you trigger a credit inquiry, which could lower your credit score.

• **Avoid cards with high balance transfer fees.** There often is a fee to transfer a balance to a low-intro-rate card. It typically is worth paying this fee only when transferring a four-figure or larger balance, and only when the fee is capped at no more than $100.

Note: The "catch" in many of these offers is that there is no cap on the transfer fees.

Example: Many card companies charge a 3% balance transfer fee with no cap. Therefore,

Curtis Arnold, founder and CEO of US Citizens for Fair Credit Card Terms, Inc., which educates consumers about credit cards, based in Little Rock, Arkansas. Its Web site, CardRatings.com, features consumer reviews of credit cards. Arnold is author of *How You Can Profit from Credit Cards* (FT Press).

if you're moving a large amount of money, the transfer fee may negate the 0% introductory rate.

•**Follow the card's rules to the letter.** Your low introductory rate could turn into a much higher "default rate" if you are even a single day late with a payment. Set up automatic payments or pay your bill the day it arrives, to avoid problems.

There is some danger that you could get stuck with a big balance on a high-rate card if you cannot qualify for another low-rate introductory offer before your current one expires. If you prefer a simpler, lower-risk approach, apply for a card that offers a low fixed interest rate for the life of the transferred balance.

DOUBLE UP

There's no rule saying that you can have only one credit card from a given card issuer. In fact, it may be to your advantage to have more than one.

If you receive a very appealing card offer from a credit card issuer with which you already have an account, go ahead and apply. If you are approved and are given a low credit limit on the second card, ask the card issuer to "reallocate" your credit limit from the card with less attractive terms to the one with more attractive terms. Reallocation is not an application for new credit—it's just a consolidation, so the card issuer often will do this without even performing an additional credit check. Some issuers won't grant a reallocation, so ask before you apply.

Example: You have a $10,000 credit limit on a Discover Card (800-347-2683, *www.discovercard.com*) that charges a 17.99% interest rate, and you are approved for a $2,000 credit limit on a new Discover Card with a 15-month introductory rate of 0%. Have most or all of your credit limit from the original card reallocated to the low-rate card.

Inexperienced customer service reps sometimes do not understand what customers mean by credit reallocation. If you have trouble, ask to speak with someone in the credit or balance-transfer department, and if that fails, ask to speak to a manager.

BUYER PROTECTION

Some cards provide buyers with various types of protection for purchases of items, but few cardholders take advantage…

•**Price protection.** Citi Diamond Preferred Card (800-456-4277, *https://creditcards.citi.com*) offers this guarantee for most non-Internet items. If you buy an item with the card, then see it advertised in print within 60 days for less than the amount you paid, you will get a refund of up to $250.

•**Purchase security.** If a covered item purchased with a card that provides this guarantee is accidentally damaged or stolen within 90 days, you are covered up to a certain dollar amount.

Example: Chase Visa cards cover up to $500 per occurrence (877-682-4273, *www.chase.com*).

•**Return protection.** If you try to return a covered item within 90 days and the store won't take it back, you can get a refund for the purchase price up to certain limits.

Example: American Express provides refunds up to $300 per item and up to $1,000 annually.

GET CASH BACK

With rewards cards, the credit card company pays you for your business.

There are many different types of rewards cards. Cash-back cards, which give you a cash rebate ranging from 1% to 5% of what you spend, provide the most useful reward and tend to be the easiest to use.

Examples: Blue Cash Preferred from American Express is a great cash-back card for big spenders—6% rebates for categories such as groceries, 13% at gas stations and department stores and 1% elsewhere. Chase Freedom Visa is a better choice for those who use their credit cards less frequently. It rebates 5% in selected categories that rotate quarterly.

To make cash-back cards work…

•**Do not carry a balance on these cards.** They usually have high interest rates.

•**Select a cash-back card that matches your spending habits.** Some provide more cash back on gas purchases, others at specific merchants.

•**Read the fine print to find out if the program caps your annual cash reward, and stop using the card when you reach the cap.**

- **Do not let the rewards encourage you to spend more than you otherwise would.**

Frequent-flier cards are less appealing. Today's crowded flights make rewards seats difficult to obtain.

Exception: A card that offers a large number of miles up-front just for signing up for the card (or soon thereafter) might be worth applying for. You may even be able to cancel the card as soon as you receive your miles and before any annual fees begin.

Example: Citi Gold/AAdvantage Visa Signature Credit Card offers 40,000 miles on American Airlines if the cardholder spends just $3,000 in the first three months. It has no annual fee in the first year.

When a Credit Card Is Not a Credit Card

Not all cards bearing the name Visa or Master-Card are credit cards. Some are debit cards.

- **Credit cards.** When you charge a purchase to your credit card, the bank extends you credit until the bill is paid. At most banks, no interest is due if you pay in full by the due date. But interest is levied on any amount outstanding after that date.

- **Debit cards.** A debit card works like a check. An amount charged to your debit card is immediately withdrawn from your account. No credit is advanced.

ADVANTAGES OF A DEBIT CARD

- **It is more acceptable than a check at many merchant outlets.**

- **It is ideal for people who do not want credit.** A debit card limits the shopper to the amount that is available in the account.

What Visa and MasterCard Don't Tell You

Robert A. Bennette, former banking correspondent, *The New York Times.*

One Visa card or MasterCard could be very different from another Visa card or MasterCard. What counts is the bank that issues it.

The MasterCard and Visa organizations do not issue credit cards themselves. They provide a clearing system for charges and payments on the cards and license banks to use the Visa or MasterCard name. It is the issuing bank that determines the interest rates and fees.

A bank's name on a credit card does not necessarily mean that it is the bank actually issuing the card. Issuance of credit cards is a high-risk, low-profit business. Seldom does a small bank issue its own.

Generally a small bank acts as an agent for an issuing bank. The agent bank puts its name on the card, but it is the issuing bank that actually extends the credit.

Aside from costs, this can be important if the cardholder encounters an error. The correction might have to be agreed upon, not by a friendly local banker but by an unknown, larger institution, perhaps in a different state.

Choosing which card to take is becoming more difficult, because some of the nation's largest banks have begun active solicitation of customers throughout the US. Individuals must be especially careful about accepting any offer that might come in the mail.

A recently discovered quirk in the federal law allows federally chartered out-of-state banks to ignore state usury laws that limit the amount of interest or fees that the issuing bank may charge on its credit cards. In Arkansas, for example, state usury laws prevent local banks from charging more than 10% interest on credit card balances. But a federally chartered out-of-state bank, in lending to Arkansas residents, may charge whatever its home state allows.

Even within individual states, the terms on credit cards can vary widely.

Aside from the actual rates and fees, individuals must carefully check the fine print of their contracts. Most banks, for example, do not charge interest on balances stemming from purchases until the customer is billed for them. If the bill on which the charges first appear is paid in full by the stated due date, there is no interest charge to the holder.

But some banks, those in Texas, for example, begin charging interest as soon as they receive the charge slip and make payment to the merchant. Thus, interest begins accumulating even before the cardholder receives the bill. These interest charges continue until the bank receives payment from the customer.

Use Credit Cards with Travel Agents

It's better to use credit cards when working with a travel agent. They minimize difficulties if the agent goes into bankruptcy. *Reason:* The credit card company immediately becomes the middleman—and the financial solvency of the travel agent may no longer be an issue.

Always Check Credit Card Statements

Check credit card statements carefully to match charged amounts on your receipts.

To avoid overcharges: Be sure the statement gives correct tips at restaurants as well as the correct date and time for hotel checkout or rental car return.

Also: If you sent your previous payment in time but were charged a late fee, call the issuer to cancel it. If the issuer gives you a hard time

correcting this or any error, ask for $25 compensation for the time you waste.

Edward Mendlowitz, CPA, partner, WithumSmith+ Brown, CPAs, 1 Spring St., New Brunswick, New Jersey 08901. *www.withum.com*

Credit Card Debt Strategy

Debt payoff is getting harder. Some credit card issuers are increasing interest charges for people in debt-workout programs. In the past, creditors reduced or eliminated interest for people working out debts, so they had a better chance of getting back their money. Now, card issuers are going in the opposite direction.

Self-defense: If you are getting into credit card debt trouble, switch as much of your balance as possible to an issuer that cuts rates for debtors or call your issuer and ask for a lower interest rate if you agree to a strict payment schedule.

Stephen Brobeck, executive director, Consumer Federation of America, Washington, DC.

Cancellation Caution

When you cancel a credit card, be sure it's listed as closed on your credit report. If the report still lists the account as open, your ability to borrow may be reduced. After canceling a card, ask for written verification that it has been canceled. A month later, ask for a copy of your credit report. If the report still shows the account as open, inform the credit bureau and send it a copy of the verification letter showing the account to be closed. By law, credit bureaus must verify disputed information with the source within 30 days.

Gerri Detweiler, author of *The Ultimate Credit Handbook* (Plume). *www.gerridetweiler.com*

Beware of Lower Credit Limits

Credit card issuers are slashing credit limits by up to 50% with little warning.

Self-defense: Avoid using more than 20% of the credit available to you—better yet, stay under 10%. Your credit score, which helps determine whether you qualify for various loans and at what rates, is partly based on the percentage of your available credit that you use.

Curtis Arnold, founder and editor of CardRatings. com, which educates consumers about credit cards, Little Rock, Arkansas.

Your Liability for Lost Or Stolen Credit Cards

Your liability for unauthorized use of your credit card is sometimes limited—and then only if the card company has informed you of the rules and provided you with a postage-paid notification form to use if the card is lost.

Once you have reported the card missing, you are not liable for its use—even if someone makes a purchase with the card five minutes later.

Suggestion: When you phone or mail notification of loss, have a witness, and note the exact time.

Although liability is strictly limited, lost cards can be a problem, especially if you have a lot of them. You have to report and replace each one. In addition, your credit standing can be damaged if someone runs up big bills in your name, and your cards could be canceled if you make a habit of losing them or don't report promptly. *One solution:* Credit card protection services. Just call the service and report your cards missing, they will take care of notifying all card issuers and getting replacements. In addition, they insure against the $50 potential liability, which might be substantial if you have a lot of cards.

Credit Card Cautions

There's a risk with debit cards—if lost or stolen, unauthorized use of your bank-automation card leaves you liable for the first $50 if the card is reported stolen within two days of loss or theft. It goes up to $500 if you delay beyond two days, and becomes unlimited if you wait until 60 days after the bank statement reporting unauthorized use is mailed. That makes the convenience of a debit card much more costly than a credit card, which limits your liability to $50 tops and charges you nothing if a loss is reported in time to flag it before use.

Check your credit card statement against your receipts. It's very easy for a dishonest store owner to run off several slips when you present your card and submit them later for payment.

Be sure that it's your card that the store clerk returns. Accidental switches do happen. The number of switches is increasing. It's not costly, but it can be inconvenient, especially if you're traveling.

You are not automatically responsible for any of the credit card charges accrued by family members, even if they're using a family card. *Example:* An executive's son continued to use his father's credit card after he was told to return it. Under a Federal Trade Commission ruling, the father had only to inform the credit card issuer that the card was being used without permission. Having done so, the father would be responsible for only the next $50 charged.

Credit Counseling Can Help

Seek credit counseling if you are at or near the credit limit on each of your cards... you don't know how much you owe and are scared to find out...you use your credit cards not just for convenience but because you don't have enough money to buy things, whether they are necessities or not...you are hiding the true cost of your purchases from your spouse or family. To find a credit counselor, go to the Web site of the National Foundation for Credit Counseling, *www.nfcc.org.*

Greg McBride, CFA, senior financial analyst, Bankrate.com, 11760 US Hwy. 1, North Palm Beach, Florida 33408.

Credit Card Billing Errors

The error may be a charge for goods you never bought, never received or rejected...a failure to credit a payment...a mistake in amount...or any item on which you want a clarification.

To protect your rights, you must notify the card company of your objection, in writing, within 60 days after your bill was mailed.

• **Do not just telephone—this is not considered proper notice.** If you do phone, follow up with a letter within the 60-day period.

• **Do not just write your objection on the invoice—this isn't proper notice either.** Use a separate sheet of paper and include your name, address, account number and what you object to on the bill.

The card company must acknowledge your notice within 30 days. *And, within two billing cycles (but not more than 90 days), it also must either...*

• **Correct the bill and send you notice.** If the correction doesn't match your figures, the company must explain the difference, and if you request, furnish documentary evidence, or...

• **Send you a written explanation of why it thinks the bill is correct.** On request, it must furnish documentary evidence. If you claim the goods weren't delivered, the company must give you a written determination that they were "delivered, mailed or otherwise sent" before it can charge you.

During this period you don't have to pay the disputed amount and the company cannot...

• Make any attempt to collect it.

• Revoke your card or accelerate payment.

• Report you as delinquent to any credit bureau.

Caution: Although you do not have to pay the disputed amount, you must pay at least the minimum due on any undisputed balance. If you don't, the company can accelerate your debt, revoke your card or report you as delinquent, on the basis of the undisputed amount.

Penalties: If the company fails to comply with all requirements, it forfeits the first $50 in dispute even if it turns out that the bill was correct. In addition, you can sue for any actual damages—for example, damage to your credit if the company improperly reports you as delinquent.

Note: The Fair Credit Billing Act applies only to consumer credit—credit for "personal, family, household or agricultural purposes." It doesn't apply to business credit cards.

14

Personal Money Management

How to Keep Your Friendly Banker from Robbing You Blind

If you are a person of average means and assets, your bank will rob you of well over $100,000 during your lifetime. You will pay more than you should for your mortgages, credit cards and other loans. You will be cheated out of a fair return on your savings and bank IRA deposits. And along the way, you will be outrageously overcharged in fees and penalties for every service your bank provides.

BANKERS ARE NOT YOUR FRIENDS

Bankers are, in fact, your worst financial enemies. The community banks—which once weighed a loan applicant's character above his collateral—are being squeezed out by a handful of big banks. These huge institutions cater to major corporate accounts and are scarcely regulated by the government, which depends on their financing to keep it afloat.

The banks' attitude toward small customers is simple—our way or the highway.

BASIC RULES

• **Do business with one of the smaller banks in your market area,** where you will have most leverage in negotiating more favorable terms.

• **Comparison shop each banking service among at least three institutions.** After you find the best deal, try to negotiate for even better terms.

Forget about finding a one-stop financial supermarket. You may wind up at Bank A for a checking account, at Bank B for a savings account and at Bank C for a mortgage. Anyway, banks do not value your loyalty. They value only your money—and the more of it they can take from you, the better they like it.

The mortgage is the largest investment most people ever make—and the one where banks take greatest advantage. Most people

Edward F. Mrkvicka, Jr., president of Reliance Enterprises, Inc., a national financial consulting firm, Marengo, Illinois.

333

decide on a mortgage based on whether they can afford the monthly payments. They rarely consider—nor do banks openly disclose—that at prevailing interest rates, home owners repay $2 to $4 for every dollar they borrow over the standard 29- or 30-year term. In other words, a $100,000 mortgage could cost them as much as $400,000.

Advice: Accelerate your payments against the mortgage's outstanding principal. A negligible increase in your monthly payment—perhaps 4%—can save you 25% or more of the amount you ultimately repay the bank, and shorten your obligation to 20 years or less. While some experts advise keeping the longer term for its tax advantages, this is a big mistake for the great majority of consumers. Even if you are in the 25% tax bracket, every dollar of unnecessary interest will still cost you 75¢ after taxes—money you could be investing for your own benefit rather than the bank's.

OTHER MORTGAGE SCAMS

• **The adjustable rate mortgage (ARM) represents the banking industry at its worst.** It is a blatant marketing gimmick—complete with the deceptive come-on of an initial "discounted" rate—that fleeces the most vulnerable and overextended. The ARM was created to ensure that banks might skim the absolute maximum from their borrowers, no matter where interest rates head. The risk is virtually all yours. (It is also possible, of course, that interest rates will fall—but since bankers control the rates, rates will always fall more slowly than they rise.)

Unfortunately, the prime interest rate will tend to increase in reverse proportion to our economy's health. In other words, your mortgage payment soars just when it is most likely that you may lose your job or business. Even if you hold steady, there's a fair chance you won't be able to afford the larger payments. *Consider:* If your ARM is based at 7.5% interest and then rises to 10.5%, your interest costs have actually risen by 30%—not the innocuous sounding "three percentage points" advertised by your bank. On a $100,000 mortgage, that could translate to several hundred dollars more a month—a prescription for foreclosure.

Advice: Stick to a fixed-term mortgage, unless you are certain you will be selling your house before your ARM interest rate can substantially increase.

• **Negative amortization mortgages are special ARMs** that allow for fixed monthly payments regardless of interest-rate fluctuations.

What most customers don't understand (and what most bankers fail to make clear) is that the bank may be siphoning their equity into its profit center. If the mortgage rate rises, the difference between what you pay each month and what you owe is assessed against a balloon payment, usually due in five years.

At the end of the balloon, you may actually owe more than you did when you took out the loan. Aside from pocketing your interest payments, the bank now owns a substantial portion of your down payment.

Worst case: When you need to refinance the loan after paying off the balloon, your increased mortgage needs may exceed the property's appraised value. After the banks turn you down, you may have no option except to sell the house—at a loss.

Advice: Avoid this one at all costs.

• **Reverse mortgages** are supposed to enable people (mainly the elderly) to stay in their homes when they are no longer able to afford upkeep expenses. The borrower receives a monthly check from the lender, either for a set term or until the borrower dies. The loan balance plus interest is repaid by the sale of the house.

In most cases, however, it is a gigantic rip-off. After 30 years of monthly mortgage payments, the home owner trades in all that equity for five or 10 years of moderate income.

An "open-term" reverse mortgage allows for permanent residence until death, but it is available only on premium homes in excellent condition. And if something unexpected happens to the elderly home owners, the bank has hit a bonanza.

• **Home-equity credit lines represent new packaging for an old, dog-eared product**—the second mortgage. While interest on them remains tax deductible (for lines up to

$100,000), that advantage is quickly wiped out by fees for the application, credit check, appraisal and closing among others. For every dollar you save in taxes (versus an unsecured personal loan, for example), you may pay the bank $2 in fees.

Since your home equity may be your most liquid asset, you should save it for true emergencies. Any other purpose (to finance a car or home improvement, for example) represents an unacceptable risk...if you default on the loan, after all, you could be faced with foreclosure.

How to Calculate Your Net Worth

List all your assets at their actual or estimated fair market value. Then list all your liabilities—all the money you owe, including credit card debt and mortgages. Your net worth is your total assets minus your total liabilities.

Check your net worth every January to monitor your progress.

Added benefits: Because it lists your assets and liabilities, a net-worth statement can serve as a prepared financial statement when you apply for a loan...and it is a good measure of your available emergency money.

Barbara O'Neill, PhD, CFP, and author of *Saving on a Shoestring: How to Cut Expenses, Reduce Debt, Stash More Cash* (Berkley Books).

Bank Scam

Safe-deposit box rental bills are likely to be higher. *Reason:* Some banks are adding premiums for safe-deposit box insurance coverage. *Problem:* Tricky invoices hide the fact that the insurance policy and fee are optional—not mandatory. *Self-defense:* Pay only the rental fee and any tax. Include a note with your bill declining the insurance. Also, check with your bank and ask about increased rates. *Important:* Insure your safe-deposit box valuables with a rider on your homeowner's insurance policy.

Edward F. Mrkvicka, Jr., president of Reliance Enterprises, Inc., a national financial consulting firm, Marengo, Illinois.

How to Avoid Fights Over...Bank Accounts— Yours/Mine/Ours

Jonathan Rich, PhD, clinical psychologist in private practice in Irvine, California, *www.psychologicaltesting. com.* He is author of *The Couple's Guide to Love & Money* (New Harbinger), which he was inspired to write after seeing money become a frequent source of conflict among his clients.

Bank accounts are among the most common sources of strife for couples. Should there be a joint account...multiple individual accounts...and how do you decide the amount that each person contributes and how much discretion each person has over spending?

Even for couples who don't generally disagree over spending, having just one checking account is often not the best choice because it is difficult to keep track of the balance. And for couples who tend to disagree over spending—watch out! Having one account just adds fuel to the fire by exposing every bit of spending to both partners.

Solution: Use a joint checking account for truly necessary or shared expenses, such as the mortgage, utility bills, car payments, insurance and basic groceries...and set up a personal checking account for each partner to use for his/her discretionary spending.

Important: Contributions to the joint account must come first. To do this, have all regular income—paychecks, Social Security benefits, pension payments, etc.—deposited into the joint checking account and only later divert some remaining money into individual checking accounts. *How to use these accounts...*

• **Joint account.** Seek middle-ground compromises when the inevitable differences of opinion arise about which expenses are shared expenses.

Example: A couple agrees that most food bills are a shared expense. But the husband enjoys high-end delicacies, while his wife is just as happy with more affordable fare. This couple might have to agree that certain foods, or a certain percentage of the overall monthly food bill, will be paid for out of the husband's discretionary account.

• **Personal accounts.** Maintaining these personal accounts cuts down on squabbles about spending by segregating discretionary purchases from shared expenses and perhaps even keeping them private.

Why this helps: A discretionary purchase—whether it's football memorabilia or antique dolls—often seems frivolous unless you're the one doing the spending. When these purchases are made from an individual rather than a joint account—with the total amount of the account "preagreed" by both partners—it can head off many disputes.

Individual accounts should be funded with whatever is left over after the joint account bills and the family's investment plans are fully financed for a given period—monthly works well for most couples. Both individual accounts should be funded with equal amounts to avoid feelings of unfairness.

To maintain harmony, couples need to realize that the funding of *both* discretionary accounts might have to be reduced or suspended if *either* partner sustains an unexpected expense or income setback.

KEEPING TABS

When two people spend money out of the same joint account, it is all too easy to bounce a check. For married couples, bounced checks do not just trigger hefty bank fees, they often trigger fights about which partner is to blame.

Accurate record-keeping is key. Spouses need to be vigilant about keeping the checkbook up to date by recording all deposits, checks written and other withdrawals in the checkbook register.

Online banking can be a big help. Log on to the account at least once a week to make sure that the balance is where it should be and that each purchase has been recorded in the check register. You will have fewer bounced checks, and there will be less finger-pointing if a check does bounce. Still, spouses need to warn their partners when they plan to make large withdrawals from joint accounts and when they notice that the balance is dangerously low.

Couples would be wise to hold meetings once a week or once a month to discuss bank accounts and other financial topics. Aim to treat these sessions like business meetings, with no sarcasm or personal attacks allowed.

It is perfectly reasonable to have one partner take full responsibility for the mechanics of paying the bills and balancing the joint account checkbook. If this is the case, the other partner can take full responsibility for a different chore in order to avoid feelings of unfairness.

Tricks Banks Play With Interest Rates

Lawrence T. Jilk, Jr., former chairman of National Penn Bancshares, quoted in *The Journal of Commercial Bank Lending*.

Banks teach their loan officers a number of strategies to get an extra ¼% or even ½% from borrowers. *Recognize some of their tricks...*

• **Doing the negotiating at the bank,** which is familiar territory to the banker but intimidating to the borrower.

• **Not mentioning the rate at all,** but simply filling it in on the note.

• **"Since you need the money today, let's write it up at X%.** Then we can talk later about changing it." The banker hopes you'll never bring it up again. He certainly won't.

• *Flat statement:* **"The rate for this type of loan is X%."** (Never true except for small consumer loans. There is always room to negotiate.)

•**Postponing the rate discussion for as long as possible,** hoping the borrower will weaken under deadline pressure.

•**Ego-building.** Bank president stops by during negotiations.

•**Talking constantly about how little the interest costs after taxes.** And comparing it with finance-company rates, secondary-mortgage rates or the cost of equity capital.

The banker looks at the company's account as a package, including loans, average balances maintained and fees for service. *Borrower options:* Trade off higher average balances for a lower interest rate on borrowings, or vice versa.

The borrower is at a disadvantage because he or she probably negotiates a loan only once a year or less, while the banker does it full-time. So prepare carefully for negotiations.

GOOD TACTICS FOR THE BORROWER

•**Ask the interest rate question early—** in your office, not his. Don't volunteer suggestions.

•**Negotiate everything as a package—** rate, repayment schedule, collateral, compensating balances. The banker's strategy will be to try to nail down everything else and then negotiate interest rate when the borrower has no more leverage and no room to maneuver.

What Banks Don't Tell You

Banks like to publish their effective annual yield, whereas money market funds advertise only the simple interest rates. This conceals the fact that money-market funds compound interest on a daily basis. If a bank and a money market fund pay the same rate, the bank will appear to offer more by advertising the effective rate.

Also, some banks say they let you draw on all checks immediately, provided you put up another bank account as collateral. *Catch:* If a check backed by a six-month certificate bounces, the bank may break into the certificate before maturity. If this happens, you will have to pay an interest penalty.

How Private Are Your Bank Records?

When it comes to providing information to nongovernmental sources, each bank establishes its own rules regarding the information it will make available. Ask your bank to explain its policies. Some can provide a written privacy statement.

Many banks refuse to disclose any information about you to a private individual unless there's a court order. But most banks will be very open in supplying information to credit bureaus and other genuine grantors of credit, such as department stores. They certainly will if you list the bank as a credit reference. Generally, the bank will give such information over the telephone if it is familiar with the calling institution. It might, however, ask for a written request if it does not have a standing relationship with the inquirer.

Some banks disclose…

•**Whether your checking account is good** or whether there have been overdrafts.

•**Whether it has loaned you money,** how much, for how long and whether or not you have made your payments on time.

•**The size of your savings account.** Bank officials will talk of "high four figures," or "low five figures," and so on.

•**What kinds of loans you have with the bank**—mortgage, personal, auto.

Banks keep credit agencies up-to-date about your loan payments and the amount of credit available to you. This information pertains to lines of credit on credit cards as well as other credit lines and actual loans.

The Bank of America has a typical policy. "We will respond to a recognized business or a credit-rating bureau," reports one of their vice presidents.

On an installment loan, the Bank of America will disclose the approximate size of the monthly payment and the remaining balance on the loan. On a practical level, it would be impossible for the bank to single out individual accounts on which it would not give out any information.

337

If a merchant calls a bank to determine whether your check is good, or if a credit card is good for a certain amount, the bank will usually tell the merchant. Department stores' computer terminals often provide the same kind of information, disclosing whether the amount involved can be covered by the account. But the computers usually do not give the exact amount in the customer's account.

Can you prevent a bank from giving out this information? For the most part, it is impossible to prevent disclosure of this information unless you do business with a small bank that knows you well.

Problem: Most banks have this information on computers and the technology has not been applied to isolate individual accounts to block the dissemination of such information. Many people want their banks to supply information to credit grantors because this enables them, the individuals, to obtain additional credit more easily.

If you choose a small bank, however, especially one that is not automated, it is possible that the bank may agree not to give out information about you to anyone unless ordered to do so by a court.

Best Money Market From Banks

The best type of money market account offered through banks is one that pays interest from day of deposit to day of withdrawal.

Avoid: Daily-collected-balance accounts, which pay interest only after checks that you deposit clear the bank accounts on which they are drawn…and low-balance compounding, which pays only on the lowest balance during the time period.

The Complete Idiot's Guide to Making Money on Wall Street by Christy Heady, syndicated financial journalist (Alpha Books).

How to Spot a Forged Check

Thieves make their living by being tricky. *But you can outsmart them if you know what to look for…*

• **See if the check has perforations on one side.** A false check often has four smooth sides, since the forger cuts them with a paper cutter after printing.

• **The code numbers printed on a legitimate check reflect no light.** They are printed in magnetic ink, which is dull.

• **About 90% of all hot checks are drawn on accounts less than one year old.** The numbers in the upper-right-hand corner of the check indicate the age of the account. Be suspicious of those that are numbered 101-150 or 1001-1050 (the starting numbers).

Frank W. Abagnale, world-famous expert on white-collar crime and president of Abagnale & Associates, Washington, DC. He is author of *The Art of the Steal* (Broadway).

Better Interest Income

Get a higher interest CD by buying one from a nonlocal bank. All bank certificates of deposit are federally insured up to $250,000, so you do not give up safety for a higher rate CD.

You can find many high-rate CDs and money funds in Sunday newspapers. But you may do even better on the Internet. *Check the lists at…*

• **bankrate.com,** *www.bankrate.com.*

• **BanxQuote**, *www.banxquote.com.*

• **iMoneyNet, Inc,** *www.imoneynet.com.*

Also check into buying a CD through your stockbroker. This may be worthwhile for the simplicity of having a broker search for you—and because brokers can resell CDs at market price before maturity.

Plus you can invest more than $250,000 and the brokerage firm will spread your investment among more than one CD. This will keep you fully insured.

Barbara Weltman, attorney in Millwood, New York. *www.barbaraweltman.com.* She is author of several books, including *The Complete Idiot's Guide to Starting a Home-Based Business,* 2nd edition (Alpha Books).

How Safe Is Your Safe-Deposit Box?

Don't assume that when you put your valuables in a safe-deposit box there is no further need for worry. Safe-deposit vaults in banks get robbed in real life as well as in the movies. *Then the questions arise:* Who is responsible—and for what? Is the bank insured for the loss? How does the bank or the insurance company know what was actually in your box?

If the bank does have insurance, it may cover only damage to the bank, not losses sustained by box renters. The bank may choose not to put in a claim on its own insurance, denying responsibility for any losses. In actual practice, banks will usually attempt to reimburse their safe-deposit box holders after a robbery, for public relations purposes, but there are no guarantees. If the bank's insurance won't cover the claims made, the individual box holder may have trouble collecting, especially if he/she is unable to prove what was inside the box.

To protect yourself, do the following...

• **Purchase your own protection** through a rider on your homeowner's policy or a separate policy. (Rates may depend on the vault security system at your particular bank.)

• **Make a complete list of all the valuable items in your box,** documenting each as fully as possible. The documentation should include photographs, appraisals and receipts. Don't keep the list in your safe-deposit box.

• **Keep copies of all the important documents in your box** at home or at your attorney's office.

• **Do not keep cash in a safe-deposit box.** Cash is almost impossible to insure.

Cash Found in Decedent's Safe-Deposit Box

What was the source of any cash in a safe-deposit box or in your home or office? In the absence of proof to the contrary, the Internal Revenue Service may consider any unexplained cash to represent previously untaxed income. This presumption can be refuted if there is credible evidence. For example, there may be a letter to your executor stating that Social Security checks or horse-track winnings (reported) will be converted into cash, to be kept in the box as an emergency fund. Correspondence can identify cash as having been found money, which has been turned over to the police department and later given back to the finder when no claimant appeared.

John J. Tuozzolo, associated with the firm Collins, Hannafin, Garamella, Jaber & Tuozzolo, PC, 148 Deer Hill Ave., Danbury, Connecticut 06810.

When Holder of Safe-Deposit Box Dies

The late Jay A. Jones, vice president of Williamsburgh Savings Bank and president of the New York Safe Deposit Association, New York.

A safe-deposit box may not be the best place to keep items you want a spouse or child to inherit with the least taxation or red tape. In planning for your family's future, it is important to know the laws concerning safe-deposit boxes.

When a key holder dies: The box may be leased by a single renter or by two renters (called co-lessees). In some states, the box is immediately "sealed" by the bank for appraisal of its contents by local tax authorities when one renter dies.

• **How do banks know when a key holder has died?** Most of the time, they don't know.

In a small town, a death would often be general knowledge. And upon hearing of the death, the bank would seal the box. However, in a large city, it is unlikely that the bank would know unless someone informed it.

• **How do you get into a box once it has been sealed?** The executor of the estate must go to court for letters of administration in order to claim the contents of the box. If there might be a will in the box, the court issues a will search order. This directs the bank to witness the opening, along with the local tax authorities.

The will is then personally delivered by the bank to the court. It is wise for the executor to get a will search order even if he/she has already found a will. There might be a later will in the box. The court can also direct the removal of other important papers, such as insurance policies, death certificates and military records.

Joint ownership: People tend to assume that the co-lessee of a safe-deposit box automatically inherits the contents when the other lessee dies. This is not true. Joint rental of a safe-deposit box is not like a joint bank account. It resembles the rental of an apartment by roommates. When one roommate dies, the other does not automatically inherit all of the property in the apartment unless this is specifically provided for in the will.

• **How does inheritance work when a safe-deposit box is involved?** The same way as when a box is not involved—according to the will. The co-lessee on a box has no more right to inherit its contents than anyone else. If there is no will, the courts might or might not interpret co-ownership of a box as reflecting the intention of the deceased to leave the box's contents to the co-lessee, depending on the relationship between them.

• **Is there any way to set the box up so that the co-lessee inherits?** Not with absolute certainty, unless there are no other heirs who might contest it. Clear inheritance depends primarily on the contract both renters sign with the bank when they rent a joint box. Some banks include a clause in their contract when the renters are husband and wife. It

reads: *The box is the joint property of both and upon the death of either passes to the survivor, subject to estate taxes, if any.* However, since even this clause may not hold up in court if there is no will to back it up and other heirs have strong claims, many banks do not include an inheritance clause in their rental contracts. Others won't rent joint boxes at all to avoid litigation.

• **What happens if the other key holder cleans out the box before the sealing?** It depends on the situation. If there are heirs who feel entitled to some of the box's contents, they are likely to sue if they can prove that the co-lessee had access. However, access may be difficult to prove, because some banks throw away nightly the access slips indicating who entered their safe-deposit boxes that day. Some states require that these access slips be kept. Others don't.

It's very difficult to prove that a key holder took assets that didn't belong to him, especially if he claims that the box was empty when he opened it, but if the tax commission does prove illegal removal of assets, penalties can be heavy.

• **What is the best way to set up a joint safe-deposit box?** If there are several heirs to an estate, it is a good idea to rent the box in a single name, with the other key holders as deputies rather than co-lessees. "Deputy" is the bank's term for power of attorney. He has complete access to the box during the lifetime of the lessee.

The deputy has no rights to enter the box after the lessee's death. The will should determine who inherits the contents. In any joint safe-deposit box rental, read the contract you sign with the bank to see what it says regarding inheritance.

The bank and executor are responsible for the following…

• **The bank is not responsible for the contents of the box after the death of a key holder** unless the bank was put on notice about the death. The bank can be held responsible if the deceased had bank accounts. If, after his death, the bank accepted papers regarding the bank accounts of the deceased, it can be held liable for not checking to see if he also had a safe-deposit box.

• **The executor has no automatic access to the safe-deposit box and is not responsible for its contents** until authorized by the court. He is then responsible for distributing them according to the will.

If your family has a business, renting a safe-deposit box in the name of your corporation can assure you continued access after the death of a family member. Corporations never die. They just keep on electing new officers, and the box will not be sealed when an officer dies. To take out a safe-deposit box in a corporate name, you must show the bank papers proving that there is an actual corporation in existence.

Found Money

Find a lost pension through the Pension Search Program of the federal Pension Benefit Guaranty Corporation (PBGC). It has names of thousands of people owed millions of dollars in pensions. This money often comes from employers that went out of business while pensions were PBGC-insured.

Write the PBGC Pension Search Program at 1200 K St. NW, Washington, DC 20005...or check the Internet at *www.pbgc.gov.*

Barbara Weltman, attorney in Millwood, New York. www.barbaraweltman.com. She is author of several books, including The Complete Idiot's Guide to Starting a Home-Based Business, *2nd edition (Alpha Books).*

Common Money-Management Mistakes

Withholding too much in taxes from your paycheck. That is like giving the IRS an interest-free loan. Ask someone in your company's benefits department to help you calculate

the correct amount, or consult your tax preparer. *Another smart strategy:* Pay off your credit card debts, which can cost about 15% in interest that is not tax deductible.

Stuart Kessler, CPA, former managing director, RSM McGladrey, Inc., 1185 Avenue of the Americas, New York City 10036.

Pros and Cons of Electronic Filing

Did you know that electronic tax return filing can cost extra? The fee is paid to the party that transmits your file to the IRS. But electronic filers get faster refunds—usually within three weeks, compared with six weeks for paper filers. Electronic filing has fewer typographical errors, since your return goes directly to IRS computers. The IRS lists several companies that offer tax preparation and online filing for free. *More information:* Contact the IRS at 800-829-1040 or go to *www. irs.gov.*

Randy B. Blaustein, Esq., senior tax partner, R.B. Blaustein & Co., 155 E. 31 St., Suite 15L, New York City 10016.

401(k) Checkup Time

Ross Levin, CFP, founding principal and president of Accredited Investors, Inc., a financial planning firm, 5200 W. 73rd St., Edina, Minnesota 55439.

January is when most investors make significant changes for the year to their 401(k) plans and other retirement accounts.

Here's how I typically advise investors to manage the money they already have in their plans—*and* the new money they will be contributing...

• **Take a hard look at your plan's pie charts.** Take your 401(k) plan's suggested allocation for someone your age seriously.

While such allocation pie charts tend to be on the conservative side, they at least give you a benchmark from which to work.

Then calculate carefully how many years you have until retirement—the time when you will actually have to tap into the amount you've saved...and your tolerance for risk.

Once you've decided how much should go into stocks, bonds and cash, you must rebalance your invested assets. *Best:* Do this once a year.

Such an investment strategy keeps you buying low...and selling high.

•**Size up the funds in which you're invested.** Your time horizon is probably longer than you think. This is because the horizon doesn't end at retirement but when you expect to need the money.

Stay heavily invested in stock funds—but pick the best stock funds available. *Factors and questions to consider...*

•The performance of each fund in which you're invested versus its benchmark.

•The amount of cash a fund has attracted over the past three years. As funds get bigger, their performances tend to fall off—especially when investing in small-cap funds.

•Has the fund manager changed? Give the new manager one year to prove himself/herself. If the fund's performance weakens, consider selling.

•Has each fund's investment philosophy stayed the same? You picked the fund because you liked the manager's approach to investing. If that approach has changed, consider another fund closer to what you want.

•**Stick with stocks for money already invested in the plan.** Continue to invest for growth—emphasizing price appreciation over time. Over the long term, the assets that will grow most are stocks. *My allocation for existing money in the plans of investors with 15 years or more until they'll need the assets...*

•35% in large-cap index or growth-and-income funds.

•25% in international funds.

•20% in small-cap stock funds.

•20% in fixed income investments.

I'm against using money market funds for the fixed income portion of your plan. You give up all potential for capital gains, and the return is too low.

Better: Bond funds, preferably short-term. The return is higher than a money market fund, and the shorter the term of the bonds in the fund, the less volatility.

Even better: Guaranteed Investment Contracts (GICs)—if your plan offers them.

Reason: You lock in a guaranteed interest rate for the year, no matter how low rates go. And you are spared the price volatility of the bond market.

•**Use a different allocation for new contributions.** It's even more important to ignore market volatility with the new money you are adding to your plan.

Because you keep adding new money to the plan in monthly increments, you are dollar-cost averaging as you go. When the market is low, your contribution buys more shares.

My allocation...

•One-third large-cap stock fund—index or growth-and-income.

•One-third international fund.

•One-third small-cap stock fund.

Then, once a year, rebalance your portfolio to meet the "existing money" allocation mentioned earlier.

401(k) Reminder

Always list a beneficiary for your 401(k) plan. If you do not, most plans make your estate the beneficiary.

Problem: This may delay payment to your heirs and result in additional estate taxes and probate costs. If you are married, federal law requires that your spouse receive your entire 401(k) benefit, regardless of whom you name as beneficiary, unless your spouse provides a written consent for you to name someone else as your beneficiary.

Ted Benna, president, 401(k) Association, Potomac, Maryland.

Second-Mortgage Checklist

Margot Robinson, GRI, CRS, Juner Properties, Stamford, Connecticut.

Sometimes it's difficult for home owners to sell their home without giving the buyer help with the financing. *Typical dilemma:* The buyer can't qualify for a full first mortgage at the bank. He or she asks the seller to help close the gap by taking back a second mortgage for the balance of the purchase price.

Problems: Many sellers have been hurt by incautious secondary financing arrangements. The buyer can't come up with the payments, so the seller must go through costly foreclosure proceedings. In many cases, the seller ends up with nothing—the bank holding the first mortgage takes all proceeds from the forced sale.

To minimize the risk before agreeing to any secondary financing...

• **See a lawyer.** Don't sign papers without first getting sound legal advice. No reputable broker will urge a seller to get involved in secondary financing unless the seller has relied on an attorney for advice.

• **Get a credit check on the prospective buyer.** A strong, creditworthy buyer is the best protection an owner-financier can have. If you're working with a real estate broker, the broker will run the check for you. If not, you can tell a credit company and have the company run that check. Or, the bank holding the first mortgage might help.

• **Avoid very short-term balloon mortgages.*** The balance of the second mortgage should not be due for at least three to five years. If you give only a one-year balloon and interest rates are worse in a year, you'll have put the buyer—and yourself—in an impossible position. If he can't come up with the money or refinancing, you'll have to force a foreclosure.

• **Have someone in the area watch the property** to make sure that the buyer is

*The buyer makes small monthly payments for a limited time, then makes one large ("balloon") payment of the full amount due.

maintaining it properly. Run-down property can hurt you badly.

• **Prepare to take steps should the buyer fall behind in his payments.** Banks, for a service charge, will collect mortgage payments for you. *Alternative:* Sell the second mortgage. This is usually done at a discount, so you'll take a "loss," but you might be better off in the long run.

Some advice: Keep it clean. Consider dropping your selling price before you accept secondary financing.

Pros and Cons of Home-Equity Loans

Second mortgages, often called home-equity loans, can be a flexible and attractive means of raising fairly large amounts of money.

A convenient wrinkle in the second-mortgage business is the ability to write checks against a line of credit secured by the borrower's equity interest in his or her home. An individual can get a large loan for almost any purpose merely by writing a check.

Moreover, the interest rate on the loan will probably be lower—possibly considerably lower—than it would be if the borrower had obtained an ordinary personal loan. Generally, the interest rate on a second mortgage (because it is secured by residential real estate) is one to two percentage points lower than the interest rate on a personal loan.

A borrower should be aware, however, of some of the dangers inherent in second mortgages. First of all, the borrower is using his home to collateralize the loan. If for some reason the loan cannot be repaid as originally planned, there is the possibility that the house will be lost.

Considering this risk, a potential second-mortgage borrower should think carefully about what he plans to use the loan for. Is it prudent to put a lien on a home to take a vacation paid for by writing a check against a second-mortgage credit line?

Second mortgages have a very legitimate role to play and should be considered carefully, especially when large amounts of money are needed—paying for a child's education or an addition to a home, for example, or dealing with a large medical bill.

Potential second-mortgage borrowers should shop carefully. Different institutions may offer substantially different kinds of second mortgages and also a wide range of interest rates.

A critical element is the amount of money needed. Some lenders set relatively low limits, such as $50,000 or $60,000, while some will go several times higher.

Of course, the amount an individual can borrow under a second mortgage is limited by the equity he or she holds in his home. That is the appraised value of the property minus the amount owed under the first mortgage. The second mortgage allows the borrower to obtain cash for the increased value of his property and for the amount of principal he has paid on his first mortgage. He can thus "unlock" the frozen cash equity in his home.

Key consideration: Is the loan fixed rate or variable rate? Usually the initial interest rate on a fixed rate second mortgage is higher than it is on a variable rate loan.

Reason: On a fixed rate loan, the lender is assuming the risk of a rise in interest rates. Even if rates were to rise dramatically, the interest paid by a fixed rate borrower remains unchanged. On a variable rate mortgage, however, the borrower assumes this risk, or at least a substantial part of it.

Therefore an individual should consider the purpose of the loan in deciding whether to opt for a rate that is fixed or variable. If the loan is for a long-term purpose, such as adding an extension to a home, it might be wise to take a fixed rate loan, viewing the initial higher interest rate as a form of insurance against a sharp rise in interest rates in the future. If interest rates were to drop sharply, the fixed rate loan could be refinanced.

Warning: Check for prepayment penalties, and shop around to see which lender's offer is the least onerous.

Variable rates are usually better suited for loans that the borrower expects to pay off in a relatively short period. Loans used for investments could be expected to generate enough cash flow to at least keep up with sharply rising interest rates.

Borrowers also should be careful about so-called balloons. These are second mortgages that fall due within a few years, usually three to five. But the repayment schedule might have been calculated on a basis of up to 20 years. Thus, at the end of, say, five years, although very little might have been paid on the principal, the lender could demand immediate and full repayment. If that were to happen and the borrower could not raise the needed money, he might lose his home. It is therefore essential that the contract have a clause requiring the borrower to renew the loan. *Note:* It is critical that you borrow from a reputable lender. The last thing most well-established financial institutions want to do is take over your home. They will always try to work things out if the going gets tough. That is not always the case with unknown lenders.

If your needs are special, many second-mortgage lenders will try to devise a program that fits your requirements. For example, they might agree to postpone payments for a specified period of time.

The Best Mortgages for Different Life Stages

William Pivar, attorney and professor emeritus of business and real estate at the College of the Desert in Palm Desert, CA. He is author of numerous real estate books, including *Real Estate Investing from A to Z* (McGraw-Hill).

It is possible for home buyers to customize loans to suit their needs. With greater opportunities, however, comes greater confusion.

Here are recommendations for the type of mortgage you should consider if you're in the following stages in life…

UPWARDLY MOBILE

• **5/25 loan.** The best mortgage for someone who is likely to be transferred in three to five years or likely to trade up to a bigger home in five years is a 5/25 loan. For the first five years, a 5/25 loan offers a fixed rate that is about one percentage point lower than a 30-year fixed rate.

It has a one-time adjustment after five years—for the next 25 years—to a rate that is about one percentage point above the prevailing 30-year fixed rate.

Advantage: A 5/25 loan gives you a lower starting rate, and unlike an Adjustable Rate Mortgage—which can change from year to year—that lower rate is set for five years.

Alternative: If you think you'll be moving after five years, opt for a 7/23 loan instead. You'll pay a rate that is about one-quarter point higher than a 5/25 loan, but you'll lock in for an extra two years. If you know you'll be living in the home for less than 10 years, don't pay a lot of points—or cash up front—to get a lower rate.

Rates vs. points: Points and up-front fees are based on percentages of the loan. Higher points often mean a lower rate of interest… lower or no points would mean a higher interest rate. If you intend to live in a home for a long time, you would be ahead by paying points and obtaining a lower interest rate. If you plan to sell in a few years, a no-point loan at a higher interest rate would be better.

GRADUALLY UPWARDLY MOBILE

• **10/1 loan.** A 10/1 loan is great for someone who is fairly certain that 10 years from now he/she will be earning significantly more —but isn't sure what will happen during the years in between. With a 10/1 loan, your rate is fixed for the first 10 years at a rate about one-quarter point lower than a 30-year fixed rate—so for the first 10 years, you have a discounted fixed rate.

After 10 years, the 10/1 loan converts into a one-year ARM, and you can refinance if rates have dropped or stay with the ARM. Even if rates are higher after 10 years, your earnings will likely be higher as well, enabling you to afford a higher rate.

THE LAST-TIME BUYER

If you're buying a home to live in for at least 20 years, get a 15-year fixed rate mortgage. You'll save an average of one-half point on the interest rate. By paying a few hundred dollars more per month, you could save more than $100,000 on finance charges over 30 years.

Alternative: If you're stretching a bit to buy the home, get a 30-year mortgage. If your circumstances improve, consider prepaying it so you'll discharge the debt in 15 or 20 years.

Trap: Some loans have prepayment penalties.

Which One to Choose?

Pay the points or a higher mortgage rate? The answer depends on how long you plan to live in the house. Points—an up-front cash payment at closing—will get you a lower rate.

Two strategies: First ask the lender for rate quotes with points and without (also called "par" pricing). Second, look at monthly payments. Divide the monthly savings from lower rates into the cost of points. That will tell you how long you need to own the house to save money with points.

More information: Have a discussion with your financial adviser.

Keith Gumbinger, vice president and analyst at HSH Associates, a fee-based mortgage-data service, 51 Route 23 South, Riverdale, New Jersey 07457.

Check on Your Home Appraisal

Home appraisals may set values too low because of new rules designed to prevent overestimates of value. A low appraisal can make it difficult to get a loan. The rules, which ban mortgage brokers (and others who may profit from a loan) from choosing appraisers, are meant to prevent appraisers from feeling pressured to come up with higher values. But real estate agents and some appraisers say that the change means banks are using third parties to pick appraisers and are seeking the lowest-cost appraisals possible. That is leading to using inexperienced appraisers who are not familiar with the market.

What to do: If the appraisal of a home you want to buy comes in lower than you consider reasonable, ask the bank for a second appraisal and offer to pay for it.

USA Today

It Pays to Use a Mortgage Broker

Keith Gumbinger, vice president and analyst at HSH Associates, a fee-based mortgage-data service, 51 Route 23 South, Riverdale, New Jersey 07457.

Almost two out of every three home loans are arranged by a mortgage broker. Mortgage brokers typically work with dozens of financial institutions. They can offer a wider menu of options than individual lenders can, such as mortgage products that might not be available in your area or obscure types of loans that might prove advantageous to you.

Borrowers with poor credit who might never get a loan from a bank or savings-and-loan directly often can find one through a mortgage broker.

FINDING A MORTGAGE BROKER

Be careful when choosing a mortgage broker—the industry is poorly regulated. Brokers may offer come-on rates or provide inadequate documentation of loan terms. Some scam artists demand up-front fees, then walk away with your money.

• **Start with recommendations.** Ask for suggestions from friends and family. Also talk to bank lending officers and other lenders to find out what sort of mortgage is typical for someone in your situation.

Helpful: The Association of Mortgage Professionals maintain a database of its members on its Web site, *www.namb.org.* Type in your area or zip code to find a list of local brokers.

• **Ask brokers for references.** Find out what kind of experiences other borrowers have had with the broker. How responsive was he/she? Were there problems with the process or outcome?

• **Do a background check.** Contact your local Better Business Bureau and state mortgage broker association to find out if a broker has been the subject of any complaints. The National Association of Mortgage Brokers also lists state groups on its Web site.

Other good sources for general mortgage information: Fannie Mae, 800-732-6643, *www. fanniemae.com…www.mortgage-calc.com…*or my company, HSH Associates, *www.hsh.com.*

SECURING THE LOAN

Don't expect a broker to give you more than one quote. While he may, his job is to find you the best rate for the kind of mortgage you want.

By law, a broker has to give you a written estimate of closing costs after you apply for a mortgage. Many also will give you an estimate beforehand if you ask.

Important: Don't forget to ask about the commission. Most mortgage brokers take less than 1% of the loan as a fee. But if you have bad credit or other circumstances that make getting a mortgage difficult, you will probably have to pay more.

PROTECTING YOUR RIGHTS

• **Ask a lawyer to look over any contracts** before you sign them.

• **Know who is processing the loan** and how to contact that person. Don't depend on the broker to see that the loan is processed in a timely fashion.

New Law Makes Reverse Mortgages More Attractive

Tyler Kraemer, Esq., a Colorado Springs–based attorney specializing in real estate, finance and estate planning. He is coauthor of *The Complete Guide to Reverse Mortgages* (Adams Media).

The weak real estate market makes this a poor time to sell a house, and suddenly cautious lenders are making home-equity loans more difficult to obtain. Reverse mortgages are a third way for older home owners in need of cash to access the equity tied up in their homes. (Reverse mortgages typically are available to home owners age 62 and older.)

When a home owner takes out a reverse mortgage, he/she essentially converts a portion of his home equity into cash. The home owner can receive cash in a lump sum, monthly payments, a line of credit or some combination. When the home is sold, the loan must be repaid. Any remaining equity goes to the borrower or his heirs.

During the home owner's lifetime, no payments are due unless he moves out. Plus, no income verification is necessary to qualify for a reverse mortgage.

The catch: The biggest complaint with reverse mortgages has always been that they are expensive. Historically, up-front fees could run 5% to 6% of the home's value, and all major reverse mortgage programs have adjustable interest rates, so rates can go higher.

What's new: The federal *Housing and Economic Recovery Act of 2008*, includes provisions that make Home Equity Conversion Mortgages (HECMs), by far the most common type of reverse mortgage, somewhat more attractive…

•**Loan origination fees on HECM reverse mortgages** are now capped at 2% of the first $200,000 of the home's value, and 1% of the remainder, with an overall cap of $6,000. This cap could save borrowers perhaps $1,000 to $2,000 compared with previous fee schedules.

•**The potential size of HECM reverse mortgages is increased.** In the past, home owners could borrow no more than $363,790, and often the amounts were lower still, depending on home values in the region. The current national limit is $625,500.

•**Reverse mortgage lenders are barred from engaging in certain questionable sales practices.**

Example: Reverse mortgage lenders are prohibited from requiring the purchase of annuities and certain other financial products in connection with reverse mortgages—a strategy that rarely works in the home owner's favor.

Caution: Even with the new laws, reverse mortgages are a pricey way to obtain money. A home owner should consider all other options before getting a reverse mortgage.

Investment Scam Self-Defense

Learn about investing so you know what sounds too good to be true—and probably is. Find out how the salespeople you speak with are paid—that can influence their recommendations. Only buy mutual funds from well-known investment groups. Never buy an investment over the phone from a salesperson you don't know. Don't make decisions under pressure—legitimate investments will be there after you've had a chance to think about them.

Jane Bryant Quinn, syndicated personal-finance columnist, writing in *Newsweek*.

Hot Online Tip

Here's an online investing edge for frequent traders—open accounts with two brokers. When volume or online "outage" prevents access to one account, use the other.

Best: Open one account with a major player, such as E*TRADE (*www.etrade.com*)... and another with a smaller broker. The major Internet brokers have phone access—so you should be able to trade when electronic systems are jammed.

Busiest trading times: Weekdays around 9:30 am and 4:00 pm Eastern time—when the stock exchanges open and close.

Frank Lallos, former senior brokerage analyst at Gomez Advisors, a consumer Internet-commerce research group in Lexington, Massachusetts.

How to Select a Discount Broker

David L. Scott, professor emeritus of finance, Valdosta State University, Valdosta, GA, is author of *David Scott's Guide to Investing in Common Stocks* and *David Scott's Guide to Investing in Mutual Funds* (Houghton Mifflin).

Just because a firm calls itself a discount broker doesn't mean it really is. *Rule of thumb:* Commission fees should be at least 50% to 75% less than at a full-service firm, or you should continue searching.

In fact, there's an enormous variation in fee structures among brokers and even among discounters. Some brokers offer extremely low rates only for large trades but slim discounts for small transactions. Others do precisely the opposite...and some are in-between.

Shrewd investors should consider accounts at different discount brokers in order to benefit from the lowest fees for different-sized transactions.

Smart traders also know that in the discount brokerage business everything is negotiable. To keep a good client, discount brokers regularly offer fees that are below their published rate sheets, just as the big, full-service brokerage houses do. But you have to ask for these better deals.

While there's no substitute for comparison shopping, discount brokers with a single office generally offer lower fees than do the large national brokers with many offices (and a lot of overhead).

In the best Wall Street tradition some discounters offer free investment advice to their best clients—but again, only if the client asks. The single-office brokers with 800 numbers sometimes do this, and it may be possible for the client who trades at the local office of a national discount broker to develop a similar rapport with a particular trading agent.

Important limitations: Tax-shelter syndications are traditionally part of the full-service brokerage function. A smaller number of discount brokers offer these syndications.

If a discount broker doesn't offer these services, an investor should search elsewhere.

• **Trading.** Nearly all reputable discounters trade stocks and bonds as well as options. Some firms offer lower rates for over-the-counter trades.

• **Securities deposit.** Discount brokers should either hold the security being purchased or deliver it to the client at no charge. Avoid brokers who insist that the client take delivery or those which charge a delivery fee.

• **Insurance.** SIPC insurance, which insures a client up to $500,000, is standard industry practice, just as it is at the full-service brokers. Some have an extra insurance charge of up to $2.5 million per client.

• **Cash balances.** All cash from sales or dividends should be automatically reinvested in a money market fund. Sometimes this is done only upon client request. Investors with large cash balances should shop for a brokerage that reinvests this cash immediately.

• **Margin trading.** The usual rate for both discount and full-service firms is ½% to 2% over the broker call rate (which is based on the prime rate), depending on the amount borrowed. The more borrowed, the lower the rate.

• **Keogh and IRA plans.** Some plans are free, but most charge $25 to open the account plus a $25 annual service fee. Some firms charge more.

Most good brokers are willing to take the time to tell a prospective client what services they provide. *Bad sign:* If the phone isn't answered quickly, the broker may be understaffed or overworked. In the long run, this will waste a considerable amount of your time.

Spotting the Traps in Earnings Figures

Peter de Haas, former senior portfolio strategist, PGGM Investments, The Netherlands.

Figures on company earnings are deceptive. They are useful guides only to investors who interpret them correctly.

• **Retained earnings for some American companies can be overstated by significant amounts.** *Example:* $1 in after-tax profit shrinks to just 60¢ after 40% is subtracted to adjust for the effect of inflation on depreciation and costs. Another 40% might then be deducted in order to pay out a dividend.

• **The real corporate tax rate is elusive.** *Reason:* Inflation boosts costs, resulting in inventory profits and underdepreciation of plant and equipment. *Advice:* Have more confidence in the earnings reports of companies that use last in, first out (LIFO) inventory accounting methods that make adjustments for inflation.

• **Return on equity is often one-fourth of the reported percentage.** *Reason:* Profits are nearly halved by inflation. But the book value might almost double when current prices are used to calculate.

In most cases, it is not worth trying to make a quick trade based on a quarterly report. *Reason:* There is almost always a correction that brings the stock price back to where it was before the report. *When to trade:* After the price settles back.

WHAT TO FOCUS ON

• **Deviation** in the long-term trend of a company's earnings.

• **Changes in net margin.** If sales move ahead but income is level, watch for a trend toward lower profits. And vice versa.

• **Underlying changes,** such as currency fluctuations, tax rate and number of shares outstanding. These factors can all affect earnings per share.

Translating the earnings figures into the price/earnings (P/E) ratio is even trickier because the price of a stock is based on anticipated earnings, but the ratio is calculated on earnings in the previous 12 months.

Brokers are quite shameless about recommending one stock to a client as a good value (because the P/E ratio is low) and another as an excellent growth stock (because company prospects are so exciting that the P/E ratio is meaningless).

Rationale for buying low-multiple stocks: There is less downside risk in a declining market. And they have higher upgrade potential in an advancing market.

Rationale for buying high-multiple stocks: If the company really grows by 40% a year for the next 10 years, paying 40 times earnings is acceptable. Current earnings of $1 compounded for 10 years at a 40% rate amounts to nearly $30 of earnings 10 years from now. Even if the P/E ratio falls to 10 by then, the stock will have gone up more than seven times in value (from 40 to 290).

Bottom line: Keep a clear head when earnings, earnings forecasts and P/E ratios are being loosely presented as reasons to buy now.

Hollywood's Top Money Managers Tell All

Todd Morgan, Bel Air Investment Advisors LLC, a State Street Global Advisors Company, 1999 Avenue of the Stars, Suite 2800, Los Angeles 90067. *www.belair-llc.com*

The advisors at my firm manage approximately $6 billion for a number of clients, many of whom are prominent in the entertainment industry. They created their wealth by taking risks in their professional lives. But when it comes to their investments, they are quite conservative.

Like anyone who works hard today, our entertainment-related clients are so busy with their careers that they don't have time to manage their investments on a day-to-day basis. They are cautious with their money because they are never sure what their next project will be—or when it will arrive.

Here are our golden rules of investing when your goal is to preserve the wealth you've built up…

• **Huge risk is a fast way to lose money.** Many people ignore the dangers of risk in their quest to achieve outsized returns. They just assume that taking big chances is part of what investing is all about.

But taking more risk than your age, time horizon or need for income can handle puts your assets in tremendous jeopardy.

Example: If you lose 50% of the amount you invest, you then need to earn a return of 100% just to break even.

• **The asset allocation you choose determines your financial fate.** We carefully evaluate how to divide our clients' money between stocks and bonds.

Key factors in the decision: The client's age…how much he or she is willing to tie up in securities for long periods of time…and how much income he needs from investments.

Examples: We suggest that people in their 40s and 50s invest 65% of their portfolios in stocks and the rest in bonds if they don't need the money for at least 10 years.

But we recommend that people in their early 60s put only 40% to 50% in stocks and the rest in bonds because they will likely need steady income, don't have as long an investment time horizon and won't be able to tolerate volatility.

Be prepared: It is not uncommon for the stock market to have one or two corrections of 5% to 10% a year.

Self-defense: Before you invest a sizable amount of money in stocks, ask yourself how you would feel if that investment immediately shrank by one-fifth. If such a decline would hurt your financial plans over the next five years, limit your exposure to stocks.

To determine the proper diversity, we study each client's total financial picture.

Example: We have a new client in his early 50s who is very wealthy but who has always kept all his money in Treasury securities. Now he says he wants to switch it all into stocks.

While we don't doubt that he means what he says, we also don't think he could withstand a sharp stock market correction.

There's no way we would put 100% of his money into stocks. Instead, we would perhaps put 40% of his portfolio in stocks—to give him a chance to get used to the market.

If he had no need for income, we might eventually put 80% of his portfolio in stocks—provided he had a very long time horizon.

• **Stick with large-cap, blue-chip stocks.** We look for companies that are industry leaders with global franchises and that have minimum market capitalizations of $5 billion to $10 billion. These are world-class companies that we think are going to be around for a long time and tend to be less volatile over the short term.

We look for companies that are able to deliver consistent revenue and earnings growth, practice conservative accounting, have solid management teams with a history of doing right by their shareholders. We also make sure that they avoid such things as acquisitions that dilute profits and growth.

• **Don't fiddle with your portfolio or get hooked on trading.** An important reason to avoid constantly buying and selling stocks is that when you sell at a profit, you have to pay taxes. That leaves you with less money to reinvest than you would have if you made the same return but didn't sell.

When we buy a core stock, we expect to hold it for at least three years. Some positions in our clients' portfolios have been held for six or seven years.

• **Don't wait until stock prices decline to buy.** Just stay focused on your long-term goals. As long as you're buying stocks of great companies and holding them for three years or longer, the question of whether the current price is up or down a few points is irrelevant.

When a client comes to us with a lump sum, we don't hold on to his money and wait until the market drops to invest it.

Instead, we tend to put a small portion into the market right away. Then we like to invest additional amounts over the next few months.

• **Stick with top-quality bonds for your income requirements.** We don't want to take risk with the bond portions of our clients' money.

The goal in the bond portion is the preservation of capital and the creation of income. So we don't buy high-yield junk bonds to achieve higher returns.

Generally, the minimum municipal bond rating we will consider for our clients is A, and the average credit quality of our municipal bond portfolios is closer to AA.

To figure out how much of their portfolios we need to allocate to bonds, we ask our clients how much annual net income they need to live on.

Example: If a client told us today that he needed $500,000 a year, we would put $10 million into bonds with a variety of maturities and look for an average annual rate of return of about 4.75% after taxes. Since most of our clients are in the top tax brackets, we favor tax-free municipal bonds.

CORE PORTFOLIO

We have about 30 stocks in our core portfolios. We concentrate on a handful of sectors—consumer products, health care, financial services and technology—that we think have great long-term growth prospects.

The Art of Selling Short

Short selling is the process of borrowing common stock from an investor who holds it and selling it with the hope of profiting from a decline in price. In that case, the borrower replaces the stock at a lower price. This type of transaction is viewed as highly risky by most individual investors. But, although it is not recommended that investors jump into short selling, with more knowledge, much of the risk is removed.

Insight: A study of security-price movements shows that security prices—taken as a whole—tend to move down about as far as they move up over long periods of time. But oddly, even during the worst-performing investment environments, prices are still going up two-thirds of the time. *Implication:* Stock prices move downward twice as fast as they go up. If prices fall faster than they rise, then money can be made very quickly—hence the appeal to a short seller.

Psychological negatives: Short selling is a concept that has been maligned by many people. Investors are suspicious of advisers who recommend it. *Reason:* We get most of our investment information from the media. But much of what appears to be business "news" are really public-relations handouts that present corporations in a glowing light. For this reason most business communications are too optimistic.

The following are the practical benefits of using a short sale...

• **As a speculation.** This will benefit an individual if the market or an individual stock declines. Most people who think the market is too high and expect a decline merely refrain from buying stock. Although there is justification, that doesn't help capital grow. It merely protects it. A short sale might enable the investor to make money grow in a weak market. Naturally, you can't select just any stock to short in a bear market, just as you can't buy just any stock in a bull market. Selection of the correct security is crucial. *Logical choice:* A company whose raw-materials costs are soaring in price but that is unable to raise prices because of customer resistance. Although most investors would just eliminate such a company from their holdings, a venturesome person might not only sell his or her shares but also short some of them.

• **As a portfolio hedge.** An investor who is uncertain about the intermediate-term outlook for the stock market might arrange a portfolio that is 80% long and 20% short. Those proportions could be adjusted, depending on the investor's uncertainty or pessimism. Since stocks decline faster than they rise, some shorting might afford some protection during uncertain times.

• **As a "transactional hedge."** Within a single industry, better managed companies tend to rise faster than their peers during a good cycle for the industry, and poorer companies tend to fall faster during weak periods. *Possibility:* Being long on the shares of the strongest company in the group and going short on the weakest company.

• **To defer taxes.** This is also called "shorting against the box." If an investor has made a big gain in a single year and wishes to defer it, he might short the equivalent number of shares he already owns. The investor may close out the short sale by delivering his own shares in the year he wishes to take the gain without paying any commission. The original short sale serves to guarantee the profit at the price the shares were sold short, whereas the gain need not be declared until the year in which the entire transaction is terminated (assuming all the necessary tax rules are satisfied). Because tax laws in this area are highly complex, check with a tax professional before employing this strategy.

• **Short sale combined with an option eliminates risk.** Most people fear short selling because the stock might run away on the upside. Few stocks, though, go straight up. Still, with the advent of listed call options a short position can now be protected through purchase of a call option. It establishes a limited liability on the short sale.

Example: An investor decides he wants to short XYZ at $50 but is worried that the stock might advance sharply. If XYZ has a call option with an exercise price of $50, he may then purchase that option to protect his short. If he buys a six-month call for $600 and his worst fears are realized (say, the stock goes up to $70 per share), he may at any time until the option's expiration date exercise the call option at $50 and deliver the stock against his short position. *The only loss:* The amount he paid for the option, plus commissions on the transaction—substantially less than the potential loss if he hadn't purchased the option.

• **Variations.** There are dozens of other possibilities for combining short sales and options. They range from aggressive trading to low-risk portfolio hedging with a maximum risk of $50 plus commissions. It is the conservative way to short.

Short-Selling Alert

Short selling no longer predicts market trends. Short interest, which is widely reported around the 20th of each month, tells how many shares have been shorted—sold in the expectation that stock prices will drop. In the past, short interest of one-and-a-half to two times daily market volume meant strong bearish sentiment—typically near a market bottom. But short interest now runs five, six, even seven times daily volume, because of complex hedging activities by professional traders. There is no clear correlation between those activities and future market moves.

Norman Fosback, editor and publisher, *Fosback Fund Forecaster* (Fosback Forecaster, Inc). 20967 Blanca Terrace., Boca Raton, Florida 33433. *www.fosback.com*

Online Scams

Online stock fraud is increasing—as scam artists realize the Internet offers an easy, inexpensive way to reach thousands or millions of people. Scam artists usually send spam—junk e-mail. Or they go into investment chat rooms and talk a stock's value up or down.

The Securities and Exchange Commission (SEC) polices online scams, but it is challenging to keep up with fraud in a medium of instant communications.

Self-defense: Never buy or sell a stock based on tips you find on the Internet—it's safer to do your own research. If you suspect a scam, contact the US Securities and Exchange Commission at *www.sec.gov.*

Richard H. Walker, former director, division of enforcement, Securities and Exchange Commission, quoted in *Kiplinger's Personal Finance*, 1100 13th St. NW, Suite 750, Washington, DC 20005. *www.kiplinger.com*

The Best Day To Sell Stocks!

Friday is the best day to sell stocks. *Reason:* Historical data show that stocks generally rise more on Fridays than on any other day of the week. The rule holds especially for stocks with the lowest market capitalization (price times total number of shares outstanding). Moreover, those shares consistently outperform most higher valued shares throughout the month of January. *To take advantage of these trends:* (1) Add to your portfolio in late December. (2) Sell large capitalization stocks at the very end of a week.

Norman Fosback, editor and publisher, *Fosback Fund Forecaster* (Fosback Forecaster, Inc). 20967 Blanca Terrace, Boca Raton, Florida 33433. *www.fosback.com*

Timing a Stock Split

Stock splits are not necessarily a bullish sign. *General rule:* Stocks that split usually outperform the market only before the announcement. After the announcement, the stock performs no better than average.

How to Avoid Selling Too Soon

Investors who are nervous about the direction of stock market movement can adopt the following method to avoid selling securities just as the market may be gathering upside momentum…

• **Each week, record the number of issues making new highs** for that week on the New York Stock Exchange. (These and other key data are recorded in *Barron's*, among other sources.)

• **Maintain a moving four-week total** of the number of issues making new highs on the New York Stock Exchange.

• **Presume that the intermediate uptrend is intact** for as long as the four-week total of issues making new highs continues to expand. Investors can hold long positions in most issues without fear until the four-week total turns down.

This method is not foolproof, but in a 53-year period there has never been a market decline that wasn't foreshadowed by at least one week's notice in this indicator.

Timing and Tactics, Ventura, California.

When Not to Listen to Your Broker

The few words the average investor finds hardest to say to his or her broker are, "Thanks for calling, but no thanks." There are times when it is in your own best interest to be able to reject the broker's blandishments.

• **When the broker's *hot tip*** (or your barber's or tennis partner's) is that a certain stock is supposed to go up because of impending good news. *Ask yourself:* If the "news" is so super-special, how come you (and/or your broker) have been able to learn about it in the nick of time? Chances are by the time you hear the story, plenty of other people have, too. Often you can spot this because the stock has already been moving. This means that insiders have been buying long before you got the hot tip. After you buy, when the news does become "public," who'll be left to buy?

• **When the market is sliding.** When your broker asks, "How much lower can they go?" the temptation can be very great to try to snag a bargain. *But before you do, consider:* If the stock, at that price, is such a bargain, wouldn't some big mutual funds or pension funds be trying to buy up all they could? If that's the case, how come the stock has been going down? It's wildly speculative to buy a stock because it looks as if it has fallen "far enough." Don't try to guess the bottom. After all, the market is actually saying that the stock is weak. That is the fact, the knowable item.

• **When he tells you that a stock is "averaging down."** It's a mistake for the broker (or investor) to calculate that if he buys more "way down there," he can get out even. The flaws are obvious. The person who averages down is busy thinking of buying more just when he should be selling. And if a little rally does come along, he waits for his target price "to get out even"—so if the rally fades, he's stuck with his mathematical target.

Stock market professionals average up, not down. They want to buy stocks that are proving themselves strong, not those that are clearly weak.

Stocks vs. Mutual Funds

Investing in individual stocks may be more profitable than investing in mutual funds. *Reason:* Management fees charged by all mutual funds. Even in no-load funds with low costs, management fees cut into returns every year. *Also:* Mutual funds buy and sell stocks when their managers decide to—you have no say in when to take a profit or a loss. When you own individual stocks, you are in full control.

Bill Staton, chairman, Staton Financial Advisors, LLC, and publisher of *Bill Staton's E-Money Digest*, 2431 Hartmill Court, Charlotte, North Carolina 28226. *www.statonfinancial.com*

Big Advantage with Index Funds

Use an index fund as the core of your mutual fund portfolio now.

Broad-based index funds, such as The Vanguard 500, perform well over long time periods partly because they incur much lower costs.

They aren't actively managed, so they don't pay for managers' salaries, research, etc. Index funds also have lower *tax* cost, which is a benefit for taxable accounts.

Actively managed funds earn taxable gains on trades that are taxed to shareholders each year. But index funds, which don't trade stocks as often, produce few such tax liabilities.

Result: The combination of lower costs and tax savings give index funds a head start over other funds.

Sheldon Jacobs, founder and consultant, *The No-Load Fund Investor Newsletter. www.noloadfundinvestor.com.*

Mutual Funds' Hidden Investment Fees

William E. Donoghue, chairman of W.E. Donoghue Co., Inc. and publisher of *The Donoghue Plan Action Gram. www.donoghue.com*

Mutual funds have a responsibility to disclose their fees fully. That is required by the securities laws. But not all mutual funds structure their fees the same way.

Front-end-load fees are easy to spot. The front-end commission to a broker runs up to 8½%. In a few cases, the performance of a particular fund may justify that fee, but generally fees should be avoided. That can easily be done by buying a no-load mutual fund.

Back-end loads are less obvious. Although details are in the prospectus, the stockbroker may tell you it is a no-load fund. However, the investor winds up paying a back-end load if he or she takes his money out of the fund before a specified period of time, usually five years.

Bottom line: If you are buying a fund from either a broker or an insurance agent, you can be sure there is a commission somewhere.

Management fees: Look for a fund's 12b-1 plan. That is the section of the securities law that permits the use of the fund's assets to pay for distribution. Some funds pay and some don't. Paying for distribution is not necessarily an evil. You have to decide for yourself.

Evaluating fees: The reporting of yields on mutual funds is formulated net of all management fees. If you had a choice of a fund paying 11% after a 1% management fee or one that paid 9½% after a ½% management fee, you would obviously want the one that yields 11%, despite its higher management fee. You always want the one that nets more.

Some fund shareholders have instituted suits against funds, insisting that their management fees are too high. That is silly. If the return is very high, the shareholders should be satisfied. If it is not, they should take their money out—a vote with cash. A management that is doing a good job deserves a good profit. *Perspective:* Management fees can be warranted by good performance, but brokerage commissions are easy to avoid if you don't need hand-holding.

IRAs: Most mutual funds charge an annual fee for custodial duties—and a fee for setting up the account. The custodial fee is a pass-along because of charges by the bank's trust department, which provides the accounting services required by the IRS.

Frequently the largest expense for IRA investors is the transfer fee incurred if they wish to change their IRA from one brokerage or fund to another, from a broker to a mutual fund, etc. *The problem:* This entails a change in trusteeship (the bank providing the custodial service). And that can be costly as well as time-consuming. Believe it or not, it often takes months. *Reason:* Those trusteeships were set up with the belief that the accounts would be held there until retirement. The trustees never expected to give up these accounts quickly. To discourage transfers, they require all kinds of information and material from the investor...and they charge heavily for making the transfer.

Better transfer method: Roll over your IRA account instead of transferring it directly. In a rollover you close your account and take personal possession of your IRA money for up to 60 days. You are allowed one rollover per year. All funds, brokers, and trustees are set up to do this easily. Rollovers are faster than transfers, and at most firms they are less expensive.

Another way to avoid transfer fees: Use a no-load family of mutual funds. Then when you are unhappy with the stock market, you can switch into another type of investment fund free of charge...and switch, and switch...

Banking alternative: Banks don't charge fees for setting up IRAs, since they are trustees for themselves. There is, however, a hidden fee. Banks give a lower rate of return on your money. The differential between what an investor can expect to earn in bank certificates of deposit and a growth stock mutual fund over a 10- to 20-year period is very large. *Our estimate:* Banks will average 10%, while growth stock mutual funds can average 20%.

When to Get Out Of a Mutual Fund

Doug Fabian, president, Fabian Investment Resources, a mutual fund advisory service in Huntington Beach, California, and is the editor of the newsletter, *Successful Investing. www.fabian.com*

To check your fund holdings for "lemons," look at the quarterly Lipper Analytical Services mutual fund data. These are reported in many newspapers and financial publications. *Guidelines to use...*

• **Make proper comparisons.** Measure your fund's performance against funds with a similar investment objective.

Example: Don't compare against the Standard & Poor's 500 Index unless yours is an index fund with the same objective.

• **Use meaningful time periods.** Check your fund's relative performance against its peer average for one year, three years and five years.

Reason: Any fund manager can have a bad quarter, and that's not necessarily a reason to dump the fund.

First cut: Funds that have been underperforming for all three periods.

Second cut: Funds that are marginal performers—or worse—and charge more in annual fees than the average in their peer group. *Benchmark:* The average fee for a domestic stock fund is 1.34%.

Third cut: If you are fairly heavily invested in growth, capital appreciation or index funds where you have substantial profits but are concerned about a market correction, lower your risk by moving some of those assets into balanced funds and/or growth-and-income funds.

Caution: Consider the tax consequences of any sale carefully.

Mutual Fund Trap

Poorly performing mutual funds rarely "turn around" the way poorly performing stocks sometimes do.

Trap: The manager of a poorly performing fund isn't going to become more skillful after making a series of poor investments. And as investors leave the fund, its expense ratio will go up, further reducing returns and making a recovery even less likely.

Best: Don't buy a fund with a poor track record expecting it to turn around. If you are in such a fund now, don't wait for it to turn around. Take your loss and invest elsewhere.

Jonathan Clements, former columnist for *The Wall Street Journal* and author of *25 Myths You've Got to Avoid—If You Want to Manage Your Money Right* (Touchstone). *www.jonathanclements.com*

Advice from a Top Financial Planner

Ross Levin, CFP, founding principal and president, Accredited Investors Inc., 5200 W. 73rd St., Edina, Minnesota 55439.

Owning too many funds leads to overlapping investments, high fees and paperwork overload. *To streamline your fund holdings...*

•**Identify must-have holdings.** Before dropping funds from your portfolio, reestablish what portion of your assets to devote to stocks and bonds.

Investors' stock/bond allocation...
In their 40s—80%/20%
In their 50s—75%/25%
60s and beyond—70%/30%

Then decide what types of funds you must own to maximize returns and minimize risk.

Most investors need only five funds to properly diversify assets...

Large-cap value.
Large-cap growth.
Small-cap value.
Small-cap growth.
International fund.

•**Identify your excess funds.** You may own funds that were hot last year but haven't performed well over the past five years. Your portfolio may be missing small-cap and international funds that are important for long-term diversity.

•**Keep funds that live up to their promise.** Ask each fund what percentage of its portfolio is dedicated to stocks that fit its original mission. There has been a great deal of deviation recently.

Example: Some mid-cap fund managers have been buying shares of large companies to boost their performances.

Funds that are worth keeping should have at least 90% of their assets invested in stocks that match their missions.

•**Sell shares in funds with similar missions and assets.** Choose the fund that has been most consistent over the last three to five years. Then reinvest the assets in your five core funds according to your original allocation.

In a Hurry to Sell?

If trying to sell mutual fund shares in a hurry and the toll-free line is busy, try the fund's regular listed number. If that number is tied up and the fund has an office in your area, go there in person. If there is no office close by, keep calling outside of normal office hours or try calling other offices in small towns.

Also: Many funds have 24-hour lines, and some will accept orders via the Touch-Tone phone pad or through their Web sites.

Advance planning: Call your fund today to find out if it will accept orders by fax. If so, get the fax number in case you need it later.

Important: Confirm that your order was executed correctly by thoroughly checking your next statement.

Paul A. Merriman, founder, Merriman Berkman Next, Inc., and advisor at *www.fundadvice.com*, both in Seattle.

Watch Your Arithmetic When Municipals Are Cashed In

Many owners of municipal bonds pay more tax on appreciated value than they should.

Trap: The increase in the value of the bond is not all capital gain. The IRS has held that any increase in value that is attributable to the discount given when the bond was originally issued is really interest income.

Benefit to taxpayers: The interest accrued on a municipal bond is tax free.

Reality: A municipal bond is rarely held by the same person from the day it is issued until the day it matures, which may be many years later. It is much more likely that the bond will be traded several times during that period. And the price of a bond issued at discount will tend to rise as its maturity date approaches.

Tax treatment: The amount of the discount is attributed to the owners of the bond evenly over the bond's life.

Example: A bond issued at a $300 discount has a 30-year term. The discount is attributed (or amortized) at the rate of $10 a year. So a person who holds the bond for two years may sell it for a $20 profit and have no taxable gain.

Complications: The price of the bond may be affected by many other factors. And a price change resulting from another factor, such

as a change in interest rates, will result in a gain or loss that is capital in nature. But a taxpayer who properly amortizes the original issue discount will benefit—regardless of whether the bond is sold for a gain or a loss.

Reason: The taxpayer adds the amortized discount to the price he paid for the bond when he computes his profit or loss on the subsequent sale.

Result: If the bond is sold for a profit, the taxable gain is reduced. But if the bond is sold for a loss, the available loss deduction is increased. Of course, as with all tax issues, check with the IRS or your tax professional to ensure you're complying with any recent changes in the code.

Don't Be Fooled

Read the fine print first in investment ads. The fact that an ad has tiny type at the bottom tells you the investment is complex—no matter what the headline says. Whenever an ad grabs your attention, ask yourself if you understand the risks and assumptions. If you don't, pass up the investment.

Example: Municipal bond ads that promote the taxable equivalent yield for people in the 35% bracket are really saying they may not be appropriate for people in lower brackets.

John Markese, PhD, president, American Association of Individual Investors, 625 N. Michigan Ave., Chicago 60611. *www.aaii.com*

Junk Bonds: Don't Let the Name Fool You

Junk bonds are riskier than Treasury bonds or investment-grade corporate bonds (rated BBB or above). *The reward:* They produce better returns for investors. Many institutions (pension funds and insurance companies) aren't allowed to buy bonds rated lower than A, so the market prices them inefficiently.

The typical high-yield "junk" bond can yield, at a minimum, 350 to 450 basis points (3.5% to 4.5%) more than US Treasury bonds—6.5% a year or more.

If you're afraid of high-yield bonds, consider this: The scariest thing in the world is buying an AAA bond at par (face value). You have paid for everything good that can ever happen to your investment. If the bond goes up much in price, the company will call it (that is, buy it back from you), and if it goes down, you may have to take a loss, or wait out the bond's maturity. But if you buy a B bond, any number of things can happen. Many high-yield bonds are issued at 85% or so of face value, so there's room for the price to go up. *Another possibility:* Instant upgrade through merger.

If the issuing company goes bankrupt, all is not lost by any means. You may lose some interest and some sleep, but if you are willing to wait awhile and don't panic, you can still do well. There was more money lost on the downgrading of Ford's bonds from AA to A than on all the bankruptcies of B bonds in 10 years put together.

The volatility of interest rates makes the prices of high-grade bonds gyrate, and that makes junk bonds even more attractive. Low-grade bonds tend to trade like stocks, so they have always fluctuated in price. (Many are even convertible to stock.) That is part of what gave junk bonds their image problem. People think bonds shouldn't be volatile. When even the high-grade bonds are fluctuating in price the risk/reward ratio shifts still more in favor of lower grade credits.

How to invest in junk bonds: As always, the key to success is to do homework and to spread risks. Most individuals should not buy one or two issues of B-rated bonds. Although the risk on a broadly based portfolio is minimal relative to the yield differential, the risk on any single issue could be catastrophic. By diversifying, you reduce the risk of a thermonuclear event in your portfolio.

If you can afford to buy an assortment of high-yield bonds issued by different companies in different industries, that's great. For smaller investors, there are a dozen or so high-yield bond mutual funds that have diversified portfolios and will do your homework for you. *Typical minimum investment:* $1,000.

Remember: You can make money only if you're careful. Returns can be substantial, but you can never forget they're called junk bonds for a reason.

How to Play the Junk Bond Market

John Rekenthaler, vice president, Research and New Products, Morningstar, Inc., an independent fund rating service and publisher, 225 W. Wacker Dr., Chicago 60606.

If you're going to play the junk bond game, you have to know the rules—and the tricks. *For example…*

• **Invest in junk bonds only after you have invested in the basics.** Junk bonds are a second-tier investment. They are for investors who have already invested at least two-thirds of their portfolios in large-cap stocks, Treasury bonds and investment-grade bonds, which have credit ratings of BBB or higher.

• **Invest in a no-load junk bond fund rather than in individual issues.** Funds hold a diversified portfolio of high-yield bonds.

• **Before choosing a fund, compare its record and manager.** Consider only those funds that have performed in the top half of all junk bond funds over the past three and five years. This information is available free on our Web site, *www.morningstar.com.* Then make sure the current manager was responsible for that record.

• **In a bull market, be wary of choosing top-performing funds.** Their yields almost always fall hardest in a bear market.

Hours When Experts Do Their Trading

Popularly traded issues show distinct tendencies during the course of the day. *Reason:* Traders tend to buy and sell at certain hours. *Astute investors can take advantage of these patterns...*

• **Day traders often buy early in the morning** or on evidence of overall stock market strength that day. If the market is weak, traders will sell short at the earliest opportunity. Positions on the New York exchange are normally equalized between 3:30 and 3:45 pm there.

• **On stronger days,** expect temporary weaknesses in the issue at about 3:30, when most traders close out their long positions. Buyers should try to place orders during this period. Sellers should wait until just near the close, when prices often recover. (Another point of market weakness is between noon and 1 pm)

• **On weaker days,** short sellers should expect some price recovery at about 3:30 pm when some traders are covering their shorts.

Guide to Stock Market Indicators

It's important to be familiar with common market terminology. *Here are a few terms you should know to better understand stock market indicators...*

• **Speculation index.** Divide the weekly trading volume on the American Stock Exchange (in thousands) by the number of issues traded. Calculate the same ratio for New York Stock Exchange trading. Divide the AMEX ratio by the NYSE ratio to calculate the speculation index.

To read the index: Strategists believe the market is bearish when the index is more than .38 (and especially so if it rises to .38 and then falls back). Less than .20 is bullish.

• **Member short selling.** Divide the number of shares NYSE members sell short each week by total NYSE short selling.

To read the index: It is bearish when readings of .87 are reached. A reading below .75 is very bullish, particularly if it lasts several weeks.

• **New highs–new lows.** The market is usually approaching an intermediate bottom when the number of new lows reaches 600. The probable sign of an intermediate top is 600 new highs in one week, followed by a decline in number the next week.

• **NYSE short interest ratio.** The total number of outstanding shares sold short each month divided by the average daily trading volume for that month. A strong rally generally comes after the ratio reaches 1.75.

• **Ten-week moving NYSE average.** Compute the average NYSE index for the previous 10 weeks. Then measure the difference between last week's close and the average.

How to read it: When the gap between the last weekly close and the 10-week average remains at 4.00 or below for two to three weeks, investors can expect an intermediate advance. Market tops are usually near when the last week's index is 4.00 or more above the previous 10-week average.

• **Reading the indicators together.** Only once or twice a year will as many as four of the five indicators signal an intermediate bottom, but when four do, it is highly reliable. The same is true for intermediate tops.

All indicators available weekly in *Barron's.*

How Professionals Spot Low-Priced Stock That May Bounce Back

Robert J. Ravitz, principal, David J. Greene & Company, New York City.

Value has little to do with telling a good company from a bad one. A top-quality large company that is selling at a high price/earnings multiple is less attractive than a lesser quality company that is selling at a depressed price in terms of its past and future earnings power, working capital, book value and historical prices.

WHAT TO LOOK FOR

•**Stocks that have just made a new low for the past 12 months.**

•**Companies that are likely to be liquidated.** In the liquidation process, shareholders may get paid considerably more than the stock is selling for now.

•**Unsuccessful merger candidates.** If one buyer thinks a company's stock is a good value, it's possible that others may also come to the same conclusion.

•**Companies that have just reduced or eliminated their dividends.** The stock is usually hit with a selling wave, which often creates a good buying opportunity.

•**Financially troubled companies** in which another major company has a sizable ownership position. If the financial stake is large enough, you can be sure that the major company will do everything it can to turn the earnings around and get the stock price up so that its investment will work out.

There are opportunities, also, in stocks that are totally washed out—that is, situations where all the bad news is out. The stock usually has nowhere to go but up.

HOW TO BE SURE A STOCK IS TRULY WASHED OUT

•**Trading volume slows to practically nothing.** If over-the-counter, few if any dealers are making a market.

•**No Wall Street research analysts are following the company anymore.**

•**No financial journalists,** stock market newsletters or advisory services discuss the company.

•**Selling of the stock by company's management and directors has stopped.**

SIGNS OF A TURNAROUND

•**The company plans to get rid of a losing division or business.** If so, be sure to learn whether the company will be able to report a big jump in earnings once the losing operation is sold.

•**The company is selling off assets** to improve its financial situation and/or reduce debt.

•**A new management comes on board** with an established track record of success with turnaround situations.

•**Management begins buying the company's stock** in the open market.

•**Also, be sure to follow the Form 13D statements filed with the SEC.** (A company or individual owning 5% or more of a public company must report such holdings to the Securities and Exchange Commission.) If any substantial company is acquiring a major position in a company, it's possible a tender offer at a much higher price is in the wind.

Signal That a Large Block of Stock Is About to Be Dumped

Very frequently, knowledge that a large block of shares of a particular stock is up for sale can influence the decision on whether to buy or to sell those securities. For example, you might postpone or permanently avoid purchasing shares about to come under institutional liquidation. Or you might choose to sell before a competing large sell order becomes operative.

While mutual funds and other institutions don't advertise that they plan a liquidation prior to actual sale, such information, not infrequently, manages to leak out, and this often puts a sizable dent in the stock's price. There are usually hints available to the alert investor that a liquidation of the block is imminent.

The major indication that a block is coming up for sale lies in a sudden shrinkage of the trading range of the issue in question. For example, a stock might usually demonstrate an average trading range of perhaps a full point or point and a half between its daily high and low in a typical trading day. If, for two or three days, this trading range shrinks to, say, one-tenth to three-eighths of a point, you might anticipate a block is coming up for sale at near current market levels or below.

The shrinkage may represent awareness on the part of knowledgeable floor and other traders that a large sell order exists and an unwillingness to bid up for the stock until the overhead supply, which is immediately forthcoming, is fully liquidated.

For more information, go to *www.nasdaq.com*.

Four Reasons To Fire Your Adviser

Jack Waymire, cofounder of Paladin Registry, an Internet company that matches investors with financial advisers (*www.paladinregistry.com*). He was president of money management firm Lexington Capital Management for 21 years and is author of *Who's Watching Your Money? The 17 Paladin Principles for Selecting a Financial Adviser* (Wiley).

It's not your financial adviser's fault that the economy hit the skids in 2008, but he/she may deserve the boot if any one of the following is true...

• **The adviser disappeared.** Your calls weren't returned or your meetings were repeatedly canceled. Some advisers dodge difficult conversations with clients who have lost big bucks—but that's when clients need their help most.

• **Your portfolio underperformed appropriate benchmarks over several years.** If the stock portion of your portfolio performed roughly as well as the Standard & Poor's 500 Index during the five-year bull market, it should not have lost much more than the S&P 500 during the bear market. Use the Nasdaq Composite Index as your measuring stick if you have an aggressive portfolio of small-caps. And use an appropriate bond index, perhaps one of the Barclays Capital bond indices, to judge the fixed-income portion of your portfolio (visit *http://ecommerce.barcap.com/indices*).

• **Your portfolio was riskier than was appropriate for you.** If you are retired or near retirement, or you told your adviser that you wanted a conservative portfolio, a significant portion of your money—30% or more—should have been invested in bonds or cash. And no more than a few percent should have been in any one stock.

• **Your adviser offered no constructive advice as the market declined.** If your adviser's only guidance during the rout was "just hang in there—the market will turn the corner soon," there is no need to hang on to him. The financial world changed last year, and your adviser should have been suggesting ways in which your portfolio and financial plan should have changed in response.

Examples of good advice: Sell off some weak securities that lost money to reduce taxes... select stocks and sectors well-positioned for a rebound.

Protecting Paper Profits When the Market Dips

There's a way to safeguard paper profits against the stock market dropping without selling out entirely. It's called covered option writing. *How covered option writing works...*

Sell short one 100-share call option for every 100 shares of stock owned. If the stock goes down, the option will go down, too. Then there'll be a profit when the investor buys it back at a loss, or when it expires worthless. If the stock goes up (providing more paper profits), the option will go up, too. The investor must then buy it back (that's a cash loss, not a paper loss). Otherwise the option will be exercised, which means the investor is forced to sell the stock at the option exercise price.

The technique is a bit complicated, but many brokers are familiar with it and will guide the investor. Be aware that this is a hedging strategy for uncertainty. If an investor feels sure the market will drop, he or she probably should sell his stocks outright.

• *Points to remember:* Covered option writing gives only limited downside protection. If the market drops faster than 10% in six months (which could happen), this program loses money. And the cost of getting this protection is that the investor gives up most of the additional profits he'd make if the market goes higher.

How to Tell When a Fast-Rising Industry Is Topping Out

There's a typical pattern—initial price gains attract wide public speculative interest, which finally gives way to sharp price declines. The declines often trap inexperienced or unwary investors.

How to recognize when such groups may be topping out prior to a sharp price drop…

• **The industry group already has had a very sharp run-up.**

• **Very heavy trading volume.** Stocks in this group dominate the list of most actively traded stocks.

• **Near the top of the rise,** the stocks gain and lose in substantial price swings. But little ground is gained in the process.

• **Price/earnings multiples for the group soar far above historical norms.**

• **Heavy short selling appears.** Early short sellers of the stocks are driven to cover by sharp rallies. Their covering of shorts adds fuel to late rallies within the group. (Short sellers who enter the picture later, however, are likely to be amply rewarded.)

Trading options that work for professionals: Extreme caution first and foremost. Close stop-orders are placed on any long and/or short positions taken. Short sales are entered into only after these issues have shown signs of fatigue and of topping out, and then only after recent support levels have been broken. Wait for a clear sign that the uptrend has ended before selling out.

How Bear Market Rallies Can Fool You

Bear market rallies may often be sharp. They're fueled in part by short sellers who are rushing to cover shares. However, advances in issues sold short sometimes lack durability once short covering is completed. *Details…*

• **Bear market rallies tend to last for no more than five or six weeks.**

• **Bear market advances often end rapidly** —with relatively little advance warning. If you are trading during a bear market, you must be ready to sell at the first sign of weakness.

• **The first strong advance during a bear market** frequently lulls many analysts into a false sense of security, leading them to conclude that a new bull market is under way. The majority of the bear markets don't end until pessimism is widespread and the vast majority is convinced that prices are going to continue to decline indefinitely.

• **Although the stock market can remain "overbought" for considerable periods of time during bull markets,** bear market rallies generally end fairly rapidly. This typically occurs as the market enters into overbought conditions. An overbought condition happens when prices advance for a short time at a rate that can't be sustained.

One way to predict a decline—using the advance-decline line as a guide: Each day, compute the net difference between the number of issues that rise on the Big Board and the number that decline. A 10-day total of the daily nets is then maintained. During bear markets, be careful when the 10-day net differential rises to +2,500 or more. You should be ready to sell immediately once this figure is reached and starts to decline. The decline will usually indicate that the advance is beginning to weaken.

This may prove to be the last opportunity to sell into strength.

The patterns seen during one-day reversals occasionally take place early in intermediate advances, with the backoff representing a test of previous lows. If such action appears prior to significant market gains, do not sell.

Instead, you should buy during any near-term weakness. The market will probably resume its rise.

However, if such a trading pattern occurs following a period of several weeks or months of rising prices, the odds increase that a genuine one-day reversal is occurring. Then you must take protective action.

Three Ways to Spot a Market Decline Before It Starts

Strong market moves can frequently end in one- or two-day reversal spikes. Those spikes often provide advance warning of significant market turning points. *Here are a few signs that show when a market decline may be coming…*

•**The market will rise sharply in the morning** on very high volume running at close to 15 million shares during the first hour of trading.

•**From 10:30 am (Eastern time) on,** the market will make little or no progress despite heavy trading throughout the day.

•**By the end of the first day,** almost all the morning's gains will have been lost, with the market closing clearly toward the downside. Occasionally this process will be spread over a two-day period.

Steps to take: When you see the pattern, either sell immediately or await the retest of the highs that were reached during that first morning. Such a retest often takes place within a week or two, on much lower trading volume.

Making Profits on a Stock Split

C. Colburn Hardy, *Trader's Guide to Technical Analysis* (Traders Library).

When a stock splits, the average profit to an investor is 20%. But the greatest profits are generally made in three to six months before the split is announced. The general pattern is that the price stays high for two days after the split announcement and then declines. *To spot a candidate for a split, look for…*

•**A company that needs to attract** more stockholders, diversify or attract additional financing.

•**A takeover candidate** (heavy in cash and liquid assets) whose management holds only a small percentage of the outstanding shares. (Companies with concentrated ownership rarely split stock unless there are problems with taxes, acquisitions or diversification.)

•**A stock price above $75.** A split moves it into the more attractive $35 to $50 range.

•**A stock that was split previously** and price has climbed steadily since then.

•**Earnings prospects so strong** that the company will be able to increase dividends after the split.

Likely prospects are over-the-counter companies with current earnings of $2.5 million, at least $2 million annually in preceding years and less than one million shares outstanding (or under 2,000 shareholders). A stock split is necessary if management wants to list on a major exchange.

Techniques For Evaluating Over-the-Counter Stocks

C. Colburn Hardy, *Trader's Guide to Technical Analysis* (Traders Library).

Growth potential is the single most important consideration when evaluating stocks. Earnings increases should average 10% over the past six years when acquisitions and divestitures are factored out. Cash, investments, accounts receivable, materials and inventories should be twice the size of financial claims due within the next year.

In addition, working capital per share should be greater than the market value of the stock (an $8 stock should be backed by $10 per share in working capital). Long-term debt should be covered by working capital, cash or one year's income. And the balance sheet should show no deferred operating expenses and no unreceived income.

The criteria for final selections include ownership by at least 10 institutions and public ownership of between 500,000 and one million shares, with no more than 10% controlled by a single institution. There should also be continued price increases after a dividend or split, and a strong likelihood of moving up to a major exchange. (A good sign is strong broker and institutional support.)

Over-the-counter stocks you should try to avoid are those of companies expanding into unrelated fields, where they lack the required management experience and depth, and stock selling at prices far below recent highs.

This sign of loss of investor support can take months to overcome.

Best Time to Invest in Newly Listed Stocks

Market Logic.

Most investors believe that a stock will rise in price as soon as it moves from an over-the-counter listing to the New York Stock Exchange. That's rarely true. *What actually happens…*

• **The prices of such shares tend to run up sharply** on the smaller exchange in the year preceding the NYSE listing. Foreknowledge of listings may or may not be available to shareholders, however, and you can't necessarily presume that you'll benefit from this information.

• **During the average nine-week period** required for the NYSE to consider applications for listing, stocks that move from the over-the-counter markets usually outperform other stocks. If you hold such an issue, keep it until the listing procedure is completed.

• **Once listing has been achieved,** expect the price performance of such issues to fall to below average. Weakness is usually particularly acute during the first six weeks following listing, and this weakness can linger for as long as a year.

Hold or buy as soon as applications for an NYSE listing are made, but plan to sell when the application is approved. *Be careful:* A few issues will rise in price even after listing is complete, and some will fall during the period just prior to listing.

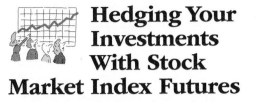

Hedging Your Investments With Stock Market Index Futures

Malcolm "Mac" Fellman, former first vice president, Prudential Securities, New York City (now Wachovia Securities, Charlotte, North Carolina).

There is an opportunity for people to call a turn in the stock market without having to pick and choose individual stocks. At times it is easier to call a turn in the market than to determine the individual stocks to "bet" on. Since it's just as easy to be short on a commodity as it is to be long, an investor can just short one of the indexes if he or she thinks the stock market is going to move downward. An investor doesn't have to choose specific stocks to short.

Right from the beginning, it was obvious to everyone that these were going to be viable contracts. They have attracted both speculators—the traditional commodities traders—and more-conservative equities investors who can use the futures contracts to hedge their investments.

Attraction for speculators: Enormous leverage can be obtained on the initial outlay of cash. Each contract is valued at the index multiplied by 250. For instance, with the S&P 500 index at 155, the value of the S&P futures contract would be $38,750. *Margin requirements:* 10%, or, in this example, $3,875. But for each dollar the index moves up or down, the speculator makes or loses $250, according to how he was positioned.

Obviously, this leverage factor can work either for or against the investor. That potential for volatility and the possibility of a margin call frighten some people. It is the same as the margin calls for gold and silver futures contracts. An investor will be called to add to his margin requirement if the market gets out of his trading range and moves against him. Actually, stock market index futures are even more risky than gold and silver futures contracts, since there are no limits on the contract's movements as there are in gold and silver.

For that reason, brokerage houses insist that potential buyers of any futures be high-net-worth individuals.

Hedging opportunities: Besides speculating on which way the market might be blowing, there are some savvy uses of stock market index futures for the moderately large equities investor. *For example...*

For the investor with a sizable portfolio—say, in the $1 million range—who is worried that the stock market is moving down and is in for a serious correction, there is great opportunity in selling the index short. If the investor is correct, and the market falls, he will profit from the position in the futures contract while he loses money on some of his stocks. This is especially true if the investor wishes to take a capital gain at the end of a year and has not been holding many of his stocks long enough. This way there is profit at a lower tax...and the investor is able to qualify for the holding period on his stocks.

For many individuals, accumulating a good, balanced portfolio takes a long time and a lot of thinking. Selling the index short against an equities portfolio ensures investors of not having to upset that balance. And they aren't later forced into selling those stocks into a weak market where they must take panic prices if the market is falling fast.

If an investor shorts the index instead of selling his stocks and there is a false start—the market appears to be plunging and then turns back upward—it is much easier to "cut bait and run" with a stock market index contract than it is to buy back stocks once you have sold them. And you'll save a great deal in commissions if you substitute shorting the future for selling the stocks.

Buy hedge: On the opposite side of the fence, people can go long the index-futures contract as a hedge. By definition, a hedge in the futures market is taking a position opposite that of your inventories. Thus if you buy a futures contract, you are holding no stocks, but you are anticipating a future purchase.

For example, you have a strong feeling that the market will make a major bullish move, but your cash-flow situation is poor. Although you have the money, it is tied up in various money market instruments. You wish you had the money in hand to put into the stock market. At that point it is a hedge to buy the futures contract. If you are correct, you will have to pay more for any stocks you want to buy when your instruments come due a few months later. On the other hand, you will have made at least a comparable amount of profit on the futures to make up for the higher prices. *Point:* You have fixed the cost of your purchase when the market is just beginning to take off.

For foreign investors: Going long the stock market indexes can be a good substitute when you can't get your money out of your country quickly enough to participate in a stock market rally.

An unusual use of the sell hedge: When there is a possible merger of two corporations, and one of the participants asks you to tender stock. In many cases, the merger doesn't materialize, and the stock value has gone down by the time it is finally released. You could have sold a stock market futures contract short against the stock you tendered. *Condition:* If the merger is so dramatic that it affects the entire stock market in one way or another (which has happened in a few cases). This could cause the contract to move in an unusual way.

To learn more about index futures: *An assortment of web sites detail the specifics about the new index futures...*

• **Stock Market Savvy: Investing for Your Future.** This is a free educational program designed for middle school and high school students. Investor education materials are also available online at *www.nyse.com*. At the site, click "US Equities," then search "Educational Materials."

• **Kansas City Board of Trade.** *www.kcbt. com*

• **CME Group.** *www.cmegroup.com*

What Makes "The Dow" Tick and How It Can Fool You

The Dow Jones Industrial Average is computed by adding the prices of the 30 stocks that comprise the average

and dividing the total by a divisor, published every Monday in *The Wall Street Journal*, that changes periodically to reflect stock splits.

As a result of this method of computation, the higher priced issues in the Dow contribute more to the average than do lower priced ones.

Were each of the 30 components of the Dow to gain 8 points on average, or 240 points in total, the Dow would rise by approximately 1,818 points (240 divided by 0.132). Of course, this is unlikely, since the higher priced issues are more likely to show wider fluctuation than the lower priced issues, on a point-change basis.

A deceptively rising Dow: Very frequently, bull markets end with the Dow rising to new heights, but investors don't make that profit. Such situations come about when one or two influential issues (like IBM or GE) rise to new highs, pulling up the averages significantly because of their weight. However, the rest of the list is faltering, but their troubles are buried in the computation of the Dow Industrials Average. *Result:* A deceptive rise in the Dow, luring in investors, although the bulk of the market is either standing still or falling.

Remedy: Track either the Advance-Decline Line, which shows how many issues on the New York Stock Exchange are actually rising and falling, or check on how many components of the Dow Industrials Average are actually contributing to its rise. The Advance-Decline Line figures are published daily in *The Wall Street Journal*.

Questions and Answers About Convertible Bonds

Paul Singer, formerly president of Braxton Associates, New York City.

When are convertibles a good investment? When convertibles are undervalued, they can be much more attractive than either a straight bond or the underlying common stock. *Best choice:* From time to time, you can find a convertible bond that has as high a yield as a straight bond. You get the equity kicker for nothing. *Why this happens:* Since many people don't understand convertibles, the market is thin and there are often valuation discrepancies.

When should a convertible be converted into a common stock? Only when the stock sells well above its redemption price. Further, take into account the interest-rate payment date of the bond. Convertibles generally pay interest semiannually. In the interim, the interest is accrued. However, if you convert a bond before interest is payable, you could lose up to six months' interest, especially since the bond interest is usually greater than the stock's dividend. If you want to liquidate a convertible-bond position, you can do it by selling the bond or by converting into the resulting stock. Check both ways to see which is more profitable. Be wary of lost interest upon conversion.

How do you measure the value of a convertible? First: Compare the yield of the bond with the yield of the stock.

Next: Compare the current price of the bond with the redemption price. There is a high likelihood of redemption of the bond by the issuing company when the stock is selling for much more than the redemption price. At such time, the convertible will not sell at a premium to its stock value. Find out if there are any special provisions that could affect the value of the bond, such as the expiration of the conversion privilege, which is sometimes set before the bond matures.

What happens to convertible bonds when interest rates increase or decrease dramatically? Convertible bonds are interest-sensitive, but not as much as straight bonds. Other things being equal, they would rally if interest rates decline and drop if interest rates rise.

How can you reduce the risk of owning convertible bonds? Look for undervalued convertibles and hedge them by shorting stock against it. There are other hedging techniques that make use of options.

Where do I find more information? You may want to subscribe to leading convertible-bond publications...

• **Value Line Convertible Survey,** which is available online by subscription, *www.value line.com.* 800-634-3583.

A convertible bond is convertible into the common stock of a company. It generally carries a lower interest rate than a straight bond because of this kicker. *Evaluate...*

• **Its attractiveness as straight, subordinated debt.**

• **Its long-term warrant** (which allows you to buy the underlying stock at a specific price or an indefinite time period).

• **The right of the company to redeem the bond and when.**

Why Small Caps?

Small-cap stock funds are the best investments for people with at least a 20-year time horizon, despite their short-term volatility.

Surprising: Over two decades, small-cap funds actually have higher returns than large-cap funds. Overall, small-caps' worst 20-year time period was better than large-caps' worst 20-year period.

Important: Small-cap funds outperform only if you continue investing in them. Plan to put the same percentage of your income into small-cap funds each year.

Sherman Hanna, PhD, professor of consumer sciences, Ohio State University, Columbus, and coauthor of a study on funds.

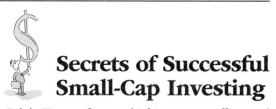

Secrets of Successful Small-Cap Investing

Ralph Wanger, former chief investment officer and lead manager of the Acorn Fund. He is author of A Zebra Among the Lions: Ralph Wanger's Investment Survival Manual *(Simon & Schuster). www.columbiamanagement. com*

Successful investors have a strategy that dictates what types of stocks they want to own, and they stick to their guns. *I've always sought small-cap companies that have...*

- **Products that investors can easily understand.**

- **A dominant market position in whatever they make.**

- **Limited themselves to one or two lines of business.**

- **Entrepreneurial management.**

Small-cap value stocks tend to rebound following a year in which these equities underperformed other types of stocks.

I look for stocks of small, sound, undervalued companies with products or services that are in demand both here and abroad. A small company is—by my definition—any company that has a market capitalization of less than $1 billion.

In a tough, competitive business environment, the companies that survive and prosper will be those that find and exploit their own special niches. You can find such companies by asking your broker to request them from the firm's analysts.

A niche can be geographical, such as that enjoyed by a regional bank, utility or railroad. Or it can be technological—meaning it is based on patents or know-how. Sometimes the niche is simply a marketing technique—the ability to sell a product or service at least a little bit better than rivals.

What I don't want are "me-too" companies that rank fourth or fifth in their industries.

Managers of great small companies are better than larger companies at responding to change. They have the aggressive spirit that is needed to succeed, and they can push harder than more-mature companies with layers of management bureaucracy.

Best of all, small companies are not under the hot lights of Wall Street analysts. You can uncover things about small companies that others don't know yet. As a result, the prices of small-company stocks are frequently undervalued.

- **Hold the stock of small companies for five years or more.** In our experience, the sound economic values of good small companies are eventually reflected in their stock prices...but you must be patient.

A small company's stock price will often rise as the company...

...grows and earns more.

...repurchases its own stock.

...is revalued in the marketplace as analysts who once denounced the company as an ugly duckling suddenly see it as a swan.

- **Know your risk tolerance.** It's important to realize, though, that small companies are riskier investments than large companies. They may be dependent on one or two people or products, and it's always easier for Wall Street to sink a tugboat than to sink a battleship.

But the greater the risk, the greater the opportunity to make money. Each investor has to evaluate his or her tolerance for risk.

Stock funds like mine that concentrate on small-company stocks are volatile, and investors should have no more than one-third of their portfolios invested in these types of stocks or funds.

- **Don't overpay for a small-cap value stock.** When you invest, you want good, growing companies. But you don't want to pay too much. *Examples...*

- I seldom buy "supergrowth" stocks because their high rise-in-earnings estimates rarely come true.

- I also avoid value stocks of companies that have high stated book values (net worths) but that may, in fact, be very sick.

  Example: A company's book value may be inflated by outmoded assets, such as open-hearth steel furnaces.

- I look for growth at a reasonable price over the next five years.

Insider-Selling Signals

Don't overreact to insider selling. Corporate insiders frequently have good reasons to raise cash. Insider selling is simply a signal to take a closer look at a stock—not a reason to panic.

Example: If insiders sell while a stock's price soars, that probably means nothing. But if they sell while it goes down, that can be a bad sign. And if they sell when the price is not moving much, that could be a signal of coming changes in the company.

Helpful: Use Web search engines to track insider-selling reports.

Example: Using the search engine *http://finance.yahoo.com*, enter a stock's symbol. Then under the "Ownership" banner, click on "Insider Transactions" to see details of insider sales.

Bob Gabele, formerly a principal research analyst with First Call/Thomson Financial.

Before Jumping into a Commodity Pool...

Commodity pools have many attractions for the speculatively inclined investor who wants the leverage of commodity trading but also wants to cut some of the risk. *Before investing...*

• **Look for performance consistency over at least five years.** Pools that have outstanding records are often successful for only a relatively brief period. Monthly or even annually computed returns can vary from excellent to terrible.

• **Be wary of a pool that pays the manager more than 5% in commission.**

• **Make sure the pool is getting a favorable commission rate** if it's organized by a brokerage house. Although the typical brokerage house does provide a commission discount to its pool, these discounts are often minimal compared with what can be achieved elsewhere. So compare the commission expenses of the various pools.

Bargain Homes for Sale: How to Find a Good Deal at a Foreclosure Auction

Ralph Roberts, who has sold more than 10,000 homes during 30 years as a real estate agent. Roberts, based in Sterling Heights, Michigan, has personally purchased hundreds of homes at foreclosure auctions and is author of *Foreclosure Investing for Dummies* (Wiley). *www.ralphroberts.com*

More than 200,000 homes per month are going into foreclosure nationwide, according to Internet real estate marketplace RealtyTrac. Many of them are being sold at foreclosure auctions.

Should you buy your next home this way? Possibly, but take care. While you can get a great deal—some foreclosed properties sell for less than half their assessed value—not all auctioned homes are bargains, and complex auction rules can trip up novices. *What you need to know...*

WHICH AUCTIONS TO GO TO

When people picture real estate auctions, they typically think of what is known as sheriff's auctions, also called trustee auctions or courthouse auctions. These are conducted by a government entity and feature recently foreclosed-upon homes. But they can be extremely hazardous for novice bidders, who may run into unwelcome surprises.

Much better: Bid at "live auctions," large-scale real estate auctions run by major auction companies. Here, unlike with many of the sheriff's auctions, you can inspect homes prior to the auction...obtain a mortgage to finance your purchase...and never have to deal with owners forced out by foreclosure. But you may pay up to 30% more than at a sheriff's auction.

Helpful: Review the auction's terms and listing descriptions to confirm that the properties you bid on are free and clear of all liens. Live auctions usually are well-advertised in local newspaper real estate sections.

HOW TO PREPARE

In the weeks before bidding at a live auction…

• **Get preapproved for a mortgage.** Mortgage lenders often are on hand at live auctions to provide quick financing—but there's no guarantee that they'll give you a loan. Obtaining mortgage preapproval prior to the auction gives you time to shop around for attractive loan terms.

• **Work with a buyer's agent** who is very experienced with foreclosure auctions. This agent can help you identify soon-to-be auctioned homes that meet your criteria…and help you decide how much to bid. Buyer's agents receive their commissions from the seller, so there's no reason not to work with one.

• **Identify three or more homes that you like in upcoming auctions**—not just one that you love. Falling in love with one home encourages overbidding. Pick neighborhoods you love, then visit all homes up for auction in those areas.

• **Examine homes carefully before bidding.** Homes bought at auction are purchased "as is"—you can't lower your offer later if a home inspector discovers a problem. If there's any hint that significant repairs will be needed, assume the worst and adjust your bid accordingly.

• **Before an auction, set a maximum bid for each property you like.** Ask a friend to accompany you to the auction, and instruct this friend to stop you if you try to exceed these maximums.

Helpful: In this market, consider setting your maximum at between 50% and 75% of the home's "State Equalized Value" (sometimes called its "Assessed Value"). The city or county assessor's office can provide this figure. Stay at the low end of this range if your local real estate market is weak and you can be patient.

Buying a Foreclosed Home

If you want to buy a foreclosed home, look for listings on specialized Web sites, such as *www.realtytrac.com*. Buy from a bank if possible—banks will clear outstanding liens, and you can inspect their foreclosed homes before purchase. Before you bid, ask a contractor for an estimate of how much renovations will cost. Bid low—about 20% below market price, even if the bank is asking for more. Be prepared to wait—the process can take up to three months. *Helpful:* Have multiple properties in mind, and get financing preapproved before you make a bid.

Money

Buyer, Beware

Steer clear of investing in insurance viaticals. Though they promise guaranteed returns of 18%, 24%, 40% or even 60% from buying out the life insurance benefits of a terminally ill policyholder, there's no federal agency regulating the industry and there are no licensing requirements for those who market them.

If the insurance company underwriting the policy goes bust, you may be out of luck. Also, the "terminally ill" policyholder could live much longer than expected, greatly reducing your actual return—perhaps even below what you'd earn from much safer fixed-income investments.

Martin D. Weiss, PhD, chairman, Weiss Group, Inc., 15430 Endeavour Dr., Jupiter, FL 33478, and publisher and contributing editor of Safe Money Report. www.weissresearchissues.com

Why You Should Not Invest Like Warren Buffett —Smarter Plays for Individual Investors

Vahan Janjigian, editor, Forbes Growth Investor, 60 Fifth Ave., New York City 10011. He is author of Even Buffett Isn't Perfect (Portfolio).

Warren Buffett ranks as one of the greatest investors of all time. Over more than three decades, his Berkshire Hathaway Inc. has purchased dozens of stocks and businesses. During that time, the company has outperformed the Standard & Poor's 500 Index by a wide margin. Buffett achieved his record by following a disciplined investment strategy. He waits years for stocks to sell at discounts. Buffett does not hesitate to hold cash if nothing meets his exacting standards.

Seeing his record, many investors seek to mimic Buffett's style. When the master buys a stock, the imitators also make the purchase. While there is much to learn from Buffett, those who seek to copy him should beware. Buffett's approach is difficult to implement, and even the master himself has made mistakes while using the strategy. *Some trademark Buffett tactics that most investors should avoid...*

***Mistake:* Holding a concentrated portfolio.** Academics have long argued that investors should own a wide variety of stocks and other assets. That way, if some holdings fall, others may rise. Buffett understands the scholarly research, but prefers to hold "concentrated" positions, keeping big stakes in just a few industries. Altogether, Berkshire derived one-fourth of its revenue and half its profit from one industry—insurance.

Buffett's success can be traced to his concentrated approach. But most investors should tread more carefully. In fact, Buffett says most investors should diversify extensively. Many part-time investors should stick with mutual funds. A sound approach is to buy an index fund, such as one that tracks the S&P 500. While funds may never outpace the best stock pickers, the index trackers never finish at the bottom of the standings.

***Mistake:* Buying nothing but cheap stocks.** Stocks are often thought of as being from one of two categories—growth stocks, which have growing earnings and price multiples that are higher than average...and value stocks, which have little or no earnings growth and relatively low prices. Buffett does not fit neatly into any one camp. His portfolio includes some stocks that may be considered "growth" and others that fit into the value category.

Some investors may want to follow his example of holding growth and value. By owning both, you can diversify a portfolio because growth and value sometimes move in different directions. But for long-term investments, I prefer putting more than 50% of assets in value stocks. According to research by Eugene Fama, PhD, professor of finance at the University of Chicago, and Kenneth French, PhD, professor of finance at Dartmouth, value stocks tend to outperform growth over long periods. The best performance comes from stocks that are in the cheapest 10% of the market as indicated by their price-to-book ratios. This is the share price divided by the book value, a measure of a company's assets minus its liabilities. Fama and French found that during the 27 years ending in 1990, the cheapest 10% of stocks returned 21% annually, compared with the most expensive 10%, which returned 8% annually.

***Mistake:* Investing only in big companies.** Because his company is huge, Buffett finds it more convenient to buy big companies. Otherwise, to put Berkshire's assets to use, he would need to own a great many small companies and it would be difficult to watch so many as closely as he would like. The result would be an unwieldy portfolio that would be too hard to manage. But ordinary investors should hold at least some small-company stocks. According to Fama and French, the smallest stocks in the market produce the biggest returns. During the 27-year study, the smallest 10% of stocks grew more than six times, while the largest 10% returned less than half as much.

***Mistake:* Favoring losers.** As a value investor, Buffett often buys unloved stocks, picking up shares that have fallen. He shuns growth stocks that have been embraced by the markets. But investors seeking to build diverse portfolios should include at least some growth stars as short-term holdings.

When stocks have climbed for six months, they have tended on average to continue climbing for the next 12 months, according to a study by Narasimhan Jegadeesh, PhD, professor of finance at Emory University, and

Sheridan Titman, PhD, professor of finance at the University of Texas.

Investors who take advantage of the short-term moves of growth stocks must be prepared to trade quickly. Studies indicate that after 12 months, the growth stars begin to lag.

Mistake: **Holding for life.** After buying a stock, Buffett holds it indefinitely. If the shares climb sharply, he still won't sell. And if the company doesn't show earnings growth, he still hesitates to sell. Buffett often refrains from selling because he believes that it is difficult to tell the right time for unloading a stock. Rather than making mistimed moves, he holds.

Because most investors, especially those near retirement age, can't wait the decades that Buffett is prepared to wait, they can't be so patient. Expensive shares with shaky earnings can deliver disastrous short-term results.

Before buying a stock, Buffett estimates its intrinsic or fair value. This requires projecting the company's cash flow into the future and then "discounting" it to the present using an appropriate interest rate that takes the risk of the investment into consideration.

Measuring fair value precisely isn't easy, but there are ways to estimate when a stock's price has become too rich. Start by comparing the stock's price-to-book ratio (p/b) to those of the company's competitors. If the stock commands a relatively high multiple, then it could be priced above fair value.

Additional check: Compare the stock's current p/b to those from the past. When a stock's p/b exceeds its typical historical level, it is another sign that the price may be too high.

Mistake: **Sticking with what you know.** Buffett prefers buying companies that are easy to understand. Until recently, he bought only US companies. He still has very little international diversification.

Unlike Buffett, most investors should use more international diversification. Their portfolios should include shares from the emerging markets of Asia and Latin America. Overseas markets don't always move in lock-step with Wall Street.

The ABCs of IPOs

Linda Killian, CFA and portfolio manager, Renaissance Capital, Two Greenwich Plaza, Greenwich, Connecticut 06830. *www.renaissancecapital.com*

The down economy has made a number of companies second guess going public, but IPOs are still an option for investors. Yet even with all the recent hype surrounding such IPOs as Facebook (one of the largest in history), these shares can be difficult to obtain by individual investors.

HOW IPOs WORK

When a company first decides to go public, it selects an underwriter, which controls the issuance of shares. The underwriter then sets a price for the stock and sells the stock to its best clients in advance of its being traded publicly.

The sale of the stock by the underwriter to the public is called the Initial Public Offering (IPO). The price set by the underwriter is sometimes less than the price at which the IPO will trade initially on the stock exchange. This is called the IPO discount, and it is why IPOs can be sought after by institutions and individuals.

HOW TO INVEST

There are several ways individuals can participate in an IPO…

•**Sign up with a brokerage that is a major IPO underwriter.**

To find out which brokerages underwrite which deals, visit the Web site *www.renaissance capital.com/research*.

But just because you are a client at a brokerage doesn't necessarily mean that you have a shot at buying the stock of a company that is going public.

In order to do that, you have to be one of the brokerage's better customers—meaning, someone who trades frequently, has a high account balance, etc.

•**Sign up with the right small brokerage.** Another way to participate in an IPO is to become a client of a brokerage that specializes in underwriting IPOs in the sectors you favor and want to invest in.

Or you can sign up with a regional brokerage that underwrites IPOs.

Examples: William Blair (800-621-0687)... Raymond James (800-647-7378).

- **Put in a bid with a discount/online broker,** such as Fidelity Investments. Generally, these brokers reserve IPO shares for customers who meet certain qualifications (large account balances, frequent trading activity, etc.).

- **Buy the shares once they start trading.** Once the stock begins trading on the stock exchange, any investor can buy shares. However, investors should be cautious about jumping right in. Hot IPOs can shoot up in price on their first trading day, only to fall back later.

By waiting a few weeks to buy the stock of a company that has just gone public, you stand a much better chance of paying less for the shares.

SIGNS OF IPO QUALITY

Not all IPOs are worthwhile investments. *Here's what to look for...*

- **Large *spin-offs* of established companies.** A spin-off is a division of a public company that becomes independent by selling its own stock. The larger the division, the more shares are issued and the greater your chances of buying stock in the new company.

Most large spin-offs have established track records and histories of delivering higher annual earnings.

Many large spin-offs make particularly good IPOs because they are often good businesses that are not dependent on the parent company.

- **Clean preliminary prospectus.** Pay close attention to the section called "Management Discussion and Analysis of Financial Conditions." This section explains where the company's revenues come from and how the money is spent. Also read the section called "Risk Factors," which discloses potential problems. *What to look for...*

  - The company expects to issue additional stock to finance operations. This means the initial offering isn't expected to raise enough money to meet the company's future needs.

  - Management that holds a significant amount of stock. While every deal is structured differently, we like companies in which the average percentage of stock retained by management is at least in the high single digits.

Throw Out The Old Rules About Money

Ric Edelman, chairman and CEO of Edelman Financial Services LLC, a financial advisory firm that manages more than $10 billion in assets, Fairfax, Virginia. *Barron's* has chosen him for seven straight years as one of America's 100 top independent financial advisers, ranking him number one in 2012. Edelman has written seven books, including *The Truth About Money* (HarperBusiness). *www.ricedelman.com*

Wh   hen it comes to finances, the conventional wisdom often is your enemy. What everyone knows to be true is typically what trips you up.

The advice I give my clients often is unconventional—it sounds and feels unfamiliar and typically in sharp contrast to what they commonly hear—but I believe it is exactly the right thing to do in these turbulent times, and it has paid off for my clients over and over...

MORTGAGE MYTH

Conventional mortgage wisdom: Pay off your home mortgage as soon as possible using extra payments.

My unconventional wisdom: Keep a long-term mortgage, typically 30 years, regardless of your age or income, even if you can pay it off sooner.

Why it's smarter: Owning your home outright saddles you with some pretty significant disadvantages nowadays, such as a lack of liquidity. Every dollar you give to the bank is one that you will never get back until you sell your home. You may need that money if you lose your job unexpectedly or have a large medical expense. Making extra payments is like stuffing money into a mattress—it doesn't reduce the interest rate on the mortgage. All it does is reduce the amount of time that you will be making payments and the amount of interest you end up paying (assuming that you don't sell the home or refinance before the mortgage runs out). And the less that you are paying in interest, the less you can claim for tax deductions.

Instead, put that money to work in a diversified investment portfolio, possibly one composed of a mix of passively managed "index" funds to keep expenses low.

RETIREMENT PLANNING NO-NO

Conventional IRA wisdom: Convert your traditional IRA to a Roth IRA. Although you have to pay income tax on the money you convert now, your withdrawals in retirement, including your gains, will be tax-free.

My unconventional wisdom: Forget about Roth IRAs, which are designed to get you to pay taxes earlier.

Why it's smarter: Converting to a Roth IRA does nothing to increase your wealth. For example, I had a client in the 25% federal income tax bracket with a $100,000 IRA. If he converted the IRA to a Roth, he would have to pay tax and would be left with $75,000. Say the Roth doubled in 10 years thanks to shrewd investments. It would be worth $150,000. Instead, say the same client sticks with the traditional IRA and it doubles in 10 years to $200,000. After paying taxes, my client would wind up with $150,000, the same amount but without the hassle, assuming that he still is in the same tax bracket at the end of those 10 years.

Also, Congress may well decide to tax Roth IRA withdrawals in the future or make them subject to the Alternative Minimum Tax (AMT).

WRONG PENSION CHOICE

Conventional pension wisdom: If you retire with a pension, choose the "joint and survivor" option that companies often offer. It pays you income for as long as you live and keeps paying after you die for as long as your spouse lives.

My unconventional wisdom: Set up your own "joint and survivor" plan.

Why it's smarter: Accepting the "joint and survivor" option means that you get as much as 25% less in each monthly pension payment. Instead, opt for the highest monthly pension payout or an up-front lump-sum payout, and purchase a life insurance policy, naming your spouse as beneficiary. If your spouse dies first, you can cancel the insurance and keep collecting the higher payout for the rest of your life.

LONG-TERM-CARE CAUTION

Conventional long-term-care advice: Purchase long-term-care (LTC) insurance with lifetime benefits, which pays for at-home health care or nursing home or assisted-living care as long as you live. It's very expensive, but you won't have to rely on family members for care or spend down your assets, so your children will inherit more.

My unconventional wisdom: Opt for five years of LTC benefits rather than lifetime benefits.

Why it's smarter: The average nursing home stay is less than three years, and fewer than 12% of people who enter a nursing home stay more than five years. I've found that a policy offering five years of benefits often (but not always) is sufficient, and premiums are as much as 50% less.

Consider adding on a shared-care rider. This lets you use the benefits offered by your spouse's policy if you exhaust your own benefits.

FLAWED INFLATION FIGHTER

Conventional inflation-fighting wisdom: Treasury Inflation-Protected Securities (TIPS), whose principal is adjusted based on inflation, are the ideal investment to help protect your portfolio from inflation.

My unconventional wisdom: You can't rely on TIPS to protect your portfolio from inflation.

Why it's smarter: If inflation soars, no one knows whether TIPS actually will work as an effective hedge. We have never experienced a prolonged inflationary period since TIPS were introduced a little more than a decade ago. If interest rates rise more quickly than the inflation rate rises, that would increase the yield offered by new Treasury bonds, possibly making them more attractive than TIPS and possibly driving down returns on TIPS mutual funds. High unemployment continues to stifle one of the main drivers of inflation—rising wages. If inflation remains low, you actually could lose money in TIPS.

529 PROBLEM

Conventional college-savings advice: The best way for grandparents to contribute to a grandchild's education is a 529 college savings plan. These state-operated plans are designed to help families set aside funds for future college costs by offering tax breaks.

My unconventional wisdom: Most grandparents should skip 529 plans.

Why it's smarter: There's no assurance that your grandkids will need the money. They might win scholarships or not go to college at all. What's more, their parents might incur problems of their own, such as divorce or job loss, causing them to raid the account that you helped fund. Another drawback is that 529 plans limit options for investing money. Most important, you may need that money yourself for health-care or other expenses. *Better:* Talk to your estate-planning attorney about setting up a tax-free trust for your young grandchild, and stipulate that it remain untouched until the child reaches retirement age. Over the long run, that will serve the child much better than your contributions to a college fund.

How to Really Read Financial Reports

Thornton L. O'Glove, former securities analyst and author of *Quality of Earnings* (Free Press).

The growing complexity of corporate finance and changes in accounting standards can make it difficult for even the most sophisticated and experienced investor to judge a company's health accurately from its financial reports.

However, we have come up with simple ways to translate the increasingly garbled language of financial reports. *What we watch…*

• **Annual reports.** Compare the latest report with the two previous ones. Though the chairman's letter usually portrays the company in a positive way, the best way to measure management integrity is to watch what was promised in years past and see how those promises turned out.

If the chairman's letter is so optimistic that he or she would be better suited to work as a Florida sunny-weather forecaster, beware. Coleco was like this. Management projected nonstop optimism all the way to bankruptcy. *Tipoff:* Any glossing-over of obvious negatives.

• **Income statements.** *Helpful:* Pay close attention to income statements in the company's financial reports. *Aim:* To see how clear the earnings statement is of nonoperating items such as deferred income tax credits, sale of assets and interest income Such earnings are real, but they're not the same as operating earnings. They may not occur again.

• **Balance sheets.** *A key element:* Debt. How much debt is short-term (due within a year) and how much is long-term? Too much short-term debt can squeeze the company's operating flexibility by hurting cash flow.

For most industrial companies, a balance of 40% debt and 60% shareholders' equity is about right. Above 40% of total capital debt can become worrisome.

• **Footnotes to financial statements.** These tie in with and further explain the income statement and the balance sheet. Always read them, because they often contain information you can't get anywhere else. *Example:* Details about lawsuits against the company that could represent big future liabilities.

Know When to Hold 'Em

Many people think that if they sell a stock before the date on which it pays a dividend, they will lose the value of the dividend.

Reality: Technically, a stock's price drops by the amount of a dividend when it is paid.

375

So, if a stock is priced at $20 and it then pays a $2 dividend, the stock's price afterward will be $18.

Result: You get the same value for the stock whether you sell it before or after it pays its dividend ($20 versus $18 plus a $2 dividend).

Trap: If you hold stock only to avoid losing the dividend, it could drop in price in the meantime, and then you would lose money.

Charles B. Carlson, CFA, editor, *DRIP Investor,* 7412 Calumet Ave., Hammond, Indiana 46324.

Investing in Diamonds

Unless you're in the business, diamonds are a bad investment. *Why:* Most of us buy at retail (at a markup of 100%) and have to sell at wholesale. *What your diamond is worth:* About 20% of the appraised value. *Also:* Diamonds are not really rare. Some dealers have artificially maintained the rarity of diamonds by withholding them from the market. But this monopoly is currently breaking down. *Possible result:* A collapse of world diamond prices.

Good investment stones: Rubies, emeralds, sapphires and high-quality colored diamonds (especially red). These are naturally rare.

 # What a Greenback Is Worth If Part of It Is Missing

Worn and torn paper money will be replaced by the Department of the Treasury depending on how much of the bill is still intact. No matter how little of the bill is left, send it to the Treasury. Their decisions are often arbitrary, so it pays to make an effort.

Avoid Big Money Mistakes—Yes, Ignore Your Intuition

Morton D. Davis, PhD, professor emeritus of mathematics, City College of New York, New York City. He is author of *The Math of Money: Making Mathematical Sense of Your Personal Finances* (Copernicus).

From paying off the mortgage on a house to buying stock—most people make big money decisions based on intuition. Yet they seldom look at the numbers. To demonstrate how intuition can lead anyone astray, I have applied principles of mathematics to four situations.

AT THE APPLIANCE STORE

You buy a dishwasher for $600 and agree to pay for the purchase with 13 consecutive monthly payments of $50—$650 in all. You figure that if you're paying $50 in interest for a one-year loan, your interest rate is 8.33% ($50 ÷ $600 = 8.33%).

Reality: If the loan really were for one year at that interest rate, you would be able to keep the money for a full year before repaying any part of it.

Instead, your first payment, including interest and principal, is due immediately, and you must make additional payments each month until the loan is paid off. Worse still, you owe interest for the full year on the original $600 you borrowed—even though the amount you owe diminishes each month. Even in your final payment, which reduces the unpaid balance of the loan to zero, you are paying interest on the full $600. The effective interest rate goes up each month as the unpaid balance declines.

My calculations show the real annual rate of interest on that loan—repaid month-by-month—is 17.36%.

With each payment, you borrowed money for an average of six months. Yet you paid for a one-year loan—about double the nominal interest rate of 8.33%. Using a credit card with a rate of 17% or less would have been better.

IN THE
STOCK MARKET

Investment experts talk about "undervalued" stocks. The idea is that these stocks can be bought at bargain prices now—and sold at a profit when they return to their "proper" prices.

Reality: The only "proper" price for a stock is what an investor will pay for it. Growth and value managers expend great effort calculating what a stock *might* sell for next month or next year, yet active investment managers seldom beat the market.

Strategy: Put the majority of your investments in a low-cost, broad-market index fund. You won't have to worry that a given stock is overvalued, undervalued or fairly valued.

Should You Follow
Your Financial Adviser?

The Wall Street Journal

If your financial adviser goes to a new firm, find out why. If you might want to move your account, you may have to reach out and contact your former adviser—firms often forbid advisers who leave from actively soliciting former clients.

Contact the person at your current firm who informed you, and ask some key questions—such as whether there has been a lot of turnover or if issues facing the firm could have caused your adviser to leave.

If you get empty assurances that everything will be fine, that could be a red flag about the credibility or future of the firm. You want specific information—for instance, that your adviser left to start his/her own firm.

What to do: Decide whether the firm or the adviser matters more to you. Consider whether a new adviser at the same firm will meet your needs or whether you want to follow your previous one.

Getting Robbed
By Your Bank?
How to Slash the
Outrageous Fees

Edward F. Mrkvicka, Jr., president of Reliance Enterprises, Inc., a national financial consulting firm, Marengo, Illinois.

The key to bringing down many banking costs—and even boosting interest rates on savings—is developing a relationship with your local banker. No small bank will risk losing a large account because of a quibble over one-half of a percentage point in interest or a $25 monthly service fee. While Internet banks might charge less for checking, resolving problems can be a nightmare because you can't find out who is in charge or where records are kept.

Compare costs for services you need by calling at least three local banks. *Shortcut:* Go to *www.bankrate.com* and click "Checking & Savings" under "Compare Rates."

To slash annoying banking costs…

OVERDRAFTS

The average fee for a bounced check is $35.00.* Even with overdraft protection, you will be charged a fee plus interest.

Solutions…

●**Ask the bank to refund the overdraft charge.** Many banks will oblige if you only make a mistake occasionally.

●**Avoid triggering overdraft.** Many charges result from debit cards as husbands and wives make purchases without telling each other. Use credit cards instead. Pay them off promptly to avoid interest charges.

●**Ask for "free" overdraft protection.** When you overdraw your account, the bank will phone and give you a day—or more—to cover the shortfall at no charge.

Caution: Customers who frequently trigger overdrafts may lose this consideration.

MINIMUM BALANCE

*According to a survey of bank checking-account fees by Bankrate.com.

This fee averages $6 to $11 per month if your account falls below the minimum—for even just one day. The average minimum needed to avoid this fee is about $3,000 at most traditional banks.

Solution: Choose an account that has little or no minimum. Many banks offer truly free checking with no minimums for senior citizens and students.

INTEREST ON INSTALLMENT LOANS

If you take a three-year installment loan to buy a car, don't think that the interest costs will decline over time, as with a mortgage. In many cases, you will continue to pay interest on the initial amount throughout the loan's term.

Solution: Insist on a simple interest single-payment loan that allows for monthly payments or a simple interest installment loan. Most banks make simple interest loans but don't necessarily volunteer this information.

Example: If you had a 48-month car loan for $10,000 at 10.25%, you would save $138.87 over the life of the loan with simple instead of traditional interest.

UNNECESSARY INSURANCE

When you take out a loan, bank officers often try to sell you expensive *credit life and disability insurance*, which pays off the loan should you die or makes monthly payments should you become disabled.

Some automatically write insurance into loan documents and don't discuss it with customers. Customers are afraid of disrupting the closing, so they don't question the extra charges.

Solution: Don't buy loan insurance from the bank. In the event of your death, it pays off only your loan balance. If you choose to protect a $10,000 four-year car loan, earmark $10,000 of your term life insurance policy for this purpose.

To compare term insurance rates, ask an independent agent or go to *www.insure.com* or *www.term4sale.com.*

If unauthorized insurance is included in your loan documents, ask that it be removed before proceeding with the closing.

CASHIER'S CHECKS

Many banks charge between $5 and $10 for cashier's checks.

Solution: Get a money order from the post office for between $1.10 and $1.50.

DELAYS IN CREDITING YOUR ACCOUNT

Many banks say they will not clear an out-of-state check for three business days. Some checks take even longer.

Your bank receives payment for most checks from anywhere in the US within 24 hours. Banks impose a waiting period and only count business days, not calendar days, so they can get free use of your money.

Solution: Ask for a brochure describing your bank's check-clearing policy. Direct deposits should clear immediately. If you need immediate access to cash, even from out of state, ask your banker to arrange it.

Home Buyer's Planning Mistake

A man withdrew funds from his 401(k) plan account to help purchase a new home. He was under age 59½, but didn't pay the 10% penalty on early withdrawals. This was because he claimed the exception to the penalty for "first-time home buyers."

Mistake: The IRS and Tax Court pointed out that the penalty exception applies only to distributions from IRAs—not to distributions from 401(k)s and other employer-sponsored qualified retirement plans. Thus, they imposed the penalty.

Better: A person who wants to use funds in a qualified plan can first make a rollover of the funds into an IRA—and then withdraw them from the IRA, claiming the penalty exception. Even better, borrow from the 401(k) to avoid any current tax.

Joseph Jones, TC Summary Opinion 2003-153.

How to Use Home-Equity Loans

Gary Schatsky, JD, president of ObjectiveAdvice.com, fee-only financial-planning firm in New York City, and chairman emeritus of National Association of Personal Financial Advisors.

Equity built up in your house can cushion financial setbacks, such as job loss, costly medical procedures or necessary repairs.

Interest on home-equity lines of credit now are around 4.5%, making these loans an excellent source of capital for necessities. Ask for a home-equity line of credit with no fees and an interest rate at or below prime. *Smart moves...*

•**Apply for a line of credit** while the bank considers you a good risk. You can decide later how much, if any, to borrow. You only need to pay interest on the money you borrow. Even then, the interest may be tax deductible.

Caution: Only use the line of credit for a significant need or emergency.

•**Pay back the money as soon as possible.** If you borrow heavily and the prime rate soars, your payments will soar, too. If you can't pay the loan within two to five years, consider refinancing your mortgage to get the money.

•**Avoid teaser loans.** These often have low introductory rates that rise substantially after several months.

For rates, call several banks near you or search online.

Simple Ways to Deduct Your Loss

To deduct a loss on the sale of your home, convert part or all of it to business or rental use before you sell it.

Losses on the sale of a primary residence are not deductible—but if you are renting out your house or using even part of it for business when you sell it, losses become partly deductible, based on what percentage of the home was used for rental or business purposes. Only losses after conversion are deductible. *More information:* Consult a financial adviser or tax professional.

Randy Gardner, CPA, professor of tax and financial planning, University of Missouri, Kansas City, and coauthor of *101 Tax Saving Ideas* (Wealth Builders).

Shrewd Ways to Protect Your Assets From Creditors

Gideon Rothschild, Esq., CPA, partner in the law firm Moses & Singer LLP, 405 Lexington Ave., New York City 10174. *www.mosessinger.com*

You have a legal right to set up your affairs in a way that protects your property from unexpected claims—as long as you're not defrauding existing creditors.

New asset protection opportunities have recently arisen, but there are also a few unanswered questions to keep in mind.

DOMESTIC SELF-SETTLED TRUSTS

In a handful of states, you can put your own money in a trust for yourself and have those assets protected from creditors. In those states, you can set up a trust for yourself—a "self-settled trust"—manage the money, receive the income, have access to principal, and block creditors from laying claim to the assets in the trust.

States that allow these asset-protection trusts include: Alaska, Colorado, Delaware, Missouri, Nevada, New Hampshire, Oklahoma, Rhode Island, South Dakota, Tennessee, Utah, Virginia and Wyoming.

Caution: There are no court decisions addressing whether *nonresidents* can set up a self-settled trust in one of these states to gain asset protection. It may require US Supreme Court review to ultimately settle the issue.

Bottom line: There's no downside to a nonresident seeking asset protection in one of these states—other than the cost of setting up the trust. If a court permits creditors access to funds in the trust, the nonresident is no worse off than if the trust had not been set up in the first place. And there is a possibility that a court may uphold asset protection for nonresidents. Setting up such a trust creates a significant obstacle for any creditor, giving you negotiating leverage when settling a claim.

FOREIGN TRUSTS

Off-shore trusts (set up in another country) are also an effective way to protect assets from creditors. Foreign courts do not have to honor US court judgments.

Caution: Several US courts have recently imposed civil contempt orders against debtors whose foreign trusts were set up after claims were made against the debtors. In such cases, the debtor is ordered to pay a US judgment with funds in the foreign trust or face an undetermined amount of jail time. Whether this trend will continue remains to be seen.

WILLS AND LIVING TRUSTS

You have an opportunity to create asset protection for your family when making your estate plans. Parents often set up trusts for their children to run until the children attain a certain age. However, it may be advisable to let assets remain in the trust indefinitely to protect against your children's future creditors or divorce claims.

Suggestion: Draft the terms of the trust to give an adult child maximum control over the funds without losing asset protection. This can be done by allowing the child to replace a trustee with someone who will cooperate with his/her wishes. The trustee can be permitted to purchase assets, such as a vacation home, which the child can use and enjoy without exposure to creditor or divorce claims. In order to avoid potential tax problems—as well as a perception that the child controls his own trust—it's a good idea to make sure the replacement trustee is not someone who is related to or under the direct control of the child.

FLPs AND FLLCs

Family limited partnerships (FLPs) and family limited liability companies (FLLCs) can be used to provide a measure of asset protection. A creditor of a limited partner cannot obtain assets from the FLP. The creditor can only get a "charging order"—a right to any distributions made to the limited partner.

Result: Assets can then remain within the family—a creditor can only receive distributions when and to the extent they are made.

Note: Where assets have been transferred to FLPs in an attempt to hinder or delay the claims of creditors, family limited partnerships do not protect assets from attachment by creditors.

529 TUITION PLANS

All states now allow college savings through tax-advantaged accounts called 529 plans. Contribution limits and other rules for these plans vary by state. However, 529 plans may be the best way to shelter funds from creditors.

About a dozen states have legislated that 529 plan funds are protected from claims against *both* the person contributing the funds as well as the beneficiary. Other states protect those assets for either the contributor or the beneficiary. This protection exists even though a contributor retains control over the funds and can recoup them (albeit by paying a 10% penalty).

The limits of asset protection are high…

• **Contribution limits are substantial**—most plans have total (rather than annual) contribution limits, usually exceeding $100,000. Visit *www.savingforcollege.com* to find out about the contribution limits for each state. Or call the state education department for any state in which you are interested.

• **Contributors who set up plans for a beneficiary** can avoid gift tax on contributions up to $65,000 ($130,000 if a contributor's spouse joins in the contribution) by averaging the gift over five years to take advantage of the $13,000 annual gift tax exclusion.

• **Contributors are not subject to any income limitations**—wealthy individuals can make contributions. They can even set up accounts for their own benefit (sometimes referred to as "solo 529 plans").

Assets enjoy deferral of tax on income until withdrawal *and* no there is tax on earnings if the distributions are used for qualified education costs.

Bonus: With few exceptions, there is no bar to a nonresident setting up a 529 plan in another state, so factor in asset protection when selecting which 529 plan to use. As is the case with domestic self-settled trusts, it is not yet known whether the state law where the plan is adopted will determine whether the account is protected.

Caution: It is not clear whether funds in 529 plans would be protected if the contributor or beneficiary has to file for bankruptcy protection. Federal bankruptcy legislation that has yet to be enacted may end up creating an exemption for 529 plans.

QUALIFIED RETIREMENT PLANS AND IRAS

Qualified retirement plans, including 401(k) accounts and IRAs, are protected from the claims of creditors under federal law.

Exceptions: A state court can issue a qualified domestic relations order (QDRO), directing that payments from a plan be made to a former spouse, dependent, or other person as "alternate payee." The IRS can also put a levy on funds in an IRA for back taxes.

Are Emotions Driving Your Investments? Four Traps to Avoid

Richard Geist, EdD, clinical instructor in psychology, department of psychiatry, Harvard Medical School, Boston, and founding member of the Massachusetts Institute for Psychoanalysis, where he is on the faculty. He is president of Institute of Psychology and Investing, Inc., a consulting firm in Newton, Massachusetts, and author of Investor Therapy *(Crown Business).*

Most of us know that many investors base decisions on emotion rather than logic. The trouble is that few of us believe we're among them.

To find out how much emotion influences your investments, look back over your stock and mutual fund trades for the past year, and note the reason for each purchase and sale. If trades were motivated by the headlines of the

day or your eagerness to make a quick profit, chances are emotion played a key role.

Good news: Once you recognize that emotions are guiding your decisions, you can take steps to separate them from investments. Alternatively, you can choose stocks and funds suited to your particular psychological bias.

Here are several psychological traps and how to deal with them...

HERD MENTALITY

It's only human to follow winners. In investing, those are the people who have made money. Unfortunately, by the time an investment sector posts strong returns, there's often little advantage left to plowing money in.

Solution: When an investor herd goes in one direction, look for opportunities in stocks and funds that are left behind. Today, these include companies that recently have had problems but have solid fundamentals—such as good management, a healthy market share, low debt and a history of earnings growth over the last decade.

IMPATIENCE

It's impossible to predict the ideal time to sell a stock, but impatient investors are notorious for selling just before a stock takes off.

Test your own patience: Are you reluctant to start reading long books? In conversations, are you annoyed when people don't get to the point? If you answered "yes" to either question, there is a good chance that you are an impatient investor.

When you look back over your trading record for the past 12 months, check the price of each position you sold three to six months after you sold it. (If you can't find past transaction statements, ask your financial institution for copies or download them from its Web site.) If you regularly sold shares that continued to rise in price, impatience may have played a role.

Solution: Add up the profits you could have made by holding on longer. Merely seeing the total may be enough to cure you.

If you simply can't break the habit of selling shares prematurely, consider buying stocks that *should* be sold for a quick profit.

These often are in companies that take advantage of new trends—especially technology stocks. If shares in cutting-edge companies rise, the increase is likely to be fast. Holding these risky stocks long after their initial rise can be a mistake if the fundamentals don't support the gain, although there certainly are exceptions to this rule.

FEAR OF LETTING GO

This is the opposite of impatience. It means hanging on to shares long after you should have sold them.

When you look at your trades of the past year, check the price of stocks three and six months before you sold them. Look also at the stocks you own now, and compare current prices with share prices three and six months ago.

If you find that you consistently hang on to shares after they rise and then fall, it is likely that you're afraid of selling.

Why might this be? *One possibility:* If your costliest mistakes always seem to occur at certain times of the year—for instance, near the anniversary of a painful event, such as the loss of a loved one—the memory could be subconsciously influencing your investment behavior.

Solution: Continue to keep records of your trades, and periodically note profits that you missed because you hung on too long.

If this doesn't stop you from keeping losing stocks, stick with stock funds that have performed well in both up and down markets. By following this strategy, you won't be hurt by your fear of letting go.

Helpful: Free fund-screening tools are available at *www.morningstar.com*. If you don't have a computer, research funds at a public library computer.

OVERREACTING TO NEWS

Don't let headlines determine your stock trades. Individual investors are rarely knowledgeable or dispassionate enough to profit from the news.

Example: Airline stocks suffered after the September 11 disaster as many investors worried about a drop in tourism. Yet few individual investors got out of the stocks quickly enough to contain their losses.

Professional investors interpret and react to news more quickly than most individual investors. As a result, stock prices are affected by news before most individuals have time to respond. In fact, several fund managers did buy airline stocks right after September 11, 2001, and then sold them when they rebounded.

Solution: Before buying or selling a stock, ask yourself whether the decision is influenced by a news event. If it is, review the company's fundamentals—management, competitive position and outlook for its industry sector. Go ahead only if the fundamentals justify the trade.

Think twice before buying or selling shares purely on the basis of trends you see on financial news Web sites in a day's first hour of trading.

Make More Money—How to Get the Best Financial Advice

Donald B. Trone, president and founder of the Foundation for Fiduciary Studies, which operates in association with the University of Pittsburgh in Sewickley, Pennsylvania. He is coauthor of two manuals for the financial planning industry, *Procedural Prudence* (Veale & Associates) and *The Management of Investment Decisions* (McGraw-Hill). In 2003, he was appointed by the US Secretary of Labor to represent the investment counseling industry on the ERISA Advisory Council.

Anyone can call himself/herself a financial adviser or consultant—a stockbroker, insurance agent, accountant, even a layperson who is good with numbers. In the past five years, the number of financial advisers has risen by almost 40% as consumers—hurt by the last bear market and intimidated by retirement planning—seek professional help.

Unfortunately, financial advisers aren't required as a general rule to act solely in your best interest—a standard known as "fiduciary responsibility."

Common: An adviser may not recommend the best mutual fund for you, but rather the best one for you that also pays him a commission.

Who you choose depends on your needs.

Example: Whether you want someone to draw up a financial plan or provide ongoing investment services.

DECIDING WHAT YOU NEED

To find the right money coach…

• **If you need broad financial guidance—** such as help setting up a portfolio that you will mostly oversee yourself…a plan to pay for your children's educations…a retirement plan…estate planning and tax planning—go with a fee-only planner who has a certified financial planner (CFP) designation.

Fee-only advisers do not accept commissions. CFPs are required to pass a certification exam, have at least three years of financial-planning experience, adhere to a code of ethics, earn continuing education credits and pledge fiduciary responsibility.

Typical cost: One-time fee of $1,000 or more for a comprehensive plan.

Resource: Two associations can make referrals—The Financial Planning Association (800-322-4237, *www.fpanet.org*)…and the National Association of Personal Financial Advisors (800-366-2732, *www.napfa.org*).

• **If you want a professional to help manage your portfolio** on an ongoing basis, look for a chartered financial analyst (CFA). CFAs undergo rigorous training in stock and bond analysis, financial accounting and portfolio management. They are required to pass a certification exam, adhere to a code of ethics and pledge fiduciary responsibility.

Important: Never give an adviser full discretion over your portfolio, no matter how trustworthy he seems. You should receive at least a phone call or an E-mail when a trade is going to be made.

Typical cost: A fixed percentage of assets under management—0.5% to 2% annually for ongoing market advice and investment recommendations. For example, annual fees for an all-bond portfolio may average 0.5% of assets versus 1.5% for a mix of stocks and bonds.

Resource: For referrals to CFAs, go to *www.cfainstitute.org* or call 800-247-8132.

Important: If you have less than $300,000 in your portfolio, it can be difficult to find a financial adviser to manage it because it is not cost-effective for them.

Alternatives…

• **Use a financial planner who charges hourly rates,** typically $100 to $300 per hour. For referrals, contact Garrett Planning Network (866-260-8400, *www.garrettplanningnetwork. com*), a network of planners who charge by the hour. Or get recommendations from your attorney or accountant.

• **Consider the advisory services offered by large, no-load mutual fund companies.** They provide low-cost individualized portfolio advice by CFPs. For example, at Fidelity (800-343-3548, *www.fidelity.com*), counselors will manage a handpicked selection of Fidelity and non-Fidelity funds for clients who have at least $50,000 under management. Fees range from 0.25% of assets to 1.7%. Similar services are available from Vanguard (800-523-7731, *www.vanguard.com*) and T. Rowe Price (800-225-5132, *www.trowe price.com*).

SIZING UP CANDIDATES

• **Conduct a background check of prospective advisers and their firms.** You should work only with firms registered with the SEC. They are subject to government supervision.

Go to *www.sec.gov/investor/brokers.htm*. Search for the firm you want to investigate, and examine the firm's Form ADV. It contains information on the education and professional backgrounds of the firm's principals, types of clients, compensation, amount managed and disciplinary history.

You can find the same information through the Financial Industry Regulatory Authority (800-289-9999, *www.finra.org/Investors/Tools Calculators/BrokerCheck/*). Any reputable adviser will make his ADV form available to you without your even having to ask.

• **Conduct a 30-minute, in-person interview with each candidate.** (You should not be charged for this.) Ask if the adviser frequently works with other financial specialists on behalf of clients and would therefore be amenable to working with your professionals. For example, if your estate plan is complex, you already may be working with an insurance agent and an estate lawyer.

Find out if the financial adviser will handle your account personally or farm out your assets to managers whom he supervises (you'll need to check the backgrounds of those managers, if that's the case)...how much time you can expect with him...and whether you can monitor your account online.

Ask if he will provide a comprehensive analysis of your financial situation, including specific recommendations—he should present you with a sample.

Ask about the firm's typical client, and gauge whether his/her needs are similar to yours. For instance, the firm might deal primarily with corporate executives who need help with stock options or retired people who want to maximize investment income. Ask to see actual performance figures for the clients whose goals are similar to yours.

• **Speak with at least two of the adviser's references.**

Questions to ask: Did the financial adviser educate you on complex financial issues? Did he carefully follow your directives? In particular, did he understand how aggressive/conservative a portfolio you wanted? Did he ever make mistakes or disappoint you? What did he do about it?

• **Once you are ready to hire a firm, get a written policy.** *It should include...*

A promise that the adviser will act as your "fiduciary."

List of potential conflicts of interest regarding product-based commissions and a reasonable explanation of how they are addressed.

Explanation of the fee structure, what constitutes billable work and how fee disputes will be resolved-for instance, if the stock market drops and you make a quick call asking for advice. In this case, an adviser earning an asset-based annual fee should not charge for taking your call.

15
Insurance and You

Long-Term-Care Insurance...Essentials

The risk is real...about 11% of those turning age 65 can expect to spend a significant amount of time in a nursing home.

The cost of nursing home care is high. The average cost for a year's stay is over $85,000 today—but in a number of areas in the country it can top $200,000.

How are you going to cover such a huge expense if the need arises? *The answer depends on your income and net worth...*

• **The "poor"**—and those who spend down their assets to become poor—can usually rely on Medicaid to cover the cost of a nursing home stay.

• **The "wealthy"** can afford to use their incomes to pay for such care without affecting their assets or the standard of living for other family members.

• **Those in the middle**—individuals with a net worth, say, of between $500,000 and $5 million—should consider buying a long-term-care policy.

There are a variety of factors to weigh in deciding whether to buy a long-term-care policy, and when. *For example...*

CAN I AFFORD IT?

Premiums for long-term-care policies aren't cheap. They can run between $2,000 and $10,000 a year for those under age 70, and as much as $15,000 or even $20,000 a year for those 70 and older. Like life insurance policies, the younger you are when you take out the policy, the lower your premiums will be.

Caution: Premiums for long-term-care policies are considered "level premiums"—that is, they don't increase as you age. *However—* the insurance company has the right to increase the premiums for a whole *class* of policies. This could happen with long-term-care policies as

---

Lee Slavutin, MD, CLU, chairman of Stern Slavutin-2 Inc., insurance and estate planners, 530 Fifth Ave., New York City 10036. *www.sternslavutin.com*

insurance companies gain more experience and find they've underpriced them.

Cost of the premium depends on…

- **The person's age when the policy is first purchased.**
- **The dollar benefit per day.**
- **The period for which benefits will be paid**—three years, five years, life.
- **The "elimination period"**—the time before benefits will start.
- **Other factors,** such as a cost-of-living adjustment to the daily benefit.

Today, the people who can afford it are taking the maximum daily benefit available ($500) and are choosing lifetime policies (instead of those running for three, five or 10 years).

TYPES OF POLICIES

The type of policy you buy really depends on what you can afford.

The best policies: Lifetime coverage for the maximum benefit ($500 a day, depending on the company)…with a short elimination period.

But if you find the cost of such coverage prohibitive, consider a more modest policy, say $200 a day, for a shorter period than life, or with a longer elimination period.

In comparing policies offered by different companies, there are nuances to consider that can affect your choice.

Example: Be sure you understand how each company counts days of care for purposes of the elimination period. Say someone needs three days of care per week. Does this count as an entire week for the elimination period or will it take seven calendar days to equal one week for the elimination period?

- **Get professional help.** Use an insurance professional who can guide you through the intricacies of long-term-care insurance.
- **Experience counts.** Stick with an insurance company that has experience with long-term-care policies, such as Genworth, Travelers, John Hancock, Fortis and Unum.

Tax break: A portion of the premiums can be treated as a deductible medical expense based on your age, thereby offsetting some of the cost for those who itemize their medical expenses.

Note: States may offer tax breaks. For example, New York has a 20% tax credit for long-term-care premiums.

CAN YOU AFFORD NOT TO?

If you are in the middle—not rich and not poor—you may not accumulate enough through savings to pay for nursing home care. If you are in this situation, you should consider buying a long-term-care policy.

Example: At age 60, you buy a $100 per day benefit at a cost of $519 per year—a three-year policy with a 90-day elimination period.

Then assume at age 80, you require nursing home care. You would have paid $10,380 over the 20 years of coverage.

Had you used that same $519 each year to invest for an after-tax return of 6%, you have only $20,237 after 20 years.

This would cover just 203 days in the home (at $100 a day). The policy would cover 1,095 days.

WHEN TO BUY A POLICY

Those who are 55 years old or older should start to look seriously at long-term-care policies.

Note: In recent years an increasing number of employers have offered this coverage as an employee benefit.

If you don't have employer-provided coverage, then look into individual coverage. The younger you are when you start the policy, the lower your premiums will be.

But if you buy at 55, won't you be paying premiums for 20 or 30 years before needing benefits, if ever? Does that make sense?

While your chances are better than 50% that you'll never put in a claim, should you need to do so, you're likely to come out ahead financially if you have a policy.

Suppose a 55-year-old woman buys a policy to provide $250 a day for a lifetime if needed (with a 90-day elimination period). She would pay $3,452.20 a year in premiums.

Example: If she needs long-term care after just *one year* of paying premiums, she would recover her entire outlay in just 14 days in a nursing home of average cost.

Five years of premiums would be recovered in 69 days, 10 years in 138 days. And—20 years in 276 days.

Even if this 55-year-old were not to need any benefits until age 85, her 30 years of premiums would be recovered in 414 days.

Low-Priority Insurance Policies

Slice-of-life insurance policies such as mortgage life insurance, credit life insurance (to pay off installment loans on a car, furniture, etc.) and flight insurance should be low-priority items in the family budget. More important—and more economical—are comprehensive life insurance policies that cover a family's total financial needs no matter how the major breadwinner dies. A renewable term-life insurance policy large enough to pay off the mortgage, the car loan and business debts, and to cover college costs for the children is far better than a series of special policies to cover individual situations.

J. Robert Hunter, insurance director, Consumer Federation of America, 1620 I St., NW, Suite 200, Washington, DC 20006.

How to Get Your Insurance Company to Pay Up

J. Robert Hunter, insurance director, Consumer Federation of America, 1620 I St., NW, Suite 200, Washington, DC 20006.

Don't give up if you have trouble getting a fair claims settlement from your health insurance company. There are a number of steps you can take to fight the insurer's decision to refuse your claim.

First: Resubmit another medical insurance claim form about 30 days after the refusal. Very often, a company randomly denies a claim... and just as randomly approves the same claim when it comes in again. It does no harm to try for reimbursement of a doctor's bill by submitting your insurance forms a second time.

Second: If that does not work, contact the insurer and request, in writing, a full explanation of the refusal to pay. Sometimes the denial-of-benefits statement is filled with numeric or alphabetic codes that are undecipherable by a layperson. Request a clear explanation. There should be no ambiguity as to why a health insurer will not pay the benefits that you think are called for in the contract.

Third: Once you are given the insurance company's rationale for turning you down, you have a couple of other weapons in your arsenal...

...the insurer cannot give you an alternative reason for the refusal after you refute the initial one.

...when the refusal is based on a rule against paying for experimental treatment, you can marshal evidence from your doctor and others that the treatment was, in fact, the treatment of choice—and therefore should be covered by the policy.

Fourth: If it becomes necessary to appeal, start within the company. Write directly to the president—whose name can be found in insurance directories at your local library... or call the company and ask.

Enclose copies of all relevant documents... claims forms, medical receipts, responses from the insurer, notes of telephone conversations and any backup materials.

Caution: Never send any originals, since you may need them for future action.

Fifth: If you get nowhere at the company level, write to your State Insurance Department. Every state now has a section set up to assist consumers with complaints. You can reach them by checking directory assistance for a toll-free number.

With the correct department and address, again mail copies of the relevant documents and ask for a response. The Insurance Department won't take your side in every dispute, but it can obtain an answer from your insurance company in situations where you have been stonewalled or treated unfairly.

Ultimate weapon: File a suit against the insurer in small-claims court, or in a regular court if the amount at stake is too large to be handled by the small-claims court.

If you go to regular court, you'll need a lawyer, preferably one who takes the case on a contingency basis, where the fee is a percentage of what you ultimately recover. You can handle a small-claims case yourself. Also, if the insurer's behavior is particularly abusive, you may be able to collect punitive damages from such a suit.

Real case: A man was conned into trading in his health policy for another on the basis that the second policy was substantially improved. Yet when he filed a claim, he found the new policy paid 40% less in benefits than the old one. He sued the insurance company for fraud...and wound up collecting over $1 million in punitive damages.

Bottom line: Carefully review your policy before filing claims for illness or injury.

Go to your corporate benefits manager or insurance agent with any questions about coverage and costs. By knowing exactly what you can expect from your policy, you won't be surprised when the reimbursement check arrives. And in the event that the insurer sends you the wrong amount, you will be ready to take whatever action is necessary to obtain the money you deserve.

One Insurance *Not* to Get

Private pension plans (PPPs) are just variable life insurance policies with fancy sales pitches. Brokers may highlight a PPP's big selling point—the ability to borrow from it tax free.

What your broker won't tell you: Cash value is low in the early years due to high brokers' commissions—you'll lose money if you want to cash out. If you borrow, your money is effectively committed to *cash-value*

life insurance—not always the best investment option.

Trap: If the loan lapses, you face a big tax bill—loans get added back to the cash value to determine taxable gain.

Better alternatives: Cheap, guaranteed, convertible, level-premium term insurance and no-load mutual funds, such as Vanguard's index funds (800-523-7731).

Glenn Daily, a fee-only insurance consultant in New York City. www.glenndaily.com

Most Common Mistakes When Buying Life Insurance

James H. Hunt, life actuary, Consumer Federation of America in Washington, DC, and former commissioner of banking and insurance for the State of Vermont.

In addition to offering protection for your family, life insurance can also be a good investment. But life insurance policies are complicated, and without facts and comparisons it's easy to spend a lot of money for the wrong coverage.

The most common mistakes to avoid and recommendations on what you should buy...

Mistake: To buy life insurance when you have no dependents. Agents tend to create needs where none really exist in order to sell policies. If you are single, you don't need life insurance.

Mistake: To buy insurance for which you receive solicitations by mail. It's most often a bad bargain for most people.

Mistake: To buy life insurance for your children. Unless there's some extraordinary reason, there are better ways to save money.

Mistake: To put money into a cash-value life insurance policy at the expense of funding a tax-deductible IRA or 401(k) plan. (Cash-value policies are whole life, universal life, variable life or any form of life insurance that contains a savings element.) Be cautious about variable life. It has very high built-in expenses. If you want a cash-value policy, buy universal or whole life—provided you know how to choose the right policy and company and intend to keep the policy for at least 15 to 20 years. Otherwise you'd be a lot better off with term insurance.

Mistake: **To buy a cash-value policy from a high-pressure salesperson.** Keep in mind that agents make five to 10 times as much commission selling you a $100,000 cash-value policy as a term policy for the same amount. So you should always be alert to the hard sell for such policies.

Mistake: **To buy life insurance and not disability insurance.** People may automatically buy life insurance without realizing that a long-term disability can be an even worse financial event for their family than dying. If you're disabled, you not only lose your income, but you are still incurring expenses. You don't have to buy disability insurance if you're covered at work. However, only 30% of workers have such coverage. Everyone is covered by Social Security disability, but it's very restrictive, especially for white-collar workers.

Mistake: **To buy riders on your policy**— such as the accidental-death benefit or the additional-purchase option. These should be treated like options on a car—high-profit items that are best avoided.

Example: Double indemnity. Contrary to popular belief, you're not worth more dead in an accident than dead otherwise.

Controversial rider: The waiver of premiums in case of disability. You don't need it if you're covered for disability. If you become disabled, you'll have enough money to keep up your life insurance premium.

The safest and best insurance protection is the purchase of annual, renewable term insurance. A nonsmoking male can buy $250,000 coverage for about $300 or less a year at age 30 and $350 or less at age 40. Women pay about 15% less, smokers 50% to 100% more, depending on their age. For a family with one wage earner and group insurance at work, at least five times annual income is one rule of thumb.

Compare any cash-value or term policy you're thinking of buying with the policies sold by USAA Life* of San Antonio, Texas. Salaried representatives at its home office sell by phone. It usually has the best values on whole-life, universal-life and term insurance. *Alternative:* Ameritas,** which also offers second-to-die policies. USAA doesn't. Some policies are so complicated that it's impossible to figure out exactly what you're getting without a special computer program.

Example: If a universal-life policy says it pays 7%, that may be figured on whatever is left after a lot of expenses. You have to compare it with what you would have earned if you'd bought term and invested the difference. Assuming you hold the policy 20 years, 7% may turn out to be more like 5½%.

Reevaluate your older policies. If your old policy is a term policy, you should assume you can replace it with a lower priced policy, at least if you're a nonsmoker. If your old cash-value policy doesn't pay dividends, it probably should be replaced. If it does pay dividends, you'll be better off keeping it, especially if it has a low policy-loan interest rate.

*www.usaa.com...**www.ameritas.com

Life Insurance Test

Add up your assets—IRAs, savings, investments, etc. Subtract the amount that will be needed for estate taxes, mortgages, children's education, etc. If the balance won't generate enough income to support survivors, you need more life insurance. *Best buy:* Annual term insurance. Don't forget disability insurance. At age 50, you're more likely to be disabled than to die suddenly.

The late P. Kemp Fain, Jr., Asset Planning Corp., Knoxville, Tennessee, quoted in *Dun's.*

What Life Insurance Companies Don't Tell You

The late Venita VanCaspel Harris, certified financial planner.

Buying the wrong kind of life insurance is one of the major reasons people fail to become financially independent. *The other major reasons:* Investment procrastination. Lack of financial goals. Ignorance of what to do with money to accomplish those goals. Failure to apply tax laws to advantage.

LIFE INSURANCE TRAPS TO AVOID

• **A policy that does not use a current mortality table.** Many premiums are still being paid and policies are still in force based on the American Experience Table. That's the death rate from the days of Abraham Lincoln. Another table, the 1941 Commissioner's Standard Ordinary (CSO) table, was devised before penicillin was discovered. The current CSO table is based on a 2001 mortality study. If you have a policy based on an old table, you may be paying as much as 300% more than you need to because you are on the wrong table.

• **Cash-surrender policies.** Many consider them to be one of the greatest frauds in our country today. Insurance companies convince people that these are worthwhile because they give you a level premium on a whole-life policy and you can borrow your cash value. *Reality:* Insurance is based on a mortality table, and all the funny banking in the world won't change that. The companies are willing to give you a level premium on whole life because you are overpaying until you reach age 72. Then you can underpay when you don't need the insurance anyway. *Parallel:* Would you go to the telephone company and say, "Could I overpay my bill for each of the next 30 years for the privilege of underpaying after age 72?"

On the cash-value side, you would never go to a bank that takes away everything you deposit the first year and then charges you to deposit money in the account. Then if you want to borrow, it charges 5½% for your own money. And if you die, the insurance company can keep the money. No one would open that kind of bank account. Neither should you accept such terms from an insurance company.

Principle: People are willing to believe they can combine a living estate and a dying estate. In reality, these are incompatible. Insurance should be bought as an umbrella in case you die before building up a life estate. Don't ever consider it a method of building up your net worth (or "living" estate).

• **Dividend participating policies.** These are not really dividends. They are partial returns of an overcharge. Again, people believe that they can combine nest eggs for life and for death. A controversial Federal Trade Commission report says that if you keep a policy for an average period, you would receive 1.3% on your money. That means it takes 55.4 years for $1 to become $2.

Worse: If you hold the policy under five years, you could have a negative interest as high as 18%. Holding for 10 years could produce a negative 4%.

• **Insurance that is in your pension plan.** The incidental costs are much higher than most people are led to believe. After all, your pension plan is for living, not for dying.

BETTER METHODS OF INSURING

If you can pass a physical, you get a lower price per thousand on insurance if you switch to annual renewable term or 10-year deposit-level term.

Which to choose: If you know you are going to need insurance for the next 10 years, there is merit in the 10-year deposit-level term, since your premiums will be level for 10 years. However, realize that you are being overcharged in the beginning and undercharged at the end. But by making a deposit, you do get a discount on the rates you pay.

Best: If you believe you will soon start making enough to take care of your family out of your living estate (the money you build up out of investments over a lifetime), you will want to drop your insurance incrementally as your estate grows.

How to manage it: If you have a dependent who requires $1,000 a month if you die, then you need an estate of $200,000 (at a 6% return a year—half of that at 12%). If you have only $20,000 in your living estate, you need a $180,000 death estate (or insurance policy). As you build up your living estate, you can annually decrease your death estate. When your living estate rises to $50,000, then your death estate should go down to $150,000. Naturally, you may want to adjust this in accordance with inflation. However, your goal is to be self-insured so that benefits don't hinge on death.

Insurance should be viewed as a way to buy time before you build up your own future.

How to Choose A Life Insurance Company

Joseph M. Belth, PhD, editor of The Insurance Forum, *Box 245, Ellettsville, Indiana 47429.*

Most people now know that they need to purchase life insurance from a reputable insurance company.

But exactly how do you evaluate the financial condition of a company? And how do you choose among several that are established, healthy and reliable?

Here are five steps consumers can take to select the best insurer for their needs…

Step 1: **Determine how much life insurance you need.** Selecting a life insurance company is only one major decision you must make—and it's not the first one.

Before researching insurers, you'll need to determine the financial needs your family would face in the event of your death. There is no formula that will apply to everyone, because family circumstances vary widely.

But in addition to your expenses, assets, debts and short-term income needs, you will have to consider several difficult, personal questions in order to calculate your family's long-term needs.

Examples: Would your spouse work following your death? Would he or she sell your current home in order to move to a less costly one or have to move in with relatives?

Step 2: **Decide what kind of life insurance you wish to buy.** The variety of life insurance products on the market can be overwhelming to consumers. Most insurance companies can offer dozens of policies that can be further altered with riders, or optional clauses.

Helpful: The life insurance needs of almost any family can be met with one, or some of each, of just two types of policies—term and cash-value insurance.

• **Term insurance has no cash value or savings component.** It carries a relatively low premium for a large death benefit. Premiums increase with age…and as the policy is renewed.

• **Cash-value insurance**—straight life, universal life, variable life, etc.—accumulates cash value each year as premiums are paid. Premiums generally stay level for the duration of the contract.

Step 3: **Select several financially healthy insurers.** In order to do this, consumers must rely on professional rating firms, because the evelation process is complex.

Five rating firms use their specialized knowledge to publish ratings of life and health insurance companies: A.M. Best Company, Standard & Poor's Corp., Moody's Investors Service, Duff & Phelps Credit Rating Co. and Weiss Research.

Consumers should check all ratings that are available on the companies they are considering. Do not rely on what an insurer says about its own ratings.

Caution: While each firm generally does a good job evaluating insurers, they are not perfect. Each uses its own criteria, so the ratings are not uniform.

Example: An A+ is the highest rating from Weiss, the second highest from Best and the fifth highest from Standard & Poor's and Duff & Phelps.

Look for companies that have received very high ratings from at least three ratings services.

***Step 4:* Investigate the pricing of the policies you are considering,** and rule out all that are not reasonably priced.

To determine whether a policy is reasonably priced, it is necessary to obtain a large amount of information about a policy and make comparisons with certain benchmarks. This policy information includes premiums, cash values (if any), death benefits and dividends (if any) for each year.

Pay close attention to figures that are guaranteed by an insurer, as opposed to illustrations—or those that are not guaranteed.

It is not practical to search for the cheapest policy, since there are numerous factors that affect premiums.

***Step 5:* Compare the provisions of the candidate policies.** Life insurance policies are complex legal documents, and their provisions can vary widely. *Some examples of the provisions to examine...*

•**Does the company pay interest on the death benefit** between the date of death and the date of the settlement check?

•**Does the company reimburse the beneficiary** for any unearned portion of any premiums paid prior to death?

•**On a term policy,** what are your rights regarding renewability? How about convertibility to another type of policy?

•**What are your rights** with regard to borrowing against the policy? Cashing it in?

•**What are the provisions** of the policy's incontestability clause and suicide clause?

PERSONAL ADVANTAGE

On close comparison, one or more policies will emerge as superior.

It will be up to you to decide which provisions are most important to you and which you are willing to pay for.

A New Policy May Be Better Than an Old One

Buying a new policy may be cheaper than reinstating a lapsed one if you're considerably older now. Age is only one factor in setting premiums. Of equal or greater importance are fluctuations in the interest rate. The higher the rate, the lower the premium. Generally, higher interest rates may lower premiums more than your increasing age may raise them.

Christopher Collins, CLU, Tomorrow's Money, Lincoln, Nebraska.

Health Insurance— Choose Wisely

Bruce S. Pyenson and Jim O'Connor, principals with Milliman USA, an actuarial consulting firm. Mr. Pyenson is coauthor of *J.K. Lasser's Employee Benefits for Small Business* (John Wiley & Sons).

Most health insurance is provided through group policies available in the workplace. But there are millions of people who are self-employed or between jobs who have to find individual coverage on their own. Medicare also offers different coverage options.

While there are plenty of good policies out there, finding one that fits your needs takes some digging. New options provided by the 2010 Affordable Care Act will become available in 2014. Meanwhile, a government website, *www.healthcare.gov,* can direct you to existing options in your state.

SIZE UP YOUR NEEDS

The health-care needs of families with young children are different from those of singles starting new jobs...couples without children...and empty nesters. Families with infants want a full range of preventive care that covers everything from routine vaccinations to ear infections. Healthy singles may only need bare-bones coverage for unexpected catastrophes.

In these days of managed care, there are four basic types of coverage...

HEALTH MAINTENANCE ORGANIZATIONS (HMOs)

A very prevalent type of group coverage, HMOs provide comprehensive medical care through networks of physicians. Typically, you pay $5 or $10 per in-network doctor visit and don't have to fill out forms after each appointment or worry about meeting a deductible requirement.

If you have a special health problem, you typically must first consult your primary care physician—also known as the *gatekeeper*. This physician may treat you or may refer you to a specialist. If you decide to use an out-of-network specialist or hospital, coverage—if any—is limited.

With limited choice about which doctors and hospitals to use and limited access to specialists, these plans are usually the most economical. Your out-of-pocket costs are fairly low for the wide range of coverage you get.

Best for: People with children who are new to a community—they have no relationships with physicians or hospitals. Also good for people with children whose current physician and hospital are part of the HMO network.

PREFERRED PROVIDER ORGANIZATIONS (PPOs)

These types of policies—which are more expensive than comparable HMOs—give you the ability to go outside the plan network for your medical care. Most PPO plans don't have a gatekeeper system, so you usually don't need approval to see specialists.

If you see a physician within the network, you get one level of benefits (usually 80% of a claim is covered). If you see a physician outside the network, you get another, lower level of benefits (only 60% to 70% of the claim might be covered).

Best for: People who want more choice about health-care providers...and whose doctors are part of the PPO network.

INDEMNITY POLICIES

These plans pay benefits no matter what doctor or hospital you go to. Such traditional policies appeal to people who have lived in the same community for a long time and have established ties to physicians and hospitals. While they guarantee you the most latitude in terms of choosing your health-care providers, indemnity plans are also the most expensive. Sometimes people who want the flexibility of an indemnity policy opt for high deductibles of as much as $10,000 to reduce monthly premiums.

"ANY DOCTOR" POLICIES

These hybrid plans use a PPO approach for hospitals but allow you to see any licensed physicians you wish. They are cheaper than indemnity policies but more expensive than full-fledged PPOs.

Best for: People who feel comfortable with the hospitals in the PPO network but want the flexibility of using any doctor they choose.

FINDING THE BEST PLAN

• **Research what is available in your state.** Because each state regulates insurance, choices will be limited. Not all insurance companies offer policies in all states. And a company's policies may be different in different states.

If your car and homeowner's insurance is with a company that sells through a network of agents, start by calling your agent.

If you belong to a professional or trade group or a college alumni association, find out if these organizations offer special health policies for members. Such policies often cost less than individual policies but more than group policies. If you have chronic health problems, these policies can be a good deal since you may not be able to get an affordable policy on your own.

• **Determine what different types of policies will cost you.** Call two major companies that write health insurance nationwide.

For HMOs: Aetna (800-872-3862)...United HealthCare Group (877-311-7848).

For PPOs, "Any Doctor" and indemnity: Assurant Health (800-800-1212)...Mutual of Omaha (800-775-6000).

Simplify your search by using the Internet. Two sites that provide up to 20 different premium quotes are *www.insure.com* and *www.insweb.com*.

Be sure to get the answers to some crucial questions…

• **Does the plan cover maternity, mental health and substance abuse?**

• **What are the rules concerning preexisting conditions** (health problems you had before taking out the policy)?

• **Ask the insurer about rate increases.** You want to know how often and by how much insurers boost their premiums each year. Ask what the increases have been for the past several years. Some companies charge very low initial rates but then raise premiums by a large amount. Rate increases are currently running 10% to 15% a year. If your insurer is boosting rates by 30% or more annually, it's time to shop around.

• **Find out if customers are satisfied.** Get the names of current HMO members. Ask if they've experienced delays in obtaining membership cards, problems communicating with physicians, difficulty getting pharmacies to accept their coverage, trouble getting doctor's appointments quickly or trouble getting prompt referrals to specialists.

You can also call your state insurance or health department (they usually are listed in the state government pages of your telephone directory). Some states develop statistics that indicate complaint ratios of HMOs.

If you have an established doctor, you might also call him or her for feedback on the plan you are considering, particularly for HMOs.

You Can Avoid a Physical Exam

Insurance medical exams are quietly being abandoned by insurance companies, even for $100,000 to $200,000 term insurance sales, according to a major insurance broker. The reasons are the high cost of the exams and the poor reliability of the information given by those seeking insurance. Even the best exams, say the insurers, protect them only for about six months anyway. Now they often rely on a medical history taken by the insurance broker. They may also request an electrocardiogram and a chest X-ray.

Secrets to Fast Payment from Your HMO

William M. Shernoff, senior partner at the law firm Shernoff Bidart Echeverria Bentley LLP (*www.shernoff. com*), which represents policyholders who are seeking claims payments from insurance companies and HMOs, 600 S. Indian Hill Blvd., Claremont, California 91711. He is author of *Fight Back & Win: How to Get Your HMO and Health Insurance to Pay Up* (Capital Books).

The larger the dollar amount of a claim filed with an HMO, the less likely the HMO is to pay for all—or even most—of the claim.

No matter how frustrated you become with the HMO, don't give up. Managed-care companies count on most people to accept their decisions on claims, even if the companies are wrong.

Here's how to get satisfaction on your medical claims…

• **Take an active role in the claims process.** Unlike conventional—or indemnity—insurance policies, in which you personally file your claims, HMOs handle your claims for you.

But if anything goes wrong—such as an HMO doctor's office neglecting to file the right forms or paperwork being improperly filled out—the HMO may deny the claim or delay payment for it. *Helpful…*

If your case is not routine: Ask the HMO to send you copies of all the claims that have been filed on your behalf. Review them, and promptly forward any missing information to the HMO's home office.

Don't be afraid to contact the claims examiner who is assigned to your case. Ask the examiner to explain any decision that you believe is unfair. If you're not satisfied, move up the chain of command and contact the examiner's supervisor.

With a complex medical problem that will require ongoing treatment: Establish a personal relationship with the case manager (who oversees the examiner) in charge of your paperwork.

As a participant in the HMO, you have the right to see how the case manager has written up your problem—and what the HMO has recommended to your physician. When HMO employees know that you are taking an active role in your care, they are less likely to put up roadblocks.

• **Don't take the company's first *no* as the final answer.** File an immediate appeal in writing.

Important: Carefully follow the complaint procedure outlined in your HMO handbook.

Explain why you feel your benefits were wrongfully denied...and clearly state what action you want your HMO to take.

To protect your future legal rights, include the following sentence in every letter that you write to the HMO...

"This appeal relates only to the denial of the benefits in question. It does not constitute, and shall in no way be deemed an admission, that I am limited in my right to pursue a 'bad faith' remedy in state court."

Send your complaint letter by registered mail, return receipt requested—even if you are not required to do so. It's amazing how often HMOs claim they never received communications from patients...so you should have proof to the contrary. Request a written response within 30 days.

Set up a folder for all the paperwork on the grievance, and track on a calendar each step of the complaint process and when the HMO's responses are due.

• **Go straight to arbitration if you feel you are not getting a fair hearing.** The *internal* appeals procedures set up by HMOs may not be as impartial as they seem.

Some are biased in favor of the health plan because decision makers in the appeals process are not likely to disagree with their fellow employees.

The HMO's appeals process is not your only remedy. You also have the right to arbitration, an independent process conducted by third parties who are not usually beholden to the HMO. The sooner you can get your appeal heard in this setting, the better. Your HMO handbook lists the arbitration entity.

• **Get another medical opinion from doctors outside your HMO.** If your HMO doctor is reluctant to order a costly or experimental test or procedure that you're convinced you need, get a second, or even a third, opinion—even if you must pay for it out of your own pocket.

If these outside doctors agree with you, ask them to write to the HMO on your behalf. The aim is to establish a written record that supports your case, should you later appeal.

• **Get documentation for using a non-affiliated emergency room.** Most people who seek care in an emergency room that is not affiliated with their HMO network do so when they are away from home.

If you must visit a nonaffiliated emergency room, request a letter from the facility documenting that you had a real medical emergency. The letter should also state that you could not be transferred to a facility in the HMO network without endangering your health.

• **Make as much noise as possible.** Start in your own company's human resources department with the person who is the official liaison with the HMO. Then contact local consumer hot lines and consumer affairs reporters at television stations and newspapers.

Also complain to your local, state and federal elected officials—your mayor, state representatives and US senators. It's also wise to contact your Better Business Bureau and state attorney general.

Complain to the regulators. Contact the appropriate state regulatory agency—usually the Department of Insurance or the Department of Corporations—and ask about the procedures for filing a complaint against the HMO. Many states have waiting periods, but in some emergency cases a complaint may be filed and heard within 72 hours. Be sure to let your HMO know that you are contacting the state regulator.

If you are covered by both an HMO and Medicare, you can also appeal to the MAXIMUS Federal Services, 3750 Monroe Ave., Suite 702, Pittsford, NY 14534-1302. 585-348-3300, *www.medicareappeal.com.*

If the Center for Health Dispute Resolution rules in your favor, you can then have the HMO provide appropriate care and treatment or have the HMO pay for the care and treatment you received in the interim.

If you lose, you can then file a complaint with the Administrative Law Justice division of Medicare.

• **Seek legal redress if necessary.** If your claim is modest, file a claim in small-claims court. You don't need a lawyer, and the odds of winning are good. Your case will probably be heard within six months.

If you have a major claim, look for a lawyer who specializes in "bad faith" cases against insurance companies and HMOs. You're best off hiring an attorney who works on a contingency basis. This means the attorney gets nothing if you lose but takes at least one-third of any amount you recover from the HMO.

Short-Term Health Protection

Short-term health insurance can protect you between jobs. It may also be suitable for recent college graduates over age 26 who are no longer covered by their parents' insurance...and for Medicare beneficiaries traveling abroad and not covered by other policies.

Cost depends on copays, deductibles and coverage limits. *Important:* Renewal is not automatic—you must reapply at the end of each coverage period.

Limitations: Coverage may be limited to 180 days within a year...short-term policies do not cover maternity costs—except the cost of complications associated with birth...not all states allow the sale of short-term health insurance.

Roy Diliberto, former president, Financial Planning Association, Denver.

Get Medigap Insurance

Medicare patients who expect to be dropped by their HMOs—a growing trend—should apply now for traditional Medicare insurance. Also apply for Medicare gap insurance (Medigap). That may take as long as three months to take effect. *Downside:* Paying $50 to several hundred a month for Medigap. *Upside:* More choice among medical practitioners...and an opportunity for better care than from a cost-cutting HMO. *Note:* Nobody can be turned down for Medicare. Medigap has limitations on renal disease and hospice care.

Frank N. Darras, former partner at the law firm Shernoff Bidart Echeverria Bentley LLP (*www.shernoff.com*), which represents policyholders who are seeking claims payments from insurance companies and HMOs, 600 S. Indian Hill Blvd., Claremont, California 91711.

Medigap Traps...and How to Avoid Them

Robert M. Freedman, partner, Mazur Carp Rubin & Schulman, PC, elder law and elder care consultants specializing in estate planning, 1250 Broadway, New York City 10001.

Most Americans age 65 and older enroll in Medicare as their primary health insurer.

But Medicare was not designed to provide comprehensive coverage, and the gaps leave policyholders liable for potentially huge medical expenses.

To cover the gaps, about two-thirds of Americans enrolled in Medicare purchase supplemental coverage, or "Medigap insurance."

Choosing a supplemental policy has become simpler since federal regulations standardized Medigap plans in 1992. Insurers may now offer 10 plans, labeled A, B, C, D, F, G, K, L, M and N. (In Massachusetts, Minnesota and Wisconsin Medigap policies are standardized in a different way.) Consumers can easily compare costs. But there are still many variables to consider when choosing a Medigap policy. *Here are the most important...*

• **Which plan is right for you?** The new standardized Medigap policies allow you to choose a package of benefits to suit your needs and budget.

Plan A is the most basic and least expensive.

Plans B, C or D will meet the needs of most seniors.

In some cases, you may have to pay for a benefit you don't need in order to get those you do.

Example: All but the most basic plans cover foreign travel emergencies—whether you want the coverage or not.

When comparing plans, note that certain benefits are really not worth much. Be realistic about which out-of-pocket medical expenses you are willing to pay for yourself.

• **How much does Medigap insurance cost?** Medigap plans have been standardized —but prices and levels of service have not.

Example: You may find a lower rate from a mail-order company that doesn't have to pay agents' commissions, but you might prefer to pay a slightly higher premium to buy from a local agent who will help file your claims.

Most insurers base their premiums on the buyer's age and state of residence. Rates are generally uniform for men and women. United HealthCare, under contract with AARP, charges a fixed premium per plan regardless of a policyholder's age, but adjusts premiums by state.

Insurers may also have different intervals between premium increases, different rules governing conversion and renewability or different maximum benefit limits.

Not all insurers offer all 10 plans, and not all states have adopted the standardized system.

Shop around! Annual premiums can vary enormously from one insurer to another.

• **When should I buy a Medigap policy?** If you are 65 or older, you can qualify for any Medigap policy without regard to preexisting conditions for the six months after you enroll in Medicare Part B. There may be, though, a six-month exclusionary period for coverage of these conditions.

• **What if I already have coverage?** Many people already own one of the hundreds of Medigap policies that were on the market in the past, or have insurance through an employer plan. There is no need to switch to a standard plan if you are happy with your coverage. It is now illegal to sell duplicate or unnecessary Medigap coverage to any person, so if you do decide to switch, you will have to surrender your old policy. You may have to requalify to upgrade.

If you are covered by an employer or older Medigap policy, call your benefits manager or insurer to check on the future of your coverage.

Reason: Many employers have been cutting back on retiree health benefits, including group health plans that once paid many non-Medicare-covered benefits. And many insurers are discontinuing their older Medigap plans now that the new plans are on the market.

Catch: Insurers are not required to offer coverage that is comparable to their discontinued products. Result...many retirees are suddenly faced with the need to find new Medigap coverage.

Frequent problems: A policyholder is offered an opportunity to convert an old Medigap policy to a new plan—but the insurer only offers Plans A and B, and the coverage is inferior to the old plan. Or, if the replacement policy has a new benefit, the insurer can impose a waiting period for coverage.

The policyholder decides to switch to a new insurer. If accepted by a new company, there is no waiting period for coverage of preexisting conditions...but insurers can turn down applicants with preexisting conditions.

Solution: Some providers, including AARP, usually don't consider an applicant's health.

• **Are there alternatives to Medigap policies?** Medicare Part B participants are eligible to enroll in health maintenance organizations (HMOs) if they live in a plan's service area. However, if you belong to an HMO, you probably don't need Medigap insurance.

The majority of states have a new and possibly less expensive type of private Medigap insurance called Medicare Select. Participants in this plan agree to use a selected group of health-care providers. The insurer picks the group, which may include a local managed-care organization.

Medigap coverage for prescription drugs may not be as good as coverage under Medicare Part D—consider changing your Medigap policy so that you obtain prescription drug coverage separately (through Medicare Part D).

There are also Medicare Advantage Plans that eliminate the need to carry a Medigap policy.

•**What is not covered by Medicare and Medigap insurance?** When calculating your potential medical expenses, remember that Medicare/Medigap policies do not cover eye care, dental services, hearing aids, routine checkups—procedures deemed not medically necessary—and, perhaps most important, long-term nursing home or custodial care.

Traps in Company-Provided Disability Insurance

William M. Shernoff, senior partner at the law firm Shernoff Bidart Echeverria Bentley LLP (*www.shernoff. com*), which represents policyholders who are seeking claims payments from insurance companies and HMOs, 600 S. Indian Hill Blvd., Claremont, California 91711. He is author of *Fight Back & Win: How to Get Your HMO and Health Insurance to Pay Up* (Capital Books).

It's not unusual for people who receive life insurance at work to supplement their policy by buying additional coverage.

Yet relatively few bother to calculate whether the company's disability insurance will cover their financial needs if they are out of work for an extended period of time. They simply assume that the company's benefits are sufficient.

In fact, employer-sponsored disability insurance is very often woefully inadequate.

Many employers purchase the minimum amount of protection for employees, and most employees are unaware of how easy it is for insurers to wriggle out of paying them.

In most cases, a company's short-term-disability policy will pay only 70% of your salary for between 13 and 26 weeks.

Long-term-disability insurance usually begins after 26 weeks, paying only 60% of your salary—and then up to only $60,000 a year.

TRAPS

•**There may be a gap of as much as three months** between the time short-term disability ends and long-term coverage begins.

•**Disability income is taxable unless you have purchased your own coverage,** so you'd actually take home even less. The amount of additional coverage that you need depends on your monthly living expenses—and how much of your savings is available for such purposes.

Here's how to tell whether you need additional coverage, and what to look for when shopping for a supplemental insurance policy...

•**Estimate what your monthly expenses would be** if you were unable to work for 90 days or longer. Once you've arrived at this figure, determine what your take-home benefit would be. If the monthly sum is too low to meet your needs, you should buy additional coverage to make up the difference.

Buying your own policy also has two other advantages...

•**You can take an individual or supplemental policy with you if you change jobs.**

•**The younger you are when you purchase the policy,** the lower the fixed premium will be throughout the time you own it.

Before you buy—understand the plan's definition of disability. Most insurance contracts have more restrictive standards for defining disability than do most states. This is due to a loophole in the federal Employee Retirement Income Security Act (ERISA), which overrides state laws and prevents insurance companies from being sued in state courts for damages.

Although most states say you are legally disabled if you cannot perform the substantial tasks of your work with any regularity, many insurance policies define disability as the inability to perform any of your work-related tasks now or ever again.

Example: A paralyzed surgeon who is unable to operate on patients but can still read or dictate medical reports would be considered disabled by most states, but not by many insurers.

• **Beware of "offset" clauses.** These allow the insurer to deduct from your monthly benefit any income you already receive from other sources, such as workers' compensation or Social Security. These deductions can cut your monthly insurance benefit in half.

• **Not all "lifetime" policies are the same.** Many actually pay for only a certain period (usually one or two years) if you are disabled from your occupation. They will pay over a lifetime only if you can prove that you are disabled from working at any occupation.

Many high-earning professionals have lost the lifetime benefits they thought they were entitled to because the insurer proved that they could perform a low-wage job.

Example: A bedridden executive could still work in telephone sales.

• **A lifetime policy offers little protection if your job or coverage is terminated due to a disability.** According to certain state laws, it is illegal for an employer or insurer to cut off a policyholder's benefits if he or she contracts a disease or suffers an accident. But this frequently happens to policyholders, anyway, because they have little legal recourse in these matters due to the ERISA loophole.

Example: There was a recent case in which an employer was permitted to dramatically reduce an employee's AIDS benefit after the employee discovered that he had the disease.

As a result, most group coverage offered by an employer is illusory. If you lose your job due to disability, your employer can terminate your lifetime coverage after one year.

• **Look for a policy that does not tie coverage to the cause of a disability.** Many policies will pay only if you are disabled by an accident, not a sickness. Some insurers have even been known to unjustly convert accident claims to sickness claims to avoid paying out.

Example: An insurer may say that injuries from an accidental fall were really caused by dizziness due to an underlying condition such as arthritis, sunstroke or high blood pressure.

SELF-DEFENSE

• **Buy a policy that considers you disabled if you can't do the important tasks of your own job.** Until legislation closes the ERISA loophole, it is preferable to buy non-cancelable, guaranteed-renewable disability insurance. You can do this on your own or through a professional or church group that offers such a policy.

• **Be prepared for disputes.** Even with individual policies, it is not uncommon for disputes to occur between policyholders' doctors and insurers' doctors over the extent of a disability.

Most insurers send disability cases to "independent" medical examiners for review. But these doctors are usually far from independent, since they receive a large volume of work from the insurer. While many review cases in good faith, they must work with the definition of disability supplied by the insurer, even if it is contrary to state law.

Solution: If your disability claim is denied, enlist the help of your physician. Also, get a truly independent second opinion and consider seeing an attorney.

• **Those who can't afford the premium for a new policy** should save some money each month to be used in case they become disabled. Be sure to save enough to cover any gap between when short-term disability ends and long-term coverage begins.

• **At work, require your company's insurance agent to sign a written statement.** *It should say:* "If you become disabled, even if your employer terminates you because of your disability, we will keep paying your claim for the period specified in the policy."

• **Don't forget to protect your home.** Mortgage insurance policies are usually sold in such a way that policyholders believe that their mortgage payments will be made for life if they become disabled.

Trap: These policies are often limited in time, say for just two years. If you have a 30-year mortgage and are permanently disabled, two years of mortgage payments won't prevent you from losing your home.

Solution: Make sure the insurance policy is for the life of the mortgage—or find a disability policy that pays a high enough benefit to meet your needs.

How to Buy Disability Insurance

You can generally get coverage up to 50% of your income. Policies cover all illnesses not specifically excluded. This includes psychiatric disabilities. Pregnancy is usually excluded, but not complications from pregnancy. *What to look for in a policy...*

• **Noncancelability.** As you get older, you're more susceptible to disabilities, and they last longer. You can get a policy that's noncancelable to age 65, with the option to renew if you keep working.

• **Cost-of-living clause.** This pays additional benefits when the cost-of-living index goes up. The annual adjustment is usually limited to 6%, although some policies pay more than this. There's also usually an upper limit, such as twice the original benefit.

• **Waiting period.** One- to six-month periods are common. Choose as long a period as you can. Why? You'll get higher coverage for the same premium. With a short waiting period, you may be paid for some illnesses you could probably ride out without help; but you'll get proportionately less in time of real need if you're hit by catastrophic long-term disability.

• **Definition of disability.** You want a policy that defines disability as inability to work at your regular occupation. Also, the policy should pay for illness that first manifests itself while the policy is in force. This protects you if you have a condition (such as heart disease or cancer) that you don't know about when you buy the policy.

• **Residual-disability benefits.** A residual-benefit clause pays partial benefits if you can work part-time or at a lower paying job. *Example:* A violinist who lost the use of his fingers from arthritis took a teaching job at a lower income. He could collect a percentage of his disability benefit equal to the percentage of his lost income.

Leonard B. Stern, president of Leonard B. Stern & Co., insurance and consulting firm, New York City.

Disability Insurance for Homemakers

Full-time homemakers can now get insurance that allows them to hire replacement help if they become disabled. About one-third of the country's largest disability insurance firms now offer such policies. Rates are based on age and coverage.

American Council of Life Insurers, Washington, DC. *www.acli.com*

Property Insurance Trap

Traditional policies pay only the "actual cash value" of an item that's lost, stolen or destroyed. *Example:* A sofa purchased five years ago for $600 is destroyed in a fire. At today's prices a comparable replacement costs $900. But the cash value of that five-year-old sofa—if you tried to sell it secondhand—is only, say, $150. So all you could collect under a traditional policy is $150.

Replacement-cost insurance seems to be an attractive alternative. But in practice, most of these policies pay off only the smallest of either replacement cost, repair cost or four times the actual cash value.

In the example, the payout would be $600, four times the actual cash value. And the policyholder would be $300 short of the price of a new sofa. *Cost of coverage:* About 15% higher premiums on a typical homeowner's policy, 25% higher for condominium and co-op owners and 40% extra on a tenant's policy.

Covering Computer Equipment

Computer equipment, like any other household possession, is covered by home insurance policies. *Exception:* Expensive equipment may necessitate upgrading of your present policy. And if you use the computer for business, consider a separate business policy to cover damage, theft or destruction of data.

Insure Your Home–Based Business

Home–based businesses are only minimally covered by traditional homeowner's insurance. Most will not cover computer-stored information, paperwork, accounts receivable or other business elements.

Self-defense: Expand existing homeowner's policies to provide business coverage if your business is considered incidental—usually defined by insurers as generating less than $5,000 in annual gross income. *Cost:* $50 to $100/yr. For larger home-based businesses, buy a business owner's package that works with your homeowner's policy. *Cost:* $250/year and up.

Scot McCartney, independent insurance agent, Ardsley, New York.

Umbrella Policies: How to Protect Against Catastrophes

Leonard B. Stern, president of Leonard B. Stern & Co., insurance and consulting firm, New York City.

In a litigious society, if you have substantial assets you are fair game for lawsuits and heavy damage judgments simply because you do have those substantial assets.

Homeowner's insurance and automobile insurance policies offer basic liability coverage for injuries and damage caused by you or your family (even your pet) and by your car or small boat. (Larger boats and many recreational vehicles require separate policies.) These policies cover accidents that happen on your property as well. You pay higher and higher premiums as you raise the limits of your liability coverage.

However, the amount you owe when you are sued for damages is determined by the courts, not by the limits of your insurance coverage. Judgments have skyrocketed in the past decade. If you are not prepared, a judgment can be financially ruinous. The more you own—houses, jewelry, boats, cars, investments—the more you can be expected to pay.

MINIMUM LIABILITY RECOMMENDATIONS

• **Automobile bodily injury.** $100,000 per person, $300,000 per accident.
• **Automobile property damage.** $25,000 per accident.
• **Boat owner's liability.** $100,000 per occurrence.
• **Homeowner's liability.** $100,000 per occurrence.

ENTER THE UMBRELLA

If your net worth is a great deal more than these minimums, you need more protection. This is where umbrella liability insurance becomes useful. An umbrella policy provides excess coverage for all your primary liability insurance.

Example: A guest is injured at a party around your swimming pool. The courts award him $300,000 for medical costs and lost pay. Your homeowner's policy has only a $100,000 liability limit. The umbrella policy covers the $200,000 gap. And then your car goes out of control and plows into a new addition on a neighbor's house. The courts assess the damage at $40,000. Your car insurance pays a maximum of $25,000. Again, the umbrella policy picks up the $15,000 shortfall.

COST OF UMBRELLA POLICIES

Personal umbrella liability insurance is sold in increments of $1 million of coverage. Premiums generally start at around $200 a year. More than 75 companies now offer this blanket coverage for personal (rather than business) liability. *Biggest difference in policies:* Requirements for minimum-liability coverage in primary home-owners, car, boat and recreational vehicle contracts. Each personal umbrella liability policy has its own conditions, definitions and exclusions, too. In shopping around, look for a policy that includes all your family's potentially hazardous activities.

Interesting bonus: Personal umbrella policies give primary coverage for one area of liability not touched on by other general types of liability insurance—slander and libel.

Bottom line: Personal umbrella liability insurance is designed to protect individuals with substantial property, who are vulnerable to lawsuits and costly judgments. For them it is inexpensive insurance against catastrophic losses in court.

Canceled Check Is Proof That Fire Insurance Is Paid for, Right? Wrong!

Fire and casualty policies should be in hand (on file) before the full premium is paid. One firm, after finding its plant burned to the ground, didn't have the policy it had paid for. Though it produced the canceled check to the broker, its claim was disallowed. The wise course is to buy insurance as you would an automobile—give the broker a small deposit, but don't pay up until the policy is delivered.

Cut Your Car Insurance Costs

Jack Gillis, director of public affairs at Consumer Federation of America, 1620 I St., NW, Suite 200, Washington, DC 20006. He is author of *The Car Book* (Gillis).

Despite declining auto insurance rates, 75% of car owners haven't changed their insurance policies—or even inquired about doing so—within the last five years.

Here's how to pay less for your insurance coverage…

•**Compare policy rates on the Web.** This process takes about a half hour. First look at the sample rates charged by all insurers that do business in your state.

•*www.insure.com* provides a link to every state insurance department. At the home page, enter your state in the box labeled "insurance in your state."

Once you have a benchmark rate, visit a site that can locate policies with the lowest rates.

•Insweb (*www.insweb.com*). You type in the information about your driving history. Then this Web site sifts through the insurance companies in its database to find the ones that have the lowest prices. This service is free.

•**Shop aggressively every two years.** Different insurers target certain types of drivers at different times and then offer lower rates based on how closely you fit their preferred "top tier" profiles.

You're a candidate for a lower insurance rate whenever…

•Points are removed from your license.

•One of your vehicles is removed from your policy.

•Your kids no longer drive your car.

•Your car is no longer used for commuting.

•**Maximize your policy's discounts.** Discounts can cut your premium in half. Most insurers offer as many as 20 different discounts. Most don't tell you about all of them unless you specifically ask. *Helpful…*

•Antitheft devices •Air bags
•Antilock brakes •Car-pool drivers

- Low mileage
- Nonsmokers
- Graduates of driver-training courses
- Multiple policies
- No accident in three years
- Older drivers who don't drive at night

• **Ask insurance companies if they offer low-rate group policies.** More insurers now offer organizations group policies that have discounted rates for members.

Examples: Retirement organizations, alumni associations, credit unions...and some credit card issuers, too.

• **Eliminate unnecessary coverage.** Increasing your monthly deductible from $200 to $500 could reduce your collision and comprehensive premiums by as much as 30%.

Consider eliminating collision and comprehensive coverage if your car is completely paid off...more than four years old...or worth less than $4,000.

To research car values: National Automobile Dealers Association (*www.nada.com*)... or Kelley Blue Book (*www.kbb.com*).

• **Buy a less desirable—or safer—car.** Buying a model that is a favorite with thieves or statistically in frequent accidents can send your premiums sky-high.

For cars with high theft rates: The National Insurance Crime Bureau (*www.nicb.org*).

For cars with the highest safety ratings: Insurance Institute for Highway Safety (*www.iihs.org*).

When You Are Hit By the Uninsured (Or Underinsured) Motorist

Richard P. Oatman, assistant claim counsel for Aetna Life & Casualty, Hartford, Connecticut.

An accident with an uninsured or underinsured motorist can be financially ruinous. As part of your own policy, underinsured (in some states) and uninsured motorist's coverage is obtainable to deal with such accidents.

UNINSURED COVERAGE

Most states have statutory requirements that automobile liability insurance policies include uninsured motorist's coverage.

• **Financial-responsibility limits.** The law requires that uninsured motorist's coverage be provided in an amount mandated by the state. These financial-responsibility limits vary.

• **Getting more coverage.** Usually you can buy coverage up to your liability limits. *Example:* If you carry $300,000 in liability, you can get the same amount in uninsured coverage.

• **Proof of fault.** Under uninsured coverage, your company has to pay you only what the other party is legally liable for. So the other party must be proved to be at fault.

• **Comparative negligence provisions.** In some states, if the other driver is proved to be somewhat at fault, you can recover proportional damages from your own insurance company.

• **Making a claim.** You are placed in an adversarial position with your own insurance company. You must prove the extent of the injury, establish its value and negotiate with your own carrier to settle. If you can't reach a settlement, most claims will go to arbitration, not to court.

• **Limits.** Most mandatory uninsured motorist's protection covers only bodily injury. Property damage is covered under your collision insurance, after the deductible. (As with any collision claim, your rates may go up after filing.)

UNDERINSURED COVERAGE

This type of coverage is becoming more and more popular. Some states require that underinsured coverage be offered. In others, it is optional. *With underinsured coverage...*

• **You must first recover the maximum amount** from the other party's liability policy before you can collect on your own policy.

• **As with uninsured coverage,** you are in an adversarial position with your carrier and must prove that the value of your injury has exceeded the liability limits of the other party's policy.

Important: Uninsured motorist's coverage will not pay you if the other driver has any insurance at all, no matter how inadequate.

PEDESTRIAN ACCIDENTS

You will be covered by your uninsured motorist's coverage just as if you were in a car at the time. If you don't own a car, you might be able to get coverage under the policy of a family member in your immediate household who does own one. If neither you nor anyone in your family has coverage, you can apply to a fund that some states maintain to cover such accidents or pursue a court action directly against the responsible party.

Children Can Sue Insured Parents

A child could sue his or her parents for damages from an auto accident caused by the parents' negligence. (The doctrine of parental immunity from lawsuits is waived in negligence cases to the extent to which the parent is covered by insurance.) The court noted that the insurance company could have protected itself by adding an appropriate clause to the policy.

Ard v. Ard, 414 So. 2d 1066 (Fla.).

No-Hit Protection

Auto insurance policies are required by state law to cover hit-and-run accidents. One driver wrecked her car when another vehicle veered at her, forcing her off the road. The other car then sped off. But the insurance company refused to pay for the accident because the damaged car was not actually hit by the other one. So the car's owner sued. *Court's decision:* A hit-and-run accident is any accident caused by a person who runs

away. There doesn't actually have to be a hit involved. The insurance company had to pay.

Su v. Kemper/American Motorist Insurance Cos., R.I. Sup. Ct.

Health Insurance For You...for Your Business

Alan Mittermaier, president, HealthMetrix Research, Inc., a company that assists older adults in finding the right health-care providers, Box 30041, Columbus, Ohio 43230. www.medicarenewswatch.com

Many business owners avoid buying the type of health insurance they need because they're adequately covered under a spouse's insurance plan. Or—they simply give their own health care low priority because other business matters seem much more important.

Trap: Without adequate health insurance, you put yourself, your family and your business at unnecessary risk.

Fortunately, despite recent rises in health insurance costs, there are still ways to find affordable coverage tailored to your needs. *How to do it...*

SHOP FOR SPECIAL GROUP POLICIES

You may be eligible for various types of advantageous group coverage—even if your business is a sole proprietorship. That can be a big advantage, because groups buy coverage in bulk and pass a large portion of the savings on to individual policy holders.

Groups that often provide health insurance to members include...

• **National and state associations of business owners.**

• **Professional associations.**

• **Chambers of commerce.**

Members can nearly always purchase health insurance at a lower cost through these organizations than by buying it directly from the insurance company. The savings can be so great—typically 10% to 30%—that it easily offsets the cost of membership.

Option: Using the same policy for yourself and your family that the company offers—or is considering offering—to its employees. Even though you may want better coverage for yourself and your family than what you can afford for your employees, the insurance company that provides the company with group coverage is likely to offer a discount on a supplemental policy for you.

HMO OR INDEMNITY POLICY?

As a general rule, HMOs are less expensive than conventional indemnity plans. But—for business owners, there are two possible disadvantages. An HMO, for example, typically does not offer policy options that you can find by shopping around at indemnity insurance carriers. *Example:* A higher cap on lifetime benefits.

Also, if you don't live in or near a metropolitan area, there may be no HMOs to choose from.

NEW WAY TO SHOP

If group coverage isn't practical, there's little alternative to buying individual coverage for you and/or your family.

Consult an agent who represents more than one health insurance carrier.

An even more efficient way to compare policies is to use the growing number of Web sites that help make comparisons. The sites let you compare premiums and coverage from hundreds of insurance carriers. There's no charge for this information.

Typical sites ask you to key in such personal data as age, weight and health condition, as well as the price you want to pay and the type of coverage you're looking for. Some give you nearly instant online quotes for several carriers …others have an agent contact you by phone… and still others E-mail the information to you.

My favorite: Quotesmith.com, a service that compares premiums and coverage from more than 300 carriers and replies online, usually within a minute or two. Check it out at *www.insure.com.*

Online insurance quotes are especially useful because insurance agents don't always understand the needs of business owners, who require coverage that will protect them and their business during a prolonged illness.

Young businesses have different needs than older ones.

In this case, online services can help by letting you quickly compare policies that cover specific medical conditions and different levels of benefits.

COMPARING POLICIES

Regardless of how you find potentially suitable policies, compare them for more than just premiums and general extent of coverage. Look also at deductibles, copayments, lifetime benefit caps, coverage of existing medical conditions and restrictions on consulting specialists.

Mistake: Trying to save money by buying a policy with high deductibles but relatively low caps on lifetime benefits.

Very high deductibles—$5,000, or even $10,000—may make sense if you can easily afford them. But many owners of smaller businesses would find it very difficult to cover this cost. Owners should generally look at policies that protect them and their families during catastrophic or prolonged illnesses. That includes high caps on lifetime benefits.

A cap of even $1 million might seem more than adequate, for example, but many catastrophic conditions require medical care that can quickly exceed that amount. Similarly, it usually pays to look for a policy with a single annual deductible rather than a deductible for each illness.

Reason: If you or family members suffer from multiple hospitalizations, deductibles can quickly reach a level that may be difficult to pay if you're also sustaining a business.

Before deciding on the premium level that you can afford, consult your tax adviser about what portion of premiums may be tax deductible under recent federal law.

Once you find a policy that suits your needs, take a close look at the insurance company itself—unless you already have firsthand knowledge of it. While the majority of carriers are solvent and reputable, today's health-care industry is rapidly changing. That means many new companies are starting up, and some older ones are faltering.

To check out an insurance company: Phone the insurance commission in the state where the carrier is headquartered. Ask for information on customer complaints and financial status.

Since it is normal for almost any company to have a few customer complaints, make a comparison by asking for the complaint record of several other carriers in addition to the one you're considering.

Caution: An insurance company doesn't necessarily have to be insolvent to be in poor financial condition.

Ask each company you are considering about problems with financial reserves. That's the key indicator of the health of insurance carriers, and state insurance commissions routinely report on problems. Many commissions also post such information on their Web sites.

An alternative source for insurance company ratings is TheStreet.com, *www.thestreet. com/insurers.*

16

Points of Law

Collecting on a Judgment

After getting a judgment, many people find that they have spent much time and money and gone to a lot of trouble to get a worthless piece of paper. Estimated projections of the percentage of judgments that are collected in full are very low—according to some lawyers. Few people are willing to go to the trouble and expense of pursuing a reluctant debtor. To make winning a judgment worthwhile, it is important to know what to do and what to avoid.

BEFORE YOU SUE

The biggest problem with judgment collection is suing the wrong entity. For instance, Joe at Joe's Garage puts a defective part into your car. You sue Joe but later find out that the XYZ Corporation owns his shop. Even though Joe owns every piece of stock in XYZ, your judgment is not collectible out of the corporation's assets.

SOME GUIDELINES FOR A SUCCESSFUL SUIT

• **Don't sue a firm just because its name is on a sign outside a place of business,** or the person you assume owns the business. Always check further. *Example:* A large national fast-food chain has a number of restaurants in New York City that are not owned by the chain but by another large food corporation.

• **Check with the local county clerk's office,** business-licensing bureau, department of consumer affairs or police department to find out the actual name in which the business is registered.

• **Sue where the assets are.** The service person who did the damage, the franchise owner, the corporate owner or the parent corporation may all be liable if you can prove wrongful involvement. Sue whichever entity or entities have enough assets to pay your judgments. You can sue more than one.

Kenneth D. Litwack, attorney in private practice in Bayside, NY, and formerly the director of the Bureau of City Marshalls and former counsel for the New York City Sheriff.

FINDING ASSETS

Unless your judgment is against a well-established corporation, you may have to deal with a debtor who will not pay voluntarily. Hiding assets is the most popular method of avoiding payment. These assets must be uncovered in order to collect.

• **If you have ever received a check from or given a check to the debtor,** you may have a clue to the whereabouts of the debtor's bank account.

• **If you have a judgment against someone who owns a home,** check the county's home-ownership records in that area of residence.

• **If you have won a judgment against a business,** go personally to the business location to see what equipment and machinery are on the site.

• **If the judgment is large enough,** hire an agency to do an asset search. Before paying for a professional search, find out what the agency is actually going to do to uncover assets and what results you can realistically expect to achieve.

• **Watch out for fraud.** To avoid creditors, an unscrupulous company will often go out of business in one name and start up the same business the next day with a different name—on the same location and with the same equipment. To collect on your judgment you will need a lawyer to prove that the transfer of assets took place for the purposes of fraud.

HOW JUDGMENTS ARE COLLECTED

Judgments can be forcibly collected only by an enforcement officer (a local marshall, sheriff or constable) or sometimes the court clerk. You are responsible for informing the officer where to find the debtor's assets.

COLLECTION PROCEDURES

• **Property execution.** The officer seizes any property that is not exempt and sells it at auction to pay the debt.

• **Income execution.** The officer garnishes a debtor's salary. You may collect 10% to 25% of take-home pay, depending on state law. For an income execution, you must tell the officer where the debtor works.

COLLECTIBLE PROPERTY*

• ***Exempt from collection:*** Household and personal items, including furniture, stoves, refrigerators, stereos, TVs, sewing machines, clothing, cooking utensils, tools specifically used for a person's trade.

• ***Collectible items:*** These include motor vehicles, valuable jewelry, antiques, real estate, bank accounts, business equipment, stocks, bonds and the like.

• **A home lived in by the debtor is exempt up to a certain amount** (which varies from state to state). *The major problem in collecting on a home:* Many are jointly owned by married couples, which limits the creditor's right to have the house sold if the debt is only against one of the parties. But if only the debtor owns it, you can have it seized, sell it and return the exempt amount.

OUT-OF-STATE COLLECTIONS

Under the US Constitution, judgments are reciprocal from one state to another. If you have a judgment against an individual or business in one state that has assets in another, you or your lawyer can have the judgment docketed (registered) in the state in which the business is located or the state in which you wish to collect. The judgment is then viable in both places at the same time and can be collected in either. A judgment can be good for as long as 20 years, depending on the jurisdiction, and in some instances can be renewed by the court for an equal amount of time.

GETTING HELP

• **Legal help is recommended** if you are suing for an amount that exceeds the small-claims-court limit. After you win the judgment, your lawyer may arrange an asset search for you or recommend an agency to do one.

Collection agencies are not recommended. They deal mostly with large accounts and not with one-shot cases. *Also:* A collection agency can only dun a debtor in a formal, legalistic way to convince him to pay voluntarily. After assets have been uncovered, only an enforcement officer can actually collect.

*These are general guidelines. Details vary from state to state. Check with the local marshal or other enforcement officer for more information.

About Company Lawyers

If you're asked to discuss something about your job with the company attorney, you can't assume that all statements you make will be kept confidential. As a matter of fact, in most cases the lawyer would be violating his duty to his client (the company) if he even reminds you that your statements may be reported to company officials.

Exception: If the lawyer has represented you on some personal matter, such as drafting your will or handling some traffic tickets, then he or she might have a duty to explain the situation to you and point out that he is not representing you in this instance.

American Bar Association Journal

Lawyer–Client Caution

Lawyer–client privilege may be lost if a third party sits in on the conversation. *Trap:* When a complicated financial matter is to be discussed, the lawyer may want an accountant or a banker, for example, to sit in. But since the third party cannot claim the lawyer–client privilege, confidentiality is lost. *Better way:* Have the lawyer hire a financial expert to sit in as an employee, or have the lawyer talk to the expert separately.

Nonclients Can Sue Lawyers

The owner of some shares of restricted stock needed a letter from a law firm in order to sell his shares. It took 10 months for the firm to issue the letter. Meanwhile, the price of the shares dropped significantly. But when the shareholder sued for damages caused by the delay, the lawyers thought they had a solid defense. *Their argument:* We were the lawyers for the company whose shares were being traded, not for the shareholder. Since the shareholder was not our client, we did not owe him any duty. He has no basis for suing us.

Court: The shareholder is entitled to sue. He need not be a client to recover if he can show that the firm deliberately favored some shareholders by promptly issuing the letters that let them sell their stock while delaying the issuance of letters to others.

Singer v. Whitman & Ranson, 186 NYLJ 35, at 12.

When to Sue a Lawyer For Malpractice

The legal profession is entering its own malpractice crisis. The number of suits against attorneys being brought by clients is increasing, and the availability of malpractice insurance is decreasing.

Ground rules for considering a suit against your lawyer…

• **Where malpractice is charged in connection with litigation,** the client must show that the litigation would have ended with a result more favorable to the client if it were not for the attorney's neglect.

• **Where the attorney fell below the standards of skill and knowledge** ordinarily possessed by attorneys under similar circumstances, expert testimony is needed to support this charge. And the standard may be affected by specialization (which raises the standard of care required), custom and locality. Locality and custom can't lower the standard, but they may be used as a defense to show that the procedure or law involved is unsettled.

Some of the best ways to avoid malpractice charges…

• **See that there is good communication between lawyer and client.**

• **Avoid a situation where a lawyer is handling serious matters for personal friends.**

The tendency is to deal with friends in a more casual, informal way.

• **The attorney should give an honest opinion of each case, good or bad.** The client shouldn't press him for a guarantee as to the result.

• **All fee arrangements should be specified in writing.**

• **The attorney should spell out the scope of his responsibilities,** including appeals, and a limit should be placed on costs.

• **The agreement should provide for periodic payments** unless the matter is one involving a contingency fee and for withdrawal if there is a default in payment.

Cost of Bankruptcy

The court fee for a Chapter 7 action—a straight discharge of debt—is $306. The more complicated Chapter 13 bankruptcy is $281, and Chapter 11 is $1,213. Attorney's fees vary by case and location.

Robert H. Bressler of the law firm Bressler and Lida, New York.

Avoid Lawsuit Loans

If you are a plaintiff in a personal injury lawsuit, think twice about obtaining a presettlement cash advance. Someone who obtains one repays the advance only after receiving a favorable settlement. Most lenders will offer cash advances between $500 and $25,000.

Major drawback: Some companies charge a fixed fee, but others charge as much as 15% a month from the date the check was issued. You could end up owing fees that exceed the amount of the cash advance. While firms justify the fees because of the risks they face, in reality these companies offer money only in cases when the plaintiff almost certainly will win. If you have no other way to obtain cash and want

a presettlement advance, get offers from several firms and select the one that charges the least. Also ask your lawyer to review the terms.

Aaron Larson, attorney in Ann Arbor, MI, who specializes in civil appellate cases and litigation consulting.

Helpful Resource

Download forms (wills, powers of attorney, etc.), find a lawyer, use the extensive directory of legal information and services at *www.alllaw.com*.

Durable Powers Of Attorney

Peter J. Strauss, Esq., senior counsel in the law firm of Epstein, Becker & Green, PC, New York City, and a fellow of the National Academy of Elder Law Attorneys. He is coauthor of The Complete Retirement Survival Guide: Everything You Need to Know to Safeguard Your Money, Your Health, and Your Independence (Checkmate Books).

Suppose an accident or illness robs you of your ability to look after your money. What will happen? Can someone do it for you?

Trap: If you don't make arrangements for money management before you run into trouble, your family will have to get a court to appoint a guardian to handle your affairs. This is time-consuming and costly. Depending on where you live, it could cost $2,000 to $5,000—and significantly more if anyone contests the guardianship.

You can prevent the need to go to court by having your lawyer put together a legal document called a "durable power of attorney," in which you name someone to handle your affairs in the event you become unable to do so.

THE BASICS

In a *durable power of attorney*, you name someone to act as your agent (also called an *attorney in fact*) to make your bank deposits, pay your bills, file your tax returns and handle your other financial matters. It's called *durable power* because it remains effective even though you become incapacitated. You can name a single agent or multiple agents. You can name your spouse and one of your children for this role.

Caution: Specify in the document whether multiple agents can act independently of one another or must act together. As a practical matter, independent action is simpler. But you can require the agents to agree with each other for certain actions, such as making gifts of your property.

Whom you should name as your agent: The person you name must be someone you have complete confidence in. While the agent holds a fiduciary position that requires he or she follow certain rules of conduct, there's no court looking over the agent's actions.

It's generally a good idea, of course, to name someone who's good at handling money. Trustworthiness, though, is more important. The agent can always seek financial advice from an accountant or other financial adviser.

Important: Name a successor agent, too—in case the first named agent is no longer able to act.

HOW TO CREATE A DURABLE POWER OF ATTORNEY

You can use a preprinted one- or two-page form available in most stationery and office supply stores.

Caution: Be sure the form is the current version approved under your state's law.

The form contains a long list of basic powers provided under state law, including power to...

- **Sell your home.**
- **Make retirement plan benefit choices.**
- **Buy and sell stocks,** bonds and mutual fund shares.
- **Initiate lawsuits on your behalf.**

Additional powers: You may want to supplement the powers listed in a printed form with others.

Example: If your finances are complicated but you want to keep your property in your name for now, you may want to set up a trust which is unfunded. You can give your agent the power to fund the trust you've set up if you become incapacitated.

Other supplemental powers may include...

- **Creating, amending or revoking a trust.** In addition to funding a trust you've already set up, your agent may be able to create or change a trust. Not all states permit this action. States that do require the power to be clearly spelled out in the power of attorney and existing trusts may also have to include language allowing an agent to amend or revoke them.

- **Gift giving.** You can empower your agent to make gifts to himself and his family —something that can be beneficial for your estate planning.

It's generally not a good idea to make this power open-ended (there's a possibility that if he dies before you, the IRS could charge that he had a general power of appointment over all of your property and his estate would then be taxed on all of your assets).

Limit the power to the annual gift tax exclusion ($14,000 in 2013) or, if you've routinely been making gifts, to this level of gift giving. For larger gifts, exercise of the power should require consent of a third party.

After you've included the powers you want and named the agents to act on your behalf, make sure the form is properly signed (executed).

What constitutes proper execution varies from state to state.

After execution: Send a copy to each bank, brokerage firm and other financial institution you deal with asking whether they'll recognize the power of attorney in the event of your incapacity. Some states require banks to recognize them or face penalties. By getting a letter from each institution as to whether it will honor your power of attorney, you'll be able to overcome objections or take other action before it's too late.

Alternative: Have a lawyer draw up a durable power of attorney for you. Since the form is fairly simple, the cost is modest—or is part of the overall fee that you will be charged for planning. The lawyer will make sure that the form includes all special powers for your situation and that the form meets your state's law.

SPECIAL CONSIDERATIONS

Now that you know the basics, you may have special circumstances to address...

• **Property owned in more than one state.** If you have homes in New York and Florida, for example, be sure to have forms drawn up in each state. This will ensure that the forms are drafted and signed in accordance with each state's laws.

• **Psychological barrier.** If you're not comfortable with giving up control of your money, use a *springing power of attorney*. This is available in many (not all) states. The form is signed now, but comes into effect only upon the occurrence of a specified event.

   Caution: Make sure the event is measured by an objective standard. For example, don't make the event just "disability," because this term is ambiguous. Instead, make the event a written certification by one or two physicians that you are unable to manage your affairs.

• **Your agent is a nonfamily member.** While a relative will act as your agent without any compensation, a nonfamily member, such as your accountant, will generally expect payment for services. Be clear about the fees. Specify your arrangement in the document itself or in a side letter.

Be sure the power of attorney authorizes the agent to write checks to himself so there's no fiduciary conflict.

• **Revoking the power.** When you recover, you can end the agent's power to act on your behalf. This is called a *revocation*. Keep track of all financial institutions and others who have copies of your power of attorney so you can notify them of your revocation.

OTHERS IN FAMILY

If you have aging parents, suggest that they sign durable powers of attorney if they haven't already done so.

Uncharitable Charities

Generous people who donate to charities like to think they're helping a philanthropic cause and people in need. Very often this is not the case. Often the only cause being helped is the charity itself— or its officers.

Problem: There are no federal guidelines specifying the amount of funds charities must channel toward their cause. As long as some of the money raised goes to the charity's cause the organization can still call itself a charity. Because of "creative" accounting practices used by charities and professional fund-raisers, it is often difficult for donors to assess how well a particular charity is performing.

Background: According to the standards developed by the Council of Better Business Bureaus, each charity must apply at least half of all income to its particular activities. Fund-raising activities are not to absorb more than 35% of the contributions received by the charity. Because of incompetence or outright fraud, many charities flout these guidelines.

To protect yourself: Before donating to a charity, contact the local Better Business Bureau or the state charities registration office in your area. In addition, it is important to obtain examples of how the charity has benefited the cause during the past years. If you're told what it plans to do…remember, big plans for the future do not count!

The Washington Spectator

17

Crime Prevention

Financial Aid for the Mugging Victim

Financial compensation programs for mugging victims are available throughout the US. This compensation can cover both medical expenses and lost earnings. However, most of these programs utilize a means test that eliminates all but lower income victims from compensation. In addition, the victim's own medical unemployment insurance must be fully depleted before state compensation is granted.

• **Workers' compensation may cover you** (up to two-thirds of your gross earnings in New York State) if you were mugged on the job or on your way to or from company business during your workday. It will not cover you while traveling from home to work and back.

• **Homeowner's policies may cover financial losses suffered during a mugging.**

• **Mugging insurance is an idea whose time has come.** This insurance is available in New York. It covers property loss, medical care and mental anguish. If successful, this type of coverage may become available in other states.

• **A lawsuit may be successful if it can be proved that the mugging was the result of negligence.** *Example:* The celebrity Connie Francis was attacked in her room at a major motel chain. She won $2 million in damages by proving that the motel's security system was inadequate.

• **The Office for Victims of Crime (OVC) provides resources.** A division of the US Department of Justice in Washington, DC, this federal agency is a national clearinghouse for emerging victim issues and resources, which are available around the clock. Crime victims have access to a criminal justice library, information specialists to answer questions,

Lucy N. Friedman, PhD, former executive director, Victim Services, a domestic-violence prevention agency, New York City.

products and online services. Contact 800-851-3420 or go to *www.ojp.usdoj.gov/ovc/ovcres/ welcome.html*.

Personal Protection For Executives

A bodyguard may be advisable if your company is becoming very controversial or getting involved in an area that is receiving a great deal of attention. Otherwise, unless an executive has gotten a personal threat, violence against executives is so rare that personal protection isn't necessary.

Oliver B. Revell, former manager of the FBI's criminal investigation operations, quoted in *Personnel Administrator*.

How to Outsmart Muggers

Ken Glickman, former consumer editor, *Bottom Line/ Personal*, Stamford, Connecticut.

Getting mugged these days is a real and personal threat, not something that happens only to other people. Not only must you prepare yourself, but your entire family should be taught how to act to survive an attack. If only one member of a group that is held up responds badly, all of you might be hurt.

Fortunately, most muggings are simple robberies in which neither the criminal nor the victim is hurt. However, the possibility of violence is always there.

First rule: Cooperate. Assume that the mugger is armed. No matter how strong or fit you are, you are no match for a gun or knife. *Remember:* Your personal safety is far more important than your valuables or your pride.

SPECIFIC RECOMMENDATIONS

•**Follow the mugger's instructions to the letter.** Try not to move too quickly or too slowly—either could upset him/her.

•**Stay as calm as possible,** and encourage companions to do the same.

•**Give the mugger whatever he asks for.** Don't argue. But if something is of great sentimental value to you, give it to him, and then say, "This watch was given to me by my grandfather. It means a lot to me. But if you insist, I will give it to you."

•**When he has all he wants of your valuables,** ask him what he wants you to do while he gets away—stay where you are, lie face down, whatever. If he dismisses you, leave the scene immediately, and don't look back. Don't call the police until you are in a safe place.

Most criminals are not anxious to hurt you. If there is no violence, the police are not likely to pursue the offender. Mugging is like a job to many practitioners. If you respond in a businesslike way with a minimum of words and gestures, it will probably be over quickly and without injury.

SOME IMPORTANT DON'TS

•**Don't reach for your wallet in a back pocket without first explaining what you plan to do.** The mugger might think you are reaching for a gun.

•**Don't give him dirty looks or make judgmental remarks.**

•**Don't threaten him with hostile comments.**

•**Don't be a wise guy or a joker.** Even smiling is a dangerous idea. He may think you are laughing at him.

•**Don't try any tricks like carrying a second empty wallet to give to a mugger.** This common ruse could make the mugger angry. Some experts even recommend that you carry at least $25 with you at all times to keep from upsetting a mugger. Muggers are often as frightened and inexperienced as you are, which is why it is important not to upset them.

If you're assaulted, scream *Fire!* People are more likely to come to your aid than if you shout *Help!*

Limiting Larceny Losses

The two safest places for a wallet are in the jacket breast pocket and front pants pocket. Insert the wallet sideways so it's harder for a pickpocket to remove. Leave unnecessary credit cards at home. Don't put all your money in the same pocket. Always have some cash to give to a mugger. Don't keep your keys with your wallet or with any other form of identification.

Crime Prevention Manual for Business Owners and Managers by Margaret Kenda. AMACOM.

Pickpocket Deterrents

Pickpockets work in pairs. One is the stall and the other the pick. The stall distracts the targets by bumping into them or otherwise detaining them. The pick takes advantage of the moment of confusion to lift a wallet or a purse. Pickpockets carry newspapers in their hands to conceal the stolen goods. They stand too close to you. And they wear caps to keep people from seeing their eyes, which makes future identification more difficult.

Precautions: Men should not carry their wallets in their back pockets. Women should keep their bags zippered shut. Hold the bag under your arm. When you're walking with someone else, keep the bag between the two of you.

Andrea Forrest, president, Preventive Security Services, New York.

How to Catch a Thief

If you witness a crime in progress, report it immediately. Waiting even a minute or two makes it nearly impossible to catch the perpetrator in the act. In general, most crimes last only a few minutes.

Instant Revenge Against Obscene Phone Caller

Forget blowing a whistle into the receiver or slamming down the phone—this only serves to antagonize the pest.

Better: Electronic voice boxes, available with a preprogrammed joke script by comics such as Henny Youngman and Jackie Mason. Hold it up to the phone, press a button and have the last laugh. Available through many novelty mail-order houses.

Breaking In on a Burglary

If you walk in on a burglar by accident, just asking an innocent question may defuse potential violence. *Example:* "Oh, you're the guy who's supposed to pick up the package, aren't you?" If at this point the burglar tries to run away, it's smart to step aside.

Crime Prevention Manual for Business Owners and Managers by Margaret Kenda. AMACOM.

If an intruder is in your house when you arrive, resist the temptation to yell or otherwise provoke a confrontation. You then become an obstacle to the burglar's escape, escalating the chances that you may be hurt. *Better:* Go as quickly and quietly as possible to a neighbor's and call the police from there.

How to Protect Yourself from Crime (DIANE Publishing).

How to avoid walking into your home while a thief is there: Leave a $10 or $20 bill conspicuously placed, near the door. If the bill is gone when you walk inside, someone else may be there. Leave at once and call the police.

Venture

Where to Hide Your Valuables

Bill Phillips, lock expert who writes on security and safety issues. He is author of *Home Mechanix Guide to Security: Protecting Your Home, Car & Family* (John Wiley & Sons).

To decide where to hide valuables, you need to understand exactly how burglars operate. The worst room to use is the master bedroom—the place where most people like to hide things. Thieves are likely to start right there. Burglars usually know just where to search both in the master bedroom and in other rooms—including the kitchen, where they are almost sure to check the cookie jar.

But thieves are in a hurry. They rarely spend more than 20 minutes in a house. You can take advantage of a burglar's haste to get away before he is detected by storing valuables in stealth devices. These hiding places take a thief a long time to locate.

• **The wall outlet safe* has a tiny compartment, and it requires installation.** But if you choose a color and style indistinguishable from your real outlets, there's little likelihood of its being detected. The sockets accept plugs, so you can plug in a combination

*These and other stealth devices are available at home improvement centers, some hardware stores and from a number of security catalogs.

battery/outlet clock radio with a light-up dial and actually run it on batteries. Or, you can install the outlet safe in a child's room. This is usually the last place thieves look, but also the place people don't like to hide valuables lest children get at them. They won't, though, if the fake outlet is behind a piece of furniture. And a thief probably won't, either—especially if you insert convincing child-safety clips in the sockets.

• **The flowerpot safe.** A real, plastic flowerpot with a hollowed out hidden compartment within. The compartment is no larger than a small juice glass, but it makes a pretty safe place to keep a necklace and earrings or other valuables, as well as a few large bills.

• **Book safe.** Especially effective if you have lots of real books to hide it among. *Recommended:* Models hollowed out from actual books. You can't order these by title, but unlike a wooden fake book this model will age exactly like a real book.

• **Safe cans.** *These are facsimiles of popular canned products:* Shaving creams, cleansers, spray cans, etc. As stealth devices they are well-known to thieves. But they come in a wide variety of designs, and new ones appear all the time. *Best:* Spend extra money for a weighted model, since one that feels too light could betray its real use.

18

Computers and The Internet

How to Watch TV on Your Computer

Watching TV shows via computer has become as easy as browsing the Web. *Here are the advantages and best options to watching TV on your computer...*

Advantages: Shows can be viewed whenever you want. They typically include fewer commercials than on TV or no commercials at all. You might even be able to cancel or cut back on your cable subscription and save hundreds of dollars a year. Available shows range from recent episodes of *60 Minutes* and *House* to decades-old episodes of *The Donna Reed Show* and *Father Knows Best* to highlights from sporting events.

BEST OPTIONS

•**Clicker.com.** The best way to find TV shows is through the Web site Clicker.com. Just enter the name of a program, and hit "Find" to link to any episodes available online. Or browse Clicker.com's more than 12,000 show listings, which include a total of more than 750,000 episodes. Expect to find recent episodes of most current network and basic cable programs online for free. Older episodes of current shows and episodes of pay cable shows often are available, too, but there might be a charge. Access to older programs no longer on the air is spotty but improving rapidly.

Warning: Some Clicker.com listings that appear to be full episodes are brief video clips. These often display run times of just a minute or two.

You also can go directly to sites that carry many old and/or new shows...

•**Hulu** (*www.hulu.com*) offers, for free, recent episodes of most shows on ABC, Fox and NBC (not CBS), such as *The Simpsons* and *Modern Family*, and classic shows, including *The Mary Tyler Moore Show* and *The Bob Newhart Show*. Hulu rolled out *Hulu Plus*,

Harry McCracken, founder and editor of Technologizer. com, a Web site offering news and reviews of high-tech products, Internet sites and related topics, based in Daly City, California. *www.technologizer.com*

with access to additional episodes of current shows, not just those that aired recently, for $7.99 per month.

- **CBS** (*www.cbs.com*). Free episodes of many of the network's current shows are available with a reduced number of commercials. Some classic CBS shows are there, too, including *Perry Mason* and *The Twilight Zone*.
- **TV Land** (*www.tvland.com*) offers episodes of classic TV shows for free.

Examples: Gunsmoke…The Andy Griffith Show.

- **Netflix** (*www.netflix.com*). Sign up for one of the cheapest Netflix services—the $7.99-per-month one-DVD-at-a-time plan—and you also receive unlimited access to *Netflix Watch Instantly*, through which you can view a wide range of movies and television shows online with no additional fees.

Examples: 30 Rock…The Dick Van Dyke Show…The George Burns and Gracie Allen Show.

- **Apple iTunes** (*www.apple.com/itunes*) and Amazon Video on Demand (*www.amazon.com/videoondemand*) offer a wide range of TV shows, including HBO and Showtime programs, but at a price—typically 99 cents or $1.99 per episode. These pay services often feature additional episodes that no longer are available for free online.

Simple Solutions For Common Computer Problems

Joshua Gulick, former editor for *Smart Computing* magazine, a monthly publication featuring computer tutorials, buying advice and related articles, Lincoln, Nebraska. He has written for various computer publications, including *PC Today, Computer Power User* and *Processor. www.smartcomputing.com*

Computers are complex devices, but certain computer problems are surprisingly simple to solve. Troubleshooting these problems on your own could save you a repair bill—and often the expert's solutions are so simple that you find yourself saying, "I should have thought of that!" *Here's what to try when your computer tries your patience…*

Problem: The computer will not turn on.

What to try first: A loose power cord is the most likely culprit—but not just where the computer plugs into the wall or power strip. What many users fail to check is the other end of the power cord, the one that connects to the computer. Push the end of the power cord that connects to the computer firmly into its socket. If the computer is a laptop, there might be a third connection to tighten as well, where the power cord meets the external power adapter—the small box located midcord. Try to turn the computer on again once all of these connections have been made firm.

If that doesn't work: Plug another electrical device into the outlet or power strip that you're using to power the computer. If this device won't power on either, the problem probably is the power strip, a circuit breaker or a wall switch controlling the outlet, not the computer.

If none of this works, your computer might have a problem with its power supply, a component that distributes power to other components inside the system, such as the hard drive. A repair shop can test this in minutes.

Problem: The computer loses its Internet connection.

What to try first: Unplug your modem's power cord. Also unplug your network router, if you have one. Let these devices sit unpowered for one full minute, then plug them back in and wait a minute or two as they restart. Now refresh your Internet browser to see if the connection has returned.

If that doesn't work: Check your modem and router for reset buttons. If you find them, press them both, wait a minute or two, then see if the connection has returned.

If it hasn't, call your Internet service provider's tech-support line—this phone number should be on your bill. Explain the problem, and ask for assistance. A representative might inform you that service temporarily is down throughout your region. Otherwise he/she should walk you through possible solutions.

Problem: The Internet slows way down.

What to try first: If there are multiple computers in your household, see if someone else is downloading or streaming a TV show or movie…uploading pictures…downloading music files…or making a video phone call. If so, your Internet speed should improve as soon as this ends.

If that doesn't work: Your computer might have a virus. Update your security software, and use it to run a scan. If you do not have security software, use the free online scan offered by computer security software maker Kaspersky (*http://usa.kaspersky.com*, select "Free Virus Scan" at the top of the page).

Problem: A Web site won't accept your password.

What to try first: Check whether your keyboard's caps-lock light is lit. If it is lit, press the keyboard's caps-lock button to turn it off, then reenter your password. Many password fields are case-sensitive and reject passwords that are accidentally entered in all capital letters.

If that doesn't work: Look for a link on the Web site labeled "Lost Your Password?" or something similar. Click this, and follow the directions to reset or retrieve your password.

Problem: The computer is on but not responding to any commands.

What to try first: Confirm that your keyboard and/or mouse cables still are properly connected to your computer. If you have a wireless keyboard and/or mouse, make sure that the transceiver is plugged firmly into the computer. If it is, reset the keyboard and/or mouse's wireless connections by pressing the connection buttons typically found on the bottoms of these devices. If that doesn't work, try changing the batteries in the mouse and keyboard.

If that doesn't work: Restart the computer by pressing and holding the power button for five seconds.

Problem: The DVD or CD drive won't open.

What to try first: Straighten a paper clip, slide it into the small hole on or near the door of the disk drive and push gently. The door should open slightly. Once this door is open a bit, you slowly can pull it open the rest of the way without damaging the computer.

If that doesn't work: Restart the computer.

Problem: You're buried by dozens of pop-ups whenever you go online.

What to try first: Your browser's pop-up blocker might be disabled. To turn it back on…

In the Internet Explorer browser, select "Pop-Up Blocker" from the Tools menu, then select "Turn On Pop-Up Blocker" if this is offered. (If your pop-up blocker already is on, you will instead be given the option "Turn Off Pop-Up Blocker." Do not select this.)

In the Mozilla Firefox browser, select "Tools," then "Options," then "Content," and click the box next to "Block Pop-Up Windows" if it is not already checked.

In the Safari browser, select the "Safari" menu, then choose "Block Pop-Up Windows" if not already checked.

If that doesn't work: Your computer might be infected with *adware*, a form of computer virus that displays advertisements. Update your security software and run a scan, or use Kaspersky's free online scan, mentioned above.

Problem: A program is chronically crashing or freezing.

What to try first: If rebooting doesn't help, then updating the program often solves the problem. Open the program, select the "Help" pull-down menu, then look for the option labeled "Update" or "Check for Updates" and follow the directions. If you don't see a menu listing like this, visit the software publisher's Web site and see if updates are available in the "Support" section.

If that doesn't work: Uninstall the program, then reinstall it. However, do not uninstall unless you are certain you have the installation disk or can download the program online for free.

Problem: It takes much longer than it used to to start the computer.

What to try first: Viruses might be causing this slowdown. Update your security software and run a full system scan, or use Kaspersky's free online scan, mentioned above.

If that doesn't work: Remove anything nonessential from the list of programs that start up each time you start your computer. To do this in Microsoft Windows, click the Windows "Start" button—the Start button is the on-screen button that lets you open a program or shut down your computer, not the actual power button on the computer itself. Select "All Programs" from the menu that appears, then select the "Startup" folder from this list. Right-click on programs in this folder that you don't need to run each time the computer starts, then select "Delete." This will not delete the program from your computer but will simply drop it from the list of programs launched at start-up, likely reducing start-up times.

Mac owners: To select programs that you don't want to start automatically, choose "System Preferences," click "Accounts," then "Login Items."

The Facebook Payoff

Sherrie A. Madia, PhD, director of communications, external affairs, at The Wharton School of the University of Pennsylvania, Philadelphia. She teaches social media and communications strategies to students and corporate clients and is coauthor of The Social Media Survival Guide *(Full Court).* www.socialmediasurvivalguide.com

Facebook has more than 1.1 billion monthly active users—that's right, over a billion. So it's a great way for businesses and organizations to find new customers/members, strengthen connections with existing ones and conduct market research. *Here's how…*

FIRST THINGS FIRST

To launch a Facebook page for your business, you first need to set up a personal profile for yourself if you don't already have one. Follow the directions on *www.facebook.com* to set up that profile. Next, click on "Create Ad" at the very bottom of the page. On the Facebook Advertising page, click on the Facebook Pages link, then on the green "Create a Page" button, and follow the directions to start an official page—also called a fan page—for your business. You will need to choose the category, select a name for your page and complete the detailed information. The key thing to remember with profiles and pages is that profiles are for people and pages are for businesses.

Establishing a page for a business on Facebook—or on a similar site, such as MySpace or LinkedIn—is just the first step, however. Your business's page will require ongoing attention and a well-thought-out strategy to truly benefit your business.

PROVIDE VALUE AND PROVIDE IT OFTEN

Add new content to your business's Facebook page at least once a week. Failing to do so could create the impression that you are not attentive to your customers. If you go on vacation or are too swamped with work to provide new content for a while, explain this on the page and say when the new content will resume.

No more than 20% of the content you put on your business's Facebook page should be obvious attempts at marketing. When Facebook pages read like extended advertisements, potential customers leave and never come back. Most of your content should be attempts to provide the page's visitors with something of value.

Three ways to provide value…

•**Give insider advice in your area of expertise.** Post articles or videos explaining how to use your company's products or supplying other do-it-yourself guidance.

•**Offer to answer questions or respond to complaints.** This shows potential customers that you are service-oriented, knowledgeable and willing to stand behind your products and services. But do this only if you can monitor your Facebook page regularly and respond to questions and complaints within a few days. Slow response times to questions and complaints will only anger existing customers and scare off potential new ones.

•**Supply discounts or coupons.** Providing special savings is the single best way to lure traffic to a business's Facebook page. Many companies offer a discount or coupon code when you sign up to become a fan of the page. This is a great way to drive traffic, increase fans and provide immediate value.

HUMANIZE YOUR COMPANY

Your company's Facebook page should not read like it is written by a businessperson—it should read like it is written by a person who happens to own a business. Let customers into your life a little. People who feel they know you personally are more likely to feel a bond with your company and consider it trustworthy.

Examples: Provide a few details about your family or how you spend your time away from work. Mention your participation in local community organizations. Offer your personal opinion on issues related to your profession.

KNOW YOUR READERS

Market research firms charge thousands of dollars to figure out who customers are and what they want, but Facebook can supply this information to you for free.

When other Facebook users join your company's Facebook page, click on their images and learn what you can about them from their Facebook pages. The more you know about your customers, the easier it will be to sell to them. You might even notice patterns in the things that your customers tend to enjoy or the places they tend to live that could help you target marketing campaigns.

Example: You notice that a handful of customers who have joined your business's Facebook page also have joined the Facebook page of a seemingly unrelated business across town. That business might have additional customers who would be interested in what you do, and vice versa. Perhaps the owner of that business would let you put a flyer in his/her window or a stack of business cards by his register if you let him do the same.

If your competitors have Facebook pages, read up on those who have joined their pages, too. You might learn something about the potential customers your company is failing to reach.

From time to time, solicit the opinions of visitors to your Facebook page. What do they think of the products and services that you currently provide? What do they want from your business that they're not getting? This can trigger loyalty-building interaction with customers and provide valuable feedback.

Example: Clothing retailer The Gap recently unveiled a new logo on Facebook—but it received such an overwhelmingly negative response that the company squelched the redesign. With-

out this Facebook feedback, The Gap would have wasted millions promoting a new logo that its customers didn't like.

PROMOTE YOUR PAGE

Add "Visit Our Facebook Page" and the page's user name to your receipts and invoices. Print your page's user name on your business card and your other marketing materials.

Make use of your other networks in conjunction with Facebook. Twitter can be particularly powerful in getting a message out quickly to your target group's cell phones when you have a last-minute deal, an exclusive special or a limited-time offer. Twitter will allow your Facebook fans to get the message first.

CREATE A FACEBOOK AD

Allocate a portion of your marketing budget to Facebook ads. (To create a Facebook ad, click the "Create Ad" link at the bottom of the Facebook page, then click the green "Create an Ad" button.) Facebook ads can be a great way to target niche groups at a relatively low cost. Facebook ads can be targeted very specifically, based on user interests, age and geographic regions.

One of the beauties of the Facebook ad is that creating the content can be done in moments, and Facebook even will provide suggestions for ad content—such as how to use photos and keywords—based on the Web site address that you provide.

Set your Facebook ad spending caps (the total amount you're willing to spend per day on Facebook advertisements) low until you are certain that your ads are effective.

Also, choose the "Pay for clicks" billing option. With this, you pay only when Facebook users click the ad to visit your Facebook page or Web site. This costs more than the "Pay for Impressions" options (where you pay each time your ad appears on a computer screen whether it's clicked or not) but often is more cost effective.

Unlike traditional ad campaigns, which may lock you in for six months or more, elements in Facebook ads (such as content and targeting) can be modified at any time and can be turned off entirely at any point.

Check Your E-mail

Your e-mail account may not have been compromised, even if friends tell you that they have received spam from your address. Spammers can "spoof" your address, meaning that your e-mail address appears as the return address, even though it was sent from someone else's (the spammer's) account. However, if you are concerned that someone may have accessed your account, change your password and notify your e-mail provider's customer service. A representative may be able to investigate the matter further to make sure that no one is accessing your e-mail account.

Research editor David Boyer is *Bottom Line/Personal's* resident computer guru, 281 Tresser Blvd., Stamford, Connecticut 06901. *www.bottomlinepublications.com*

No "Autocomplete"

Turn off "autocomplete" on your Internet browser for more security. Most modern browsers are able to remember what you type into forms—passwords for Web sites, credit card information, your address, etc. This can save time when logging into a site or making a purchase, but it can cause problems if your computer is stolen or someone else uses it. Disabling this feature differs from browser to browser. Search the "Help" file on your browser for instructions.

Research editor David Boyer is *Bottom Line/Personal's* resident computer guru, 281 Tresser Blvd., Stamford, Connecticut 06901. *www.bottomlinepublications.com*

Personal Web Profile

Create a site all about you without having to know all the intricacies of Web page development. At *http://businesscard2.com* you can create a free account and then create your site. You can use the site to tell people about your interests, job and other activities. You also can link the site to your social networks (Facebook, Twitter), recent photos or videos, blog posts, etc.…and you can post ways for people to get in touch with you. The sites enable you to make great electronic business cards and signatures for e-mails.

Research editor David Boyer is *Bottom Line/Personal's* resident computer guru, 281 Tresser Blvd., Stamford, Connecticut 06901. *www.bottomlinepublications.com*

Easy PDF Creation

If you want to create a document that virtually any computer can view, create a PDF. One of the easiest ways to do this is with a program called *PrimoPDF* (*www.primopdf. com*). It lets you create a PDF from more than 300 different file types (*Word, Excel,* etc.) with one button. The basic version is free.

Research editor David Boyer is *Bottom Line/Personal's* resident computer guru, 281 Tresser Blvd., Stamford, Connecticut 06901. *www.bottomlinepublications.com*

Which Netbook Is Right For You?

Cisco Cheng, lead analyst for laptops and netbooks at PCMag.com, New York City.

If your needs for a laptop computer are modest and you don't want to spend more than $500, a netbook might be the answer, especially now that the latest generation offers vastly improved computing power.

Advantages: Netbooks weigh two to three pounds, about half the weight of many standard laptops…generally cost $250 to $500, hundreds less than laptops…and can run on battery power for seven hours or more, up to 30% longer than laptops. Although netbooks have some drawbacks, they're more than adequate for basic computer functions, including e-mailing…surfing the Internet…and storing hundreds of pictures. *To choose the right one…*

THREE QUESTIONS

•**Do you do a lot of typing?** Most netbooks have keyboards about 10% smaller than standard laptops and smaller screens (10 inches measured diagonally versus 13 or more inches). Some designs are much more comfortable than others, so try specific models before you buy.

•**Do you need an internal DVD/CD player?** Internal players are standard on laptops but missing in netbooks. If you need to use discs to install store-bought software or to play DVD rentals, or you want to burn discs to save data, photos and videos, you would need to add a portable DVD drive.

•**Do you need additional speed?** Many more netbooks will offer a dual-core processor, which provides at least 30% more power and speed than a standard single-core processor. This should increase the price by $50 to $100.

Nevertheless, if you need powerful video or gaming software, netbooks typically don't have enough computing power or a big enough screen. Consider a powerful laptop or a desktop computer.

Virus Scanner

If you have a file that you think might harbor a virus, trojan or other type of malware, go to *www.virustotal.com* and upload the file. The site will thoroughly analyze the file with nearly 40 different antivirus engines using the most up-to-date virus-detection information and give you reports from each. Free.

Research editor David Boyer is Bottom Line/Personal's resident computer guru, 281 Tresser Blvd., Stamford, Connecticut 06901. www.bottomlinepublications.com

Tame Computer Cords

A tangle of cords behind your computer looks bad and can be confusing—but with a little effort, they can be brought under control. The easiest solutions are to bind cords with the twist ties that you use to close garbage bags or with rubber bands or binder clips. If you search online for "cord organizers," you'll find many solutions starting at about $2.50. It's

also a good idea to label cords, so if you need to unplug a certain device, you can find its cord instantly. You can write on a piece of paper and tape it to the cord, or search online for "cord labels" (they start at about $4.50 for 100).

Research editor David Boyer is Bottom Line/Personal's resident computer guru, 281 Tresser Blvd., Stamford, Connecticut 06901. www.bottomlinepublications.com

USB Drive

Ultraslim USB drive with four gigabytes of memory is about the size and thickness of a credit card, so you can keep it in your wallet. PC and Mac compatible.

Information: SlimData, *www.slimdatausb.com.*

Cost: $24.99.

Research editor David Boyer is Bottom Line/Personal's resident computer guru, 281 Tresser Blvd., Stamford, Connecticut 06901. www.bottomlinepublications.com

Video Calls to Friends And Family

Tom Merritt, host of This Week in Tech's "Tech News Today." He previously was executive editor of the technology news Web site CNET, a division of CBS, wrote CNET's "The Real Deal" consumer technology how-to column and was executive producer of TechTV's Web site. http://twit.tv/tnt

When AT&T demonstrated a picture phone at the 1964 World's Fair, the device was greeted with oohs and aahs. Nearly half a century later, video calling is finally easy enough that it can play a big role in your communications.

Picture and sound quality tend to be quite good. Computer-to-computer video calls usually are free—even internationally. *How to get it going...*

CALLING WITH A COMPUTER

The best way to place video calls is through your computer, although that means both parties must have the same video-calling service set-up. The software required is free and easy to use. You'll need a high-speed Internet connection and a Webcam that is either built in or installed.

If your computer does not have a Webcam, consider buying a Logitech Webcam Pro 9000 ($99.99 list, *www.logitech.com*). It provides good picture quality and works well with the major video-calling programs.

There are three major video-calling services…

• **Skype** is the most popular, in part because it's very easy to install and use. Once it's set up, you just select the person you want to reach off a list you create and click "Video Call." (On a Mac, select the person, click the green phone button, then the blue video button.) If the person you are calling has Skype turned on, his/her computer will ring like a phone, but you might want to send an e-mail or call in advance so that the person knows to expect your video call.

To install Skype, visit *www.skype.com*, click "Get Skype" and follow the directions. Skype's software will help you add names to your contact list. Unlike the other video-calling services, Skype also lets users place ultra-low-cost voice-only calls from their computers to any traditional phone.

• **Apple iChat.** Apple's video-calling program is very much like Skype, but it's available only on Apple computers. You can use an Apple MobileMe, AOL AIM or Google Talk account. Some newer Apple computers allow you to add special effects, such as fish floating across the screen or the Eiffel Tower in the background, and up to four callers can take part in a video conversation at once. If your Apple computer doesn't have iChat, you can add it by downloading the free version available through CNET (*http://download.cnet.com/mac*).

• **Google Video Chat.** Sign up for a free Gmail e-mail account (*http://mail.google.com*), and click "Settings" at the top of the screen. Next, select "Chat," then "Learn more" from the "Voice and video chat" section, and "Install voice and video chat." To place video calls, just click the name of anyone in your Gmail account contact list and then click the video camera icon next to his name.

Which of the three services should you use? You might want to set up two or all three of

them and then, at any given time, use whichever one that a particular contact tends to use.

VIDEO CALLS WITHOUT A COMPUTER

It is increasingly possible to place video calls without a computer…

• **Call from your phone.** Apple's iPhone 4 has a feature called FaceTime that allows you to video-chat with someone on another iPhone 4 (but only over WiFi networks) by tapping a button on the screen (*www.apple. com*). The Ojo Personal Video Phone, which connects to a home Internet router (*www. ojophone.com*), and the Saygus VPhone smartphone (*www.saygus.com*) have the ability to place video calls. Skype offers cell-phone–based video-calling software for smartphones. And the HTC EVO 4G phone from Sprint (*www.sprint.com*) allows you to install an application that lets you make video calls.

• **Call from your TV.** Some LG (*www. lg.com*), Panasonic (*www.panasonic.com*) and Samsung (*www.samsung.com*) high-end HDTVs comes with the ability to place Skype video calls if you purchase a Webcam designed for the TV. An Internet connection is required. Some Panasonic Viera models feature WiFi wireless Internet capabilities, while others must be connected via cable.

Is Google Making Us Stupid? What the Internet Is Doing to Our Brains

Nicholas Carr, journalist based in Boulder, Colorado, whose writings about the social, economic and business implications of technology have appeared in *The New York Times*, *Wired*, *The Atlantic* and elsewhere. He previously served as executive editor of *Harvard Business Review* and was a principal at Mercer Management Consulting. His book is *The Shallows: What the Internet Is Doing to Our Brains* (Norton). *www.nicholasgcarr.com*

The Internet is changing our brains. Neurologists and psychologists have discovered that our brains process Internet pages differently than they do printed pages.

That can affect how much we learn when we read—and even alter our brains themselves.

The human brain "rewires" itself depending on how it is used, an ability neurologists refer to as "plasticity." An experiment by UCLA psychology professor Gary Small, MD, showed that spending one hour per day on the Internet for just one week alters our neural pathways. That neural rewiring could have unfortunate consequences.

Example: For the past five centuries, reading books has helped train human brains to concentrate intently over extended periods of time, an ability that has helped our species produce ideas and inventions. If we abandon books in favor of the Internet, our ability to maintain focus and think up new ideas might diminish.

Other consequences of Internet use and what we can do about them…

INTERRUPTION SYSTEM

When we read online, words are not the only information coming at us. There usually are eye-catching advertisements alongside the text and hyperlinks in the text in case we wish to jump to different Web pages on related topics. We might have our e-mail program open and a Facebook feed, too, alerting us each time a new message arrives. Even when a printed book is transferred to an electronic device connected to the Internet, it turns into something very much like a Web site, with links and other digital enhancements.

These distractions don't just slow our reading, they also make it less likely that we will understand and retain new knowledge.

Example: Canadian researchers asked 70 people to read a short story on a computer screen. Some read traditional text, while others read a version containing hyperlinks. Only 10% of those who read the traditional text reported any difficulty following the story—versus 75% of people who read the hyperlink version. Those who read traditional text did so faster, too.

Simply ignoring online distractions does not work. We can choose not to click a hyperlink or open an e-mail message—but ironically, the fact that our brains must make this split-second decision to not be distracted is in itself enough of a distraction to break our concentration.

Reading books often is portrayed as a passive activity when compared with surfing the Web, but the truth is, we think more deeply when we read printed pages than when we read Internet pages. The "quiet space" afforded by the printed page lets us mull over what we read. That quiet space usually doesn't exist online, so we're less likely to form reasoned conclusions about the validity of what we read or to create unique ideas by combining the new information we read with things we already know.

What to do: When you wish to give your full attention to online or eReader text, close your e-mail program, your Facebook page and any other competing information feeds on the screen. Also, use software and settings that minimize interruptions. Free, easy-to-use programs *Instapaper Text* (*www.instapaper.com/text*) and *Readability* (*www.readability.com/addons*) strip away most, though not all, of the distractions from Web sites, leaving mainly straightforward text. Or use the *Safari 5* Web browser, which has a "Reader" button in the address field that works similarly (*www.apple.com/safari*).

LESS IS READ

The Internet puts more information than ever at our fingertips—yet evidence suggests that it actually leads us to read and rely upon a smaller set of information resources, encouraging uncreative group thinking.

The trouble is that the Internet does not just provide information. It also subtly evaluates it for us. Search engines typically sort their results in order of popularity, and few of us scan past the first page of results.

Example: A study by James Evans, PhD, a sociologist at the University of Chicago, found that the increased availability of academic research online has led academics to read and reference a narrower set of articles when they write journal articles. The Internet allows them to identify which prior journal articles are most popular with their peers and most related to their own research, and they often ignore the rest.

True, the most popular Web pages and articles are likely to be the most useful—but reading obscure authors, ideas and opinions has value, too. When we read things that most other people have not read, we increase the odds that we'll have original ideas.

The ease and speed with which we can find specific facts online carry a hidden cost, too. Prior to the Internet, we often had to dig deep into newspapers, magazines and books to find the facts we needed. These days, search engines such as Google direct us to the desired snippet of data in seconds. Once we've found the fact that we are after, we usually stop reading. That's unfortunate, because the time we previously had "wasted" searching through lots of resources gave us a chance to stumble across other important or interesting facts or ideas.

What to do: Scan beyond the first page of results when you use a search engine to explore a topic of interest. This at least gives you a chance to learn more than what almost everyone else interested in the topic already knows.

When an Internet search for a piece of information leads you to a compelling article, book or Web site, jot down its name, then explore it more fully when you have some free time.

LESS SOCIAL INTELLIGENCE

The Internet is no longer confined to our desktops. eReaders, smartphones and even vehicle dashboards increasingly allow us to bring the online world wherever we go—a trend that will accelerate in the years ahead.

The danger of digital distractions while driving already is well-publicized. Less discussed is the potential danger that such portable distractions pose while we're just sitting around with friends or loved ones. Preliminary research by the Brain and Creativity Institute at the University of Southern California suggests that the distractions created by the use of mobile Internet devices make it less likely that we will fully grasp the psychological states of those around us. The weaker our grasp of other people's moods, the less able we are to show appropriate empathy, weakening the bonds that hold together human communities, families and friendships.

What to do: Turn off digital devices when you spend time with others, or at the very least, silence the chime notifying you when phone calls or new messages arrive. Even if you don't stop in the middle of a conversation to check incoming text messages or e-mails, that chime alone could be enough of a distraction to inhibit your ability to focus on your friends' feelings.

19

Tax-Cutting Tactics

Using the Internet to Cut Your Taxes

N
ow it is possible to obtain free tax information that before was only available by paying a tax professional to get it for you—that is, if you could get it at all.

FREE FROM THE GOVERNMENT

• **IRS Web site,** *www.irs.gov,* is the most important tax Web site of all. *It offers a huge array of resources...*

• Forms and publications. No more trips to the IRS office or waiting for tax forms to arrive by mail.

• Local resources. Get help from your local IRS office that you may not know is available.

Examples: Free tax counseling for seniors ...schedules of problem-solving days...small-business workshops...citizen advocacy groups...and much more.

• Latest news. The IRS's E-mail letter provides national tax news and news of your local IRS district.

• Tax research. Official IRS regulations, rulings, procedures and announcements, along with the IRS manual and many other official documents.

• Questions answered. Submit questions to the IRS through its Web site. Receive responses via E-mail.

This is just a sampling. The IRS site is well worth examining in detail.

• **US Tax Court,** *www.ustaxcourt.gov.* Learn how to use the Court's "small tax case procedure" to contest a tax bill involving up to $50,000 (excluding penalties and interest) per year—without a lawyer...and under simplified rules. This site also lists Tax Court decisions issued since 1995.

• **State and local tax agencies.** A great many of these agencies are now on the Internet. You can find a comprehensive listing at

James Glass, New York–based tax attorney.

427

www.taxsites.com/state.html. This site also lists many local taxpayer advocacy groups, which can assist individuals and local businesses.

ANSWERS FROM PROFESSIONALS

One of the best features about the Internet is that you can use it to get your questions answered by tax professionals—*for free.* These groups are a great starting point for tax research, but you should still contact a tax professional.

• **Tax newsgroups.** These are open, ongoing discussion groups that anyone can join. *The two major newsgroups for US taxes are…*

• *misc.taxes.moderated.* This has a number of tax professionals as "regulars" who answer questions from anyone. A tax professor moderates the group, screening questions so discussion is polite and focused on practical tax issues.

• *misc.taxes.* This group is not moderated, so "anything goes."

Newsgroups are not part of the World Wide Web. To reach them, go to an Internet search engine like Google or Yahoo! and enter the name of the newsgroup.

A complete, searchable archive of all the messages that have appeared in these groups is also available on the Web at *http://groups.google.com.* And—visit the Usenet Info Center Launch Pad, *www.ibiblio.org/usenet-i/home.html.*

• **E-mail discussion groups.** If you want to focus on a specific tax issue, you can join one of many specialized Internet discussion groups that are hosted by professional groups and universities. Questions and comments are submitted via E-mail to a moderator, who compiles them in a document that is E-mailed to all group members.

Top discussion forum: An excellent range of discussion groups is hosted by Tax Analysts. Go to *www.taxanalysts.com* and sign up for a free trial. The site covers dozens of different topics, including estate taxes, real estate, insurance and pensions. There's also an archive of past messages for each group.

TAX-FILING HELP

You don't have to buy software every year to prepare your tax return and keep records. Some Web sites do it for you. *The best…*

• **TurboTax® for the Web,** http://*turbotax. intuit.com,* is the online version of the popular TurboTax return-preparation software.

• **H&R Block TaxCut for the Web,** *www. hrblock.com,* offers services to help you prepare and file your federal and state tax forms electronically. Ideal for students and those with simple tax returns.

MORE RESOURCES

Still more useful sources of free tax information on the Web…

• **Nolo legal encyclopedia,** *www.nolo.com/ legal-encyclopedia.*

• **Fairmark Press Tax Guide for Investors,** *http://fairmark.com.* Includes one of the most extensive explanations of Roth IRAs, as well as tax news and discussion boards on investment tax subjects.

• **US Tax Center,** *www.irs.com.* Includes lists of frequently asked questions as well as perhaps the broadest collection of links to tax discussion groups, taxpayer organizations and other tax resources.

What's the Best Tax Year?

Calendar-year companies with seasonal businesses should consider adopting a fiscal year for tax and financial reporting purposes. *The year can end on the last day of any month and be timed so that…*

• **The financial statement looks best**—high cash and low receivables.

• **The company has more time** to take inventories and utilize internal controls.

• **The company gets more attention from its tax advisers** (since it does not have to have its return prepared during the advisers' busiest season).

IRS permission is required and can usually be obtained by filing Form 1128. The IRS seldom objects to a switch when there's a good business reason behind it.

COMMON FISCAL YEAR-ENDS

Manufacturing
Building supplies ....June
Electrical equipment ....September
Meat packing................................October
Office equipment ....June

Wholesaling
Auto accessories............................January
Groceries ....June
Plumbing supplies ....February
Paper...June

Retailing
Books...June
Department stores.........................January
Furniture & appliances.......................June
Hardware.......................................January

Services
Building contractors.....................February
Real estate agencies ....September
Garages..September
Warehouses .... March

Tax-Wise Timing For Start-up of S Corporations

New S corporations must adopt a calendar year. An exception is made only where there is a strong business purpose for the use of a fiscal year. Furthermore, if there is more than a 50% change in ownership, then a calendar year must be adopted or the S status ceases.

If the stockholders are confident that the period of losses will be brief, they should time the start-up so that the first taxable year will be very short. For example, start the business in September and the first fiscal year will only be three or four months. The stockholders get the benefit of the losses during the brief start-up period. Then they can terminate the Sub S status for the second fiscal year beginning January 1.

This can be most applicable to a service business that started as an unincorporated organization, keeping its books on the accrual basis. In that case, the accounts payable are negligible as most of the expenses are labor.

In a service business on the accrual basis, taxes are paid on profits represented by accounts receivable. As an example, let's say that such profits in the first year's accounts receivable amounted to $50,000—the profit equals that amount, and taxes are paid on it.

At this point the business is restructured as an S corporation on the cash basis. But the old organization keeps collecting the cash on its existing accounts receivable, while the new Sub S company pays all expenses. Assume that three months' expenses come to approximately $50,000, and that billed but uncollected accounts receivable also come to $50,000. Cash to pay the bills of the Sub S company can be generated by transferring the $50,000 in accounts receivable collections from the old organization as an investment in the new business. Meanwhile, however—at least for the roughly 90-day period during which no cash collections are coming into the Sub S from its own new accounts receivable—the new company reports a loss.

S Corporation Magic

Barry D. Sussman and Martin Galuskin, partners, Milgrom, Sussman, Galuskin & Co., CPAs, Edison, New Jersey.

The present tax law has greatly expanded the number of ways in which Subchapter S corporations can be used to cut business and personal taxes. *The following rules make it possible to use S corporations...*

• **In syndications and other money-raising ventures.**

• **In tax-shelter arrangements subject to passive-loss rules.**

• **As a tax-cutting tool for personal investments.**

An S corporation combines the tax benefits of personally owning a business with the legal protection of the corporate form. The income and deductions of the firm flow directly to the shareholders in proportion to their stockholdings that are to be claimed on their personal tax returns.

For example, business losses can be used to cut the tax on shareholder salaries. But at the same time, shareholders have personal protection from corporate liabilities (such as lawsuits and unsecured debts).

An S corporation can receive most of its income from investments in the form of rents, dividends and interest. An S corporation's stock can bear different voting rights.

Tax shelters: Until now, the typical tax shelter has been arranged as a limited partnership. The shelter business (such as oil drilling or equipment leasing) incurs losses in its early years, which flow through to the partners and offset other passive income.

Drawback: Each limited partnership must have at least one general partner who has unlimited liability for the shelter's debts. The remaining partners are limited partners who are liable only up to the amount they invest. But since limited partners can't have any regular input into the management of the business, they have little say as to how their money is being spent. Furthermore, it's difficult to get out of a partnership because partnership interests aren't freely transferable.

S corporation advantages: Tax benefits flow through to investors in much the same way as in a partnership, and the same shelter advantages (subject to passive-loss rules) result. *But in addition…*

•**The corporation protects all the investors** from personal liability.

•**Since shareholders can be executives and managers of the firm,** they can control how their money is spent.

•**Shares of stock may be much easier to sell or give away** if the investor wants to get out.

Business opportunities: Because most businesses incur tax losses during their start-up phase, syndicators and entrepreneurs can attract investors by starting up a new business in the S corporation form. The flow-through of losses will offset income from other shelters.

Similarly, a large, established business that wishes to expand (by purchasing new equipment or real estate, for example) can have some of its executives and shareholders form an independent S corporation to acquire the new property. The company can then lease the property on terms that are arranged to be advantageous to it and the new firm's shareholders.

Personal tax planning: Because an S corporation may have passive income, it's possible for a top-bracket investor to incorporate his or her personal portfolio. Shares of stock without voting rights may then be given to (or placed in certain trusts for) other family members. At the same time, by keeping all the voting shares of the S corporation's stock, the taxpayer retains complete control over the investments. The same tactic is available to the top tax bracket owner of a family business.

Restrictions: There's no limit to the assets or revenues of a company that elects S corporation status. But the company can have no more than 100 shareholders (family members are counted as one). Another corporation other than a tax-exempt organization (charity) can't be a shareholder.

Although an S corporation's losses extend to its shareholders, the amount of losses a shareholder can claim is generally limited to the amount he paid for his stock plus the amount of any loans he made to the company. Excess losses can be carried forward and deducted from the company's future income.

The loss-limitation rule means that S corporation status may not be best when company losses result from heavy interest payments on borrowings for which the shareholders aren't personally liable. *Example:* Real estate tax shelters, when a mortgage is secured by the property alone. *Tactic:* Shareholders can increase their deduction limit by substituting themselves for the company as the party primarily liable on the loan. (They're then assumed to have reloaned the borrowed amount to the company.) If the business is successful, they will never have to pay off the loan out-of-pocket. And since the owners of a closely held company are usually required to guarantee its major debts personally anyway, the substitution doesn't really increase their liability, even in the worst case.

There are other technical rules that apply to S corporations, making it necessary to consult with a tax professional to see if an S corporation election is a good idea in your case. But don't overlook the flexible planning opportunities that result from the liberalized new law.

Even an established company that's highly profitable may gain by electing S status...

• **The election eliminates corporate income tax at the federal level** and sometimes at the state level as well.

• **Income can be collected by shareholders at favorable rates** if they have tax benefits or offsetting losses from other investments (such as tax shelters).

• **S status eliminates the risk of two common IRS challenges,** namely, that the company pays unreasonably large salaries, or has accumulated too much in business earnings.

A firm that expects to lose money can elect S corporation status to pass its losses through to its owners. It can then return to regular corporate status when it returns to profitability.

Normally, S corporation status can't be elected more than once every five years.

must show that without the buyout its business will be in jeopardy.

HOW THE RULE WORKS

• **Winner.** A company produced a patented product under license. But the conduct of one of the shareholders upset the patent owner, who threatened to cancel the license agreement if the shareholder was not removed from the company. So the company bought the shareholder out and deducted the cost. *Court of Appeals decision:* Without the license, the company would have been out of business. So there was an overriding business motive for the deal, and the deduction was ruled okay.

• **Loser.** A company wanted to close an unprofitable subsidiary. But it was contractually committed to buy out the interest of the subsidiary's manager first. *IRS objection:* The company business was healthy on the whole. The fact that the company had made a bad investment in the subsidiary did not entitle it to specially favored tax treatment. *The court's decision:* The fact that there was some business motive for the deal did not outweigh the fact that it was a purchase of capital stock. The deduction was disallowed.

Winner: *Five Star Mfg.,* 355 F.2d 724 (5th Cir.). Loser: *Harder Services,* 67 TC 585.

Buying Out a Shareholder and Deducting the Cost

One of the worst things that can happen to a closely held company is trouble among the shareholders. Buying out the dissenting shareholders can be very costly.

Some companies have tried to minimize the cost of a buyout by deducting it as a business expense. *Problem:* Company stock is a capital asset, and the cost of a capital asset is generally not deductible. *Opportunity:* Show that there is a compelling business reason for the buyout. The elimination of friction among shareholders is not enough. The company

Interest Deductible... Principal, Too

Employee stock-ownership plans (ESOPs) are a tax-saving means of corporate financing. *The essence:* A firm sets up a plan, which borrows money from a bank on a note guaranteed by the corporation. Then the plan uses this to buy stock from the corporation. The corporation makes annual contributions to the plan in cash or stock, for which it gets tax deductions. The contributions are used to pay off the bank loan. In effect, the corporation raises capital with tax-deductible dollars.

The ESOP can be used as a personal financial-planning tool for the shareholder-owners of a close corporation who are otherwise locked into the corporation.

If the corporation redeems part of their shares in an ordinary way, they're almost certain to be taxed at ordinary income rates. And that transaction will be treated as a dividend distribution (which the shareholder pays taxes on) rather than as a sale or exchange taxable at capital gains rates.

The corporation itself faces a major problem on redemptions. It must accumulate the necessary funds. They can be accumulated only out of after-tax dollars.

By interposing an ESOP, the picture changes dramatically. The shareholders have a market for their shares—the ESOP. The plan buys their shares with deductible contributions made with pretax dollars.

If there isn't enough money in the ESOP at the time to effect the purchase, then the plan borrows money from a bank in the procedure outlined above.

The same approach may be used by the shareholder's estate as a means of realizing cash on stock held by the estate, without getting dividend treatment.

Insurance angle: The ESOP, as an alternative to borrowing to raise cash to purchase stock from the estate, may, according to current thinking among practitioners, carry life insurance on a key shareholder. If the corporation itself were to carry such insurance to facilitate redemption, the premiums paid wouldn't be tax deductible. By interposing an ESOP, the premiums effectively become tax deductible, since they're paid by the plan out of tax-deductible dollars contributed to it by the company.

Other benefits: The shareholder-executive will be able to participate in the plan himself/herself and enjoy its benefits…

• **His company will make tax-deductible contributions to the plan.**

• **He won't be taxed until the benefits are made available to him.**

• **He'll get favorable tax treatment on lump-sum distributions** through a special averaging formula.

• **The payout is required to be made in company stock** and he won't be taxed on the unrealized appreciation in the stock over the cost to the plan until he sells the stock.

Chief problem: Valuation of shares on a sale to the ESOP. Another is the necessary distribution of corporate information to the employee-shareholders. If corporate progress isn't to the liking of employees, expect worker dissatisfaction.

The concepts are new, but the idea is one well worth exploring.

Loopholes Everywhere

Edward Mendlowitz, CPA, partner, WithumSmith+Brown, CPAs, 1 Spring St., New Brunswick, New Jersey 08901. *www.withum.com*

Some federal tax loopholes are created intentionally to attract private investors into fields the government can't cope with. *Example:* Tax credits for investors in low-income housing. Other loopholes are accidental, created by flaws in the writing of legislation. *The best of these loopholes…*

• **Tax-favored long-term capital-gains loophole.** Capital gains are taxed as low as 0% for some individuals, while ordinary income is taxed at a top rate of 39.6%.

• **Education savings bonds loophole.** Interest on US savings bonds issued after December 31, 1989, that are cashed in to pay for educational expenses is tax-free income for certain taxpayers. *Main restrictions…*

• Applies only to people who buy the bonds after reaching age 24.

• Interest exclusion is phased out for joint filers whose adjusted gross income (AGI) in 2013 is between $112,050 and $142,050 (for single filers, $74,700 and $89,700).

• **Early-withdrawals-from-IRA-accounts loophole.** The 10% penalty tax on withdrawals before age 59½ from IRAs does not apply if the money is taken out in the form of an annuity—that is, in a series of payments over one's life expectancy or the joint life expectancies of a couple. This loophole can be put to good use if there is a fair amount of money in your IRA, say $100,000, from the rollover of a company pension plan.

Best Tax Loopholes

Edward Mendlowitz, CPA, partner, WithumSmith+ Brown, CPAs, 1 Spring St., New Brunswick, New Jersey 08901. *www.withum.com*

Taxes have become much more complicated in recent years. The stomping ground for tax professionals remains—loopholes. There are always loopholes. *Here are the best...*

• **Pension and profit-sharing plans.** Probably the very best tax shelters. Amounts put into a pension plan are deductible by the business. Neither the original amount contributed nor any of the earnings are taxed until actually paid to the individual (presumably after retirement, when the person will be in a lower tax bracket). For a business owner/officer, this amounts to a bonanza. The owner can put a share of the business profits aside for his retirement and see the government contribute a sizable additional amount (equal to the taxes saved by deducting the contribution).

• **For the self-employed.** The limits for qualified retirement plan deductions are the same as those that apply to company-sponsored qualified plans. This is a tremendous benefit for people who have unincorporated businesses, but new rules applicable to all plans require much more coverage for employees.

• **Charity loopholes.** Instead of giving cash to charity, give securities that have increased in value. You get a charitable deduction for the present market value of the securities and you avoid paying tax on the gain. *Deferred giving:* Get an immediate income tax deduction for a gift that won't be completed until sometime in the future by setting up a charitable remainder trust. In the meantime, you or your beneficiaries can enjoy the income from the assets you put into the trust.

• **QTIP trusts.** You don't have to leave property outright to your spouse to take advantage of the estate tax marital deduction. By setting up a Qualified Terminable Interest Property Trust (QTIP trust), you can provide an income for your spouse for his/her lifetime, get an estate tax deduction for the amount put into the trust and control who gets the trust assets when your spouse dies.

Handle Big Gains

Matthew Levitan, vice president and director of financial services for a major brokerage firm in New York City.

Stock market gains. Gains on real estate sales. Gifts and inheritances. Bonuses. Pension-plan distributions. There are many ways you can get windfalls, and all are taxed differently.

CAPITAL GAINS

Anytime you sell a capital asset (stocks, bonds, real estate) for a profit, you have a capital gain. But only assets held more than one year qualify for favorable capital gains tax rates.

Look for built-in losses in your portfolio. Did you buy oil stocks a year ago when they were at their peak? If you sell, those losses can help shelter your other gains.

REAL ESTATE ANGLES

If you sell your house, you don't pay on a gain up to $250,000 ($500,000 on a joint return and surviving spouses who sell within two years of the other spouse's death) if you owned and used the house as your principal residence for two out of five years before the date of sale. You can also defer tax on commercial property—if you swap with someone else rather than selling.

GIFTS AND INHERITANCES

Gifts are easy—the recipient pays no tax. For example, if your uncle gives you a $2,000 wedding present, you don't have to pay taxes on it. *Exception:* Capital gains on property you receive as a gift. Say I bought XYZ stock for $10 and gave it to you when it was worth

$30. When you sell the stock, you pay tax on that $20 gain, as well as on any gain that has arisen since you received it.

Protect your beneficiaries. Rather than give away highly appreciated assets, keep them in your estate. When you die, the cost basis of everything in your estate is revalued to market value. When your beneficiaries sell the property, they will be taxed only on any gain that has arisen since they inherited it.

Although inheritances are tax free to the recipient for federal income tax purposes, states may impose a 10% to 12% inheritance tax. The only way around this is to have the will probated in a state with low or no death taxes (Nevada and Florida are favorites). But the person making the will must be a resident of that state. You may not have to spend more than six months of the year in the state to be considered a resident. The authorities will look at the broad picture to decide where you belong. *Examples:* Where are you registered to vote? Which state is your driver's license from?

BONUSES

If you can see a bonus coming ahead of time, you may be able to elect deferred compensation if your company allows it. That avoids paying tax until you actually get the money. (Your company may even pay you interest while you wait.) *Caution:* You must make the election before you have a right to the money.

If your employer has "cafeteria-plan" benefits, take tax-free fringes. *Examples:* Medical benefits, pension contributions, group term life insurance. The plan must not discriminate among employees. *Also:* See if your company's stock-option plan qualifies for incentive stock option (ISO) treatment. If so, you pay tax only when you sell the stock, not when you exercise the option—and even then at capital gains rates. Be aware of any potential impact of the alternative minimum tax (AMT) when exercising ISOs.

LUMP-SUM DISTRIBUTIONS

You have a clear-cut choice with lump-sum payments from a retirement plan. Either take the money now and pay tax on it now or roll it over (transfer it directly) into an IRA and pay tax as you receive the income.

Corporate Tax Loopholes For Business Owners

Edward Mendlowitz, CPA, partner, WithumSmith+ Brown, CPAs, 1 Spring St., New Brunswick, New Jersey 08901. *www.withum.com*

Understanding the various corporate tax loopholes can make a difference. *Here are a few of the best...*

•**Timing loophole I.** Partnerships, S corporations and personal service corporations are generally required to use a calendar year. For these entities, it's no longer possible to get certain officer salary deferrals by having the company on a fiscal year while the owners are on a calendar tax year. *Loophole:* The deferral ability continues to be available to regular C corporations that are not personal-service corporations.

•**Timing loophole II.** Arrange your own leveraged buyout after you have become a legal resident in a low-tax state such as Florida. *Reason for a leveraged buyout:* You need personal funds, but all your money is tied up in the business. The company borrows the money then distributes it to you. *Reason for moving to Florida:* To avoid paying state income tax on the money you get in the buyout.

•**Size loophole.** Regular corporations generally can't use the cash method* of accounting if the business has average annual gross receipts of more than $5 million (although there are special rules for certain corporations with gross receipts up to $10 million). *Loophole:* If special rules don't apply, split the business into a number of corporations, each with annual sales of under $5 million.

*Cash method: You report as income only the money actually received, not the accounts receivable.

• **Profit loophole.** Corporations (other than "small corporations") are required to pay Alternative Minimum Tax on a certain amount of book profit. *Loophole:* Consider changing the method of reporting so that the company's financial statement will more closely agree with its tax return on book-profit items.

• **Incorporation loophole.** Elect Subchapter S status for your business. S corporations generally pay no corporate taxes. Instead, income, deductions and credits are passed through to the shareholders and reported on their individual income tax returns.

Deductible Gambling Losses

John J. Tuozzolo, associated with the firm Collins, Hannafin, Garamella, Jaber & Tuozzolo, PC, 148 Deer Hill Ave., Danbury, Connecticut 06810.

With luck, you might win big. But winnings are taxable, and winnings of $600 or more must be reported to the Internal Revenue Service.

The tax on winnings can be cut by claiming all your gambling losses, but few people document their losses. *Result:* A person who scores a big win may wind up paying tax on the winnings without getting any benefit from his/her losses. He may wind up paying extra tax even if he *lost more than he won* over the entire year.

Better way: Keep tabs on your winnings and losses. The IRS recommends wagering tickets, canceled checks, credit records, bank withdrawal statements and credit receipts as proof. An accurate diary is also recommended.

Bottom line: Gambling losses for the year are deductible as an itemized deduction to the extent of your gambling winnings for the year. So if you are planning to be lucky at all this year, keep records for the *entire* year.

Avoiding a Gain on Insurance Proceeds

When property is destroyed by fire or accident, the insurance proceeds may give you a taxable gain. But you can avoid being taxed on the gain by reinvesting the proceeds in similar property within two years (three years if the property is real estate used in business).

Make sure that the first replacement property you pick is the right one. Recently, a taxpayer avoided tax by designating a replacement property, then filed an amended return to designate a different property that was more attractive.

IRS ruling: Even though the replacement period had not expired, it was too late. The first pick was final.

Income-Shifting Opportunities

Edward Mendlowitz, CPA, partner, WithumSmith+ Brown, CPAs, 1 Spring St., New Brunswick, New Jersey 08901. *www.withum.com*

It's hard for taxpayers today to spread income among the family as a tax-saving device. The options have been cut back for shifting income from higher tax bracketed family members to those with lower tax brackets (so the income is taxed at the lower rate).

Giving income-producing assets to a child may not reduce the family's overall tax. Unearned income (income other than wages or salary) of a child who is not age 24 by the end of the year and who are full-time students will be taxed at the parent's tax rate.

LOOPHOLES

• **Give generously to children beyond the "kiddie tax."** Income from gifts to children at this age is taxed in the child's lower tax bracket.

Strategy: In the year your child is going to turn 19 if not a full-time student, or 24 if a full-time student, start giving him or her gifts so he can accumulate money for college. As long as your child is this age by the close of the tax year, he is exempt from the rules.

Smart gift: Appreciated securities that you were thinking about selling. Give them to your child and let the child sell the securities. The gain will be taxed at the child's lower tax rate rather than at your higher one.

• **For children subject to the "kiddie tax," take advantage of the $2,000 allowance in 2013.** The first $1,000 earned on an income-producing gift may be offset by the child's standard deduction. The next $1,000 that is earned on income-producing property given to your child is taxed at his lower tax rate.

• **Hire your children in your business.** Salary earned by children of any age is shielded by the standard deduction of up to $6,100 in 2013. The children must really work for you, and you must pay them a reasonable wage.

Double advantage: Your business gets a deduction for the wages. Your child, depending on how much he earns, will pay little or no tax in his low-income bracket. And sole proprietorships don't have to pay Social Security tax for the owner's child under age 18.

• **Refinance your home to pay for your child's education.** Interest on student loans is deductible only up to a limited amount and only by those people whose income is below modest limits.

Loophole: Convert this nondeductible interest into a deduction. *How:* Take out an equity loan on your home and use this money instead of a student loan to pay for college. You can deduct interest on a home-equity loan of up to $100,000, provided that sum doesn't exceed fair market value less acquisition debt.

• **Give "deferred income" gifts to children subject to the "kiddie tax."** These are gifts for which taxable income won't have to be reported for many years, preferably until the child is beyond the "kiddie tax." *Examples...*

• Low-income securities. These usually don't pay large dividends over the years, but will appreciate in value and sell at a large profit by the time the child passes the "kiddie tax" age.

• US savings bonds. Your child won't have to pay tax until the bond is cashed in (unless the child elects to report each year's income as it is earned).

AND DON'T FORGET THE OLD FOLKS

• **Buy a home for your parents.** Elderly parents are likely to be in a lower tax bracket and wouldn't get much of a tax benefit from the purchase of a small home or condo. Consider buying the home or condo and renting it to them. This will create tax deductions for you while you are providing them with a place in which to live. You can only deduct up to $25,000 of losses from the home. However, this $25,000 loss allowance is phased out on Adjusted Gross Income from $100,000 to $150,000.

• **Give appreciated securities instead of cash to your parents if you are supporting them.** They can cash in the securities in 2013 and pay no tax on the appreciation if they are in the 10% or 15% tax bracket on other income.

Caution: A large gain could push your parents into a higher tax bracket.

First Home...Your IRA... And the Tax Law

Lisa N. Collins, CPA/PFS, former vice president and director of tax services, Harding, Shymanski & Co., PC, 21 SE Third St., Suite 500, Evansville, Indiana 47708.

Under the law, people under age 59½ may take up to $10,000 from an IRA without having to pay the 10% early withdrawal penalty, if the money is applied toward the purchase of a first home.

While first-time home buyers do not typically have $10,000 in an IRA, a few who have rented for a while may have put away that much money. Or perhaps they have changed jobs and rolled a company pension plan over into an IRA.

Parents and grandparents to the rescue:
This new right to withdraw penalty-free is not restricted to the home buyer.

Parents and grandparents can withdraw up to $10,000 from their own IRAs and apply the money to the first purchase of a principal residence by their child or grandchild.

Older people often like to help the younger generation with the down payment on their first house or condo.

The price you pay: Of course, income tax will have to be paid on the money that is withdrawn. Only the penalty is avoided.

Caution: The house purchase must take place within 120 days of the IRA withdrawal.

A Partial Tax Break Is Better Than None

People who sell their homes after living in them less than two years will be allowed a partial tax break on any profits if the sale is due to a job change, health reasons or unforeseen circumstances.

The law does not spell out what "unforeseen circumstances" might be. That is to be done later in IRS regulations, and presumably the requirements will be stricter than, "I didn't like the rock music my neighbor played."

Still, as with many fuzzy areas of law, it would not be surprising to see litigation over such claims.

People who move for one of those reasons will be entitled to a prorated tax break, based on the length of residence.

Lisa N. Collins, CPA/PFS, former vice president and director of tax services, Harding, Shymanski & Co., PC, 21 SE Third St., Suite 500, Evansville, Indiana 47708.

How Hiring Your Kids Can Shelter Income

If you have children old enough to work and responsible enough to earn their pay, you can cut thousands of dollars off the family tax bill by putting the kids on your payroll. The wages you pay will be shifted from your tax return to the children's returns, where as much as $11,100 a year for each child can escape tax entirely.

In 2013, a child can earn $11,100 without paying any federal income tax by utilizing...

• **The standard deduction $6,100** (annually indexed for inflation), plus...

• **The $5,000 that can be invested** in a deductible Individual Retirement Account (IRA).

If the child earns more than this amount during the year, the excess will be taxed at the lowest tax rates.

The benefits are almost as great, even if the child has substantial income of his or her own—for instance, a trust fund from grandparents. In that case, he already pays taxes (at your rates, until he is at least 24 if a full-time student) and has used up $1,000 of his standard deduction. But the balance of the standard deduction and the $5,000 IRA deduction are not available for "passive" income (interest, dividend, etc.). If, however, you put the child on the payroll, he can earn up to the standard deduction amount, apply it to these two items and pay no tax on the money. The wages are "earned" income and qualify for the standard deduction and IRA. *Bonus:* The income earned on the IRA funds is sheltered from current tax.

The wages you pay can be generous, but must not be unreasonably high for the kind of work the child does. And the child must have genuine duties. *Recommended:* Have the child keep a log showing the hours he's worked and what he's done.

Meet the obligations of an employer. As a sole proprietor, you won't have to withhold and pay Social Security taxes if the child is under age 18, but any state or local payroll taxes may apply. You do not have to withhold income tax as long as the child files Form W-4, certifying that he had no tax liability the previous year and expects none for the current year.

"Child Labor" and the IRS

A professor paid salaries to his children for helping out with his correspondence, filing, answering telephones and cleaning. They did all the work at his home.

Tax Court: Deduction allowed for the filing and correspondence, but since his home wasn't a "home office," the cleaning wasn't deductible. And the telephone-answering salary wasn't deductible because there were no records separating personal calls from business calls.

L. J. Moriarity, TC Memo 1984-249.

Nepotism Pays

Irving L. Blackman, CPA, retired founding partner, Blackman Kallick, LLP, 10 S. Riverside Plaza, Chicago 60606. *www.taxsecretsofthewealthy.com*

A favorite tax-planning tactic is to have a minor child work for the family-owned business. The first $6,100 in 2013 earned by the child is tax-free, and further income is taxed at low rates. In addition, the company gets a deduction for the child's salary. Now a dramatic taxpayer victory shows just how effective this tactic can be.

The facts: The taxpayers owned a mobile-home park and hired their three children, aged 7, 11 and 12, to work there. The children cleaned the grounds, did landscaping work, maintained the swimming pool, answered phones and did minor repair work. The taxpayers deducted over $17,000 that they paid to the children during a three-year period. But the IRS objected, and the case went to trial.

Court's decision: Over $15,000 of deductions were approved. Most of the deductions

that were disallowed were attributable to the 7-year-old. But even $4,000 of his earnings were approved by the court.

Key: The children actually performed the work for which they were paid. And the work was necessary for the business. The taxpayers demonstrated that if their children had not done the work, they would have had to hire someone else to do it.

Tax Shifting in the Family

A husband and wife owned property that the husband used in his business. The husband paid his wife rent for using her half of the property and treated the rent as a business expense.

The couple then filed separate returns. The rent was deducted on the husband's return as a business expense and treated as income on the wife's return. But since the wife was in a much lower tax bracket, the result was a net tax savings.

IRS ruling: The arrangement is OK.

IRS Revenue Ruling 74-209.

Dangerous Family Loans

Parents who don't press their children to repay money they've lent them can fall into a trap. *Recent example:* A father lent his child $500,000. In return, he got an interest-bearing note payable on demand. But three years later, the father still hadn't demanded repayment of the loan.

Problem: At the end of those three years, the father was legally barred (by the statute of limitations) from enforcing the debt.

Result: The loan plus interest automatically turned into a taxable gift to the child.

Intra-Family Loans

The IRS disallowed the deduction a taxpayer claimed for interest paid on a loan from his brother.

IRS: The loan was not genuine because there was no repayment schedule or security.

Tax Court: The taxpayer had signed a document acknowledging the debt and promising to pay interest at a set rate. This was enough to establish a genuine loan, even though there was no specific repayment schedule. The interest was deductible. *Catch:* The taxpayer could not deduct the interest paid on similar loans he received from his sister and mother because there was no written document evidencing the debt.

Badi Zohoury, TC Memo 1983-597.

Good News for Home Owners

An IRS rule lets more taxpayers escape capital gains when selling homes they have lived in for less than two of the prior five years.

Taxpayers can prorate excludable capital gains—$250,000 ($500,000 jointly)—if the two-year test isn't met for reasons that include death of a household member...divorce or separation...job loss resulting in unemployment benefits...multiple births from the same pregnancy.

Laurence I. Foster, CPA, PFS, consultant and former partner in the accounting and advisory firm of Eisner LLP, New York City.

Moving? Consider Capital Gains Rules

Not only do many US states have different income tax rates, they also have different rules for taxing capital gains. *For example, if you move to...*

•**A high-tax state like California, Massachusetts, or New York,** you may want to take a capital gain before the move.

•**A low-tax state like Florida,** which has no income tax, you may want to defer taking a gain until after you move.

Opportune timing of a large gain around a move may save you thousands of dollars—and may even pay for the move.

For more information, visit the "Retirement Living Information Center" at *www.retirement living.com.*

Barbara Weltman, attorney in Millwood, New York. *www. barbaraweltman.com.* She is author of several books, including *The Complete Idiot's Guide to Starting a Home-Based Business,* 3rd edition (Alpha).

Multiple Family Support

Suppose you're chipping in with other family members to support a dependent relative. It may seem that no one is entitled to a dependency exemption because no one member of the group provided more than half of the dependent's support.

Election: If all of you sign a Multiple Support Declaration (Form 2120), you can take turns claiming the dependency exemption for the relative you're supporting.

Requirements: The people signing, as a group, must provide more than 50% of the dependent's support. And the person who is claiming the exemption must furnish more than 10% of the support.

Edward Mendlowitz, CPA, partner, WithumSmith+ Brown, CPAs, 1 Spring St., New Brunswick, New Jersey 08901. *www.withum.com*

When a Widow Can File a Joint Return

Awidow or widower with dependent children living at home can qualify as a qualifying widow(er) and file using advantageous joint-return tax rates for each of the two taxable years after the year in which the spouse died. Check filing status box 5 on Form 1040.

Buying Relatives' Tax Losses

If you are a high-bracket taxpayer and have a relative with little or no taxable income, consider taking advantage of a tax-law provision that allows you, in effect, to acquire your immediate relatives' deductible losses.

How it works: If a member of your immediate family sells property to you at a loss, that loss can't be deducted. But when you turn around and sell that property, you don't have to pay tax on any gain unless the gain is more than your family member's loss. Even then, only the portion of the gain that exceeds the previous loss is taxable.

Example: John White's mother is very ill. She has some steady income from dividends and receives a modest pension. But her deductible medical expenses are so high that her taxable income is zero. Her portfolio includes 100 shares of Consolidated Conglomerate that she bought at $35 a share. The current price is $11. If Mrs. White sells on the open market, she'll have a $2,400 loss that won't save a penny in taxes. If John buys the stock, he can hold on to it until the price recovers. And although he bought the shares at $11, he won't have a taxable gain until the stock hits $35 again.

Added twist: John can give his mother a note for the purchase price of the stock with a reasonable interest rate, say 10%. The money can help defray Mrs. White's medical costs, while John gets an interest deduction.

Who can do it: This special rule applies on any transaction between you and your parents, grandparents, children, grandchildren, brother, sister or any corporation in which you own more than 50% (by value) of the shares.

How Marriage May Save You Money on Taxes

John J. Tuozzolo, associated with the firm Collins, Hannafin, Garamella, Jaber & Tuozzolo, PC, 148 Deer Hill Ave., Danbury, Connecticut 06810.

The privilege of filing a joint federal income tax return is available only to people who are legally married. In some years, filing a joint return is advantageous. In others, it isn't.

Usually a joint return works out better. But there are a couple of situations in which separate returns can save taxes. *Consider filing separately in these situations…*

•**The spouse with the lower income has very large medical expenses.** The expenses may be deductible on a separate return. On a joint return they would have to exceed 10% of the couple's combined adjusted gross income (AGI) to be deductible (7.5% if either spouse is 65 or older).

•**One spouse has large casualty losses.** If spouses file separate returns, the loss is reduced by only 10% of the income of the spouse who is claiming the loss. On a joint return, casualty losses must be reduced by 10% of combined AGI.

Warning: Don't file separate returns unless you've figured the tax both ways and are certain you'll benefit by filing separately. Remember, the rates paid by married people filing separately are the highest that anyone pays.

ESTATE TAX SAVINGS

A major tax advantage of being married is the "unlimited" marital deduction for gift and estate taxes. An unlimited amount of cash or other assets can be left by one spouse to the other completely free of federal estate tax as long as the property goes to the survivor without strings attached.

Trouble with the IRS

If you've been having trouble with the IRS—for example, say you owe back taxes from a business that failed—it may be a good idea to file this year's return listing your spouse's name first. The IRS's computers are programmed to pick up the Social Security number of the spouse whose name appears first on the return. By filing under your spouse's name, there's a good chance that your refund won't be held up.

Edward Mendlowitz, CPA, partner, WithumSmith+ Brown, CPAs, 1 Spring St., New Brunswick, New Jersey 08901. *www.withum.com*

Neglected Loopholes For Divorced Couples

Edward Mendlowitz, CPA, partner, WithumSmith+ Brown, CPAs, 1 Spring St., New Brunswick, New Jersey 08901. *www.withum.com*

Divorce settlements reached in anger, or by picking numbers out of the air, can have disastrous tax consequences. All too often the IRS ends up with too big a piece of the pie. But this won't happen to a couple who carefully work out in advance the tax implications of their settlement.

ALIMONY LOOPHOLES

Alimony paid under a divorce decree or a written separation agreement is deductible by the husband and taxable to the wife. But child support, lump-sum property-settlement payments and the wife's legal fees (if paid by the husband) are not deductible, and they don't have to be reported as income by the wife. *The loophole:* In a properly worded agreement, the legal fees can be made deductible by including them as alimony.

If the husband agrees to pay the wife's divorce lawyer, estimate the fee and add that amount to the alimony to be paid to the wife. The husband can then deduct the amount—as alimony. The wife includes it in her taxable income and uses the funds to pay her lawyer.

INCOME AFTER TAXES

Where the husband has a large taxable income and the nonworking wife has little or none, it makes sense to have all payments treated as alimony. *Reason:* Income is shifted from the husband's high tax bracket to the wife's lower bracket.

In negotiating a settlement, the parties must calculate the income that each will have after taxes. *Factors that affect after-tax income...*

• **The parent who has custody is entitled to claim the children as dependents** for tax purposes. He/she may waive this right by filing a consent to allow the exemption to the other parent. A copy of the consent to waive the exemption must be attached to the non-custodial parent's return.

• **A parent who has a child living with him** can file tax returns at lower head-of-household rates.

• **Both parents might have head-of-household filing status.** This could happen if the younger children live with the mother, but an older child, who is away at college, lists his father's home as his regular residence and stays with him when home on vacation.

• **Child support normally stops when the kids become independent.** Alimony often goes on until the spouse receiving it remarries.

• **Professional fees for advice about the tax aspects of a settlement are deductible.** However, fees for nontax services cannot be deducted. Make sure your advisers submit two bills, one for tax services and the other for nontax matters.

ALIMONY TRAPS

Alimony must be paid as a result of a written agreement or a court order. Otherwise, it won't be deductible.

Informal payments that a husband gives his wife after he moves out of the house, but before there is any written agreement or court order, are not deductible. *Solution:* Get a formal written agreement from the wife that amounts paid to her as alimony during negotiations are taxable to her. To protect her position, state in the agreement that she is not giving up the right to demand bigger payments later.

441

Vague wording: Too often judges don't consider tax consequences when wording an order. Vaguely worded orders that don't specify the exact nature of the payments simply invite the IRS to interpret the language in their favor. Always check the wording of the order carefully.

Reporting requirements: The spouse who claims an alimony deduction must show the Social Security number of the spouse receiving the alimony on his or her return or face penalties. The payee spouse must provide the number. *Penalty for failure of either spouse:* $50.

THE LAST JOINT RETURN

Even though they're separated, a couple who are still legally married on the last day of the year have the right to file either a joint return or as married filing separately.

Pitfall: Failing to provide in the separation agreement that a joint return will be filed and that both spouses will sign it. Without such an agreement, the husband's income will be taxed at the highest rates. If a couple agrees to file a joint return, they should also agree in advance how they will apportion the tax owed or share the tax savings.

IRA benefit: The spouse receiving the alimony can treat it as earned income for IRA purposes. *Maximum benefit for a nonworking divorcée in 2013:* $5,500 ($6,500 if age 50 or older by year end.)

Tax Considerations for Divorcing Couples

Sidney Kess, attorney and CPA. He has taught tax law to more than 725,000 tax professionals and is coauthor of *1040 Preparation and Planning Guide* (CCH Inc).

It is important for couples involved in a matrimonial dispute to seek the advice of a knowledgeable tax professional. *Special tax considerations...*

•**Changing tax rates.** While alimony is still fully deductible by the spouse who pays it, lower income tax rates diminish the value of the deduction. Husbands, who tradition-ally pay alimony, may balk at making alimony a big part of the divorce settlement. And because of the increased tax on capital gains, they may be more disposed to give low-basis, appreciated property, such as the family home, stock and interest in a business, etc., to the other spouse as part of the settlement. *Reason:* The spouse who gives the property would avoid paying tax on the gain. The spouse who receives the property could sell it and have the gain taxed at 23.8% (zero in 2013 if she is in the 10% or 15% tax bracket on other income). The tax savings would then be factored into the amount of the settlement.

•**Reduced value of home-mortgage interest deductions,** caused by lower income tax rates, may be an additional incentive for one spouse to give up his/her interest in the family home.

•**Increased exemptions for dependents** makes the right to claim children as dependents after a divorce a more valuable bargaining chip.

The spouse who is awarded custody today of the children is automatically entitled to claim the dependency exemptions. But these can be signed over to the noncustodial spouse. Spouses may consider trading dependency exemptions for increased child support. *Flip side:* High-income spouses may not want dependency exemptions, since the exemptions could cause the spouse to pay more income tax.

•**Medical expenses.** Either divorced parent can treat a child as a dependent for purposes of claiming medical-expense deductions. *Planning point:* Have the low-bracket spouse pay the medical expenses. That way, more of the expenses are likely to be deductible.

•**Legal fees.** The portion of a divorce lawyer's fee that is for tax advice is deductible (if separately stated on the bill) as a miscellaneous deduction. But you may claim miscellaneous deductions only to the extent that they exceed 2% of your Adjusted Gross Income. *Planning point:* Bunch your miscellaneous deductions into the year you pay the divorce lawyer so that as much as possible of the bill will be deductible.

• **Alimony complication.** There's a recapture rule to prevent nondeductible property-settlement payments from being deducted as alimony. Excess up-front alimony payments (those that exceed the limits set by the law) must be added back into income by the spouse who paid them. *Bottom line:* Get expert tax advice on your divorce settlement.

Co-op Alimony

When a married couple separated, he got title to their co-op. She got the right to live in the apartment rent-free. He agreed to pay all maintenance charges and assessments to the cooperative. Alimony? The IRS said the payments were taxable alimony to the ex-wife (and were deductible by her ex-husband). She said the payments benefited her husband because they enabled him to hold on to his investment.

Tax Court: The IRS was 99% right. Except for a small part of the payments that resulted in a tax benefit to the husband (the portion that went for real estate taxes and interest on the co-op mortgage), the payments were taxable alimony to the wife and deductible by her former husband.

Doriane Grutman, 80 TC No. 18.

Estimated Tax Planning

When year-end approaches, individuals often find themselves facing an estimated tax penalty for underwithholding. *To avoid this:* Have your employer withhold the necessary additional tax before the end of the year. The total amount withheld will be prorated by the IRS over the entire year.

Example: You had originally calculated your estimated-tax liability to be $4,000. You paid $1,000 for each of the first three quarters and plan to pay the final $1,000 on January 15. But it now becomes clear that you should have figured on an estimated tax of $6,000 and paid $1,500 each quarter. *Solution:* Have the extra $2,000 withheld from your salary before the year ends. Then $500 (one-fourth of the amount withheld) will be credited against your estimated tax liability for each quarter. *Result:* The penalties will have been avoided. *Important:* If you simply add that $2,000 to your last quarter's estimated tax payment, you'll still face penalties for the first three quarters.

Suggestion: If the additional liability is the result of some end-of-the-year income you didn't anticipate, you may be able to take advantage of an exception to the underestimation penalty provisions. There is one other exception that you may be able to qualify for, particularly if last year's tax bill was lower than this year's. Review these with your adviser.

Getting Maximum Protection from Your Accountant

David Ellis, former editor, *Bottom Line Retirement*, Stamford, Connecticut.

Something's wrong if all you've been getting from your accountant is a tax return every April and a bill. An accountant who isn't coming up with new suggestions each year for you to mull over and discuss with him or her is not doing anything for you.

MORE THAN THE BASICS

Beyond taxes: The advice you get from a first-rate accountant will not be limited to your needs this year. He will be planning for the long term, for your retirement and after. Nor will his advice be limited to tax preparation and tax savings. *Expect from your accountant:* An evaluation of your insurance coverage, the pros and cons of various types of life insurance, guidance in retirement and estate planning, personal financial statements for bank loans or divorce settlements, evaluations of investment advice from other professional services, help with record keeping for your business and help in getting credit.

Look to your accountant for objectivity. For example, expect him to explain to you the advantages and disadvantages of various kinds of life insurance without recommending any specific company or policy. Expect him to explain the risk in any investment or aggressive tax strategy and to avoid recommending particular investments (such as a specific tax-shelter program).

IS HE DOING HIS JOB?

A crackerjack accountant knows his clients. He's looking for ways to transfer knowledge and experience. When he puts a tax-saving plan into action for Smith, he remembers that Jones is in a similar situation and might benefit from the plan.

Your accountant is doing his job when…

• **You are kept informed of changes in the tax law.**

• **Periodically, you are asked if there have been any changes** in the information originally provided to him, especially your personal data.

• **It is clear that your file has been reviewed** before your session with him.

• **He regularly presents tax-planning suggestions** even if they were rejected in the past. *For example:* Isn't it time you reconsidered getting into a tax shelter? Have you done any more thinking about a gift program for your children?

• **His advice is objective and within his range of competence.** Beware of an accountant or any financial adviser who is dogmatic about a specific investment.

A TWO-WAY STREET

There are a number of things you can do to get the most from your accountant…

• **Keep him informed about changes** in essential personal and financial data. For example, if you don't tell him that you've started to support an aged parent, he isn't likely to recommend setting up a way to use gifts to support your parent.

• **Organize information as efficiently as possible.** This saves his time and your money. If he sends you an income tax questionnaire, use that to organize the necessary information.

• **Be sure the information is complete.** The bane of an accountant's existence is to find out about deductions the client forgot to mention—after the tax return has been prepared.

CHANGING FIRMS

The best way to find a new accountant is through recommendations from satisfied clients. When you switch accountants, the greater knowledge and capability of the new one should be obvious.

You can judge a new accountant by the number of questions he asks you. How probing is he? How creative? Avoid an accountant who gives off-the-cuff advice without knowing anything about your personal financial situation.

Gift Giving

You can give more stock shares if you make gifts after the stock market has dropped significantly. In 2013, anyone can give a maximum of $14,000 per year tax-free to anyone else—a couple can give $28,000. When the market is down, it takes more shares of stocks or mutual funds to reach the limit, so you can give away more of your assets and create a bigger potential gain for the recipients.

The Wall Street Journal

Tax Loopholes for Home Owners

Gerald J. Robinson, former counsel to the law firm Carb, Luria, Glassner, Cook & Kufeld, New York City... Lisa N. Collins, CPA/PFS, former vice president and director of tax services, Harding, Shymanski & Co., PC, 21 SE Third St., Suite 500, Evansville, Indiana 47708.

It's common knowledge that the Tax Code is more generous to home owners than to tenants. Deductions for mortgage interest, real estate taxes and casualty losses amount to hidden tax subsidies for home ownership. *Some other well-known tax benefits...*

• **Anyone who sells a principal residence can avoid tax on gain** up to $250,000 ($500,000 on a joint return). *Requirement:* The home must have been owned and used as a principal residence for two out of five years before the date of sale.

UNCOMMON TAX ANGLE

Opportunity: For people who want to sell and not buy a new home. People who are temporarily out of the home-ownership market are real winners under the law.

Example: A few local employers send employees overseas, generally for a few years. Often the employees rented out their homes while they were away. *Reason:* If they sold their homes, paid a capital gains tax and invested the balance, they might not have enough to buy equally nice houses when they returned home. Now, a better strategy for employees sent overseas for a few years is to sell and be 100% invested in the market.

Opportunity: For people who remarry after divorce or widowhood...there is considerable flexibility. People who are divorcing have flexibility, too.

Tax considerations no longer dictate personal choices. For years, when two older people were getting married and combining households, they saw their clergyman, then saw their accountant to find out what to do about selling the extra home. Do they sell before or after they are married? The answer depended on individual circumstances. If both were over age 55, we had to ask if either had used the one-time $125,000 exclusion. If so, then the other needed to sell before the wedding or forfeit his or her right to the exclusion.

Now people planning to remarry don't have to worry about that anymore. They can sell whenever is most convenient, before marriage or after, and if they want to sell both homes and buy a new one—unless they have very large gains—that will generally make sense, too.

Rehabilitate A Building

There are tax advantages for qualified realty rehabilitation expenditures—expenditures that are bound to increase in popularity under the latest incarnation of the tax code.

There are two tiers of tax credit: Twenty percent for rehabilitations of certified historic structures and 10% for rehabilitation of non-residential buildings that were first placed in service before 1936. The expenditures during a two-year period must be more than the greater of $5,000 or the adjusted basis of the property. (The credits are phased out for taxpayers with adjusted gross income above $200,000 and disappear altogether when adjusted gross income reaches $250,000.)

Credits are even available for expenditures incurred by lessees, provided that at the time the rehabilitation is finished, the remaining lease term is at least 27½ years for residential property or, for nonresidential property, at least 39 years.

There are tests, naturally, regarding just what qualifies as rehabilitation. For example, for structures other than those certified as historic, the test is whether at least three-quarters of both the outside walls and the internal framework remain in place. If your building was standing even before Jesse Owens took all the gold at the 1936 Olympics, you may want to redo it for an extra 10% credit.

445

Vacation-Home Loophole For Business Owners

If you own a vacation home, consider having your own company rent it from you to hold one or more business meetings or conferences there.

Key: When you rent a home or vacation home out for 14 or fewer days during the year, the rental income you receive is totally tax free—you don't even have to report it to the IRS. This is true even if your own corporation rents it from you. And your company gets to deduct the rental as a business expense.

Safety: Charge a fair market rent, and document the business purpose of the rental.

James Glass, New York–based tax attorney.

Real Estate Confidential

Randy Bruce Blaustein, Esq., senior tax partner R.B. Blaustein & Co., New York City. Mr. Blaustein is author of *How to Do Business With the IRS* (Prentice Hall).

Through a sale and leaseback of the house, children in high tax brackets can help support their parents and at the same time improve their own tax picture.

How it works: The children buy the house from the parents, using an installment sale, and then rent the house back to the parents. (The installment payments can be set larger than the rental payments, increasing the parents' cash flow.) Since the place is now the children's rental property, they can deduct depreciation, mortgage interest and operating expenses. The parents' gain on the sale may be entirely tax free because of the home-sale exclusion ($250,000 on a single or $500,000 on a joint return). *Note:* Installment-sale treatment will be denied if the children resell to a third party within two years.

Alternate tax saver: Buy a condominium for your parents and rent it to them at fair market rent. You can deduct depreciation, operating expenses, interest, etc.

Planning point: Go over the numbers very carefully. It doesn't always make tax sense to charge rent and take depreciation and operating expenses. You may be better off simply deducting real estate tax and mortgage interest, especially if your income is too high to allow you to deduct the operating losses.

Caution: Watch the passive-loss rules which may limit deductions.

Renting Out Your Vacation Home

Sam Starr, CPA, PricewaterhouseCoopers, Washington, DC.

If you have a vacation home and want to pick up some extra cash by renting it out when you aren't using it, you need to know the tax rules. They severely restrict the deductions you can claim as expenses. You can't ignore the rules. Your tax return (Schedule E) specifically asks if you deduct expenses on a vacation home. Except for "qualified rental periods," the rules apply to any dwelling (including trailers, houseboats, co-ops, etc.) used for part of the year and rented for part. (The rules also apply if you rent out rooms in your home.)

PRIMARY RULES

If the vacation-home rules apply, you can't deduct more than the amount of rent you receive. Losses are not allowable. *In addition, you must deduct expenses in the following prescribed order...*

1. Taxes and mortgage interest that are attributable to the rental period. (You can deduct the balance on Schedule A.)

The IRS says you must prorate on the basis of actual use. If you use the home for one month and rent it for two (and close it down for the rest of the year), you must then allocate two-thirds of interest and taxes to the rental period.

The Tax Court, however, has ruled that you can prorate during the course of the year. If you rent for two months, you allocate 2/12 of taxes and interest to the rental period. This helps the taxpayer. You get these deductions whether you rent or not. So the less interest and taxes you deduct from rental income, the more you can deduct for other costs and depreciation.

2. Operating expenses, such as repairs, electricity, water, etc., are prorated on the basis of use. If you use the home for one month and rent it for two, deduct two-thirds of operating costs.

3. Depreciation is prorated on the basis of use, like operating costs. This is your best deduction. You couldn't claim it if you didn't rent the home. (This also applies to operating expenses.) In addition, it costs you nothing out-of-pocket. Remember, though, that you can't show a loss. If you received $2,000 in rent and deducted $1,900 for interest, taxes and other costs, you can take off only $100 for depreciation, no matter what the actual figure may be.

Example: You use the house for one month and rent it for three months. Total rent is $2,000. Interest and taxes for the year are $1,000. Under the IRS rule, you allocate ¾ ($750) to the rental period; under the Tax Court rule, you allocate ³⁄₁₂ ($250). If operating costs are $800 and depreciation is $2,000, you can deduct ¾. Here's how your figures would look for your tax return:

	IRS rule	Court rule
Income	$2,000	$2,000
Expenses:		
Interest & taxes	$ 750	$ 250
Operating expenses	600	600
Depreciation, limited to	650	1,150
Total expenses	$2,000	$2,000
Schedule A deductions (interest and taxes)	$ 250	$ 750

WHEN YOU CAN AVOID THE RULES

If you rent out your house for 14 days or fewer, you don't have to report the income. Usually only trivial sums are involved. However, if your home is in an area where some annual event shoots up rents for a week or two (Mardi Gras, the Kentucky Derby, a big tennis or golf tournament), you can pick up meaningful tax-free dollars.

If personal use of the vacation home is fewer than 15 days or less than 10% of the number of days rented during the year, whichever is greater, the vacation-home rules don't apply. You can deduct all expenses, even when this gives you a tax loss. Any such loss would be a passive loss, deductible only against passive income, except that $25,000 might be deductible under the rental-loss exception. Check with your tax adviser.

Another problem if you show a tax loss: The so-called "hobby loss" rules will apply. In general, this means that the losses could be challenged by the IRS under the presumption that activities generating losses in three out of five consecutive years may not be engaged in for profit. So if you use the place for a month (30 days) and rent it for nine months (about 275 days), consider leaving a few days early to come within the 10% limit.

You must always prorate expenses, no matter how short the period of personal use. *Example:* You use the house for only five days and rent it for 50. You deduct 50/55 (or ¹⁰⁄₁₁) of total depreciation and operating costs.

Figuring personal use: You count every day the house is used by you, your family or anyone else you allow to use it, unless that person rents for fair value. Lending the place to friends counts as personal use. You can't evade the rule by charging nominal rent.

You do not count days you visit the house to open or close it or to attend to maintenance, repairs and the like.

Renting to relatives: At one time all rental to relatives, whether of a vacation home or of regular rental property, was considered subject to vacation-home rules.

Now, however, the rules for relatives are exactly the same as those for anyone else provided that you charge normal fair market rents. But you must be prepared to prove it. The IRS is always suspicious of transactions between relatives.

Profit motive: Even if you meet the days-of-use test, the IRS may still disallow any tax losses on the grounds that you were not renting the property with the purpose of making a profit or gain.

The Tax Court upheld the IRS ruling that the entire transaction (purchase, rental, etc.) was entered into for personal reasons, not for profit or gain. All losses were disallowed.

Note: Despite the decision described above, buying a retirement home before actually retiring may be a smart move. First, it's possible the IRS won't disallow your losses. Second, you can deduct at least the amount of income received, so you won't owe any taxes. Third, if the property is likely to increase in value, you'd have a strong argument that the property was held for purposes of gain, despite the initial losses. Finally, if you do show a profit for at least three of any five consecutive years, it will be presumed that you are renting for profit.

Tax Rules on Educational Scholarships

Educational scholarships are generally not taxable, except to the extent that they include room and board. *Exception:* If the recipient is required to perform services (such as teaching) as a condition of getting the money. Some or all of it may be considered taxable compensation for services rendered.

Scholarships are not counted in determining child support. If you provide half or more of the support for your child's education, you can claim a dependency exemption.

When a State Refund Is Tax Free on Federal Return

A state income tax refund is taxable only if the state tax was deducted on your previous federal return and the deduction reduced your federal taxes. If you didn't itemize on your federal return last year, you don't have to pay tax on the state refund when you file your

federal return this year. Even if you did itemize last year, a portion of your state refund may have been nontaxable.

SHORTCUT FOR FIGURING THE NONTAXABLE PORTION

• **Find out your standard deduction** for last year.

• **Find your total itemized deductions** and subtract your state income tax deduction.

• **Compare the result of the subtraction** with your standard deduction. If the subtraction result is lower than your standard deduction, the difference between the two figures is the nontaxable portion of your state tax refund. If it's higher, your state refund is fully taxable.

IRS Revenue Ruling 79-15, 1979-1 CB 80.

Life Insurance Dividends

No income tax is due on dividends paid on life insurance policies. This is true whether you receive a check or have the dividends applied against next year's premium. Dividends are viewed as a refund that reduces the cost of your policy, not as part of your income.

Embezzler's Spouse Innocent

A man escaped paying any penalty even though he filed a joint return with his wife, who was an embezzler. *Reason:* He didn't significantly benefit from the embezzled funds. And she had complete control over the family finances.

Dependency Loopholes

You can claim a dependency exemption for unrelated individuals. But these dependents must live with you for the entire year, and your relationship can't violate local morality laws. They can't be your dependent's dependent (e.g., your girlfriend's child).

Another loophole is that, in many cases, greater overall tax savings result if parents claim a newly married daughter as a dependent than if she files a joint return with her husband in the first year of their marriage.

Smart Gift Giving

Well-planned gifts to family members can help preserve wealth by cutting estate and income tax. *Here's how you can do it...*

Each year you can use your gift tax exclusion to make tax-free gifts to as many different recipients as you wish...to children, grandchildren and in-laws. The limit in 2013 is $14,000 to each recipient ($28,000 each if you split gifts with your spouse).

In addition, there is a lifetime gift tax exemption amount of $5.25 million in 2013. So a married couple can plan to use their two exemptions to pass during their lifetime.

How to do it: The simplest way to make gifts is to make full use of your annual gift tax exclusion each year. Over a number of years these gifts—and the investment earnings on them—can add up to big-dollar amounts.

David S. Rhine, regional director of family wealth planning, Sagemark Consulting, division of Lincoln Financial Advisors Corp., registered investment adviser, 395 W. Passaic St., Rochelle Park, New Jersey 07662.

New Baby Loopholes

Edward Mendlowitz, CPA, partner, WithumSmith+ Brown, CPAs, 1 Spring St., New Brunswick, New Jersey 08901. *www.withum.com*

There's nothing wrong with buying rattles and silver cups for your new baby, but these gifts lack the built-in tax advantages that other gifts provide. So—mix and match. *Example:* A pink rattle and a custodial account.

First: Get a Social Security number for the baby right away. Without it you can't open a bank or brokerage account in the child's name or even buy savings bonds.

Next: Consider implementing some of the following strategies that are designed to help newborns and their families whittle down their tax bills...

Loophole: Contribute to a 529 savings plan for the baby. There are no income limits on eligibility to contribute to the plan and earnings on contributions are tax deferred. If withdrawals are used to pay qualified higher educations costs, then they are fully tax free.

Extra break: Contributors can use a special gift tax rule to contribute five times the usual annual gift tax exclusion amount ($14,000 in 2013) without any gift tax. For example, a parent or grandparent can contribute up to $70,000 to the plan in 2013 with no gift tax concern.

Trap: Like any other savings-type account, there are no guarantees that investments will perform as anticipated. A better choice for those who want to ensure that money will be available to pay tuition when needed should opt for a 529 prepaid tuition plan—through a state plan or the private plan in which more than 275 fine institutions participate (go to *www.independent529plan.org* for details)

Loophole: Put your baby to work—as a model or "actor." Children can have earned income—income from work—of up to $6,100 before owing any tax in 2013. Beyond that, earnings up to $8,925 are taxed at 10% and earnings up to $36,250 are taxed at only 15% and up to $5,500 of earnings can be contributed to a Roth IRA.

Loophole: Buy tax-favored investments in the baby's name. You can reduce taxes owed on a baby's investments by putting the money into zero-coupon or regular municipal bonds or bond funds, which pay tax-exempt interest. These investments are suitable until the child is no longer subject to the kiddie tax.

Another good alternative: Growth stocks that pay little or no dividends, such as Internet stocks.

Loophole: Report US savings bond interest annually. When your child receives US savings bonds as gifts, elect on his first tax return to report the bond's interest annually rather than let it accumulate. (File a tax return for the child right away even though you are not required to do so.)

Reason: The baby will owe no tax so long as the interest paid on the bond does not exceed $1,000 a year and is the child's only unearned income. That way, when the child passes the kiddie tax limit and cashes in the bonds, no taxes will be due.

Loophole: Shift future income to the child. While income shifting is not a good idea because most of a young child's income is taxed at the parent's bracket, do consider shifting assets that will produce income in the future.

Example: Put S corporation stock or a limited liability company interest that produces little current income but has future growth potential into a trust for the baby. The appreciation will be taxed at the child's lower rates when he is age 18 or older. *Bonus:* The assets are no longer in the parents' taxable estate.

Loophole: Update your wills to name a guardian for your child in case both of you die. *Reason:* If a guardian isn't named in the parents' wills, the court will appoint one—usually a relative. But the court won't necessarily name the relative that you would choose.

Strategy: You can name two guardians in your will, a "guardian of the person," to care for the child and a "guardian of the property," to look after the child's money if you don't want the same person doing both.

Charitable Contribution Loopholes

Edward Mendlowitz, CPA, partner, WithumSmith+ Brown, CPAs, 1 Spring St., New Brunswick, New Jersey 08901. *www.withum.com*

The Tax Code gives taxpayers bigger breaks for certain kinds of charitable contributions than for others. *Here are some smart ways to maximize the tax benefits of charitable giving…*

Loophole: Donate appreciated securities instead of cash. Giving cash is an expensive

way to make a donation because you're giving money that has already been taxed.

Better: Give securities that have gone up in value since you bought them. You can get a tax deduction for the full market value of the securities and you avoid capital gains tax on the securities' appreciation.

Caution: You must have owned the appreciated assets for more than 12 months to get the full write-off. Otherwise, your deduction will be limited to your basis (tax cost) in the securities.

Limits: Annual deductions for gifts of appreciated property are limited to 30% of your adjusted gross income. (The excess can be carried forward up to five years.)

Loophole: Deduct membership dues paid to a charity to the extent you receive nothing in return. If you do receive something in return, its value must be subtracted from the gift.

Example: If you receive a magazine subscription, the value of that subscription is subtracted from the dues to calculate your charitable deduction. The same is also true when you receive items of nominal value, such as jackets or shirts.

Loophole: Get tax breaks for doing volunteer work. You can't deduct the value of your time or the services you provide as a volunteer, but you can deduct many expenses. *Examples…*

• **You can deduct actual out-of-pocket costs,** including any supplies you buy.

• **When you host a fund-raiser,** the cost of invitations, food, drink, and other expenses is deductible.

• **You can deduct any driving** you do for a charitable organization (14 cents a mile) plus tolls and parking fees.

• **When you attend a convention** of a qualified charity as a chosen representative, you can deduct unreimbursed expenses including meals and lodging.

• **Travel costs are deductible** if you take an active role in leading a trip for a tax-exempt group, such as the Boy Scouts.

Loophole: Deduct contributions to a religious organization for after-school educational programs. The supplementary schooling is not in lieu of a secular education nor is it parochial school education. Rather, it is religious training for a young child. The only benefit is an "intangible religious benefit," which has no financial value in terms of reducing charitable donations.

Caution: The IRS has not ruled on this issue, and tax practitioners differ on whether to take the deduction.

Loophole: Set up your own charitable foundation. Contributions of appreciated securities are tax deductible. You control the timing and method of distribution, and to whom, as long as the recipient is a fully recognized charity (search for IRS Publication 78, *Cumulative List of Organizations,* at *www.irs.gov.* You can even pay yourself (or family members) a reasonable salary for operating the foundation.

Caution: Contributions to charities must equal a minimum of 5% of foundation assets each year. Also, contributions, once made, cannot be used for any other purpose.

Taxpayer Loopholes You Need to Know

Barbara Weltman, Esq., attorney in Millwood, New York, author of *J.K. Lasser's 1001 Deductions and Tax Breaks* (Wiley) and publisher of *Big Ideas for Small Business*, a free monthly e-newsletter. *www.barbaraweltman.com*

You may think that you don't stand a chance in fighting the IRS, but you would be wrong. Taxpayers can be successful. *Here are some recent disputes that resulted in taxpayer victories that can help you in your future handling of similar tax matters and reduce your taxes…*

A TAX BREAK WITHOUT RECEIPTS

A gain on the sale of a personal residence is determined by comparing the sale price with the cost basis, which includes the original price that the owner paid for the home and the costs of capital improvements made over the years. However, many home owners fail to keep records and receipts proving the amount spent on these improvements. Can they be estimated?

In April 2002, Louis Greenwald bought a home in Santa Barbara, California. He made various improvements to the home but retained only some of the invoices. He sold the home in 2005 for $2,650,000. He reported a capital gain of $638,802. His cost basis reflected improvements totaling $387,735.

IRS Position: The gain was $356,515 more than he claimed because he could not substantiate most of the improvements.

Tax Court: The court applied the Cohan doctrine, under which a court can allow a claimed expense even if the taxpayer cannot fully substantiate it. But this requires what the court called an "evidentiary basis" for claiming the expense. The Cohan doctrine typically is used for unsubstantiated travel and entertainment expenses, but the court said that it could and would apply the doctrine to improvements to a residence. It allowed all but $950 of Greenwald's claimed improvements because he was able to list what they were and to estimate how much each cost.

What to do: Even though receipts were not necessary in this case, it's best to keep them, and you should maintain an ongoing record of capital improvements to your home to minimize the gain on an eventual sale. Find a list of improvements to track in IRS Publication 523, *Selling Your Home*, at *www.irs.gov.*

Louis Greenwald, TC Memo 2011-239

VOLUNTEERS MUST PROVE EXPENSES TO CLAIM DEDUCTIONS

Volunteers can claim a tax deduction for out-of-pocket costs—these costs are considered a charitable contribution—but the costs must be substantiated.

In a recent case, Jan Elizabeth Van Dusen of Oakland, California, cared for a total of 70 to 80 feral cats under a foster-cat program. She paid for their food, veterinary bills (for tests, treatment, vaccines and surgery) and other pet supplies totaling $12,068. She had receipts, credit card bills and other documentary proof of her outlays. In 2004, she claimed those costs for a tax deduction.

In another case, Tawana Bradley of Louisville, Kentucky, acting as a volunteer coach for a football cheerleading squad, paid for pizza, party favors and other supplies for a squad party totaling $162.27. She had receipts. In 2006, she claimed this cost for a tax deduction.

IRS Position: Volunteer expenses are subject to the same substantiation rule as cash contributions—they must be proven by canceled checks or bank statements, which these two taxpayers did not have.

Amounts of $250 or more also must be substantiated by a written acknowledgment from the charity.

Tax Court Ruling: Volunteer expenses up to $249 can be substantiated by receipts, credit card slips and other documentary proof—they are acceptable substitutes for canceled checks. Although Van Dusen was able to declare only a small portion of her expenses, the ruling set a precedent for other cases, such as Bradley's.

Caution: If the amount to be deducted is $250 or more, you do need a written acknowledgment from the charity, just as if you had made a cash donation.

Lesson: Learn the substantiation rules for charitable donations (go to IRS Publication 526, *Charitable Contributions*, at *www.irs.gov*) to claim the full extent of your out-of-pocket costs.

For example, track vehicle mileage incurred on behalf of charitable activities so that you can deduct mileage at the rate of 14¢ per mile.

Jan Elizabeth Van Dusen, 136 TC No. 25 (2011); Tawana Bradley, TC Summary Opinion 2011-120

PROVING THAT A BUSINESS IS NOT A HOBBY FOR TAX PURPOSES

An activity that loses money may be treated as a hobby by the IRS—meaning that expenses in excess of the business's income are not deductible—unless the taxpayer can demonstrate that there is a "profit motive."

In one recent case, Peter Morton, co-founder of the Hard Rock Cafe, owned or controlled several businesses related to his Hard Rock brand. One was an *S corporation* (a corporation that does not pay federal income tax) that owned a Gulfstream jet. This S corporation never made money.

IRS Position: Losses from the S corporation that owns the plane are nondeductible because the S corporation represented a hobby activity.

Federal Claims Court: The determination of whether a taxpayer has a profit motive (and therefore is not engaged in a hobby activity) can be based on the "aggregation" of business activities—treating them as related activities—rather than considering the businesses as entirely separate. In this case, Morton's various corporations were interrelated in terms of their activities—and all furthered the Hard Rock brand. As detailed by flight logs, he used the plane for personal and business travel, including the promotion of the Hard Rock brand and activities related to the Hard Rock Hotel and Casino in Las Vegas. Since his use was in furtherance of his corporate "brand," it supported his overall profit motive and so was not a hobby activity.

Lesson: You don't have to be a mogul (or own a jet) for this ruling to help you. What it means is that you can maintain separate but related companies—even small companies—while aggregating them only for the tax purpose of demonstrating a profit motive.

Morton v. United States, No. 08-804C (Fed. Cl 2011)

20

Tax Deductions

How to Deduct Your Vacation

here are several ways to get tax deductions for vacation travel. One is to plan a trip that concentrates on business as its primary purpose. Even if a trip is essentially personal, it's often desirable to tack on business activities and get a partial write-off. And sometimes you can combine good works with leisure and get a charity deduction for the cost of your travel.

BUSINESS VS. PLEASURE

Basic rule: When business and personal activities are mixed, traveling expenses are deductible if the primary purpose of the trip is business. *Included:* All fares, room and meals and incidental expenses such as phone calls, laundry and local transportation.

Whether a trip is primarily business or personal depends on various factors. *Key question:*

Is this a trip that would not have been made but for the business activities that were planned? The amount of time you spend on each activity is an important indicator of the primary purpose. But you can spend a reasonable amount of time on recreation without changing the primary focus of the trip.

OVERSEAS TRAVEL

If you spend more than one week outside the US and more than 25% of the days you're away are not business days, your write-offs are reduced. *Amount of the reduction:* A percentage of the write-offs equal to the percentage of nonbusiness days.

When traveling overseas, a business day is a day in which...

• **Your principal activity during normal business hours is business.** *Note:* Even if you spend more time on nonbusiness activity than on business, the day can still be a business day. *Important:* Don't cram all your business

Edward Mendlowitz, CPA, partner, WithumSmith+ Brown, CPAs, 1 Spring St., New Brunswick, New Jersey 08901. *www.withum.com*

appointments into a single day. Spread them out over the course of your trip.

And even a day on which you don't do any business at all can be counted as a business day, provided...

• **You're traveling to or from a business destination.**

• **You would have done business but circumstances beyond your control,** such as a blizzard or a strike, kept you from doing so.

• **It's a weekend or holiday** that's preceded and followed by days on which you actually do business.

BUSINESS TRAVEL ESSENTIALS

Keep a simple diary showing what your principal business activities were each day. *It should include...*

• **Who you saw.**

• **When and for how long you met.**

• **The business purpose of the meeting.**

For business entertainment, include the place you met and the amount of the bill, as well as a receipt if the bill is over $75.

ALTERNATE STRATEGY

If you can't make business the primary purpose of your trip, see whether you can arrange to travel on behalf of a recognized charity. It may take some imagination, but this tactic has worked in a variety of situations. *Examples...*

• **Lay delegates to a church convention,** attending in an official capacity.

• **American Legion convention delegates.**

• **A safari to bring back specimens for a museum.**

• **Members of the National Ski Patrol.**

Not useful: Conventions that are open to all members of the sponsoring organization unless you are designated to fulfill some special role in the proceeding.

To qualify for this type of write-off, the benefit to the sponsoring charity must be primary.

SUGGESTIONS

• **Arrange in advance** to represent the organization in some official capacity.

• **Document the relationship** between your trip and the organization's goals.

• **Show what tangible benefit** the organization is getting from your trip.

• **Have the charity reimburse** a small part of your costs, if possible.

Discuss travel plans with your tax adviser as early as possible. Innovative tax planning is your adviser's business. Focus on how to make the trip deductible and how to maintain the kind of records you'll need. And have a good trip.

• **Ship travel can be an asset** on a combined business-vacation trip. *Reason:* Days spent in transit count as business days in the allocation formula. *Example:* A two-day business meeting in Paris followed by a two-week European vacation. If you fly (one day each way), only 22% is deductible (two business days plus two travel days out of a total of 18 days away). But if you sail (five days each way), 46% is deductible (two business days plus 10 travel days out of a total 26 days away).

State Taxes Can Lower Federal Taxes

State and local taxes can reduce your federal taxable income in a variety of ways. *Here are a few examples...*

• **Real estate taxes are deductible, of course.** Many people own vacation homes or land held for investment. Real estate taxes on these properties are deductible along with taxes on your personal residence.

If you bought or sold a home during the year, the real estate tax deduction is shared between buyer and seller. It's based on the length of time each held title. You can usually find out how the taxes were prorated by looking at the closing papers for your house.

• **State and local income taxes.** You are allowed to deduct all the state or local income tax withheld from your pay even if you expect part of it to be refunded when you file your state or local return. Beyond that, if you filed a return last year that had a balance due, that balance is deductible on this year's federal return provided you paid it this year.

Did the IRS audit you this year? If it did, and if you ended up with a balance due, you probably got a bill for additional state income tax as well. (The IRS exchanges audit information with state taxing authorities.) If you paid any back state income tax this year, don't forget to deduct it on your federal return.

- **State and local sales taxes.** For 2013, you can opt to deduct your sales taxes if you do not deduct state and local income taxes. The deduction can be based on your actual receipts, showing taxes paid, or by relying on IRS tables.

- **Other taxes.** If you live in a state with a disability tax, or one where employees have part of the unemployment tax withheld from their pay, you can add that to your state income tax deduction.

Auto registration fees are deductible in some states. If the amount of the fee is based on the value of the vehicle, you can deduct it. In some states a portion of the fee is based on value. That portion is deductible. *States with vehicle fees partly or fully deductible:* AL, AR, AZ, CA, CO, GA, IA, IN, KY, LA, MI, MN, MO, MS, MT, NE, NH, NV, SC, WA, WY. Any other personal-property tax or fee based on the property's value is also deductible. *Examples:* Fees for boats and motorcycles.

Deduct a Boat as A Second Home

Can a person qualify his/her boat as a second home in order to get an interest deduction for the loan used to finance its purchase? If so, how?

The answer is yes. The IRS has ruled many times that a boat can qualify as a residence. And under standard IRS rules, a property qualifies as a residence if it is used by the owner as such for the greater of either 14 days during the year or 10% of the total days during which it is leased to outsiders. Thus, if you're not in the practice of leasing out your boat, it seems that a simple two-week vacation trip taken in it will qualify it as a second home.

Also important: To qualify as a residence, the boat must include both cooking and bathroom facilities.

Capital Losses Loophole

Capital losses are fully deductible against capital gains. However, $3,000 of ordinary income (e.g., salary) can be offset by capital losses in excess of capital gains in any single year. Unused losses can be carried over into future years.

Home-Office Deduction

More people can deduct a home office. The law lets an office be deducted if it is needed for keeping records for a business primarily conducted elsewhere—an exception to the general requirement that a home office be the principal place where the taxpayer conducts a business. However, to use this rule, you cannot have another office outside your home.

Barbara Weltman, an attorney in Millwood, New York. *www.barbaraweltman.com.* She is author of several books, including *The Complete Idiot's Guide to Starting a Home-Based Business,* 3rd edition (Alpha).

Timing Your Deductions

John J. Tuozzolo, associated with the firm Collins, Hannafin, Garamella, Jaber & Tuozzolo, PC, 148 Deer Hill Ave., Danbury, Connecticut 06810.

Medical costs are deductible to the extent that they exceed 10% (7.5% if you are 65 or older) of adjusted gross income. The figure is 10% for casualty and theft losses.

Strategy: Maximize tax benefits by piling two or more years of deductions into a single year (thus topping the limits). It may seem as though you have little choice as to when to take these deductions. But often there is a choice. That's because these items are not deductible until it is clear that they will not be compensated for, by insurance or otherwise. Even if the chance of an insurance recovery seems remote, you should file a claim. Otherwise the IRS can deny the deduction on the grounds that the insurer might have paid off.

When you want a deduction immediately, process your insurance claim as quickly as possible. Pressure the insurer for a quick response so you get either the money or the deduction right away. It may even be worthwhile to offer the insurer a compromise in order to get a quick determination.

If you feel that you will be in a higher tax bracket in a future year, you can delay the deduction by processing your insurance claim in a very deliberate manner. Take your time collecting relevant information and ask for clarifications. The insurance company is not likely to hurry you.

Also: Seek reimbursement for your loss from other related parties. Put your requests in writing. Even if there is little chance of their coming through, the possibility that they might will help justify your delaying the deduction until a later year.

When Tax Treatment Depends on Which Credit Card You Use

The general rule is that you only get a tax deduction in the year you actually pay for a deductible expense. But there's an important exception when you pay with a credit card. For tax purposes, payment is considered made on the date of the transaction, not on the date you pay the credit card company. You can sign now and deduct this year but pay next year.

Medical and dental expenses paid by credit card are deductible in the year you sign for the charge rather than in the year you pay the credit card company. You can boost your deductions this year by putting year-end medical expenses on your credit card.

Caution: If you charge a deductible expense on a credit card issued by the company supplying the deductible goods (or services), you can't take a deduction until the credit card bill is paid.

Example: If you have a prescription filled at a department-store pharmacy and charge it on a credit card issued by the store, you can't deduct the cost of that medication until you get the bill and pay it. But if you charge the same prescription on a credit card issued by a third party, such as MasterCard or VISA, you can deduct it right away.

Wonderful Deductible Moving Expenses

The expenses of a job-related move are deductible whether or not you itemize your other deductions. *Requirements...*

• **The distance between your new place of work and your old principal residence** must be at least 50 miles farther than the distance from your old residence to your old place of work.

• **You must work at least 39 weeks during the 12-month period** immediately after your arrival in the new work location. This work need not be for a single employer, nor do the 39 weeks have to be consecutive.

Deductible moving expenses include...

1. Travel expenses, including lodging, for the taxpayer and his/her family while en route to the new location.

2. The cost of moving household goods, personal effects and automobiles owned by yourself and members of your household.

John J. Tuozzolo, associated with the firm Collins, Hannafin, Garamella, Jaber & Tuozzolo, PC, 148 Deer Hill Ave., Danbury, Connecticut 06810.

Neglected Medical Deductions

You can deduct medical bills paid for a person who qualifies as a dependent, even though you can't claim a dependency exemption for that person, provided that you paid more than half that person's support in either the year the bills were run up or the year they were paid. A similar rule applies to married couples. You can deduct bills paid now for a former spouse as long as you were married when the bills were incurred. You can deduct medical costs paid for your child if you are divorced and the child lives with and is a dependent of your divorced spouse.

• **Weight-reduction programs to improve your general health are not deductible,** even when recommended by a doctor. But a weight-reduction program prescribed as treatment for hypertension, obesity and hearing loss was ruled deductible. *Key:* The program was prescribed to treat specific ailments.

IRS Letter Ruling 8004111.

• **A transplant donor can deduct surgical, hospital and laboratory costs and transportation expenses.** So can a prospective donor, even if found to be unacceptable. If the recipient pays the expenses, the recipient gets the deduction.

IRS Revenue Ruling 68-452; IRS Revenue Ruling 73-189.

• **Removing lead-based paint and covering areas within a child's reach** with wallboard to help prevent and cure further lead poisoning are deductible expenses. But paint removal and wallboard for areas beyond the reach of the child are not—nor is the cost of repainting.

IRS Revenue Ruling 79-66.

• **A clarinet and lessons are deductible medical expenses** when prescribed to cure teeth defects.

IRS Revenue Ruling 62-210, 1962-2 CB 89.

• **Both the installation and the operating cost of a home-computerized visual alert system** to offset a taxpayer's deafness are deductible as medical expenses.

IRS Letter Ruling 8250040.

Also deductible: Whiskey prescribed for heart disease.

How to Beat the 10% Limit on Your Medical Deductions

Edward Mendlowitz, CPA, partner, WithumSmith+ Brown, CPAs, 1 Spring St., New Brunswick, New Jersey 08901. *www.withum.com*

Everyone has medical expenses and everyone now faces a tough limit on deducting them—you can only deduct those expenses that are in excess of 10% of your adjusted gross income. But there are ways to beat the limit.

• **Double up.** Maximize your medical deductions by bunching payments in alternate years. If you're not going to meet the 10% threshold this year, defer paying medical bills until next year, when your combined expenses may put you over the limit.

On the other hand, if you're clearly going to meet the limit this year, stock up on medicine and drugs, pay outstanding medical and dental bills before year-end and consider having planned dental work and voluntary surgery done (and paid for) this year rather than next.

• **Hold off.** If you don't plan to itemize your deductions this year, postpone paying medical bills until January. You'll get no deduction for them this year, while next year you might.

• **Drugs.** Only prescription drugs and insulin can now be deducted as medical expenses. *Tip:* Many over-the-counter drugs can also be bought on prescription. Ask your doctor for prescriptions for patent drugs you use. *Trap:* The price, as a prescription, may be higher.

• **Dependents.** You are entitled to include in your deductions medical expenses you pay on behalf of a dependent. *Bonus:* You can deduct medical expenses for a family member who meets all the requirements for being claimed as your dependent except that he or she has too much income. *Suggestion:* Make your support dollars do double duty by paying the medical bills of someone you're helping to support. Those payments could get you both a dependency deduction and a medical-expense deduction.

•**Life care.** The medical-expense portion of a lump-sum life-care fee paid to a retirement home for a parent is fully deductible as a medical expense in the year the fee is paid. You may be better off taking a deduction now for future medical care rather than making annual payments.

•**Separate returns.** It is sometimes advantageous for a married couple to file separate returns when one spouse, but not the other, has heavy medical expenses. On a joint return, medical expenses must exceed 7.5% of a couple's combined adjusted gross income. But if separate returns are filed, only the income of the spouse with the big medical bills is considered for the deduction limit. (The only way to tell for sure whether it's better to file jointly or separately is to work out the figures both ways.)

•**For bosses.** Owners of closely held C corporations, especially those with a few other employees, may avoid the 10% limit by setting up a company medical-reimbursement plan. As long as the plan covers all employees and does not favor those who are highly compensated, the company can reimburse its employees (including officer-stockholders) for their actual medical bills. The reimbursed amounts are tax deductible by the corporation and are not taxable income to the employees. The 10% limit does not apply. *Caution:* The IRS can rule that the plan is discriminatory if it favors highly paid employees. If this happens, the value of the benefits will be taxed to the recipient.

Doctor's orders: Obvious medical expenses include prescription drugs, doctor, dentist and psychiatrist bills, hospital costs and laboratory fees. *Less obvious expenses include…*

•**Transportation costs back and forth to the doctor's or the dentist's office,** by cab, train or bus. If you drive, you can deduct as a medical expense either your actual car expenses or the IRS allowance of 24¢ per mile in 2013 (plus tolls and parking, whichever method you use).

•**Lodging.** A patient and an individual accompanying him can each deduct up to $50 per night of lodging expenses—but not meals—on a trip to an out-of-town hospital facility to get necessary medical care.

•**Marriage counseling** is deductible if performed by a licensed psychologist or psychiatrist. So is sex therapy.

•**Home improvements that are medically required** are deductible to the extent that they do not increase the value of your property. (If a pool for an arthritis sufferer costs $10,000 to install and increases the value of the house by $6,000, the deduction is usually limited to $4,000.) Improvements required to accommodate a disability (e.g., ramps) are fully deductible, regardless of any increase to the home's value.

•**Travel simply for a change of scenery is not deductible.** But trips recommended by a doctor to treat a specific ailment are deductible. *Example:* A trip to Arizona by an asthma victim or by someone whose postoperative throat condition is aggravated by cold weather.

•**Stop-smoking program** (including the cost of prescription drugs to alleviate nicotine withdrawal), but not over-the-counter nicotine patches and gum.

•**Weight-loss programs prescribed by a doctor** as treatment for a specific medical condition, such as hypertension, are deductible. *Not deductible:* Weight loss to improve general health, appearance and well-being. Get a letter from your doctor recommending a specific program as treatment for a specific disorder.

Also deductible if prescribed by a doctor as treatment for a specific medical condition are…

•Speech therapy.

•Health club visits.

•Special filters for air conditioners…ionizers to purify the air…and filters to purify drinking water.

•Special foods taken in addition to your normal diet.

Other deductible medical expenses include…

•Birth-control pills, abortions that are legal under local law, vasectomies.

•Acupuncture, hearing aids, eyeglasses, contact lenses, dentures and braces.

•Orthopedic shoes, medically required shoe lifts, support hose and surgical belts.

Tax Credit on Dependent Care

Suppose your mother lives with you and you support her. She becomes severely ill for several months and you hire a private nurse to take care of her while you're working. Should you claim a medical deduction, or take the dependent care credit, or both?

You can take your choice—figure out which gives you the biggest tax savings. Or you can split the expense between the two. For example, if you spent $5,000, you might allocate $3,000 to the dependent care credit (the maximum allowable) and claim the $2,000 balance as a medical-expense deduction. But you can't get a credit and a deduction for the same money.

Mother Aid

A son paid his mother's medical expenses with money he withdrew from her bank account under a power of attorney. The IRS disallowed the son's deduction for these expenses, saying the money was really the mother's. But the Court of Appeals allowed the deduction. The money was legally his—a gift from his mother to him.

John M. Ruch, CA 5, 82-4463.

Deductions for Special Schools

Two children suffering from language learning disabilities were sent to a special school.

Costs were $1,800 above regular tuition. The school had no staff psychiatrists or psychologists, and no doctor had prescribed that the children be sent there. The IRS refused the $1,800 as a medical deduction. The Tax Court reversed. Although the children didn't need medical treatment, their disorders were severe enough to make normal education impossible. The teachers, though not medical personnel, were trained.

Lawrence F. Fay, 76 TC 408.

Recently, the IRS ruled that special schooling for a child with dyslexia was a deductible medical expense.

IRS Letter Ruling 2005 21003.

How to Avoid the 2% Floor for Miscellaneous Deductions

Richard Lager, former partner, Grant Thornton, CPAs, 1900 M St. NW, Washington, DC 20036. *www.grantthornton.com*

Miscellaneous itemized deductions include expenses that are directly connected with the production of investment income, such as...

1. Fees for managing investment property.
2. Legal and professional fees.
3. Fees for tax preparation and advice, investment advice and financial planning.

Problem: Most taxpayers are unable to deduct any investment expenses on Schedule A because their total miscellaneous expenses don't exceed 2% of their adjusted gross income.

Solution: Put as many expenses as possible out of reach of the 2% floor by accounting for them elsewhere on your return. *Possibilities...*

•**Schedule C.** Report nonwage miscellaneous income, such as that earned from consulting, lecturing or speaking engagements, on Schedule C as business income rather than as "other income" on Schedule A. The expenses you incur in producing that income are deductible on your Schedule C, where they are not subject to the 2% floor.

- **Schedule E.** Expenses of earning rent, royalties or other income that is reportable on Schedule E are deductible on Schedule E, where they are not subject to the 2% floor.

- **Adjust the cost of assets.** Add all the expenses of acquiring a capital asset to the asset's cost. This will reduce the amount of capital gain you must report when you eventually sell. Although this approach doesn't give you a current deduction for the expenses, it does reduce the tax you pay on the gain.

- **Bunch payment of expenses** so that you get two years' worth into one year and exceed the 2% floor in at least one year.

Home Improvements

If you make a capital improvement to your home for medical reasons, you get a medical deduction, but not for full cost. It must be reduced by any increase in the resale value of the property. *Example:* Your wife has a respiratory illness. On her doctor's orders, you install a central air-conditioning system at a cost of $12,000. The new system increases the value of your home by $8,000. You can claim a deduction of $4,000. You can also deduct, in full, the costs of operating, maintaining and repairing the system.

Medically required home improvements, such as elevators, air conditioners and swimming pools, qualify in part as deductible medical expenses. In order to get the deduction, the taxpayer making the improvement must have a property interest in the home. *Recent ruling:* A polio victim who had a specially designed swimming pool installed at his parents' home could not deduct part of the cost. Although he lived in the house, he had no ownership interest in it.

IRS Letter Ruling 8249025.

Hotel Stay Not Deductible

An asthmatic was told by her doctor to stay in air-conditioned rooms. When her home air conditioner broke down, she spent the night in a motel. *IRS ruling:* Although the cost of operating the home air-conditioning system might be a deductible medical expense, the motel bill was not deductible. *Reason:* No medical care was furnished at the motel.

IRS Letter Ruling 8317035.

Charitable Donations

Edward Mendlowitz, CPA, partner, WithumSmith+ Brown, CPAs, 1 Spring St., New Brunswick, New Jersey 08901. *www.withum.com*

The easiest way to make a charitable donation is by a check. But other kinds of gifts to public charities can also produce large tax savings and may accomplish the same charitable objectives at less cost.

- **Donate appreciated assets (stocks, bonds, real estate) rather than cash.** If you've held the property for more than a year, you're entitled to a double tax benefit. You can deduct the full market value of the property as a charitable contribution, and you avoid paying capital gains tax on the appreciation. *Deduction limit:* 30% of your adjusted gross income. Any excess is deductible in the five succeeding tax years.

- **Set up a charitable remainder trust, preferably with securities that have gone up in value.** Most commonly, this kind of trust pays you a fixed amount of income each year until your death and then distributes the remaining assets to charity. *Loophole:* You get a tax deduction now for a gift the charity won't receive until sometime in the future. In the meantime, you continue to have the use of the money.

Example: A man of 55 sets up a charitable remainder trust with securities that cost him $25,000 but are now worth $50,000. He reserves an income of $3,000 a year for life. *Tax benefits:* An immediate charitable deduction of nearly $20,000 (the present value of the charity's remainder interest). And even though this deduction is based on the stock's current value, no tax has to be paid on the appreciation.

Fund the trust with municipal bonds and you will also avoid paying tax on the income you receive from the trust. If you set up the trust with very long-term municipal bonds, your yield might well exceed current money-market rates. And it's completely tax free.

• **Contribute to a pooled income fund.** Many charities maintain investment funds called pooled income funds. The fund "pools" the contributions of individual donors, each of whom has retained the right to receive an income for life from their contributions. *Tax loopholes:* Similar to those of a charitable remainder trust. *Investment benefits:* Funds are diversified. You get the benefit of professional management without having to pay for establishing and administering a trust. *Drawback:* Pooled income funds are not permitted to invest in municipal bonds or other tax-exempt securities.

• **Charitable lead trusts are the reverse of charitable remainder trusts.** Instead of providing you with an income, the charity gets the income from the trust assets for a certain number of years, usually eight to 10. When the trust's term is over, the assets are returned to you. *Loophole:* You get a big up-front tax deduction for the value of the charity's income interest.

Lead trusts make a lot of sense for high-earning taxpayers who intend to retire in a few years. The trust gives them a big tax deduction in an earning year, lets them continue to provide for their favorite charity and gives them the security of knowing that the trust assets will be available for their own use during retirement.

• **Community trusts.** Another way to get maximum tax benefits from your charitable donations is to set up a fund in your own name through a recognized public charity that will serve as a conduit to other charities that you recommend. *Loophole:* You get a deduction when you set up the fund without the

pressure of having to name specific charities at that time. Set up the fund and get big tax deductions in high-income years—for example, the years just before retirement. In the years after your retirement, the fund will make donations in your name to the various charities that you suggest. *Problem:* You can't order the charity that is administering the fund to make donations. You can only suggest the beneficiaries. But the administering charities usually do follow a donor's suggestions.

• **Gifts of life insurance.** The mere act of naming a charity as the beneficiary of a policy on your life will not provide you with an income tax deduction. To guarantee a deduction, you must give up all ownership rights in the policy. *Loophole:* Have the charity own the policy, and make annual contributions to the charity. The charity will use its own money to pay the premiums. You will get a current income tax deduction for your annual gifts, and you will have given the charity a very large gift—with the proceeds payable on your death.

Fair Market Value Defined

The fair market value of property donated to charity means the price paid in a market transaction by the ultimate user. If, for example, you donate used furniture to charity, its value is not the price a used furniture dealer pays you, but the price at which the dealer sells it to a customer.

Goldman, 388 F.2d (6th Cir.), aff'g 46 TC 126.

Personal Deduction for Corporate Donation

A way for owners of closely held companies to use company funds to get a charitable deduction on their personal income tax returns is for the owner to give the charity stock in his company. Subsequently, the company redeems the stock from the charity. *Advantage:* A 100% owner would not give up any ownership interest in the company, since his interest in the company after the charity's stock is redeemed would still be 100%.

How a bailout works: The owner makes an informal agreement with the charity to offer the stock for redemption shortly after the charity receives it. The owner gives the stock to the charity. He takes a deduction on his personal return for the fair market value of the stock. A week or so later, the company redeems the stock from the charity. If the transaction is handled properly, the stock's redemption will not be taxed as a dividend to the owner.

Caution: The agreement with the charity must be informal. The charity must not be under a binding obligation to let the company redeem the stock. It must have the legal right to retain the stock or to sell it to an outsider.

Tax rule: Normally if a 100% shareholder in a closely held company has some of his stock redeemed, income from the redemption will be taxed to him as a dividend. But the IRS has agreed that a redemption will not be considered a dividend if it is handled by an informal prearranged plan with a charity. Such a transaction must be structured properly to ensure the desired tax results. Check with your accountant or attorney.

Tom C. Klein, CPA, 450 Seventh Ave., New York City 10123. *www.tckcpa.com*

Bargain Sale To Charity

A business owner sold some of his company's stock to a charity for less than its market value. The charity, to obtain usable cash, intends to have the company redeem the stock at market value.

IRS: The owners can claim a charitable deduction for the discount he gave on the price of the shares.

Benefit: The owner gets to deduct a cash payment that will be made by the company.

IRS Letter Ruling 8307134.

Family Gift Trap

If you help a family member to make payments on his home mortgage, neither of you may be able to deduct the interest.

Trap: To deduct the interest, you must actually pay and be legally obligated to pay it. If you're not named on the mortgage, you are not legally obligated to pay and can't deduct the payments you do make. The family member you're helping can't deduct the payments either, because he/she is not making them.

Solutions: Make cash gifts to the family member, who can then use them to make payments and claim the deduction, or…if you want to claim the deduction yourself, acquire a partial interest in the home to become jointly liable on the mortgage.

Market Value of Donated Land

Three people donated adjacent tracts of land to a university. They valued the tracts as one when determining the property's market value. This increased the value and their charitable deductions. But the IRS said the tracts should be valued separately. *Tax Court:* The university intended to use the three tracts as a single property, on which it planned to build a research facility. So it would have to pay the higher price to buy similar land in the market. The higher deduction was justified.

Charles Ivey, TC Memo 1983-273.

Maximum Deduction On Donated Land

When you donate property to charity, your maximum deduction may be less than the property's market value.

Recent case: A partnership owned valuable real estate. One of the partners gave his interest in the partnership to a charity and claimed a $180,000 deduction. The IRS challenged it.

Court of Claims: The property was subject to a mortgage. Moreover, the other partners had to be paid off before the charity could liquidate its holdings. So the net value of the charitable contribution was only $1,000.

Dan L. Beaird, Ct. Cl., No. 491-80T.

Art Donations

The IRS challenges and eventually alters more than half of the art appraisals it receives to justify deductions for gifts to museums and other nonprofit institutions. And yet according to the IRS, properly prepared appraisals are readily accepted.

What makes the difference? A good appraiser who documents the figures with research. Such experts charge by the hour, not a percentage of the appraisal figure, and provide the essentials for substantiating the deduction.

They include…

• **A careful description of the piece of art,** including the size, medium and artist and the date and place of origin.

• **A statement of the work's condition,** including the relative importance of flaws and imperfections.

• **Research establishing the authenticity of the work** and the historical significance of the artist.

• **Documentation of recent sale prices of similar pieces of art** and/or works by the same artist.

Important: Record the date, place and price of purchase.

The Collector-Investor.

• **The gift of a painting to a nonprofit retirement center** entitled its donor to a charitable deduction for the painting's full fair market value.

IRS ruling: The charity's use of the painting was related to its charitable function. The center displayed works of art in its public areas to keep the residents alert and to encourage their arts-and-crafts activities.

IRS Letter Ruling 8247062.

Rules for Deductible Donations

Donated household items can be deducted only if they are in "good" condition—but the IRS has not defined what that means. If a donated item is not in good condition but is still worth more than $500, you must get a qualified appraisal at the time of the donation. If a total donation exceeds $500 even though no one item does, IRS form 8283, *Noncash Charitable Contributions*, must be filed, explaining when the items were acquired, at what cost, what the fair-market value is and how the value was determined. *Information:* Consult your tax adviser.

Sidney Kess, Esq., CPA, New York City, and coauthor of *1040 Preparation and Planning Guide* (CCH).

Charity Traps

Anselmo donated 461 colored gems to a museum and claimed a charitable contribution for their retail value. But the IRS objected. *Tax Court:* If Anselmo were to sell the gems, he would have to do so to a wholesale dealer. So he was entitled to a deduction only for their lower wholesale value.

Ronald Anselmo, 80 TC 872, aff'd, CA-11, 85-1 USTC.

The cost of tickets to a benefit performance for a charitable organization may not be deductible. The cost of tickets to a concert or show is deductible to the extent that it exceeds the going rate for tickets to similar events. That is because you cannot deduct a contribution when you get something of equal value in return. So if there's no premium built into the price of the tickets, there's no deduction.

Give Money to Charity And Keep Earning Interest on It

It's possible to give money to charity, take a deduction and still receive interest for life. It's called a charitable remainder trust. The trustees can agree to pay the donor a percentage of the principal every year. Or a fixed number of dollars. Or the trustees may pool the gift with others and pay a pro rata share of the earnings of the combined fund. The payments continue as long as the donor lives.

The full contribution is not deductible. The deduction will be the actuarially determined value today of the money at some time in the future, when the charity gets full use of it. It depends on the giver's age. For a man of 55, it would be 42%. For a woman of 55, 34%.

If the property has appreciated, the calculation is based on current value, and there's no capital gains tax. But in the case of a gift of appreciated property, the deduction can't be more than 30% of adjusted gross income. The usual limit is 50%. (Any excess can be carried forward.)

Most charities have already set up the procedures and paid the lawyers; there shouldn't be any fees. But you can't change your mind. It must be a permanent transfer of ownership.

Give a House to Charity And Keep Living in It

It's possible to give a home to charity but continue to live in it for as long as either spouse lives. Then the charitable organization takes title and possession. It works for vacation houses or any other real estate, but not for personal property (paintings, jewelry, etc.).

The catch: The tax deduction for the charitable contribution is less than the full value of the property. It's some fraction of the value, determined by an actuarial calculation according to life expectancy. Since the charity won't get the property until sometime in the future, the present value of the gift is less than the full value of the property.

Example: A home is donated by a 70-year-old man and his 68-year-old wife, with provision that they keep the house as long as either one lives, then it goes to the charity. In the year of the gift, they would get a charitable deduction for 41.5% of the value of the house.

Leftover Oil for Charity

Home owners who convert from oil to gas heat may be able to get a charitable deduction for the oil left in their tanks.

IRS ruling: Home owners who had the unused oil removed from their tanks by a utility company, which then delivered it to a local charity, were allowed a deduction for the retail price of the oil at the time the gift was made.

IRS Letter Ruling 8134209.

Deductible Antidrug Campaign

After two of his children fell victim to drug addiction, a taxpayer dedicated himself to stamping out drugs in the community. He worked with law-enforcement agents, providing money for informants and for purchases from pushers. The Tax Court ruled that he was entitled to a charitable deduction for his expenses, as they were directly related to state law-enforcement services, even though his motivation was strictly personal.

Sherman H. Sampson, TC Memo 1982-276.

Religious Activities Can Be Deducted

All out-of-pocket expenses of volunteer work for your church are deductible (but not the value of your time). Say you provide auto transportation for a church group. You can deduct either your actual out-of-pocket car expenses or the IRS standard mileage allowance. Whichever you choose, parking and tolls are deductible.

Deduction Rules for Volunteer Work

How can a couple get a deduction for all the time one spouse puts into volunteer work for charity?

Unfortunately, they can't deduct the value of the spouse's services. But they can deduct all out-of-pocket expenses, such as luncheons and dinners, transportation (including car use at 14¢ per mile), parking fees and tolls, telephone calls and uniforms, such as those worn by Red Cross volunteers. Meals and lodging are also deductible when the work required the volunteer to be out-of-town overnight.

Thrift Shops and Charities

A charitable organization allowed the operator of a thrift shop to use the charity's name in return for a total of 20% of gross sales. The IRS ruled that donations to the thrift shop were not deductible; they were neither "to" nor "for the use of" the charity.

Nondeductible Promise

A taxpayer claimed a charitable deduction for a promissory note she had given to a charity. The IRS disallowed the deduction and the courts agreed.

Decision: A promise to make a gift is not deductible. The taxpayer must wait until she actually sends the charity money before she can take a charitable deduction.

Nancy J. O'Neil, CA-9, No. 82-4128.

Voluntary Alimony Payment Not Deductible

Before the divorce, a husband paid his wife "temporary" alimony for five months before a state court fixed spouse support. The IRS disallowed this deduction because it wasn't paid pursuant to a separation agreement or divorce decree.

Tax Court: For the IRS. For the husband to deduct alimony payments, the wife must be required to include them in income. But wives don't have to include predivorce payments that aren't made under a written separation agreement or a support order.

Kirk A. Keegan, Jr., TC Memo 1997-359.

Cohabitation Penalty

A husband who continued to live in the same house with his estranged wife pending their divorce was ordered by the court to pay all mortgage and utility costs. The husband deducted these payments as alimony.

Tax Court ruling: No deduction. Alimony payments are deductible only when a couple is living separated and apart. Living estranged in separate parts of the same house does not constitute separation within the meaning of the tax law.

Alexander Washington, 77 TC No. 44.

Fixed-Amount Alimony

Support payments a husband made under an agreement to pay his separated wife whatever it took to maintain her former standard of living may be deductible by the husband even though the agreement did not set a specific dollar amount.

Tax Court: The IRS was wrong to automatically deny the husband a deduction simply because the agreement didn't fix a sum. The tax law on separation agreements says nothing about fixing a sum.

Patience C. Jacklin, 79 TC 340.

Verbal Alimony

Additional payments a separated husband made to his wife under a verbal modification of their written separation agreement were not deductible as alimony.

Reason: To be deductible, payments to a separated spouse must be required under the terms of a written separation agreement. Verbal agreements won't do.

Eugene H. Bishop, TC Memo 1983-240.

Fine Points of Alimony

A separated couple hasn't gone through any court proceedings and isn't planning to. Does he get any deductions for the money he sends to help support her and the kids? Is it considered alimony?

If there is a written separation agreement between the husband and wife, he can deduct amounts specified as alimony. If there are children, the custodial spouse has the right to claim dependency exemptions for them, unless he or she formally waives the right to the exemptions.

• **A husband agreed to give his wife property valued at more than half of their combined net worth.** But the divorce papers did not describe any part of the settlement as alimony. When the husband claimed an alimony deduction for his monthly payments, the IRS said they were a nondeductible part of the property settlement. The husband appealed and the Tax Court issued a split decision. The payments were alimony to the extent that the wife received more than half of the marital estate.

Robert H. Hall, TC Memo 1982-605.

• **A divorced wife was injured in an accident and confined to a convalescent home.** Her ex-husband agreed to pay the costs even though they came to more than the alimony specified in the divorce agreement. The wife's conservator wrote a letter spelling out the agreement and sent it to the home, with a copy to the husband, who paid the money and deducted it as alimony. The Tax Court held that the conservator's letter satisfied the requirement that alimony payments be made under a written agreement. The husband hadn't signed it, but his actions proved he accepted and ratified it.

Alimony-Suit Expenses

The cost of suing to protect your right to receive taxable alimony is deductible as an expense for the production of income. *Also deductible:* Litigation costs of suing for an increase in taxable alimony.

Elsie B. Gale, 191 F.2d 79.

Personal Interest and Mortgage Interest

Jerry Williford, partner, Grant Thornton, 175 W. Jackson Blvd., Chicago 60604. *www.grantthornton.com*

To get the greatest tax benefit for your interest costs, you should know how to handle each interest charge.

Personal interest, which includes charges incurred on credit cards, car loans, personal loans and the like, is not deductible (other than mortgage interest and student loan interest, within limits).

Interest paid on a mortgage on your primary residence or a second home is deductible. *Limit on deduction:* $1 million of mortgage debt on original purchase plus capital improvements.

There is also a way to get around the deduction limit on personal interest. An individual who has partially paid off the mortgage on his or her home may obtain a home-equity loan and use the cash obtained to make personal purchases (items such as a car, boat, new furniture, etc.). Since the interest paid on the refinancing is deductible, the home owner in effect gets an interest deduction for a personal loan.

Limit: The interest deduction on a home-equity loan is limited. The amount of a new loan incurred after October 13, 1987, must not exceed the fair market value of the home up to a limit of $100,000.

EXAMPLE

A taxpayer bought a house 20 years ago for $80,000. He later spent another $25,000 adding an extra room and other improvements to the house. The house has also appreciated in value by $40,000 so that it's now worth $145,000 on the market. The remaining mortgage debt is $40,000.

Based on these facts, the taxpayer will be able to deduct all the interest on a home-equity loan of up to $100,000. The new loan doesn't exceed fair market value ($145,000) less acquisition debt ($40,000).

PLANNING POINT

• **Many home owners may be careless about keeping records** concerning the cost of home improvements. But now these records are important. If your records aren't complete and up-to-date, it's important to pull them together now.

• **If you own more than one second home,** you can deduct only interest that's paid on one of them. But you get to choose which home you'll claim a deduction for, and you can change your designation each year (for example, if you increase the interest paid on one home by refinancing it).

Interest-Deduction Loophole

If you borrow money from your margin account and use the money for personal purposes (for instance, to take a vacation), the interest is personal interest and not deductible. But if you use the money to buy stock, the interest is investment interest (fully deductible up to the amount of your investment income for the year).

To get full deductions for interest on money borrowed for personal use, sell some of the stock you currently own, use the proceeds to take your vacation and buy the stock back on margin. Your margin-interest charges will be fully deductible investment interest (assuming that you have enough investment income to cover it). *Caution:* Keep records that clearly show where borrowed money came from, what it was spent on and all interest payments you make.

Edward Mendlowitz, CPA, partner, WithumSmith+Brown, CPAs, 1 Spring St., New Brunswick, New Jersey 08901. *www.withum.com*

All About Interest Deductions

Prepaid interest is not deductible in full in the year you pay. *Recent case:* A taxpayer bought a building in October. His mortgage called for a first-year interest-only payment, due when the deal was closed. He deducted the total payment on his tax return. The IRS disallowed nine-twelfths of his deduction. The Tax Court agreed. Prepaid interest must be prorated.

Joseph A Zidanic, 79 TC 651.

•**Zero interest equals 10%.** A taxpayer bought a house for one-third down with the balance to be paid over seven years in equal monthly payments of principal only. No interest was charged. *IRS ruling:* The home buyer can claim an interest-expense deduction of 10% of his annual payments. *Rationale:* When no interest is payable in an installment sale, the IRS assumes for tax purposes that interest at 10% is incorporated into the deal. (*Note:* The seller must include 10% interest as taxable interest income each year.)

IRS Letter Ruling 8228113.

•**Mortgage-interest deductions were lost to a separated husband who no longer lived in the house,** even though he paid support to his wife and she paid the mortgage. *Reason:* He could not prove that she made the mortgage payments with funds that he gave her. *Better way:* The husband could have made the payments himself and kept the deduction.

IRS Letter Ruling 8246073.

Proper Appraisal of Casualty Cost

Allan I. Weiss, national director of tax services, and Thomas P. Donnelly, partner, Pannell Kerr Forster, CPAs, New York City.

A casualty loss (fire, theft, accident, etc.) is usually easy to prove from police and fire department records, insurance reports or witnesses' statements. But proving the amount of the loss can be tricky. And there are rules restricting the amount of the deduction you can take.

•**Stolen or destroyed property.** If the property has risen in value (e.g., jewelry, works of art, some buildings), you can normally deduct its original cost. The best proof of the cost is a sales slip. *Second best:* Insurance records or appraisals made at the time of purchase. *Next:* Statements of the purchaser or other knowledgeable person. Often none of these are available, especially if the property was received as a gift. The only solution is to describe the property as fully as possible and get expert testimony on what the price would have been at the time of purchase. For inherited property, you can deduct the value at the time of the inheritance. *Best proof:* The valuation used for estate tax purposes.

If the stolen or destroyed property has depreciated in value (e.g., automobiles, household furnishings), you can deduct the lower of the original cost less depreciation or its actual market value—not the cost of buying a new or used car or new or used furniture. For automobiles, *Blue Book* value is a common measure. If you claim more, you'll need proof, such as a mechanic's testimony that your car was in unusually good condition or had low mileage. For household items such as furniture, clothing and TV sets, you can deduct the original cost less depreciation, based on the estimated life of the property and its actual age or value, whichever is less.

If you had a large-scale loss, such as the loss of a home by fire, try to list every item you can possibly think of. Even if individual items have small value, the aggregate may be extremely large. If some of your household goods were far above average in value (e.g., a large wardrobe of expensive clothing), get records or statements from the stores you deal with. If you don't have invoices for everything, you can show a pattern of expensive purchases.

• **Damaged property.** You can deduct the difference in market value before and after the damage (but not more than the original cost). One method of proof is to get an appraisal. Cost of repairs may also be a measure of damage—provided the repair just restores the property to its previous condition. Remember to reduce the amount of the loss by any insurance or other reimbursements.

All About Casualty-Loss Deductions

A tornado blew down 12 trees on a taxpayer's 10-acre wooded property. The IRS disallowed the taxpayer's casualty-loss deduction of $28,000 for the loss of the trees. Its reasoning: There are so many trees that the loss of 12 couldn't make a difference in the value of the property. The taxpayer, however, had a tree expert value each lost tree according to its size, species, condition and location in relation to the house. Tax Court decision: The taxpayer was entitled to a $20,000 casualty-loss deduction for the reduction in the property's value.

Thomas R. Bowers, TC Memo 1981-658.

• **All the trees on a home owner's new property died from a lethal yellowing disease shortly after he moved in.** The disease started by insect infestation and took about six months to kill the trees. The Tax Court disallowed the home owner's casualty-loss deduction because the loss wasn't sudden enough. *Home owner's appeal:* The event precipitating

the disease—insect infestation—was a sudden event. *Court:* No deduction. A loss attributable to disease does not constitute a casualty loss.

John A. Maher, CA-2, No. 81-5561.

• **A casualty deduction for earthquake damage to a building could include the cost of repairs,** even though the repairs were not made. The Tax Court agreed with testimony on lowered market value given by an appraiser, who said prospective purchasers would either demand that repairs be made or insist that the price be lowered by the amount the repairs would cost.

Paul Abrams, TC Memo 1981-231.

• **Unusually heavy winter rains altered the soil density under a taxpayer's new house.** The house settled and was damaged extensively in the process. But the IRS and the courts disallowed a casualty-loss deduction for the damage. *Reason:* Although the rain was heavy, it was not unforeseen. The ordinary action of the elements on a poorly constructed house does not qualify for a casualty loss, the court said.

Sheldon Portman, CA-9, No. 81-4433.

• **A mid-Atlantic–state taxpayer whose car engine froze during a period of extreme cold** could not claim a casualty-loss deduction for the damage. *IRS reasoning:* Very cold winter weather was not extraordinary and nonrecurring in the taxpayer's state. And to qualify as a casualty, an event must be unexpected or unusual.

IRS Letter Ruling 8247060.

Deducting Points on a Home Mortgage

In 1983, an individual bought a home using a 29-year mortgage. He paid three points to finance the purchase and another four points to obtain a lower interest rate over the life of the loan. The home owner deducted the three points in 1983. He also deducted ½₉ of the four points in 1983 and in each year since. In 1986, he took out a new mortgage and paid off the old one.

IRS ruling: The home owner can deduct the remainder of the four points immediately. The old loan has been completely paid off, so all interest on it is deductible as paid.

IRS Letter Ruling 8637058.

Deduct Fees for Advice on Taxes and Investments

Legal fees for advice about the taxation and management of investments are deductible, but subject to the floor on miscellaneous deductions of 2% of adjusted gross income (AGI). However, fees for legal advice that results in the sale of an investment currently cannot be deducted as an investment expense. The legal fees must be capitalized (that is, they must be added to the cost to determine your profit in the resale).

What to do: Make sure your lawyer gives you an itemized bill showing how much he charged for general investment and tax advice and how much for handling the sale of an investment.

Paul W. Learner, TC Memo 1983-122.

The beneficiary of a trust could deduct fees he paid an attorney to keep him informed of the handling of trust property, even though the beneficiary received no income in the year he paid the fees. The Tax Court said the fees were ordinary and necessary expenses in connection with the production of income.

Hobart J. Hendrick, 35 TC 1223.

Little-Known Computer Deduction

If you use a personal computer to manage your investments, you can deduct related costs as investment expenses.

Examples: Internet costs…the cost of investment software. Software is deductible over three years, but may be written off sooner if it has a shorter useful life…that is, if you buy a new version each year.

Your computer can also be depreciated to the extent it is used to manage investments. Investment expenses are miscellaneous expenses, deductible to the extent they exceed 2% of Adjusted Gross Income.

Richard J. Shapiro, Esq., former tax partner, Ernst & Young LLP, 5 Times Sq., New York City 10036. *www.ey.com*

Nontaxable Income Expenses Are Not Deductible

If a taxpayer incurs expenses for investment advice, accountants' fees, safe-deposit–box rentals, etc., that apply to both taxable and nontaxable income, he or she can deduct only the expenses (or percentage of expenses) allocable to taxable income. Failure to establish the allocation can jeopardize the entire deduction.

Deductible IRA Fees

An IRS official has confirmed that the start-up costs and custodial fees that brokerage firms and mutual funds charge IRA account holders are tax deductible as a cost of producing income. The fees do not reduce the amount an individual can contribute to an IRA. No penalty will be charged if the fees put you over the annual contribution limit.

Deducting the Cost of a Home Safe

The cost of a home safe bought to store securities and other financial investments as well as jewelry and personal effects is partially deductible through depreciation deductions. The part of the safe's cost relating to the production of taxable income—storing securities and income-producing financial instruments—can be deducted as it is depreciated. *Not depreciable:* That part of the cost allocated to personal use—that is, storing jewelry and personal effects.

IRS Letter Ruling 8218037.

Protect Yourself from The IRS When You Make a Loan

Whatever risks you take on when you make a loan, you need not risk trouble with the IRS when it comes to deducting bad debts.

It's important to look before you lend. A careful review of the options often shows that other, more tax-wise methods of employing capital can be used instead of loans. *Reason:* Taxpayers who have money to lend are likely to benefit most from tax deductions or credits. Loans, however, offer no direct tax benefits to lenders.

Strategy: Consult a tax professional about ways to get more advantageous tax treatment by becoming a partner, a shareholder, an equipment lessor or a landlord instead of assuming the role of lender. These and other options can serve the same purpose as loans, while providing you with considerable tax benefits.

• **Protective measures.** Businesslike lending practices offer you the best means of supporting bad-debt deductions in case the IRS questions them. *Guidelines...*

• Document all aspects of the loan. *Include:* A formal note, your reasons for lending, what steps you took to collect both interest and principal, how you arrived at the conclusion that the debt was worthless. *Goal:* To prove that you intended the transaction to be a loan—that you expected repayment in full.

• Determine the borrower's creditworthiness. For individuals, use credit reports. For businesses, use both credit ratings and debt/equity ratios. *Alternative:* A copy of a commercial lender's loan approval.

• Lend at a "reasonable" rate of interest. *What's reasonable:* Using the AFR rate is both expedient and safe. IRS releases AFR rates on a monthly basis.

• Use fixed-term loans rather than demand loans. *Why:* By definition, term loans clearly indicate when payment is due. They emphasize your intention to be repaid. This fine point can work to your advantage if the IRS questions your bad-debt deduction.

• **Proof of worthlessness.** Be prepared to prove that a bad debt is worthless. *How:* Retain all relevant documents and receipts (copies of return-receipted letters, lawyer's letters, loan-payment checks returned for insufficient funds by the borrower's bank, etc.). Also retain any evidence of the debtor's insolvency, bankruptcy or disappearance. Save envelopes marked "Refused" or "Unable to Deliver." These can be used as proof of a debtor's disappearance.

Strategy: Since worthlessness is generally a subjective determination, your actions should demonstrate reasonableness. Although it may be perfectly reasonable to rely solely on telephone calls and letters to collect, say, a $100 debt, limiting yourself to the same steps for a $10,000 debt just doesn't make sense. Whatever seems "unreasonable" is more likely to be disallowed by the IRS.

• **Family loans.** Loans to relatives invariably prompt IRS questions. The closer the relation, the closer the IRS will scrutinize the transaction. *Trap:* If the IRS denies your bad-debt deduction and rules that your "family loan" was really a gift, there may be gift tax consequences. *Note:* If you guarantee a loan made to a family member by a bank or third party and are forced to pay it back, this may also be treated as a gift. Check with your tax adviser about how to handle family loans.

• **Not deductible.** *Nondeductible losses result in each of the following situations...*

• Monies owed but never paid (such as salaries owed to employees or rents owed to landlords) can't be deducted as bad debts. *Rule of thumb:* You can't get a bad-debt deduction for amounts not previously reported as income.

• Loans that were worthless when made are not deductible.

• Unrepaid loans to political parties or to candidates for elective office generally cannot be deducted as bad debts by individuals and nonbank corporations. *Caution:* Check with your tax adviser about the very limited exceptions allowed by law.

Capital-Loss Trap

If you have stock or other property that has gone down in value, do not sell it to your spouse, child (or other descendant), parent (or other ancestor), brother, sister or any corporation, trust or organization that you control. If you do, you will probably not be allowed to deduct the capital loss.

Weekend Farmer's Costs Are Deductible

Reversing the Tax Court, the US Court of Appeals ruled that a weekend farmer's hope that his farming activities would produce a profit when he began full-time operations entitled him to deduct his current losses. The fact that he could not make a profit from his weekend activities did not mean that he

lacked a profit motive for operating the farm. His expectation of making a profit in the future and his lack of a recreational motive justified his deduction.

Melvin Nickerson, CA-7, 82-1323.

Expense for Future Income Is Deductible

A taxpayer took a 50-year lease on undeveloped land on which he intended to build and operate an office building. He deducted the first-year lease payments as a business expense. But the IRS denied his deduction, arguing that since the building hadn't yet been constructed, the taxpayer wasn't in business. *Tax Court:* The lease payment was deductible as an expense incurred for the production of future income—though not deductible as a business expense. The fact that the taxpayer wasn't actively engaged in business didn't cost him his deduction.

Herschel Hoopengarner, 80 TC 538, aff'd CA-9, 745 F.2d 66.

Medical-Exam Loophole

Medical examinations are usually included with the rest of your medical expenses— they are only deductible to the extent that the total of all your medical expenses exceeds 10% (7.5% if you are 50 or older) of your adjusted gross income (AGI).

Loophole: When the medical exam is taken because it's required by your current job or potential employer, it's counted as a miscellaneous expense. These expenses are deductible to the extent that the total miscellaneous deductions exceed only 2% of your AGI.

Bigger Travel Deductions

Mix pleasure with business to get bigger travel deductions or reimbursements from your employer.

Key: You can't deduct the cost of meals and lodging for pleasure days added to a business trip—but you can deduct costs for pleasure days that are nonworkdays (holidays, weekends) that fall between workdays.

Example: You plan to visit friends in San Francisco over Labor Day weekend. If you travel to San Francisco, work there the preceding week, stay the weekend and then go home, you'll get no deduction for the weekend. But if you work in San Francisco the Thursday and Friday before the weekend and on the Tuesday and Wednesday after it, you can deduct your weekend costs or get a tax-free reimbursement for them.

Irving L. Blackman, CPA, retired founding partner, Blackman Kallick, LLP, 10 S. Riverside Plaza, Chicago 60606. *www.taxsecretsofthewealthy.com*

Best Tax Shelter in America Is a Business Of Your Own

There's no feeling in the world like owning your own business. *An added bonus is the tax benefit it can provide...*

•**Deductible executive dining-room and living quarters.** Meals furnished by a corporation to a shareholder-employee are tax free to the employee if furnished for the business convenience of the corporation. This includes meals furnished on the corporation's premises so that the employee will have more working time or so that there will be a responsible person on hand at all times to provide supervision or handle business communications.

If the business is large enough to warrant it, a separate executive dining room may be set up. The cost of the meals will be deductible by the corporation and not taxable to the executives, including shareholder-executives, if business decisions take place during the meal either among the executives themselves or with customers, suppliers or consultants invited to dine.

Living quarters may be provided on a tax-deductible basis for the corporation and tax free to the shareholder-employee if the corporation requires him or her to live on the premises for a good business reason. This might apply to a shareholder serving as a hotel, motel, farm or ranch manager. It might also apply to the manager of a nursing home, hospital or funeral home and other occupations requiring close and more or less continual availability in connection with the business.

•**Personal use of deductible company car.** The use of a company car, especially a luxury car, can be a valuable fringe benefit. The expenses of the car, including depreciation, are deductible by the corporation and not taxable to the shareholder-employee if it is used for company business. The IRS has informally taken the position that if the car is used primarily for business, income will not be imputed to the user because he takes the car home on weekends and makes incidental use of it for nonbusiness purposes.

If a shareholder-executive is given the use of two cars and it is clear that one of them is being used by the executive's spouse for nonbusiness purposes, he will be taxed on the value of the use of the car. But his tax liability will be less than the cost of renting a car, and most likely less than it would cost him to buy, finance and maintain the car on his own. If the extra car is treated as extra compensation, the attending expenses are deductible by the corporation as compensation, subject to the overall limitation of reasonableness. If treated as dividend income to the shareholder, it would not be deductible by the corporation.

•**Deductible chauffeur.** The cost of a chauffeur may be deductible by the corporation and not taxable to the shareholder-employee if deemed an "ordinary and necessary expense," sometimes translated as "appropriate and helpful."

•**Capital loss transformed into ordinary loss.** A special form of stock (Section 1244 stock), within limits, permits an ordinary loss rather than a capital loss if the business turns sour.

If the stock qualifies, an ordinary loss of up to $50,000 per year ($100,000 on a joint return) may be taken. This may be spread over several years. Whether or not a loss is anticipated, stock should be issued under the aegis of Section 1244 to qualify for such treatment. Briefly, the requirements are that it be common stock of a domestic small-business corporation and the total it has received for stock (including Section 1244 stock) doesn't exceed $1 million. For the five years prior to the loss, the corporation must have derived more than 50% of its gross receipts from sources other than rents, royalties, interest, etc.

• **Bailout loophole for family members.** Income tax and estate tax considerations generally make it desirable for family members to hold stock in a close corporation. The family head may wish to give them money to buy stock from the corporation, or they may already have their own money to buy in.

There are two good reasons why it may be desirable for family members to acquire their stock directly from the corporation as soon as the corporation is set up…

1. The stock will be cheaper at that time than later, assuming that the corporation succeeds, and…

2. The rules governing corporate redemptions are less restrictive when the stock is acquired directly from the corporation rather than by a transfer from the family head or other family member.

If the stock is acquired from a family member, it must be held for at least 10 years before it can be redeemed to yield capital gains. This 10-year requirement does not apply if the stock is acquired from the corporation. Thus, it will be possible for the holder to bail out corporate earnings and profits as capital gains whenever the need arises or when it is desirable to do so.

• **Leasing assets to your own corporation.** The fact that the corporate form is selected as the basic means of conducting a business enterprise does not mean that all of the physical components of the enterprise need be owned by the corporation. Indeed, there may be legal, tax and personal financial planning reasons for not having the corporation own all the assets to be used in the business.

Whether the corporation is to be the continuation of a sole proprietorship or partnership or a wholly new enterprise, decisions can be made about which assets owned by the predecessor or acquired or used in the corporation are to be owned by the corporation and which assets are to be made available to the corporation through a leasing or other contractual arrangement. For the assets that go to the corporation, decisions must be made about how they are to be held and on what terms they are to be made available to the corporation.

There are several possible choices. *The assets may be owned by…*

1. An individual shareholder or some member of his family,

2. A partnership, limited or general, in which family members participate or

3. A trust for the benefit of family members.

A separate corporation is still yet another possibility. However, the risk of being considered a personal holding company and incurring penalties due to passive income (including rent and royalties) may make this impractical.

Normally a leasing arrangement is used for the assets to be made available for corporate use. Assuming that the rental is fair, it would be deductible by the corporation and taxable to the lessor. Against the rental income, the lessor would have possible deductions for interest paid on loans financing the acquisition of the asset, depreciation, maintenance and repairs, insurance and administrative costs.

These deductions and the credit might produce a tax-free cash flow for the lessor. When depreciation and interest deductions begin to run out, a high tax bracket lessor might find that he is being taxed at too high a rate on the rental income. At this point he may transfer the leased property to a lower-tax bracket family member. He might also consider a sale of the property to his corporation, possibly on installment terms to reduce the impact of tax liability. This sale would serve to extract earnings and profits from the corporation at favorable tax rates. At the same time, it would give the corporation a higher tax basis for the asset than it had in the hands of the lessor, thus increasing the corporation's depreciation deductions. This, of course, would reduce the corporation's tax liabilities and benefit the shareholders—the lessor included, if he is a shareholder.

You Must Establish a Tax Home

A salesman spent most of his time on the road but rented a room in his sister's home in the same city as his company's main office. The Tax Court ruled that this was his "tax home," and he could deduct expenses while away. But where another salesman, in almost the same situation, did not pay his sister any rent for the room, the IRS ruled that he had no "tax home" to be away from. Hence, no deduction.

Sapson, 49 TC 636; Rev. Rul. 73-529.

Educational-Expense Trap

Your kids have reached school age and your wife wants to resume her career. She plans to take some brush-up courses first. Are they deductible?

Educational expenses are deductible only if related to a taxpayer's trade or business. What your wife should do is get a job first—then take the courses. A part-time job will do—just as long as she can show that she is currently engaged in an occupation to which the courses are related.

Alternative: Check to see if her expenses qualify for an education tax credit.

Loss of Apartment Security Deposit Is Deductible

A taxpayer who was transferred to another city lost the security deposit on his old apartment. Can he get a tax deduction?

Yes—deductible moving expenses include the cost of getting out of any leases on his previous residence—as well as the cost of finding a new one, such as real estate brokers' fees. (But not the security deposit on the new apartment...presumably he'll get that back someday.)

Withdrawal Penalties Are Deductible

A couple cashed in a certificate of deposit (CD) before maturity and the bank charged a penalty. Is it deductible on their tax return?

Yes—early withdrawal penalties are deductible and are subtracted from gross income to arrive at adjusted gross income.

Deduct Hobbies, Salaries And More

Sidney Kess, Esq., CPA, New York City. He has taught tax law to more than 725,000 tax professionals and is coauthor of *1040 Preparation and Planning Guide* (CCH).

The best way to reduce taxes is to start a sideline business. When you own a business, you can deduct contributions to a tax-favored Simplified Employee Pension (SEP) plan or other qualified retirement plan, in addition to whatever retirement benefits your regular employer already provides.

You also are able to claim other *extraordinary* tax-saving deductions. *Some of the best taxpayer victories over the IRS of all time show how a sideline business pays off…*

• **Deduct your hobby.** The Tax Court says an activity does not become nondeductible just because you enjoy it. It may be easier than you think to qualify your favorite hobby as a business that provides big tax deductions.

All you have to do is show that you have a genuine intention to make a profit. You do not actually ever have to make a profit. Any loss you incur becomes fully deductible against other income, such as salary from a regular job.

So your new sideline/former hobby can become a legitimate tax shelter…with your enjoyment of it subsidized by the IRS. *Winners…*

• **Woman who admitted that she painted for pleasure** but also tried to sell her paintings at shows.
Gloria Churchman, 68 TC 696.

• **Accountant/songwriter who copyrighted his songs** and hired a band to play and promote them.
Bernard Wagner, TC Memo 1983-606.

• **Engineer/actor who took acting lessons,** joined the Actors' Guild and then went out on theatrical auditions.
J. Thomas Regan, TC Memo 1979-340.

• **Rental agent/author** who made a conscientious but unsuccessful effort to sell his books.
Joseph and Florence Sheban, TC Memo, 1970-163.

Of course, the IRS may be suspicious if you suddenly deduct your long-time hobby as a business. Hobby losses are on the IRS watch list of common errors. *But a winning case shows how to do it…*

• **Probation officer/longtime stamp collector** tried to deduct his collecting as a business. Both the IRS and Tax Court said no because he had poor records and didn't operate in a businesslike manner.

Then he registered a name for his stamp business, obtained a credit card in the name of the business, took a formal inventory and started keeping full records of transactions.

He claimed business deductions again, and the Tax Court said yes because he was acting

in a manner that indicated a desire to make a profit. So his actual $5,000 loss became fully deductible.
Eugene Feistman, TC Memo 1982-306.

An intention to make a profit in the future can justify deductions now for your sideline.

• **Executive** who lived in a city bought a farm and renovated it on weekends. He lost money on it for 10 years. But because he intended to earn retirement income from it in the future, his current losses were deductible against his salary.
Melvin Nickerson, 700 F2d 402.

• **Deduct salaries paid to children.** Once you have a business, you can deduct salaries paid to those who work for it—including your own very young children.

You then take your deduction at your high tax bracket rate, while they receive their earnings at a low or zero tax bracket rate. All you need to do is show that the children do real work and are paid a reasonable rate. *Winners…*

• **Seven-year-old child** could receive a deductible salary for doing cleanup chores for his father's business.
Walt E. Eller, 77 TC 934.

• **Doctor's four children** could be paid deductible salaries for doing secretarial chores for him at home, such as filing.
James A. Moriarity, TC Memo 1984-249.

Even better: A child's earned income can fund a Roth IRA for the child that may earn tax-free investment income for the child's whole life.

HOME DEDUCTIONS

Do not overlook home deductions that become available from being in business…

• **Deduct more interest for home loans.** You probably know you can deduct mortgage interest on up to $100,000 of home-equity borrowing. But you can also deduct interest on borrowing more than $100,000 if you use the borrowed funds for business or investment purposes.

The excess interest can qualify as deductible business or investment interest in spite of the home-equity deduction limit.
IRS Letter Ruling 9335043.

Opportunity: Once you have a business, you can use the extra home-equity borrowing to finance it, deducting the interest.

• **Claim home-office deductions** to deduct formerly nondeductible household expenses attributable to your office.

Examples: Insurance, repairs, utilities and depreciation—a no-cash-cost expense that saves cash tax dollars.

More people than ever before now can claim the home-office deduction. New law lets it be claimed by people who need a home office for administrative or management activities of a business for which there is no other fixed location. Formerly, the office had to be the principal place at which a business was conducted. *Deductions are allowed when...*

• **Only *part* of a room is used as an office.** An office must be used exclusively for business operations—but there's no requirement that it be a whole room.

George Weightman, TC Memo 1981-301.

• **Both spouses use an office for work,** but only one spouse qualifies for the deduction because the other has a regular office.

Max Frankel, 82 TC 318.

It is even easier to claim deductions if your office isn't physically attached to your home—such as if it is in a freestanding garage or a gardener's shed. It is not necessary to prove the garage is your principal place of business.

• **A person could deduct a separate office that he built next to his vacation beach house,** even though it couldn't be deducted as a home office because he had a regular office elsewhere.

Ben Heineman, 82 TC 538.

• **A lawyer could deduct half the rent he paid** to himself for an office he used in a building that he co-owned with his wife (because half the rent legally benefited his wife, although they filed a joint return). The same amount was then taxable to him as rental income—but he received a net tax benefit because converting the business income into rental income allowed him to take other real estate-related deductions.

D. Sherman Cox, TC Memo 1993-326.

Little-Known Ways to Write Off Commuting Expenses

Barbara Weltman, attorney in Millwood, New York. *www.barbaraweltman.com*. She is author of several books, including *J.K. Lasser's 1,001 Deductions and Tax Breaks* (Wiley).

It's a well-known tax rule that ordinary commuting costs are nondeductible personal expenses. This rule applies to both employees and self-employed individuals.

Employees who are reimbursed by their employer for nondeductible commuting costs are taxed on this benefit.

But the IRS has recognized that some situations are out of the ordinary. In such cases, commuting costs may be deductible.

Self-employed individuals can deduct these costs in full on Schedule C.

Employees can write off deductible commuting costs as unreimbursed employee business expenses. They are deductible only to the extent that they exceed 2% of adjusted gross income (AGI).

ACCOUNTABLE PLANS

Alternatively, employees who are reimbursed under an accountable plan* for their otherwise deductible commuting costs are not taxed on such reimbursements.

Benefit: From the employer's view, deductible commuting costs paid under an accountable plan are not subject to payroll taxes—Social Security, Medicare, unemployment.

TRIPS OUT OF TOWN

If you're away from home on business, local transportation costs for travel between your hotel and all business calls throughout the day are deductible. So if you work in Atlanta and fly to San Francisco on business, taxi fares or BART tickets to see clients in that city are deductible business expenses.

*The employee substantiates travel costs to the employer and returns excess reimbursements within 120 days.

OUT-OF-TOWN ASSIGNMENTS

If you have a regular place of business within the metropolitan area in which you live and work, travel costs to and from assignments outside the area are deductible. It doesn't matter how short or long these assignments last.

Caution: The IRS hasn't provided guidance on what constitutes a "metropolitan area."

TEMPORARY ASSIGNMENTS

Traveling to and from the office or other regular work location isn't deductible. But travel costs to and from temporary work assignments within the metropolitan area in which you work and live are deductible.

"Temporary" means assignments that are not expected to last more than one year and do in fact end within that time ("one-year rule").

Example: You work for a consulting firm that assigns you to a client's offices for three months. The job finishes up in two months. The assignment is considered temporary, so your travel costs to and from the client's offices are deductible.

WORK ASSIGNMENT HIATUS

What happens if you have a temporary assignment, but you are reassigned to the same location? According to the IRS, a break of three weeks or less between assignments is not considered significant.

Result: The separate assignments are considered together for purposes of the one-year tax rule.

But breaks of seven months or more would be considered significant. Thus, successive assignments to the same location separated by a break of seven months or more would not be counted together in determining whether the one-year rule is met.

Whether breaks lasting between three weeks and seven months—the safe harbors used by the IRS—are considered significant is anybody's guess. These safe harbors are gleaned from private IRS rulings. Future rulings may provide further guidance on this question.

INFREQUENT ASSIGNMENTS

What about regular assignments to the same location on an infrequent or sporadic basis?

The IRS says that separate assignments do not have to be aggregated in certain cases for purposes of the one-year rule. If you're not expected to work more than 35 full or part days at a work location within the year, then the assignment is considered temporary.

So an assignment to a work location lasting just one or two days every month would be considered temporary (travel there doesn't exceed 35 days) even though the overall assignment exceeds one year.

But an assignment to a work location of one day each week wouldn't be considered temporary (total days for the year would exceed 35 days).

HOME OFFICE

If you claim a home office deduction—establishing that your home is the principal place of business for you—then all travel costs to and from other locations related to the business are deductible.

Strategy: Increase your business mileage by making your first and last stops of the day at the post office.

Caution: Employees who work from home can only claim a home office deduction if this work arrangement is for the convenience of the employer.

21

Tax Strategies for Investors

Deduct! Defer!

he year-end rallying cry for most investors should be, "Deduct! Defer! Deduct losses this year and defer income to next year."

Your investment decisions should be governed by the current market outlook for your holdings, not by tax savings. Get professional tax advice...individual situations create vastly different tax consequences. Also, many year-end strategies involve complicated tax rules. Consult your tax adviser before undertaking such transactions.

• **Defer current income** through the purchase of utilities whose dividends are expected to be partially or wholly recognized as return of capital.

• **Defer capital gains** through installment sales. Under an installment sale, a pro rata portion of the gain is taxed each year. *Warning:* Installment sales cannot be used for publicly traded securities and should not be attempted without the help of a tax expert.

• **Defer income to next year** by purchasing short-term unit trusts or one-year government securities. *Suggestion:* Liquidate money market assets and reinvest the funds in a pooled fund that is composed of six-month vehicles (CDs, bankers acceptances, Treasury bills). There will be no tax liability this year because interest isn't paid until maturity.

• **Deduct losses this year.** Offset capital gains and capital gain distributions with capital losses. Then deduct excess capital losses from ordinary income on a dollar-for-dollar basis up to $3,000. Capital losses beyond $3,000 can be carried forward to future years.

• **Deduct losses in bonds or securities** through tax swaps, or doubling up. These techniques will turn a current paper loss into a deductible loss.

Doubling up involves buying an equal number of shares at today's prices of stock on which you have paper losses. After 30 days, you sell your first purchase. This gives you a

---

Alfred F. Palladino, corporate vice president and resident manager of a major brokerage firm in New York City.

deductible loss that does not violate the wash-sale rules.

• **Deduct margin interest.** *Caution:* The tax code disallows interest-expense deductions on money borrowed to finance tax-free investments…it also denies interest deductions until income is realized. Seek advice from your tax expert.

Seek Out Tax-Effective Mutual Funds

Barbara J. Raasch, CPA, CFP, partner in the personal financial counseling practice of Ernst & Young LLP, 5 Times Sq., New York City 10036. She is a coauthor of *Ernst & Young's Personal Financial Planning Guide, 5th Edition* (John Wiley & Sons). *www.ey.com*

Taxable gains and losses realized within mutual funds over the year are distributed to their shareholders, usually just before year-end.

The increase in the difference in tax rates imposed on long-term and short-term gains makes the nature of the gains earned within a fund more important than before.

Tax-effective funds will tend to trade their holdings infrequently (have low turnover) so that realized gains are fewer and tend to be long term. They may also try to take losses before they become long term, to preserve their deductibility. (Index funds are among the most tax effective, since their turnover is near zero.)

In contrast, a tax *in*effective fund will incur many high-tax-rate, short-term gains.

Timing: Taxable gains are distributed to fund shareholders who are owners of record on the fund's "dividend date," usually in the last weeks of December.

Learn the dividend dates of the funds that you own—and are considering buying.

If you are planning to revise your fund holdings at year-end, sell fund shares *before* the dividend date, and buy fund shares *after* the dividend date, to avoid the taxable distribution.

Income Investments vs. Capital Gains

If your portfolio includes both income-producing investments and capital gains investments, and you own both taxable investment accounts and tax-deferred retirement accounts, try to move your income-producing investments into the retirement accounts and capital gain investments into the taxable accounts.

Using this planning strategy, you obtain tax deferral for current income, tax-favored rates for long-term gains and the possibility of deducting investment losses.

If you move income-producing investments into retirement accounts now, you'll avoid paying tax on them for the rest of the year.

Barbara J. Raasch, CPA, CFP, partner in the personal financial counseling practice of Ernst & Young LLP, 5 Times St., New York City 10036. She is a coauthor of *Ernst & Young's Personal Financial Planning Guide, 5th Edition* (John Wiley & Sons). *www.ey.com*

Deduct Stock Losses Without Selling Your Shares

Examine your portfolio for stocks and securities that have gone down in value. Their sale will produce losses that can be used to offset capital gains and other taxable income. *Problem:* You may not want to sell the securities. What should you do? *Use one of the following strategies that allow you to lock in losses while substantially retaining your current investment position…*

1. Double up by purchasing a matching amount of the same securities you already own. Hold the new lot for 31 days, then sell the old lot. You get your tax losses on the sale of the old lot, yet emerge with the same investment you started with. Your tax losses may far outweigh the cost of carrying a double position for 31 days.

2. Sell and buy back the same securities, but be sure to wait 31 days before making the repurchase. Again, you get your losses while retaining your position. *Caution:* If you don't wait the full 31 days before making the repurchase, the loss won't be recognized.

3. Repurchase similar securities immediately after you sell the old ones. You don't have to wait 31 days to secure your losses. What is considered similar? (1) Stock of a different company in the same business. (2) Bonds of the same company with a slightly different maturity date and coupon rate.

Smart Investors

When you make a new investment, it's important that you break down the cost between what is and what isn't deductible.

Deductible subject to the 2% limit: The cost of an investment counselor's advice, management fees, amounts paid for investment-related publications, fees charged by a lawyer or accountant for advice and insurance that protects your investment.

Not deductible: Any costs that are directly related to buying or selling the investment. These must be capitalized—added to the price of the investment to reduce your capital gain (or increase your capital loss) when you sell it or otherwise dispose of it.

Trap: A broker, lawyer or accountant may provide both deductible and nondeductible services on the same deal. For example, when a broker recommends an investment, a lawyer provides a legal opinion of it and an accountant estimates its tax impact, the fees involved are deductible. But when a broker charges a commission on a purchase, a lawyer handles the closing papers and an accountant adjusts your books to reflect the purchase, the fees involved are nondeductible capital costs.

Advice: Always have your professional advisers provide itemized bills that spell out what's deductible.

Tax-Free Interest

Savings bonds are popular baby gifts. Plan to file a tax return for the baby's first year if your child is given them. On that return you can elect to report the bond's interest annually rather than let it accumulate. *Loophole:* The election to pick up the interest annually will result in a very small tax (as long as it's not over $2,000 a year in 2013—perhaps higher in future years). If you let the interest accumulate, when the child is past the kiddie tax age and wants to take the money out, he'll have to pay tax on as much as 24 years of interest.

Bigger Write-Offs for Money Lost in New Business

Edward Mendlowitz, CPA, partner, WithumSmith+ Brown, CPAs, 1 Spring St., New Brunswick, New Jersey 08901. *www.withum.com*

Tax law provides a very favorable opportunity for those who invest in starting up a small business. If both investors and new companies follow a few simple rules, they can be certain that if the business fails, investors can be protected through an ability to deduct their loss against ordinary income rather than taking it as a capital loss. The provision is not new, but it has been streamlined and liberalized in recent years.

An ordinary income deduction is better than a capital loss. Capital losses of any size can be used to offset capital gains. But if the net result of all capital transactions is a loss, it can be deducted from ordinary income only at the rate of $3,000 per year. The remainder can be carried forward and used in later years. But, even so, it would take over eight years to write off a $25,000 loss.

Any unused capital losses expire at the taxpayer's death. Thus if an older investor realizes a large loss, he or she may find it impossible to take advantage of all of it.

Accordingly, a provision for turning all kinds of capital losses into ordinary income losses is very valuable. And that's what is offered by Section 1244 of the Internal Revenue Code.

How the investor deducts the losses: The basic feature of Section 1244 is that the annual $3,000 limit on capital losses that may be used to offset ordinary income does not apply. Section 1244 capital losses can be deducted from ordinary income up to $50,000 a year ($100,000 for a married couple filing jointly). Losses in excess of these amounts are then treated the same as other capital losses.

There is no lifetime limit on Section 1244 losses. Accordingly, if a corporation is failing, a better strategy than immediate liquidation might be to keep it (barely) alive for several years and sell part of the stock every year in order to take deductions far in excess of the one-year limit.

It is important to realize that the investor cannot deduct the corporation's operating losses against his taxable income, as he would with a Subchapter S corporation. He can deduct his capital loss on the sale of the stock, but not until he sells it or can show that it is worthless.

How a corporation can qualify under Section 1244: To safeguard its investors, a company must meet the following requirements...

1. The total capital contributed (that is, the amounts paid to the company by its stockholders when they buy newly issued stock) may not at any time exceed $1,000,000. (Retained earnings are not counted toward this limit.) The stock may be sold in a single transaction or in several transactions spread over a period of time. And it may be sold in a private sale or a public offering.

2. The corporation must operate a business. It cannot be a passive-investment vehicle owning real estate or securities or a tax shelter.

3. It is no longer required that the corporation have a written plan covering the offering.

4. Stock issued in exchange for personal services does not qualify under Section 1244. To meet the test, the stock must be issued for money or property.

Gratuitous benefit: Section 1244 is one of the very few provisions of the tax law that has no disadvantages and costs nothing to use. Obviously if the business prospers, Section 1244 will never be used, but that is hardly something to complain about.

Tax Surprise for Fund Investors?

Tom Roseen, senior analyst, Lipper, a division of Thomson Reuters Inc., Denver. He is author of *Taxes in the Mutual Fund Industry* (Lipper).

A tax shock could surprise many mutual fund investors. Even if your fund's value has plunged 40% or more with the stock market, it may deliver a capital gains tax bill to you at year-end.

The volatile stock market has led many investors to cash out of their stock fund shares, forcing some funds to sell appreciated investments to redeem these shares.

Trap: When a fund sells appreciated investments, it realizes taxable capital gains on those investments that are passed through to its shareholders. This is true even if the overall value of the fund's own shares has fallen.

These taxable gains are distributed to shareholders when the fund makes taxable distributions.

This is especially a problem if the fund is cashing in stocks that soared during the five-year bull market.

Even worse: Fund distributions can include short-term gains and nonqualified dividends taxed at ordinary income tax rates up to 39.6%.

Biggest mistake: Buying shares in a fund just before it pays a taxable distribution. If you wait until after the fund distributes gains and dividends ("goes ex-dividend"), you avoid the immediate tax bill.

TO MINIMIZE THE TAX HIT

Not all mutual funds are in this tax-trap-creating situation. For example, if your fund's managers sold investments that declined in value, the fund may have realized enough losses to offset its gains and keep shareholders from receiving a taxable distribution. *Planning...*

• **Learn the expected distribution of any mutual fund** you own or in which you might invest. Many funds make distributions in December but provide estimates in mid- to late November. Funds typically post estimated distributions on their Web sites—if not, call the fund management to inquire.

• **Learn the fund's ex-dividend date.** If it will distribute significant taxable gains, consider buying shares after that date. Or, if you own shares in such a fund and will continue to do so, sell shares in other funds (or stocks) that have lost value to "lock in" those losses.

Reason: Losses can be used to offset gains or up to $3,000 of other income. Unused losses can be carried forward to offset gains and up to $3,000 a year of other income in future tax years.

Caution: Don't make investment moves solely for tax purposes. That's one of the easiest ways to make a bad investment mistake.

Mutual Fund Tax Loopholes

Edward Mendlowitz, CPA, partner, WithumSmith+ Brown, CPAs, 1 Spring St., New Brunswick, New Jersey 08901. *www.withum.com*

Mutual funds are not particularly tax friendly, and the taxes you pay can trim gains substantially. Savvy investors and their advisers can find many ways to save taxes on their fund investments, however. *Now you'll know them all, too...*

Loophole: Hold funds that are not tax efficient in your IRA, 401(k) plan or other tax-deferred retirement plan.

Funds that aren't tax efficient have high turnover rates and distribute large amounts of short-term capital gains to shareholders each year. These distributions are taxable, unless the fund is held in a tax-deferred account. Then income earned by the fund builds up and compounds tax free until you begin making withdrawals.

Loophole: Maximize fund profits by carefully tracking any dividends that you reinvest in the fund.

Keep a permanent file folder for each fund you hold, and keep copies of the quarterly and annual statements you receive from the fund company in the folder.

Reason: You must pay tax each year on any dividends from your fund—even if you receive no cash from the fund because you automatically reinvest the dividends in additional fund shares. If you don't keep track, you will pay tax on the dividends twice. That is—when dividends are paid and again when you sell those shares.

Key tax saver: Add reinvested dividends and capital gains distributions to your tax cost (basis) in your fund shares. Because capital gains taxes are owed on the difference between the selling price and your tax cost, increasing the tax cost reduces your tax bill.

Example: You invest $2,000 in ABC Fund. During the three years you own it, the fund pays $500 of dividends that you reinvest. When you sell the shares for $3,000, you owe tax on gain of $500—not $1,000.

Loophole: Increase the yield earned from municipal bond investments by buying funds that own private purpose munis.

Interest paid by private purpose municipal bonds is free from regular tax but subject to the alternative minimum tax (AMT). To compensate, they pay slightly higher yields than regular municipal bonds.

So investors who do not owe the AMT can earn more from their municipal bond portfolio.

How to do it: Read the fund's prospectus before you invest in tax-free municipal bond or money market funds to find out how much of the portfolio is invested in private purpose municipal bonds.

Loophole: Buy mutual funds all year—except in November and December.

By law, funds may distribute any capital gains earned during the year, and they must distribute any dividends received from the stocks and bonds in their portfolio. When you buy shares in a fund that will soon pay dividends, you are paying tax on the money you invested, since you paid more for the shares due to that as-yet-unpaid dividend.

Loophole: You can save taxes by analyzing a fund's capital gains exposure before you buy any shares.

While funds must distribute their dividends and interest to their shareholders every year, nothing prevents funds from building up long-term gains in their portfolios. So two funds that look identical may produce very different after-tax returns when they sell the shares that they own.

Example: Because of appreciation, a fund's value may include as much as 50% of capital gains appreciation. So if the fund manager sold $1 million of shares, shareholders would receive their proportionate share of $500,000 in long-term capital gains. Another fund's value might comprise only 10% of capital gains. Here the tax bite would be lower.

What to do: Call the fund or look for the capital gains exposure in analyses prepared by Chicago financial publisher Morningstar Inc. or other fund data providers.

Loophole: Time fund purchases so you can deduct your losses.

Under the "wash-sale" rule, you can't deduct a loss when you sell shares in a fund and have bought shares in the same fund 30 days before or 30 days after the original sale. Your loss will be deferred until the second batch of shares is sold.

Caution: Investors who have elected to reinvest dividends automatically and who sell only part of their holdings will continue to "buy" shares by way of reinvested dividends after the sale. They must remember to defer the amount of loss equal to the reinvested dividends.

Loophole: Minimize your taxes by choosing the most favorable method of calculating your gains.

The IRS requires you to use the FIFO (first in, first out) method to figure your gain on mutual fund sales—unless you elect a different method. FIFO assumes that the shares you

sold were the first ones you bought—usually the ones with the lowest cost and highest built-in gains.

Better: The *specific identification* method. When you can identify the shares you're selling, you can pick which ones to sell to control the amount of tax you pay. Keep detailed records when you buy fund shares—purchase date, amount paid, price per share and number of shares—so you can sell those that will produce the lowest taxable gain. When you sell them, designate in writing which shares are to be sold by the date of purchase.

How to Keep Much More Of Your Investment Gains

Janice Johnson, CPA, JD, financial services consultant in New York City.

No matter how well your investments perform, it's the money you keep after taxes that counts.

Here's how to avoid the most common investment mistakes that result in higher taxes—and how to keep more of your gains.

MOST COMMON MISTAKES

Mistake: **Not identifying specific shares being sold.** You probably own shares of a stock or a fund that you bought at different times and prices.

If so, you have the opportunity to sell specific shares that produce the least amount of taxes. If you don't identify specific shares being sold (at the time of the sale), the IRS will assume you're selling the first shares you purchased—which may not be best for you.

Example: You bought shares of the same stock at different times, paying first $10, then $20, then $30 per share. Today the stock trades at $25, and you intend to sell some of your shares. But the tax effect per share can be a $15 gain, $5 gain or $5 loss, depending on which shares you sell.

By selecting the most expensive shares to sell —in this case, the ones that cost $30—you can take a $5 loss deduction per share.

Check whether you need long- or short-term gains or losses—look at the holding period of the various lots of stock you own. Holding more than one year gets you long-term treatment.

If you don't identify the specific shares being sold, the IRS will say you sold the $10 shares first and impose tax on the $15 gain per share.

Of course, if you have realized net losses so far for the year, you can sell the least expensive shares first to take the biggest gains tax free, sheltering them from tax with the losses.

Mistake: **Neglecting deductible fees.** Many investors now have *wrap fee accounts*, which simplify broker fees by imposing a single fee that covers all investment advice and transactional costs.

Wrap fees and other investment expenses are deductible as miscellaneous expenses. But the total of these expenses is deductible only if it exceeds 2% of your adjusted gross income (AGI). This limit may reduce or eliminate your deduction for the fees.

Better: Ask your broker for a statement saying how much of your total wrap fee is for transactions related to actual buying and selling of shares. These costs are added to the basis of the shares to reduce your gain or increase your loss.

Mistake: **Not minimizing interest paid on borrowings.** Investors often put more effort into maximizing the interest rates they receive than reducing the interest rates they pay.

Example: Many investors neglect to use low-cost margin loans against their investments. These loans are available from your broker. Instead, they run up high rate consumer loan debt.

People often seem to avoid margin borrowing because they associate it with risky *margin investing*—which is borrowing to invest.

But it isn't reckless to use margin loans to pay off higher rate debt. You wind up with the same amount of debt either way, but you'll pay less interest and the interest is deductible to the extent of investment income.

Mistake: **Having too many accounts with different brokerages.** Over the years, many people accumulate a growing number of investment accounts. Some of these accounts are likely to have small amounts in them. *But there's a triple cost to owning so many accounts...*

• **Investments are harder to monitor** and manage when they are in several accounts.

• **Duplicate fees are charged** for all the services.

• **Tax paperwork is multiplied** when you receive numerous statements.

Better: Consolidate all your various investments into a small number of easy-to-manage accounts at one broker.

Mistake: **Making charitable gifts with cash raised by selling stock.** This is one of the simplest but most costly and common mistakes that investors make.

Much better: Donate appreciated shares to a charity, and let the charity sell them. When you donate appreciated shares that you have owned for more than one year to charity, you get a deduction for their full market value—without ever paying any capital gains tax on their appreciation. The charity (a tax-exempt organization) then can sell the shares tax free to raise cash. The IRS gets nothing.

But if you sell the shares yourself, the IRS takes capital gains tax first. Only what is left after taxes will be available to give to the charity.

Mistake: **Not matching gains against losses all year long.** Minimize taxes on investments by matching gains against losses.

Try to achieve net long-term capital gains in one tax year—taxed at up to 23.8%. Use both long- and short-term capital losses in another year to offset short-term gains— taxed at your maximum ordinary income tax rate of up to 39.6%.

• **Use the 30-day rule.** When you have gains, you can sell securities that have lost money to offset them. Then, after 30 days, you can repurchase the same securities that you sold at a loss to restore your original investment position.

You also will have eliminated the tax on the gain. *Caution:* If you buy back the same securities within 30 days, directly or through an IRA, the loss will be disallowed.

Or you can immediately repurchase similar

securities, such as shares of another fund with the same investment objectives as the one you sold, without losing the loss write-off.

●**Or avoid the 30-day rule.** When you already have losses, you can sell other securities at a gain and then immediately repurchase the same securities. No 30-day rule applies.

You take your gain tax free, restore your original investment position and increase your tax basis in the repurchased shares so any future gain on them will be correspondingly reduced.

Mistake: **Paying off the mortgage on a home too soon.** Many people start prepaying the mortgages on their homes without thinking of all the long-term consequences.

Key: Mortgage interest is generally fully tax deductible. But this is true only of mortgage debt used to buy or remodel a home.

Once you finish paying off a mortgage, only $100,000 of home-equity loan borrowing produces deductible interest.

Beware: In the future, you may need a source of funds to pay children's college costs. But you won't be able to borrow on a tax-deductible basis against the full value of your home because you paid down your mortgage too soon.

Alternative: Consider using the funds that you would use to prepay your mortgage to start a new investment account. If you need cash in the future, you'll have the account and a larger amount of deductible borrowing in place.

With the use of a home-equity loan, you can borrow the full equity value of your home and deduct the interest payments up to $100,000 of the borrowing.

This strategy also is likely to be more profitable than prepaying a mortgage. Mortgage rates today are low, and mortgage interest is deductible.

Prepaying a mortgage may not save much after taxes, while the alternative investment account may produce substantial returns.

Traps to Avoid When Buying A Franchise

Franchising now accounts for nearly one-third of all US retail sales. But if you are thinking of taking a crack at investing in a franchise, look hard before you leap.

While only 5% of franchises fail, according to surveys by the US Department of Commerce, a lot are only moderately successful. But, realize that there are still plenty of pitfalls for the unwary.

Trap: **Thinking anyone can be a franchisee.** There's no one profile of the ideal franchisee, but you're not likely to succeed if you are either a loner or a person who likes to call all the shots.

Reason: You have to be able to listen and interact with the policies and procedures of the franchisor. Every franchisee has to do things the same way. That's the whole logic behind a franchise.

Trap: **Buying a franchise because of a traumatic life change**—divorce, being fired, etc. An upheaval in your life can give you a needed push in that direction, but it shouldn't be the major reason for taking such a large economic step.

The only valid reason to buy a franchise: You really want to go into business for yourself.

Key: Family support. Without it you're behind the eight ball from the start.

Trap: **Thinking of the franchise as just another job.** It isn't. You have to be willing to take on the responsibility of managing your own business, and that's far from a 9-to-5 proposition. You can run a franchise into the ground if you don't give it your all.

Trap: **Picking a franchise that's not suitable for you.** *Better:* Figure out what you like…and what you do best.

Example: If you enjoy working with your hands, you might choose an automotive-services business. If you shine at sales and marketing, a retailing operation might be the right ticket.

***Trap:* Investing in an unproven concept.** You don't have to pick the top franchisor in the field, but a franchise must have at least a couple of successful units operating to be worthy of your consideration.

There are advantages and disadvantages to going with a relatively new concept. You may get a better financial deal, but the risks are also greater. You must weigh the pros and cons.

***Trap:* Not considering a lot of franchise possibilities before making a final choice.** About 1,100 companies in more than 75 industries—from accounting and tax services to bodybuilding salons—sell franchises today. Most of the important franchisors are listed in *The Franchise Opportunity Guide.**

Study the book, note the companies you're interested in...and pick a location where you'd like to live. Take your time studying the material. Concentrate for at least three to six months on finding the franchise that's just right for you.

***Trap:* Failing to check out the franchisor thoroughly.** Once you've narrowed the list, go see the most promising prospects. Ask each company for a copy of the franchise offering circular. By law, the company must give one to prospective buyers. This document provides a wealth of vital information, including history of the business, names of top executives, financial statements, the cost of becoming a franchisee and a list of current franchisees.

If the chemistry between you and the franchisor personnel is not good—forget it. The relationship is very similar to a marriage...but even more difficult to get out of.

Ask the franchisor...

• **When did you award your first franchise?**

• **Is it still in business?**

• **How many franchises have failed?** Where and why?

• **How many franchises do you plan to open** over the next 12 months?

*Available from The International Franchise Association, 1501 K Street, NW, Suite 350, Washington, DC 20005, or online at *www.franchise.org*.

• **Do any of your company's operations** in the same type of business compete with your franchisees?

• **Is the franchise territory exclusive** or non-exclusive?

• **Do you provide aid in financing?**

• **Do you provide site-selection help?**

• **In the event of termination,** what rights do I have?

• **What are my renewal rights?**

• **What are the restrictions on resale?**

• **Is there a policy of mandatory reinvestment**—i.e., a certain percentage of profits that must be reinvested for future growth?

• **Does the franchisor have right of first refusal?**

• **Does the company have to approve the person** I might pick to sell to?

Questions to ask other franchisees...**

• **How long have you been in business?**

• **What kind of support do you get from the franchisor?**

• **Did you initially get adequate training,** good systems and clear manuals?

• **Did the franchisor help you when you needed support** because of unexpected hardship—a death in the family, for instance?

• **Did the franchisor help if it took you longer** to adjust than expected?

• **If you didn't like the business at first,** what did the franchisor do?

• **Did it try to help?**

• **Is the franchisor keeping its end of the bargain,** meeting all your expectations?

• **How long did it take to reach the break-even point?**

• **How long did it take you to recoup your investment?**

• **Is your franchise profitable now?**

• **Are the profits as great as you expected?**

• **Is the franchisor alert to changes in the marketplace** and quick to change with them?

**Meet with as many other franchisees as you can.

487

• **What do you like the most about the franchisor?**

• **What do you like least?**

***Trap:* Failing to develop your own business plan.** Ask yourself, "What am I going to do?" Draw up a balance sheet, including what you're going to live on while the new business is not supporting you.

***Trap:* Not seeking advice from competent professionals.** Don't sink a large amount into a franchise and then stint on a few thousand dollars for expert legal and accounting advice.

A good lawyer knows what the trouble spots are likely to be and can spare you a lot of heartache down the road. A good accountant can make sure you are adequately capitalized and help with financial projections.

You need an OK from both before you sign up for anything.

***Trap:* Being too impatient for profits.** Realize it takes time to build up a business to the point where you can take money out.

It's a mistake to draw down—too early—profits you should be reinvesting to build a super-successful franchise.

New IRS Rules on Reporting Profits And Losses

Mark Luscombe, CPA, JD, principal federal tax analyst for CCH, a global provider of tax, accounting and audit information, based in Riverwoods, Illinois. He is developments chair of the partnership committee, American Bar Association tax section, and coauthor of a biweekly tax strategies column for *Accounting Today*.

A recent law requires your investment broker to track and report more of your investment information to the IRS. Although that likely means higher taxes for many investors, the extra tracking could save money for some.

Until now, the IRS relied solely on investors to report how much profit (or loss) they made on the sale of stocks, bonds and mutual fund shares. You would report the dollar value of any sale on your income tax form and subtract

your cost basis—how much you originally paid for the shares. But cost basis often has been tricky to figure out, especially if you have accumulated shares at different prices over many years…if you have to make adjustments for reinvested dividends and mutual fund capital gains distributions…or if a company had spin-offs or mergers since you bought the stock. The IRS estimates that inaccurate record-keeping by investors regarding investment profits and losses costs the federal government as much as $25 billion a year in tax revenue. In some cases, investors may have paid more than they had to because they didn't want to perform complex calculations for alternative versions of cost basis.

What's changing: The recent law requires your brokerage firm to track and automatically report directly to the IRS your cost basis on any sale.

Here are answers to some commonly asked questions…

• **Does the law affect all kinds of investments?** Brokerages started tracking and reporting profits and losses starting January 1, 2011, on stocks, including foreign stocks, real estate investment trusts (REITs) and exchange-traded funds (ETFs) that own foreign securities…January 1, 2012, on mutual funds, domestic ETFs and dividend-reinvestment plans (DRIPs)…and January 1, 2013, on individual bonds.

The calculations must include stock splits, reinvested dividends and company mergers. Brokerages do not have to report gains or losses for investments bought prior to these dates.

• **Do I need to do anything to be in compliance with the new law?** As in the past, you need to report profits and losses on the sale of any securities in a given year on IRS Form 1040 Schedule D when you file your tax return. Also, because the federal government allows you to calculate your cost basis—and your resulting profits and losses—in several ways, you need to tell your brokerage firm which method you want it to use. The options…

• Specific-share identification allows you to designate the most expensive shares to sell first, resulting in a smaller capital gain.

•First-in, first-out method assumes that you are selling your oldest shares first.

•Average cost method averages the cost over all your shares.

If you don't specify a method, the broker will use the default method, which for stocks is first in, first out…for funds, the average-cost method.

•**What happens if my cost-basis calculations differ from what my brokerage firm sends me?** Contact the firm to resolve the discrepancy, which might reflect a mistaken calculation by the brokerage or by you or just two different methods of calculation. If necessary, have your firm file an amended 1099 Form with the IRS with the correct cost-basis amounts.

Roth IRAs

A revision to the tax law created a nonde-ductible Roth IRA.

•**Amounts contributed to a Roth IRA can be withdrawn tax free and penalty free** at any time. So you can tap it before age 59½ for tax-free funds.

•**Retirement distributions from a Roth IRA will be totally tax free,** provided the five-year holding period is met.

•**Mandatory distributions are not required** from a Roth IRA at age 70½.

These rules mean that a Roth IRA effectively can be used as a flexible tax-free investment account.

In 2013, you can make a full $5,500 contribution ($6,500 if age 50 or older by year end) to a Roth IRA, if AGI is less than $112,000 if single or $178,000 if married filing jointly. There are no longer income requirements when converting a traditional IRA to a Roth IRA.

Edward Mendlowitz, CPA, partner, WithumSmith+Brown, CPAs, 1 Spring St., New Brunswick, New Jersey 08901. *www.withum.com*

Direct Donations

Donations from IRAs directly to charities are allowed for people age 70½ or older—in amounts up to $100,000, according to the new tax law. The amount of the charitable gift is excluded from taxable income but cannot also be claimed as a tax deduction.

What to do: If you do not itemize deductions and want to make a charitable gift, consider doing it directly from your IRA. Consult your financial adviser for details.

Kiplinger.com

Investors Can Profit More

There are two specific ways you can gain more from your investments. First, long-term capital gains are taxed at a preferential rate—up to 23.8% (0% for those in the 10% or 15% tax bracket).

Second, "passive losses" (for example, from limited partnerships) are not deductible, except as an offset against "passive income" (the anti-tax-shelter provision).

Here are investments that look good under these rule…

•**Buying your own home may be the best investment you'll ever make.** First of all, you'll have a place in which to live. And you get tax deductions, not available to people who rent, for real estate taxes and mortgage interest. You can sell the home and exclude gain up to $250,000 ($500,000 on a joint return).

Advantage: The deduction for most consumer interest (on car loans, credit cards, etc.) is not deductible. Home owners, however, can obtain cash—not exceeding $100,000 for such purposes—through home equity loans for which interest is deductible.

• **Real estate investment trusts (REITs) and the new real estate mortgage-investment companies (REMICs)** receive favorable treatment under the new tax-reform law and may become the hottest investments in the field.

• **Real estate limited partnerships are still good,** but only if they produce positive cash flow and income. If you already have investments that are producing passive losses, it's important to find investments that produce offsetting passive income.

• **Municipal bonds with high yields are available.** And the exemption from state and local taxes is important to investors in the higher tax brackets and in high tax states.

• **US Series EE and I Savings Bonds are attractive, especially to conservative investors.** Series EE and I bonds come in denominations as small as $50. Like all Treasury securities, they're exempt from state and local taxes. And you have the option of deferring federal taxes until the bonds are cashed. Moreover, interest on bonds purchased in 1990 or later may be tax free if used to pay educational costs.

INVESTING FOR RETIREMENT

• **Qualified retirement plans for the self-employed are still great investments.** The new law now allows owners to take plan loans that were previously viewed as prohibited transactions.

• **401(k) plans.** Contributions are limited (in 2013, you may put in $17,500, or $23,000 for those age 50 or older by year end), and the rules on withdrawals have been tightened. But contributions are still effectively tax deductible and will accumulate tax free until withdrawn. If your employer has a 401(k) plan, take advantage of it.

• **IRAs.** Many taxpayers may not be able to make deductible contributions because they are covered by their company's retirement plan and their income is over a threshold amount. They can, however, make nondeductible contributions to take advantage of tax-free accumulation. Even better, they may be eligible to make Roth IRA contributions.

Example: Two thousand dollars invested in an IRA at 8% will grow to more than $9,500 in 20 years. If annual taxes had to be paid on the income, the investment would grow to only slightly over $6,000.

22

Fighting the IRS

Solve Your Tax Problems In Advance

Many financial decisions turn on tax consider- ations. But what if you are not sure of the tax consequences of your decision? *For example...*

• **You're considering an exchange of property,** but only if the exchange is ruled tax free.

• **A modification of a divorce settlement is proposed.** How will it affect the status of payments?

• **You're working out an arrangement to defer compensation.** But if it doesn't meet all the tax requirements, you could find your- self being taxed on income you won't receive for years.

• **You want to know if a scholarship is tax free.**

• **A family member needs extensive phys- ical therapy.** Can you build a swimming pool and deduct the cost as a medical expense?

You can't make a sound decision until you know how the IRS will view the transaction.

The solution: Get a private-letter ruling. Any taxpayer (or authorized representative) can get an IRS ruling on the tax effect of most proposed transactions. The IRS charges a fee for these rulings. Corporations have used this pro- cedure most often. A ruling is equally available to an individual. And it applies to tax questions involving estates, trusts and gifts, as well as to personal income taxes.

TAX PROTECTION

If you get a favorable ruling in advance, your tax position is fully protected. Even if other taxpayers are treated differently, or if the IRS changes its mind, the ruling in your case will not be changed retroactively except in unusual circumstances. (*Note:* A private-letter ruling is binding on the particular transaction it covers. Similar situations involving other tax- payers will probably be treated the same way, but not necessarily.)

The IRS gives you a chance to talk the situation over before a ruling is issued. If it appears that some aspects of the transaction may lead to adverse tax results, you can modify or amend your proposal to come up with a plan that will qualify for the ruling you want. *Caution:* There's no point in asking for a ruling if you're sure it will go against you. Study the rulings issued to other taxpayers with similar problems. These rulings are all published, and you can find them through several tax services. Also, your accountant or attorney can probably talk with IRS people and sound them out informally.

Letter rulings generally can't be appealed. You can appeal to the courts only after a return has been filed and tax assessed.

HOW TO GET A RULING

There is no prescribed form. Send a letter to the Internal Revenue Service. The IRS will generally get in touch with you within 21 working days. *Include in your letter...*

• **A complete statement of all the facts.**

• **A carefully detailed description** of the transaction.

• **Names, addresses and taxpayer identification numbers** of all persons involved.

• **Copies of all relevant documents.**

• **An explanation of the transaction's business purpose.** ("Business" includes personal and commercial financial dealings.)

• **A statement of which ruling you are asking for.**

• **Citation of authorities (regulations, decisions, etc.).**

• **Arguments supporting your position.**

• **Whether the issue, or an identical issue,** is being examined, litigated, etc.

• **A request for a conference to discuss the matter.**

• **The location of the district office that has jurisdiction.**

• **A penalty of perjury statement.**

• **Some of the confidential information** (names, addresses, etc.) is deleted before publication of IRS rulings. You should state which information you want deleted and why.

OTHER REQUIREMENTS

You must put everything in writing. If you supply any information verbally, it must be confirmed in writing within 21 days or the IRS will not consider it. If the IRS requests additional information, it must be submitted in writing. Information must be complete. If you leave out or misstate material facts, the ruling could be invalidated.

CONFERENCE

You're entitled to a conference with the IRS. Ask for it when you submit your original letter. The conference is more informal than a hearing. You'll get a chance to argue your position with IRS representatives and see what their opinion is likely to be.

This is the time to find out what objections, if any, the IRS has to your proposal and what changes are necessary to make it acceptable. You or your representative may well be able to come up with modifications to the proposed transaction that will lead to a favorable ruling.

Safe strategy: If the IRS's reaction is negative and you can't come up with an acceptable modification, withdraw your request. Having no ruling at all is better than having an unfavorable one. *Reason:* You must attach any unfavorable ruling to your tax return.

When the IRS will not rule: There are some issues the IRS will not rule on, either by law or as a matter of policy. *Examples:* Purely hypothetical questions, or certain issues involving determinations of fact. *Other major "no-ruling" issues...*

• **The prospective effect of estate taxes** on the property of a living person.

• **Issues on which there are court decisions** the IRS may be planning to appeal.

• **Issues on which no regulations have yet been issued** (unless the application of the law itself is obvious).

• **The effect of pending legislation.**

• **Whether a proposed action would subject** a taxpayer to criminal liability.

Last-Minute Filing Tips

Tom C. Klein, CPA, 450 Seventh Ave., New York City 10123. *www.tckcpa.com*

Don't forget to sign. Both husband and wife must sign a joint return. Be sure to put your name and Social Security number on every form and every piece of paper attached to the return—if they get separated, they may never find their way back.

Check your arithmetic. Make sure you used the right tax table. Mistakes will delay your refund. If you owe money, you may be charged interest.

Tip: Round figures to the nearest dollar. You'll make fewer errors.

Put forms in order. The return on top (Form 1040), then Schedules A, B, C, etc., followed by numerical forms in order.

Don't forget the following forms if they apply…

• **Form 2210, if you owe more than 10% of the total tax.** Use the form to figure whether you owe a penalty or come within one of the exceptions (e.g., your current-year tax payments at least equal last year's tax).

• **Form 6251 (Alternative Minimum Tax).** If you are liable for the alternative minimum tax, you must file Form 6251. It applies if you have tax-preference items, such as accelerated depreciation or intangible drilling costs, or claim certain large itemized deductions, such as state and local taxes.

• **Form 4684, for casualty and theft losses.**

• **Form 8283, if you gave more than $500 in property to charity.** This is a statement showing the nature of the property, valuation, etc.

Answer all questions or check the correct boxes…

Your occupation: You can use general terms like executive or administrator.

On Schedule B (Interest and Dividends): Questions on foreign bank accounts or trusts.

On Schedule C (Self-Employed): Questions on accounting methods and home-office use.

On Form 2441 (Child-Care Credit): Questions on employees hired to work in your home.

Attach all W-2 forms from employers. But you can file without a W-2 if you have to. Attach an explanation of why the form is missing, along with any evidence of wages paid and taxes withheld, such as a final pay stub.

Put on enough postage when you mail the return. If it comes back you could be hit with a penalty for late filing. Don't use a postage meter. The date may be unacceptable as proof. If you're worried about proving you filed on time, use certified mail. Better yet, deliver the return to the IRS personally and get your copy receipted.

Extensions: If you aren't able to file on time, you can get an automatic six-month extension by filing Form 4868 no later than April 15th.

Caution: You get an extension of the time to file, not the time to pay. Estimate the tax due and send it in with Form 4868 (if you pay by credit card on-line or by phone, no form is required). If your estimate is too low, you'll be charged interest. If you're too low by more than 10%, you may be subject to a penalty.

Unanswered Questions Cause Problems

Income tax returns with unanswered questions are considered no returns. That means the statute of limitations never expires and you can be audited no matter how many years have passed. Unanswered questions can also delay refunds, result in interest charges and call attention to your return by IRS agents (since the computer automatically spits out the return). If a question doesn't seem to apply to you—Do you have any foreign bank accounts? Do you claim a deduction for an office in your home? Just answer "no," but answer.

Dealing with the IRS

Peter A. Weitsen, CPA, partner, WithumSmith+Brown, CPAs, 1 Spring St., New Brunswick, New Jersey 08901. *www.withum.com*

There are ways to make the IRS bureaucracy work for you and work efficiently. But you must know how the system operates and where to call or write to get results.

COLLECTION NOTICES

Problem: Even though you've written the IRS an answer to its collection notice, the notices keep coming. You get a second notice, and a third one and then one that says, "Past Due Final Notice (Notice of Intention to Levy)." This final notice (sometimes it's the third in a series) is the one to watch out for. *Trap:* The IRS can seize your bank account without first having an IRS employee meet with you. They can notify you by mail and then automatically take money from your account.

Self-defense: If you get such a final notice, immediately call the phone number given on the notice and explain that you've already written to them and you don't owe tax. The collection-division employee who answers the phone at that number has the authority to put a hold on collection action if given a good reason. Unfortunately, not all of them will take that step.

Loophole I: If the person who answers your call isn't receptive, excuse yourself and call back. You won't get the same person. There's a decent chance that your second call will be answered by someone who is willing to put a hold on the levy.

Loophole II: You can delay collection action on a tax deficiency you're protesting by filing a claim for a refund. The refund claim will cause the IRS to automatically put a hold on collection action. This is a smart move if you've missed the deadline for filing a Tax Court petition.

Late-Filing Excuses That Work

Any person who fails to file a federal income tax return without obtaining a filing extension faces the prospect of stiff tax penalties. But penalties can be avoided if the taxpayer acts quickly to present the IRS with an adequate late-filing excuse. *Here are some excuses that usually work...*

- **The death or serious illness** of an immediate family member.
- **Incapacitating illness** of the taxpayer himself/herself.
- **Absence of the taxpayer from home** due to circumstances beyond his control.
- **Destruction of the taxpayer's records** due to circumstances beyond his control, such as fire or flood.
- **A competent tax adviser told the taxpayer** that a tax return wasn't necessary.
- **The IRS failed to provide the taxpayer with necessary forms** after he requested them to do so in a timely fashion.

To present the excuse, the taxpayer should file the overdue return as quickly as possible, with an explanation of the delay attached. If the IRS is satisfied the taxpayer acted reasonably under the circumstances, it will abate any penalty. But the IRS is not required to accept any excuse, so expedient action by the taxpayer is a must.

Taxpayers who face penalties for misfiling returns or misreporting income will do the best they can to come up with a good explanation. Some excuses work—others don't.

EXCUSES THAT WORK

- **Reliance on bad IRS advice from an IRS employee or an IRS publication.** If the advice came from an employee, you must show that it was his or her job to advise taxpayers and that you gave him all the facts.
- **Bad advice from a tax professional can excuse a mistake** if you fully disclosed the facts to the adviser. You must also show that he was a competent professional, experienced in federal tax matters.
- **Lost or unavailable records will excuse a mistake** if the loss wasn't the taxpayer's fault and he makes a genuine attempt to recover or reconstruct the records.
- **Incapacity of a key person can be a legitimate excuse for filing late.** *Examples:* Serious illness of the taxpayer or a death in his immediate family.

EXCUSES THAT DON'T WORK

• **Pleading ignorance or misunderstanding of the law** generally does not excuse a mistake. *Exception:* Where a tax expert might have made the same mistake.

• **Someone else slipped up.** You are personally responsible for filing your tax return correctly. You can't delegate that responsibility to anyone else. If your accountant or lawyer files late, for example, you pay the penalty.

• **Personal problems don't carry much weight with the IRS.** For example, don't expect to avoid a penalty by pleading severe emotional strain brought on by a divorce.

Easy Ways to File For Extensions

Irving L. Blackman, CPA, retired founding partner, Blackman Kallick, LLP, 10 S. Riverside Plaza, Chicago 60606. www.taxsecretsofthewealthy.com

Better late than never is not a good idea when filing your tax return. Each year more and more Americans face April 15 without the complete information they need to file a proper return. *Frequent problem:* Partnership data from tax shelters is missing. Some promoters are months late in sending out the K-1 schedules that contain individual partners' tax information. What should you do?

Fortunately, there is an easy answer—file extension Form 4868 on or before April 15. The extension automatically gives you until October 15 to file. But it does not give you extra time to pay. The form requires that you estimate the tax you still owe and send it in with your extension request.

Not filing your tax return when due is an expensive disaster. You must pay interest from the due date of the return to the date the tax is finally paid.

There are two additional penalties. The first is a penalty for failure to pay on time. It is .5% per month on the net amount of tax due, up to 25%. This penalty can be avoided if, when you file your return (having gotten a proper extension),

the balance of tax still due doesn't exceed 10% of your total tax liability and you pay the balance with your return. The failure-to-pay penalty goes up to 1% a month after you receive an IRS notice to pay tax. There is an even stiffer penalty for failure to file your return on time. This penalty is 5% per month (for each month or fraction of a month), up to 25% maximum.

Example: Joe Lately mails his return on June 4, along with a $10,000 check for the tax he owes. Since Joe had not filed an extension request, the IRS bills him for the interest plus a $1,100 penalty (5% for one full month plus 5% for a fraction of a month, or 10%, plus .5% for two months for failure to pay). If Joe had filed Form 4868, the most he would pay would be interest plus the .5% penalty for two months (1% x 10,000 or $100).

If you can't pay: Some people put off filing their returns because they owe a sizable balance that they can't pay right away. This is not a good idea. For one thing, the penalties will be much higher ultimately. And putting off filing because you can't pay is probably the most common way that people fall into the trap of not filing at all. That can be disastrous. It may even lead to criminal charges.

How to handle it: You can choose to charge the balance owed to your credit card, but you'll pay a convenience fee ranging from 1.89% to 3.93%, depending on the authorized company that processes the payment. Or you can request an installment agreement (attach Form 9465, *Installment Agreement Request,* to your return). If the amount owed is under $10,000 and certain conditions are met, you have up to three years to complete your payment to the government.

Taxpayer Penalizes IRS For Lateness

You file your tax return in February and get a refund check in May—but no interest. Does the government owe you interest on the money?

No. The government doesn't have to pay interest if it sends your refund within 45 days of the date the return was due—April 15—not 45 days from the date you filed it. But if it doesn't get the refund out within the 45 days, it has to pay interest all the way back to April 15 even if it's only one day late.

No Penalty for Late Filers

Late tax filers may escape penalties because the IRS has *no way of checking* whether or not a person filed an extension request on time. The General Accounting Office (GAO) reports that the IRS has no procedures for tracking Form 4868 extensions and that "as a matter of policy," it generally does not assess failure to file penalties because of this lack. The GAO also reports that, in many cases, taxpayers avoid penalties by producing copies of extensions that were "purportedly" filed on time even though the IRS has no record of them.

Hidden Treasures in Your Old Tax Returns

Steven L. Severin, CPA, tax partner with Deloitte & Touche LLP, Seattle.

It's surprising how often people pay more income tax than they have to. Overlooked deductions, alternative (money-saving) ways of computing tax liability, little-known exemptions and credits—there could be big dollars in missed tax-saving opportunities on your old returns, up to three years old in most cases.

You can still get refunds you overlooked the first time around by filing an amended return (Form 1040X). The procedure is simpler and safer than most people realize.

All the form requires is some basic identifying data, an explanation of the change that's being made, and a recomputation of the tax. You don't have to redo the entire return. And the IRS will figure out how much interest it owes you.

The IRS does not automatically audit you just because you've filed for an additional refund. But it is useful to thoroughly document the basis for amending your return. The clearer it is, the less likely it will be looked at twice.

What if there's a problem area on your return that's unrelated to the item you're amending? For example, you've just found out that you could have claimed a dependency exemption and a large medical deduction for your mother-in-law, whose nursing home bills you were paying two years ago. However, you deducted a lot of travel and entertainment business expenses that year, and you'd have a hard time pulling those records together if the IRS decided to check them.

In practice, the possibility that the IRS will even look at such an unrelated area of your return is low. But you can make things even safer by working with the statute of limitations. *How:* You wait to file until a week or so before the deadline for requesting a refund. The same deadline applies to the IRS. It can't assess additional tax unless you failed to report more than 25% of your income or committed tax fraud.

The worst that could happen, in the unlikely event that the IRS does examine other areas of your return and finds a deficiency, is to apply that deficiency against the refund you've requested. It can't bill you for additional tax due.

The deadline is three years from the original or extended due date of the original return.

Here are items to look for…

•**Medical expenses for medical dependents.** You can sometimes deduct, for tax purposes, medical expenses you've paid on behalf of someone for whom you can't claim a dependency deduction because he has too much gross income. That person must have met all the criteria for being claimed as a dependent, except that his own income was too high. You must have provided more than one half of the total support for a medical dependent.

• **Exemptions.** Occasionally, someone who's not a member of your household could have been claimed as a dependent if he is related to you, received more than half his support from you, lived in your home for the entire year and didn't have too much nonexempt income of his own.

• **Shared support.** Several people may have been contributing to support someone, with no single person contributing more than half of that person's support. With the consent of the others, one member of the group can claim a dependency exemption if the group as a whole provides more than half the support.

• **Miscellaneous possibilities.** Job-hunting expenses, noncash charity contributions or subscriptions to business investment and tax publications.

Once you've filed your return, it takes three to six months to get your refund. You are entitled to interest from the due date of the return. The IRS will figure out the various interest rates that applied back to when your original tax return was due.

Don't get impatient. One taxpayer hadn't gotten his refund from an amended return when he filed the next year's regular return. So he just subtracted the money he figured the IRS owed him. That maneuver cost him some heavy underpayment penalties. The two transactions were treated separately.

Whistle-Blowers

Whistle-blowers now eligible for up to 30% of monetary sanctions collected in securities fraud cases. These incentives are part of the financial-regulation overhaul and come in reaction to multibillion-dollar fraud cases in recent years, including the Ponzi scheme carried out by Bernard Madoff. They apply in cases where a tipster provides information to the Securities and Exchange Commission (SEC) that leads to fraud sanctions of more than $1 million, including fines and ill-gotten profits. Previously, whistle-blowers

were eligible for only 10% of any fine and only in cases involving insider trading. For more information, go to *www.sec.gov/complaint.shtml.*

John Nester, public affairs director, Securities and Exchange Commission, Washington, DC.

Winning the IRS Audit Game

James Brennan, CPA, former partner and director of IRS practice and procedure, Ernst & Young. *www.ey.com*

Nobody wants to suffer an IRS tax audit. But with care and preparation, you can reduce your risk of facing an audit—and minimize the cost and inconvenience of an audit even if you do face one.

Best defense: Start by minimizing your audit risk and head off an audit before it arises.

• **Avoid errors on your tax return that will draw IRS attention.**

• Attach all required schedules, forms and documentation to your return.

• Completely fill out all sections that you are required to fill out.

• Sign your return, and provide the required Social Security or taxpayer ID numbers.

Properly filed returns are processed automatically. Any mistake you make, however, will draw *human* attention from IRS personnel who may begin asking questions about it. If after filing your return, you discover that you *did* make a mistake, correct it by filing an amended tax return, IRS Form 1040X.

Refund snag: If you file an amended tax return claiming a large refund, this can draw extra attention from the IRS. This may be no problem if the rest of your return is "bullet-proof." But if there are large "gray area" items on your return, you might not want to risk closer examination.

Self-defense: One way to handle this is to delay filing your refund claim until the three-year statute of limitations is soon to expire. Amending a return does *not* extend the limitation period. Accordingly, if the IRS decides to examine a claim for refund after the statute of limitations on assessment has expired, the item claimed could be denied in whole or in part by an offset of tax due to other items in the original return. However, in general, the IRS would not be able to assert a deficiency. Delaying the claim filing will ultimately delay the receipt of your refund, but the IRS will pay interest on the refund it approves.

• Add written explanations for unusual items. If you claim large deductions or other unusual items on your tax return, IRS computers may flag it for examination. But by attaching an explanation of the unusual items, you can reduce the risk of a full audit.

If your explanation convinces the IRS that the unusual item is legitimate and that there's nothing to be gained from examining it, the IRS will move on.

• Answer IRS correspondence diligently. Every year, the IRS sends out millions of notices inquiring about specific items on tax returns. *Examples...*

• If 1099s don't match the figures shown on your tax return, the IRS may send a letter asking you to explain the difference.

• The IRS may request information to determine if certain income reported on a return is subject to self-employment tax.

Goal: Satisfy the IRS inquiry right away so it doesn't expand. Give the IRS a timely, full answer. Make it easy for the IRS agent who receives your response to understand it. Include a copy of the IRS notice you received, a clear explanation of your situation and copies of all documents you need to support your position.

By not drawing IRS attention to your return, and quickly resolving questions, you can minimize audit risk.

MANAGING AN AUDIT

There is always a chance that you will be called for an audit, even if you minimize your audit risk. But if you find yourself facing an audit, you can minimize its likely cost—in both tax adjustments and inconvenience—with sound preparation and by understanding the audit process.

Useful: IRS Publication 1, *Your Rights as a Taxpayer.* It is available free at 800-TAX-FORM (800-829-3676) or from the IRS Web site, *www. irs.gov.*

When you receive an audit notice from the IRS—if the examination is an "office examination"—it will state the items on your tax return that the IRS wants to look at. And it will set a time and a place for the audit to take place.

If that date is inconvenient for you—you need more time to prepare or have some other conflict—you can ask to reschedule. The IRS will be reasonable about meeting your request if you have reasonable grounds for making it. Do *not* ask to postpone an audit just to delay.

Strategy: Your goal should be to answer the IRS's questions about the specified items quickly and clearly—and prevent the IRS inquiry from spreading to other areas. *How...*

• Bring to the audit the records needed to document the items mentioned in the audit notice and *only* those records. Do not bring all your records and give the auditor a chance to thumb through them.

• Answer the auditor's questions, but volunteer nothing else. Avoid conversation about your finances, business or personal life that could strike the auditor's curiosity.

• Prepare and organize records. If your records look complete and organized, the auditor may feel he has little to gain by going through them. But if they look incomplete and disorganized, he may feel that closer scrutiny will pay off.

• Keep the auditor on the topic. The auditor is supposed to ask questions only about the items listed in the audit notice. If he seems to begin "fishing" with questions about other matters, respectfully ask what the questions have to do with the items under examination.

Caution: The auditor has the right to expand the examination, so question any inquiries in a manner that does not imply you are hiding something.

• Don't guess at answers. If you are not sure of the answer to a question, say, "I'll have to get back to you," rather than make a guess that could be wrong.

•**Ask the auditor to put all requests for information in writing.** This prevents misunderstandings and creates a record that keeps the IRS from later claiming it asked you to provide certain information when in fact it didn't.

•**Have a professional, businesslike attitude.** If you act as if you have something to hide, the auditor may conclude that you do. The last thing you want to do is personally antagonize an auditor.

Key decision: *The Taxpayer Bill of Rights* gives you the right to be represented at an audit by a professional, such as a CPA, an attorney or an accountant. In most cases, you don't have to meet the auditor—if you don't want to. A professional will be better able to handle complicated tax issues than a layperson. Even if the items in an audit notice are simple, a professional may help prevent the audit from expanding into other areas.

A professional will be better able to say, "I don't know" to an auditor's questions, when you might feel compelled to give an answer. After the professional says, "I don't know," the auditor may drop the issue. If not, the professional will have time to carefully prepare an accurate answer that addresses the auditor's concerns—while your answer probably would have been improvised.

Relevant: Question whether an auditor's inquiries are relevant to the issues in the audit notice or relevant to the entire tax return itself. Many laypeople don't have the knowledge or nerve to do this.

Unproductive: Telling an auditor when his inquiries would be unproductive.

Example: A professional may get an auditor to drop his questioning of a deduction by showing that other factors would prevent its disallowance from affecting the bottom line tax bill. You might not know about the other factors.

When deciding whether to pay a professional to represent you in an audit, consider the dollar amount of the items in the audit notice and the potential liability on other items should the audit spread to other areas of your tax return.

AUDIT'S END

At the audit's end, you will get a notice that either finds "no change" is called for or that lists proposed adjustments to your return. You can accept the adjustments and pay the tax due or you can take your case to the IRS Appeals or Tax Court. *First...*

•**Meet with the auditor's supervisor** if you think the auditor's report contains obvious mistakes that should be corrected before going any further.

•**Obtain the auditor's notes and work papers,** either by request or under the *Freedom of Information Act,* to understand his position and to help build your case for appeal.

APPEALING

If an audit goes against you, you still have the chance to reduce your tax bill by going to the IRS Appeals Division.

Key: Unlike IRS auditors, Appeals Officers are authorized to negotiate compromise settlements while considering "the hazards of litigation."

Best: If you've represented yourself through the audit to this point, it is best to hire a professional to handle the appeal.

Careful legal arguments are more important at Appeals. And because Appeals involves negotiations, you want an experienced negotiator on your side to get the best possible deal for you and to let you know when you've obtained it.

Beware of Services Claiming to Help Settle Tax Debts for Less

Services that claim to help settle tax debts for less than the full amount usually are fraudulent. Only the IRS can agree to let you pay less tax than you owe—and it accepts no more than 25% of so-called Offers in Compromise (OICs). People with OICs may lose all or almost all their savings, property, home equity, cars and future income.

What to do: If you will have trouble paying what you owe, you can request installment payments by filing IRS Form 9465 if the amount is $25,000 or less, or Forms 433F and 9465 if the amount is more than $25,000. If the amount is $10,000 or less, IRS consent is automatic. You will be charged a fee and interest for the plan, plus possible penalties.

Information: *www.irs.gov*

Kiplinger's Personal Finance, 1729 H St. NW, Washington, DC 20006.

IRS Hit List

Ralph J. Pribble, former IRS field agent, tax consultant/preparer, Foster City, California.

Doctors and dentists tend to be very high-priority targets. *Items IRS agents look for:* Dubious promotional expenses. If the same four people take turns having lunch together once a week and take turns picking up the tab, a close examination of diaries and logbooks will show this. Agents also take a close look at limited partnership investments, seeking signs of abusive tax shelters. And they take a dim view of fellowship exclusions claimed by medical residents. *Other target occupations...*

• **Salespeople.** Outside and auto salespeople are particular favorites. Agents look for and often find poorly documented travel expenses and padded promotional figures.

• **Airline pilots.** High incomes, a propensity to invest in questionable tax shelters and commuting expenses claimed as business travel make them inviting prospects.

• **Flight attendants.** Travel expenses are usually a high percentage of their total income and often aren't well documented. Some persist in trying to deduct pantyhose, permanents, cosmetics and similar items that the courts have repeatedly ruled are personal rather than business expenses.

• **Executives.** As a group they are not usually singled out. But if the return includes a Form 2106, showing a sizable sum for unreimbursed employee business expenses, an audit is more likely. Of course, anyone whose income exceeds $50,000 a year is a high-priority target just because of the sums involved.

• **Teachers and college professors.** Agents pounce on returns claiming office-at-home deductions. They are also wary of educational expense deductions because they may turn out to be vacations in disguise.

• **Clergy.** Bona fide priests, ministers and rabbis aren't considered a problem group. But if W-2s show income from non-church employers, the IRS will be on the alert for mail-order ministry scams.

• **Waitresses, cabdrivers, etc.** Anyone in an occupation where tips are a significant factor is likely to get a closer look from the IRS nowadays.

Many people, aware that their profession subjects them to IRS scrutiny, use nebulous terms to describe what they do. Professionals in private practice may list themselves as simply "self-employed." Waitresses become "culinary employees," pilots list themselves as "transportation executives." But there's a fine line here. Truly deceptive descriptions could trigger penalties. And if the return is chosen for audit, an unorthodox job title for a mundane profession could convince the agent that you have something to hide. Then he'll dig all the deeper.

Taxpayer Victories

Recent taxpayer victories over the IRS in court can help you cut your tax bill. *Opportunities...*

• **IRS pays $5,000 to taxpayer for altering document.** The IRS submitted to the Tax Court a list of facts regarding a tax dispute that it said it and the taxpayer had "agreed upon." But when the taxpayer's lawyer examined the list, he found that it *differed* from what he actually had agreed to. An IRS agent at first testified that she didn't know who had altered the document—then admitted that she had.

Tax Court: The IRS was ordered to pay $5,000 to the taxpayer as a sanction. The IRS wasn't defaulted only because the altered facts weren't important with regard to the merits of the case.

David K. Straight, TC Memo 1997-569.

• **Bankruptcy wipes out tax bill.** A person didn't file tax returns for several years, until the IRS assessed taxes for those years and the Tax Court determined the amount of tax due. Then he filed late returns showing that amount as due—but *didn't* pay the tax. Two years later, he declared bankruptcy and the tax bill was discharged. But the IRS objected that taxes can't be discharged unless they are reported on a valid tax return and noted that the individual hadn't filed his tax returns until after it had assessed taxes against him.

Court: Nothing in the law requires that tax returns be filed before a tax assessment is received to be valid. The individual had waited the required two years after filing them to declare bankruptcy, so the discharge of the tax bill stands.

John C. Pierchoski, Bankr. WD Pa., Adv. No. 97-2414-BM.

• **Taxpayer gets to keep $637,000 mistaken refund.** Leroy Stanley settled a tax dispute by making a payment to the IRS. The IRS miscredited the payment and sent him a $637,000 erroneous refund. The IRS didn't realize its mistake until more than two years later. Then it demanded the refund be returned.

Court: To recover the refund, the IRS either had to reassess the tax before the statute of limitations expired or sue for the return of the refund within two years. But it had missed both deadlines—so Stanley keeps the money.

Leroy P. Stanley, Fed. Cir., No. 97-5002.

• **Trust saves family home from the IRS.** A couple put their home in a trust for their five-year-old son, then continued to live in it. Later, the IRS assessed a tax bill against them and tried to collect the taxes against the home.

The IRS argued that the trust was fraudulent because the couple owed a tax debt when it was set up—and that the trust was a sham because the couple still used the home as their own.

Court: The trust was set up to assure the home would pass to the child, which was a legitimate purpose. The tax debt that existed when the trust was set up had since been paid, and so was irrelevant. The trust's terms meaningfully restricted how the couple could use the home, so it was not a sham. Thus, the trust was valid—and the home was beyond the reach of the IRS.

In re: Eugene T. Richards, Jr., Bankr ED Pa., No. 97-14798DWS.

• **Mere attempt to commit tax crime isn't punishable.** A husband and wife secretly took $400,000 from a corporation they owned, disguising their actions and not reporting the money on their tax returns. But the IRS found out and charged them with tax evasion.

Court of Appeals: The couple had committed no offense, even though they had tried.

Background: Their corporation had no accumulated profits—so the money they took out of it was merely a return of what they had previously put into it through equity contributions and loans. Thus, the couple owed no tax on the withdrawals even though they *thought* they did and tried to evade the tax. "Bad intentions, alone, are not punishable."

US v. James D'Agostino, CA 2, No. 97-1336.

• **Getting professional advice saves penalties.** Two sisters underreported the tax they owed on more than $3 million of income they received, and the IRS imposed negligence and substantial understatement penalties against them. But they protested that they had relied on the advice of a tax attorney.

Court of Appeals: Obtaining professional advice refutes the charge of negligence. "Due care does not require unsophisticated individuals to independently reexamine their tax liabilities after taking the prudent step of securing advice from a tax attorney." The penalties are lifted.

Tracy P. Streber, CA 5, No. 96-60443.

• **Interest on improper loan is deductible.** A doctor borrowed $130,000 from the retirement plan of the medical corporation he owned to invest in another business. The IRS later ruled the loan improper and told him to repay it with interest. The doctor did so and deducted the interest he paid. The IRS denied the deduction because the loan was improper to begin with.

Tax Court: Interest that is paid on a loan used to carry an investment qualifies as deductible investment interest. The doctor had in fact paid such interest, so he gets the deduction.

French E. Hickman, TC Memo 1997-545.

• **Loan to keep favorite restaurant open is deductible.** Kenneth and Carol Bauer enjoyed frequent dining at their favorite restaurant. When the restaurant ran into financial problems, the couple made a loan to the restaurant's owners, who were friends of theirs. But the restaurant went out of business and the loan wasn't repaid. The Bauers then claimed a bad-debt deduction for their loss. But the IRS disallowed the deduction. It said the loan was not genuine because it hadn't been documented, bore no interest and had been made to friends.

Tax Court: The Bauers had made four previous loans on similar terms, and all had been repaid. This showed the loan was genuine, so the deduction was allowed.

Kenneth R. Bauer, TC Memo 1998-133.

• **Owner not liable for corporation's unpaid taxes.** Larrie Blasberg was the sole owner of a corporation that went out of business owing $67,000 in taxes. The IRS levied on his personal assets to collect the tax bill.

Court: A corporation is a separate taxpayer from the individual who owns it. The IRS had not shown that Blasberg had used the corporation improperly in any way, so it had no reason to hold him personally liable for its taxes. The levied-upon property must be returned to him and the IRS must pay his legal expenses.

Larrie S. Blasberg, S.D. Fla., No. 94-1844-CIV-DAVIS.

• **Attorney–client privilege expanded.** Only documents prepared in anticipation of litigation are protected by attorney–client privilege. But the litigation can be only "potential," says a new court decision.

Facts: A company considered making a deal that would produce a large tax loss. Its lawyer feared that the loss would invite a legal challenge from the IRS, so he hired an accountant to analyze it. Then the company went ahead.

The IRS did challenge the deal and demanded to see the accountant's work papers. The company said it was protected by attorney-client privilege—but the IRS answered that it wasn't privileged because the papers were prepared before the deal took place, when no litigation was possible.

Court: The papers were prepared in anticipation of litigation nonetheless, so they were privileged.

Monroe Adlman, CA 2, No. 96-6095.

• **IRS has burden of proving taxpayer's worth.** The IRS believed an individual was not reporting income taken from his business, so it reconstructed his income for three years by calculating his net worth at the start of the period and how it changed. The individual protested that the IRS's figure for his initial net worth was wrong. But the IRS answered that if this was so, it was up to the individual to prove otherwise.

Court: For the individual. The IRS's computation of initial net worth was arbitrarily based on "an absence of evidence," so it was not presumed to be correct. In such cases, the IRS has the burden of showing net worth with "reasonable certainty"—it can't just assume what it wants to reach its conclusion.

Jung K. Yoon, CA 5, No. 97-60252.

Top Filing Mistakes... According to the IRS

No matter how careful you are in preparing your annual tax return, it's easy to miss something. *Here are some common errors...*

Error: Miscalculating medical and dental expenses. The deduction is based on adjusted gross income (AGI). Figure your AGI on your 1040 before calculating your medical-expense deduction.

Error: Taking the wrong amount of earned income credit. Use the tables in the 1040 instruction booklet to avoid mistakes.

Error: **Entering the wrong amount of tax from the tax tables.** Be sure to use the table that applies to your filing status (married filing jointly, single, etc.).

Error: **Confusing Social Security tax and federal income tax.** Form W-2 shows both. Be sure to use the right figure for income tax withheld.

Error: **Making a mistake in calculating the child- and dependent-care credit.** Use Form 2441 and be sure to check your math. Then check it again.

Error: **Incorrect refund of balance due.** Verify your math. Compare the tax you owe with the amount you have paid through with-holding and estimated tax payments.

Error: **Failing to claim the earned in-come credit.** Refer to the instructions in the tax package if your income is low, and especially if you have a child. *Note:* EIC now applies not only to those with children.

Error: **Making a mistake in figuring the taxable amount of your Social Security benefits.** Use the Social Security benefits work sheet in the instruction booklet.

IRS Tax Topic 303. www.irs.gov

All About IRS Notices

The first thing to do when you get an IRS notice is to understand what it means. The notice may not be anything to get excited about—for example, the automatic notice the IRS sends when you file an amended return.

Never ignore an IRS notice for payment, no matter how wrong the notice is. Respond quickly, within the time limit given on the notice. Once the IRS computer has you target-ed, you'll continue to get threatening notices until you do something to take the problem out of the system.

• **Don't panic and pay without first check-ing the figures on a payment notice.** The IRS may have made a mistake.

• **Avoid trying to straighten out mistakes in person at your local IRS office.** The clerk you deal with won't be able to resolve the problem—you'll be wasting your time. Contact your local service center instead.

• **Keep copies of your letters to the IRS.** You may need a copy if the service center loses your letter and says you didn't respond in time.

• **Put your Social Security number on every letter you send the IRS.**

• **See your tax adviser if sizable amounts of money are involved** or if you have the slightest question about the notice. Send your adviser a copy of the notice and copies of all your correspondence to the IRS, to keep his files up-to-date.

Never Meet an IRS Auditor At Your Home

Once inside your home, an auditor may question elements of your lifestyle and open up entire new areas to investigate.

Best: Have a professional handle any meetings with an auditor. Assign him or her power of attorney, and tell the IRS to send him all questions. *Caution:* Accountants can be forced to testify against you in court. Lawyers cannot. So if you are seriously worried about anything the IRS is investigating, it may be wiser to hire a lawyer.

Randy B. Blaustein, Esq., senior tax partner, R.B. Blaustein & Co., New York City.

Two Kinds of Tax Audits

An office audit usually concerns only a few items on your return. These items are checked off in the notification let-ter, which also sets an appointment for you to appear at an IRS office. A field audit is a more general examination. The letter asks you to make an appointment for an agent to come to your home or business.

PREPARING FOR AN OFFICE AUDIT

The notification letter usually gives you two or three weeks to prepare for the audit. The items the IRS is interested in are checked off or written in on the back of the letter.

• **If the items checked off can be readily documented by canceled checks and receipts,** you may be able to resolve the issue by mail. Make a copy of the documentation and send it in. But first call the agent and tell him you're mailing the proof. He'll tell you how to address the envelope so it won't go astray. Hopefully you'll eventually get a letter back from the agent advising you that your return has been accepted as filed—examination closed.

• **The letter of acceptance may take months to come.** If you send the information in and hear nothing for a couple of months, chances are it has been accepted.

• **If the questioned item is something that really cannot be answered by mail,** you or your representative must assemble your documentation and keep your appointment.

• **Ask for a postponement** if the date in the notification letter does not give you time to prepare thoroughly. Auditors are very cooperative when you call up and ask for a short delay.

Important: You have to present substantiation only for items that are checked off in the letter. Take only this documentation to the audit. Don't answer questions about items not checked off. Another notification letter is required for items you were not told to prepare for.

PREPARING FOR A FIELD AUDIT

In a field audit, your entire return is open for examination. When you telephone the agent to set up an appointment, ask him what he's looking for. You may be able to narrow down the issues. Have documentation ready. While the agent can ask for proof of all items on your return, he has only a limited amount of time.

If the documentation you give him in the first meeting doesn't satisfy him, ask him to list the questions he still has and set a second appointment.

Three Kinds of IRS Audits

You've filed your tax return and everything seems to be in order. Then you find out you're being audited. *Here's what to expect...*

CORRESPONDENCE AUDIT

Some IRS audits are more thorough than others. The least thorough is a correspondence audit. Here, the IRS seeks to test compliance with perhaps one item on either a regional or national basis. For example, the IRS may send out hundreds of letters asking for verification of energy-credit expenditures. When you receive this notice, simply mail in the appropriate documentation to support your deduction.

Technically, this inquiry constitutes an audit. Once it takes place, there is very little chance that the rest of your return for that particular tax year will ever be audited. If the IRS should decide that it wants to audit your return at a later date, it must go through a formal "reopening procedure"—which is rarely done. The obvious advantage of the correspondence audit is that if the IRS does not select an area in which you may be vulnerable, it will never know that it could have made other adjustments to your return that might have resulted in more tax.

OFFICE AUDIT

The next level of audit is the office audit. This examination is handled at a local IRS office. Typically, one or two deductions on your return will be questioned. Barring special circumstances, such as suspicion of fraud or gross errors in other areas of the return, the audit will not be extended to other issues. The primary advantage of the office audit is that it is generally conducted by individuals who lack the sophistication in tax matters needed to recognize more significant issues. The training and method of operation at the office-audit level consists of telling the examiner (called a tax auditor) exactly what to look for in a given issue. The audit will be conducted mechanically and "by the book."

FIELD AUDIT

These audits are conducted by the best educated employees at the IRS, known as revenue agents. They are usually assigned the tax returns of businesses and wealthy individuals. An audit conducted by a revenue agent is usually quite complete, and although he or she will not examine every item in depth, he will attempt to cover many areas. One of the jobs of the revenue agent is to identify promptly areas with the potential for extra tax dollars and then to spend time developing the tax issues.

The chances of having the IRS uncover unreported income or disallow deductions that are either personal or otherwise not deductible are more likely at the field audit than at any other type of IRS examination. It is unwise to try to handle a field audit yourself because the potential adverse ramifications can be severe —even if you think you did everything right. A sharp revenue agent can be quite creative when it comes to interpreting the Internal Revenue Code in the government's favor. Your ability to survive such creativity is enhanced by having an experienced practitioner representing your interests.

Audit Ploy to Avoid

Readers of popular tax services are frequently advised to confront IRS auditors with such a stack of bills and receipts that the overwhelmed agent will assume, in frustration, that the proof he wants is somewhere in the pile. This is bad advice. An experienced auditor will recognize this ploy at once. And as one court said recently, "Merely presenting an 'avalanche' of receipts falls woefully short of meeting the [substantiation] requirements…"

Lynch, TC Memo 1983-173.

If an IRS Agent Comes To Your Door

The IRS recently issued instructions to be followed by auditors making field visits to a taxpayer's home or place of business. *Rule:* Agents may enter private premises "only when invited in by the rightful occupant." The IRS is concerned about the growing number of taxpayer lawsuits for violation of privacy rights.

Manual Transmittal 4200-471.

Before Investing— Study Audit Fees

For advance warning of company problems, study the company's audit fees. The fees are reported in a firm's Securities and Exchange Commission filings. If audit fees grow suddenly, that could mean the auditors have found something requiring additional accounting attention…or see risks of future problems.

What to do: Examine similar-sized companies in the same industry. If one has a much higher audit fee than others, look carefully at the reasons before investing in that firm.

Jonathan D. Stanley, PhD, CPA, assistant professor of accounting, College of Business, Auburn University, Auburn, Alabama, and leader of a study of SEC filings from 2000 to 2007, published in *Auditing: A Journal of Practice & Theory.*

Audits the IRS Forgets to Do

Asking the IRS to transfer your case to another district may be the key to avoiding an audit. Don't expect the IRS to admit it, but transferred cases often fall through the cracks and never get worked on even though the taxpayer has been notified of the examination. Delays caused in processing the case file between districts, combined with the fact that the case is likely to go to the bottom of the pile when it is assigned to a new agent, may bring help from the statute of limitations. Rather than asking the taxpayer to extend the statute of limitations, as is the usual practice, many agents are inclined to take the easy way out and close transferred cases without auditing them.

Ms. X, former IRS agent, author of How to Beat the IRS *(Boardroom Classics).*

What to Do If You Haven't Kept Good Records

Under the law, a taxpayer has the burden of proving his/her deductions. If you haven't kept good records, get duplicate receipts from the people you paid money to. *Alternatives:* Sworn affidavits, copies of canceled checks from your bank (usually available for a fee).

Under IRS guidelines, agents will generally give you adequate time to come up with proof if they believe you're making a good-faith effort to cooperate.

Most agents will allow only what you can substantiate under the circumstances. The balance is negotiable. Always present a plausible story to explain your lack of records. *Example...*

"I realize I didn't follow the law 100%, but I couldn't because I had to do so much traveling and there was so much illness at home that I had to take care of. I'm willing to take a reasonable disallowance and prove the illnesses."

What records you should have:

Itemized deductions are a common IRS target. *Here's the information you'll need to support your numbers...*

MEDICAL EXPENSES

- **Doctor and dentist bills.**
- **Copies of prescriptions.**
- **Doctor's letter describing the illness** and treatment to justify travel costs.
- **Copies of premium invoices** and policies to prove medical insurance coverage.

TAXES

- **Copies of state and local returns.**
- **Tax bills and receipts** (property tax).

INTEREST

- **Copies of promissory notes.**
- **Mortgage amortization tables.**

CONTRIBUTIONS

- **Letters from the organization** that prove the donation.
- **Appraisals or other proof of value.**

CASUALTY LOSSES

- **Police or fire department reports.**
- **Description of property** and proof of ownership.
- **Appraisals to establish value.**
- **Itemized list of stolen/**destroyed items.
- **Documented insurance recovery.**

PROFESSIONAL FEES

- **Invoices or letters** itemizing services and detailing percentage of tax-deductible work.

Stuart R. Josephs, former tax partner, BDO Seidman, San Diego, CA.

INADEQUATE RECORDS NOTICE

That's what you'll get from the IRS after an audit if you haven't kept proper records to substantiate your income and deductions. Despite poor record keeping, you can often work out a satisfactory settlement—the IRS may take your word on a lot of things if it's reasonable. But don't try it twice. One taxpayer was charged with fraud when he made the same "mistakes" two years later. The government said he had received an inadequate records notice, so he must have known exactly what was wrong.

Your Taxpayer Rights

Margaret M. Richardson, regional director, Legg Mason, Inc., Baltimore, Maryland. *www.leggmason.com*. She is a former commissioner of the Internal Revenue Service.

Rights for some taxpayers were significantly expanded by the *IRS Restructuring and Reform Act.*

Most people file their tax returns uneventfully and never have a problem with the IRS. But for those who do incur a problem, dealing with the IRS can be traumatic. The taxpayer rights added by this legislation might help you resolve any problems you experience with the IRS—with less cost and upset.

• **More IRS officials on your side.** The Taxpayer Advocate Service (TAS) serves as the independent representative of taxpayers' interests within the IRS.

The law created a National Taxpayer Advocate with local offices to deal directly with taxpayers. Local Taxpayer Advocates now report directly to the National Taxpayer Advocate in Washington, DC, rather than to local IRS District Directors.

The Taxpayer Advocate Service is supposed to monitor the performance of the IRS, identify problems incurred by taxpayers, recommend system improvements to help taxpayers and make legislative proposals to Congress. It also has the power to cut IRS red tape to solve problems with IRS bureaucracy that taxpayers haven't been able to resolve through normal channels.

Examples: Missing refunds, miscredited payments, erroneous or unexplained tax notices and so on.

Emergency help: The law also allows the Taxpayer Advocate to provide emergency help to stop an imminent IRS collection action—such as a property seizure, levy or lien.

Request such emergency help by filing IRS Form 911, *Request for Taxpayer Advocate Service Assistance.* Obtain Form 911 by calling the TAS at 877-777-4778 or going to its Web page, *www.irs.gov/advocate.*

This site provides…

• **Addresses and phone numbers** for all local offices of the TAS.

• **Form 911,** ready to be downloaded and filed, along with the new rules specified by Congress for determining when relief will be granted.

• **Copies of IRS Publication 1,** *Your Rights as a Taxpayer,* and highlights of *The Taxpayer Bill of Rights 2.*

• **The Taxpayer Advocate's *Annual Report to Congress,*** which details the problems that taxpayers most frequently incur and the Taxpayer Advocate's recommendations for dealing with them.

• **Help for "innocent spouses."** Congressional hearings on IRS reform highlighted the problems of persons who unwittingly become liable for tax bills incurred by former spouses. *Two provisions now help innocent spouses…*

• The IRS now has authority to grant relief from a tax obligation as a matter of fairness—even when no provision of the Tax Code authorizes such relief.

Example: When one spouse was unaware that the other spouse took money earmarked to pay taxes and used it for other purposes.

This gives IRS personnel discretion to act in the interest of justice in cases where, in the past, their hands were tied by their duty to follow the letter of the law.

• The law allows a divorced, widowed or separated spouse to limit liability on a joint tax return. The person elects "separate liability" based on his/her share of the items on the return.

Without this election, each spouse can be held separately liable for all the taxes due on a joint return.

Helpful: IRS Publication 971, *Innocent Spouse Relief,* explains the rules. Obtain it by calling 800-TAX-FORM (800-829-3676) or from the IRS Web site, *www.irs.gov.*

• **No more interest and penalties on late-assessed taxes.** Interest and penalties on an individual tax return are frozen if the IRS fails to provide a tax liability notice within 36 months after the return is filed.

This ends the risk that if the IRS delays examining your tax return for years, a huge bill for interest and penalties will result.

• **Pay tax bills in installments.** The law validates an IRS program that lets taxpayers automatically obtain installment-payment agreements for tax bills of up to $10,000 that they can't afford to pay.

The failure-to-pay penalty also is cut in half —from 0.5% to 0.25% per month—for persons who use installment agreements.

To obtain an agreement, you must agree to pay off the overdue tax within three years and must have properly filed all returns owed and paid all taxes due during the prior five years.

• **Expanded tax adviser–client privilege.** The new law extends the protections of attorney–client privilege to cover the dealings of all tax professionals who are authorized to practice before the IRS with their clients.

Examples: CPAs, enrolled agents, enrolled actuaries.

This rule can prevent the IRS from summoning a tax adviser's work papers and using them as evidence against the adviser's client.

The expanded privilege has limits: It applies only in civil cases, not criminal cases, and it does not apply against state or local tax authorities.

Also, attorney–client privilege itself is subject to many limitations. It does not apply to all dealings between an attorney and a client.

Generally, it applies only to those dealing with—or anticipating—litigation. And privilege is lost for documents officially seen by any third party other than the attorney or client.

• **"Burden of proof" shifts to the IRS in court disputes.** After a taxpayer has met specified record-keeping requirements and has cooperated with the IRS during a tax examination, the burden of proof in a court shifts from the taxpayer to the IRS.

Danger: Persons who have heard of this provision may mistakenly believe that it applies to IRS audits. However, it does not.

• **Defenses against liens and levies.** The law requires that taxpayers must receive written notice of their rights regarding all IRS liens and levies.

Example: The IRS must provide written notification that a taxpayer has the right to request a hearing before an impartial appeals officer within 30 days after the IRS issues a notice of lien or levy.

In the hearing, the taxpayer can require that the IRS consider alternative collection action, such as an installment-payment agreement.

If a hearing is requested, the proposed collection action may not take place until after the appeals officer has made a finding. After that, the taxpayer has another 30 days to challenge the appeals finding in court. During that period, the IRS may not act.

These provisions only formalize rules the IRS had previously adopted on its own. But the requirement of written notice can prevent taxpayers from being victims of "surprise" liens and levies and better enable them to respond to the IRS with a timely, effective defense.

Proof of Charity

The IRS has imposed tough substantiation rules for charitable contributions. *For cash gifts:* Taxpayers must have a canceled check, receipt or other written evidence showing the amount, date of the gift and the charity's name. For gifts of $250 or more you must have a receipt from the charity. *For gifts of property:* A receipt and a reliable written record about the property will be required. The receipt must include the taxpayer's name, the date and location of the gift and a detailed description of the property. For property over $500, you must use Form 8283. Written appraisals are necessary for property gifts worth $5,000 or more.

Prop. Reg. Sec. 1.170A-13.

IRS Power to Get at Financial Records

The IRS can compel production of any records of a taxpayer's financial dealings—not only from banks and brokers but also from department stores, etc. *Objective:* To find out if the taxpayer is spending more than the income he reported on his return. If he is, he may be asked to explain where he's getting the money—and to pay taxes on it.

How to Protect Yourself From Excess IRS Interest Charges

Peter A. Weitsen, CPA, partner, WithumSmith+Brown, CPAs, 1 Spring St., New Brunswick, New Jersey 08901. *www.withum.com*

When the IRS comes up with a deficiency as the result of an audit, the taxpayer is given a waiver to sign and mail back to the service. According to the tax law, if the IRS doesn't demand payment of the tax bill within 30 days after the waiver was executed, interest on the deficiency stops running.

Problem: The IRS has been charging some taxpayers interest right up to the date of billing, which is often several months after the waiver was signed and returned. This extra interest can be several hundred dollars more than you should pay.

What to do: Carefully check interest charges before paying the deficiency bill. Interest should be charged for the period beginning with the due date of the return and ending 30 days after you sign the waiver and mail it back to the IRS. Pay the tax you owe and the interest that you determine to be correct. Clearly explain in an accompanying letter how you arrived at your figures, including a detailed computation of the correct interest. *Note:* Pay the deficiency bill within 10 days after you get it. If you don't, interest will start running again.

Stopping IRS Interest

Audited taxpayers can stop interest from building up on proposed tax liabilities (while preserving their right to contest the auditor's findings in Tax Court) by depositing the contested amount with the IRS. *Conditions:* The deposit must be made before the IRS sends a statutory notice of deficiency—a 90-day letter. The taxpayer must say in writing that the payment is "a deposit in the nature of a cash bond." *Drawback:* If the taxpayer wins in court, the IRS doesn't have to pay interest on the refunded deposit.

IRS Revenue Procedure 82-51.

How to Appeal a Tax Auditor's Decision— And Win

The best place to settle a tax dispute with the IRS is at the audit or examiner level. However, if you don't reach a satisfactory settlement there, you can request an IRS appeals division hearing. If you document your appeal with sound facts or a good legal argument, you have an excellent chance of winning at least some reduction in your tax bill without having to go to court.

In dollars, the appeals division settles about 50¢ to 60¢ for the taxpayer, per tax dollar dispute.

WHY APPEALS PAY OFF

• **Experienced hearing officers.** Appeals are handled by highly trained and experienced IRS personnel called appeals officers. Most are CPAs and/or attorneys who have experience as revenue agents. They can generally tell when an auditor has been unreasonable.

• **Settlement authority.** Appeals officers have broad settlement authority—their mission is to resolve tax disputes, without litigation, in a way that is fair and impartial to both the government and the taxpayer. Unlike auditors, who are bound by IRS rulings and record-keeping requirements, appeals officers can settle disputes on the basis of hazards of litigation. This concerns the government's chance of winning or losing if the case goes to court.

If, for example, the appeals officer feels that the government has only a 20% chance of winning in court, he or she will settle for an 80% reduction in the tax increase proposed by the auditor. If the officer feels that the government has a 70% chance of winning, he'll offer you 30¢ on the dollar to settle the case.

Best chance of settling: Legal issues where the IRS's position has been rejected by the courts. Auditors will follow the service's position despite taxpayer victories in the courts. But an appeals officer will look at both sides and settle depending on how well he thinks the IRS would make out in court. *An issue the IRS has a bad record on in the courts...*

• **Is rent paid under a gift-leaseback arrangement** a deductible business expense?

TAX SHELTERS

If you're looking for settlement of a tax-shelter case beyond your out-of-pocket expenses, you can only get it at the appeals level. Auditors can't offer you more than your out-of-pocket costs even though the IRS has labeled the shelter a "settlement vehicle." But you may be able to convince an appeals officer that the economic reality of the investment exceeds the tax benefits you received.

WINNING STRATEGIES

To win a good settlement in the appeals division you must have a strong factual case or a good technical (i.e., legal) argument. The game is to convince the appeals officer that you will beat the IRS in court—if the case goes to court. *Pointers...*

• **Present new facts at the start of your session with the appeals officer**—facts that were not available to the auditor or that the auditor wouldn't accept. *Aim:* Convince the appeals officer that the agent sped through the audit or rigidly applied the tax law.

• **Be prepared to horse-trade with the appeals officer,** to concede issues you're weak on in return for concessions on other issues.

• **The appeals division can partially settle a case.** For instance, it can agree to settle two out of five issues in dispute. The other three you'll have to take to Tax Court.

• **Nuisance settlements are not allowed.** If your chances of winning in court are greater than 80%, the appeals officer must give you the full amount in dispute. He can't extract 20% from you just to save you the cost of going to court.

When You Can Decline an Audit

Under their own rules, the IRS will not audit you if the same item was examined in the past two years and no change was made by the auditor. *Problem:* Audit invitations are computer-generated. If you get an audit notice but you fall within the two-year rule, call the IRS and request cancellation of the audit.

Louis Lieberman, former IRS agent, Great Neck, New York.

What to Do If the IRS Comes for You—Twice As Many Tax Audits Now

Mark S. Heroux, JD, former senior trial attorney and special assistant US attorney with the IRS Chief Counsel's office. He is a partner in the tax services group at Baker Tilly Virchow Krause, LLP, Chicago, one of the largest accounting firms in the US. He specializes in IRS procedures and dispute resolution. *www.bakertilly.com*

IRS audits have more than doubled in the past decade. The number of taxpayers targeted is likely to continue to increase in the years ahead as the federal government tries to boost tax revenues to close its huge budget deficit.

High earners, small-business owners, the self-employed and those with offshore accounts face the greatest risks—but an audit can happen to anyone.

Most audits are simple "correspondence exams"—an IRS computer identifies a math error…mismatched data…a missing form…or some other straightforward mistake. Once you are contacted by the IRS, you mail in the additional payment or information requested and the matter often is resolved without further fuss.

You face a much more significant audit if the IRS requests a meeting. Although many taxpayers choose to handle this on their own, it is best to hire an experienced tax attorney, certified public accountant (CPA) or enrolled agent (who is required to pass a test to represent taxpayers in dealing with the IRS). This could cost from a few hundred to a few thousand dollars, depending on the experience level of the professional you hire, the complexity of the audit and where you live. Costs could climb even higher if there are appeals or the case goes to court.

Helpful: If you can't afford to hire representation, ask local law schools if they have a free or low-cost tax clinic that can provide representation.

Whether you work with a representative or go it alone, it pays to be aware of IRS agents' latest tactics…and the often-overlooked tools available to you.

THE TRICKIEST TECHNIQUES

•**The surprise phone call.** Prior to 2009, audit notifications almost always were sent through the mail. Now IRS agents sometimes contact taxpayers by telephone out of the blue to tell them that they are being audited. The shock of this call may cause a taxpayer to say more than he/she should.

What to do: If you receive such a call, take down the IRS agent's contact information, say that you are represented by a tax preparer or tax lawyer (or that you may hire one) and that this representative will be in contact. Say nothing else—you have a legal right to consult a tax adviser before responding to IRS questions. And be aware that in some cases, the caller could be a scammer posing as an IRS agent in hopes of obtaining sensitive data, so don't supply personal information.

•Inflexible deadline. The IRS requires taxpayers to respond to most audit notices within just 15 or 30 days. Those deadlines have become increasingly inflexible in recent years.

Example: Fail to respond to a correspondence exam notice within 30 days, and the disputed amount becomes a final assessment to be handled by the collection department, making it very difficult and expensive to challenge the IRS's position—even if you can prove that the IRS is wrong.

What to do: Always contact the IRS by the deadline on the notice, and ask what in particular the IRS wants to cover. Do so by certified mail so that you have proof of when your reply was received. If you intend to hire a representative, do this as soon as possible so that your rep has time to respond.

•**Casual chitchat.** Anything you say to an IRS agent can be used against you, and agents increasingly are trained to get taxpayers to say things they shouldn't.

Example: An auditor swapped fishing stories with the owner of a part-time boat charter business, then asked whether the business ever was likely to make money. The owner jokingly replied that he loved fishing so much that he didn't really care if it did. The agent said this quip showed that the business was just a hobby, and the owner's tax losses were disallowed.

What to do: If you work with a representative, politely refer all questions from the IRS to your tax pro—even questions that seem innocuous. Let your representative meet with the IRS without you unless the representative specifically advises you to accompany him. If you do not hire a representative, politely avoid small talk. Respond to financial queries by writing down the questions and promising to provide the requested information as soon as possible. Supply these answers in writing to reduce the possibility of misspeaking or saying too much, and keep a copy.

THE SHREWDEST STRATEGIES

It isn't easy to take on the IRS, but taxpayers and their representatives do have some tools at their disposal…

•**Ask to speak with a manager—twice.** If you can't see eye-to-eye with the agent handling your audit, you have the right to speak with the agent's "team manager." Unfortunately, team managers generally stand behind their agents' rulings. If this happens, ask to speak with the team manager's manager—the "territory manager." Territory managers tend to be more reasonable and flexible than lower-level IRS employees and sometimes overrule low-level agents' decisions.

• **Turn the IRS's strict deadlines against the IRS.** Send certified letters to the agent handling your audit. These letters might ask questions about your audit or provide information requested by the auditor. If 30 days pass without any reply to your letter—as often happens—you have the right to request the free assistance of the IRS Taxpayer Advocate Service (877-777-4778, *www.irs.gov/advocate*). The Advocate Service can spur the IRS to action when it is dragging its feet or stand up for taxpayers when the IRS is not following its own rules. Most important, enlisting the Advocate Service's help encourages IRS agents to treat you kindly—agents typically tread with caution when this watchdog is looking over their shoulders.

• **Request a Fast-Track Settlement (FTS) if your audit involves a gray area of tax law.** The FTS option lets you enter the IRS appeals process even before the initial audit has ended. That could work in your favor if your audit involves a gray area of tax law. Why? An agent who handles an initial audit typically rules against the taxpayer if there is any chance that the taxpayer owes money… but IRS appeals officers take into account the odds that the IRS may lose if the case goes to court. Thus appeals officers are much more likely to back down or compromise when it's unclear which side the tax law favors.

Example: An IRS agent questions whether you "actively participated" in a business. What constitutes active participation is a legal gray area.

You could wait until after the initial audit to appeal, but that likely would leave the audit hanging over your head for many months and inflate your representative's bill if you hire one. A tax pro should be able to advise you as to which issues fall into legal gray areas.

Warning: If an FTS makes sense in your case, request it as soon as the agent handling your audit indicates that he/she intends to pursue what seems like a gray-area tax issue. An IRS policy makes this fast-track process unavailable once the agent handling the initial audit sends a 30-day notice officially ruling on an issue.

• **Request a face-to-face penalty-reduction meeting.** The IRS attempts to impose penalties almost every time it concludes that a taxpayer has underpaid his taxes. In most cases, those penalties are unjustified. Penalties generally are called for only when taxpayers knowingly fail to pay taxes, not when they make honest mistakes.

Agents who specifically handle penalty abatements are far more likely to reduce or eliminate penalties when they have looked the taxpayer—or the taxpayer's representative—in the eye and heard in person an explanation of how the underpayment was accidental.

Nonpayment Surprise

Can't pay your taxes? Don't worry, you won't go to jail. Nonpayment isn't a crime unless you intentionally squirrel away assets to evade taxes. The worst that will happen to someone who legitimately can't pay is that the IRS will constantly inquire about his or her financial status and will try to seize, whenever possible, salary and bank accounts. Because of the volume of cases it has, the IRS often stops actively pursuing collection after a few years.

23

Retirement Planning

Money for Life—A Fresh Look at Annuities

Annuities have long been considered an investment that insurance salesmen push on unsophisticated clients, not something that smart investors seek out. While annuities may offer tax-deferred earnings and, often, a relatively secure stream of retirement income, many of them also tend to feature steep fees and commissions, inflexible distribution rules and impenetrable complexity.

Example: Many investors who purchased "variable" annuities in the 1990s thought they were obtaining an ultra-safe investment...until they endured steep losses from 2000 through 2003, when the stock market plunged.

Yet some annuities can have a place in a wise investor's portfolio. They can serve as a welcome safe haven in a time of stock market and real estate volatility. They can reduce the odds of outliving retirement savings in a time of shrunken nest eggs. They can offer an opportunity to defer taxes. And in recent years, several of the more reliable insurance companies have made a few changes that tackle some of the drawbacks.

Instead of simply relying on the advice of a commissioned insurance or investment professional, start by reviewing the various types of annuities listed below. Shop for the best terms using the buying strategies provided here or hire a fee-only financial planner to help.

Annuities often are discussed as if they were a single type of investment. *In fact, there are several different types of annuities, each appropriate for different investors and investment goals...*

VARIABLE ANNUITIES

What they are: Variable annuities essentially are a way to invest in mutual funds

Robert Carlson, JD, editor of *Retirement Watch*, personal finance newsletter based in Waldorf, Maryland. He is chairman of the board of trustees of the Fairfax County Employees' Retirement System and author of *Invest Like a Fox...Not Like a Hedgehog* (Wiley). *www. retirementwatch.com* except that the funds' earnings are tax-deferred and withdrawals can be scheduled as monthly payments that are guaranteed to continue for as long as you (or your spouse… or someone else designated) live. Many of the variable annuities sold these days also feature a component that limits potential capital losses. This feature is an attempt by insurance companies to attract investors who were scared off by the losses suffered in variable annuities a decade ago. Unlike some annuities, variable annuities do not offer a guarantee about the amount that you will receive during retirement when you purchase the product. The size of the distributions depends largely on the performance of the mutual funds you select within your annuity.

Problem: *High fees.* The typical variable annuity charges annual fees in the neighborhood of 2%, and some charge 3% to 4%. Onetime commissions of 5% or more are common, too, as are surrender fees of 5% to 6% or more if you attempt to withdraw money in the years immediately after investing. Also, investment gains within the variable annuity are taxed as income when the money is withdrawn, not as capital gains, and withdrawals made prior to age 59½ are subject to a 10% penalty.

Appropriate for: High-tax-bracket investors younger than 55 who have maxed out 401(k)s and IRAs for the year, who wish to do even more tax-deferred investing and who will not need this money for at least 15 to 20 years. It takes decades of tax-deferred growth for the advantages of variable annuities to outweigh their additional fees.

Buying strategy: If you do purchase a variable annuity, do so through a large, low-fee mutual fund company or discount broker, such as Fidelity Investments, Charles Schwab or Vanguard. These tend to charge lower fees and commissions than do commissioned agents. Select aggressive investments within the variable annuity, and do not withdraw this money for at least a decade, preferably two decades or longer.

IMMEDIATE ANNUITIES

What they are: Immediate annuities operate much like traditional pensions. In exchange for a lump-sum payment, you will receive a fixed amount each month, quarter or year for the rest of your life…or the rest of your spouse's life…or for some predetermined number of years, depending on the distribution option you select.

Problem: *Low returns.* The fixed payment you receive from an immediate annuity is based in part on prevailing interest rates at the time the annuity was purchased. A 60-year-old man who puts $50,000 into an immediate annuity, for instance, currently could receive a monthly income of just $250 for the rest of his life.

Immediate annuities also are likely to reduce the size of the estate you leave to your heirs, particularly if you die relatively young. Some immediate annuities do make payments to heirs when the annuity purchaser dies within a predetermined time frame, but adding such a provision further reduces the size of the distributions that the annuity owner receives during his/her life.

Appropriate for: Retirees who want an ultrastable source of income with no market risk and/or retirees who fear that they might outlive their savings, perhaps because they come from families whose members tend to live long.

Buying strategy: If the security of an immediate annuity appeals to you, wait to buy. Interest rates are likely to rise in the coming years, increasing the distributions offered by immediate annuities. The distributions you receive also will increase the older you are when you purchase your annuity.

If you don't want to wait, at least "ladder" your way into presumably rising rates, putting only 20% of the total amount you intend to invest into an immediate annuity this year, then adding an additional 20% in each of the coming four years. One place to obtain annuity quotes is *www.immediateannuities.com.*

Alternative: Longevity annuities, a relatively new product that has become available in recent years, are similar to immediate annuities. Rather than make payments immediately upon the purchase of the annuity, however, longevity annuities do so only when the annuity buyer reaches some advanced age—often 75, 80 or 85.

Buyers who die before this age receive nothing, but those who live long enough receive much, much more per month than from an immediate annuity. A longevity annuity is a viable option if you fear that you will outlive your money but your financial situation seems secure for the first 15 or 20 years of retirement.

Example: A 65-year-old woman currently would receive a monthly income of around $130 from a $25,000 investment in an immediate annuity—but she could receive $1,169 starting at age 85 from a longevity annuity.

EQUITY-INDEXED ANNUITIES

What they are: Equity-indexed annuities (EIAs) are deferred annuities, so their distributions do not begin immediately but rather at some pre-determined future date. The size of distributions is determined in part by the performance of an underlying stock market index—often the Standard & Poor's 500 stock index or the Russell 2000 Index. But unlike index funds, EIAs come with safeguards against losses—there's usually a guarantee that the principal won't decline much or at all in value, plus a guaranteed minimum annual return of 2% to 3%, so your investment could make money even in years when the underlying index falls. There's often a death benefit, too—a designated heir receives a check if the annuity owner dies before receiving some predetermined amount.

Problem: Complexity. Insurance companies that offer EIAs use extremely complicated formulas to calculate these annuities' returns. That makes it very difficult for investors to compare EIAs or to predict how much they can expect to earn from one. Investors should not expect to receive the full returns of the underlying index—EIA returns generally are capped at about 6% per year. On top of this, steep EIA annual fees, surrender fees and commissions eat into profits.

Appropriate for: Conservative investors who seek stock gains but who do not want to risk losses.

Buying strategy: Ask the financial pros you speak with for data on the past 10 years of annual returns on the EIAs that they recommend. Compare those past returns to get some idea as to which EIAs truly offer the best returns and/or lowest risks. Also, compare commissions and annual fees.

CHECK RATINGS

Don't buy annuities issued by an insurer rated lower than A by A.M. Best (*www.ambest.com*) or Moody's (*www.moodys.com*). A low-rated insurer is more likely to fail.

Tax-Time Relief

If your Social Security benefits are subject to income tax, you can voluntarily elect to have the tax withheld from them by the Social Security Administration (SSA). That way, you won't have to come up with cash to pay the tax on April 15. Call the IRS at 800-829-3676 and ask for Form W-4V, or go to the IRS Web site at *www.irs.gov*. Fill out the form and file it with your local SSA office.

Edward Mendlowitz, CPA, partner, WithumSmith+ Brown, CPAs, 1 Spring St., New Brunswick, New Jersey 08901. www.withum.com

Retirement Savvy

Plan your retirement date carefully if you have a traditional *defined benefit* pension plan. Formulas usually base the amount you get on length of service, wages and interest rate at the time you retire. Some plans credit you only for the last *completed* year of work, so you may want to work a *full* final year.

For lump-sum options: Know the date your company changes the interest rate used to figure the benefit. Base your exit date on whether the rate is likely to go higher or lower. The lump-sum amount is higher if rates go down...lower if rates go up.

Note: These factors do not arise in defined-contribution plans, which are more typical.

Avery E. Neumark, Esq., CPA, director of employee benefits and executive compensation, Rosen Seymour Shapss Martin & Co., a New York–based accounting firm.

Two-Month Interest-Free Loan from Your Own IRA

Generally, IRA borrowings are prohibited. But it is possible to move funds from one IRA to another, as long as the transfer is completed in a 60-day period.

Benefit: You have use of the funds for 59 days.

Warning: The exact amount you take out of the first IRA must be placed in the second one within the 60 days. And you can use this device only once a year.

IRA Procrastination Doesn't Pay

Make your full contribution on the first business day in January of the tax year rather than on the April 15 deadline of the following year. (For example, a working couple contributing just $6,000 in January of the tax year will have $75,000 more after 30 years—at an 8% return—than they would if they waited the extra 15½ months.)

Gold Coins And IRAs

Uncle Sam's minted gold coins are the only collectibles that can be included in an individual retirement account.

Cost: The spot price of gold plus about a 55% premium (less-than-one-ounce coins carry a higher charge).

Big IRA Tax Trap

Steven G. Lockwood, tax attorney and president, Lockwood Pension Services, Inc., New York City, writing in *Ed Slott's IRA Advisor,* 100 Merrick Rd., Suite 200E, Rockville Centre, New York 11570.

An IRA may be taxed at rates as high as 80% after the IRA owner's death if proper planning is not done—so it can be a big mistake to try to provide for heirs by leaving them IRA savings.

Tax traps: IRAs are fully subject to federal estate tax at rates as high as 40% maximum rate in 2013. Funds withdrawn from IRAs by heirs also will be subject to federal income tax at rates as high as 39.6%. And state and local estate and income taxes may apply—creating a combined tax rate as high as 80%.

Planning mistakes: *Not worrying about estate taxes on an IRA because…*

• **You know you can leave it to a spouse estate tax free.** *Snag:* The IRA will be taxed when your spouse dies.

• **Only a total of assets up to $5.25 million (in 2013) can be left free of estate tax.** *Snag:* "Hidden" assets, such as life insurance proceeds, retirement accounts and appreciation in a home, may push you over the limit.

Best: Meet with an estate-planning expert to plan how to minimize the tax bill. *Ideas…*

• **Consume IRAs, or leave IRAs to charity for an estate tax deduction,** and instead bequeath to heirs capital gains assets they can take income tax free with stepped-up basis.

• **Set up an estate-tax-free life insurance trust** with single life insurance or second-to-die life insurance to pay estate taxes that will be due on IRA savings at death.

Ensure IRA Heirs Get Their Share

If you want your IRA to pass to the heirs of a beneficiary who dies before you, make sure your IRA beneficiary forms clearly state this. (Most don't.)

Problem: Say you name two or more of your children as beneficiaries of your IRA and one dies before you. That child's family may receive nothing from the IRA. All the funds will go to your surviving children.

What to do: File a special beneficiary form with your IRA trustee to give the heirs of a deceased beneficiary a share of the IRA.

Seymour Goldberg, Esq., CPA, Goldberg & Goldberg, PC, 100 Jericho Quadrangle, Jericho, New York 11753.

The Deferred Commercial Annuity Trick

Irving L. Blackman, CPA, retired founding partner, Blackman Kallick, LLP, 10 S. Riverside Plaza, Chicago 60606. *www.taxsecretsofthewealthy.com*

Few people have heard of the deferred commercial annuity (DCA), which is a completely legal personal tax shelter that can contribute greatly to an individual's retirement wealth.

How it works: An individual pays one or more premiums to an insurance company in exchange for the right to receive annuity payments beginning at some future date. The insurance company then invests the premium proceeds and credits the earnings to the investor's account.

TAX BENEFITS

• **Earnings accumulate in the account tax free until they are distributed.** They can thus be reinvested later to produce more tax-free earnings.

• **When the annuity is paid, a portion of each payment is tax free.** That's because a portion of each payment represents a return of the original premiums. Tax is due only on the earnings of the premiums that are paid out.

• **If the annuity is paid after the recipient retires,** the portion of the annual payment that is taxable will probably be taxed at lower rates.

A DCA can be set up in addition to an IRA, and there is no limit to the amount of money you can put into it. DCA contributions are not deductible the way IRA contributions are, but a DCA is still such a good deal tax-wise that the government does not want you to begin collecting payments from one too soon. So withdrawals from a DCA taken before age 59½ are subject to a 10% penalty.

Early-Withdrawals-from-IRA-Accounts Loophole

The 10% penalty tax on pre-age 59½ withdrawals from IRAs does not apply if the money is taken out in the form of an annuity —that is, in a series of payments over one's life expectancy or the joint life expectancies of a couple. This loophole can be put to good use if there is a fair amount of money in your IRA, say $100,000, from the rollover of a company pension plan.

Edward Mendlowitz, CPA, partner, WithumSmith+ Brown, CPAs, 1 Spring St., New Brunswick, New Jersey 08901. *www.withum.com*

Social Security Card Secret

Few people know it, but the first three digits of a Social Security number are a code for the state in which the card was issued. This code, which can be used to confirm a place of birth or an employment history, is not public knowledge. However, many private detectives have the key to the code and will crack the Social Security number for a fee.

The late Milo Speriglio, director and chief of Nick Harris Detectives, Inc.

Five Kinds of Pay That Are Exempt from Social Security Taxes

One type of pay is wages paid that are to a child under 18, when the parent's business is a proprietorship. Wages paid by a corporation are subject to tax. *The others...*

• **Loans taken out from the company by an employee or shareholder.** But be sure the loan is fully documented so that there is no doubt about its legitimacy. If the IRS concludes that the loan will not be paid back, tax will be imposed. The loan must carry an interest rate equal to 110% of the applicable federal rate at the time of the loan. The IRS will announce this rate monthly.

• **Health insurance payments made into an employee accident,** health or medical reimbursement plan.

• **Educational benefits that add to an employee's on-the-job skills.**

• **Moving-expense reimbursements when a move is job related,** the new job location is at least 50 miles farther from the worker's former home than the old job, and the worker stays at the new job site for at least 39 weeks during the next year.

Consultants Don't Always Have to Pay Social Security Taxes

A retired executive continued to work for his company as a consultant and a member of the board of directors. The IRS said he had to pay Social Security taxes on the fees the company paid him. *Tax Court decision:* For the executive. He was not self-employed in the trade or business of being a consultant and board member. *Key facts:* The executive had agreed not to work for any other company after retirement. He did no work for any other company. His duties as a director took up about six hours of his time each year.

Fred W. Steffens, TC Memo 1981-637.

Bigger Social Security Income for Wife Who Never Worked

Making your wife a partner in your business could boost her ultimate Social Security retirement benefits. As a partner, the wife now has self-employment income. When she reaches retirement, her benefits will be based on that income. This could far exceed the 50% of her husband's retirement benefits that she would get if she had no earnings of her own on which to compute her Social Security entitlement.

John J. Tuozzolo, associated with the firm Collins, Hannafin, Garamella, Jaber & Tuozzolo, PC, 148 Deer Hill Ave., Danbury, Connecticut 06810.

Social Security Secret

Collecting Social Security early can pay off. Even though benefits are reduced, you won't lose out—at least not for a long time. *Example:* If full benefits are $750 per month for retiring at age 65, you can get reduced benefits of $600 a month by retiring at age 62. You'd have to collect full benefits for 12 years to make up the $21,600 you'd receive during the three years of early payments.

Changing Times

Protect Your Social Security Rights

Barbara Weltman, attorney in Millwood, NY. *www.barbaraweltman.com*. She is author of several books, including *The Complete Idiot's Guide to Starting a Home-Based Business* (2nd edition. Macmillan).

Check the amount of annual earnings recorded under your name and number in the Social Security Administration's files every three years. It's harder to correct mistakes after this.

Why? You may have thrown out your own earnings records once the three-year limitation period on IRS audits has expired.

How to check your records: Review the statement sent to you three months before your birthday. If you don't receive a statement, request Form SSA-7004, *Request for Social Security Statement.* (Get Form SSA-7004 by calling 800-772-1213. Or download the form from its Web site at *www.socialsecurity.gov.*)

If you find a mistake: Suppose the statement says you earned $5,000 in 2010 when, in fact, you earned $50,000—call the number on the statement (800-772-1213). If the problem cannot be corrected over the telephone, you may be instructed to write to the Social Security Administration.

• **Ask SSA to update your statement immediately.**

• **Ask them to send you a new statement** so you can confirm that the correction has been made.

Social Security Secrets For Those Under 65

Dan Wilcox, disability program specialist, Social Security Administration, Disability Programs Branch, New York.

It's your right as a working person to apply for disability insurance from the Social Security Administration if at any point you're unable to work because of a mental or physical disability. Before applying, you should know how the system works, who is eligible and what kind of medical criteria a decision is based on. When dealing with any government agency, the more you know before you walk in, the better are your chances of walking out with what you want.

There are two disability programs under Social Security. One is the needs-based program, Supplemental Security Income Program. SSI is basically a nationalization of welfare benefits for the unemployable. The other, which applies to working people, is the basic insurance program that you pay into as the FICA tax—old age and survivors disability insurance (OASDI).

Although the disability criteria for acceptance are the same under both programs, you don't have to prove financial need for OASDI. You're eligible if you've worked and paid into the system for 20 quarters out of the last 40 (five years out of the last 10) and have the necessary years of work credit, depending upon your age. If your last day in the system was 10 years or more ago, you're not eligible for disability benefits now, though you may eventually be eligible for retirement benefits.

Benefits are based on what you've paid into the system.

The system works as follows…

• **The first step.** File an application with your local Social Security office. You'll be interviewed by a claims representative, who will ask you some basic questions about your disability. *For example:* What is the nature of it? When did you stop working? How does it interfere with your daily activities and ability to work? Which doctors and hospitals have treated you?

You'll be asked to sign medical releases so Social Security can obtain information from your medical sources. The interviewer will also note any evidence of your disability that he observed.

• **This material is sent to a trained disability examiner at a state agency,** who will contact your medical sources.

•**If the medical information you have submitted isn't sufficient,** the agency will send you to a consulting specialist, at the government's expense, and this information will become part of your file.

•**If you've met the medical disability requirements** (which are extremely stringent), you'll be granted benefits. But you can still be found disabled even if you don't meet the medical requirements. Age, past work experience and education are also taken into account. Anyone over 50 is put in a special category because his vocational outlook is less favorable. A 55-year-old construction worker with minimal education who suffers from mild heart disease might be eligible—he can't do his past work and probably wouldn't be able to find another job. Another construction worker of the same age and disability, but with more education and skill, might be expected to find light or sedentary work. The approach is individualized throughout the process.

•**The final eligibility decision is made and signed by the disability examiner,** together with a physician who works for the state (not the consulting physician).

•**If benefits are denied,** you can either appeal the decision or reapply.

Social Security's definition of medical disability: The inability to do any substantial, gainful activity by reason of any medically determinable physical or mental impairment that can be expected to result in death, or that has lasted or can be expected to last, for a continuous period of not less than 12 months. To meet the definition, you must have a severe impairment that makes you unable to do your previous work or any other gainful work that exists in the national economy. *How to prove it...*

•**It's crucial that your doctor submit very precise medical information,** including all test results—the same kind of information a doctor would use in coming up with a diagnosis and treatment plan. Social Security won't accept your doctor's conclusions. It wants the medical evidence that led to the conclusion.

•**Social Security has a long list of impairments under which your disability should fall.** The listing, broken down into 13 body systems, covers about 99% of the disabilities that people apply for. This listing outlines exactly what tests must be met for eligibility. *Examples:* An amputee is eligible only if he has lost both feet, both hands or one hand and one foot. Angina pectoris victims must show certain results on a treadmill test and/or a number of other listed tests. *Helpful:* You and your doctor should take a look at the listings before you apply. If your doctor answers in sufficient detail, you might avoid a visit to the agency's consulting physician.

FILING AN APPEAL

When benefits are denied, a notice is sent. A brief paragraph explains the reason in general terms. At that point you can go back to the Social Security office and file for a reconsideration, which is simply a review of your case.

If the reconsideration is denied, you can take your case to an administrative law judge within Social Security's Office of Hearings and Appeals. You don't need a lawyer for this hearing, but many people do have one. At the hearing you present your case, review the evidence in your file, add other relevant evidence and personally impress the judge. The reversal rate at this level is fairly high (40% to 60%).

If denied at this hearing, you can go to the Appeals Council and then up through the courts. The chances of reversal improve at each level. Most people just go up to the administrative law judge level. If they're turned down there, they file a new claim and start all over. Often delay works in a claimant's favor, since disabilities may worsen over time.

• **Look into state disability programs.** If your disability is temporary, you might be covered by your state. State programs bridge the gap for people who have been disabled for less than a year. *Be aware:* Many state disability programs and private insurance companies require that you apply for Social Security first before you can collect from them.

• **File soon.** Don't wait until you've been disabled for a year. There's some retroactivity (up to 12 months), but the sooner you file, the better.

• **Call the Social Security office before going in.** You can save yourself a lot of trouble. Find out first what you should bring with you and which are the best days and times to come in.

• **Ask at your local Social Security office for the Listing of Impairments,** or look them up in the library. Request the Code of Federal Regulations—see 20 CFR 404 and 20 CFR 416.

When You Retire as A Consultant

A longtime executive of a company plans to retire but also plans to continue working for the company as a consultant. As a consultant, he'll be paid an hourly rate. The amount of consulting work to be done isn't fixed. *IRS ruling:* The retired executive will be considered to have separated from service with the company in spite of the fact that he'll continue to do consulting work. Thus the payout from his company's retirement plan will qualify as a lump-sum distribution and get favorable tax treatment.

IRS Letter Ruling 8635067.

Financing a Retirement Home

Maureen Tsu, CFP, San Juan Capistrano, California, quoted in *Where to Retire*, 5851 San Felipe St., Suite 500, Houston 77057.

When buying a retirement home, a key decision you will have to make is whether to purchase it with cash or finance it with a mortgage.

Many people prefer the security of buying with cash and then not owing any debt on their home.

Drawback: Using so much cash may leave you cash poor and limit the lifestyle you can afford in retirement.

Contrast: Buying a home with a mortgage can leave you with more spendable cash. The debt on the home can be paid off or refinanced upon your death.

ISSUES IF YOU DECIDE TO FINANCE WITH A MORTGAGE...

• **Can you obtain tax benefits from deducting mortgage interest?** Do you have enough total deductions to itemize deductions? Are you in a high enough tax bracket to make it worthwhile?

• **Can you invest the cash saved by buying with a mortgage** to earn a higher after-tax rate of return than you will pay on the mortgage?

• **Are you willing to have your estate deal with the debt on your home by selling it,** or by having heirs refinance it at your death?

ISSUES IF YOU BUY WITH CASH...

• **Will you have a way of tapping your equity in the home** to raise cash in an emergency?

• **After spending cash on the home,** will you have enough money to enjoy a comfortable retirement lifestyle?

• **Will your estate eventually have to sell the home for cash**—so that you might as well take the cash while you are alive by financing the home?

Best: Consider these issues before you retire, while you are still working. You will have more options and a stronger credit standing to make any arrangement you finally choose.

Get Back the Tax Paid on Excess Social Security Benefits

If you paid tax on Social Security benefits that you received, then were told you had to repay some of the benefits because you had too much income during the year, is there any way you can get back the tax you paid?

Answer: Yes. File an amended tax return, Form 1040X, for the year in which you paid the tax. On it, report your accurate income total for the year—excluding the benefits you had to repay. You'll get your refund.

Retire in Alaska

Alaska is a tax haven for retirees who don't mind the cold. There's no state income tax or sales tax. Residents also share profits of the state's oil industry, receiving annual disbursements that ranged from $1,964 in 2000 to $1,281 in 2010. Residents age 65 and over receive generous exemptions from property taxes and are exempt from car registration fees. Some cities, including Anchorage have no local sales tax.

R. Alan Fox, former editor, *Where to Retire*

All About "Top-Heavy" Retirement Plans

A "top-heavy" retirement plan, whether maintained by a corporation, a partnership, or a sole proprietorship, does not qualify for beneficial tax treatment unless certain conditions are met.

Meaning of top-heavy: More than 60% of the plan's benefits go to key employees. *These are:* Officers of the company, over-5% owners, over-1% owners earning more than $150,000 and employees with the 10 largest ownership interests in the company.

To qualify a top-heavy plan for tax purposes, the employer must…

• **Vest* benefits faster.** Either 100% vesting after three years of service or six-year graded vesting (with even faster vesting for employer matching contributions).

• **Provide minimum benefits for non-key employees.** In determining these minimum benefits, Social Security can't be taken into account. *For a pension plan:* The benefit must be at least 2% of pay for each year of service (but not more than 20% of average annual compensation). *For a profit-sharing plan:* 3% of the pay.

*A benefit is "vested" when the employee's right to that benefit can't be forfeited.

How Safe Is Your Pension?

The late James E. Conway, president of The Ayco Corporation, Albany, New York.

Be proactive with your retirement plans. *Here's how to check on the safety of your retirement income…*

For employees of public companies: Basic information is included in the firm's annual report. Usually the size of a firm's unfunded pension liability and the size of its past service liability are disclosed in footnotes. More detailed information is available in the financial section of the firm's 10K report, filed with the Securities and Exchange Commission.

For employees of private companies: Everyone who is in a qualified plan (one approved by the IRS under the Code) has the right to obtain information about his or her pension from the trustees of the plan. They may be either internal or external trustees. The average person may not be able to decipher the information. If you can't, then take it to a pension expert, actuary, lawyer or accountant for an analysis. Whether you are examining pension information of public or of private firms, you are seeking the same sort of basic information.

The size of a company's liability for retirement payouts is not as important as the assumptions about funding these liabilities. Like a mortgage, these obligations don't exist 100% in the present. Concern yourself with how the company expects to fund its liabilities.

TYPES OF LIABILITIES

• **Unfunded pension liabilities.** The amount a firm expects to need over the next 20 to 30 years to supply vested workers with promised pension benefits. These figures are derived from various actuarial assumptions.

• **Past service liabilities.** Created when a company raises its pension compensation. For instance, a company may have been planning to provide 40% of compensation as a pension. One year it may raise that to 45% and treat it retroactively.

TROUBLE SIGNS

• **A poor record on investing.** Compare the market value of the assets in the pension with their book value. If book value is more than market value, the trustees have not been investing wisely. *Point:* If the fund had to sell those assets today, there would be a loss. I would also get a bit nervous if the fund is still holding some obscure bonds or other fixed-income obligations issued at low rates years ago.

• **Funding assumptions are overstated.** Actuaries have a myriad of estimates on how long it takes to fund pension plans and what rate of return a company will get.

WHAT TO LOOK AT

• **Time frame.** This should not be too long. If the firm is funding over 40 years, I would want to know why and how, since 10 to 20 years is more customary. *Reason:* We don't have a crystal ball, and the investment world will be different in as little as 10 years from now. Assumptions made on 40 years may not hold up at all.

• **Rate of return.** If a company assumes a conservative 6% to 7% or less right now, you can be comfortable. If the assumed rate is 10% or more, I would want to know how it plans to meet that expectation for the entire fund over the long run.

• **Salary and wage scales.** The company should be assuming an increase in compensation over years. Most plans have such provisions. It must start funding now for future salary increases.

• **Assumptions about the employee turnover rate.** These should be consistent with the historically documented turnover of the company. If a firm has a very low turnover rate and assumes a 4% turnover, the company will be underfunded at some time. Estimates should be conservative.

To assess your own status in a corporate pension plan, see what benefits you are eligible for. Many people have the illusion that they are eligible for a maximum pension after only a few years. In truth, companies couldn't afford to fully include people who have such short service. They may offer some token pension for such service. But most people are not fully covered until they have worked for the firm for 10 or even 20 years, and then they might be covered only to the extent of their accrued pension to date, not the full pension expected at normal retirement. With so much job-hopping in the past two decades, an individual's pension-fund status may be much less than imagined.

Employees of troubled or even bankrupt companies need not panic. Trustees of the plan have an obligation to the vested employees. The assets of the plan are segregated, and no creditor can reach them. In fact, as a creditor the corporate pension plan can grab some corporate assets under certain circumstances. And if there has been gross mismanagement of pension funds, stockholders of a closely held company can be held personally liable.

The Mistakes in Retirement Can Be Avoided

Alexandra Armstrong, CFP, chairman, Armstrong, Fleming & Moore, Inc., financial advisers, 1850 M St. Suite 250, Washington, DC 20036. She is coauthor of *On Your Own: A Widow's Passage to Emotional and Financial Well-Being* (Kaplan Professional Co).

When it comes to retirement planning, what are the mistakes people make most often? The most common one is waiting too long to plan for retirement. Sometimes, a couple in their early 60s comes in and wants to know how things will look when they retire at age 65. All I can do is look at their financial assets and their current spending...and speculate what their situation will be when they retire. It certainly doesn't leave much time to accumulate assets.

What puts blinders on such people? A company pension plan? A feeling they have a house and enough to live on? No. Usually it's fear that they do not have enough...so they refuse to look at the facts.

When people wait that long to start their retirement planning, how can you help? First, cut back on current spending and save more—fast. Most people don't budget because they hate counting every penny. If you're going to crash-save for retirement, you simply have to do it.

Aside from saving more, what else can late-starters do? Change where they plan to live when they retire. Moving to a less expensive part of the country is one of the best ways to get by on less in retirement.

Caution: Make your move for sound reasons...not merely because it's somewhere you spent a few pleasant vacation weeks. If you don't know anybody who lives in that community before you move, that could be a big mistake. Too often what happens is that retired people sell their homes...buy in the new place...discover they don't like it...but can't afford to move back home.

What's the smart way to make such a retirement move? Test out a community. Rent out your current home for a year...and rent where you think you might like to move.

Caution: Don't make your move based on where your children live. There's the risk that a relationship with children that's great long-distance may not be so great when you live close to one another.

What other big retirement mistake is being made? Taking money out of an IRA too soon. Many people start taking money out at age 59½ because that's the first time they can withdraw from an IRA without facing a 10% penalty.

Unless your IRA is your major source of retirement income, you don't have to start withdrawing from retirement accounts until the year after you turn 70½. The longer you compound that money without paying current taxes on it, the better off you will be. During those 12 years, you could double your money.

What about planning to live on Social Security and a company pension? Don't count too much on either Social Security or your pension. More and more of Social Security will be taxed and may not be indexed to inflation—or it may be discontinued. And most company pensions are fixed. The monthly pension check may be worth only half as much in real dollars within 10 years after retirement. Think seriously about saving some of that pension income during your early retirement years because you may need that money later on.

What's the most common mistake you see in investing retirement money? Too many people invest entirely, or primarily, in fixed-income securities once they retire. That was fine when people retired at 65 and died at 70. Now they retire at 60 or earlier and live to 90-plus.

People used to figure their expenses would go down when they retired. But the reality for people who have to live on retirement income for 10, 20 or 30 years is that their expenses will go up.

Therefore, you want to invest to produce a rising stream of income during retirement. Think of total return...with your capital and your income stream continuing to build while you're retired.

What about long-term-care insurance, to pay for a nursing home, as part of retirement planning? A catastrophic illness requiring a nursing home stay can quickly deplete retirement savings unless you have insurance to cover your costs.

If you have over $1 million in assets, you can probably use this if you need long-term care at home or in a nursing home. If your assets are $100,000 or less, you'll probably qualify for Medicaid to handle those expenses.

People in their mid-50s can generally find good long-term-care insurance for about $2,000 a year that will pay $150 a day plus up to 3% a year inflation adjustment...for 3 years. These policies are much improved over those first offered years ago. Premiums are deductible within limits.

Last-Minute Saving Strategies

Ray Martin, CFP, president of CitiStreet Advisors LLC, advisory unit of CitiStreet LLC, 1 Heritage Dr., Quincy, Massachusetts 02171.

There is no quick fix for decades of not saving for retirement. *But it is possible to make some moves now that will help cash-strapped 50-somethings finance a comfortable retirement...*

• **Run the numbers** to find out exactly how big your shortfall is. *Useful free calculators...*

• Choose to Save's Ballpark Estimate, *www.choosetosave.org/ballpark*

• Smart Money's Retirement Worksheets, *www.smartmoney.com/personal-finance/retirement.*

• **Keep saving.** Contribute the maximum allowed to your company-sponsored retirement plan, especially if your employer matches your contributions.

The maximum 401(k), 403(b) or 457 plan contribution allowed in 2013 is $17,500.

For 2013, the catch-up limit is $5,500.

Are you self-employed? You can contribute as much as $51,000 in 2013 to a qualified retirement plan account. Since the contribution is tax-deductible, the government subsidizes about one-third or more, depending on your tax bracket.

• **Eliminate big-ticket expenditures.** Cutting back on new clothes, restaurant meals and fancy vacations can easily save you as much as $1,000 a month. If you invest that $1,000 at 8% a year, you will have $185,000 at the end of a decade.

But that still isn't enough to fund a comfortable retirement. *Focus on these cutbacks...*

If your children are still in college, have them shoulder at least part of their tuition bills.

If they haven't started college yet, have them live at home and attend a less costly public university or community college for the first two years. After that, they can transfer to a private university and take out loans to pay for it.

These moves can save you $100,000 or more per child over four years.

With decades of earning power ahead of them, your children are better positioned than you to pay off these debts.

• **Downsize the family house.** If you have lived in your house for more than five years, you will have accumulated a significant amount of equity. Selling your current house and moving to a house or condo that's smaller will unlock equity that could be used to help finance your retirement. Assuming you unlock $150,000 and it earns 8% a year, it would grow to $333,000 after a decade.

You could also consider renting instead of buying. By eliminating bills for your mortgage, home insurance, maintenance, repairs and property taxes, much more of the cash flow you free up by selling your house becomes available for retirement investments.

• **Don't chase extraordinary returns for outsized risks.** Create a diversified portfolio even though you are behind schedule. In the late 1990s, many people thought diversification was outmoded—until they were stung by the meltdown in the technology sector. A prudent allocation for someone approaching retirement is 70% stocks for future growth and 30% bonds for current stability. It's also a good idea to divide the stock portion between large-, mid- and small-cap funds.

Reason: The same portfolio manager often runs several funds within the same family. Investments may overlap even among funds with different objectives.

Overlap is not a problem with bond funds, which are much more uniform in terms of performance within categories. Here, the best approach is to buy the funds with the lowest expenses.

If your tax bracket is 25% or less, consider a short- to intermediate-term *corporate* bond fund. If you are in a higher tax bracket, consider a short- to intermediate-term *municipal* bond fund.

Retirement Tax Break Helps Low-Income Earners

The *Credit for Qualified Retirement Savings Contributions* can reimburse up to 50% of the first $2,000 of retirement-plan contributions by reducing tax owed. It is separate from the usual IRA or 401(k) tax breaks. It cannot be used by people who are not subject to income tax for the year…and is graduated according to income. Singles earning up to $29,500 in 2013…joint filers earning $59,000…and heads of household earning $44,250 may be eligible if they contribute to a qualified retirement plan. See IRS Form 8880 (800-TAX-FORM, *www.irs.gov*) to determine how much of the credit you can claim.

Catherine Collinson, president, Transamerica Center for Retirement Studies, Los Angeles. *www.transamerica center.org*

Index